Communications
in Computer and Information Science 160

Andrzej Kwiecień   Piotr Gaj
Piotr Stera (Eds.)

Computer Networks

18th Conference, CN 2011
Ustroń, Poland, June 14-18, 2011
Proceedings

 Springer

Volume Editors

Andrzej Kwiecień
Piotr Gaj
Piotr Stera

Silesian University of Technology
Institute of Informatics
ul. Akademicka 16
44-100 Gliwice, Poland

E-mail: {andrzej.kwiecien, piotr.gaj, piotr.stera}@polsl.pl

ISSN 1865-0929   e-ISSN 1865-0937
ISBN 978-3-642-21770-8   e-ISBN 978-3-642-21771-5
DOI 10.1007/978-3-642-21771-5
Springer Heidelberg Dordrecht London New York

Library of Congress Control Number: 2011929183

CR Subject Classification (1998): C.2, H.4, D.2, H.3.4-5, D.4.6, K.6.5

Typesetting: Camera-ready by author, data conversion by Scientific Publishing Services, Chennai, India

Printed on acid-free paper

Springer is part of Springer Science+Business Media (www.springer.com)

Preface

Information technology is a science which focuses mainly on methods and ways of data transmission. The continuous and very intense development of IT results in the fast development of the methods and technologies of data transmission. Computer networks, as well as the entire field of IT, are the objects of regular changes, which are caused by the general technological advancement, and also the influence of new IT technologies. New methods and tools of designing and modelling computer networks are constantly being extended. First of all, the scope of their application is extended thanks to the results of new research and application proposals, which were not even taken into consideration in the past. These new applications stimulate the progress of scientific research, as the broader use of system solutions based on computer networks results in a large number of problems, both practical and theoretical. This book is the result of the above considerations, and consists of 50 chapters referring to the broad spectrum of issues and problems.

Generally speaking, the content can be divided into the following subject groups:

- Molecular networks
- Network issues related to nano and quantum technology
- New technologies related to computer networks
- Fundamentals of computer networks architecture and programming
- Internet networks
- Data security in distributed systems
- Industrial computer networks
- Applications of computer networks

The first group refers to the new technologies used in computer networks, with particular reference to nano, molecular and quantum technologies.

The second subject group comprises chapters devoted to new and typical technologies related to computer network structure. A good example may be the chapter "Design of the Stimulation Model of the Web Server."

The next group consists of chapters which concern the fundamentals of computer networks, their architecture and programming. The chapter entitled "Analysis of Time Measurements in Network Systems Using Decomposition on Subprocesses" can be given as an example.

The fourth group covers a variety of topics related to the Internet in its broad meaning, such as the "Comparative Analysis of IP-Based Mobility Protocols and Fast Handover Algorithms in IEEE 802.11-Based WLANs."

Another group of chapters focuses mainly on data security in distributed systems. It is a very essential thematic group, because of the constant risks involved in the appropriate and secure operation of information technology systems.

This issue is presented in the paper "Flow-Based Algorithm for Malware Traffic Detection."

The chapters referring to the range of problems connected with use and analysis of industrial systems are included in group number six. This issue is fundamental from the point of view of the structure and industrial application of distributed real-time IT systems. An example is the chapter "Network Integration on the Control Level."

The last group describes the problems faced in the general application of computer networks. "Self-Adapting Algorithm for Transmission Power Control in Integrated Meter-Reading Systems Based on Wireless Sensor Networks" is one of the chapters that presents this issue.

On behalf of the Program Committee we would like to take this opportunity to express our thanks to all the authors for sharing their research results and for their assistance in creating this monograph. We believe this book is a valuable reference on the computer networks area. We would also like to thank the members of the international jury for their participation in reviewing each paper twice.

April 2011   Andrzej Kwiecień
                                                                        Piotr Gaj

Organization

CN 2011 was organized by the Institute of Informatics, Silesian Univeristy of Technology (SUT), and supported by the Committee of Informatics of the Polish Academy of Sciences, Section of Computer Network and Distributed Systems in technical cooperation with the IEEE organization.

Institute of Informatics
Silesian University of Technology
ul. Akademicka 16
44-100 Gliwice, Poland
e-mail: cn@polsl.pl
web: http://cn.polsl.pl

Executive Committee

All members of the Executing Committee are from the Silesian University of Technology, Poland.

Honorary Member	Halina Węgrzyn
Organizing Chair	Piotr Gaj
Technical Volume Editor	Piotr Stera
Technical Support	Aleksander Cisek
Technical Support	Arkadiusz Jestratjew
Technical Support	Jacek Stój
Office	Małgorzata Gładysz
WEB Support	Piotr Kuźniacki
IEEE PS Coordinator	Jacek Izydorczyk

Program Committee

Program Chair

Andrzej Kwiecień	Silesian University of Technology, Poland

Honorary Members

Klaus Bender	TU München, Germany
Zdzisław Duda	Silesian University of Technology, Poland
Andrzej Karbownik	Silesian University of Technology, Poland
Jerzy Rutkowski	Silesian University of Technology, Poland
Stefan Węgrzyn	IITiS PAN Gliwice, Poland
Bogdan M. Wilamowski	Auburn University, USA

Program Committee Members

Anoosh Abdy	Realm Information Technologies, USA
Tülin Atmaca	Institut National de Télécommunication, France
Win Aung	National Science Foundation, USA
Leszek Borzemski	Technical University of Wrocław, Poland
Markus Bregulla	University of Applied Sciences Ingolstadt, Germany
Tadeusz Czachórski	Silesian University of Technology, Poland
Andrzej Duda	INP Grenoble, France
Alexander N. Dudin	Belarusian State University, Belarus
Jean-Michel Fourneau	Versailles University, France
Natalia Gaviria	Universidad de Antioquia, Colombia
Roman Gielerak	University of Zielona Góra, Poland
Jürgen Jasperneite	Ostwestfalen-Lippe University of Applied Sciences, Germany
Jerzy Klamka	IITiS Polish Academy of Sciences, Gliwice, Poland
Demetres D. Kouvatsos	University of Bradford, UK
Stanisław Kozielski	Silesian University of Technology, Poland
Henryk Krawczyk	Gdańsk University of Technology, Poland
Kevin M. McNeil	BAE Systems, USA
Nihal Pekergin	Versailles University, France
Piotr Pikiewicz	College of Business in Dąbrowa Górnicza, Poland
Bolesław Pochopień	Silesian University of Technology, Poland
Mirosław Skrzewski	Silesian University of Technology, Poland
Kerry-Lynn Thomson	Nelson Mandela Metropolitan University, South Africa
Oleg Tikhonenko	IITiS Polish Academy of Sciences, Gliwice, Poland
Bane Vasic	University of Arizona, USA
Sylwester Warecki	Freescale Semiconductor Inc., USA
Tadeusz Wieczorek	Silesian University of Technology, Poland
Grzegorz Zaręba	University of Arizona, USA

Referees

Anoosh Abdy
Tülin Atmaca
Leszek Borzemski
Markus Bregulla
Tadeusz Czachórski
Andrzej Duda
Alexander N. Dudin
Jean-Michel Fourneau
Natalia Gaviria

Roman Gielerak
Jürgen Jasperneite
Jerzy Klamka
Demetres D. Kouvatsos
Stanisław Kozielski
Henryk Krawczyk
Andrzej Kwiecień
Piotr Pikiewicz
Bolesław Pochopień

Mirosław Skrzewski
Kerry-Lynn Thomson
Oleg Tikhonenko
Bane Vasic
Sylwester Warecki
Tadeusz Wieczorek
Grzegorz Zaręba

Sponsoring Institutions

Technical cosponsor of the conference: IEEE Poland Section.

Table of Contents

π-local Operations in Composite Quantum Systems with Applications to Multipartite Entanglement

Roman Gielerak and Marek Sawerwain

Institute of Control & Computation Engineering
University of Zielona Góra, ul. Podgórna 50, Zielona Góra 65-246, Poland
{R.Gielerak,M.Sawerwain}@issi.uz.zgora.pl

Abstract. A coordinate-wise description of the multi-local operations performed on multi-partite quantum systems is presented. A particular application of the result presented to the maximally-entangled cluster decomposition of a general multi-partite quantum states is given together with their ZG QCS environment implementations as well.

Keywords: quantum entanglement, multi-partite entanglement, detection of entanglement, numerical simulations.

1 Introduction

The major role played by the phenomenon of entanglement, originally discovered and discussed in the very early days of quantum theory [1,2] in several quantum information processing tasks is well known. However, only in the case of bipartite systems our present understanding of entanglement seems to be reached a satisfactory level of qualitative and quantitative as well knowledge [3,4,5,6]. The situation concerning entanglement of quantum systems composed of several, spacely separated subsystems is much less explored as the problems arising are more technically involved than in the bipartite case. The importance of multipartite entanglement can be illustrated by several illuminating examples. A class of the so called graph states used in one-way computation models [9] and fault-tolerant topological quantum computation [10] model as well are both good examples for this. Multipartite entangled photons are being essential resources used in the present version of QKD protocols [11,12]. For the purposes of quantum communications tasks a multipartite entangled states can serve as a quantum communication channels.

The main aim of the present contribution is to demonstrate certain computational tools which might be very useful in analysing multipartite entanglement. In the next section an analytical approach to compute in a coordinate-wise way the action of a multilocal operations on a globally given quantum state will be presented. These computational results in Sect. 3 will be then applied to localise maximally-entangled clusters for a given quantum multipartite states. As the corresponding computations are rather very tedious we have utilised them by

A. Kwiecień, P. Gaj, and P. Stera (Eds.): CN 2011, CCIS 160, pp. 1–10, 2011.

performing them in the recently developed Zielona Góra Quantum Computing System (ZG QCS or QCS) environment [13,14].

2   Local Operations in Composite Systems

Let us consider a quantum system $\mathcal{H}$ composing of separated N subsystems $\theta_i, i = 1 : N$. The corresponding Hilbert spaces of states $\mathcal{H}_i$, each of finite (for simplicity mainly) dimension n_i and the corresponding sets of states will be denoted as $E(\mathcal{H}_i)$. The space of states of the global composite system Θ is according to quantum physics rules $\mathcal{H} = \mathcal{H}_1 \otimes \mathcal{H}_2 \otimes \ldots \otimes \mathcal{H}_N$ and has dimension $D = n_1 \cdot n_2 \cdot \ldots n_N$.

Let $\mathbb{I}_N = \{1, 2, \ldots, N\}$ and let $\mathrm{Par}(\mathbb{I}_N)$ be the space off all partitions of the set $\mathbb{I}_N$. A typical element of $\mathrm{Par}(\mathbb{I}_N)$ will be denoted as π and $\pi = (\pi_1, \ldots, \pi_k)$, where $\pi_i \subset \mathbb{I}_N$, $\pi_i \cap \pi_{i'} = \emptyset$ for $i \neq i'$ and $\bigcup_i \pi_i = \mathbb{I}_N$. We say that $\pi = (\pi_1, \ldots, \pi_k)$ is finer, than $\pi' = (\pi'_1, \ldots, \pi'_l))$ iff for $i \in \mathbb{I}_k$ there exists $j \in \mathbb{I}_l$ such that $\pi_i \subseteq \pi'_j$. This notion introduces then the partial order in the space $\mathrm{Par}(\mathbb{I}_N)$ denoted as α. The maximal element $\pi_{\max} = \{\mathbb{I}_N\}$ and the minimal one $\pi_{\min} = \{\{1\}, \ldots, \{n\}\}$ are easily detected. For a given $\pi = (\pi_1, \ldots, \pi_k) \in \mathrm{Par}(\mathbb{I}_N)$ we denote $\mathcal{H}^\pi = (\mathcal{H}_{\pi_1}, \ldots, \mathcal{H}_{\pi_k})$, where $\mathcal{H}_{\pi_k} = \bigotimes_{i \in \pi_k} \mathcal{H}_i$. A physical operation OP acting on $E(\mathcal{H})$ will be called elementary π-local operation iff there exists a sequence of physical operations $(\mathrm{OP}_{\pi_1}, \ldots, \mathrm{OP}_{\pi_k})$ each acting on $E(\mathcal{H}_{\pi_i})$ and such that $\mathrm{OP} = \bigotimes_{i=1:k} \hat{\mathrm{OP}}_{\pi_i}$, where $\hat{\mathrm{OP}}_{\pi_i}$ are natural embeddings of OP_{π_i} into the space $\mathrm{OP}(\mathcal{H})$. In many typical applications a global state $\rho \in E(\mathcal{H})$ and a π-local operations OP are given in terms of OP_{π_i} and the question is to calculate the action of OP and therefore of OP_{π_i} on the state ρ and this is the main aim of this subsection.

Let $\mathcal{M}_{n \times m}(C)$ stands for the space of C-valued matrices of size $n \times m$. Let a family of such matrices $A_i \in \mathcal{M}_{n_i \times m_i}(C)$, $i = 1 : N$ be given and let $A = A_1 \otimes \ldots \otimes A_N \in \mathcal{M}_{n_1 \cdot \ldots n_N, m_1 \cdot \ldots m_N}(C)$. The following (presumably well known) result gives the value $A(i, j)$ of matrix element of A in term of the local indices $(i_\alpha, j_\beta) \in \mathbb{I}_{n_1} \times \mathbb{I}_{m_1}$.

Proposition 1. *Let $A_i \in \mathbb{M}_{n_i \times m_i}(\mathbb{C})$ for $i = 1 : N$ and let $A = A_1 \otimes \ldots \otimes A_N$. Then for any $i \in \{1, \ldots, n_1 \cdot \ldots \cdot n_N\}$, $j \in \{1, \ldots, m_1 \cdot \ldots \cdot m_N\}$ there exist an unique N-tuples*

$$
\begin{aligned}
\underline{\alpha} &= (\alpha^1, \ldots, \alpha^N), \alpha^k \in \{1, \ldots, n_k\} \\
\underline{\beta} &= (\beta^1, \ldots, \beta^N), \beta^k \in \{1, \ldots, m_k\}
\end{aligned} \tag{1}
$$

and such that

$$
A(i, j) = A_1(\alpha^1, \beta^1) \cdot \ldots \cdot A_N(\alpha^N, \beta^N) \tag{2}
$$

where

$$
\begin{aligned}
i = \ &(\alpha^1 - 1)n_2 \cdot \ldots \cdot n_N \\
&+ (\alpha^2 - 1)n_3 \cdot \ldots \cdot n_N \\
&+ \ldots \quad \ldots \quad \ldots \quad \ldots \\
&+ (\alpha^{N-1} - 1)n_N + \alpha^N
\end{aligned} \tag{3}
$$

$$j = (\beta^1 - 1)m_2 \cdot \ldots \cdot m_N$$
$$+ (\beta^2 - 1)m_3 \cdot \ldots \cdot m_N$$
$$+ \quad \ldots \quad \ldots \quad \ldots \quad \ldots \tag{4}$$
$$+ (\beta^{N-1} - 1)m_N + \beta^N$$

Proof. It follows from the associativity of the Kronecker product together with the version of the ancient theorem about dividing integers with rest. The details can be found in [15].

A constructive route to determine the corresponding N-tuples $\underline{\alpha}$ and $\underline{\beta}$ in the above proposition also follows directly from the proof. A several examples demonstrating how this works will be given now.

Example 1. (The case of pure states)
Let $N = 2$ and $|\psi_1\rangle \in \mathcal{M}_{1 \times n_1}(C)$, $|\psi_2\rangle \in \mathcal{M}_{1 \times n_2}(C)$. Then $|\psi\rangle = |\psi_1\rangle \otimes |\psi_2\rangle \in \mathcal{M}_{1 \times n_1 n_2}(C)$ has the coordinates $|\psi\rangle(i) = |\psi_1\rangle(\alpha^1) \cdot |\psi_2\rangle(\alpha^2)$ where $i = (\alpha^1 - 1)n_2 + \alpha^2$ and $\alpha^1 \in \{1, \ldots, n_1\}$, $\alpha^2 \in \{1, \ldots, n_2\}$. The coefficients α^1 and α^2 can be determined by dividing the number i by n_2 with the remainder.

Example 2. Let $N = 3$ and $A_1 \in \mathcal{M}_{n_1 \times m_1}(C)$, $A_2 \in \mathcal{M}_{n_2 \times m_2}(C)$, $A_3 \in \mathcal{M}_{n_3 \times m_3}(C)$. Then $(A_1 \otimes A_2 \otimes A_3)(i, j) = A_1(\alpha^1, \beta^1) A_2(\alpha^2, \beta^2) A_3(\alpha^3, \beta^3)$ where

$$i = (\alpha^1 - 1)n_2 \cdot n_3 + (\alpha^2 - 1)n_3 + \alpha^3$$
$$j = (\beta^1 - 1)m_2 \cdot m_3 + (\beta^2 - 1)m_3 + \beta^3 \tag{5}$$

are uniquely determined.

Let $(E_{i,j})$ stands for the system of canonical unit-matrix, i.e. $(E_{i,j})(k, l) = \delta_{ki} \cdot \delta_{lj}$. Then the system $(E_{\alpha_1, \beta_1} \otimes \ldots \otimes E_{\alpha_N, \beta_N})$ forms a basis in the space $\otimes_{i=1}^N \mathcal{M}_{n_i, m_i}(C)$.

Any linear map $\mathrm{Op} : \mathcal{M}_{n \times m}(C) \to \mathcal{M}_{n \times m}(C)$, called sometimes a superoperator, can be parametrised by the (super)-matrix representation in the considered canonical basis (E_{ij}):

$$\mathrm{Op}(E_{ij}) = \sum_{k,l} \mathrm{Op}_{i,j}^{[k,l]} E_{kl} \ , \tag{6}$$

and therefore for $A \in \mathcal{M}_{n \times m}(C)$:

$$\mathrm{Op}(A)(k, l) = \sum_{i,j} A(i, j) \mathrm{Op}_{i,j}^{[k,l]} \ . \tag{7}$$

For any k-tuple $\sigma = (i_1, \ldots, i_k) \subset \mathbb{I}_N$ we consider the corresponding two-partite partition $\pi^\sigma = (\sigma, \sigma^c)$, where $\sigma^c = \mathbb{I}_N \setminus \{\sigma\}$. For any partition $\pi = (\pi_1, \ldots, \pi_k) \in \mathrm{Par}(\mathbb{I}_N)$ we can define a notion of π-locality in the product $\otimes_{i=1}^N \mathcal{M}_{n_i, m_i}(C)$. A superoperator Op acting in the space $\otimes_{i=1}^N \mathcal{M}_{n_i, m_i}(C)$ is called π-local operation iff there exists a sequence of superoperators Op^{π_i}, each acting in the space $\otimes_{\alpha \in \pi_i} \mathcal{M}_{n_\alpha, m_\alpha}(C)$ and such that

$$\mathrm{Op} = \otimes_{i=1}^k \hat{\mathrm{Op}}^{\pi_i} \ , \tag{8}$$

where $\hat{\mathrm{Op}}^{\pi_i}$ are natural embeddings of Op^{π_i} to the space $\mathrm{End}(\otimes_{i=1}^N \mathcal{M}_{n_i, m_i}(C))$.

Now let us take $\rho \in E(\mathcal{H})$ and let us assume that some π-local operation Op^π is performed on ρ. The question is how to compute the effect of this action on ρ providing only the local information on Op^π is available. For this purpose we perform the following steps:

Step 1. If ρ is represented in the canonical basis $(E_{ij})_{ij}$ of the global space $\mathcal{H}$ then use Proposition (1) and pass to the corresponding representation in the product basis $(E_{\alpha_1\beta_1} \otimes \ldots \otimes E_{\alpha_n\beta_n})$:

$$\rho = \sum_{\substack{\underline{\alpha}=(\alpha_1,\ldots,\alpha_N), \\ \underline{\beta}=(\beta_1,\ldots,\beta_N)}} \tilde{\rho}(\underline{\alpha}|\underline{\beta})E_{\underline{\alpha}\underline{\beta}} \quad \text{where} \quad E_{\underline{\alpha}\underline{\beta}} = \otimes_{i=1}^N E_{\alpha_i\beta_i} \ . \tag{9}$$

Step 2. Let Op^σ be a superoperator acting in the space $\otimes_{i\in\sigma}\mathcal{H}^i$ and let Op^σ stands also for its matrix representation in the product basis $\otimes_{i\in\sigma}E_{k_i,l_i}$. Then:

$$\hat{\text{Op}}^\sigma(\rho)(i,j) = \sum_{k_\sigma,l_\sigma} \text{Op}^\sigma\binom{k_\sigma,l_\sigma}{i_\sigma,j_\sigma} \cdot \tilde{\rho}(k_\sigma \vee l_{\sigma^c}, i_\sigma \vee j_{\sigma^c}) \tag{10}$$

where the multindices $\underline{\alpha}$ and $\underline{\beta}$ are given from Proposition (1) and $(\alpha_\sigma \vee \alpha_{\sigma^c}) = \underline{\alpha}$, $(\beta_\sigma \vee \beta_{\sigma^c}) = \underline{\beta}$ are the corresponding decompositions of them.

Step 3. For a general $\pi = (\pi_1,\ldots,\pi_k)$-local operation $\text{Op}^\pi = \hat{\text{Op}}^{\pi_1} \otimes \ldots \otimes \hat{\text{Op}}^{\pi_k}$ apply reapeditely step 2 above.

Example 3. Let us compute the action of the partial transposes corresponding to the partition $\pi = (\{1,3\},\{2\})$. Let us consider the action of $\hat{T}_2 = \mathbb{I}_{(1)} \otimes T \otimes \mathbb{I}_{(3)}$ on a given tripartite state $\rho \in \mathcal{M}_{n_1\cdot n_2\cdot n_3, m_1\cdot m_2\cdot m_3}(C)$. Owing to the extremely simple action of the operation $\hat{T}_2$ and using the previous computations we have:

$$(\hat{T}_2\rho)(i,j) = \rho(i^\star,j^\star) \tag{11}$$

where

$$\begin{aligned} i^\star &= (\alpha^1 - 1)n_2 \cdot n_3 + (\beta^2 - 1)n_3 + \beta^3 \\ j^\star &= (\beta^1 - 1)m_2 \cdot m_3 + (\alpha^2 - 1)m_3 + \alpha^3 \ . \end{aligned} \tag{12}$$

3 Maximally Entangled Cluster Decomposition of Quantum States

Let Θ be N-partite quantum system as in previous section. For a given $\rho \in E(\mathcal{H})$ and $\pi = (\pi_1,\ldots,\pi_k) \in \text{Par}(\mathbb{I}_N)$ we will say that ρ is π-separable iff

(i) there exists a decomposition

$$\rho = \sum_\alpha \bar{p}_\alpha \bigotimes_{i=1:k} \hat{\rho}^\alpha_{\pi_i} \ ; \quad \hat{\rho}^\alpha_{\pi_i} \in \text{Ent}(\mathcal{H}_{\pi_i}) \ , \tag{13}$$

where $\text{Ent}(\mathcal{H}_{\pi_i})$ is the space of maximally entangled states on $\mathcal{H}_{\pi_i}$, providing $|\pi_i| > 1$, and for $|\pi_i| = 1$ case $\text{Ent}(\mathcal{H}_{\pi_i}) = E(\mathcal{H}_i)$,

(ii) π is finest partition of $\mathbb{I}_N$ for which (13) holds.

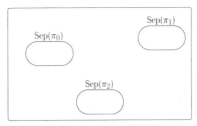

Fig. 1. The decomposition $E(\mathcal{H}) = \bigcup_{\pi \in Par(\mathbb{I}_N)} \mathrm{Sep}\ (\pi)$

In particular: a state $\rho \in E(\mathcal{H})$ is maximally separable (separable for shorthand) iff it is π_{MIN}-separable a state $\rho \in E(\mathcal{H})$ is maximally entangled iff ρ is π_{MAX}-separable. A dual notion is that of π-entanglement. A state $\rho \in E(\mathcal{H})$ is π-entangled iff ρ is π-separable. Let us denote by $\mathrm{S\mathring{e}p}(\pi)$ the set of all π-separable states in $E(\mathcal{H})$. Then $E(\mathcal{H}) = \bigcup_{\pi \in Par(\mathbb{I}_N)} \mathrm{S\mathring{e}p}(\pi)$, $\mathrm{S\mathring{e}p}(\pi) \cap \mathrm{S\mathring{e}p}(\pi') = \emptyset$ for $\pi \neq \pi'$ each component $\mathrm{S\mathring{e}p}(\pi)$ is convex.

After taking the closure of $\mathrm{S\mathring{e}p}(\pi)$ the arising set $\mathrm{Sep}(\pi)$ of π-separable states is compact, convex subset of $E(\mathcal{H})$, topologically equivalent to the product space $\otimes_{i=1:|\pi|} E(\mathcal{H}_{\pi_i})$.

Proposition 2. *Let $\mathcal{H} = \mathcal{H}_1 \otimes \dots \mathcal{H}_N$ and let $\rho \in E(\mathcal{H})$. Then there exists an unique $\pi \in Par(\mathbb{I}_N)$ such that ρ is π-separable.*

A constructive approach to the explicit localisation of the corresponding $\pi = (\pi_1, \dots, \pi_k) \in Par(\mathbb{I}_N)$ for a given $\rho \in E(\mathcal{H})$ is given by dividing the set $\mathbb{I}_N$ into two disjoint pieces and then applying the appropriate 2-partite methods. However there are two main difficulties in order to determine π in a computationally feasible way. As is well known in general the problem of determining whether a given two-partite state ρ is entangled or separable is NP-hard problem and although an exhaustive routine based on semi-definite programming methods is known [16,17,18] and their computer implementations are available [19] the estimation how much of the computer resources (time mainly) it take for a particular ρ may be hardly available and often leads to untreatable situation. The second of the mentioned difficulty is the question how to perform the analytical division of a given state $\rho \in E(\mathcal{H})$ into portions belonging to the corresponding partitions $\pi = (\pi_1, \pi_2) \in Par(\mathbb{I}_N)$. And this is the point where our result help.

The following algorithm describes a systematic process of finding partition $\pi = (\pi_1, \dots, \pi_k)$ for which an analysed state $\rho \in E(\mathcal{H})$ is π-separable. The notations used in the formulated Algorithm (Fig. 2) below is the following:

- 2p-Oracle function: It is assumed that an oracle for determining whether a given state ρ of any bipartite system is entangled or separable is given. As we have mentioned above, in principle, although the problem is NP-hard there do exists such oracles, the methods of semi-definite programming are example of such an oracle. Such an oracle is assumed to be for our disposal and is denoted as 2p-Oracle(ρ,σ,σ^c) with values TRUE if the bipartite system obtained by partitioning into (σ, σ^c) is in entangled state ρ and NO if the two-subsystems, indexed by σ and σ^c are in the separable state ρ.

- Systematically generating two-partitions list functions:
  - first_part – function generating first two-partite division of the system considered and then analysed by 2p-Oracle,
  - get_next_part – function generating next two-partite division depending on output given by 2p-Oracle.
- Final output is given by partition π giving the maximally-entangled cluster decomposition of the state ρ and successively constructed in DetMinClusterEnt partitions.

Several separability criteria known in the bipartite case can be generalised to cover the multipartite systems case as well. However none of them, as in the bipartite case is of definite character, at least from the computational point of view. As an example we mention here a generalised t-positivity criterion.

Let $\rho \in E(\mathcal{H})$ be a $\pi = (\pi_1, \ldots, \pi_k)$ separable state. Then, for any partial transposition $T_{\pi'}; \pi' = (\pi'_1, \ldots, \pi'_l)$ is any partition of $\mathbb{I}_N$ such that $\pi \prec \pi'$, $T_{\pi'}(\rho) \geq 0$ and $T_{\pi'}$ is of the from $\mathbb{I}_{N \setminus \pi'_\alpha} \otimes T_{\pi'_\alpha}$.

Thus any considered partial transposition $T_{\pi'}$ has the form of π-local operation. But in real application it is rather very tedious process to compute effectively the action of any of $T_{\pi'}$ on a particular ρ until the method described in the previous section has been introduced.

Example 4. Let us consider the case of tri-partite system and let $\rho \in E(\mathcal{H}_1 \otimes \mathcal{H}_2 \otimes \mathcal{H}_3)$ be given. Then the possible two element partitions of $\mathbb{I}_3$ are given as 2-Par$(\mathbb{I}_3) = \{(\{1\}, \{2, 3\}), (\{2\}, \{1, 3\}), (\{3\}, \{1, 2\})\}$. Providing ρ is completely

```
input  :  L : ∅ and Q : H = H₁ ⊗ H₂ ⊗ ... ⊗ Hₙ, n = k₁ · k₂ · ... kₙ,
          ρ ∈ E(H₁ ⊗ H₂ ⊗ ... ⊗ Hₙ) where kᵢ = dim Hᵢ, Hᵢ ≅ C^{kᵢ}
output:  L : π ∈ Par(𝕀ₙ) such that ρ is π-separable

DetMinClusterEnt( L, Q )
    s := number of qudits encoded in Q
    if (s > 1)
        first_part(e, {1, 2, 3, ..., s})
        while gen_next_part(e, {1, 2, 3, ..., s}) do
            if( 2p-Oracle( Q, e_{e₀}, e_{e₁} ) = NO )
                DetMinClusterEnt( e_{e₀}, Q_{e_{e₀}} )
                DetMinClusterEnt( e_{e₁}, Q_{e_{e₁}} )
                break while
            else
                if (¬∃ b₀, b₁ ∈ L that (e_{e₀} ⊂ b₀ ∧ e_{e₁} ⊂ b₁))
                    L := L ∪ {n, e_{e₀}, e_{e₁}}
                else
                    remove b₀ and b₁ from L
                    L := L ∪ {n, e_{e₀}, e_{e₁}}
                end if
            end if
        end while
    end if
    return L
```

Fig. 2. Separable or Entangled? General n-partite states

separable the action of all possible partial transpositions: $T_1 \otimes \mathbb{I}_{2,3}$, $\mathbb{I}_1 \otimes T_{2,3}$, $T_2 \otimes \mathbb{I}_{1,3}$, $T_{1,3} \otimes \mathbb{I}_2$, $T_3 \otimes \mathbb{I}_{1,2}$, $T_{1,2} \otimes \mathbb{I}_3$ with self explained notation, should preserve the positivity of ρ as any breaking of positivity will be the signal that ρ is partially entangled state. Using the method of previous section it is easy matter then to calculate the listed partial transposition like $\mathbb{I} \otimes T_{2,3}(\rho)$ and others. However it is only the necessity type criterion as there exists a plenty of entangled states which pass all the listed positivity preservation tests.

Remark 1. In fact any positive but not completely positive maps can be taken instead of transposition map. A multipartite version of the corresponding bipartite case results of Horodecki's type [20,21] can be proved as well.

4   Some Numerical Experiments with QCS System

The use of the algorithm depicted on Fig. 2 can be demonstrated by the problem of tracing evolution of entanglement when executing a quantum algorithm. Because of limitation of technology, it can be realised nowadays only by using a software simulator of quantum computation models. The Zielona Góra team created recently package called QCS [14] which is one of widely available simulators of quantum computations models, additionally by the use of Python language it is easy to build suitable and rich variety of tools to perform several numerical (and symbolic) experiments.

The possibility of detection and tracing of entanglement will be demonstrated by using simulation of unitary gate in the one-way quantum computation model (termed as 1WQC). The 1WQC is a model of quantum computation, in which measurements play a key role. The one-way quantum computation model was introduced in [22] and extensively discussed in [23], the contribution [9] contains review of the basic features of 1WQC.

Firstly, we recall the Pauli operators (I, X, Y, Z) and the Hadamard gate denoted by H:

$$I = \begin{pmatrix} 1 & 0 \\ 0 & 1 \end{pmatrix}, \ X = \begin{pmatrix} 0 & 1 \\ 1 & 0 \end{pmatrix}, \ Y = \begin{pmatrix} 0 & -i \\ i & 0 \end{pmatrix}, \ Z = \begin{pmatrix} 1 & 0 \\ 0 & -1 \end{pmatrix}, \ H = \frac{1}{\sqrt{2}} \begin{pmatrix} 1 & 1 \\ 1 & -1 \end{pmatrix}. \tag{14}$$

We use the Pauli operators as gates in simulations of 1WQC to correct errors which can appear in the measurement process of qubits in a cluster.

In 1WQC we mainly use a measurement procedure in several different bases (including the standard base). Most often used in 1WQC is basis:

$$B(\varphi) = \left\{ \frac{|0\rangle + e^{i\varphi}|1\rangle}{\sqrt{2}}, \frac{|0\rangle - e^{i\varphi}|1\rangle}{\sqrt{2}} \right\}. \tag{15}$$

We note that for $\theta = 0$ the basis (15) corresponds to the standard X basis.

The important ingredient of 1WQCS is the controlled phase gate (CPhase gate or short CZ) which introduces to a given system entanglement between two qubits. It is the 4×4 unitary transformation which flips the phase of the second

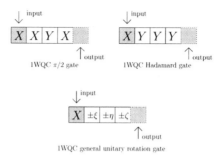

Fig. 3. Examples of measurement patterns for an unitary one qubit gates: Hadamard and $\pi/2$ phase gate. The pattern for general rotation gate is specified by the Euler angles ξ, η, ζ.

qubit if the first qubit is in state $|1\rangle$ and does nothing if the first qubit is in $|0\rangle$. The CZ gate is given in the matrix form as

$$
\text{CPhase} = \begin{pmatrix} 1 & 0 & 0 & 0 \\ 0 & 1 & 0 & 0 \\ 0 & 0 & -1 & 0 \\ 0 & 0 & 0 & -1 \end{pmatrix}. \tag{16}
$$

Simulation of the action of an one-qubit unitary gate is realised by the application of several measurements in different bases. Three most basic examples has been presented at Fig. 3. Naturally, quantum register in this case is represented by the vector state instead of density matrix.

Implementation of the simulation of 1WQC and tracing the evolution of entanglement requires the creation of an appropriate Python script for the mentioned QCS package. Figure 4 shows most important snippet of script which performs whole experiment. The function responsible for the detection of entanglement is called det_ent_by_par. Because this function is executed after each step in the process of simulation then the size of area which contains entanglement can be easily detected.

Basis steps of script code depicted in Fig. 4 can be summarised as follows ($\mathcal{M}$ represents the measurement process in base (15)):

1. set parameters for simulation of Hadamard gate, $a = \pi/2$, $b = \pi/2$, $c = \pi/2$, prepare the computation cluster Q (five qubits), result of detection of entanglement cluster – $[q_0, q_1, q_2, q_3, q_4]$ – all qubits are entangled,
2. perform the measurement (in standard base) $s_1 = \mathcal{M}^{\mathcal{B}(0)}(q_0)$, result of detection of entanglement cluster – $[q_1, q_2, q_3, q_4]$,
3. perform the measurement $s_2 = \mathcal{M}^{\mathcal{B}(-a \cdot (-1)^{s_1})}(q_1)$, result of detection routine – $[q_2, q_3, q_4]$,
4. perform the measurement $s_3 = \mathcal{M}^{\mathcal{B}(-b \cdot (-1)^{s_2})}(q_2)$, result of detection routine – $[q_3, q_4]$,

q = qcs.QuantumReg(5) q.Reset() q.HadN(0) q.RotThetaN(0, 0.3) q.HadN(1) ; q.HadN(2) q.HadN(3) ; q.HadN(4) q.CPhaseF(0, 1) ; q.CPhaseF(1, 2) q.CPhaseF(2, 3) ; q.CPhaseF(3, 4) pp0 = det_ent_by_par(q) a = b = c = math.pi / 2	s1 = q.MeasureOneQubitInBBase(0, 0) pp1 = det_ent_by_par(q) a = -a * math.pow(-1, s1) s2 = q.MeasureOneQubitInBBase(1, a) pp2 = det_ent_by_par(q) b = -b * math.pow(-1, s2) s3 = q.MeasureOneQubitInBBase(2, b) pp3 = det_ent_by_par(q) c = -c * math.pow(-1, s1+s3) s4 = q.MeasureOneQubitInBBase(3, c) pp4 = det_ent_by_par(q)

Fig. 4. Script in Python language for detection of entanglement (routine det_ent_by_par) during the simulation of 1WQC realised with application of Hadamard gate

5. perform the measurement $s_4 = \mathcal{M}^{\mathcal{B}(-c \cdot (-1)^{s_3})}(q_3)$, result of detection routine – [ ] – register is in the fully separable state,
6. qubit q_4 has state after application the Hadamard gate.

5   Summary

Quantum states describing multi-partite systems are given conventionally in the standard basis of the global space of states. Such representation makes the analysis of the local operations influence on the global state rather hardly to be computable. The resolution of this computational difficulty is to pass to the corresponding multiplicative basis as we have demonstrated in this contribution. Working in such representations the action of local operations is then easy computable. In particular these method has been applied to construct maximally-entangled cluster decompositions of general quantum state. As an example of possible, future applications of the computations presented here some, interesting computer experiment has been presented showing the evolution of the corresponding maximally-entangled cluster decomposition in the course of certain quantum computations.

References

1. Einstein, A., Podolsky, B., Rosen, N.: Can Quantum-Mechanical Description of Physical Reality Be Considered Complete? Phys. Rev. 47, 777 (1935)
2. Schrodinger, E.: Die gegenwärtige Situation der Quantenmechanik. Naturwissenschaften 23, 807 (1935)

3. Nielsen, M.A., Chuang, I.L.: Quantum Computation and Quantum Information. Cambridge University Press, Cambridge (2000)
4. Bengtsson, I., Życzkowski, K.: Geometry of Quantum States: An Introduction to Quantum Entanglement. Cambridge University Press, Cambridge (2006)
5. Horodecki, R., Horodecki, P., Horodecki, M., Horodecki, K.: Quantum Entanglement. Rev. Mod. Phys., 81, 865, (2009), available also at arXiv:quant-ph:/0702225
6. Gühne, O., Tóth, G.: Entanglement detection (2008), arXiv:quant-ph:/0811280
7. Gühne, O., Seevinck, M.: Separability criteria for genuine multiparticle entanglement, arXiv:quant-ph/0905.1349v3
8. Huber, M., Mintert, F., Gabriel, A., Hiesmayr, B.C.: Detection of high-dimensional genuine multi-parite entanglement of mixed states, arXiv:quant-ph/0912.1870v1
9. Campbell, E.T., Fitzsimons, J.: An introduction to one-way quantum computing in distributed architectures. International Journal of Quantum Information 8(1-2), 219–258 (2010), arXiv:0906.2725
10. Kitaev, A.: Fault tolerant quantum computation by anyons. Ann.Phys. 303(1), 2–30 (2004)
11. Ling, A., Peloso, M.P., Marcikic, I., Scarani, V., Lamas-Linares, A., Kurtsiefer, C.: Experimental quantum key distribution based on a Bell test. Phys.Rev.A 78, 020301R (2008)
12. Scarani, V., Bechmann-Pasquinucci, H., Cerf, N.J., Dušek, M., Lütkenhaus, M., Peev, M.: The security of practical quantum key distribution. Rev. Mod. Phys. 81, 1301 (2009)
13. Sawerwain, M., Gielerak, R.: Natural quantum operational semantics with predicates. Int. J. Appl. Math. Comput. Sci. 18(3), 341–359 (2008)
14. Sawerwain, M., Gielerak, R.: Quantum computing simulator – an extendable library to perform quantum computation calculations. In: Preparation for Computer Physics Communications
15. Gielerak, R., Sawerwain, M.: Algorithm for detection of maximally entangled cluster decomposition (in preparation)
16. Doherty, A.C., Parrilo, P.A., Spedalieri, F.M.: Distinguishing Separable and Entangled States. Phys. Rev. Lett. 88, 187904 (2002)
17. Doherty, A.C., Parrilo, P.A., Spedalieri, F.M.: Complete family of separability criteria. Phys. Rev. A 69, 022308 (2004)
18. Navascues, M., Owari, M., Plenio, M.B.: Power of symmetric extensions for entanglement detection. Phys. Rev. A 80, 052306 (2009)
19. Sturm, J.F.: SeDuMi a MATLAB toolbox for optimization over symmetric cones, http://sedumi.mcmaster.ca
20. Peres, A.: Separability Criterion for Density Matrices. Phys. Rev. Lett. 77, 1413–1415 (1996)
21. Horodecki, M., Horodecki, P., Horodecki, R.: Separability of Mixed States: Necessary and Sufficient Conditions. Physics Letters A 223, 1–8 (1996)
22. Raussendorf, R., Briegel, H.J.: A one-way quantum computer. Phys. Rev. Lett. 86, 5188–5191 (2001), arXiv:quant-ph/0010033
23. Raussendorf, R., Browne, D.E., Briegel, H.J.: Measurement-based quantum computation with cluster states. Phys. Rev. A 68, 022312 (2003), arXiv:quant-ph/0301052

Quantum Information Transfer Protocols: A Model and Its Numerical Simulations

Marek Sawerwain and Roman Gielerak

Institute of Control & Computation Engineering,
University of Zielona Góra, ul. Podgórna 50, Zielona Góra 65-246, Poland
{M.Sawerwain,R.Gielerak}@issi.uz.zgora.pl

Abstract. A general concept of quantum communication networks and some fundamental properties of them are discussed. In particular case of unitary dynamics based protocols some general results were formulated. A particular case of transferring pure states in spin chains, due to XY-like unitary dynamics, has been numerically explored within the ZG QCS simulator environment and some basic features of this transferring quantum data protocols has been confirmed through an explicit computations.

Keywords: quantum information transfer, quantum spin networks, quantum circuits, numerical simulations.

1 Introduction

One of the main challenges of a recently emerged branch of quantum information processing technology is to develop an effective tools for quantum data transfers between spacely separated systems. This challenge is widely known as quantum communication technology. Several exciting developments like the teleportation based transfers of quantum data performed on the hard physical ground [1] not only mathematically, suggests the appearance of new quantum era in communication technologies. Another prominent achievement of quantum communication technology is the practical realisation of the absolute secure cryptography, known as Quantum Key Distribution [2,3,4].

In recent years several scenarios for transferring quantum data in space have been proposed and discussed [5]. The transfer of quantum data by the use of quantum dynamics and realised practically through the interacting spin systems is one of the most often discussed possibility.

It is the main aim of this contribution to study numerically the opportunity of pure quantum state transfer in linear chain of $\frac{1}{2}$-spins interacting by XY Hamiltonian. Certain capabilities, of the recently constructed computer environment for simulating several quantum computation tasks, tool which is called Quantum Computing System, has been used for this purpose and details of our simulations are presented in Sect. 4.

However, before we pass to these very particular models and results, a general perspective of the quantum networks notion will be presented in the next section. Also the so-called unitary dynamics based, transfer of states protocols are

A. Kwiecień, P. Gaj, and P. Stera (Eds.): CN 2011, CCIS 160, pp. 11–18, 2011.

formulated in full generality and some very interesting mathematical problems are pointed out there.

2   Quantum Data Transferring Networks: General Outlook

By a quantum network QN we mean structure consisting of dynamical family of quantum nodes $\mathcal{N}_i$, by which we mean a dynamical quantum systems Θ_i, the appropriate Hilbert spaces of which shall be denoted by $\mathcal{H}_i$ and the corresponding sets of quantum states denoted as $E(\mathcal{H}_i)$. Then the space $\mathcal{H} = \mathcal{H}_1 \otimes \ldots \mathcal{H}_N$ will be called the space of global states of the network QN. The quantum nodes are assumed to be separated in the space and one can associate certain dynamical graph G structure representing theirs space location and several communication channels in between individual nodes and between groups of them are also present. The network channels might be of quantum and of classical nature as well. The ensemble of all network channels will be denoted as $CH(QN)$.

The important feature of quantum network is the presence of certain local interactions of quantum nature. More precisely we can imagine that in every quantum node $\mathcal{N}_i$ a certain set of quantum operations (i.e. linear of class CP-operations) on local states can be performed. These classes of operations will be called one-node quantum operations. Additionally, we shall assume that for certain k-tuples of nodes $\mathcal{H}_i$ a joint quantum operations (that will be called local k-tuples interactions) are at a disposal of network user.

For example, if for any pair of nodes $(\mathcal{N}_i, \mathcal{N}_j)$ a certain set of interactions is given i.e. sets of allowed operations on the spaces $E(\mathcal{H}_i \otimes \mathcal{H}_j)$ is given then these operations are called bi-local operations and if only such operations are existing then the network will be called bi-local quantum network. In general, a maximal value of k for which the interactions exists will be called the degree of locality of the considered network.

The important classes of quantum networks will be defined now.

Definition 1. *A quantum network QN is called a completely entangling system iff for any completely separable initial state $\rho_{\mathrm{in}} \in E(\mathcal{H})$ there exists a protocol $\mathcal{P}$ such that $\mathcal{P}(\rho_{\mathrm{in}})$ become maximally entangled state.*

Remark 1. By a protocol $\mathcal{P}$ we mean a sequence of operations on the initial state ρ_{in} that use only the resources of QN. If only local operations are performed then the protocol $\mathcal{P}$ will be called local protocol.

Definition 2. *A quantum network QN is completely and perfectly communicating iff for any initial k-partite state ρ_{in} there exists a protocol $\mathcal{P}$ that maps the local state ρ_{in} into any of other k-element set of nodes state $\rho' = \mathcal{P}(\rho_{\mathrm{in}})$ and such that ρ' is mathematically the same state as ρ_{in}.*

A more details of these very condensed notion will be explained in the examples below.

3   Unitary Dynamics Protocols. Some Generalities

Let $(U_t)_{t\in\mathbb{R}}$ be an unitary dynamics acting on the global space $\mathcal{H}_1 \otimes \ldots \otimes \mathcal{H}_N$. From the Stone's theorem it follows that there exists an unique, self-adjoint operator H such that $U_t = \exp(itH)$. The operator H, called the total Hamiltonian operator is assumed to poses a local structure expressed by the following decomposition

$$H = \sum_{I \subset \{1,2,\ldots,N\}} H_I \tag{1}$$

where the self-adjoint H_I are acting on the local spaces $\mathcal{H}_I = \otimes_{i \in I} \mathcal{H}_i$. A number $d = \max\{|I| : H_I \neq 0\}$ is called the degree of locality of the dynamics U_t. In particular case $d = 2$ the corresponding dynamics is called bi-local dynamics.

A given (local) dynamics U_t is called entangling dynamics iff for any $\rho_{\text{in}} \in \text{Sep}(\pi_{\min})$, the set $\{t \in R : U_t(\rho_{\text{in}}) \in \text{Ent}(\pi) \text{ for some } \pi \neq \pi_{\min}\}$ is nonempty.

Using the computational methods presented in [6], several examples of the evolution of the maximally-entangled cluster decomposition of the states $U_t(\rho_{\text{in}})$ arising will be presented elsewhere. In Sect. 4 a numerical example based on the explicitly solvable quantum spin chain dynamics will be presented in details.

Proposition 1. *Let (U_t) be a bi-local unitary dynamics and such that for any pair of vertices (i,j) there exists a path on which the corresponding bi-local Hamiltonians are entangling. Then the dynamics (U_t) is entangling one.*

A given unitary dynamics (U_t) is called perfectly and completely transferring states iff preparing state $\rho_{\text{in}} \in E(\mathcal{H}_i)$ locally the unitary evolution U_t drives it after some time to the state $\rho_{\text{fin}} \in E(\mathcal{H}_j)$, $\rho_{\text{fin}} = \rho_{\text{in}}$ and for any $j \neq i$.

A formal definition is the following one. There exists $\rho_0 \in E(\mathcal{H})$ such that $\text{tr}_{\{i\}^c}(\rho_0) = \rho_{\text{in}}$ and for which $\{t \in R : U_t(\rho_0) = \rho_f \in E(\mathcal{H}) \wedge \text{tr}_{\{j\}^c}(\rho_f) = \rho_{\text{in}}\} \neq \emptyset$ and this holds for any $\rho_{\text{in}} \in E(\mathcal{H}_i)$.

If the possibility of perfect transfer is valid only for some subset of states (i.e. the set of pure states) then the corresponding dynamics is called partially transferring states.

Let Fid be a version of fidelity measure [7,8] which enables us to compare in a quantitative way the similarity in between two quantum states ρ and ρ'. It may happen that in particular situation only the transfer with some predefined fidelity precision is demanded or reachable.

An unitary dynamics (U_t) is called approximate (with Fidelity $\text{Fid} \in [1-\epsilon, 1]$) and (partially) complete transferring quantum data iff for any pair (i,j) of nodes, any $\rho_{\text{in}} \in E(\mathcal{H}_i)$ the state ρ_{in} is transmitted by U_t to the node $\{j\}$ but only with $\text{Fid}\{\rho_{\text{in}}, \rho_{\text{tr}}\} \geq 1 - \epsilon$.

The interesting question is to describe the transfer quantum data properties of a given local dynamics $(U_t)_t$ in terms of the local Hamiltonians H_I arising in the decomposition (1). The following preliminary remarks might be helpfully for this.

Observation 1. *Let $\rho_i \in E(\mathcal{H}_i)$. Then we define the probability envelope of ρ_i as $\mathcal{L}(\rho_i) = \{\rho \in E(\mathcal{H}) : \mathrm{tr}_{\{i\}^c}(\rho) = \rho_i\}$. Then, for any $\rho_i \in E(\mathcal{H}_i)$, $\mathcal{L}(\rho_i)$ is a closed, convex subset of $E(\mathcal{H})$. Moreover, for $\rho_i \neq \rho_i' : \mathcal{L}(\rho_i) \cap \mathcal{L}(\rho_i') = \emptyset$ and $\bigcup_{\rho_i \in E(\mathcal{H}_i)} \mathcal{L}(\rho_i) = E(\mathcal{H})$.*

Now, providing the underlying network structure is homogeneous the corresponding spaces $E(\mathcal{H}_i)$ and their stratifications Fig. (1) by envelopes are identical. Thus, we can see that the transfer quantum data properties are connected to certain ergodic type behaviour of U_t acting on $E(\mathcal{H})$.

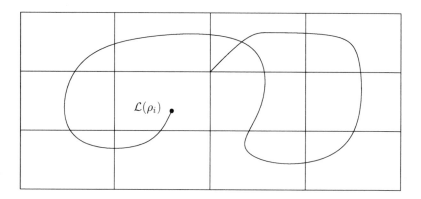

Fig. 1. Stratification of $E(\mathcal{H})$ by envelopes indexed by $\mathcal{L}(\rho), \rho \in \mathcal{H}_i$

Proposition 2. *Let the network be homogeneous and let $(U_t)_t$ be an unitary dynamics. The dynamics is perfectly and completely transferring quantum data iff starting from any $\rho_{\mathrm{in}} \in \mathcal{L}(\rho_0)$ after some time it returns to the same stratum $\mathcal{L}(\rho_0)$.*

4   Numerical Simulations

Transfer process of quantum state is possible to realise through computer simulations on a classical machines, however only for small quantum systems because of exponential size of data which are necessary to deal properly with quantum states.

In our example an unknown pure state of qubit will be transferred

$$|\psi\rangle = \alpha|0\rangle + \beta|1\rangle \quad \text{and} \quad |\alpha|^2 + |\beta|^2 = 1, \text{ where } \alpha, \beta \in \mathbb{C} \ . \tag{2}$$

Generally the transfer process (or transfer protocol) in one-dimensional chain of n qubit can be regarded as the following transformation of the state $|\Psi_{\mathrm{in}}\rangle$ into the state $|\Psi_{\mathrm{out}}\rangle$

$$|\Psi_{\mathrm{in}}\rangle = |\psi\rangle|\underbrace{000\ldots0}_{n-1}\rangle \implies |\Psi_{\mathrm{out}}\rangle = |\underbrace{000\ldots0}_{n-1}\rangle|\psi\rangle \ . \tag{3}$$

There exists a wide group of operations which can realise such task. A basic methods of realising of transfer described by Equation (3) is the quantum circuit method (others description of transfer process as operational semantics or control flow graphs are also possible [9,10]). Figure 2 depicts appropriate quantum circuit where the transfer process is realised by the set of SWAP gates and by the use of special unitary operation (in the further part of this contribution will be called as transfer operation) build from appropriate an hamiltonian which will be defined below.

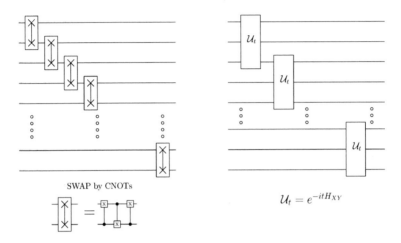

Fig. 2. Realisation of transfer of single unknown qubit state by quantum circuit using a set of SWAP gates or multiqubit $\mathcal{U}(t)$ transfers gates

The definition of XY Hamiltonian which is able to realise transfer operation was first given in the work [11]:

$$H_{XY} = \frac{1}{2} \sum_{(i,i+1)\in\mathcal{L}(G)} \left[\sigma_i^x \sigma_{i+1}^x + \sigma_i^y \sigma_{i+1}^y\right] \,, \qquad (4)$$

where σ_i^x or σ_i^y denotes Pauli's gate applied to i-th qubit.

It must be stressed that perfect transfer with fidelity equal to one with H_{XY} Hamiltonian is possible only for chains built from two or three qubit. The solution of this problem was shown in the contribution [12] where into definition of Hamiltonian H_{XY} additionally some coupling J_n was introduced. The J_n coupling constant is responsible for proper modulation of couplings between two neighbour qubits in chain

$$H_{XY} = \frac{J_i}{2} \sum_{(i,i+1)\in\mathcal{L}(G)} \left[\sigma_i^x \sigma_{i+1}^x + \sigma_i^y \sigma_{i+1}^y\right], \quad \text{where} \quad J_i = \frac{\lambda}{2}\sqrt{i(N-i)} \qquad (5)$$

The transfer process also changes the local phase, however the proper value of local phase can be restored by the use of unitary rotation. In simple cases the Pauli's operators are enough to restore local phase.

The simulation of transfer process with the QCS package will be realised by the use of the following unitary operator, for time $t \in \langle 0, \pi/2 \rangle$:

$$\mathcal{U}(t) = e^{-itH} \qquad (6)$$

where H represents one of the defined Hamiltonians in equations (4) and (5).

The state of our system built from four qubits under the transfer process has the following form

$$|\Psi\rangle = \alpha_0|0000\rangle + \alpha_1|1000\rangle + \alpha_2|0100\rangle + \alpha_3|0010\rangle + \alpha_4|0001\rangle, \alpha_i \in \mathbb{C} , \qquad (7)$$

which means that entanglement is present. Numerical simulation allows on the estimate of amount of entanglement (e.g. by using the CCNR criteria) contained.

The main elements of the corresponding Python script which are responsible for the simulation are as follows

```
q = qcs.QuantumReg( N )
q.Reset() ; q.HadN(0) ; q.RotThetaN(0, 0.6)

u = qcs.CreateXYPerfectSpinTransferUnitrayOp( N, (math.pi / 2) / P )
step = (math.pi / 2) / P

for i in range(1,P+1,1):
    // other operations e.g. CCNR test
    t=t+step ; q.MatrixApply( u )
```

The evolution of transfer protocol has been divided into P steps. After or before execution of one step, it is possible to execute additional task e.g. test for the presence of entanglement [13]. Figure (3) shows results of level of entanglement obtained by the use of CCNR criteria. Despite the different length of chain it is easy to observe that the level of entanglement is similar. Characteristic feature which can be observed is also the fact that at time equal to $\pi/2$ the level of entanglement is nearly the same. It is consequence of fact that transferred information is evenly distributed in the quantum register.

Another interesting experiment which can be realised with QCS package is introduction of a noise in the process of simulation of the evolution of Hamiltonian (5). The noise is modelled by the following equation

$$E_0(\rho) = \sqrt{1-p} \left(\bigotimes^n I \right), \quad E_1 = \sqrt{p} \left(\bigotimes^n \sigma_z \right) , \qquad (8)$$

in the literature it is often called as the fully correlated change of phase, where $P \in \langle 0, 1 \rangle$. Figure 4 shows of the result of experiment. Similar to the last example the evolution was divided into sixteen steps. The figure shows the trace distance

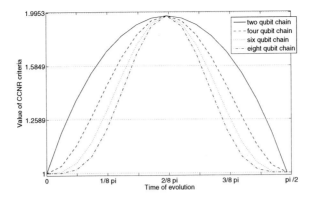

Fig. 3. Level of entanglement (calculated by the use of CCNR criteria) during the simulation of $\mathcal{U}(t)$ for $t \in \langle 0, \pi/2 \rangle$ for chains built from 2, 4, 6 and 8 qubit. The process of simulation of Hamiltonian evolution has been divided into sixteen discrete steps.

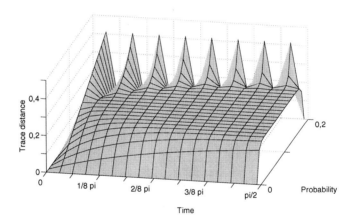

Fig. 4. Influence of noise modelled as fully correlated change of phase in the transfer protocol for the chain build with four qubits, the state of transferred qubit is approximately equal to $|\psi\rangle = 0.18|0\rangle + 0.98|1\rangle$

between states at transfer process with the presence of a noise and without presence of a noise. Even for small value of P the noise called as fully correlated change of phase introduces significant modification of state, however for $P = 1$, there are cases where the influence of noise is diminished.

5   Conclusions

There are many very important and mainly open questions of different nature behind the notion of a general quantum networks. The role of producing entanglement in the transferring quantum data protocols is one of the open problems which seems to be of principal value here. It is mainly because of exact solvability of the spin-$\frac{1}{2}$ XY 1D dynamics that some analytical results were obtained that have been confirmed by our computer experiments. However it seems to be a very interesting problem to perform such computer simulations in the case of higher spins or/and higher dimensional lattices as in these situations the corresponding analytical results are not known.

References

1. Tanaka, Y., Asano, M., Ohya, M.: Physical realization of quantum teleportation for a nonmaximal entangled state. Phys. Rev. A 82, 022308 (2010)
2. Hiskett, P.A., Rosenberg, D., Peterson, C.G., Hughes, R.J., Nam, S., Lita, A.E., Miller, A.J., Nordholt, J.E.: Long-distance quantum key distribution in optical fibre. New J. Phys. 8(193) (2006)
3. Bennett, C.H., Brassard, G.: Quantum Cryptography: Public Key Distribution and Coin Tossing. In: Proceedings of IEEE International Conference on Computers Systems and Signal Processing, Bangalore, India, pp. 175–179 (December 1984)
4. Ekert, A.K.: Quantum cryptography based on Bell's theorem. Phys. Rev. Lett. 67(6), 661 (1991)
5. Bose, S.: Quantum Communication Through Spin Chain Dynamics: An Introductory Overview. Contemporary Physics 48(1), 13–30 (2007), arXiv:0802.1224v1
6. Gielerak, R., Sawerwain, M.: π-local Operations in Composite Quantum Systems with Applications to Multipartite Entanglement. In: Kwiecień, A., Gaj, P., Stera, P. (eds.) 18th Conference on Computer Networks, CN 2011, Ustroń, Poland. CCIS, vol. 160. Springer, Heidelberg (2011)
7. Nielsen, M.A., Chuang, I.L.: Quantum computation and quantum information. Cambridge University Press, New York (2000)
8. Bengtsson, I., Życzkowski, K.: Geometry of Quantum States: An Introduction to Quantum Entanglement. Cambridge University Press, Cambridge (2006)
9. Gold, R.: Control flow graphs and code coverage. Int. J. Appl. Math. Comput. Sci. 20(4), 739–749 (2010)
10. Sawerwain, M., Gielerak, R.: Natural quantum operational semantics with predicates. Int. J. Appl. Math. Comput. Sci. 18(3), 341–359 (2008)
11. Bose, S.: Quantum Communication through an Unmodulated Spin Chain. Phys. Rev. Lett. 91, 207901 (2003)
12. Christandl, M., Datta, N., Ekert, A., Landahl, A.J.: Perfect state transfer in quantum spin networks. Phys. Rev. Lett. 92(18), 187902 (2004), arXiv:quant-ph/0309131v2
13. Latorre, J.I., Riera, A.: A short review on entanglement in quantum spin systems. Journal of Physics A: Mathematical and Theoretical 42(50), 504002 (2009), arXiv:0906.1499

An Impact of the Nanoscale Network-on-Chip Topology on the Transmission Delay

Remigiusz Olejnik

West Pomeranian University of Technology, Szczecin
Faculty of Computer Science and Information Systems
ul. Żołnierska 49, 71-210 Szczecin, Poland
r.olejnik@ieee.org

Abstract. The article presents simulation results of the topology impact on the transmission delay in Network-on-Chip models. Four topologies have been simulated and compared – ring, star, mesh and torus. It has been proven that transmission delay depends on the network topology – the lowest value was obtained for torus topology while ring topology is the worst. Moreover topologies have been compared using mean distance between the nodes as a routing metric.

Keywords: network topology, Network-on-Chip, delay analysis.

1 Introduction

Nanoscale networking is a new and still developing interdisciplinary field which consists of molecular networks, carbo nanotube-based networks, nanoscale quantum networking and network-on-chip techniques [1]. Network-on-chip is one of the techniques used in digital circuits design for a communication purpose. It is proven to be more efficient than traditonal bus concept [2]. The article describes simulation experiments which show an impact of network-on-chip topology on the overall delay in the process of data transmission between the processing cores. Four different topologies have been compared using transmission delay values and mean distance between the nodes.

2 Nanoscale Networks-on-Chip

Network-on-Chip (NoC) approach is generally used in applications with intense internal communication between processing cores. Communication is provided by point-to-point connections utilizing switches to send signals (data) from source to destination module (node/core) using intermediate modules (nodes/cores) similar to mesh networks behaviour. NoCs are similar to modern telecommunication networks – many mechanisms known in computer networks world are implemented in NoC field. Most today NoC real world implementation are dedicated to multimedia aplications [3] such as 3G telephony with simultaneous audio/video

A. Kwiecień, P. Gaj, and P. Stera (Eds.): CN 2011, CCIS 160, pp. 19–26, 2011.

data, MPEG data processing, DAB (Digital Audio Broadcasting), DVB (Digital Video Broadcasting) [2]. Traditionally Systems-on-Chip (SoC) used bus and point-to-point connections [4]. Bus is shared medium and the performance suffers from increasing traffic – more sources of traffic could incure instability. NoC approach is more scalable and could be adapted to diverse technologies. In many aspects NoC communication issues could be defined and standarized similar to well known network communication problems.

In the process of SoC prototyping we need to provide complete system design [4] – required functionality has to be achieved by linking of the modules (cores) which are connected by the bus. In NoC approach the traffic is controlled by the switches and the paths could be established between the cores (modules).

2.1   Networks-on-Chip and Traditional Networks

NoC inherits many aspects from traditional computer and telecommunication networks world. Similarly to computer networks we can describe NoC in layer model manner. Physical layer is represented by voltage levels, length and width of communication links and timing signals. Data link layer consists of packet encoding, synchronization, errors detection and/or correction algorithms. Network layer includes routing rules for packets forwarded accross the network, where decisions are made by the intermediate switches along the path from source to destination core. Transport layer is implemented as point-to-point connection.

2.2   Network Layer in NoC

Traditionally routing algorithms can be divided into two groups: static (deterministic) or adaptive. Routing algorithm in NoC has the same role as in traditional networks – to direct data from source to destination core. Depending on the nature of network traffic routing algorithms in NoC field follow traditional static or adaptive behaviour. Simulation models presented later uses deterministic X-Y algorithm [5].

3   Nanoscale NoC Topology Models and Simulation Environment

The analysis of an impact of network-on-chip topology on the overall transmission delay has been based on the simulation which was conducted in Synopsys CoCentric System Studio [6] environment run on standard PC class workstation under Red Hat Enterprise Linux 4.0 operating system.

The network has been specified in SystemC language, which is an extension to standard C++ [7]. SystemC through its signals, modules and ports specifications is a dedicated modeling and hardware description language, similar to VHDL and Verilog. Synopsys CoCentric System Studio is a simulator specialized to SoC design on many abstraction levels. Process of model composition is two-stage:

modules are created and interconnected using GUI and finally the modules are compiled. Compilation stage often is time consuming.

Simulation time in every case has been set to a value of 1500 ns.

3.1   NoC Model Specification

NoC simulation model has been built of nine identical cores (routers, switches) which had to switch (route) packets of data in the network i.e. to decide which direction should be chosen for specific packet. Every core was connected with a block that could generate and receive specified type of traffic to be sent accross the network.

Every single router uses wormhole method [8] for sending data packets. Packets are divided into entities called flits which are of constant length. First flit has a header carrying data of the destination core, so a virtual path can be created from source to destination core and all of the flits are directed the that virtual path. Having read the header and knowing its own address router determines next router on the path for all of the flits. Then it directs all of the data to selected output port. Counter of flits is initialized with the value *number of flits* and then decreased after passing each of the flits. Flits that constituted data packets has been generated randomly. Data packet has been built of eight flits and every flit consisted of eight bits. First flit carry destination address of the packet, as mentioned above. Second flit contains packet length field. Remaining flits carry information data.

The traffic in every case was identical and composed of some constant traffic sent over predefined paths and remaining random traffic.

3.2   NoC Topologies

It was decided to model four network topologies applied to NoC environment – star, ring, mesh and torus. The routers have the possibility of sending data to

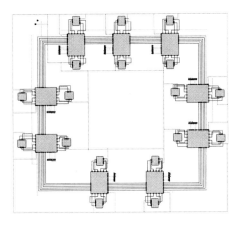

Fig. 1. NoC ring topology

any of four directions (N, W, S, E). In ring topology N and S directions are not used. Mesh and star topology also have disabled unused ports of edge routers. Moreover the router could be equipped with small buffer, although it was not implemented here.

Ring Topology. Model of NoC utilizing ring topology is depicted on Fig. 1. Addressation scheme uses only four most significant bits of address field, so it is enough to address nine nodes 0–8. Ring topology is better than bus topology in term of easier packet management. The most important disadvantage of this topology is fact that one failed router (core) makes all NoC not working. Number of connections is equal to number of cores (9).

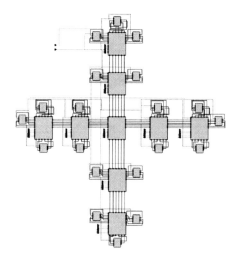

Fig. 2. NoC star topology

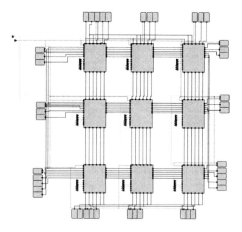

Fig. 3. NoC mesh topology

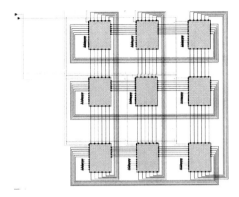

Fig. 4. NoC torus topology

Star Topology. Model of NoC utilizing ring topology is depicted on Fig. 2. It has one central node (core) which has an impact on overall reliability – its failure disconnects remaining nodes. Addressation scheme uses all eight bits. Number of connections necessary for building such network is 48.

Mesh Topology. Model of NoC utilizing ring topology is depicted on Fig. 3. It has regular shape of 3×3 cores. Addressation scheme uses eight bits – 4 most significant bits for X coordinate, remaining 4 bits for Y coordinate. That topology contains 72 connections between the cores.

Torus Topology. Model of NoC utilizing ring topology is depicted on Fig. 4. The topology is modified mesh topology with additional connections. Addressation scheme is the same as in mesh topology. Torus topology contains 108 connections.

3.3   Routing Algorithm

As stated earlier simulation models use deterministic X-Y algorithm [5] which is based on cartesian coordinates of the cores – first X coordinate is processed, then Y coordinate. Metric is a number of hops from source to destination core.

Routing algorithm has been slightly adjusted according to specific conditions in each topology. Examples of routing paths for presented topologies are shown in Table 1.

Table 1. Examples of routing paths

Topology	Route path
MESH	(0,0) → (2,2) via (1,0) → (2,0) → (2,1) → (2,2)
TORUS	(0,2) → (2,1) via (2,2)
STAR	(0,2) → (3,2) via (1,2) → (2,2) → (2,3)
RING	(8) → (3) via (0) → (1) → (2)

4   Simulation Results

During simulation experiments transmission delays has been measured – minimum, maximum, mean and standard deviation values has been collected for flits propagation. Data for every topology is presented in Table 2. Moreover routing algorithms has been compared with metric based on number of hops between source and destination core. Mean distance between the cores for varying topologies is shown in Table 3.

Table 2. Transmission delay in NoC topologies

Path	Propagation time [ns]				Path	Propagation time [ns]			
src → dst core	min value	max value	mean value	std dev	src → dst core	min value	max value	mean value	std dev
RING					MESH				
(0) → (5)	41	775	477	217	(2,2) → (1,1)	25	287	241	74
(8) → (3)	109	642	438	168	(0,2) → (2,0)	119	393	340	77
(6) → (2)	110	639	419	163	(2,0) → (2,1)	17	374	251	92
avg	—	—	**445**	—	**avg**	—	—	**277**	—
STAR					TORUS				
(2,3) → (2,1)	25	398	339	83	(0,0) → (1,1)	25	286	241	72
(0,2) → (4,2)	47	308	267	72	(0,2) → (0,1)	17	378	255	87
(3,2) → (1,2)	25	637	413	180	(2,0) → (0,2)	25	300	247	74
avg	—	—	**340**	—	**avg**	—	—	**248**	—

Table 3. Mean distance in NoC topologies

Topology	Mean distance [hops]
MESH	1.778
TORUS	1.333
STAR	2.173
RING	2.222

Graph shown on Fig. 5 displays average mean propagation time in all four topologies.

Values of mean distance between the cores are presented on the graph on Fig. 6.

Results gathered during simulation show how transmission delay vary with changing NoC topology. The lowest value was obtained for torus topology, which has the highest number of connections between the cores. The worst delay values were noticed for ring topology composed of only 9 connections. Obviously centralized topologies are worse than mesh and torus where many more connections are available. In term of distance characterized by measured metric torus topology is the best, while ring topology gave worst results.

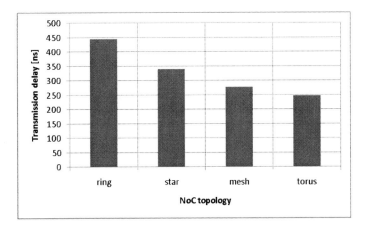

Fig. 5. Transmission delay for all NoC topologies

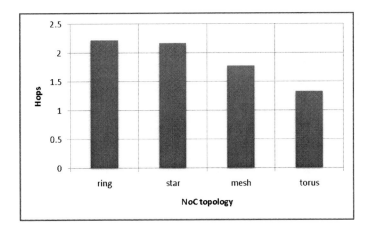

Fig. 6. Mean distance for all NoC topologies

Traffic used in simulations was composed of some static flow between designated cores and remaining part of random transmissions. It has also been proven that similar topology impact on transmission delay is valid for other static/random traffic ratios. Generally the impact of topology is independent on character of the traffic. Flits propagation delay is highly dependent on number of connections building the network.

5   Summary

One of the most important advantages of NoC principle is fact that it does not have any central coordination nor control entity which are a must in bus topology. The only decision that have to be made are on network topology and routing algorithm. Simulation experiments undertaken for Network-on-Chip topologies have shown the dependence between type of topology and transmission delay. Mean distance between the cores depends on the topology in similar way. Those conclusions are important for SoC/NoC designers when making design decisions.

Network-on-Chip is an interdisciplinary field combining computer networks techniques with digital circuits design principles and it is still growing and developing. Future directions for network-specific research could be:

- real-time traffic examining for NoC adaptability,
- different traffic classes (VBR/CBR/...) impact on NoC performance,
- overall NoC performance for varying packet parameters (length of flit etc.).

Acknowledgments. I would like to thank my graduate student, Dominik Kaczmar, who implemented my preliminary ideas of the NoC performance measurements in his master dissertation [9].

References

1. Bush, S.F.: Nanoscale Communication Networks. Artech House, Norwood (2010)
2. Benini, L., De Micheli, G.: Networks on Chips: A New SoC Paradigm. IEEE Computer 35(1), 569–571 (2002)
3. Ulacha, G., Stasiński, R., Dziurzański, P., Olejnik, R.: Lossless compression system architecture dedicated to Networks on Chips. In: Proceedings of International Conference on Signals and Electronic Systems ICSES 2006, Łódź, vol. 1, pp. 235–238 (2006)
4. Steve Lin, Y.-L.: Essential Issues In SOC Design. Springer, Dordrecht (2006)
5. Li, M., Zeng, Q.-A., Jone, W.-B.: DyXY: a proximity congestion-aware deadlock-free dynamic routing method for network on chip. In: Proceedings of the 43rd Annual Design Automation Conference, pp. 849–852. ACM, New York (2006)
6. Synopsys.com, http://www.synopsys.com
7. Open SystemC Language Reference Manual, http://standards.ieee.org/getieee/1666/download/1666-2005.pdf
8. Ivanov, A., De Micheli, G.: Guest Editors' Introduction: The Network-on-Chip Paradigm in Practice and Research. IEEE Design & Test of Computers 22(5), 399–403 (2005)
9. Kaczmar, D.: The comparison of the efficiency of networks-on-chip architectures. Master thesis, Szczecin University of Technology, Szczecin (2008) (in Polish)

The Least Squares SVM Approach for a Non-linear Channel Prediction in the MIMO System

Jerzy Martyna

Institute of Computer Science, Jagiellonian University, ul. Prof. S. Lojasiewicza 6,
30-348 Cracow, Poland

Abstract. In this paper we investigate the problem of a Multiple-Input Multiple-Output (MIMO) frequency in a non-selective channel prediction. We develop a new method for the channel prediction which is based on the Least Squares Support Vector Machine (SVM). We develop a new method for the channel which allows us to predict a signal. The proposed method is evaluated through simulation in a MIMO system under a channel prediction.

Keywords: Multiple-Input Multiple-Output systems, Least Squares Support Vector Machine, channel prediction.

1 Introduction

The Multiple-Input Multiple-Output (MIMO) [1,2] systems exploit the spatial dimension and the scattering properties of most radio channels. This technology is widespread in many technologies of wireless communications, such as WCDMA 3G systems [3], Mobile WiMAX, LTE, IEEE 802.11a, IEEE 802.11n, wireless PAN (MB-OFDM) [4], broadcasting (DAB, DVB, DMB), etc. By means of this technology the capacity of the channel is increased as well as the ability to support multiple users simultaneously [5]. The MIMO systems have also recently been developed by the various research and standarization activities such as METRA Project, 3GPP/3GPP2, and the WINNER Projects aiming at a high-speed wireless transmission and diversity gain.

The MIMO technology has been considered as a strong candidate for the next generation wireless communication systems. A MIMO system gives a high data rate without increasing the total transmission power or bandwidth compared to a single antenna system. This technology is based on the assumption that the receiver and transmitter have knowledge of the channel coefficients. In reality they must either be estimated or predicted. Some popular ways to estimate the channel are by using pilot symbols [6] and *space time block codes* (STBC) [7]. Nevertheless, both methods waste time learning the channel parameters when meaningful data can be sent.

In some papers a solution with a feedback or a partial feedback to transmission of the so-called *channel state information* (CSI) information is proposed [8].

A. Kwiecień, P. Gaj, and P. Stera (Eds.): CN 2011, CCIS 160, pp. 27–36, 2011.

To have a good CSI information some methods to estimate of the MIMO channel [9,10] were developed. In all of these technologies the MIMO channel prediction to the better spectrum utilization must be used. Additionally, these methods waste the time learning the channel characteristics when meaningful data are transmitted.

Kernel machines and the associated learning methods [11,12,13], especially the support vector machine (SVM) approach [14], represent one of the most important directions both in theory and application of the machine learning. With proper learning methods, kernel machines are known to have good generalization abilities and, more importantly, perform very well on high (or even infinite) dimensional feature spaces. In recent years, efforts have been made to signal equalization and detection for a multicarrier (MC)-CDMA system with the help of the SVM linear classification [15]. The SVM methods have also been used by Sanchez-Fernandez et al. [16] for a nonlinear channel estimation in the MIMO system. The SVM technique for a robust channel estimation in a OFDM modulation and demodulation was also used by Fernandez [17]. Nevertheless, these solutions cannot be used easily as the on-line adaptive algorithms.

The main goal of this paper is to introduce a model based on the Least Squares SVM (LS-SVM) [18] method for a channel prediction. In this model a recurrent version of the LS-SVM, as well as a quadratic error criterion of prediction was used. The adequacy of this approach was investigated by simulation in the presence of an impulse noise.

The rest of the paper is organized as follows. In the next section we formulate the MIMO received model. In Section 3 we present our solution based on the recurrent LS-SVM approach. The results of the simulation of the received SNR in the MIMO system is presented in Sect. 5. In Section 6 we give our concluding remarks.

2   The Theoretical Background

In this section we present the MIMO received model for the un-coded and beam-formed system.

We assume the existence of the un-coded and beam-forming MIMO system. For both two cases are considered: the first, in which the transmitter and the receiver have a full channel state information (CSI), and the second, when both the transmitter and the receiver have the prediction matrix.

2.1   The Un-coded MIMO System

Consider a MIMO system of N_r receiver antennas and N_t transmitter antennas as illustrated in Fig. 1.

A narrowband MIMO channel $\mathbf{H}$ can be statistically expressed with an $N_r \times N_t$ matrix as

$$\mathbf{H} = \Theta_R^{1/2} \mathbf{A}_{iid} \Theta_T^{1/2} \tag{1}$$

Mobile station   Base station

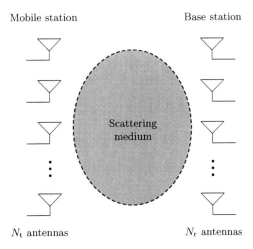

N_t antennas N_r antennas

Fig. 1. Two antenna arrays in a scattering environment

where Θ_R and Θ_T are correlation matrices for the receiver antennas and transmitter antennas, respectively, while $\mathbf{A}_{iid}$ represents an i.i.d (independent and identically distributed) Rayleigh fading channel. The basic assumption behind the correlation matrix-based MIMO channel model in Eq. (1) is that the correlation matrices for the transmitter and the receiver can be separated. That particular assumption holds when the antenna spacing in the transmitter and the receiver is sufficiently smaller than the distance between the transmitter and the receiver, which usually is true for most of wireless communication environments.

Let $y_m(t)$ denote the received signal at the received antenna. Then, the received signals at the received antenna are denoted as $\mathbf{y}(t) = [y_1, y_2(t), \ldots, y_{N_r}(t)]^T$. Similarly, the transmitted signals at the transmitter antenna are denoted as $\mathbf{x}(t) = [x_1(t), x_2(t), \ldots, x_{N_t}(t)]^T$, where $\mathbf{x}_n(t)$ is the signal transmitted at the n antenna element. The relation between the transmitter antennas and the receiver antennas signals can be expressed as

$$\mathbf{y} = \mathbf{H}\mathbf{x} + \mathbf{n} \tag{2}$$

where $\mathbf{y}$ is the $N_r \times 1$ received vector, $\mathbf{x}$ is the $N_t \times 1$ transmitted symbol vector with each x_i belonging to constelation C with symbol energy E_s, and $\mathbf{n}$ is the while noise vector of size $N_r \times 1$ with $n_i \sim \mathcal{CN}(0, N_0)$. The channel state matrix $\mathbf{H} = \{h_{mn}\}$ gives a complex channel gain between the m-th receiver and the n-th transmit antenna.

2.2   The Beam-Forming MIMO System

In the beam-forming MIMO system, the received symbols are expressed in two scenarios, when the transmitter and the receiver have full channel information

(CSI) and when they have the prediction matrix. Then, the channel matrix $\mathbf{H} = \mathbf{U} \cdot \mathbf{D} \cdot \mathbf{V}^{\mathbf{H}}$ is a singular value decomposition (SVD) where $\mathbf{U}$ and $\mathbf{V}$ are unitary matrices corresponding to the i-th non-zero singular value $\sigma_H(i)$, $(\sigma_H(1) \leq \ldots \leq \sigma_H(M))$ and $M = rank(\mathbf{H})$. Assuming that $\tilde{x} = v_1 \cdot \mathbf{x}$ we can obtain from Eq. (1) the received symbols u_1^H as follows:

$$u_1^H \mathbf{y} = \sigma_H(1)x + u_1^H \mathbf{n} . \tag{3}$$

Assuming $\tilde{u} = \mathbf{u}_1^H \mathbf{n}$ we can obtain

$$E \mid \tilde{n} \mid^2 = N_r \cdot N_0 . \tag{4}$$

Thus, the channel within a MIMO system is time-varying and can be expressed in a matrix notation as $\mathbf{H} = \hat{H} + E$. Therefore, the received symbols are as follows:

$$\hat{u}_1^H \mathbf{y} = (\sigma_H(1) + \hat{u}_1^H E \hat{v}_1)\mathbf{x} + u_1^H \mathbf{n} . \tag{5}$$

In the general case the doppler spread of the signal is greater than the pulse bandwidth. In a typical environment the MIMO channel is fast-fading [19]. Assuming a MIMO flat fast-fading transmission each sub-channel can be formulated as follows [20]:

$$h_{mn}(t) = h_{mn}(k) + jh_{mn}(k) \tag{6}$$

where in-phase component is represent as

$$h_{mn}^I(k) = \sqrt{\frac{2}{M}} \sum_{n=1}^{M} \cos(2\pi f_d k \sin(\alpha_n) + \Phi_n) \tag{7}$$

and the quadrature component can be written as

$$h_{mn}^Q(k) = \sqrt{\frac{2}{M}} \sum_{n=1}^{M} \cos(2\pi f_d k \sin(\alpha_n) + \Psi_n) \tag{8}$$

where $\alpha_n = \frac{2\pi n - \pi + \Theta}{4M}$ and Φ_n, Ψ_n, Θ are $U[-\pi, \pi]$.

3   The Multidimensional Recurrent LS-SVM

The recurrent LS-SVM based on the sum squared error (SSE) to deal with the function approximation and prediction has been proposed by Suykens and Vandewalle [21]. However, the so defined recurrent LS-SVM will not be adequate for the channel prediction in the MIMO system. It is caused by the lack of the high-dimensional reconstructed embedding phase space.

In order to extend the recurrent least squares vector machine to a multidimensional recurrent LS-SVM we introduce scalar time series $\{s_1, s_2, \ldots, s_T\}$ in the form

$$\hat{s}_k = f(\hat{s}_{k-1}), \quad k = m', m' + 1, \ldots, N' + m' - 1 \tag{9}$$

where m', N' are referred to the embedding dimension and the number of training data, respectively.

The function approximation is given by

$$\hat{s}_k = \mathbf{w}^{\mathrm{T}}\phi_i(\hat{s}_{k-1}) + b, \quad k = m', m' + 1, \ldots, N' + m' - 1, \quad i = 1, 2, \ldots, m' \tag{10}$$

where $\mathbf{w} = [w_1, w_2, \ldots, w_{m'}]$ is the output weight vector, $b \in R$ is the bias term $\phi(.)$ is the nonlinear mapping function estimated by means of using training data.

The recurrent LS-SVM can be formulated as the quadratic optimization problem:

$$\min_{w_i, b_i, e_{k,i}} \mathcal{J}(w_i, b_i, e_{k,i}) = \frac{1}{2}\sum_{i=1}^{m'} w_i^{\mathrm{T}} w_i + \frac{\gamma}{2}\sum_{k=m'+1}^{N'+m'-1}\sum_{i=1}^{m'} e_{k,i}^2 \tag{11}$$

subject to the following constraints:

$$\begin{cases} s_k^{(1)} - e_{k,1} = w_1^{\mathrm{T}}\phi_1(s_{k-1} - e_{k-1}) + b_1 \\ s_k^{(2)} - e_{k,2} = w_2^{\mathrm{T}}\phi_2(s_{k-1} - e_{k-1}) + b_2 \\ \qquad\qquad \vdots \\ s_k^{m'} - e_{k,m'} = w_{m'}^{\mathrm{T}}\phi_l(s_{k-1} - e_{k-1}) + b_{m'} \end{cases} \tag{12}$$

where $k = m' + 1, m' = 2, \ldots, N' + m' - 1$, $e_k = s_k - \hat{s}_k$. Generally, the error term here is defined as

$$e_k = x_k - f(x_{k-1}) \ . \tag{13}$$

The corresponding Lagrangian for Eq. (11) is given by

$$\mathcal{L}(w_i, b_i, e_{k,i}; \alpha_{k,i} = \mathcal{J}(w_i, b_i, e_{k,i})$$
$$+ \sum_{k=m'+1}^{N'+m'-1}\sum_{i=1}^{m'} \alpha_{k,i}\left[s_k^{(i)} - e_{k,i} - w_i^{\mathrm{T}}\phi_i \times (s_{k-1} - e_{k-1}) - b_i\right] \tag{14}$$

with respect to w_i, b_i and e_i. The solution given by the Karush-Kuhn-Tucker theorem is given by:

$$\begin{cases} \frac{\partial \mathcal{L}}{\partial w_i} = w_i - \sum_{k=m'+1}^{N'+m'-1} \alpha_{k,i}\phi_i(s_{k-1} - e_{k-1}) = 0 \\ \frac{\partial \mathcal{L}}{\partial b_i} = \sum_{k=m'+1}^{N'+m'-1} \alpha_{k,i} = 0 \\ \frac{\partial \mathcal{L}}{\partial e_{k,i}} = \gamma e_k - \alpha_{k,i} - \sum_{i=1}^{m'} \alpha_{k+i,i}\frac{\partial}{\partial e_{k+m'-i,i}} \\ \qquad\qquad \times \left[w_i^{\mathrm{T}}\phi_i(s_{k-1} - e_{k-1})\right] = 0 \\ \frac{\partial \mathcal{L}}{\partial \alpha_{k,i}} = s_k^{(i)} - e_{k,i} - w_i^{\mathrm{T}}\phi_i(s_{k-1} - e_{k-1}) - b_i = 0 \end{cases} \tag{15}$$

where $k = m' + 1, m' + 2, \ldots, N' + m' - 1$ and $i = 1, 2, \ldots, m'$.

Due to the application of the Mercer's condition [18] there exists a mapping and the LS-SVM model for the given problem, namely

$$\hat{s}_k = \sum_{i=m'+1}^{N'+m'-1} \sum_{p=1}^{m'} \alpha_{i,p} K_p(z_i, \hat{s}_{k-1}) + b_p \tag{16}$$

where $z_l = s_l - e_l$. The initial condition is given by $\hat{s}_i = s_i$ for $i = 1, 2, \ldots, m'$. Thus, the kernel function $K_p(.,.)$ can be stated as follows:

$$K_p(x_i, x_j) = \phi_p^{\mathrm{T}}(x_i)\phi_p(x_j) = \exp\left(-\frac{\| x_i - x_j \|^2}{2\sigma_p^2}\right) \tag{17}$$

where $p = 1, 2, \ldots, m'$.

4   Experimental Results

In order to test the performance of the MIMO channel prediction, we used the received signal-to-noise ratio (SNR) in the general form

$$\rho = \frac{\sigma_x^2}{\sigma_e^2 + \sigma_n^2} \tag{18}$$

where σ_x^2 is the average received signal power, σ_e^2 is the predictive error, σ_n^2 is the average noise variance. Thus, after some algebraic manipulations for the un-coded system we can obtain

$$\rho_{uc} \overset{\triangle}{=} \frac{E \| \hat{\mathbf{H}}\mathbf{x} \|_2^2}{E \| \mathbf{E}\mathbf{x} \|_2^2 + E \| \mathbf{n} \|_2^2} \tag{19}$$

and after several manipulations

$$\rho_{uc} = \frac{\sum_{i=1}^{M} E[\sigma_{\hat{\mathbf{H}}}^2(i)]}{\sum_{i=1}^{N} E[\sigma_{\mathbf{E}}^2(i)] + \frac{N_r N_0}{E_s}} \tag{20}$$

where $N = rank(\mathbf{E})$, $\sigma_{\hat{\mathbf{H}}}(i)$ and $\sigma_{\mathbf{E}}(i)$ are the i-th non-zero singular values of $\hat{\mathbf{H}}$ and $\mathbf{E}$, respectively.

The MIMO beam-forming can be formulated as follows

$$\hat{\mathbf{u}}_1^{\mathbf{H}}\mathbf{y} = (\hat{\sigma}_1^2 + \hat{u}_1^{\mathbf{H}})x + \tilde{n} \ . \tag{21}$$

Thus, after a similar technique as the one used before, we can state the received SNR for the MIMO beam-forming system

$$\rho_{bf} = \frac{E[\sigma_1^2]}{E \mid \hat{\mathbf{u}}_1^{\mathbf{H}}\mathbf{U}\mathbf{D}\mathbf{V}^{\mathbf{H}}\hat{v}_1 - \hat{\sigma}_{\max} \mid^2 + \frac{N_r N_0}{E_s}} \ . \tag{22}$$

Thus, comparing the above equation with the Eq. (19) we get the value of the prediction error σ_e^2 for the beam-forming prediction, namely

$$\sigma_e^2 = E \parallel \mathbf{Ex} \parallel_2^2 = E \parallel \hat{\mathbf{U}}^H \mathbf{E} \hat{\mathbf{V}} \mathbf{x} \parallel_2^2 \tag{23}$$

or after some algebraic manipulations

$$\sigma_e^2 = E \mid (\hat{\mathbf{u}}_1^H \mathbf{U} \mathbf{D} \mathbf{V}^H \hat{\mathbf{v}}_1 - \hat{\sigma}_{\max}) x \mid^2 \quad . \tag{24}$$

The RBF kernel with the width parameters: $\sigma = 0.5$ and the regularizotion parameter $\gamma = 500$ were selected, respectively.

The behaviour of the received SNR for the 10000 binary phase shift keying (BPSK) symbol vectors with $E_s = 1$, $N_t = N_r = 2$ is given in Fig. 2. These graphs are obtained through a simulation for the typical value of ratio E_s/N_0. This figure indicates that for a smaller value of E_s/N_0 the predicted value will be better adjusted than for a greater value of E_s/N_0. The obtained values of the maximum singular value of the error matrix and the minimum singular value of the error matrix are given in Fig. 3 and Fig. 4, respectively.

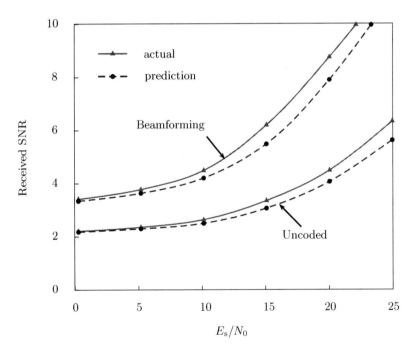

Fig. 2. Received SNR as a fubction of E_s/E_0 for un-coded and beam-forming MIMO system

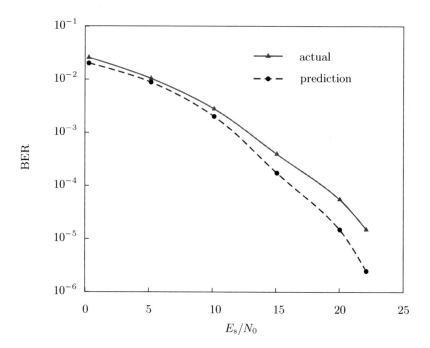

Fig. 3. Bit error rate (BER) as a function of E_s/E_0 for a un-coded 4×4 MIMO system

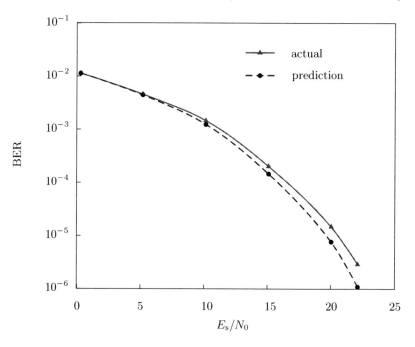

Fig. 4. Bit error rate (BER) as a function of E_s/E_0 for a beam-forming 4×4 MIMO system

5   Conclusion

The MIMO channel prediction approach that incorporates recurring into the LS-SVM method was proposed. For the un-coded and the beam-forming MIMO systems the received signal-to-noise ratio (SNR) was derived. It was shown that the beam-forming technique played a dominant role in the prediction. It allows us to obtain better values of the performance parameter of the MIMO channel prediction, such as the value of the prediction error. In the experiment the best results were achieved for the LS-SVM with the RBF kernel function. This kernel function demands the use of scaling factors for all the parameters. Despite of them it allows us to achieve a higher rate for all the data sets used in the link.

The MIMO channels with the inclusion of learning algorithms are logical further research lines, as well as simulations with different kind of noises. The introduction of other kernels in the LS-SVM method and its modification into adaptive schemes for time variant channels are also interesting possibilities.

References

1. Pedersen, K.I., Andersen, J.B., Kermoal, J.P., Mogensen, P.: A Stochastic Multiple-Input Multiple-Output Radio Channel Model for Evaluation of Space-Time Coding Algorithms. In: IEEE Vehicular Technology Conference, vol. 2, pp. 893–897 (2000)
2. Rappaport, T.S.: Wireless Communications: Principles and Practice, 2nd edn. Prentice-Hall Inc., Englewood Cliffs (2002)
3. 3GPP TR25.869 Tx Diversity Solutions for Multiple Antennas, v1.2.0 (August 2003)
4. van Nee, R., Prasad, R.: OFDM for Wireless Multimedia Communications. Artech House Publishers, Boston (2000)
5. Jindal, N., Vishwanath, S., Goldsmith, A.: On the Duality of Gaussian Multiple-Access and Broadcast Channels. IEEE Trans. on Information Theory 50(5), 768–783 (2004)
6. Hao, X., Chizhik, D., Huang, H., Valenzuela, R.: A Generalized Space-Time Multiple-Input Multiple Output (MIMO) Channel Model. IEEE Trans. on Wireless Communications 3(3), 966–975 (2004)
7. Gesbert, D., Shafi, M., Shin, D.-S., Smith, P.J., Naguib, A.: From Theory to Practice: An Overview of MIMO Space-Time Coded Wireless Systems. IEEE Journal on Selected Areas in Communications 21(3), 281–302 (2003)
8. Shahtalebi, K., Bakhshi, G.R., Rad, H.S.: Full MIMO Channel Estimation Using a Simple Adaptive Partial Feedback Method (2007)
9. Ghogho, M., Swami, A.: Training Design for Multipath Channel and Frequency-Offset Estimation in MIMO Systems. IEEE Trans. on Signal Processing 54(6), 3957–3965 (2006)
10. Biguesh, M., Gershman, A.B.: Training-Based MIMO Channel Estimation: A Study of Estimator Tradeoffs and Optimal Training Signals. IEEE Trans. on Signal Processing 54(3), 884–893 (2006)
11. Cortes, C., Vapnik, V.: Support Vector Networks. Machine Learning 20, 273–297 (1995)
12. Cristianini, N., Shawe-Taylor, J.: An Introduction to Support Vector Machines. Cambridge University Press, Cambridge (2000)

13. Schölkopf, B., Burges, C., Smola, A.: Advances in Kernel Methods Support Vector Learning. MIT Press, Cambridge (1999)
14. Vapnik, V.: Statistical Learning Theory. John Wiley and Sons, New York (1998)
15. Rahman, S., Saito, M., Okada, M., Yamamoto, H.: An MC-CDMA Signal Equalization and Detection Scheme Based on Support Vector Machines. In: Proc. 1st Int. Symp. Wireless Communication Systems, pp. 11–15 (2004)
16. Sánchez-Fernández, M.P., de Prado-Cumlido, M., Arenas-Garcia, J., Perez-Cruz, F.: SVM Multiregression for Nonlinear Channel Estimation in Multiple-Input Multiple-Output Systems. IEEE Trans. on Signal Processing 52(8), 2298–2307 (2004)
17. Fernández-Getino Garcia, M.J., Rojo-Álvarez, J.L., Alonso-Atienzo, F., Martinez-Ramón, M.: Support Vector Machines for Robust Channel Estimation in OFDM. IEEE Signal Processing Letters 13(7), 397–400 (2006)
18. Suykens, J.A.K., Van Gestel, T., De Brabantter, J., De Moor, B., Vandewalle, J.: Least Squares Support Vector Machines. World Scientific Pub. Co., Singapore (2002)
19. Rappaport, T.S.: Wireless Communications. Cambridge University Press, New York (2005)
20. Zheng, Y., Xiao, C.: Improved Models for the Generation of Multiple Uncorrelated Rayleigh Fading Waveforms. IEEE Trans. Commun. Letters 6(6), 256–258 (2002)
21. Suykens, J.A.K., Vandewalle, J.: Recurrent Least Squares Vector Machines. IEEE Trans. Circuits Systems and Systems I 47(7), 11109–11114 (2000)

The Impact of the Modified Weighted Moving Average on the Performance of the RED Mechanism

Joanna Domańska[1], Adam Domański[2], and Dariusz R. Augustyn[2]

[1] Institute of Theoretical and Applied Informatics, Polish Academy of Sciences
Baltycka 5, 44-100 Gliwice, Poland
joanna@iitis.gliwice.pl
[2] Institute of Informatics, Silesian Technical University,
Akademicka 16, 44-100 Gliwice, Poland
{draugustyn,adamd}@polsl.pl

Abstract. Algorithms of queue management in IP routers determine which packet should be deleted when necessary. The article investigates the influence of weighted moving average on the performance of the RED mechanism. The proposed average queue length calculating method is based on a difference equation (a recursive equation). Depending on a particular criterion of optimization a proper parameters of modified weighted moving average function may be chosen.

Keywords: AQM, Random Early Detection, weighted moving average.

1 Introduction

Algorithms of queue management at IP routers determine which packet should be deleted when necessary. The Active Queue Management, recommended now by IETF, enhances the efficiency of transfers and cooperates with TCP congestion window mechanism in adapting the flows intensity to the congestion at a network [1].

In *passive* queue management, packets coming to a buffer are rejected only if there is no space in the buffer to store them, hence the senders have no earlier warning on the danger of growing congestion. In this case all packets coming during saturation of the buffer are lost. The existing schemes may differ on the choice of packet to be deleted (end of the tail, head of the tail, random). During a saturation period all connections are affected and all react in the same way, hence they become synchronized. To enhance the throughput and fairness of the link sharing, also to eliminate the synchronization, the Internet Engineering Task Force (IETF) recommends *active* algorithms of buffer management. They incorporate mechanisms of preventive packet dropping when there is still place to store some packets, to advertise that the queue is growing and the danger of congestion is ahead. The probability of packet rejection is growing together with the level of congestion. The packets are dropped randomly, hence only

A. Kwiecień, P. Gaj, and P. Stera (Eds.): CN 2011, CCIS 160, pp. 37–44, 2011.

chosen users are notified and the global synchronization of connections is avoided. A detailed discussion of the active queue management goals may be found in [1].

The RED (Random Early Detection) algorithm was proposed by IETF to enhance the transmission via IP routers. It was primarily described by Sally Floyd and Van Jacobson in [2]. Its idea is based on a drop function giving probability that a packet is rejected. The argument avg of this function is a weighted moving average queue length, acting as a low-pass filter and calculated at the arrival of each packet as

$$avg = (1 - w)avg' + wq \qquad (1)$$

where avg' is the previous value of avg, q is the current queue length and w is a weight determining the importance of the instantaneous queue length, typically $w \ll 1$. If w is too small, the reaction on arising congestion is too slow, if w is too large, the algorithm is too sensitive on ephemeral changes of the queue (noise). Articles [2,3] recommend $w = 0.001$ or $w = 0.002$, and [4] shows the efficiency of $w = 0.05$ and $w = 0.07$. Article [5] analyses the influence of w on queuing time fluctuations, obviously the larger w, the higher fluctuations. In RED drop function there are two thresholds Min_{th} and Max_{th}. If $avg < Min_{th}$ all packets are admitted, if $Min_{th} < avg < Max_{th}$ then dropping probability p is growing linearly from 0 to p_{max}:

$$p = p_{max}\frac{avg - Min_{th}}{Max_{th} - Min_{th}} \qquad (2)$$

and if $avg > Max_{th}$ then all packets are dropped. The value of p_{max} has also a strong influence on the RED performance: if it is too large, the overall throughput is unnecessarily choked and if it's too small the danger of synchronization arises; [3] recommends $p_{max} = 0.1$. The problem of the choice of parameters is still discussed, see e.g. [6,7]. The mean avg may be also determined in other way, see [8] for discussion. Despite of evident highlights, RED has also such drawbacks as low throughput, unfair bandwidth sharing, introduction of variable latency, deterioration of network stability. Therefore numerous propositions of basic algorithms improvements appear, their comparison may be found e.g. in [9]. Figure 1 shows dropping functions for RED.

This paper describes another approach based on weighted moving average estimating applying high order difference equation.

This section gives basic notions on active queue management. Section 2 presents the assumed model of estimating average queue length. Section 3 discusses numerical results. Some conclusions are given in Sect. 4.

2   Theoretical Background – The Assumed Model of Estimating Average Queue Length

The proposed average queue length calculating method is based on a difference equation (a recursive equation).

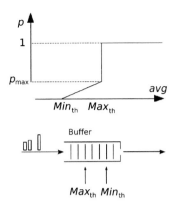

Fig. 1. Dropping functions for RED

$A(n)$ – the average length at the n-th moment of time – may be expressed using the difference equation as follows:

$$A(n) = a_1 A(n-1) + a_2 A(n-2) + \ldots + a_k A(n-k) +$$
$$+ b_0 Q(n) + b_1 Q(n-1) + \ldots + b_m Q(n-m) \qquad (3)$$

where $a_j = const$ for $j = 1, \ldots, k$, $b_i = const$ for $i = 0, \ldots, m$, $A(l)$ – average length at the l-th moment of time, $Q(l)$ – current length of the packet queue at the l-th moment.

Constraint conditions for a_j and b_i coefficients are:

$$\sum_{j=1}^{k} a_j + \sum_{i=0}^{m} b_i = 1 \wedge a_j \geq 0 \wedge b_i \geq 0 \ . \qquad (4)$$

A score function based on e.g. a mean waiting time or a total number of dropped packets may be used for obtaining the order of model (m and k values) and concrete values of equation coefficients (a_j and b_i). The minimum of the assumed score function determines the optimal model.

3   Experimental Results

The classic RED approach (were the average length is given by eq. (1) satisfies the equation of the model given by eq. (3) when only a_1 and b_0 are significant coefficients. Only one parameter – a_1 should be determined in the RED approach (because $b_0 = 1 - a_1$). This was named 1-dimesional model – $[a_1]$ ($k = 1, m = 0$).

In the proposed approach we want to take into account 4 significant parameters (a_1, a_2, b_0, b_1), so we consider 3-dimensional model $[a_1, a_2, b_1]$ ($k = 2, m = 1$) were $b_0 = 1 - a_1 - a_2 - b_1$. Basing on (3) we can calculate the average length as follows:

$$A(n) = a_1 A(n-1) + a_2 A(n-2) + (1 - a_1 - a_2 - b_1)Q(n) + b_1 Q(n-1) \ . \qquad (5)$$

Especially for selected values of a_2 and b_1 the proposed model $[a_1, a_2, b_1] = [a_1, 0, 0]$ becomes the classic RED model i.e. $[a_1]$.

To find optimal values of a_1, a_2, b_1 we used the score function based on the mean packet waiting time. The problem of obtaining the best values of parameters is equivalent to the problem of finding minimum of the trivariate score function. That was made using the well-known Hooke and Jeeves direct search method for minimization of multivariate functions.

The score function based on waiting time has many local minimums. The first we start to search the minimum with initial values near the ones recommended by classical RED authors, i.e. $[a_1, a_2, b_1] = [0.002, 0, 0]$. We found better coefficients values $[a_1, a_2, b_1] = [0.004, 0.009, 0]$ because WaitingTimeScore $(0.004, 0.009, 0) = 751.385$ is less then WaitingTimeScore $(0.002, 0, 0) = 775.605$. Figure 2 displays the comparison of queue distribution for above coefficients values. The comparison of waiting times for the same coefficients values is presented in Fig. 3.

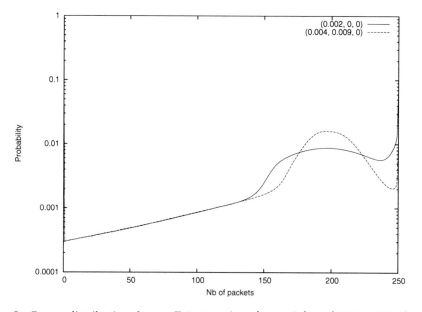

Fig. 2. Queue distribution for coefficients values $[a_1, a_2, b_1] = [0.004, 0.009, 0]$ and $[a_1, a_2, b_1] = [0.002, 0, 0]$

We found even better coefficients values than those ones mentioned before, starting from initial values $[0.08, 0.002, 0]$. The optimal coefficients values obtained using the proposed approach are $[a_1, a_2, b_1] = [0.08, 0.0014, 0.001]$ where WaitTimeScore $(0.08, 0.0014, 0.001) = 738.232$. This is the best achieved result. Figures 4 and 5 display the queue distributions and waiting times for above coefficients values.

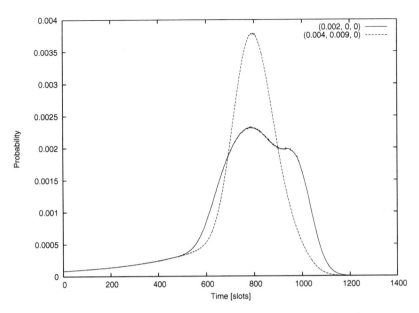

Fig. 3. Waiting times distribution for coefficients values $[a_1, a_2, b_1] = [0.004, 0.009, 0]$ and $[a_1, a_2, b_1] = [0.002, 0, 0]$

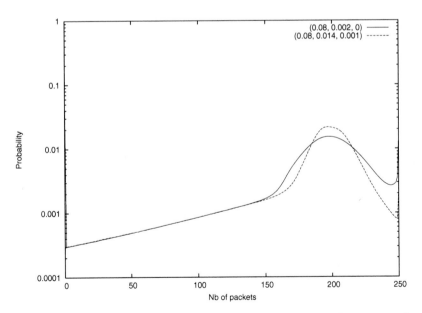

Fig. 4. Queue distribution for coefficients values $[a_1, a_2, b_1] = [0.08, 0.002, 0]$ and $[a_1, a_2, b_1] = [0.08, 0.0014, 0.001]$

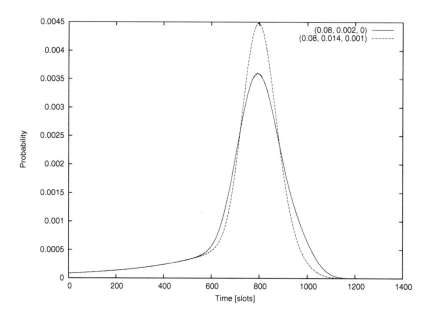

Fig. 5. Waiting times distribution for coefficients values $[a_1, a_2, b_1] = [0.08, 0.002, 0]$ and $[a_1, a_2, b_1] = [0.08, 0.0014, 0.001]$

Every step of minimum searching with evaluating the WaitingTimeScore function is equivalent to realize a simulation, and takes about 1 hour.

The simulation evaluations were carried out with the use of OMNeT++ simulation framework. The OMNeT++ is the modular, component-based simulator mainly designed for simulation of communication networks, queuing networks and performance evaluation. The framework is very popular in research and for academic purposes [10,11]. The service time represents the time of a packet treatment and dispatching. Its distributions is selfsimilar. Input traffic intensity was chosen as $\alpha = 0.5$, and due to the modulator characteristics, the Hurst parameter of self-similar traffic was fixed to $H = 0.78$. The RED parameters had the following values: buffer size 250 packets, threshold values $Min_{th} = 100$ and $Max_{th} = 200$, $p_{max} = 0.1$. Parameter μ of geometric distribution of service times (probability of the end of service within a current time-slot) was $\mu = 0.25$. We considered only high traffic load.

Finding the interesting coefficients values i.e. $[0.004, 0.009, 0]$ and $[0.08, 0.0014, 0.001]$ took 61 and 26 steps (with the predefined accuracy for each direction equals 0.0001).

Considering high dimensional models (i.e. $k > 2$ and $m > 1$) gives very small coefficients values (relative to the obtained a_1, a_2, b_1 values), so the proposed 3-dimentional model seems to be optimal (according to the assumed score function).

4   Conclusions

Many extensions of the classic RED were considered in the past. Some of them are based on modifications of the probability of packed dropping function [12,13,14,15,16].

This approach is based on the proposed simple dynamical discrete model of obtaining the average packet queue length. The linear difference equations was proposed for calculating average length. The optimal values of equation coefficients were found during minimization of the score function. The achieved results are better than results for parameter values taken from the classic RED approach (for the assumed score function based on the mean packet waiting time).

The usage of different score functions (the number of dropped packets, the mean of waiting time, the score based on mixed criterions) and different models of network traffic (BMAP, HMM) are planned to consider in the future.

Acknowledgements. This research was partially financed by Polish Ministry of Science and Higher Education project no N N516441438.

References

1. Braden, B., Clark, D., Crowcroft, J., Davie, B., Deering, S., Estrin, D., Floyd, S., Jacobson, V., Minshall, G., Partridge, C., Peterson, L., Ramakrishnan, K., Shenker, S., Wroclawski, J., Zhang, L.: Recommendations on queue management and congestion avoidance in the internet. RFC 2309, IETF (1998)
2. Floyd, S., Jacobson, V.: Random early detection gateways for congestion avoidance. IEEE/ACM Transactions on Networking 1(4), 397–413 (1993)
3. Floyd, S.: Discussions of setting parameters (1997),
   `http://www.icir.org/floyd/REDparameters.txt`
4. Zheng, B., Atiquzzaman, M.: A framework to determine the optimal weight parameter of red in next generation internet routers. The University of Dayton, Department of Electrical and Computer Engineering, Tech. Rep. (2000)
5. May, M., Bonald, T., Bolot, J.: Analytic evaluation of red performance. In: IEEE Infocom 2000, Tel-Aviv, Izrael (2000)
6. Chang Feng, W., Kandlur, D., Saha, D.: Adaptive packet marking for maintaining end to end throughput in a differentiated service internet. IEEE/ACM Transactions on Networking 7(5), 685–697 (1999)
7. May, M., Diot, C., Lyles, B., Bolot, J.: Influence of active queue management parameters on aggregate traffic performance. Technical report, Research Report, Institut de Recherche en Informatique et en Automatique (2000)
8. Zheng, B., Atiquzzaman, M.: Low pass filter/over drop avoidance (lpf/oda): An algorithm to improve the response time of red gateways. Int. Journal of Communication Systems 15(10), 899–906 (2002)
9. Hassan, M., Jain, R.: High Performance TCP/IP Networking. Pearson Education Inc., London (2004)
10. OMNET++ homepage, `http://www.omnetpp.org/`
11. Domanska, J., Grochla, K., Nowak, S.: Symulator zdarzeń dyskretnych OM-NeT++. Wyd. Wyzsza Szkola Biznesu w Dabrowie Górniczej, Dabrowa Górnicza (2009)

12. Floyd, S., Gummadi, R., Shenker, S.: Adaptive RED: An Algorithm for Increasing the Robustness of REDs Active Queue Management,
    `http://citeseer.ist.psu.edu/448749.html`
13. Zhou, K., Yeung, K.L., Li, V.: Nonlinear RED: A simple yet efficient active queue management scheme. Computer Networks 50, 3784–3794 (2006)
14. Domańska, J., Domański, A.: Active Queue Management in Linux based routers. In: IWSI (2008)
15. Augustyn, D.R., Domański, A., Domańska, J.: Active Queue Management with non linear packet dropping function. In: Performance Modelling and Evaluation of Heterogenous Networks, HET-NETs 2010, pp. 133–143 (2010)
16. Augustyn, D.R., Domański, A., Domańska, J.: A Choice of Optimal Packet Dropping Function for Active Queue Management. In: Kwiecień, A., Gaj, P., Stera, P. (eds.) 17th Conference on Computer Networks, CN 2010, Ustroń, Poland. CCIS, vol. 79, pp. 199–206. Springer, Heidelberg (2010)
17. Domańska, J., Domański, A., Czachórski, T.: Implementation of modified AQM mechanisms in IP routers. Journal of Communications Software and Systems 4(1) (March 2008)
18. Domańska, J., Domański, A., Czachórski, T.: The Drop-From-Front Strategy in AQM. In: Koucheryavy, Y., Harju, J., Sayenko, A. (eds.) NEW2AN 2007. LNCS, vol. 4712, pp. 61–72. Springer, Heidelberg (2007)
19. Domańska, J.: Procesy Markowa w modelowaniu natężenia ruchu w sieciach komputerowych. PhD thesis, IITiS PAN, Gliwice (2005)

Identification of the Web Server

Krzysztof Zatwarnicki

Department of Electrical, Control and Computer Engineering,
Opole University of Technology, Opole, Poland
k.zatwarnicki@gmail.com

Abstract. The article considers the problem of modeling the Web server operations. At first, the simulation model of the server and the way of conducting experiments making possible to obtain required simulation model parameters of real Web server is introduced. The experiment resulsts and calculated values of parameter of specified Web server are presented. In the end the program written with use of the CSIM 19 package simulating operations of the Web server is discussed.

Keywords: simulation model, web server modeling, queuing networks.

1 Introduction

Nowadays, the Internet is one of the basic media entertainment, advertisement and latest news provider. The Internet is also a driving force for a range of business activities, such as running Internet stores, auction systems, Internet banking systems and many others. The quality of Web services can be assessed by users in various ways. On one hand the interesting content presented in the service ensures growth in the number of users, on the other hand, it is important to deliver the information in specified time just right after the user requests them.

There are many methods allowing reduction of delays experienced by users. These include methods to improve the transmission conditions [1], employing more efficient hardware and software, employing caching proxy, reveres proxy and mirror servers, and also applying cluster of local [2] and/or global distributed Web systems [3]. The significant growth in methods mentioned above requires conducting research enabling evaluation and comparison of the methods before applying them in the industrial solutions.

There are few ways of efficiency evaluation of a prospective service planned in use. One of them is the method of theoretical analysis using a proper mathematical modeling. This method, for instance, is applied in requests scheduling and resources allocation in multiprocessor systems. It should be noticed that models of systems constructed in this way are usually very simplified because only those bring good results in the discussed method of analysis [4]. The existing difficulties are overcome to some extent by the simulation approach, which allows modeling of complex web services based on analysis of actual systems. In this approach software simulating operation of the clients and the Web service is designed. The

A. Kwiecień, P. Gaj, and P. Stera (Eds.): CN 2011, CCIS 160, pp. 45–54, 2011.

Web service models are most often constructed on the base of queuing networks (QN) which enable creation of models of different Web systems architectures and computer networks with required precision [5]. The big advantage of simulation methods is a low time and low financial cost of conducting researches during which number of different hardware and software solution can be evaluated.

The third method consists in building a prototype service containing real web servers [6]. Testing the work of such service can be done using benchmarks [7,8]. The major disadvantage of the discussed method is a high cost of carrying out experiments compared to the two previous methods.

Taking into account a large extent of application, elasticity, low costs and high accuracy, simulation methods are used most often for the evaluation of the efficiency and properties of the service planned. Planning the construction of a simulator it is necessary to consider how the particular elements of the service planned will be modeled.

In the article the process of identification of the Web server is shown. At first the simulation model of the server is introduced. In the next step the way, proposed by the author, of conducting experiments as well as the method of calculation parameters of simulation model and results of conducted experiments are presented. In the end the program written with use of the CSIM 19 package simulating operations of the Web server is discussed.

The issue of creation the simulation model of the Web service is the topic of several publications. It is worth to start with WWW clients' behavior models. The early works in this matter cover the issue of the HTTP object size modeling [7,9,10]. Further, the complex client's behavior model [11,12] is presented as well as client's behavior model in business service [13]. Other works concern the modeling of whole WWW services that cover the part related to client's modeling and also WWW servers, database servers, web dispatchers and wide area network [6,14,15,16,17,18]. However there are not many works related to detailed WWW server simulation models [19,20,21].

The paper is divided into four sections. Section 2 presents the concept of conducting research and obtaining simulation model parameters. Section 3 describes a simulation program and finally Sect. 4 contains concluding remarks.

2   Design of Web Server Simulation Model

Currently the most frequent applied group of simulation models are queuing networks. These models, despite many simplifications, are able to represent the dependencies among system parameters, point the bottleneck and estimate the response time in the load function. The computer system resources that bring in the biggest delays and can become potential bottlenecks are most often modeled in the simulation models. Among those resources one can distinguish procesors, hard drives and the elements of network infrastructure. Each of the resources are most often modeled in the QN as the queue consisting of waiting queue and the resource servicing the request [15]. The queue can be characterized by the function $S(n)$, which calculates the service time, where n is the number of request in the queue. The resource can be also described by the service demand denoted by D, which is the sum of service times for a request at the resource. Elaboration of appropriate simulation model consists of designing the structure of the model and designation of service demands for individual resources. It have been adopted that the simulation model of the web server is composed of resources representing the processor and the hard drive [22]. Additionally, the web server model should contain model of the cache memory stores HTTP objects. For simplification we assume that the objects are stored as a whole and the memory is organized according to the Last Recently Used policy. Figure 1 pictures the model of Web server.

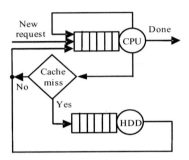

Fig. 1. QN model of the Web server

The service of the HTTP request in the web server includes the following steps: TCP connection establishment, data preparation, reading the requested object from hard drive (in case the object is not yet in the cache memory), data transmission, TCP connection tear-down. The costs connected with the requests service time can be described as follows:

1. Cost of request service on the processor:
   - TCP connection establishment and connection teardown time $D_{\text{TCP}}^{\text{CPU}}$,
   - response preparation time $D_{\text{P}}^{\text{CPU}}$,
   - data transmission time $D_{\text{T}}^{\text{CPU}}$,
2. Cost of request service on the disk D^{HDD}.

In order to build simulation model of specific web server an appropriate parameter measurements of the system must be done. The measurements of web systems parameters' may be carried out in various ways. One of the most popular way is the modification of server software to make the measurement of service time during the system operations possible [21]. However, this method has some drawbacks. First of all, the access to software source codes of the Web server is required. Moreover, the changes of the software can significantly change the way the examined system operates. This sort of modifications can increase the load of the processor and prolong the request service time. In this section another way of obtaining the web server parameters, proposed by the author, is presented. The service and service demand times for the processor and the hard drive are gained on the base of carried out experiments and with a usage of service Demand Law [5]. This law specifies the dependence of service demand time D^{Resource} from the resource utilization U^{Resource} and the throughput X of the entire system according to formula (1):

$$D^{\text{Resource}} = \frac{U^{\text{Resource}}}{X} \qquad (1)$$

The experiments were carried out with the use of a testbed consisting of client computer generating HTTP requests, the Web server and the switch. In the Fig. 2 the schema of the testbed is presented.

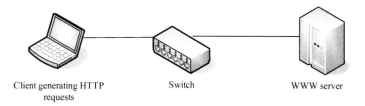

Client generating HTTP   Switch   WWW server
       requests

Fig. 2. Testbed

The Web server used in the experiments contained Intel Pentium 4.2 GHz processor, Seagate ST340810A 80 GB IDE hard drive and 1 GB of operating memory. It was working under the control of the Linux Fedora Core 6 operating system and the Apache 2.2.4 with PHP 5.1 Web server. The switch was Repotec RP-G3224E containing Gigabit Ethernet ports. As the clients' computer the IBM Thinkpad T60 with Intel T2400 1.8 GHz processor was used. The request generator software was installed on client computer. The software was written for research purposes in the C++ language with use of the CURL library [23]. It allowed sending many HTTP request in one TCP connection as well as sending each request in separate TCP connection depending on the needs.

The experiments were carried out in several stages. Firstly, the mean time $D_{\text{TCP}}^{\text{CPU}}$, which is the time the processor has to spend to establish and teardown the TCP connection was determined. In order to determine the time two experiments were conducted. In the first experiment, the clients' software was generating HTTP requests concerning the same object of size lower then 1 KB. The Web server was configured in such a way that it was closing the TCP connection each time the request service was completed. In the second experiment the client was sending request concerning the same object, but this time the Web server allowed keeping persistent connections. Therefore, each of the request were serviced within the same TCP connection. In both of the experiments the mean load of the processor as well as mean throughput were measured. The time $D_1^{\text{CPU}} = U_1^{\text{CPU}}/X_1$ is the average service demand in a function of the mean processor utilization U_1^{CPU} due to the request execution and the mean server throughput

X_1 measured in request serviced per second in the first experiment. Similarly, the time $D_2^{CPU} = U_2^{CPU}/X_2$ is a mean service demand in the second experiment. After calculating both values of time the TCP connection establishment time can be calculated according to $D_{TCP}^{CPU} = D_1^{CPU} - D_1^{CPU}$. As a result of the experiments the following values were obtained $U_1^{CPU} = 0.1433$, $X_1 = 986\,[1/s]$, $U_2^{CPU} = 0.1224$, $X_2 = 499\,[1/s]$, thus the values of service demand times were $D_1^{CPU} = 0.0001443\,[s]$, $D_2^{CPU} = 0.000245\,[s]$ and $D_{TCP}^{CPU} = 0.0001009\,[s]$.

In the next stage the response preparation time D_P^{CPU} was determined. This time consists of localization of the object time and response preparation time. In the conducted experiments client application was sending every request concerning different object which size did not exceed 1 KB. In this case, the transferred data with the HTTP response header could be put in a single frame of the data link layer protocol. The time spent by the processor on transferring the request is significantly lower than the request preparation time. The Web server was configured in a way that all requests were sent within one TCP connection. During the experiments the clients application were recording throughput X_3 and Web server processor utilization U_3^{CPU}. The response preparation time D_P^{CPU} was calculated according to $D_P^{CPU} = U_3^{CPU}/X_3$. As the result of the experiments the following average values of throughput $X_3 = 992\,[1/s]$ and the processor utilization $U_3^{CPU} = 0.1339$ were obtained while determined request preparation time was $D_P^{CPU} = 0.0001453\,[s]$.

In the next step the data transmission time D_T^{CPU}, which the Web server processor requires for sending data to the client, was determined. The data transmission time depends on the size of requested object therefore the task is to find the relation between the transmission time and the object size. Adequate multistage experiments were carried out. All experiments were similar to the one concerning response preparation time. In each one, average size of requested objects was different. The experiments were carried out for objects in size of 1, 4, 16, 64 and 512 KB. For every taken experiment the processor service demand was calculated on a basis of $D_z^{CPU} = U_z^{CPU}/X_z$, where z is the size of requested object $z = 1, 4, 16, 64, 512$, and z is in kilobytes, U_z^{CPU} is the mean processor utilization and X_z is the mean throughput in the experiment. Consecutive values $D_z^{CPU}(z)$ of the data transmission time are the differences between obtained service demands D_z^{CPU} and the response preparation time D_P^{CPU}, therefore $D_T^{CPU}(z) = D_z^{CPU} - D_P^{CPU}$. After collecting service demand time values for different object sizes, the data transmission time in the object size function can be set. This function is presented in the Fig. 3. and can be finally expressed as follows $D_T^{CPU}(z) = 0.00000429z\,[s]$, where coefficient of determination is $R^2 = 0.94$.

In the end the hard drive service demand D^{HDD} was determined. This particular time includes the time of data searching on the disk (seek time and rotational latency) and the disk transfer time. The hard drive service demand mainly depends on the size of the file requested by the client. Therefore, according to the previous, multistage experiments were carried out. In each of the experiments objects of similar sizes were downloaded and the size of requested files in each

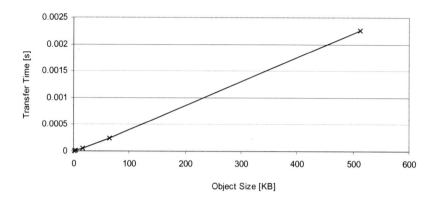

Fig. 3. Processor transfer time in object size function

experiment was different. It was adopted that objects of following sizes were downloaded: 1, 4, 16, 32, 64, 128, 512, 2048 KB. According to the previous experiments the hard drive mean utilization U_z^{HDD} and mean system throughput X_z were measured. The mean hard drive service demand was calculated according to $D_z^{\mathrm{HDD}} = U_z^{\mathrm{HDD}}/X_z$. After carrying out series of experiments the hard drive service demand was calculated on the base of obtained results. The Fig. 4 presents the mean hard drive service demand in the object size function.

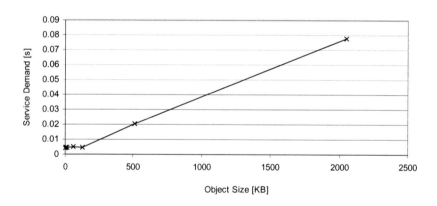

Fig. 4. Disc service demand in the object size function

Finally, it was adopted that mean hard drive service demand can be expressed as follow:

$$D^{\mathrm{HDD}}(z) = \begin{cases} 0.0045 & \text{for } z \in\, <0, 128> \\ 0.00003813125z + 0.0003808 & \text{for } z \in\, <128, \infty> \end{cases} \quad (2)$$

where z is the file size in kilobytes, and D^{HDD} is expressed in seconds. Coefficient of determination is $R^2 = 0.97$.

3   Simulation Program Modeling Operations of Web Server

A proposition of a simulation program describing the behavior of the Web server system will be presented now. The program is written in C++ language with the use of the CSIM 19 packet [24]. The packet is a library of routines, for use with C or C++ programs, which allows to create process-oriented, discrete-event simulation models. This packet is well-known and well-tested and as well as is one of the most common ones in the Web environment simulation domain [25,3,10,26]. The simulator includes the following elements: a simple request generator, the processor and the hard drive both modeled as the single waiting queue with one resource. Below a listing of the simulation program modeling of the Web server according to design presented in the previous section is introduced.

```
/*** Simulation program modeling Web server operation, ***/
/*** written in C++ with use of CSIM 19 libraries      ***/

include <cpp.h>
define CPU_TCP_Cost 0.00010097 //CPU TCP connection time
define CPU_Prepatation_Cost 0.00014533 //CPU preparation
define CPU_Transfer_Cost 0.000004291//CPU transfer time
define HDD_Factor_1 0.0045 //Disc factor 1
define HDD_Factor_2 0.00003813125 // Disc factor 2
define HDD_Factor_3 0.0003808 // Disc factor 3
define Objects_number 400 //Number of HTTP objects
facility *cpu;   //CPU queue
facility *hdd;   //Disc queue
int HTTP_Objects[Objests_number]; //Table of HTTP objects
//The main function
extern "C" void sim()
{
    double ai_time; //Interarrival time
    int r_id;       //Requested object identifier
    create("generator"); //creation of the generator process
    cpu= new facility ("cpu"); //creation of a new queue
    hdd= new facility ("hdd");
    //generation of HTTP objects
    //function must be defined by the designer
    create_HTTP_Objects(int HTTP_Objects[]);
    //generation of HTTP requests
    while(request_generator(ai_time, r_id))
    {
        //Stopping the request generation for interarrival time
        hold (ai_time);
        web_server(r_id);//sending the request to Web server
    }
    report(); //preparation of the report
}
//servicing the request on the Web server
```

```
void web_server (int r_id)
{
  create ("request"); //creation of the request process
  //inserting the request to CPU queue
  cpu->use(CPU_TCP_Cost+CPU_Prepatation_Cost);
  //checking if the object is available in the cache
  if (cache_miss(r_id)==1)
      {
          //processing the request in the disc
          if (HTTP_Objects[r_id]=< 128)
              hdd->use(HDD_Factor_1);
            else
              hdd->use(HDD_Factor_2*HTTP_Objects[r_id]+HDD_Factor_3);
  }
  //processing the transfer by the CPU
  cpu->use(HTTP_Objects[r_id]*CPU_Transfer_Cost);
}
```

In the presented example, first out of all, constants characterizing disc and processor are defined. Next variables representing processor and disk queues and the table containing HTTP objects sizes are declared. At the beginning of the sim function (the main function in the simulation program) the variable containing interarrival time and object identifier are declared. Afterwards, the request generator process and the processor and disc queues are created. Then with the use of `create_HTTP_Objects` function the table of object sizes is filled up. Further, the request generator function at the fixed interarrival time generates requests in the loop. Both of the functions define the operations of the request generator which can be build according to the model presented at [11,12]. Requests are serviced with the use of the web server function, which creates the request process, service the requests at the processor and disc queues according to model presented in the previous section.

4   Conclusion

In the article the way of building the simulation model was presented. The concept of Web server model was introduced also the way of conducting experiments, which lets to determine the server model parameters were described. With the use of service demand law the required HTTP request service demands for the processor and the hard drive were determined. For the processor we determined TCP connection establishment and connection teardown time $D_{\mathrm{TCP}}^{\mathrm{CPU}} = 0.00010097\,[\mathrm{s}]$, the response preparation time $D_{\mathrm{P}}^{\mathrm{CPU}} = 0.00014533\,[\mathrm{s}]$ and the data transmission time $D_{\mathrm{T}}^{\mathrm{CPU}}(z) = 0.00000429z\,[\mathrm{s}]$, where z is the size of requested object in KB. For the hard drive we determined only one time according to formula (2), including all other component times. In the end, the simulation program modeling the operations of described Web server was presented and discussed.

References

1. Borzemski, L.: The Use of Data Mining to Predict Web Performance. Cybernetics and Systems 37(6), 587–608 (2006)
2. Gilly, K., Juiz, C., Puigjaner, R.: An up-to-date survey in web load balancing. Springer, World Wide Web 10.1007/s11280-010-0101-5 (2010)
3. Borzemski, L., Zatwarnicki, K., Zatwarnicka, A.: Adaptive and Intelligent Request Distribution for Content Delivery Networks. Cybernetics and Systems 38(8), 837–857 (2007)
4. Czachorski, T.: A diffusion approximation model of web servers. In: Cellary, W., Iyengar, A. (eds.) Proceedings of IFIP TC6/WG6.4 Workshop on Internet Technologies, Wroclaw, Poland, October 10–11. Applications and Societal Impact (WITASI 2002), pp. 83–92. Kluwer Academic Publishers, Boston (2002)
5. Denning, P., Buzen, J.: The Operational Analysis of Queueing Network Models. ACM Comput. Surv. 10(3), 225–261 (1978)
6. Borzemski, L., Zatwarnicki, K.: A Fuzzy Adaptive Request Distribution Algorithm for Cluster-Based Web Systems. In: Proc. of 11th PDP Conf., pp. 119–126. IEEE Press, Los Alamitos (2003)
7. Arlitt, M., Jin, T.: Workload Characterization of the 1998 World Cup Web Site. Internet Systems and Applications Laboratory, HP Laboratories Palo Alto, HPL-1999-35(R.1) (1999)
8. Menascé, D., Bennani, M.: Analytic performance models for single class and multiple class multithreaded software servers. Int. CMG Conference 2006, 475–482 (2006)
9. Arlitt, M., Friedrich, R., Jin, T.: Workload characterization of a Web proxy in a cable modem environment. ACM Performauce EvaluaUon Review 27(2), 25–36 (1999)
10. Williams, A., Arlitt, M., Williamson, C., Barker, K.: Web workload characterization: ten years later. In: Tang, X., Xu, J., Chanson, S.T. (eds.) Publish info Web content, pp. 3–22. Springer, New York (2005)
11. Barford, M.: Modeling, Measurement and Performance of World Wide Web Transactions. Ph.D. Thesis (2001)
12. Barford, P., Misra, V.: Measurement, Modeling and Analysis of the Internet. In: IMA Workshop on Internet Modeling and Analysis, Minneapolis, MN (2004)
13. Cardellini, V., Colajanni, M., Yu, P.S.: Impact of workload models in evaluating the performance of distributed Web-server systems. In: Gelenbe, E. (ed.) System Performance Evaluation: Methodologies and Applications, pp. 397–417. CRC Press, Boca Raton (2000)
14. Borzemski, L., Zatwarnicki, K.: Using Adaptive Fuzzy-Neural Control to Minimize Response Time in Cluster-Based Web Systems. In: Szczepaniak, P.S., Kacprzyk, J., Niewiadomski, A. (eds.) AWIC 2005. LNCS (LNAI), vol. 3528, pp. 63–68. Springer, Heidelberg (2005)
15. Menascé, D., Almeida, V., Fonseca, R.: Business-oriented resource management policies for e-commerce servers. Performance Evaluation 42(2), 223–239 (2000)
16. Riska, A., Riedel, E.: Disk Drive Level workload Characterization. In: Proceedings of the USENIX Annual Technical Conference, Boston, pp. 97–103 (2006)
17. Zatwarnicki, K.: Neuro-Fuzzy Models in Global HTTP Request Distribution. In: Pan, J.-S., Chen, S.-M., Nguyen, N.T. (eds.) ICCCI 2010. LNCS, vol. 6421, pp. 1–10. Springer, Heidelberg (2010)

18. Zhang, Q., Riska, A., Riedel, E., Mi, M., Smarni, E.: Evaluating performability of systems with background jobs. In: Proceedings of The Symposium on Dependable Systems and Networks (DSN), Philadelphia, pp. 495–505 (2006)
19. Aron, M., Druschel, P., Zwaenepoel, W.: Efficient Support for P-http in Cluster-based Web Servers. In: Proceedings of the USENIX 1999 Annual Technical Conference, Monterey, CA (1999)
20. Casalicchio, E., Cardellini, V., Tucci, S.: Design and performance evaluation of mechanisms for mobile-devices handoff forecast. In: Proc. of FIRB-Perf Workshop on Techniques, Methodologies and Tools for Performance Evaluation of Complex Systems (in conjunction with QEST 2005), Torino, Italy (2005)
21. Cherkasova, L., Gardner, R.: Measuring CPU Overhead for I/O Processing in the Xen Virtual Machine Monitor. USENIX Association Berkeley, CA, USA, pp. 24–27 (2005)
22. Pai, V.S., Aron, M., Banga, G., Svendsen, M., Druschel, P., Zwaenpoel, W., Nahum, E.: Locality-Aware Request Distribution in Cluster-Based Network Servers. SIGOPS Oper. Syst. Rev. 32(5), 205–216 (1998)
23. CURL library documentation (2010), http://curl.haxx.se
24. CSIM19. CSIM19, Mesquite Software, 2008 Development toolkit for simulation and modeling (2008), http://www.mesquite.com
25. Andreolini, M., Casolari, S., Colajanni, M.: Autonomic request management algorithms for geographically distributed Internet-based systems. In: Proc. of 2-nd IEEE Int. Conference on Self-Adaptive and Self-Organizing Systems (2008)
26. Zatwarnicki, K.: Providing Web Service of Established Quality with the Use of HTTP Requests Scheduling Methods. In: Jędrzejowicz, P., Nguyen, N.T., Howlet, R.J., Jain, L.C. (eds.) KES-AMSTA 2010. LNCS, vol. 6070, pp. 142–151. Springer, Heidelberg (2010)

Maintenance of Custom Applications in the Grid Environment – On Basis of Oracle Enterprise Manager Grid Control and Logback Logging Utility

Lukasz Warchal and Lukasz Wycislik

Institute of Informatics
Silesian Technical University, ul. Akademicka 16, 44-100 Gliwice
{lwarchal,lwycislik}@polsl.pl

Abstract. The article presents functionality and areas of application in complex, corporate computing systems management of Oracle Grid Control. As preliminaries, the authors describe an evolutionary way the Oracle management systems were developed. Next, on basis of Grid Control application, the preset approach for building management systems is presented. Finally the authors show the plugin mechanism that allows extending Grid Control functionality to administrating of custom systems. On basis of a Logback logging utility a custom plugin development process was shown.

Keywords: grid, Oracle, Logback, logging, framework.

1 Introduction

Oracle Corporation is a company having a long established position in the market for software vendors. Although it is now the third company in the world (after IBM and Microsoft), taking into account the size of income and has a very wide range of software products, the company was mainly initially identified to the relational database server. This is a product designed for professional application – offering high flexibility configuration what allows effective use of memory resources and computing environments. Huge configuration options, both during installation and during maintenance of the database already running, have been paid for complication of administrative tasks. Application tools that supported the process of administering an Oracle database were being developed in a natural rhythm of developing the functional capabilities of the database itself and the technologies of applications developing, in particular the technologies influencing the possibility of building the graphical user interface of these applications. Initially they were console applications, dedicated to particular administrative areas (such as imports/exports data, performance tuning, etc.). An important criterion for creating these applications was their availability for different software platforms (Windows, Unix, Linux), hence the evolution of presentation layer technology was possible after the reinforcement of Java technology. At the

A. Kwiecień, P. Gaj, and P. Stera (Eds.): CN 2011, CCIS 160, pp. 55–60, 2011.

beginning Java technology was used only to implement the presentation layer in a thick client technology (called fat client as well), and the business functionality was called from the console applications. Later, these tools (such as DBA Studio) strengthened its position, setting standards and attracting many users among the database systems administrators.

The continuous increase in demand for cheap computing power and reliability of computer systems resulted in developing the concepts of grid architectures (called grid computing), where calculations and data processing can be distributed on the nodes of different architectures, which are often under the control of heterogeneous operating systems. This architecture brings particular challenges in terms of administration and maintenance. The ideal tool for administrator should allow him to manage all types of applications and infrastructure elements from one place in a unified way – this means that similar operations on different applications and systems should be implemented in a similar manner using a unified graphical user interface. Oracle's response to such demand is Enterprise Manager Grid Control system, where thanks to the three-tier architecture, the application can be run in any browser, and the mechanism of the plug-ins allows the integrations of new functionalities into the same unified graphical user interface. Description of the concept and system architecture is given in the next section.

2   Concept and Architecture

The concept of Enterprise Manager Grid Control is based on the assumption of centralized management and administration of the whole hardware/software infrastructure. By using three-tier architecture it is possible to run application on each authorized to this, computer with a web browser. Domain model on this subject has been presented in the Fig. 1.

Application Enterprise Manager Grid Control manages the constituent elements of the structure of the grid (called hosts). This is possible thanks to a software agent on each constituent element by which control is achieved by the Enterprise Manager. This diagram, for readability, shows the most frequent case, except that on one machine there are many logical partitions or virtual machines – then the agent software must be installed properly on each partition or virtual machine. Administration and management may be subject to different types of resources: application servers, database instances, operating systems, services, etc. In order to extend the functionality of a management system the corresponding plug-in (delivered by an independent supplier or developed for own needs) must be imported. One module can implement the functionality of the management of one or several types of resources. Imported modules must be deployed on selected host agents. On each machine an instance of managed type (called target instance) must be added. There is a possibility to add on one host a several instances of managed type (with different settings) – for example if one need to manage multiple instances of the database server.

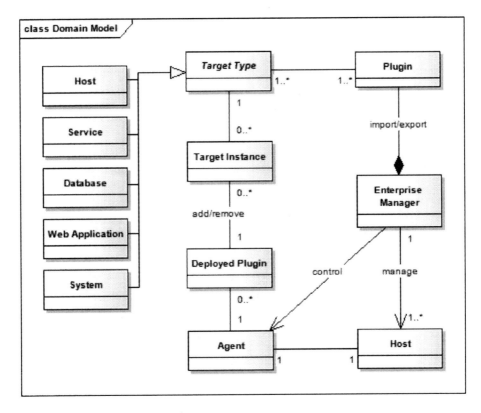

Fig. 1. Domain model of Enterprise Manager Grid Control concept

In addition to the functionality build into Enterprise Manager application, there is a possibility of extending the several available types of resources through the installation of dedicated plug-in. These modules provide both Oracle itself (eg. support for JBOSSm DB2, Tomcat, etc.), but also by independent providers (such as support for MySQL, Citrix Presentation Server, etc.). Oracle also provides tools to create plug-ins that could support custom types of resources [1]. The next section describes how to create and implement a custom plug-in utilizing data collected by Logback logging library [2].

Logback is a modern logging utility based on Java technology and is intended as a successor to very popular log4j utility. Thanks to a very refined concept it allows for building flexible software infrastructure that enables to trace such system aspects as security, efficiency and availability as well. In a complex corporate information systems, that often involving grid infrastructure, it is a very welcome feature to be able to monitor the warnings and errors reported by different applications in one place, which will present them in a unified form. What's more, administrators are able to subscribe to different types of information so that they may focus only on their interest areas of operation. All the above provides a combination of Enterprise Grid Control and Logback infrastructure.

3   Custom Plug-in Implementation Example

In this section example plug-in for Oracle Enterprise Manager Grid Control will be discussed. Its main task is to monitor and audit security events coming from custom web application, collected and stored in database using Logback logging library. Base on this information, system administrator can maintenance and change application parameters.

In each web application proper setting session timeout value is very important. If this value is too big, web server resources are used inefficient. If it is too small, user can obtain Session Timeout error. Discussed web application handles this error (if occurred) and logs corresponding information using Logback. This library is configured in a such way, that this information is stored in Oracle database – DbAppender is attached to logger instances used. Proposed custom plug-in checks number of such log entries (every 30 minutes) and if it is greater than 10 warning is reported, if greater than 20 error is reported.

Developing custom plug-in for EMGC require creating XML file called Target Type Metadata File [3] which describes new target type that instances can be monitored. In this file, the Metric elements creates list of all metrics collected for particular target type and shows how to obtain each metric. Discussed plug-in use metric build on database tables used by Logback DbAppender, as shown below[1].

```
<TargetMetadata META_VER="1.0" TYPE="sec_audit_2" TARGET_VERSION="1.2">
    <Display>
    <Label NLSID="sec_audit_label">Security Audit</Label>
    </Display>
    <InstanceProperties>
    <!-- variables -->
    </InstanceProperties>
    <Metric NAME="Response" TYPE="TABLE">
    <!-- metric responsible for exposing service availability -->
    </Metric>
    <Metric NAME="SessionTimeouts" TYPE="TABLE">
      <Display>
        <Label NLSID="WebApp">Web application</Label>
      </Display>
      <TableDescriptor>
      <ColumnDescriptor NAME="APP_NAME" TYPE="STRING" IS_KEY="FALSE">
        <Display>
          <Label NLSID="metric_app_name">App Name</Label>
        </Display>
      </ColumnDescriptor>
    <ColumnDescriptor NAME="SESSION_TIMEOUTS" TYPE="NUMBER" IS_KEY="FALSE">
        <Display>
            <Label NLSID="metric_timeouts">Num of session timeouts</Label>
        </Display>
```

---

[1] Some elements omitted for clarity.

```
      </ColumnDescriptor>
    </TableDescriptor>
    <QueryDescriptor FETCHLET_ID="SQL">
      <Property NAME="MachineName" SCOPE="INSTANCE">HOST</Property>
      <Property NAME="Port" SCOPE="INSTANCE">PORT</Property>
      <Property NAME="ServiceName" SCOPE="INSTANCE">SN</Property>
      <Property NAME="UserName" SCOPE="INSTANCE">USERNAME</Property>
      <Property NAME="password" SCOPE="INSTANCE">PASS</Property>
      <Property NAME="STATEMENT" SCOPE="GLOBAL">
        select l.arg1 as APP_NAME, count(*) as SESSION_TIMEOUTS
        from logadm.logging_event l
        where l.arg0 = 2000 group by l.arg1
      </Property>
        <Property NAME="NUMROWS" SCOPE="GLOBAL">30</Property>
    </QueryDescriptor>
  </Metric>
</TargetMetadata>
```

In QueryDescriptor element we define which fetchlet [3] (parameterized data access mechanism) will be used. In this example SQL query is used along with SQL Fetchlet.

Target Type Default Collections File is another file required to develop custom plug-in. In this XML file metric collection intervals and alert thresholds are defined. Based on this EMGC can regularly obtain monitored metrics and check defined conditions violations. Discussed plug-in collects data every 30 minutes and checks conditions described at the beginning of this section, according to its Target Type Default Collections File shown below.

```
<TargetCollection TYPE="sec_audit_2">
  <CollectionItem NAME="Response">
    <Schedule>
      <IntervalSchedule INTERVAL="1" TIME_UNIT="Min" />
    </Schedule>
    <Condition COLUMN_NAME="Status" CRITICAL="0" OPERATOR="EQ" />
  </CollectionItem>
  <CollectionItem NAME="SessionTimeouts">
    <Schedule>
      <IntervalSchedule INTERVAL="10" TIME_UNIT="Min" />
    </Schedule>
    <Condition COLUMN_NAME="SESSION_TIMEOUTS" WARNING="10"
      CRITICAL="20" OPERATOR="GE" />
  </CollectionItem>
</TargetCollection>
```

Both described XML files must be syntactically and structurally correct. To achieve this, Oracle provides ILINT tool which makes static XML validation (XML files checked with respective DTD's), dynamic validation (executing all metrics through the fetchlets). It also do some heuristic constraint checks, i.e. if too many metrics are collected (over 50) for a given target type, a warning message is obtained.

Before deploying created plug-in on agents it must be first packed into a Management Plugin Archive (MPA). This can be done with Enterprise Manager Command Line Interface (EM CLI). Below is an example of using this tool to pack discussed plug-in to MPA.

```
C:\sec_audit>emcli add_mp_to_mpa -mpa="sec_audit_2.jar" -mp_version="1.2"
  -ttd="ttd\sec_audit_2.xml" -dc="dc\sec_audit_2.xml"
Management Plug-in "sec_audit_2" version 1.2 requiring minimum OMS version
10.2.0.1 added successfully to MPA "sec_audit_2.jar"
```

Created by EM CLI JAR file can now be installed on agent machines and defined in plug-in target type instances can be created.

4   Summary

This paper presents the possibility of Oracle Grid Control and its applications in the field of management and maintenance of subsystems in a complex corporate information systems. The authors presented the possibility of extending the functionality of Grid Control on sample of Logback logging utility. The proposed solution allows to trace such system aspects as security, efficiency and availability as well.

References

1. Oracle Enterprise Manager – Extensibility Guide (March 2009)
2. Logback Home Page, http://logback.qos.ch/
3. Enterprise Manager – Connectors Integration Guide (May 2009)

Queueing Systems with Common Buffer: A Theoretical Treatment

Oleg Tikhonenko

Institute of Theoretical and Applied Informatics, Polish Academy of Sciences
Baltycka 5, 44–100 Gliwice, Poland
oleg.tikhonenko@gmail.com

Abstract. We investigate queueing systems of different types with demands having some random space requirements connected via common limited buffer space. For such systems combination we determine steady-state loss probability and distribution of number of demands present in each system from the combination.

Keywords: queueing system, space requirement, total demands capacity, buffer space capacity.

1 Introduction

We consider queueing systems with demands of random space requirement. It means that (1) each demand is characterized by some non-negative random indication named the demand space requirement ore demand volume ζ; (2) the total sum $\sigma(t)$ of space requirements (volumes) of all demands present in the system at arbitrary time moment t is limited by some constant value V, which is named the buffer space capacity of the system; (3) we also assume sometimes that service time ξ of the demand and it's space requirement ζ are dependent.

Such systems have been used to model and solve the various practical problems occurring in the design of computer and communicating systems.

The joint distribution of ζ and ξ random variables we characterize by the joint distribution function $F(x,t) = \mathbf{P}\{\zeta < x, \xi < t\}$. The buffer space is occupied by the demand at the epoch it arrives and is released entirely at the epoch it completes service. The random process $\sigma(t)$ is called the total (demands) capacity. If the value V is finite, it leads to additional losses of demands. A demand having space requirement (volume) x, which arrives at the epoch τ when there are idle servers or waiting positions, will be admitted to the system, if $\sigma(\tau - 0) + x \le V$. Otherwise (if $\sigma(\tau - 0) + x > V$) the demand will be lost.

Queueing systems with limited buffer capacity were analyzed, for example, in [1–7]. It follows from the earlier publications that we can determine a stationary demands number distribution and loss probability for the following queueing systems.

1. $M/M/n/(m, V)$ system. This notation means that we deal with like classical $M/M/n/m$ system, but the difference is that in the first system a demand

A. Kwiecień, P. Gaj, and P. Stera (Eds.): CN 2011, CCIS 160, pp. 61–69, 2011.

has an arbitrary distributed space requirement, its service time (having an exponential distribution) is independent of the space requirement and the total buffer capacity is limited by the value $V > 0$, $1 \leq n \leq \infty$, $0 \leq m \leq \infty$.

2. $M/G/n/(0, V)$ system (generalized Erlang system). This is like classical $M/G/n/0$ system with an arbitrary joint distribution of service time and demand volume and limited (by V) total buffer capacity.

3. Processor-sharing system with an arbitrary joint distribution of service time (or demand length) and demand space requirement and limited (by V) total buffer capacity.

In present paper we investigate combinations of (may be different) queueing systems connected via common limited (by V) buffer. Such models obviously can be used in computer and communicating networks designing. For simplicity we shall analyze in detail the case of $n = 1$, $m = \infty$, i. e. we consider two like classical $M/G/1/\infty$ queues connected via common buffer. The case of $n > 1$, $m < \infty$ and arbitrary number of systems can be investigated analogously. A statement allowing determination of the steady-state demands number distribution and loss probability for each of systems connected via common buffer will be presented.

In similar way can be also investigated the case of processor-sharing system connected with other queues.

2   Random Process and Characteristics

We shall use the following notation ($i = 1, 2$): a_i – the rate of demand arrival process for ith queue, ζ_i – the demand space requirement for ith queue, ξ_i – the ith queue demand service time; $L_i(x)$ – the distribution function of ζ_i random variable, $B_i(t)$ – the distribution function of ξ_i random variable; $\eta_i(t)$ – the number of demands present in ith system at time moment t; $\zeta_j^{(i)}(t)$ – the volume of jth demand present in ith system at the moment t, $j = \overline{1, \eta_i(t)}$; $\xi_*^{(i)}(t)$ – the residual service time of the demand being on service in ith system at the moment t. It's clear that $\sigma(t) = \sum\limits_{i=1}^{2} \sum\limits_{j=1}^{\eta_i(t)} \zeta_j^{(i)}(t)$.

The combination of queues under consideration can be described by the following Markov random process:

$$(\eta_i(t), \zeta_j^{(i)}(t), \xi_*^{(i)}(t), j = \overline{1, \eta_i(t)}, i = 1, 2) \tag{1}$$

The process (1) is characterized by the functions having the following probability sense:

$$P_0(t) = \mathbf{P}\{\eta_i(t) = 0, i = 1, 2\} = \mathbf{P}\{\sigma(t) = 0\} \tag{2}$$

$$G(k, 0, x, y, t) = \mathbf{P}\{\eta_1(t) = k, \eta_2(t) = 0, \sigma(t) < x, \xi_*^{(1)}(t) < y\}, \ k = 1, 2, \ldots \tag{3}$$

$$G(0, k, x, z, t) = \mathbf{P}\{\eta_1(t) = 0, \eta_2(t) = k, \sigma(t) < x, \xi_*^{(2)}(t) < z\}, \ k = 1, 2, \ldots \tag{4}$$

$$G(k_1, k_2, x, y, z, t) =$$

$$= \mathbf{P}\{\eta_1(t) = k_1, \eta_2(t) = k_2, \sigma(t) < x, \xi_*^{(1)}(t) < y, \xi_*^{(2)}(t) < z\}, \ k_1, k_2 = 1, 2, \dots \tag{5}$$

We introduce also the functions

$$W(k_1, k_2, y, z, t) = \mathbf{P}\{\eta_1(t) = k_1, \eta_2(t) = k_2, \xi_*^{(1)}(t) < y, \xi_*^{(2)}(t) < z\} =$$

$$= G(k_1, k_2, V, y, z, t), \ k_1, k_2 = 1, 2, \dots \tag{6}$$

The functions $W(k, 0, y, t)$ and $W(0, k, z, t)$ can be introduced by similar way. The demand number distribution is defined by the following functions:

$$P(k_1, k_2, t) = \mathbf{P}\{\eta_i(t) = k_i, i = 1, 2\} = W(k_1, k_2, \infty, \infty, t), \ k_1, k_2 = 1, 2, \dots \tag{7}$$

We can define the functions $P(k, 0, t)$, $P(0, k, t)$ analogously.

We are interested in steady-state demands number distribution and loss probability. Therefore let us write out the stationary analogies of the functions (2)–(5):

$$p_0 = \lim_{t \to \infty} P_0(t) \tag{8}$$

$$g(k, 0, x, y) = \lim_{t \to \infty} G(k, 0, x, y, t), \ k = 1, 2, \dots \tag{9}$$

$$g(0, k, x, z) = \lim_{t \to \infty} G(0, k, x, z, t), \ k = 1, 2, \dots \tag{10}$$

$$g(k_1, k_2, x, y, z) = \lim_{t \to \infty} G(k_1, k_2, x, y, z, t), \ k_1, k_2 = 1, 2, \dots \tag{11}$$

Now we can define stationary analogies of (6) and (7) functions:

$$w(k_1, k_2, y, z) = g(k_1, k_2, V, y, z)), \ k_1, k_2 = 1, 2, \dots \tag{12}$$

$$p(k_1, k_2) = w(k_1, k_2, \infty, \infty), \ k_1, k_2 = 1, 2, \dots \tag{13}$$

The functions $w(k, 0, y)$, $w(0, k, z)$, $p(k, 0)$, $p(0, k)$ can be defined analogously.

The functions $p(k_1, k_2)$ define the steady-state demands number distribution in the combination of queues under consideration. We can determine loss probabilities for each queue of the combination using the functions (8)–(13). Let, for example, $P_L^{(1)}$ be a loss probability for the first queue. Let us define the following function:

$$w_k^{(1)}(y) = w(k, 0, y) + \sum_{k_2=1}^{\infty} w(k, k_2, y, \infty), \ k = 1, 2, \dots$$

Then, the loss probability can be determined from the following equilibrium equation:

$$a_1 \left(1 - P_L^{(1)}\right) = \sum_{k=1}^{\infty} \frac{\partial w_k^{(1)}(y)}{\partial y} \bigg|_{y=0}$$

It means that an average number of demands admitted to the first system during a unit of time is equal (in steady state) to an average number of demands of this system, whose service was completed during this time. We have (for arbitrary queue from our combination) from the last relation that

$$P_L^{(i)} = 1 - \frac{1}{a_i} \sum_{k=1}^{\infty} \frac{\partial w_k^{(i)}(y)}{\partial y} \bigg|_{y=0}, \ i = 1, 2 \ .$$

3   The Main Statement

Further we shall use the following (convenient for our aims) notation for Stieltjes convolution

1. $\int_0^x f_1(x-u)df_2(u) = f_1 * f_2(x) = f_2 * f_1(x).$

2. $\int_{u=0}^x f_1(y_1, ..., y_{i-1}, x-u, y_{i+1}, ..., y_k)d_u f_2(z_1, ..., z_{j-1}, u, z_{j+1}, ..., z_l) =$

$= f_1(y_1, ..., y_{i-1}, *, y_{i+1}, ..., y_k) * f_2(z_1, ..., z_{j-1}, *, z_{j+1}, ..., z_l)(x) =$
$= f_2(z_1, ..., z_{j-1}, *, z_{j+1}, ..., z_l) * f_1(y_1, ..., y_{i-1}, *, y_{i+1}, ..., y_k)(x).$

3. $\int_0^x f_1(y_1, ..., y_{i-1}, x-u, y_{i+1}, ..., y_k)df_2(u) =$

$= f_1(y_1, ..., y_{i-1}, *, y_{i+1}, ..., y_k) * f_2(x) = f_2 * f_1(y_1, ..., y_{i-1}, *, y_{i+1}, ..., y_k)(x).$

Similar notations are used for a convolution of more than two functions.

By additional variables method partial differential equations for the functions (2)–(6) can be written out. From these equations we obtain the following ones for steady-state functions (8)–(12):

$$0 = -(a_1L_1(V) + a_2L_2(V))p_0 + \left.\frac{\partial w(1,0,y)}{\partial y}\right|_{y=0} + \left.\frac{\partial w(0,1,z)}{\partial z}\right|_{z=0} \tag{14}$$

$$-\frac{\partial w(1,0,y)}{\partial y} + \left.\frac{\partial w(1,0,y)}{\partial y}\right|_{y=0} = a_1p_0L_1(V)B_1(y) - a_1g(1,0,*,y)*L_1(V)-$$

$$-a_2g(1,0,*,y)*L_2(V) + \left.\frac{\partial w(2,0,y)}{\partial y}\right|_{y=0} B_1(y) + \left.\frac{\partial w(1,1,y,z)}{\partial z}\right|_{z=0} \tag{15}$$

$$-\frac{\partial w(0,1,z)}{\partial z} + \left.\frac{\partial w(0,1,z)}{\partial z}\right|_{z=0} = a_2p_0L_2(V)B_2(z) - a_1g(0,1,*,z)*L_1(V)-$$

$$-a_2g(0,1,*,z)*L_2(V) + \left.\frac{\partial w(1,1,y,z)}{\partial y}\right|_{y=0} + \left.\frac{\partial w(0,2,z)}{\partial z}\right|_{z=0} B_2(z) \tag{16}$$

$$-\frac{\partial w(k,0,y)}{\partial y} + \left.\frac{\partial w(k,0,y)}{\partial y}\right|_{y=0} = a_1g(k-1,0,*,y)*L_1(V)-$$

$$-a_1g(k,0,*,y)*L_1(V) - a_2g(k,0,*,y)*L_2(V)+$$

$$+\left.\frac{\partial w(k+1,0,y)}{\partial y}\right|_{y=0} B_1(y) + \left.\frac{\partial w(k,1,y,z)}{\partial z}\right|_{z=0}, \quad k = 2,3,\ldots \tag{17}$$

$$-\frac{\partial w(0,k,z)}{\partial z} + \left.\frac{\partial w(0,k,z)}{\partial z}\right|_{z=0} = a_2g(0,k-1,*,z)*L_2(V)-$$

$$-a_1g(0,k,*,z)*L_1(V) - a_2g(0,k,*,z)*L_2(V)+$$

$$+\left.\frac{\partial w(1,k,y,z)}{\partial y}\right|_{y=0} + \left.\frac{\partial w(0,k+1,z)}{\partial z}\right|_{z=0} B_2(z), \quad k = 2,3,\ldots \tag{18}$$

$$-\frac{\partial w(1,1,y,z)}{\partial y} + \frac{\partial w(1,1,y,z)}{\partial y}\bigg|_{y=0} - \frac{\partial w(1,1,y,z)}{\partial z} + \frac{\partial w(1,1,y,z)}{\partial z}\bigg|_{z=0} =$$

$$= a_1 B_1(y)g(0,1,*,z)*L_1(V) + a_2 B_2(z)g(1,0,*,y)*L_2(V) -$$

$$-a_1 g(1,1,*,y,z)*L_1(V) - a_2 g(1,1,*,y,z)*L_2(V) +$$

$$+\frac{\partial w(2,1,y,z))}{\partial y}\bigg|_{y=0} B_1(y) + \frac{\partial w(1,2,y,z))}{\partial z}\bigg|_{z=0} B_2(z) \qquad (19)$$

$$-\frac{\partial w(1,k,y,z)}{\partial y} + \frac{\partial w(1,k,y,z)}{\partial y}\bigg|_{y=0} - \frac{\partial w(1,k,y,z)}{\partial z} + \frac{\partial w(1,k,y,z)}{\partial z}\bigg|_{z=0} =$$

$$= a_1 B_1(y)g(0,k,*,z)*L_1(V) + a_2 g(1,k-1,*,y,z)*L_2(V) -$$

$$-a_1 g(1,k,*,y,z)*L_1(V) - a_2 g(1,k,*,y,z)*L_2(V) +$$

$$+\frac{\partial w(2,k,y,z))}{\partial y}\bigg|_{y=0} B_1(y) + \frac{\partial w(1,k+1,y,z))}{\partial z}\bigg|_{z=0} B_2(z), \; k = 2,3,\dots \quad (20)$$

$$-\frac{\partial w(k,1,y,z)}{\partial y} + \frac{\partial w(k,1,y,z)}{\partial y}\bigg|_{y=0} - \frac{\partial w(k,1,y,z)}{\partial z} + \frac{\partial w(1,1,y,z)}{\partial z}\bigg|_{z=0} =$$

$$= a_1 g(k-1,1,*,z)*L_1(V) + a_2 B_2(z)g(k,0,*,y)*L_2(V) -$$

$$-a_1 g(k,1,*,y,z)*L_1(V) - a_2 g(k,1,*,y,z)*L_2(V) +$$

$$+\frac{\partial w(k+1,1,y,z))}{\partial y}\bigg|_{y=0} B_1(y) + \frac{\partial w(k,2,y,z))}{\partial z}\bigg|_{z=0} B_2(z), \; k = 2,3,\dots \quad (21)$$

$$-\frac{\partial w(k_1,k_2,y,z)}{\partial y} + \frac{\partial w(k_1,k_2,y,z)}{\partial y}\bigg|_{y=0} - \frac{\partial w(k_1,k_2,y,z)}{\partial z} + \frac{\partial w(k_1,k_2,y,z)}{\partial z}\bigg|_{z=0} =$$

$$= a_1 g(k_1-1,k_2,*,y,z)*L_1(V) + a_2 g(k_1,k_2-1,*,y,z)*L_2(V) -$$

$$-a_1 g(k_1,k_2,*,y,z)*L_1(V) - a_2 g(k_1,k_2,*,y,z)*L_2(V) +$$

$$+\frac{\partial w(k_1+1,k_2,y,z))}{\partial y}\bigg|_{y=0} B_1(y) + \frac{\partial w(k_1,k_2+1,y,z))}{\partial z}\bigg|_{z=0} B_2(z),$$

$$k_1, k_2 = 2,3,\dots \qquad (22)$$

The following evident boundary conditions take place in steady state:

$$a_1 L_1(V)p_0 = \frac{\partial w(1,0,y)}{\partial y}\bigg|_{y=0}; \; a_2 L_2(V)p_0 = \frac{\partial w(0,1,z)}{\partial z}\bigg|_{z=0} \qquad (23)$$

$$a_1 g(k,0,*,y)*L_1(V) = \frac{\partial w(k+1,0,y)}{\partial y}\bigg|_{y=0} B_1(y), \; k = 1,2,\dots \qquad (24)$$

$$a_2 g(k,0,*,y)*L_2(V) = \frac{\partial w(k,1,y,z)}{\partial z}\bigg|_{z=0}, \; k = 1,2,\dots \qquad (25)$$

$$a_2 g(0,k,*,z)*L_2(V) = \frac{\partial w(0,k+1,z)}{\partial z}\bigg|_{z=0} B_2(z), \; k = 1,2,\dots \qquad (26)$$

$$a_1 g(0,k,*,z)*L_1(V) = \frac{\partial w(1,k,y,z)}{\partial y}\bigg|_{y=0}, \; k = 1,2,\dots \qquad (27)$$

$$a_1 g(k_1, k_2, *, y, z) * L_1(V) = \frac{\partial w(k_1 + 1, k_2, y, z)}{\partial y}\bigg|_{y=0} B_1(y), \ k_1, k_2 = 1, 2, \ldots$$
(28)

$$a_2 g(k_1, k_2, *, y, z) * L_2(V) = \frac{\partial w(k_1, k_2 + 1, y, z)}{\partial z}\bigg|_{z=0} B_2(z), \ k_1, k_2 = 1, 2, \ldots$$
(29)

Denote by η_i, σ the stationary number of demands in ith system and total demands capacity in the combination of systems consequently. Let $\xi_*^{(i)}$ be the stationary residual service time of the demand on service in ith system and $p_0^{(i)} = \mathbf{P}\{\eta_i = 0\}$,

$$g_k^{(i)}(x, y) = \mathbf{P}\{\eta_i = k, \sigma < x, \xi_*^{(i)} < y\}, \ w_k^{(i)}(y) = g_k^{(i)}(V, y), \ i = 1, 2$$

Let us write out equations for an independent $M/G/1/(\infty, V)$ system. For example, for the first queue they follow from the equations (14)–(29), if $a_2 = 0$. So, for a separate ith ($i = 1, 2$) queue of the combination with limited (by V) buffer space capacity we obtain the following equations:

$$0 = -a_i L_i(V) p_0^{(i)} + \frac{\partial w_1^{(i)}(y)}{\partial y}\bigg|_{y=0}$$
(30)

$$-\frac{\partial w_1^{(i)}(y)}{\partial y} + \frac{\partial w_1^{(i)}(y)}{\partial y}\bigg|_{y=0} =$$

$$= a_i p_0^{(i)} L_i(V) B_i(y) - a_i g_1^{(i)}(*, y) * L_i(V) + \frac{\partial w_2^{(i)}(y)}{\partial y}\bigg|_{y=0} B_i(y)$$
(31)

$$-\frac{\partial w_k^{(i)}(y)}{\partial y} + \frac{\partial w_k^{(i)}(y)}{\partial y}\bigg|_{y=0} = a_i g_{k-1}^{(i)}(*, y) * L_i(V) -$$

$$-a_i g_k^{(i)}(*, y) * L_i(V) + \frac{\partial w_{k+1}^{(i)}(y)}{\partial y}\bigg|_{y=0} B_i(y), \ k = 2, 3, \ldots$$
(32)

$$a_i L_i(V) p_0^{(i)} = \frac{\partial w_1^{(i)}(y)}{\partial y}\bigg|_{y=0}$$
(33)

$$a_i g_k^{(i)}(*, y) * L_i(V) = \frac{\partial w_{k+1}^{(i)}(y)}{\partial y}\bigg|_{y=0} B_i(y), \ k = 1, 2, \ldots$$
(34)

The following statement takes place.

Theorem 1. *Let the numbers $\hat{p}_0^{(i)}$ and the functions $\hat{g}_k^{(i)}(x, y)$ satisfy the equations (30)–(34) and the normalization condition*

$$\hat{p}_0^{(i)} + \sum_{k=1}^{\infty} \hat{g}_k^{(i)}(V, \infty) = 1, \ i = 1, 2$$

Then the functions

$$\hat{g}(k,0,x,y) = \frac{\hat{p}_0}{\hat{p}_0^{(1)}}\hat{g}_k^{(1)}(x,y), \quad \hat{g}(0,k,x,z) = \frac{\hat{p}_0}{\hat{p}_0^{(2)}}\hat{g}_k^{(2)}(x,z), \quad k = 1,2,\ldots,$$

$$\hat{g}(k_1,k_2,x,y,z) = \frac{\hat{p}_0}{\hat{p}_0^{(1)}\hat{p}_0^{(2)}}\hat{g}_{k_1}^{(1)}(*,y)*\hat{g}_{k_2}^{(2)}(*,z)(x), \quad k_1,k_2 = 1,2,\ldots$$

satisfy the equations (14)–(29) (the number $\hat{p}_0$ can be determined from the normalization condition).

The theorem can be proved by direct substitution of $\hat{g}(k_1,k_2,x,y,z)$ functions into (14)–(29) equations.

Note that the solution of the eqs. (30)–(34) has the form [8]:

$$\hat{g}_k^{(i)}(x,y) = C_i\widetilde{w}_k^{(i)}(y)L_{i*}^{(k)}(x)$$

where $\widetilde{w}_k^{(i)}(y)$ is a steady-state solution of appropriate equations for classical $M/G/1/\infty$ system, C_i is a constant value determined from the normalization condition, $L_{i*}^{(k)}(x)$ is the kth order Stieltjes convolution of the function $L_i(x)$. Therefore we have

$$\hat{g}(k_1,k_2,x,y,z) = \frac{\hat{p}_0}{\hat{p}_0^{(1)}\hat{p}_0^{(2)}}C_1C_2\widetilde{w}_{k_1}^{(1)}(y)\widetilde{w}_{k_2}^{(2)}(z)L_{1*}^{(k_1)}*L_{2*}^{(k_2)}(x), \quad k_1,k_2 = 1,2,\ldots$$

Corollary 1. *If $p_{k_i}^{(i)} = f_i(k_i,V)$ is the demands number distribution for ith independent queue, $i = 1,2$, then for the system being combination of the queues with limited by V common buffer space capacity we have*

$$p(k_1,k_2) = Cf_1(k_1,*)*f_2(k_2,*)(V)$$

where C can be obtained from the normalization condition.

It's clear that $\widetilde{p}_k^{(i)} = \widetilde{w}_k^{(i)}(\infty)$, where $\widetilde{p}_k^{(i)}$ is a steady-state probability of the presence of k demands in classical $M/G/1/\infty$ queue. Therefore we have

$$p(k_1,k_2) = \frac{\hat{p}_0}{\hat{p}_0^{(1)}\hat{p}_0^{(2)}}C_1C_2\widetilde{p}_{k_1}^{(1)}\widetilde{p}_{k_2}^{(2)}L_{1*}^{(k_1)}*L_{2*}^{(k_2)}(V), \quad k_1,k_2 = 1,2,\ldots \; .$$

4   Some Special Cases

In the present section we analyze the case of two systems with exponentially distributed service time connected via common buffer. Let μ_1 and μ_2 be the parameter of service time distribution for the first and second sytem accordingly, $\rho_i = a_i/\mu_i$, $i = 1,2$. For such combinations of queues we can obtain the next results:

$$p_0 = \left[\sum_{k_1=0}^{\infty}\sum_{k_2=0}^{\infty}\rho_1^{k_1}\rho_2^{k_2}L_{1*}^{(k_1)}*L_{2*}^{(k_2)}(V)\right]^{-1} \tag{35}$$

$$p(k_1, k_2) = p_0 \rho_1^{k_1} \rho_2^{k_2} L_{1*}^{(k_1)} * L_{2*}^{(k_2)}(V), \ k_i = 1, 2, \ldots \tag{36}$$

$$P_L^i = 1 - \frac{1}{\rho_i}(1 - p_0^{(i)}), \ i = 1, 2 \tag{37}$$

where $p_0^{(1)} = \sum_{k=0}^{\infty} p(0, k)$, $p_0^{(2)} = \sum_{k=0}^{\infty} p(k, 0)$.

The obtained relations are generally not convenient for calculation because of Stieltjes convolutions presence. They can be precisely calculated in some special cases. For example, let the ith queue demands space requirement has gamma distribution with the following density:

$$l_i(x) = \gamma_f(\alpha_i, x) = \frac{f}{\Gamma(\alpha_i)} x^{\alpha_i - 1} e^{-fx}, \ \alpha_i > 0, \ f > 0, \ i = 1, 2$$

(the parameter f is supposed the same for both queues). In this case the convolution $L_{1*}^{(k_1)} * L_{2*}^{(k_2)}(x)$ is the gamma distribution function $Y_f(\alpha, x)$ with the parameters f and $\alpha = k_1 \alpha_1 + k_2 \alpha_2$, i. e. we have

$$p(k_1, k_2) = p_0 \rho_1^{k_1} \rho_2^{k_2} Y_f(k_1 \alpha_1 + k_2 \alpha_2, V)$$

$$p_0 = \left[\sum_{k_1=0}^{\infty} \sum_{k_2=0}^{\infty} \rho_1^{k_1} \rho_2^{k_2} Y_f(k_1 \alpha_1 + k_2 \alpha_2, V) \right]^{-1}$$

In this case the relation for the first queue demands loss probability has the form

$$P_L^{(1)} = 1 - \frac{1}{\rho_1} \left[1 - \sum_{k=0}^{\infty} \rho_2^k Y_f(k\alpha_2, V) \right]$$

Suppose now that $L_1(x) = L_2(x) = L(x) = 1 - e^{-fx}$. Suppose also that $\rho_1 \neq 1$, $\rho_2 \neq 1$ and $\rho_1 \neq \rho_2$. Then, from the relations (35), (36) we obtain

$$p(k_1, k_1) = p_0 \rho_1^{k_1} \rho_2^{k_2} \left[1 - e^{-fV} \sum_{j=0}^{k_1+k_2-1} \frac{(fV)^j}{j!} \right], \ k_1, k_2 = 1, 2, \ldots$$

$$p_0 = \left[\frac{1}{(1 - \rho_1)(1 - \rho_2)} - \frac{\rho_1^2 e^{-(1-\rho_1)fV}}{(1 - \rho_1)(\rho_1 - \rho_2)} - \frac{\rho_2^2 e^{-(1-\rho_2)fV}}{(1 - \rho_2)(\rho_2 - \rho_1)} \right]^{-1}$$

The loss probabilities can be determined from the relation (37). For $i = 1$ we have

$$P_L^{(1)} = 1 - \frac{1}{\rho_1} \left[1 - \frac{p_0 \left(1 - \rho_2 e^{-(1-\rho_2)fV} \right)}{1 - \rho_2} \right]$$

and analogously

$$P_L^{(2)} = 1 - \frac{1}{\rho_2} \left[1 - \frac{p_0 \left(1 - \rho_1 e^{-(1-\rho_1)fV} \right)}{1 - \rho_1} \right].$$

5   Conclusions

In the paper we investigated combinations of queueing systems connected via common buffer of limited space capacity.

For systems with waiting places ($m > 0$) the analytical investigation is possible for the case of demands having service time independendent of their space requirement. However, such investigation become possible for systems with dependent demands space requirement and service time and without waiting places, for example, for the case of processor sharing or Erlang systems.

The advantage of the presenting approach is that it allows analysing of combination of queueing systems of different types.

The formulas obtained in the paper are not generally convenient for precise calculation, but the calculation is possible in some special cases. In other cases we can use the numeric inversion of Laplace transform [9, 10] to approximate calculations of Stieltjes convolutions.

References

1. Tikhonenko, O.M.: Queueing Models in Computer Systems. Universitetskoe, Minsk (1990) (in Russian)
2. Tikhonenko, O.: Computer Systems Probability Analysis. Akademicka Oficyna Wydawnicza EXIT, Warsaw (2006) (in Polish)
3. Alexandrov, A.M., Katz, B.A.: Non-Homogeneous Demands Flows Service. Izvestiya AN SSSR. Tekhnicheskaya Kibernetika (2), 47–53 (1973) (in Russian)
4. Tikhonenko, O.M.: Destricted Capacity Queueing Systems: Determination of their Characteristics. Autom. Remote Control 58(6), 969–972 (1997)
5. Tikhonenko, O.M., Klimovich, K.G.: Queuing Systems for Random-Length Arrivals with Limited Cumulative Volume. Problems of Information Transmission 37(1), 70–79 (2001)
6. Tikhonenko, O.M.: Generalized Erlang Problem for Service Systems with Finite Total Capacity. Problems of Information Transmission 41(3), 243–253 (2005)
7. Tikhonenko, O.M.: Queuing Systems with Processor Sharing and Limited Resources. Autom. Remote Control 71(5), 803–815 (2010)
8. Tikhonenko, O.: General Approach to Determination of Total Capacity for Queueing Systems with Non-Homogeneous Customers. In: Probability Theory, Mathematical Statistics and their Applications. The Collection of Scientific Papers (Proceedings of the International Conference in honor of 75 years Jubilee of Professor Gennady Medvedev. Minsk) RIVS, Minsk, pp. 338–343 (February 22–25, 2010)
9. Gaver, D.P.: Observing Stochastic Processes, and Approximate Transform Inversion. Operation Research 14(3), 444–459 (1966)
10. Stehfest, H.: Algorithm 368: Numeric Inversion of Laplace Transform. Communications of ACM 13(1), 47–49 (1970)

Analysis of Time Measurements in Network Systems Using Decomposition on Subprocesses

Stanisław Wideł, Jarosław Flak, and Piotr Gaj

Silesian University of Technology, Institute of Informatics,
ul. Akademicka 2A, 44-100 Gliwice, Poland
{stanislaw.widel,jaroslaw.flak,piotr.gaj}@polsl.pl
http://www.polsl.pl

Abstract. The article discusses a simple case of the statistical interpretation of measurement data representing the response time of the wireless network, when during one measuring two phenomena were observed. The measurement data were separated and the two cases of network behavior were distinguished. One case can be used to analyze the quantitative measurement of a best-effort system. The second one can be used for the worst case analysis. The problem of stationarity of the process is also discussed. A measurement series was modeled statistically.

Keywords: distribution, convolution, time measurements, ping, decomposition, network, subprocess, stationarity, non-stationarity.

1 Introduction

In examining the computer system, the time sequence [1] of its answers to some of stimuli can be observed. However, this system may consist of several subsystems. These subsystems may have different time characteristics. It is possible that different subsystems determine the different characteristics of the system, for example, the maximum value of response time or the average value. In some cases, one can attempt to extract the time characteristics of the subprocesses from time characteristics of the main processes. One of the objectives of the study is the interpretation of the measurements [2] obtained from the computer systems [3] using the probability mass function [4]. The interpretation is based on a statistical qualification of the phenomena, which result in obtaining a characteristic response of the system.

This analysis may be helpful in determining the influence of the various subsystems on the operation of the system and its parameters. It may also be helpful in determining compliance with the requirements of the system's response time, especially for the time constraints systems.

In computer systems measuring practice, it appears that even results of the simple measurements are statistically complex. One of the reasons is non-stationarity [5] of processes describing response times. The stationarity of these processes must be also examined. If the process is not stationary, which happens often in real systems, one of the approaches is an attempt to separate stationary

A. Kwiecień, P. Gaj, and P. Stera (Eds.): CN 2011, CCIS 160, pp. 70–79, 2011.

and non-stationary subprocesses from the main processes. These subprocesses can then be analyzed separately as stationary processes.

In each analysis it is important to skillfully simplify a real case observed and ignore the insignificant details from the perspective of the goal of analysis. In some cases, response time characteristics of these subsystems can be modeled, using statistical operations, even without knowing the mechanisms of action of the subsystems or tasks they carry.

Time analysis based on the analysis of probability distributions may be interesting for cases where analysis is done on a working system, especially when changes are to be set to its independent components. The ability to qualify new characteristics of the system is valuable for the proper selection of the time parameters of considered tasks.

2   Time Response Measurement

While measuring even a simple process [6,7], it appears that typically a number of different processes are measured. For example, in a network transmission using the cache, it appears that the observed times are complex and can not be described by a simple statistical relationship, because the process of writing is composed of two different mechanisms.

To show such a phenomenon, the case was chosen in which the ping RTT (Round Trip Time) was measured during debugging of the problems encountered in wireless network operation. The ping command is a common tool used for network testing. The question arises, how to analyze obtained measurement data. Time responses for the ping command realized in wireless network with the access point set in infrastructure mode, are presented in Fig. 1. The network was placed in the high-urban area and worked in the environment of the other wireless networks. There was a low traffic in the network with a few stations. The suspected reasons of high response times are interferences with other networks.

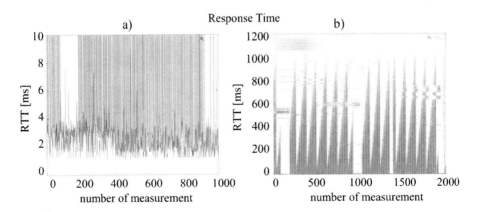

Fig. 1. Time responses for ping command realized in certain wireless network. Both graphs (a) and (b) represent the same data in the various ranges.

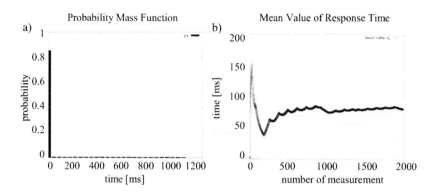

Fig. 2. (a) Discrete probability mass function, (b) The mean value of the data

The operation of the network deviates from the desired mode. Response times at certain points exceed 1000 ms. Typical response times are very small and average at 2 ms (Fig. 1).

3   Analysis of the Measurement Data

Discrete probability mass distribution function for the measurement is presented in Fig. 2a. The bars show the number of occurrences of a given response time interval. The largest is the group of samples with short response time, as shown in the first, the highest bar. The other bars show the long response times. The distribution is bimodal. One mode for normal operation and the other one for delays related to time-out after loss or problem with connection.

While observing this process, it can be concluded that the average value of the process (Fig. 2b), calculated by the Formula (1), is stabilized with the increments of the number of samples. It differs from the expected response time of the network.

$$\overline{x} = \frac{1}{n}\sum_{i=1}^{n} x_i \ .$$
(1)

On the basis of what can be seen in Fig. 1 and Fig. 2, the obtained results (reaction times) can be divided into two categories. The first one includes very short reaction times, which are very frequent. The second one includes other times, larger and not so frequent.

Separation of the measured data was made according to the criterion of response time. As the limit, the time of 20 ms was adopted. All the data below this value was assigned to the class, which was determined as the process x (Fig. 3). All the data above 20 ms was assigned to the class, which was determined as the process y (Fig. 4). So there is an assumption that response times are observed from the system z, which consists of subsystems x and y:

$$z = x + y \ . \tag{2}$$

A series of samples assigned to processes x and process y is shown in Fig. 3 and Fig. 4. The average value of the two processes is stabilized with the increments of the number of samples (Fig. 3b and Fig. 4b). So the main process is divided into two subprocesses. This division does not mean separate programs or threads, but conceptual explanation of the phenomena.

It may be found that the resulting measurement includes the two phenomena. Therefore, the measurement data were separated and two cases of the system (wireless network) behavior were distinguished. One case (process x) can be used to analyze the quantitative measurement of the system (the average response time of the system), for example the best-effort system. The second case (process y) can be used for the worst case analysis, when peak times do not depend on the typical operation of the network, but depend on the specific protocol states,

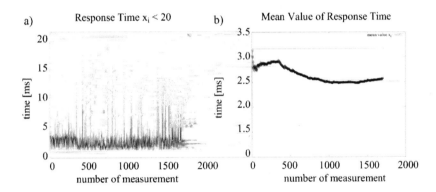

Fig. 3. (a) Samples with response times less than 20 ms, (b) The mean value

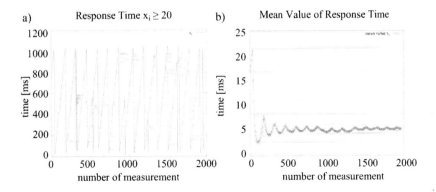

Fig. 4. (a) Samples with response times greater than 20 ms, (b) The mean value

such as protocol synchronization. A typical network performance is presented in Fig. 3. The protocol specific state in which response times are very large is presented in Fig. 4.

Considering this phenomenon from the perspective of real-time systems, it can be stated that despite the relatively small number of disruptions inserted by the process y to the process x, the maximum system response times are determined by the process y. Isolating process y and understanding the mechanism of operation of this process determines the usefulness of the process z in real-time applications.

4   Process Stationarity Analysis

Studying the time determinism and making a statistical analysis, one must also answer the question whether the system is stationary. It was assumed that the process is stationary if, for measuring of the subsequent experiments, its characteristics does not change. For the analysis carried out, particularly important is the average value. The increase of the maximum response time of the system can be also caused by non-stationarity of the process. To determine non-stationarity one must be able to compare the maximum value with the mean value of the process.

If it is assumed that the measurement data is composed of two processes x and y, it can happen that within the measure window, these two processes will have an unbalanced representation. When analyzing a particular situation shown in Fig. 5, it can be seen that there is only the process x at the beginning of the measurement. The process y starts from the measuring point greater than approximately 1300. This causes the increase of the mean value of the process. Depending on the choice of the beginning and the end of the measurement, it may happen that the process y occurs asynchronously within the observation window. Repeating consecutive measurements may end up with receiving a different mean value from measurements each time.

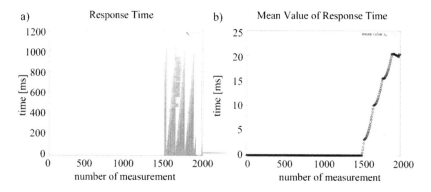

Fig. 5. (a) Samples of measured response time of non-stationary process, (b) The mean value

Without dividing the process into its components, a certain non-stationarity of the series of response time of the process can be noticed. It is the result of a sudden increase of process execution times and other events (Fig. 5). The increase of the mean value of the process execution time, calculated from the beginning of the observation, is a symptom of non-stationarity.

Any process that is observed may therefore be a non-stationary process. After the decomposition, however, it may be found that it consists of two stationary processes. One of the processes can cause non-stationarity, because it can asynchronously appear and disappear many times. Experience in observation systems shows [8] that such a phenomenon is relatively frequent. The way to solve this problem would be to extract the component processes.

5 Statistical Interpretation

For the statistical interpretation it is important to take measurements from the actual data networking systems and also the workload models, in order to reflect the real working conditions of network systems.

The properties of the measured data in terms of statistics could be described by a probability mass function. If the process is a composite of two subprocesses, the distribution of the process, resulting in a long time of observation, is a convolution of distributions of its subprocesses.

For example, it can be assumed, that the probability density function pz of system response time is a convolution of two probability density functions px and py response times of x and y. Referring to the definition of convolution [9], for continuous probability density functions the convolution can be defined as:

$$p_z = p_x * p_y = \int_0^\infty p_x\left(\tau\right) p_y\left(t - \tau\right) \mathrm{d}\tau \ .\tag{3}$$

The convolution operation is one of the most important in the field of digital signal processing. Formula (3) states that the probability pz that the random variable gets the specified value is equal to convolution of continuous probability density functions px and py. The convolution operation can be used to model the situation where two processes are executed simultaneously or sequentially (Fig. 6a). In such case the cumulative distribution function x is equal to 1 and the cumulative distribution function y is equal to 1. In considered case, however, one has made a separate classification. Events were assigned for which the response time is less than 20 ms to the process x. Events for which the response time is greater than 20 ms have been assigned by us to the process y (Fig. 6b) [10].

An approach based on the convolution does not apply to the case being modeled, because either x or y is executed. Therefore, the complete event is the sum of x and y. The probability of the sum of these events is equal to 1. So a convolution operation can not be applied to model the measured data of process z.

On the basis of the real process shown in Fig. 1, the data have been modeled in Octave program [12]. The algorithm for grading the observed measurement

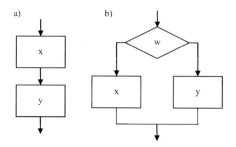

Fig. 6. (a) Sequential events, (b) Conditional events [11]

signal into classes is made intuitively. Each of the classes can be described using a generator with appropriately selected parameters or composition of random signal for the one class and deterministic signal for a second class. An important element for this statistical interpretation is the reordering procedure which shows the nature of these two classes in the measurement signal.

A simplified octave.m program:

```
#!/usr/bin/octave
p =1701;
p1 =295;
pp1=p+p1;
# Random Number Generators
# generates xt random numbers from the exponential distribution
xt = exprnd(0.35, pp1, 1);
# Elementary Matrices and Arrays operation
# yt pseudorandom values drawn from the standard normal distribution
yt = rand(pp1, 1) .* 1000;
zt = xt;
zt(p:p1+p)=yt(p:p1+p);
i =[1:(p+p1)];
# Reordering Algorithms
# j returns a random permutation of the integers
j=randperm(p+p1);
zt=zt(j);
# hh classification level value
hh=20;
# Array Manipulation
# dd reordering interval for yt
dd=[1:300];
zt3=zt(dd);
zt3(zt3 > hh) = sort(zt3(zt3 > hh));
zt([dd])=zt3;
```

Figure 7 shows the output of the program (series x, y and z) as result of statistical techniques [13] application such as distribution processing, rearrangement of series and classification [14,15]. Since the observed phenomenon is not entirely accidental, it can be seen on the original measurement series (Fig. 1) that individual values increase creating a characteristic 'teeth'. This kind of arrangement of the data was introduced in the model shown in Fig. 7. However, the difference can be noticed between a real and a modeled signal. The difference arises from the fact that the real data elements are regular and deterministic, but in modeling the pseudorandom functions are used.

A modeled process z, which is composed of processes x and y, is presented in Fig. 7. Process x determines the average response time. However, the maximum response time of the process z is not determined by the process x, but by the process y. The maximum value is determined largely by the process y, which has little influence on the average.

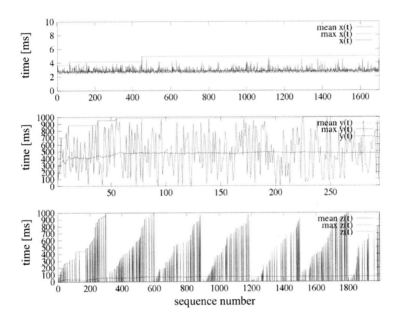

Fig. 7. Example of the model of the response time series for system $z = x + y$

6   Conclusions

Application of the analysis using statistical models requires providing relevant data to the model, which was already observed in the 80's [16]. For years, benchmark measurement techniques were developed, but these were poorly developed measurement techniques that provide data to the statistical models [17]. Providing data to the model includes such topics as the number of running processes, a quantitative value to refer to the resources, the working time of individual tasks, the utilization of individual resources, and the length of queues for resources. From the standpoint of statistical models, there are no measurement

techniques that are common in the industry and would provide data that would
make it possible to analyze these systems using modeling, as shown for example
in Formula (3).

The use of these techniques requires experience. The operation of network
systems is complex. During the measurements many phenomena are observed all
at once. The article discusses a simple case of the interpretation of measurement
data, in which at the time of one measurement two phenomena can be observed.
Therefore, the measurement data was separated and there were distinguished
two cases of behavior of a wireless network. One case can be used to analyze
the quantitative measurement of a best-effort system, and the second one can
be used for the worst case analysis.

References

1. Cox, D.R., Lewis, P.A.W.: The statistical analysis of series of events. In: Methuen's
   Monographs on Applied Probability an Statistics. John Wiley, London (1966)
2. D'Antona, G., Ferrero, A.: Digital signal processing for measurement systems: theory and applications. Springer, Milano (2006)
3. Gunther, N.J.: Analyzing Computer System Performance with Perl PDQ. Springer,
   Heidelberg (2005)
4. Józefiok, A., Nycz, T., Czachórski, T.: Pomiary czasów pracy w dużym sys-
   temie informatycznym i ich aproksymacja za pomocą wybranych rozkładów. In:
   Współczesna Problematyka Sieci Komputerowych, Conference: Computer Networks 2010, WKŁ Warsaw, Poland, pp. 59–68 (2010)
5. Papoulis, A., Unnikrishna Pillai, S.: Probability, random variables, and stochastic
   processes. McGraw-Hill, Stanford (2002)
6. Lilja, D.J.: Measuring Computer Performance: A Practitioner's Guide. Cambridge
   University Press, Cambridge (2000)
7. Mason, R.L., Gunst, R.F., Hess, J.L.: Statistical Design Analysis of Experiments.
   Wiley, Hoboken (2003)
8. Wideł, S., Machniewski, J.: Measurement and data acquisition of execution time
   from application log. In: 16th Polish Teletraffic Symposium, Łódź, September 24–
   25, pp. 145–149 (2009)
9. Mattuck, A.: Introduction to analysis. Prentice Hall, Cambridge (1998)
10. Wideł, S., Flak, J., Gaj, P.: Metoda analizy czasowej systemów czasu rzeczywis-
    tego za pomocą splotu. In: Metody wytwarzania i zastosowania systemów czasu
    rzeczywistego, WKŁ, Warsaw, Poland (2010)
11. Wideł, S., Flak, J., Gaj, P.: Interpretation of Dual Peak Time signal Measured
    in Network systems. In: Kwiecień, A., Gaj, P., Stera, P. (eds.) 17th Conference
    on Computer Networks, CN 2010, Ustroń, Poland. CCIS, vol. 79, pp. 141–152.
    Springer, Heidelberg (2010)
12. Eaton, J.W., Bateman, D., Hauberg, S.: GNU Octave Manual Version 3. Network
    Theory Ltd., UK (2008)
13. Salkind, N.J.: Encyclopedia of Measurement and Statistics. SAGE Publications,
    Kansas (2007)
14. Khuri, A.I.: Advanced Calculus with Applications in Statistics, Hoboken, New
    Jersey, USA (2003)

15. Lewis, P.A.W.: Stochastic point processes: statistical analysis, theory, and applications. Wiley-Interscience, New York (1972)
16. Lazowska, E.D., Zahorjan, J., Scott, G., Sevcik, K.C.: Quantitative System Performance, Computer System Analysis Using Queueing Network Models. Prentice-Hall, Inc., Englewood Cliffs (1984)
17. Haring, G., Lindemann, C., Reiser, M.: Performance evaluation: origins and directions. Springer, Heidelberg (2000)
18. Bendat, J.S., Piersol, A.G.: Metody analizy i pomiaru sygnałów losowych. PWN Warsaw (1976)
19. Marques de Sá, J.P.: Applied statistics: using SPSS, Statistica, MATLAB, and R. Springer, Heidelberg (2007)

A Markovian Queuing Model of a WLAN Node

Jarosław Bylina and Beata Bylina

Institute of Mathematics, Marie Curie-Skłodowska University
Pl. M. Curie-Skłodowskiej 5, 20-031 Lublin, Poland
{jmbylina,beatas}@hektor.umcs.lublin.pl

Abstract. The authors investigate one of the aspects of 802.11 standard, namely collided packet retransmission. The standard mechanism of treating collisions is presented and a Markovian queuing model of a wireless device and its behaviour during channel occupation by other devices is described. Some examples of numerical results are presented and compared with simulation results. Further possibilities of model development are also mentioned.

Keywords: IEEE 802.11, Markovian models, queuing models, analytical solution.

1 Introduction

Nowadays, there is a lot of interest in wireless networks which are developing rapidly. It is because they are very elastic and more and more efficient. Saying this, however, they still need a lot of improvement because of their innate unreliability – especially in comparison with cable networks.

A lot of contribution to the research was done (e.g. see [1,2]). Here we are to present a Markovian queuing model which represents the behavior of a wireless station in the situation of sending data. The model is similar to a Markovian model (but not a queuing one) from the paper [3]. However, the queuing model should have such an advantage that some number of such models could be composed quite easily and investigated together as a model of a system of many wireless nodes.

We present the model of the behavior of a protocol 802.11 medium access mechanism called distributed coordination function (DCF) and investigate the results of the model with the special interest in collided packets retransmission.

The outline of the article is following. Section 2 presents the manner of the modelled mechanism functioning. Section 3 describes its Markovian queuing model. Section 4 shows some numerical results and Section 5 concludes the paper.

2 Real System

The mechanism modelled in the paper, namely DCF, is a part of 802.11 standard [4]. We shortly present here its details interesting for us.

A. Kwiecień, P. Gaj, and P. Stera (Eds.): CN 2011, CCIS 160, pp. 80–86, 2011.

When a new packet is going to be sent, the medium is checked if it is busy for a fixed period of time (distributed interframe space, DIFS). If the channel is free, the packet is transmitted. However, if the channel happens to be busy, a collision control mechanism is employed. It consists of three simple steps.

- First, a backoff time is randomly chosen as an integer number of fixed time intervals σ, from $\langle 0; W-1 \rangle$ (where W is a minimal value of the contention window).
- Second, the device waits the chosen time (freezing when the channel is busy).
- Third, if the channel is free after this countdown, the packet is being sent. If it is not free, the whole procedure is repeated but the range for randomized backoff time is $\langle 0; 2 \cdot W - 1 \rangle$. If the transmission also fails this time, the drawing range becomes $\langle 0; 2 \cdot 2 \cdot W - 1 \rangle$ and so on, up to $\langle 0; 2^m \cdot W - 1 \rangle$ (that is: $2^m \cdot W$ is a maximal values of the contention window).

There are various values of the parameters for different media (for instance: $\sigma = 50\,\mu s$, $W = 16$, $m = 6$ for FHSS, or $\sigma = 8\,\mu s$, $W = 64$, $m = 4$ for IR).

3 Markovian Model

Our Markovian queuing model of such a mechanism is presented in Fig. 1. The state of the model can be described with four integers (c, k, f, s):

- $c \in \langle 0; C \rangle$ is the current number of packets in the system,
- $k \in \langle 0; m \rangle$ is the number of failed transmission attempts,
- $f \in \langle 0; 2^m \cdot W - 1 \rangle$ is the current number of time slots left to the moment of the next transmission attempt,
- $s \in \{0; 1\}$ is a flag equal to 1 if and only if the current packet is being sent.

Besides the parameters C (maximum capacity of the system), m and W (these two were described in Sect. 2), the model has also some more:

- λ is the rate of the new packet appearance in the device,
- μ is the rate of packets transmission,
- p is the the collision probability,
- η is the rate of the transition between slots f and $f - 1$.

The last parameter requires some comment. It could seem that it should hold that $\eta = 1/\sigma$. Moreover, the only one parameter suggests the exponential distribution (because it is a Markovian model) which very, very poorly approximates constant time (usually, in such a case we should approximate constant time with an Erlang distribution with a lot of phases).

However, the above paragraph would be true if the countdown were not frozen in the case of the transmission from other sources which use the same channel (see Sect. 2). In our system, the countdown can be frozen for the time of the channel occupation by other devices. So, the mean rate η of the transition between slots f and $f - 1$ must be somewhat less than $1/\sigma$ as well as it cannot be constant – thus

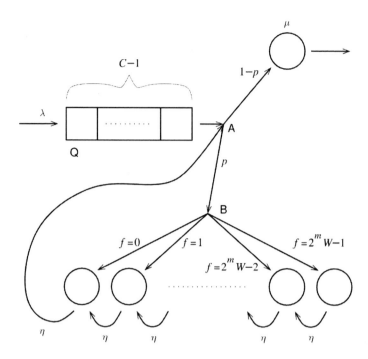

Fig. 1. The queuing model of the DCF mechanism – it is a Markovian model because all elementary transitions marked with intensities λ, μ, η have exponential distribution

the distribution is more exponential-like (being in fact an Erlang distribution, composed of a random number f – see below – of exponential distribution phases; hence the Markovian property still apply) and η depends not only on σ but also on p and μ; and thus perhaps on some more environmental characteristics (like number of interacting stations etc.).

How does our model work?

– Packets appear with an exponential distribution with the rate λ and they get to the queue Q which has a capacity $C - 1$ (there can be C packets in the system; and if there is only one, it is being processed, not waiting in the queue). It is possible only if the queue is not full, so the state of the system changes from (c, k, f, s) to $(\min(c + 1, C), k, f, s)$.
– Every packet getting out of the queue (the fork A) can be sent (with the service rate μ) if the channel is free (with the probability $1 - p$) and then the state changes as follows: $(c, k, 0, 0) \rightarrow (c, 0, 0, 1) \rightarrow (c - 1, 0, 0, 0)$.
– Otherwise, the channel is busy (with the probability p) and the packet is suspended (the fork B). It is done by randomly (and equally) drawing a backoff time (see Sect. 2) $f \in \langle 0; 2^k \cdot W - 1 \rangle$, and then the system's state changes from $(c, k, 0, 0) \rightarrow (c, \min(k + 1, m), f, 0)$.
– The last case where the packet can be in our model is the backoff loop, and here the state of the system goes from $(c, k, f, 0)$ to $(c, k, f - 1, 0)$ with the

intensity η – and eventually to $(c, k, 0, 0)$, and then back to the fork A, when the next attempt of transmission is being made.

4   Results

We were interested in overall performance of the system (not dependent on time) so we only need to compute steady-state probabilities π from a well-known equation (1) [5]

$$\pi \mathbf{Q} = \mathbf{0} \ . \tag{1}$$

Table 1. The tested models parameters (the other parameters were the same for all tests: $C = 8$, $\lambda = 20$, $\mu = 50$)

model	m	W	p	η
A0	6	16	.05	275
A1	6	16	.10	250
A2	6	16	.20	225
A3	6	16	.30	200
A4	6	16	.60	100
B	2	16	.30	200
C	6	2	.30	200
D	0	128	.30	200
E	4	64	.30	200
F	8	4	.30	200
G	4	64	.60	100
H	10	1	.60	100

Table 2. The results from the tests and simulations (percentages: $p(L)$ – packet loss probability, u – system utilization, b – ratio of backoff time to whole time spent in system)

model	analytic solutions			simulations		
	$p(L)$	u	b	$p(L)$	u	b
A0	0.11	45.32	11.51	0.92	42.11	12.41
A1	0.27	49.83	19.84	1.32	48.18	21.15
A2	3.88	64.12	39.73	4.02	61.42	40.01
A3	16.89	81.64	59.45	15.98	80.84	61.17
A4	93.37	99.99	97.44	94.18	99.97	98.03
B	12.46	80.42	56.08	11.12	82.64	55.52
C	0.30	47.82	16.36	0.13	46.63	15.26
D	70.22	99.10	87.75	73.18	98.05	89.32
E	63.15	97.98	85.09	61.00	99.03	82.18
F	1.83	54.71	28.70	3.25	59.13	31.66
G	97.02	99.97	98.91	98.13	99.99	99.08
H	60.70	91.17	82.74	62.32	90.08	80.05

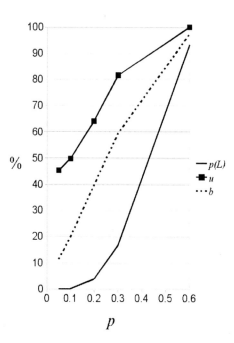

Fig. 2. The results of the tests for models A0, A1, A2, A3, A4 – $p(L)$, u, b as functions of p

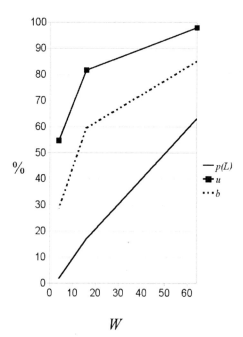

Fig. 3. The results of the tests for models F, A3, E – $p(L)$, u, b as functions of W

Because the matrix $\mathbf{Q}$ was not especially huge, we used a sequential version of a traditional iterative algorithm for such systems, namely the Gauss-Seidel method [6]. Table 1 presents parameters of some tested models. Table 2 and Fig. 2–3 shows some characteristics obtained for those parameters from analytical solution of our model. Table 2 also shows results of simulations of the system for a comparison.

The parameters were chosen quite arbitrarily, only to demonstrate various behaviors of the model and its consistency with simulation. The data for analytical solutions were generated with the use of the methods described in [7,8,9] – and solved with the GMRES as it was shown in [10,11,7,12]. The simulation was conducted with the use of a simple script randomly letting about 10^6 packets through the described model and measuring the desired characteristics.

The exemplary characteristics presented in Table 2 and Figures 2–3 (and many more results) could be very easily obtained from the vector of the stationary probabilities $\pi = [Prob(c, k, f, s)]_{c,k,f,s}$:

- the packet loss probability $p(L) = \sum_{k,f,s} Prob(C, k, f, s)$,

- the system utilization $u = \sum_{c>0,k,f,s} Prob(c, k, f, s) = 1 - \sum_{k,f,s} Prob(0, k, f, s)$,

- the ratio of the packet backoff time to whole time it spent in the system
$b = \dfrac{1}{u} \cdot \sum_{c>0,k,f} Prob(c, k, f, 0)$.

5   Conclusion and Future Work

From the tests we can see that the Markovian model and the simulation do not deviate from each other significantly, what can indicate that the model is quite useful in investigating the behaviour of such systems.

The model presented here is only an introduction and a basis for building a queuing network of such models to represent a group of such wireless stations – because our aim is to build a model of some stations, interacting by sharing a communication channel. We are going to construct it as a composition of a few models similar to presented here – what should be done with only minor modifications. In such a composed model we could get rid of the parameter p – because the state of the channel (free or busy) would depend of the current behaviour of other stations (is any of them sending or not). We could also treat better the countdown by modelling its constant time by Erlang distribution and freezing the countdown when the channel is indeed occupied.

It could let us model the behavior of wireless stations without a troublesome analysis of the collision probability [3,2].

On the other hand, there is also one more issue to improve – somewhat unrealistic (because exponential) distribution of new packets appearance. It can be changed to some self-similar process with little significant changes [13].

Acknowledgement. This work was partially supported within the project N N516 407 138 of the Ministry of Science and Higher Education of the Polish Republic (MNiSW) *Metody i narzędzia rozproszonego modelowania sieci bezprzewodowych.*

References

1. Czachórski, T., Grochla, K., Nycz, T., Pekergin, F.: A diffusion approximation model for wireless networks based on IEEE 802.11 standard (to appear in Computer Communications)
2. Wang, L.C., Huang, S.Y., Chen, A.: On the Throughput Performance of CSMA-based Wireless Local Area Network with Directional Antennas and Capture Effect: A Cross-layer Analytical Approach. In: WCNC 2004 / IEEE Communications Society, pp. 1879–1884 (2004)
3. Bianchi, G.: Performance Analysis of the IEEE 802.11 Distributed Coordination Function. IEEE Journal on Selected Areas in Communications 18(3), 535–547 (2000)
4. IEEE Standard for Wireless LAN Medium Access Control (MAC) and Physical Layer (PHY) Specifications, P80211 (November 1997)
5. Stewart, W.: Introduction to the Numerical Solution of Markov Chains. Princeton University Press, Chichester (1994)
6. Young, D.M.: Iterative Solution of Large Linear Systems. Academic Press, New York (1971)
7. Bylina, J., Bylina, B.: A distributed tool to solve Markov chains. In: Proceedings of 6th International Conference Aplimat 2007, part III, Bratislava, pp. 77–82 (2007)
8. Bylina, J., Bylina, B.: Analysis of an algorithm of distributed generation of matrices for Markovian models of congestion control mechanism. Studia Informatica 29(4B(81)), 93–102 (2008)
9. Bylina, J., Bylina, B.: Development of a distributed algorithm of matrix generation for Markovian models of congestion control and its performance analysis on a computer cluster. In: Contemporary Aspects of Computer Networks, vol. 2, pp. 251–258. Wydawnictwa Komunikacji i Łączności, Warszawa (2008)
10. Bylina, B., Bylina, J.: A review of numerical methods for solving large Markov chains. In: Proceedings from EuroNGI Workshop: New Trends in Modeling, Quantitive Methods and Measurements, pp. 75–95. Jacek Skalmierski Computer Studio, Gliwice (2004)
11. Bylina, B., Bylina, J.: The experimental analysis of GMRES convergence for solution of Markov chains. In: Proceedings of the International Multiconference on Computer Science and Information Technology, Wisła, Poland, October 18–20, vol. 5(2010), pp. 281–288, IEEE Catalog Number CFP1064E-CDR (2010)
12. Bylina, J., Bylina, B.: A Markovian model of the RED mechanism solved with a cluster of computers. Annales UMCS Informatica Lublin 5(2006), 19–27 (2006)
13. Domańska, J., Czachórski, T.: Wpływ samopodobnej natury ruchu na zachowanie mechanizmu cieknacego wiadra. Studia Informatica 24(2A(53)), 199–212 (in Polish)

Comparative Analysis of IP-Based Mobility Protocols and Fast Handover Algorithms in IEEE 802.11 Based WLANs

Jozef Wozniak, Przemyslaw Machan, Krzysztof Gierlowski,
Michal Hoeft, and Michal Lewczuk

Gdańsk University of Technology
{jozef.wozniak,gierk}@eti.pg.gda.pl, przemac@o2.pl,
michal.hoeft@gmail.com, michal@lewczuk.pl

Abstract. A rapid growth of IP-based networks and services created the vast collection of resources and functionality available to users by means of an uniform method of access – an IP protocol. At the same time, advances in design of mobile electronic devices allowed them to reach utility level comparable to stationary, desktop computers, while still retaining their mobility advantage. Unfortunately, the base IP protocol does not perform very well in mobile environments, due to lack of handover support and higher layer mobility management mechanisms. In this paper we present an overview of the most popular and promising methods of handling mobility in IPv4 and IPv6 networks, covering both ISO-OSI layer 2 low level handover mechanisms in IEEE 802.11 WLAN systems and ISO-OSI layer 3+ mobility solutions.

Keywords: IP networks, IEEE 802.11 based WLANs, handover, mobility protocols, analysis, comparison.

1 Introduction

With rapid growth of information and communication technologies during the last decade, two dominant technology trends can be observed. The first one is the Internet – an easily accessible internetwork offering numerous services based on a single network protocol – the Internet Protocol (IP). As utilization of IP protocol results in obtaining the largest possible group of potential users, service developers and providers consistently do so. This trend, which can be called "All-IP" approach, results in a uniform way in which services are provided to remote users. The second one is mobility. A rapid development of universal mobile devices, able to offer their users functionality comparable to stationary desktop computers has inevitably led to their integration with the largest available source of services – the Internet and IP protocol. Unfortunately mobility in IP network brings a number of problems, which need to be solved, if IP-based services are to be offered to end-users with satisfactory quality. Mobile users need to communicate without interruption while moving across different access networks,

A. Kwiecień, P. Gaj, and P. Stera (Eds.): CN 2011, CCIS 160, pp. 87–101, 2011.

which results not only in necessity to change points of physical network access (handover) but also in probable changes of users IP addresses. To allow a user to retain an uninterrupted access to services under such conditions, a two-tier solution is necessary: an universal, IP mobility mechanism which will counteract adverse effects of necessary IP address changes, and methods of efficient and seamless handover. To provide insight into current state-of-the-art in this area, we would like to present a description of the most promising IP-based mobility solutions being developed and deployed, complete with an overview of advanced handover solutions designed for IEEE 802.11-based networks – the most popular wireless local area network (WLAN) technology today.

2   Handover

As the mobile user moves it becomes necessary for him to change his physical point of network access. Such change can result in variety of additional requirements for the mobile node to fulfill, starting from simple change of network identification information in transmitted data frames, through performing a complete or partial association procedure with new access point, to a complete access technology change and/or change of network level addressing information (also resulting in different routing paths). The complication of handover related procedure strongly depends on the type of handover, as specified below.New technologies and applications have a strong impact on the handover requirements. The first point is the need for enhanced address concept, as in both IPv4 and IPv6 technology IP address is used both as host identifier and location information. Possible solutions are to hide address location or to include user location into addressing concept [1]. The second case enables support for not-symmetrical (upward and downward) vertical handovers in heterogeneous networks. Upward vertical handover is time-critical, because duration of small cell layer is time constrained. Heterogeneous network implies that mobile host is able to operate in any technology that is used in the network. Operation means forwarding services, support for Authentication, Authorization, and Accounting (AAA) services and quality of service (QoS) support.

Roaming and handover (or handoff) refer to different aspects of the mobility support [2]. Roaming is the network operator-based term involving formal agreements between operators that allows a mobile to get connectivity from a foreign network. Handover (handoff) refers to the process of mobile node moving from one point of attachment to the network to the other. The are several types of handover defined depending on which layers of communication stack are affected [1,3,4]:

- *Layer 2 handover* occurs when a mobile node changes access point connected to the same access router interface. This type of handover is transparent to the layer 3, although link layer reconfiguration can occur.
- *Intra-AR handover* changes access router (AR) network interface to the mobile host. In other words serving access router remains the same, but route change internal to AR takes place.

- *Intra-AN handover* takes place if the mobile node changes access routers inside the same access network (AN).
- *Inter-AN handover* occurs when a mobile node moves between two access networks. Host mobility between ANs is typically supported by external IP core. Host mobility can involve e.g. new IP address assignment.
- *Intra-technology handover* is a handover between equipment of the same technology.
- *Inter-technology handover* occurs between equipment of different technology. Note that this may involve mobile host network interface change (see vertical handover).
- *Horizontal handover* is defined as a handover in which the mobile host's network interface does not change from the IP layer point of view. In this scenario mobile host communicates with the access router via the same network interface before and after the handover. A horizontal handover is typically an intra-technology handover.
- *Vertical handover* occurs if the mobile host's network interface to the access network changes. A vertical handover is typically an inter-technology handover. However, in the special case this can also be an intra-technology handover if the mobile host is equipped with several network interfaces of the same technology. When considering vertical handover in heterogeneous system, constructed from cells of different coverage, the *upward* and *downward* vertical handovers can be defined. The upward handover is when MH moves from a access point at the lower hierarchical layer to the higher layer. The typical case can be leaving hot spot to GPRS network. The downward handover is from base station at a higher layer to the lower layer.

From the perspective of handover control the following categories can be distinguished:

- *Mobile-initiated vs. network-initiated handover.* In the first case the mobile host is the one who initiates the handover. In the latter, the network makes the initial decision to start it. For example, in IEEE 802.11 network the Access Point is able to send disassociation message for network-initiated handover. On the other hand, the Mobile Station can initiate handover when leaving the coverage of Access Point.
- *Mobile-controlled vs. network-controlled handover.* In the first case the mobile host has the primary control over handover process. In the latter case the network takes over the control.
- *Mobile-assisted, network-assisted and unassisted handover.* In the first case the information and measurements from mobile node are used by the access router in handover decision. In the second case, the access network collects data that can be used by mobile host to execute handover. Unassisted handover is a handover where no assistance is provided by mobile host or access network to each other. However, it is possible that both AN and MH make measurement on their own and decide about handover.
- *Backward vs. forward handover.* Backward handover is the one initiated by Previous Access Router (PAR) or mobile host initiates the handover via

PAR. The forward handover is the one initiated by or with support of the Next Access Router (NAR).

- *Proactive vs. reactive handover.* The proactive (i.e. expected) handover includes connection between PAR and NAR before the mobile host will connect with NAR. The reactive (also called unplanned) handover takes place if there is no signaling between ARs before mobile host moves to the new point of attachment.
- *Make-before-break vs. Break-before-make handover.* During MBB handover the mobile host can communicate with both PAR and NAR. Simultaneous communication is not possible in the BBM scenario.
- *Hard vs. soft handover.* A hard handover is when all radio links in the mobile host are disconnected before the new link (or links) is established. Soft hand-off scenario assumes that there is always at least one link connection between MH and access network. Soft handoff can utilize e.g. macro diversity.

The performance aspects of handover are as follows:

- *Handover latency* (or delay) is a time difference between when a MN is last able to send and receive an IP packet by the way of PAR until MH is able to send and receive packet through NAR. During handover the Mobile Node is unable to send or receive packets both due to link switching delay and IP protocol operations.
- *Smooth handover* aims primarily to minimize packet loss with no concern about packet delay.
- *Fast handover* strives to minimize delay with no explicit interest in packet loss.
- *Seamless handover* is a one that does not introduce any change in service capability, security or capability. In practice, some service degradation is expected.
- *Lossless handover* is the one when no user data is lost during the procedure.

3   Layer 2 Handovers – Transitions between APs in IEEE 802.11 Standard – Based WLANs

The IEEE 802.11 standard was initially published in 1997 [5] by Institute of Electrical and Electronics Engineers (IEEE). The standard has been prepared as a wireless extension of existing IEEE 802.3/Ethernet standards. Many amendments were merged into the standard since, resulting in its current, vastly extended version, named IEEE 802.11-2007 [6]. The most recent additions seem to concentrate on providing support for creating complex network systems (both homogenous and heterogeneous). Handover mechanisms, as an important element of such systems' functionality, are also being rapidly developed – layer 2 handover support procedures were described in IEEE 802.11f amendment [7]. The document introduced a way of exchanging information about Mobile Stations between Access Points. However, the extension did not gather the expected popularity and had been withdrawn. When the mobile station moves between

Infrastructure BSSs it will reassociate with AP in the new BSS, i.e. perform Layer 2 handover. To facilitate seamless handover the neighbour APs are configured to operate on different channels to overlap the coverage. The station first scans all physical channels by switching radio frequency for APs in vicinity. In the next steps the station executes 802.11 authentication and association with Access Point. The mobile station may also execute 802.1X authentication on the top of the 802.11 association. In case when the access points are under consolidated management there is a number of mechanisms designed to facilitate the handover process and help mobile client to make a seamless transition. Apart from a number of proprietary solutions (most often based on dedicated wireless network controllers) introduced by hardware developers, there is a widely recognized IEEE 802.11r standard amendment [8].

IEEE 802.11r-2008 [8] is an amendment to the IEEE 802.11-2007 standard that introduces Fast Basic Service Set Transition. The handover has already been supported under the base 802.11-1999 standard and four messages were required to connect to the new AP in the typical case. However, as the standard is extended, the number of necessary messages went up dramatically. In this situation IEEE 802.11r-2008 amendment proposes algorithms to bring the number of messages required for handover down to the level of 802.11-1999. This is expected to be achieved by limiting the number of messages in 802.1X authentication and 802.11e admission control procedures. Introduction of Fast BSS Transitions (FT) allows Mobile Station (MS) to fully authenticate only with the first AP in the FT Domain and use shorter association procedure with the next APs in the network. The amendment defines the FT Domain as the group of APs that support FT Protocol and are connected over a Distribution System (DS). The MS session i.e. security and QoS information is cached by the network. When the station associates with the first AP in the FT Domain it is now pre-authenticated with other APs in the domain. The first AP the station authenticates to, will cache its Pairwise Master Key (PMK – the starting point of key hierarchy) and use it to derive session keys for other APs. The first AP is named R0 Key Holder (R0KH) as it holds level 0 PMK (PMK-R0). When MS reassociates to the next AP in the domain, R0KH generates PMK-R1 and forwards that to the next AP, which is called R1KH. The R1KH interacts with the R0KH, rather than directly with AAA server. Next, when the MS requests R1KH to prepare reassociation with consecutive AP, R1KH communicates with the R0KH. R0KH generates PMK-R1 and forwards that to the consecutive AP. The amendment defines two methods of FT: over-the-air and over-the-DS. In the first case MS communicates over a direct 802.11 link to the new AP. In the over-the-DS method the MS communicates with the new AP via the old AP. In the Over-the-air FT protocol the Mobile Station is already associated with the old AP from the domain. At some point MS decides to reassociate with nAP sending 802.11 Authentication frame with Information Elements required by FT Protocol. The new AP responds with 802.11 Authentication frame that contains the same types of Information Elements as request. In the next step MS sends 802.11 Association Request message with FT information elements. Access

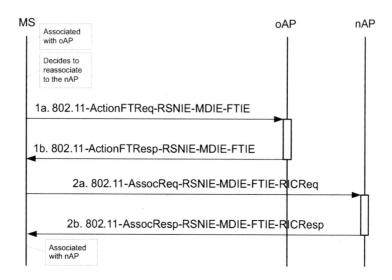

Fig. 1. Over-the-DS FT Protocol

Point responds with 802.11 Association Response message that also convey FT information elements.

Figure 1 presents Over-the-DS FT protocol version. The MS uses Action frame to communicate with the current (old) AP, providing the address of the new AP. Old AP communicates over the DS with new AP forwarding STA request. The new AP responds over DS and oAP sends Action FT Response to MS. At this step MS is authenticated with nAP. Then, MS switches the channel and begins association procedure with nAP. The type and content of information elements is the same using both methods: over-the-air and over-the-DS. The IEEE 802.11r-2008 handover performance is discussed in [9,10]. The handover with FT algorithm is much faster comparing to the legacy mode, simply because 802.1X Authentication phase can be substantially shortened.

4   IP Mobility Protocols

Apart from low-layer handover procedures regarding fast and seamless change of physical point of network attachment, a number of issues concerning IP protocol operation must also be addressed. The exact mechanisms required depend on a specific mobility type [11] – for example terminal mobility is the ability for a user terminal to access the network when the terminal moves. Another type of mobility – user mobility – is the ability for a user to access the network under the same identity when the user changes location and often includes the ability to access the network from the different terminals under the same identity. Service mobility is the ability for a user to access the service regardless of user location. All of these mobility types bring different challenges and require specialized solutions. Mobile IP introduced the concept to decouple the host and network identifiers that had been fundamental in traditional IP addressing. With the introduction of two addresses Mobile IP solved the problem of delivering IP datagrams to the mobile host that moves between networks. The base concept was later improved in multiple fields like routing optimization, handover efficiency and deployment cost. Classical MIPv4 solution contains a significant disadvantage in form of triangle routing – the data from Corresponding Node is delivered to Home Agent in MH's home network, which in turn delivers it to MH's current IP address. The Route optimization extension [12] was proposed to overcome that problem. In case of MIPv6, an extension of registration procedures allows MH to inform its corresponding nodes of its current IP address – such knowledge then permits them to transmit data directly to MH's current address, without retransmission by Home Agent. The handover efficiency oriented algorithms concentrates on optimization of data paths, which reduces transmission latency, packet loss during handover and consumption of network resources. Because of often encountered in IP systems division of network into hierarchical domains, the mobility can be divided into two broad types: inter-domain mobility and intra-domain mobility. Such an approach opens the possibility of performance optimizations. A domain is defined as a large wireless network under a single authority. Inter-domain mobility (also called macro-mobility – Fig. 2) is related to a movement from one domain to another. Such mobility most often results in complex handover procedures including full low-layer handover, full authentication, new IP address acquisition and verification, mobile node registration and radical data path change. On the other hand intra-domain mobility (also called micro mobility – Fig. 2) refers to user's movement within a particular domain. In this case many of the necessary handover procedures can be simplified – for example: fast reassociation in place of full association/authentication procedure and no IP address change. Mobile IP stays the most popular solution for macro-mobility support. It is not considered as the efficient solutions but provides the required mobility support for the infrequent movements between domains. The number of solutions strives to provide low latency handovers for micro-mobility (e.g. Cellular IP, HAWAII and TIMIP). Similarly Hierarchical Mobile IP [13,14]

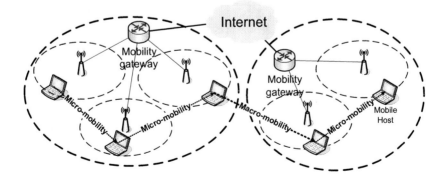

Fig. 2. Micro and macro-mobility

introduces regional mobility agent called Gateway Foreign Agent that facilitate local mobility. The different approach to decrease the handover delay is usage of link layer triggers. The Mobile IP extensions, named fast handovers [15] or low latency handovers [16], aim at forecasting handover and preparing the transition to the new Access Router (AR) before the connection to the old AR is lost. The deployment of Mobile IP requires both network architecture changes as well as changes in the mobile host protocol stack. Even though the solution is on the IETF standardization track for a long time the protocol implementations are still not widely available. For those reasons the alternative solutions are proposed. The first concept assumes that mobility can be handled completely inside the network. Thanks to that no changes are required to the current mobile hosts. Proxy Mobile IPv6 extends that concepts. The second group of protocols utilizes NAT concept that is already widely used in the IP network. The authors argue that NAT-based solution is easier to deploy with the compromise to the functionality. For example Reverse Address Translation (RAT) [17] is the macro-mobility approach based on NAT that supports only UDP traffic. On the other side Mobile NAT [18] provides both micro- and macro-mobility support and can be deployed as the Mobile IP replacement. New trend in mobility support utilizes effective cross-layer mechanisms combining low-layer (ISO-OSI layer 2) and network-layer handovers. The example algorithm – Simultaneous Handovers IEEE 802.11r for Mobile IPv6 – is described in details. The IEEE 802.21 standard will include a universal architecture that provides service continuity while a MH switches between heterogeneous link-layer technologies. The standard will also provide mechanisms for the intra-layer communication that is required for certain groups of handover algorithms. The IEEE 802.21 standard introduces Media Independent Handover (MIH) Function that is considered a shim layer in the network stack of both network node and the network elements that provide mobility support [19]. MIH Function provides abstracted services to the upper layers. There also exists a number of application level mobility solutions. They trend to perform well within bounds of their utility, which is limited to a single application or application-layer protocol. A good example of such approach is a Session Initiation Protocol (SIP) [20] and Extended SIP Mobility [21]. This protocol allows two or more participants to manage a session consisting of different media stream types and uses Uniform Resource Identifiers (URI) in place of IP addresses and provide a decent level of mobility support. The following section reviews the most popular IP mobility protocols. The summary is presented in Table 1.

4.1   Mobile IP

The IETF Mobile IP [22,23] is an oldest and the most widely known approach for mobility support in IP networks. There are two versions of the algorithm, namely for IPv4 and IPv6 protocols. Both solution are on standard track run by IETF organization. Mobile IP offers mobility support in the network layer and isolates higher layers from mobility. The key idea introduced in Mobile IP is the usage of a couple of addresses to manage user movement. Mobile host owns its own IP

Table 1. Comparison of IP mobility protocols

Protocol	Mobility Type	Handover Type	Link Detection	Registration	Address Translation
Mobile IPv6 (basic)	Macro	Hard	Router adv.	At Home Agent	Encap.
Hierarchical Mobile IPv6	Universal	Hard	Router adv.	At Mobility Anchor	Encap.
Proxy Mobile IPv6	Universal (net-based)	Hard	Events or DNAv6	At Mobile Access Gateway	Encap.
Fast Handovers	Universal	Hard	Proxy Router adv.	At Home Agent	Encap.
Cellular IP	Micro	Semi-soft / Hard	Network specific	Route Updates	No
HAWAII	Micro	Forward.&non-fw. schemes	Network specific	Path Updates	No
RAT	Macro	Hard (no TCP sup.)	Network specific	At reg. server	NAT
MobileNAT	Universal	Hard	Using DHCP ext.	At Home NAT	NA(P)T
Extended SIP	Macro	Hard (no TCP sup.)	Network specific	At SIP router	via SIP server

address which can be referred as traditional IP address. Mobile IP introduces a term of home address for such an address. Each time the mobile host connects to the network, the temporary IP address for the current network is obtained. The host stays reachable by the way of both home and temporary addresses. For Mobile IP the temporary IP address is named Care-of Address (CoA). A correspondent host addresses datagrams destined to the mobile host using its IP home address and the datagram is tunneled via Mobile IP infrastructure to the mobile node current location. Mobile IPv6 extends IP infrastructure by the concept of Home Agent (HA). HA is located in the home network, which is defined as the network that mobile IP address belongs to. In the Mobile IPv6 the MH is able to create its own CoA using its link-local address and automatic address configuration (i.e. merge subnet prefix with own hardware address). Mobile IPv4 adds also Foreign Agents (FA) that are located in any network that can be visited by the mobile host and facilitates CoA generation. Mobile IPv6 Access Routers sends periodically Agent Advertisement message (an extension of ICMP Router Discovery message [24]) with fields for mobility support. Mobile Host can solicit Agent Advertisement by sending Agent Solicitation message.

The IPv6 handover example is presented in Fig. 3 When a mobile host leaves its home IP network it detects foreign networks based on Router Advertisement messages that can be solicited. To begin data transmission mobile host updates bindings with Home Agent and corresponding nodes if any. From the perspective of the correspondent host, the mobile host is identified by its home address.

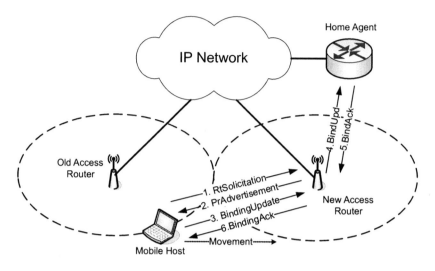

Fig. 3. Mobile IPv6 handover

When the packets are sent to the mobile host, HA intercept packet based on home address of mobile host. The Home Agent stores the registration mapping between home address of the host and its current Care-of address. The datagram is tunneled from HA to a mobile host.

4.2   Proxy Mobile IP

As opposed to Mobile IPv4 and Mobile IPv6 which are host-based mobility standards, Proxy Mobile IPv6 (PMIPv6) [25] presents a network-based approach, which lacks any kind of client-side mobility agent. Such solution brings numerous advantages, such as simplified management, ability to support legacy clients and better efficiency of radio-link utilization. PMIPv6 extends and reuses a proven MIPv6 idea, however it does not require any modification of a standard mobile node's IPv6 stack. A network-side proxy mobility agent in used in place of MIP client-side agent, and performs signaling and management on behalf of the mobile host. As a result PMIPv6 provides efficient solution without tunneling and signaling overhead on radio access link. Nevertheless Proxy Mobile IPv6 cannot be deployed as a standalone global mobility system, due to lack of standardized macro-mobility procedures and mechanisms.

Proxy Mobile IPv6 (as defined in [26]) uses two specialized network elements: Media Access Gateways and Local Mobility Anchors (Fig. 4). Media Access Gateway (MAG) is responsible for tracking the MH movements, creating bidirectional tunnel to Local Mobility Anchor and managing connectivity between MH and LMA. Local Mobility Anchor (LMA) is similar to HA in Mobile IPv6. It is responsible for maintaining routes and forwarding information for all MHs in domain.

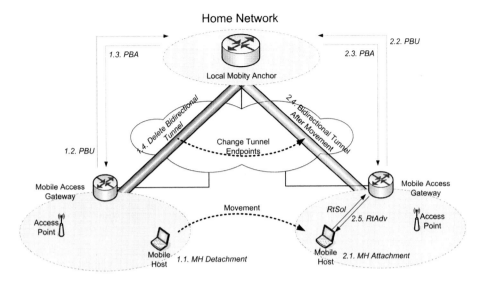

Fig. 4. Proxy Mobile IPv6 Domain

4.3 Routing Path Optimizations

The triangle routing problem was addressed by route optimization extension [12]. It adds binding update to inform the corresponding node on the current CoA. When the handover occurs the old FA communicates with the HA using binding warning. Thanks to the HA can update binding in the corresponding node. The drawbacks of the solution are the new requirements on the CN – ability to encapsulate IP packets and store CoA. Moreover, route optimization increases the signaling overhead. The extension proposed in [27] adds link and signaling cost functions to capture the trade-off between the signaling cost and processing load. The alternative approach presents DHARMA [28] that uses overlay network to select location-optimized mobility agent from the distributed set of home agents to minimize routing overheads.

4.4 Handover Performance Optimizations

The generic Mobile IP protocol does not differentiate between local and global handovers. In consequence the amount of signaling is large, especially if HA is distant from the mobile host. Moreover, MIP applies the same scheme for horizontal and vertical handovers which makes performance optimizations difficult. For those reasons micro- and macro-mobility concepts were introduced. In case of micro-mobility, MH moving inside an area called mobility domain does not need to perform all the procedures described for macro-mobility scenario when change of physical network access point becomes necessary. It is sufficient to employ much simpler signaling with local mobility support entities, which is enough to provide correct data routing to MH's public address within a given mobility domain. This approach allows reducing handover time significantly. For example Cellural IP [29] adds the micro-mobility support to the MIPv4. It also addresses a problem of MIPv4 scalability by adding local caches to support slow moving and sleeping nodes. Handoff Aware Wireless Access Internet Infrastructure (HAWAII) [30] is another micro-mobility support extension to MIPv4 that optimizes both handoff latency and data paths, by including cross-layer triggers and improved IP QoS maintenance. Another concept is used in fast handovers [15,16]. Such solutions are typically applied for intra-technology handovers and are tightly coupled with link layer protocols. Those protocols utilize the physical triggers from lower layers, like "Link Going Down" or "Link Down" to speed up the handover. The simultaneous handover discussed later is the next step to improve the handover performance. Based on the fast handovers concept, the link later and IP layers handovers are executed in parallel.

4.5   Deployment Cost Optimizations

Several alternative IP mobility protocols were introduced that address deployment issues related to the Mobile IP. Reverse Address Translation (RAT) [17] is the macro-mobility approach competitive to the Mobile IP, based on NAT procedure. It advertises easier deployment over MIP by the cost of limited functionality (e.g. no TCP session support). Mobile NAT [18] provides both micro- and macro-mobility support and can be deployed as the Mobile IP replacement. Contrary to the Mobile IP the solution is based on NAT instead of tunneling. Proxy Mobile IP also falls into that category, as it addresses the problem of MIP implementations availability for the mobile hosts. Basic characteristics of described protocols is described in the Table 1.

5   Simultaneous Handover IEEE 802.11r for Mobile IPv6

As the need to perform both low-layer IEEE 802.11 and IP-layer handover is a common occurrence, an algorithm has been proposed which allows Mobile IPv6 procedures to be executed in parallel with IEEE 802.11 procedures (Fig. 5). The algorithm shortens handover time as MIPv6 detection phase is minimized. MIPv6 handover starts as soon as 802.11 layer detects the new link and some 802.11 and MIPv6 procedures are executed simultaneously, which can decrease the handover delay up to 38% [31]. To achieve that, selected Mobile IPv6 frame formats are conveyed as IEEE 802.11 information elements and 802.11 Access Point is coupled with MIPv6 Access Router in a single device. MIPv6 Router Advertisement (RA) unsolicited messages are distributed within RAIE together with 802.11 Beacon messages. When executing active scanning MS can request MIPv6 RA by sending MIPv6 Router Solicitation together with 802.11 Probe Request. The Access Point / Access Router that supports simultaneous handover have to respond with 802.11 Probe Response that includes MIPv6 Router Advertisement. The RA is always known to the Mobile Station when either active or passive scanning method is used. When building Reassociation Request

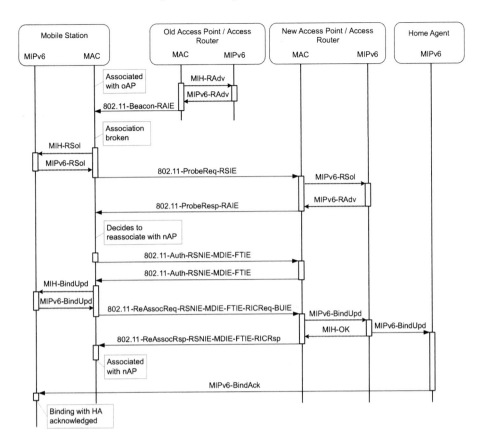

Fig. 5. Simultaneous handover IEEE 802.11r for Mobile IPv6

message the Mobile Station will sent MIH Binding Update event that is routed
to the MIPv6 protocol instance. In response, MIPv6 will send Mipv6 Binding
Update message destined to the Home Agent. The MIPv6 Binding Update message is intercepted by 802.11 protocol layer and compressed into BUIE. BUIE is
sent together with Reassociation Request message. When received at the New
Access Point BUIE is extracted to MIPv6 Binding Update and passed to the
collocated Access Router. AR confirms message reception with MIH OK event.
When event is received at MAC layer, it responds with Reassociation Response
message. New Access Router sends Binding Update to the Home Agent. The
Home Agent responds with MIPv6 Binding Acknowledge. This concludes the
handover process.

6   Conclusions

The paper introduces the handover taxonomy and describes possible implementation of the procedure. In the next steps authors perform the analysis of the

mobility support protocols at the different layers of the network protocol stack. Fast transitions for 802.11 that were standardized by the "r" working group is explained in details. IP Mobility Protocols section gives the overview of the protocols that can provide better handover efficiency (in terms of both hand-off latency and data path optimization) over the Mobile IP. The simultaneous handover methods are also presented as example of cross-layer approach to optimization of handover latency.

References

1. Festag, A., Karl, H., Schafer, G.: Current developments and trends in handover design for ALL-IP wireless networks. Technical University Berlin, TKN Technical Report TKN-00-007, Version 1.3 (August 2000)
2. Dunmore, M., Pagtzis, T.: Mobile IPv6 Handovers: Performance Analysis and Evaluation. 6NET Project, IST-2001-32603 (May 2004)
3. Reinbold, P., Bonaventure, O.: A comparison of IP mobility protocols. University of Namur, Technical Report Infonet-2001-07, Version 1 (June 2001)
4. Manner, J., Kojo, M. (eds.): Mobility Related Terminology. Draft (April 2003)
5. IEEE 802.11-1997: Part11: Wireless LAN Medium Access Control (MAC) and Physical Layer (PHY) specifications (June 1997)
6. IEEE 802.11-2007: Part11: Wireless LAN Medium Access Control and Physical Layer Specifications (June 2007)
7. IEEE 802.11f: IEEE Trial-Use Recommended Practice for Multi-Vendor Access Point Interoperability via an Inter-Access Point Protocol Across Distribution Systems Supporting IEEE 802.11 Operation. ANSI/IEEE Std 802.11f-2003 (July 2003)
8. IEEE 802.11r: Amendment 2: Fast Basic Service Set (BSS) Transition. IEEE Std 802.11r-2008 (July 2008)
9. Machań, P., Wozniak, J.: Performance evaluation of IEEE 802.11 fast BSS transition algorithms. In: 3rd Joint IFIP Wireless and Mobile Networking Conference (October 2010)
10. Chung-Ming, H., Jian-Wei, L.: A Context Transfer Mechanism for IEEE 802.11r in the Centralized Wireless LAN Architecture. In: IEEE 22nd International Conference on Advanced Information Networking and Applications (March 2008)
11. Jyh-Cheng, C.: IP-Based Next-Generation Wireless Networks: Systems, Architectures, and Protocols. John Wiley and Sons, Chichester (2004)
12. Perkins, C.E., Johnson, D.B.: Route Optimization in Mobile IP. Internet Draft, IETF, draft-ietf-mobileipoptim-11.txt (September 2001) (work in progress)
13. Fogelstroem, E., Jonsson, A., Perkins, C.: Mobile IPv4 Regional Registration. IETF, RFC 4857 (June 2007)
14. Soliman, H., Castelluccia, C., El Malki, K., Bellier, L.: Hierarchical Mobile IPv6 (HMIPv6) Mobility Management. IETF, RFC 5380 (October 2008)
15. Koodli, R.: Mobile IPv6 Fast Handovers. IETF, RFC 5268 (June 2008)
16. El Malki, K. (ed.): Low Latency Handoffs in Mobile IPv4. RFC 4881 (June 2007)
17. Singh, R., et al.: RAT: A Quick (And Dirty?) Push for Mobility Support. In: Second IEEE Workshop on Mobile Computer Systems and Applications (February 1999)
18. Buddhikot, M.M., Hari, A., Singh, K., Miller, S.: Mobilenat: A new technique for mobility across heterogeneous address spaces. MONET 10(3) (2005)
19. IEEE Comp. Society: Draft IEEE Standard for Local and Metropolitan Area Networks: Media Independent Handover Services, P802.21/D05.00 (2007)

20. Rosenberg, J., Schulzrinne, H., Camarillo, G., Johnston, A., Peterson, J., Sparks, R., Handley, M., Schooler, E.: SIP: Session Initiation Protocol. RFC 3261, IETF Proposed Standard (June 2002)
21. Wedlund, E., Schulzrinne, H.: Mobility Support using SIP. In: Proc. of Second ACM/IEEE International Conference on Wireless and Mobile Multimedia WoW-MoM 1999, Seattle Washington, USA (August 1999)
22. IP Mobility Support for IPv4. IETF, RFC 5944, http://tools.ietf.org/html/rfc5944
23. Mobility Support in IPv6. IETF, RFC 3775, http://tools.ietf.org/html/rfc3775
24. Deering, S.: ICMP Router Discovery Messages. RFC1256 (September 1991)
25. Proxy Mobile IPv6. IETF, RFC 5213, http://tools.ietf.org/html/rfc5213
26. IETF, RFC4831, Goals for Network-Based Localized Mobility Management (NETLMM). IETF, RFC 4831, http://tools.ietf.org/html/rfc4831
27. Lee, Y.J., Akyildiz, I.F.: A New Scheme for Reducing Link and Signaling Costs in Mobile IP. IEEE Trans. Computers 52(6), 706–711 (2003)
28. Mao, Y., Knutsson, B., Lu, H.H., Smith, J.M.: DHARMA: Distributed Home Agent for Robust Mobile Access. Proc. IEEE Infocom (March 2005)
29. Valko, A.: Cellular IP – A New Approach to Internet Host Mobility. ACM Computer Communication Review (January 1999)
30. Ramjee, R., Varadhan, K., Salgarelli, L., Thuel, S.R., Wang, S.Y., La Porta, T.: HAWAII: A Domain-Based Approach for Supporting Mobility in Wide-Area Wireless Networks. IEEE/ACM Transactions on Networking 10(3) (June 2002)
31. Machań, P., Wozniak, J.: Simultaneous handover scheme for IEEE 802.11 WLANs with IEEE 802.21 triggers. Telecommunication Systems 43(1-2), 83–93 (2009)

3D Web Performance Forecasting Using Turning Bands Method

Leszek Borzemski and Anna Kamińska-Chuchmała

Institute of Informatics, Wroclaw Uniwersity of Technology,
Wroclaw, Poland
{leszek.borzemski,anna.kaminska-chuchmala}@pwr.wroc.pl

Abstract. An attempt was made to evaluate Web performance by making a 3D forecast of Web site performance while resource downloading using a geostatistic simulation method Turning Bands for the first time. Data for the research were obtained in an active experiment conducted by a multi-agent measurement system MWING performing monitoring of a common group of Web sites from different agent locations. In this study we use a measurement database collected by an agent from Wrocław. A preliminary analysis of measurement data was conducted. Next a structural analysis of data was conducted and a spatial forecast of the total time of downloading data from web servers with a one-week time advance was calculated. Forecast results were analyzed in detail and then directions for further research were suggested.The article introduces the first innovative use of the Turning Bands method in the prediction of Internet performance. First results permit to find that the mentioned predictive method can be effective.

Keywords: web performance, server performance prediction, spatial forecast, geostatistics, Turning Bands method.

1 Introduction

At the time of developing Internet, in which web systems play a significant role, it is worth considering an effective way of evaluating the net performance. Another important question is Internet security which is influenced by web servers reliability and the lack of communication intervals on client-server route. From the economic point of view the problem also seems serious, the interest of net tycoons and large Internet portals, for whom it is important to win and maintain as many customers as possible, depends on Internet reliability and its best performance. Thus there arises a clear need for spatial-temporal forecasting of Internet performance which would take into account both the geographical location of web servers and the total downloading time of a given resource. Such need for forecast information arises for example when we have to choose from where we should download information resource which is available on many Internet nodes at various geographical locations to obtain the resource at the minimum (or known) time. Knowing the forecast of transfer throughput from these nodes

A. Kwiecień, P. Gaj, and P. Stera (Eds.): CN 2011, CCIS 160, pp. 102–113, 2011.

to our location will allow us to choose the node from which we can receive the resource in the shortest time [1].

Analysis of network measurements plays a fundamental role in Internet knowledge discovery. The results of such analysis can help administrators as well as casual users in studying network characteristics including forecasting of network future performance behavior. In this paper we propose to use the Turning Bands method to predict Web performance that is perceived by end users while downloading resources from Web servers. The contribution of this paper is to propose this innovative application of Turning Bands method. This forecasting method has been originally employed in geostatistics [2] and has some other applications but not still in the field of Internet/Web performance.

Networks can be measured using active or passive methods. Active measurement scheme uses a probing approach where a reaction is observed after sending a probe signal (traffic, request) whereas passive measurement scheme is based only on current network observation without any additional traffic injection [3,4,5]. This research is based on active measurements made by MWING system which is Internet measurement infrastructure developed in our Institute [6,7]. MWING has been developed to design and perform both kinds of experiments in a controlled way. The kind of experiment, its aim, time duration and the experiment itself are designed by the researcher using either basic or extended MWING functions. Designed experiment is performed within of MWING platform that employs multi-agent technology. MWING's agents can run on any Internet host performing designed measurement experiment, collecting data and storing it in local or central databases. In this work we use the measurement data collected in a world-wide experiment that has been designed and performed to monitor a performance of a group of Web servers (sites) perceived from four different Internet locations [1]. In particular, we considered data gathered by agent located in Wrocław.

The rest of the paper is organized as follows. First, we introduce the Turning Bands (TB) method. Next we present preliminary and structural data analysis of results of network measurements. After that, we present a spatial forecast of Web server performance made by means of TB method. Finally, we conclude the paper and discuss future research.

2   Turning Bands Method

This paper presents the activity methodology and the algorithm of the Turning Bands method, which will be used to calculate the area-time forecast of performance in computer network nodes. The Turning Bands method is a stereologic tool used for reduction of multidimensional simulation to a one-dimensional one started by Matheron [8,9]. The examined function was a Gaussian random function of average value equal to 0, variance equal to 1 and covariance function C continuous in domain D in $\mathbb{N}^d$. In accordance with Bochner's theorem, covariance C may be defined as Fourier transform of a positive measure (spectral measure), for example χ :

$$C(h) = \int_{\mathbb{R}^d} e^{i\langle h, u \rangle} d\chi(u) . \tag{1}$$

Moreover $C(0) = 1$, hence χ is a probability measure. After the introduction of a polar coordinate system $u = (\theta, \rho)$, where θ is a directional parameter, stretching hemisphere $\mathbb{S}_d^+$ and ρ is a location parameter $(-\infty < \rho < +\infty)$, spectral measure $d\chi(u)$ may be written as the product of distribution $d\varpi(\theta)$ and conditional distribution $d\chi_\theta(\rho)$ for given θ. After using this distribution to develop a spectral covariance C and after the introduction of onedimensional function $C_\theta(r)$, Bochner's theorem was used and thanks to this covariance function $C(h)$ can be written in the following way:

$$C(h) = \int_{\mathbb{S}_d^+} C_\theta(\langle h, \theta \rangle) d\varpi(\theta) , \tag{2}$$

where C_θ is also a covariance function. The Turning Bands method consists in the reduction of a Gaussian random function of covariance C to the simulation of an independent stochastic process of covariance C_θ. Let $(\theta_n, n \in \mathbb{N})$ be a sequence of directions $\mathbb{S}_d^+$, and let $(X_n, n \in \mathbb{N})$ be a sequence of independent stochastic processes of covariance C_{θ_n}. Random function:

$$Y^{(n)}(x) = \frac{1}{\sqrt{n}} \sum_{k=1}^{n} X_k(\langle x, \theta_k \rangle); \ x \in \mathbb{R}^d , \tag{3}$$

assumes covariance equal to:

$$C^{(n)}(h) = \frac{1}{n} \sum_{k=1}^{n} C_{\theta_k}(\langle h, \theta_k \rangle) . \tag{4}$$

It results from the central limit theorem that for very big n, the spatial distribution $Y^{(n)}$ approaches Gaussian distribution of covariance $\lim_{n \to \infty} C^{(n)}$. This limit is exactly C in the case when series $\frac{1}{2} \sum_{k=1}^{n} \delta_{\theta_k}$ is weakly convergent to ϖ. The algorithm of the Turning Bands method takes the following form:

Algorithm Turning Bands method (TB)

1. Selection of directions $\theta_1, \ldots, \theta_n$, so that $\frac{1}{n} \sum_{k=1}^{n} \delta_{\theta_k} \approx \varpi$.
2. Generation of standard, independent stochastic processes $X_1, \ldots, X_n$ with covariance functions $C_{\theta_1}, \ldots, C_{\theta_n}$.
3. Calculating $\frac{1}{\sqrt{n}} \sum_{k=1}^{n} X_k(\langle x, \theta_k \rangle)$ for each $x \in D$.

Below there is more information about particular steps of algorithm TB, while the whole Turning Bands method and conditional simulations are discussed in more detail in [10].

Step 1 algorithm TB. Generating Directions. It was assumed that ϖ has continuous density ρ on $\mathbb{S}_d^+$. If series $\frac{1}{n}\sum_{k=1}^n \delta_{\theta_k}$ is weakly convergent to homogeneous distribution on $\mathbb{S}_d^+$, then $\frac{\mathbb{S}_d^+}{n}\sum_{k=1}^n \delta_{\theta_k} p\left(\theta_k\right)$ is weakly convergent to ϖ. It results from this This means that in further considerations we can look only at the isotropic case. One of the possible solutions of the problem are weakly convergent sequences [11]. It consists in creating θ_n n as far as possible from $\theta_1, \ldots \theta_{n-1}$, simultaneously filling in $\mathbb{S}_d^+$ as quickly as possible. In the 3-dimensional case, similarly to [12], one can start with binary and ternary expansion of each integer $n = 1, 2, \ldots$:

$$n = a_0 + 2a_1 + \ldots + 2^p a_p = b_0 + 3b_1 + \ldots + 3^q b_q \ , \tag{5}$$

$(a_i = 0, 1, \ldots$ and $b_j = 0, 1, \ldots)$, to obtain two numbers u_n and v_n in the interval 0 to 1:

$$u_n = \frac{a_0}{2} + \frac{a_1}{4} + \ldots + \frac{a_p}{2^{p+1}} \ , \tag{6}$$

$$v_n = \frac{b_0}{3} + \frac{b_1}{9} + \ldots + \frac{b_q}{3^{q+1}} \ . \tag{7}$$

Then θ_n can be replaced by:

$$\theta_n = \left(\cos\left(2\pi u_n\right)\sqrt{1 - v_n^2}, \sin\left(2\pi u_n\right)\sqrt{1 - v_n^2}, v_n\right). \tag{8}$$

Step 2 algorithm TB. Defining One-Dimensional Covariance. The basic steps in defining one-dimensional covariance is determining spectral measure χ from C, and next spectral measure χ_θ from C_θ and taking its Fourier transform. Because of the fact that covariance C is isotropic, it is possible to significantly simplify the calculations where $C\left(h\right) = C_d\left(|h|\right)$ for certain scalar function C_d defined on $\mathbb{N}^+$. In this case all C_θ are equal to individual covariance function, e.g. C_1. Matheron [8] obtained the dependence between C_1 and C_d:

$$C_d\left(r\right) = 2\frac{\left(d-1\right)\omega_{d-1}}{d\omega_d}\int_0^1 \left(1 - t^2\right)^{\frac{d-3}{2}} C_1\left(tr\right) dt \ , \tag{9}$$

where ω_d stands for d-dimensional volume of the unit ball in $\mathbb{N}^d$. If $d = 3$, the formula is reduced to:

$$C_3\left(r\right) = \int_0^1 C_1\left(tr\right) dt \ , \tag{10}$$

or equivalently:

$$C_1\left(r\right) = \frac{d}{dr}\left(rC_3\left(r\right)\right) \ . \tag{11}$$

To conduct further simulation we must define covariance function K for each of the considered variable. This is done with a variogram function defined for arbitrary vector h as [13]:

$$\gamma\left(h\right) = \frac{1}{2} E\left(\left(Z\left(x+h\right) - Z\left(x\right)\right)^2\right) \ . \tag{12}$$

During the forecasting of Web performance with time advance the direction variogram is determined. In this case the direction along the time axis is selected, in this direction calculations are made for various distances $|h|$. Experimental variogram $\hat{\gamma}\left(h\right)$ is next estimated for given vector h:

$$\hat{\gamma}\left(h\right) = \frac{1}{2p} \sum_{\alpha,\beta} \left(z_x^\alpha - z_x^\beta\right)^2 \ , \tag{13}$$

where pair (x_α, x_β) is selected in such a way that $x_\beta = x_\alpha + h$, and p is the number of points which verify this relation. The obtained direction variogram is approximated with a theoretical model. There are a lot of such theoretical functions to approximate variogram, among others these are: gamma, J Bessel, K Bessel, Gaussian, spherical, cubic, power, Cauchy, exponential, nugget effect, sinusoidal, constant and linear. There is more information about variograms in [14,2,15].

Step 3 algorithm TB. Simulation of Stochastic Processes. There is wide variety of methods used for the simulation of stochastic processes with given covariance function C_1. The most commonly used methods are: spectral, dilution and migration. The methods listed above are described in more detail in [10]. The anamorphosis function is used in the transformation of Gaussian type variable y into new variable z of arbitrary distribution. Empirical Gaussian anamorphosis is represented by infinite series of Hermite polynomials [15]:

$$\varphi_k\left(y\right) = \sum_{k=0}^{\infty} \frac{\varphi_k}{k!} H_k\left(y\right) \ . \tag{14}$$

Smooth approximation of empirical Gaussian anamorphosis was obtained by cutting the expansion to K-th value. This cut expansion is called Gaussian anamorphosis:

$$\varphi^*\left(y\right) = \sum_{k=0}^{K} \frac{\varphi_k}{k!} H_k\left(y\right) \ . \tag{15}$$

Next there are attempts to match the model to draw discrete curve y in function z, calculated from data values. The anamorphosis function is reversible and it must be strictly increasing with y. This is not fulfilled in the case of polynomial expansion cut to a particular order, that is why to obtain appropriate results from φ^*, one has to define practical interval of definition φ^*, which is the largest interval in which φ^* increases with y and is limited by 2 points: $(y_{p_{min}}, z_{p_{min}})$ and $(y_{p_{max}}, z_{p_{max}})$. Moreover when Gaussian variable is determined in the whole domain of real numbers $\mathbb{N}$, i.e. it adopts arbitrary values from interval $+\infty$ to $-\infty$, the considered variables are limited (they are all positive). That is why one has to define an authorized interval limited by $(y_{a_{min}}, y_{a_{max}})$. Intersections φ^* with two horizontal lines defined by these limits, $(y_{a_{min}}, z_{a_{min}})$ and $(y_{a_{max}}, z_{a_{max}})$, are the limits of the so called absolute defined interval φ^*. It represents the interval in which the final modeled anamorphosis function adopts its value. If an absolute definition interval is wider than the practical one, the polynomial expansion cannot be used in its extreme parts; then the modeled anamorphosis has to be defined by drawing a line between $(y_{a_{min}}, z_{a_{min}})$ and $(y_{p_{min}}, z_{p_{min}})$ and also between $(y_{a_{max}}, z_{a_{max}})$ and $(y_{p_{max}}, z_{p_{max}})$. Finally the limited anamorphosis will be used in the random diagram of Gaussian curve to obtain a random graph of the original variable. A pictorial graph of Gaussian anamorphosis with interval is presented in Fig. 1.

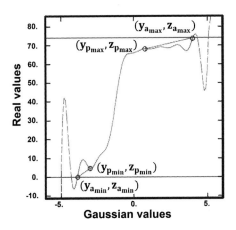

Fig. 1. Sample calculations of anamorphosis function: thickened line – experimental curve, intermittent line – final anamorphosis function, (on the basis of [16])

3   Preliminary Data Analysis

The database was created on the basis of experimental research using multi-agent system MWING [6,7,17,18], where agents were installed on local hosts of networks belonging to academic campuses in four geographical locations: Wrocław, Gliwice, Gdańsk and Las Vegas (USA). To create the discussed database, we used measurement data obtained from the agent located in Wrocław. The measured parameters referred to downloading a copy of a text document to Wrocław agent from many Web servers located among others in Europe, Asia, North America and Australia.

The measurements encompassed the period between 1st and 28th February 2009 and they were taken every day at the same time, at 11:30. The input database necessary for calculations contains the information about server (node) geographical location with which the Wrocław agent connected, the total downloading time and the time of taking the measurement.

Table 1. Elementary parameters of download times from Web servers between 1–28.02.2009

Minimum value X_{min} [s]	Maximum value X_{max} [s]	Average value X [s]	Standard deviation S [s]	Variability coefficient V [%]	Skewness coefficient G	Kurtosis coefficient K
0.11	31.18	2.68	3.55	132.46	3.52	22.07

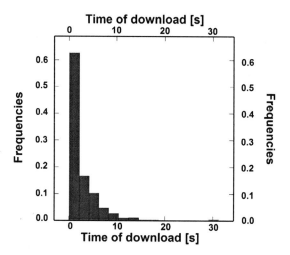

Fig. 2. Histogram of download time distribution from Web servers in February

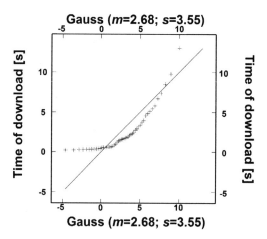

Fig. 3. Quantile graph Q-Q of performance values in nodes in February, approximated by Gaussian distribution where m is mean and s is standard deviation

Table 1 presents basic download time statistics on the discussed Web servers. Minimum and maximum values show span of data values. Additionally there is a large value of standard deviation and variability coefficient which proves the changeability of the examined process. High values of both skewness and kurtosis coefficients indicates big right side asymmetry of performance distribution. A histogram of performance distribution in the nodes of a computer network, presented in Fig. 2, is strongly asymmetric, single-wing and positively skewed. Modal class 0 – 2.15 s clearly dominates.

Figure 3 presents a comparison of download time distribution with the theoretical model. These are graphs of empirical and theoretical quantiles Q-Q. On the vertical axis there are the empirical quantiles of the considered real variable and on the horizontal axis – reference distribution quantiles. The closer to the first bisector (diagonal) there are quantile symbols, the closer the empirical distribution to the theoretical one. As one can see on the presented graph the theoretical distribution significantly deviates from the empirical one.

4   Structural Analysis of Data

4.1   Gaussian Anamorphosis

The practical interval of Gaussian values was equal $[-1.10; 2.81]$ and of real values $[0.30; 31.18]$. The authorized interval of the real variable was limited by $y_{a_{\min}} = 0.11$, $y_{a_{\max}} = 31.18$. The interval was intersected with two horizontal lines defined by these limits, $(y_{a_{\min}}, z_{a_{\min}}) = [-3.49; 0.11]$ and $(y_{a_{\min}}, z_{a_{\min}}) = [3.49; 31.18]$. These are the limits of the so called absolute definition interval in which the final modelled anamorphosis function adopts its value. During the calculations of Gaussian transformation frequency inversion model was used. The number of adopted Hermite polynomials in anamorphosis was equal to 100. Figure 4 presents the run of Gaussian anamorphosis.

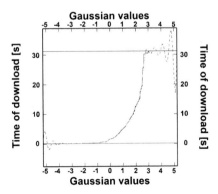

Fig. 4. Calculations of anamorphosis function used in the forecast of performance in the nodes using Turning Bands method: thickened line – experimental curve, thin line – polynomial expansion, intermittent line – final anamorphosis function

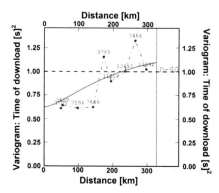

Fig. 5. Directional variogram along time axis for download times, approximated with the theoretical model of nuggets effect and Bessel

The observed gentle interval in range $[-1.10; 2.81]$ which was obtained for Gaussian values, proves good match between the adopted theoretical model and the empirical anamorphosis function of download times distribution (Fig. 4).

4.2 Variogram Model

The starting point for forecast calculation, after the initial data analysis and the calculation of Gaussian anamorphosis, is modeling the theoretical function of variogram. During the approximation of variogram model the nugget effect and Bessel functions were used. The directional variogram was calculated along the time axis (for $90°$ direction). The distance class for this variogram was $15\,\mathrm{km}$.

Figure 5 presents a directional variogram approximated with the theoretical model of nuggets effect and Bessel. The variogram function indicates a gentle rising trend.

5   Spatial Forecast of Web Servers Performance Calculated with the Turning Bands Method

The forecast model used to predict the total time of resource download from the Internet was the above presented variogram model and Gaussian anamorphosis. Additionally in the simulation the moving neighborhood was adopted, the search ellipsoid was $310.95\,\mathrm{km}$ for all three directions. Time forecasts for resource download were determined on the basis of 100 simulation realizations. A point wise type of calculation was used in the simulation. 3D forecast was calculated with one-week time advance, i.e. it encompassed the period of time between 1st and 7th March 2009. Table 2 presents global statistics of the forecasted performance values in nodes for the first week.

The values of forecasted Web servers download times presented in Table 2 are characterized with a small underestimation of data. The high value of variance coefficient (for average value above 50%) proves significant dispersion of data

Table 2. Global statistics of Web download times with one-week time advance, calculated with Turning Bands simulation method

Geostatistic parameter	Average value Z_s [s]	Maximum value Z_{smax} [s]	Minimum value Z_{smin} [s]	Variance S^2 $[s]^2$	Standard deviation S [s]	Variance coefficient V [%]
Average forecasted value Z_s	3.12	13.54	0.26	2.50	1.58	50.64
Forecast standard deviation σ_s	3.09	11.14	0.09	1.87	1.37	44.34
Maximum forecasted value $Z_{s,max}$	17.74	31.18	0.52	75.14	8.67	48.87
Minimum forecasted value $Z_{s,min}$	0.20	5.25	0.11	0.02	0.14	70.00

Table 3. Few exemplary results of spatial forecast of Web servers performance calculated with Turning Bands simulation method

URL address	Country/city	Measurement date and time	Download time [s]	Forecasted download time [s]	Forecasted error ex post [%]
www-uxsup.csx.cam.ac.uk /pub/doc/rfc/rfc1945.txt	United Kingdom /Cambridge	7 March 2009, 11:30	0.86	0.88	2.36
curl.hkmirror.org /rfc/rfc1945.txt	Netherlands /Eindhoven	6 March 2009, 11:30	1.29	1.19	7.84
plan9.aichi-u.ac.jp/ pegasus/man-2.0 /rfc/1945.txt	Japan /Tokio	5 March 2009, 11:30	5.79	5.73	1.10
paginas.fe.up.pt/~jvv /net/rfc1945.txt	Portugal /Porto	4 March 2009, 11:30	1.26	1.21	3.70
ietfreport.isoc.org /rfc/rfc1945.txt	Australia /Brisbane	3 March 2009, 11:30	5.99	6.54	9.27

and unequal distribution of web servers in the given area. This fact has direct negative influence on the forecast error. However, it may be stated that the forecast is a quite good representation of the reality of some nodes. Average, absolute, percentage, relative forecast error ex post for a few selected nodes is presented in Table 3.

The analysis of the results presented in Table 3 shows that the forecast prepared with Turning Bands method represents the download time quite well. Unfortunately due to big span of web servers in the examined area, not all of the results were characterized with good accuracy of prediction results.

The final effect of the forecast calculations is presented in Fig. 6, it is a base map for the 1st week prognosis (1–7.03.2009), it presents the download time from the Internet. The size of the cross corresponds with the download time from a given web server (in the legend the download time is given in seconds).

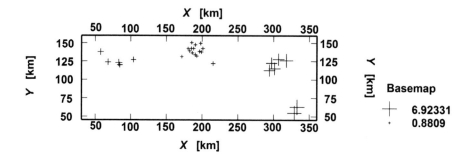

Fig. 6. Base map of download time values

Figure 6 presents the big span of Web servers in Europe, Asia, North America and Australia. Moreover the biggest Web performance is in North America and Australia.

6   Summary

The innovative application of the Turning Bands geostatistics simulation method in spatial forecasting of download time, thanks to which we can find out where there net (Internet) overloads, seems to be justified.

On the basis of conducted preliminary research, the authors claim that there is a need to work on the improvement of forecast accuracy. Web performance should be analyzed also in other area, using various measurement data and prediction lengths. However, the next step should be an attempt to use other geostatistics methods which have already been successfully used by the author to forecast loads in power transmission and distribution networks [19,20,21,22].

References

1. Borzemski, L.: The experimental design for data mining to discover web performance issues in a Wide Area Network. Cybernetics and Systems: An International Journal 41, 31–45 (2010)
2. Isaaks, E.H., Srivastava, R.M.: An Introduction to Applied Geostatistics. Oxford University Press, New York (1989)
3. Brownlee, N., Claffy, K., Murray, M., Nemeth, E.: Methodology for Passive Analysis of a University Internet Link. In: Proc. of Workshop on Passive and Active Measurements PAM 2001, Amsterdam, Holland (2001)
4. Jing, H., Dovrolis, C.: Passive estimation of TCP Round-Trip Times. ACM SIGCOMM Computer Communication Review 32(3) (2002)
5. Padmanabhan, V., Qiu, L.: Network Tomography Using Passive End-to-End Measurements. In: DIMACS Workshop on Internet and WWW Measurement, Mapping and Modeling, Piscataway, NJ (2002)

6. Borzemski, L., Cichocki, L., Kliber, M., Fras, M., Nowak, Z.: MWING: A Multiagent System for Web Site Measurements. In: Nguyen, N.T., Grzech, A., Howlett, R.J., Jain, L.C. (eds.) KES-AMSTA 2007. LNCS (LNAI), vol. 4496, pp. 278–287. Springer, Heidelberg (2007)
7. Borzemski, L., Cichocki, L., Kliber, M.: Architecture of Multiagent Internet Measurement System MWING Release 2. In: Håkansson, A., Nguyen, N.T., Hartung, R.L., Howlett, R.J., Jain, L.C. (eds.) KES-AMSTA 2009. LNCS, vol. 5559, pp. 410–419. Springer, Heidelberg (2009)
8. Matheron, G.: Quelques aspects de la montée. Internal Report N-271, Centre de Morphologie Mathematique, Fontainebleau
9. Matheron, G.: The intrinsic random functions and their applications. Adv. Appl. Prob. 5, 439–468 (1973)
10. Lantuejoul, C.: Geostatistical Simulation. Models and Algorithms, Springer-Verlag (2002)
11. Bouleau, N.: Probabilites de l'Ingenieur. Hermann, Paris (1986)
12. Freulon, X.: Conditionnement du modele gaussien par des inegalites ou des randomisees. Geostatistics Doctoral Thesis, School of Mines of Paris (1992)
13. Inizan, M.: Geostatistical Validation of a Marine Ecosystem Model Usinng In Situ Data. Technical Report S-435 Centre de Geostatistique, Ecole des Mines de Paris (2002)
14. Armstrong, M.: Basic Linear Geostatistics. Springer, Berlin (1998)
15. Wackernagel, H.: Multivariate Geostatistics: an Introduction with Applications. Springer, Berlin (2003)
16. Isatis Software Manual, 5th Edition, Geovariances & École des Mines de Paris (2004)
17. Borzemski, L., Cichocki, L., Kliber, M.: A distributed system to measure the Internet based on agent architecture. In: Borzemski, L., et al. (eds.) Information Systems Architecture and Technology, Web-age Information Systems, Oficyna Wydawnicza Politechniki Wroclawskie, Wroclaw (2009)
18. Borzemski, L., Nowak, Z.: Empirical Web performance evaluation with using a MWING system. In: Borzemski, L., et al. (eds.) Information Systems Architecture and Technology: Advances in Web-Age Information Systems, pp. 25–34. Oficyna Wydawnicza Politechniki Wroclawskiej, Wroclaw (2009)
19. Kaminska-Chuchmala, A., Wilczynski, A.: Application simulation methods to spatial electric load forecasting. Rynek Energii 1(80), 2–9 (2009) (in Polish)
20. Kaminska-Chuchmala, A., Wilczynski, A.: 3D electric load forecasting using geostatistical simulation method Turning Bands. Prace Wroclawskiego Towarzystwa Naukowego XVI, B(215), 41–48 (2009) (in Polish)
21. Kaminska-Chuchmala, A., Wilczynski, A.: Analysis of different methodological factors on accuracy of spatial electric load forecast performed with Turning Bands method. Rynek Energii 2(87), 54–59 (2010) (in Polish)
22. Kaminska-Chuchmala, A., Wilczynski, A.: Spatial electric load forecasting in transmission networks with Sequential Gaussian Simulation method. Rynek Energii 1(92), 35–40 (2011) (in Polish)

Knowledge Managemenent in the IPv6 Migration Process

Krzysztof Nowicki, Mariusz Stankiewicz, Aniela Mrugalska,
Tomasz Mrugalski, and Jozef Wozniak

Gdansk University of Technology
Faculty of Electronics, Telecommunications and Informatics
11/12 Gabriela Narutowicza Street, 80-233 Gdańsk, Poland
{krzysztof.nowicki,mariusz.stankiewicz,aniela.mrugalska,
tomasz.mrugalski,jozef.wozniak}@eti.pg.gda.pl
http://www.eti.pg.gda.pl/

Abstract. There are many reasons to deploy IPv6 protocol with IPv4 address space depletion being the most obvious. Unfortunately, migration to IPv6 protocol seems slower than anticipated. To improve pace of the IPv6 deployment, authors of the article developed an application that supports the migration process. Its main purpose is to help less experienced network administrators to facilitate the migration process with a particular target usage being SOHO networks.

Migration to IPv6 is a complex process. For the sake of simplicity, it has been split into several phases. First one is dedicated to automated network discovery that helps to gain initial knowledge about migrated networks and its services. Second step is devoted to building knowledge database about used hardware, operating systems, services and applications. It is being represented as a collection of interdependent questions with possible answers. This knowledge database is then used to provide relevant assistance for the IPv6 migration steps.

To reduce the tree structure management costs and choose only applicable elements that actually exist in migrated network, there are two proposed algorithms to create a list of questions and advices. Developed methods enable quick and easy expansion options available without any knowledge about all existing questions in base and their dependencies.

This paper presents a prototype application that is still under development. It will allow to add elements to IPv6 Migration Guide in an easy way. Used together with already developed IPv6 Migration Guide solution, it will provide significant assistance to network administrators during IPv6 enabling phase.

Keywords: IPv6, Separable Algorithm, Dripping Algorithm, IPv6 Migration Guide, multi-platform Questions Editor.

1   Introduction

Both IPv4 and IPv6 address spaces are governed by Internet Assigned Number Authority (IANA) [1]. It allocates address blocks (an /8 class of IPv4 addresses)

A. Kwiecień, P. Gaj, and P. Stera (Eds.): CN 2011, CCIS 160, pp. 114–124, 2011.

to five Regional Internet Registries (RIRs) that in turn delegate addresses to network operators. On February 3rd, 2011 IANA allocates last of the available IPv4 addresses to RIRs. Although RIRs supplies are expected to last for several months, there are no longer new addresses to replenish them. Each RIR is responsible for certain world region. Depending on the demand, some regions may run out of IPv4 addresses sooner than others. Depending on used prediction algorithm, the estimated date of first RIR will run out of IPv4 addresses is expected to happen on August 14th, 2011. The problem of the depletion of public IPv4 addresses is a very serious threat both to all operators and Internet service providers and individual users. There is a need to migrate to IPv6. This fact is confirmed by all the organizations managing the assignment of IP addresses such as IANA [1] and the RIPE.

There are many initiatives fastering the implementation of IPv6. For instance the services available via IPv6 content providers such as Google [2] and YouTube [3]. Many operators started to offer access via IPv6, such as Comcast (USA) [4], Free.fr (France) [5] or the Polish Jarsat [6]. It also should be mentioned about the forthcoming Word IPv6 Day event, when many content providers will be available include IPv6 in their services. Participation in this event scheduled for July 8, 2011 announced Facebook, Google [2], Yahoo, Akamai, Cisco, gazeta.pl and many others. Implementation of new IPv6 addresses allows a large number of telecommunications equipment allows to be visible on the Internet.

Devices, such as personal computers, small home servers, cameras, alarm systems and telephones, will be able to communicate directly and without interruption, regardless of their location. This method of communication called end-to-end, was lost in IPv4 when networks started to use Network Address Translation (NAT) solutions [7].

IPv6 provides faster transmission of packets resulting in better performance and less load in the network routers. There was also introduced QoS (Quality of Service), more expanded mechanisms for autoconfiguration or the support for IPsec [8] in the same protocol. Without the development of the IPv6 Internet technologies in the longer period of time will be impossible. We should start to implement it now to avoid higher costs, which involves adapting the network to support IPng at the last moment [9].

2   System Architecture

Migration of existing network which uses IPv4 to IPv6 is a complicated process [10]. In order to facilitate the transition through the process of changing the protocol system the IPv6 Migration Guide was developed. Guide's main goal is to help administrators to facilitate the implementation with a particular focus on SOHO networks.

There are planned two methods of a software distribution – as an application installed on Windows systems and as a component of an automatic bootable CD. The IPv6 Migration Guide will be one of the fundamental elements of the

LiveCD, which being prepared by the Future Internet Engineering [11]. Developed solution is also in addition to the IPv6 Migration Guide, going to offer a number of validation tools that are used to confirm the correctness of the migration to IPv6 [12]. LiveCD will works under the supervision FreeBSD.

Working of IPv6 Migration Guide can be divided into four basic processes. The first step includes the detection and analysis of networks, based on external scripts. In the second step it is possible to verify the information from the first step, and to provide additional answers that can not be achieved through automated network scanning. Particular questions are related to each other to not display the next question, when previous answers indicate that they are not needed in a given situation. The hierarchy of questions with dynamic dependences and well state of information about network is a base element of principal knowledge. Step three provides the necessary knowledge needed to make the real migration process. This is based on data acquired on the network from the previous action. A package of tips can be treated as assurance of knowledge accumulated in previous step. The fourth step provides opportunity to test the network settings in odder to ensure that the required steps have been made by an administrator correctly. This is the last step.

Due to the complexity of the process, the amount of data collected and processed in the second and third steps is very large. It became necessary to create a solution that provides the ability to limit viewing tips matched to the topology, technology and services available in a particular network migrated.

3   Questions and Advices Constructions

All questions and advices are stored in separated XML tags. One of the main attributes is relation called <depends>, which defines the relationship between the elements. Inside questions there are answers embedded, which have a unique name id. Because of the uniqueness of this tag it is possible to determine the answer to the question which is clearly defined. Example relationships will be presented in Fig. 1.

Building relationships was presented in the example below, where an affirmative answer to the first obvious questions about name id WinXP reads "Do you have Windows XP Professional in your network?" brings up another question that reads "Do you want to turn off all support for IPv4 and use only IPv6 in Windows XP Professional?" [13]. It was made by developing the function <depends>, which for these questions may take the following form WinXP:yes or WinXP:no, where in the first case it could display the question with id=ipv6only while in the second case its elimination.

```
<question type="single" id="WinXP" depends="system:windows">
  <content  lang="en">Do you have Windows XP Professional
      in your network?
  </content>
  <answer id="yes" lang="en">yes</answer>
  <answer id="no" lang="en">no</answer>
```

```
    <helpHtml>winVer.htm</helpHtml>
</question>

<question type="single" id="ipv6only" depends="WinXP:yes">
    <content  lang="en">Do you want to turn off all support for IPv4
        and use only IPv6 in Windows XP Professional?
    </content>
    <answer id="yes" lang="en">yes</answer>
    <answer id="no"  lang="en">no</answer>
    <helpHtml>ipv6only.html</helpHtml>
</question>
```

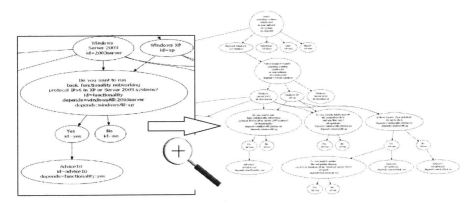

Fig. 1. `<depends>` parameters can be used to construct dependency tree. The figure shows an example subset a such tree with questions, advices and answers visualized.

A similar relationship exists with the advices that are directly related to the answers. There is also inbuilt an elimination procedure of advices that are unrelated with migrated network. In this way we avoid a situation where the administrator receives advices, which he could not use, because of the lack of understanding of their purpose and meaning.

The following example illustrates the mechanism of actions undertaken in relation to the advice of migration. For the question with **id=nat** and content "Is NAT used in your network?" [7] there are possible answers yes or no, which will mean selecting the appropriate response with id yes/no. Depending on the answers selected by the user there will be displayed an advice from the file **natAnswYes.htm**, if the relationship was **nat:yes** because of an affirmative answer, or advice from the file **natAnswNo.htm** if the answer was negative.

```
    <question type="single" id="nat" depends="system:linux">
        <content  lang="en">Is NAT used in your network?</content>
        </content>
        <answer id="yes" lang="en">yes</answer>
        <answer id="no"  lang="en">no</answer>
        <helpHtml>nat.htm</helpHtml>
```

```
</question>

<step lang="en" depends="nat:yes">
   <helpHtml>natAnswYes.htm</helpHtml>
</step>

<step lang="en" depends="nat:no">
   <helpHtml>natAnswNo.htm</helpHtml>
</step>
```

4   Proposed Solutions Algorithms

To show a simple and transparent structure of the network it was decided to use the form of a tree to illustrate its components, where the next elements in the network have the form of branches. This form is presented in Fig. 2.

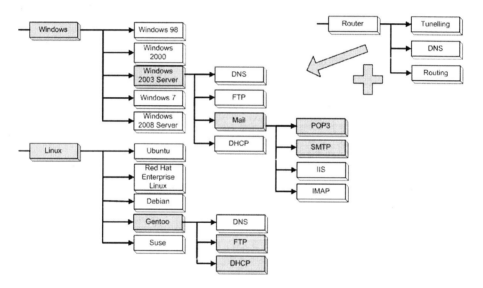

Fig. 2. Structure of the network was decided to use the form of a tree to illustrate its components. This solution is easy to understand by a large crowd of administrators who can find an analogy to the tree structure which is used in popular operating systems.

Branch delves more with details increasing in questions. The application is designed to help a users selecting the tree items that are in his network. This solution is easy to understand by a large group of administrators who can find an analogy to the tree structure which is used in popular operating systems.

Additionally this solution provides an easy way to add new questions and advices. There is no need to view trough all the questions. We can simply search key words and display only these branches in which we found our key words. Then the user, who wants to add the new question can easily check place in the display industry where he wants to add it. It is importance to add such possibility when we have a few hundred questions and advices. Otherwise, user who wants to add a new element must read all XML file and search relationships between the asked questions to find the physical location for the advice.

In order to reduce the tree of objects and select the only elements presented in the network that would launch the application there were proposed two algorithms solutions that allow to create a list of questions and advices in order to manage the displayed informations.

The principle of the first one, Dripping Algorithm with a single set, is creating a list of all the questions, where each question is marked active or inactive flag, which would find its counter part in the tag `<question>` with a `flag="active"` or `flag="inactive"`. When the second step of IPv6 Migration Guide starts only some of the questions have active flag.

Every time you give answer the application makes a search of tree branch to flags searching that should be changed so that after each of the reply is possible to change the displayed number of questions. It should also consider the case where a question depends on many others. In this case, verification is required for each question separately.

The Separable Algorithm is based on creation of two separate tables which are both for the questions and answers. At first, the reactive elements are displayed to the user while the other contains inactive elements which are at the time omitted. During running the program and loading a list of questions it follows their initial sorting.

Questions which always have to be raised up and do not have a `<depends>` tag go directly to the first (active) marker. The other questions, which have a marker go to another.

In allocating the appropriate sets of questions are followed by viewing the whole tree response. If we find the relationship back into the branch that matches the current tag is added to the dependence of the previous questions to the currently viewed. Following example explains this concept:

The dependence of the analyzed questions takes the following form:

```
<question type="single" id="functionality" depends="windowsAll:xp">(1)
```

There is dependence from the question:

```
<question type="multiple" id="windowsAll" depends="system:windows">(2)
```

And also from the answer:

```
<answer id="xp" lang="en">
```

In turn this question depends on the another:

```
<question lang="pl" type="multiple" id="system" >(3)
```

And the answer:

```
<answer id="xp" lang="pl">Windows XP</answer>
```

Summarizing, question (1) depends on question (2) directly and indirectly from the question (3). Therefore, depending on this tree looks like this:

```
system:windows -> windowsAll:xp -> functionality
```

Because of this the tag `<depends>`, in a currently browsing answer, will be automatically added a flag from the previous answer. In this case it will be the entire path that describes a particular branch of the dependent response. Added tag `<depends>` will take the following form:

```
system:windows, windowsAll:xp
```

This solution gives a guarantee that if we answer to all questions in the branch and return to the first question to change our answer, all of the questions depends on our answer in this branch will be transfered to the inactive set of questions. For example if we consider that did not have in our network any of Windows systems, all of the questions depends on this system will be transferred to the inactive set of questions, because all of these questions can not be found dependency `system:Windows`.

The Separable Algorithm with two sets is also used for management of advices displayed for the user. Its flowchart is presented in Fig. 3.

To the end of the process of giving answers there is parallel searching in all sets of advices and transferring relevant advices to the appropriate set.

Presorting of questions starts when the application is being started. Those that have tag `<depends>` are allocated to set with the inactive questions, and those that do not have a tag are allocated to the set with the active questions.

While starting the system there is an initialized counter N and a determined value of the N_{max} that equals the number of questions in a set of active questions. Then N is increased by 1 and this algorithm checked to see if $N \leq N_{max}$ and the question with the number N is displayed to the user. After answering the following set of relevant searches. If the relationship is not found in the set, there is return to the the the beginning and the increment of N. If the relationship is found, that question shall be transferred to the active set of questions and N_{max} is recalculated to succeed increment N and displayed next question. If $N == N_{max}$ there is progress to the next step.

In first order N is set to 0, then the discussed algorithm moves moved all the answers to inactive set and the increment of N. There is a created tag `<depends>` with id from question N and with selected answer to make possible search a set with the inactive answers to find a newly created question. If the tag is found the answer is moving to a new set and we increase N and check if $N \leq N_{max}$. If so, we take a new question with the number N and repeat the operation until the dependencies $N \leq N_{max}$ is true. Algorithm describes the figure below.

Between the two sets there are maintained relationships similar to the Dripping Algorithm. As a result of the answers given by the administrator, questions are moved between the sets. As a result of the above mentioned algorithm, user receives advices which are related only to his network.

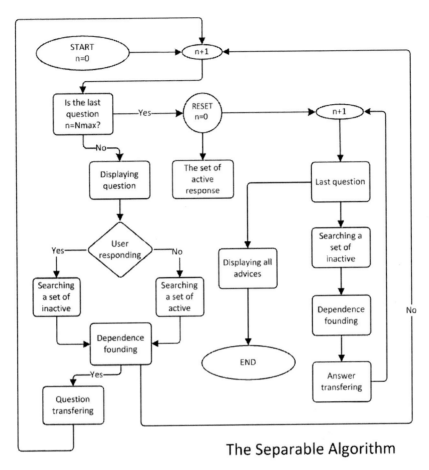

The Separable Algorithm

Fig. 3. Flowchart of the Separable Algorithm with two sets used for management of advices displayed for user

5   Research and Decision Making – Process Selection

During the initial tests in the laboratories authors was able to demonstrate that the Separable Algorithm because of the two sets of turns out to be more efficient solution in the aspect of the displaying speed. Currently, questions or suggestions transfer between two separate arrays, resulting in faster viewing them in looking for a relationship. There is no need to browse all the available questions and answers, check their flags and dependencies.

We are searching for inactive set for questions dependent on the affirmative answer, or active set in the opposite case. Using the two sets is also reflected in the speed of counting number of questions available to the user at a time. To do this, simply use the simple features built in the standard Python language [14], which was used in described solutions. Python has been used also in IPv6 Migration Guide. Past tests show the correctness of his actions [15].

Optimization activities are planned to increase, in order to improve the efficiency of the algorithm.

6   Development Plans – Extension of the Contributors Circle

The development plans of IPv6 Migration Guide predict the further development of process of making questions and advices related to migration which involves taking many relationships between contained therein essence.

With development of the available knowledge base, tracking and making correct definition of a new relationships may become problematic. Technical University of Gdansk is developing a prototype of a multi-platform Questions Editor presented in Fig. 4 with main objective to facilitate the definition of new and manage existing migration questions and advices.

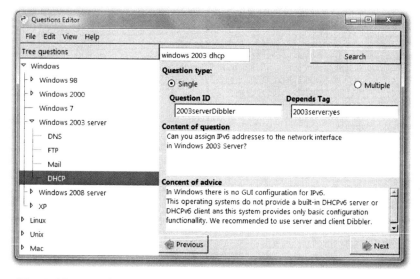

Fig. 4. Main window a prototype of a multi-platform Questions Editor [16]

It will be compatible with the solutions used in the IPv6 Migration Guide, and therefore will support the creation of the knowledge base based on XML files, handle the dependency tree of scenarios and many others.

The Questions Editor's idea is to be an intuitive application that Allows to add elements to IPv6 in easy way for every person who did not participate in its creation process.

Because of using the questions structure with analogy to the tree structure used in popular operating systems, when adding an element it is possible to quickly scan all the all the branches that match the newly designed advice, attaches the newly created questions for branch and setting a unique id or checking tag <depends> and many others.

7 Conclusions

Exhaustion of available IPv4 addresses is a serious issue for Internet expansion. This threat is reported by all organizations dedicated to the IP addresses management, such as IANA and RIPE [1]. The only viable long term solution is a migration to next generation of IP. To ease such migration, authors proposed a IPv6 Migration Guide system that assists the migration process and helps network administrators to facilitate the IPv6 deployment. Although the primary scope are SOHO networks, there are plans to expand knowledge base to other network types.

Two algorithms were proposed to create a lists of questions and advices to manage required information. Methods presented by authors enable quick and easy options expansion available without knowledge about all existing questions in base and their dependencies.

Described applications are designed to help user in migration to IPv6. To make this process easier representation structure of the network was presented in analogy to the file system used in popular operating systems. Further development plans are focused on optimization Separable Algorithm and creating specialized advices to allow use IPv6 Migration Guide in a wider aspect than originally planned.

Acknowledgment. This work has been partially supported by the Polish Ministry of Science and Higher Education under the European Regional Development Fund, Grant No. POIG.01.01.02-00-045/09-00 Future Internet Engineering.

References

1. The Official Website of IANA's IPv4 Address Report. IANA's IPv4 Address Report, http://ipv4.potaroo.netl (retrieved on February 12, 2011)
2. Access Google services over IPv6. In: The Official Website of Google over IPv6, http://www.google.com/intl/en/ipv6/l (retrieved on January 2011)
3. Marsan, C.: YouTube support of IPv6 seen in dramatic traffic spike. Network World, http://www.networkworld.com/news/2010/020110-youtube-ipv6.html (retrieved on February 11, 2011)
4. Comcast: The Official Website of Comcast IPv6, http://www.comcast6.net/ (retrieved on December 2010)
5. French ISP Free.fr IPv6: Free ISP on Wikipedia, http://en.wikipedia.org/wiki/Free_%28ISP%29#Internet_accessl (retrieved on October 2010)
6. Jarsat IPv6: The Official Website of Jarsat, http://ipv6.jarsat.pl/l (retrieved on January 2011)
7. Egevang, K.: The IP Network Address Translator (NAT). RFC 1631, IETF (May 1994)
8. Kent, S., Seo, K.: Security Architecture for the Internet Protocol. RFC 4301, IETF (December 2005)
9. Murphy, N.R., Malone, D.: IPv6 Network Administration. O'Reilly Media, Sebastopol (2005)

10. Mrugalski, T.: Metoda szybkiego wdrazania IPv6 przy wykorzystaniu DHCPv6. In: Techonologie Informacyjne Conference, Gdansk (2004)
11. Future Internet Engineering: The Official Website of Future Internet Engineering, http://iip.net.pl (retrieved on January 2011)
12. Deering, S., Hinden, R.: Internet Protocol, Version 6 (IPv6) Specification. RFC 2460, IETF (December 1998)
13. Microsoft Internet Protocol Version 6 (IPv6). Microsoft TechNet, http://technet.microsoft.com/en-us/network/bb530961.aspx (retrieved October 2009)
14. Lutz, M.: Programming Python. In: Powerful Object-Oriented Programming, O'Reilly Media, Sebastopol (2010)
15. Gajek, L., Kaluszka, M.: Wnioskowanie statystyczne. Wydawnictwa Naukowo-Techniczne, Warsaw (2000)
16. Schulzrinne, H., Volz, B.: Dynamic Host Configuration Protocol (DHCPv6) Options for Session Initiation Protocol (SIP) Servers. RFC 3319, IETF (July 2003)

Lightweight Multiresolution Jitter Analysis for Packet Networks

Przemysław Skurowski and Robert Wójcicki

Institute of Informatics, Silesian University of Technology,
ul. Akademicka 16, 44-100 Gliwice, Poland
{przemyslaw.skurowski,robert.wojcicki}@polsl.pl
http://inf.polsl.pl

Abstract. In the paper we propose a method for multiresolution jitter analysis dedicated to network transmissions where limited resources or heavy workload of devices are common situations. The concept is based on classical Gaussian pyramid – low-pass filtering and subsampling adopted to the specific application by using rectangular filtering and iterative incremental computation of incoming packet measures. The paper demonstrates computational algorithm and its computational complexity analysis for optimistic average and pessimistic scenario. Finally, possible applications of the proposal to network traffic and transmission analysis are demonstrated.

Keywords: multiresolution analysis, Gaussian pyramid, jitter analysis.

1 Introduction

In signal and image processing multiresolution or multiscale approach to data are nowadays popular technique. Such an approach offer wide possibilities of data analysis and processing usually performed by wavelet transform where the observed phenomena are located both in space/time and base function (frequency) domain. It also offers the ability to observe and analyze the data at the rough or fine detail level depending on the application needs. Wavelets due to their high computational requirements remain rather research than industrial tool in network transmission analysis. An alternative tool to the wavelets offering similar properties one can consider multiresolution (multiscale) pyramids [1] being a little bit simpler approach both conceptually and computationally. They produce signal representation on different stages at the variable levels of accuracy and as it will be shown in further parts of this paper it is possible to compute them relatively fast. So it would be possible to use such tools in real life applications such as complex traffic analysis in network servers or routers where one could consider heavy workload or limited resources of devices, moreover due to its incremental computation algorithm it would allow estimating of transmission momentary parameters and compare them between stages at the various temporal horizons. In the proposed approach there is used Gaussian pyramid with non-gaussian (moving average) low pass at the filtering step prior to the downsampling at each pyramid stage.

A. Kwiecień, P. Gaj, and P. Stera (Eds.): CN 2011, CCIS 160, pp. 125–134, 2011.

1.1   Jitter Classification

According to [2] in packet switching networking terms jitter definition is just a simple packet delay variation. Clark [3] identified three basic kinds of jitter: constant, transient and short term delay variation. There also exists one more phenomenon – slow delay change which is not jitter in fact but it is an obstacle that dejitter buffers has to deal with. The last two of them can be considered as *long term jitter*. All above types and their root causes are as follows (see Fig. 1):

- constant jitter – present in flawless transmission with roughly constant packet to packet delay variation,
- transient jitter – single packet is significantly delayed to the others. It has numerous reasons: routing table updates, packet scheduling and others,
- short term delay variation – occurring when a burst of packets has increased transmission delay. It is connected with access link congestion or route change,
- slow delay change – appearing in graph as a ramp like characteristics – Clark [3] also connects this phenomenon with access link congestion.

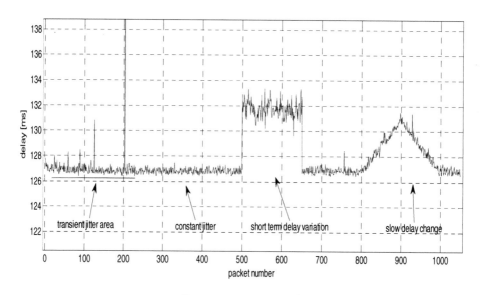

Fig. 1. Types of jitter

1.2   Jitter Estimators

There are various estimators described literature. They can be divided into two main groups D_{ap} – PDV (*packet delay variation*) related to some absolute reference value and D_{pp} – IPDV (*inter-packet delay variation*) where the preceding packet is used as a reference:

$$D_{\mathrm{ap}}(n) = t(n) - a(n) , \quad D_{\mathrm{pp}}(n) = t(n) - t(n-1) \tag{1}$$

where: $t(n)$, $t(n-1)$ is transmission delay of nth and $n^{\mathrm{th}} - 1$ packet, $a(n)$ is nominal (average) transmission time. This approach requires prior knowledge of the default transmission time, which means using local mean or median estimate. The above values are too sensitive for momentary and incidental delay changes so one can apply some local aggregating functions such as MA (*moving average*) and EWMA (*exponentially weighted moving average*) given with equations:

$$\mathrm{MA}(n) = \frac{1}{M} \sum_{m=0}^{M-1} D(n-m) \tag{2}$$

$$\mathrm{EWMA}(n) = \frac{1}{\alpha} D(n) + \frac{\alpha - 1}{\alpha} \mathrm{EWMA}(n-1) \tag{3}$$

where: D is one of delay variation measures given with Eq. (1) (these measures can be considered both in a pure form and as an absolute value), M is size of averaging window (usually 16), α is proportionality constant (usually 16).

Above formulas are used to construct estimators such as MPPDV, MAPDV or packet to packet EWMA and they will be considered in further parts of this paper. There are also proposed more sophisticated estimators like MAPDV2, SMPDV, or simple moving range statistics between selected percentiles for some recent packets (200 ms usually). All these methods quite well describe constant and transient jitter but works rather poor with short term delay variation and slow delay change which remains "invisible" for all the methods. For that reason the long term jitter cases are matter of special interest in this paper. For broad review of these algorithms see [4].

2   Multiscale Approach

2.1   Generic Pyramids

The idea behind the multiscale pyramid is that one can observe a data at various distances from local (momentary) values to long-term aggregates. Formal definition of that concept is that pyramids are *frames* (redundant bases) [5]. There are two main kinds of pyramids used: Gaussian and Laplacian applied especially in image coding. The computational scheme of both these pyramids is depicted in Fig. 2 where the original image (signal) is at zero level (G_0) of Gaussian pyramid. These are obtained by iterative low-pass filtering (LP) and downsampling previous stage signal by factor 2 ($\downarrow 2$) and in case of Laplacian pyramid by subtracting from previous stage of signal representation.

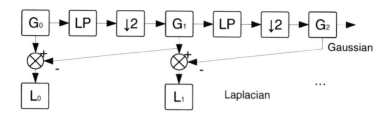

Fig. 2. Computation scheme for Gaussian and Laplacian pyramids

2.2 Proposed Solution

The proposed *multiscale binary rectangular tree* (MBRT) is intended to perform on-line analysis of network transmission therefore there the data is considered as sequence of events happening in discrete moments. In one dimensional case pyramid is reduced to a tree like structure. To reduce computational cost, the proposed algorithm is computed in incremental way using binary tree and rectangular low pass filtering by simple averaging two values from lower level of the tree.

The proposed algorithm is described using following metacode. Please note that output of multiresolution analysis has variable size at various levels but for code readability it is stored in oversized simple two-dimensional array o(K,i). The idea behind the following code is depicted in Fig. 3.

```
/*** Metacode of Multiscale Binary Rectangular Tree (MBRT) ***/
const K;                          // number of analysis levels
index=0;                          // number of received packet
do
  P = wait_and_receive_packet();
  T = compute_some_measure(P);
  O(index,0) = T;                 // store measure at 0th level
  index++;
  for k = 1..K                    // for all levels
    if ( mod(index, 2^k)==0)      // if bucket full
*     o_idx = div(index,2^k);     // remap index to kth level
*     o(o_idx,k)=(o(o_idx,k-1)+o(o_idx-1,k-1))/2;    //averaging
*     D(o_idx,k)=D_fun( o(0..index) );  // Dpp or Dap delay var fun
*     J(o_idx,k)=analysis_fun(D(0..index), J((0..index-1)));
    else
      break;                      //no use to test higher levels
    end if
  end for
while not(EOT)                    // End Of Transmission
```

In the code above there are variables that are abstract and their meaning might be unclear: P is a structure or object that is representation of packet and its parameters like arrival time or size and numeric D that is measure describing transmission like arrival- or interarrival-time (Eq. (1)) or some other that is

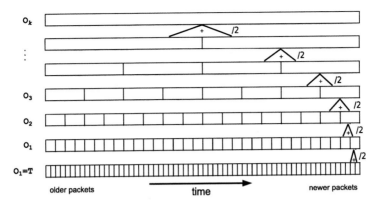

Fig. 3. Computation scheme of k levels of proposed binary tree, please note that symbols are based on the code shown above

averaged in the binary tree. Finally J is an array of results of aggregating function at each level. Functions possible to use are for example EWMA (Eq. (3)) or simple MA (Eq. (2)) over some window. MBRT can be used as 2^{k+1} size "sliding window" analysis performed with various detail levels.

2.3 Computational Complexity

In the code above there were lines marked with asterisk that one could consider as the dominant operation. They take the most time – in the half cases at least. The dominant operation is executed for every two packets plus every four plus every eight packets and so on. The average computational complexity per packet in $o(n)$ notation is:

$$o(n) = \frac{\overbrace{\dfrac{n}{2} + \dfrac{n}{4} + \dfrac{n}{8} + \dfrac{n}{16} + \cdots}^{K \text{ times}}}{n} = \frac{n\left(\sum_{k=1}^{K} \frac{1}{2^k}\right)}{n} = \sum_{k=1}^{K} \frac{1}{2^k} \ ,$$

for infinite number of levels it gets form of sum of infinite geometric series:

$$o(n) = \lim_{K \to \infty} \sum_{k=1}^{K} \frac{1}{2^k} = 1 \ .$$

For a single packet the algorithm has constant average computational complexity of $o(1)$ per packet as the sum is fast convergent to 1. Optimistic complexity occurs for odd index number when no dominant operation is performed. Pessimistic complexity occurs for every 2^K-th packet where modulo condition is fulfilled for every level then algorithm dominant operation is executed K times at every level of the tree. Summary of these considerations is collected in Table 1.

Table 1. Summary of computational complexity per packet for proposed algorithm

	pessimistic	average	optimistic
$o(n)$	K	1	0

3   Algorithm Performance

3.1   Preliminary Considerations

To verify features of the proposed solution we have briefly examined in MBRT all four cases of jitter (see Sect. 1.1). We used both delay variance measures: absolute and inter-packet variation (D_{pp} and D_{ap}) and their both values: raw and absolute. Our primary goal is to predict delay of incoming packets. The D_{pp} was our choice for further testing as it seems to be the most promising. It can be used both for estimation of jitter and to evaluate local mean transmission time by simple integration. Potentially D_{ap}, also can be used in similar manner but not so simply due to the fact that its value is affected by local transmission time estimate . In further parts of the paper we omitted absolute values of both delay variance measures D_{pp} and D_{ap} since they cannot be used for estimating long term jitter. We examined also two aggregating (estimating) functions EWMA and MA given with Eqs. (2)–(3) . All our tests were performed using one-way ping OWAMP [6] traces collected within PlanetLab [7] network. We collected numerous traces out of of which we have chosen two representative sets which we used in further parts of this paper to illustrate behavior of MBRT:

A from Poland to Germany a data set with constant transmission time and quite large jitter with numerous transient peaks (`plab2.ple.silweb.pl` – `chronos.disy.inf.uni-konstanz.de`),

B from Germany to USA an interesting data set with constant moderate jitter demonstrating all aforementioned types of jitter appearing in relatively short time (`13s.uni-hannover.de-planetlab` – `2.cmcl.cs.cmu.edu`).

3.2   Semi-synthetic Case

First, to check MBRT performance, we decided to add artificial steep and fully controlled long term jitter episodes to the data set A. They were intended for visual examination of the charts. Triangular waveform for slow delay change and rectangular one for short term delay change were added. The results for these data for 7 levels of averaging are illustrated in Fig. 4.

Using these results we have drawn following conclusions:

– averaging of source data results in smoothing the chart and in exhibiting longer term properties in the data, as it was expected,
– the higher level of the MBRT the less it is sensitive to the incidental peaks,
– EWMA is less sensitive to single peaks than MA as is gets smaller negative false values next to peak.

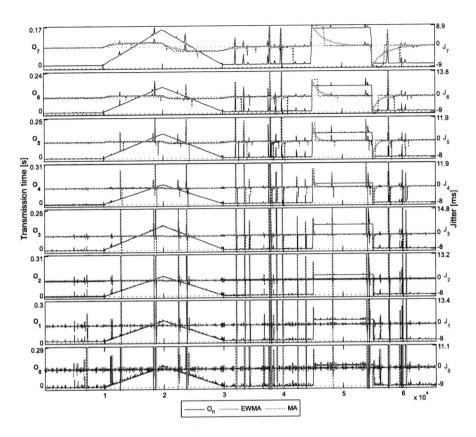

Fig. 4. Experimental results of jitter analysis in MBRT using D_{pp} for one way ping (OWAMP) based semi-synthetic data

Our next step in results analysis was to verify how the results predict successive values. As a prediction for each level we used cumulative sum of previous differences at the k level. Prediction of transmission time is given as:

$$P_k(n) = \sum_{i_k=0}^{i_k=M_k(n)} J_k(i_k) + C \qquad (4)$$

where: n, i_k – indices at 0th and k^{th} level, $M_k(n) = \lfloor (n-1)/2^k \rfloor$ – number of the last evaluated node at k^{th} level, C is summation constant which was taken as a median value for transmission time in whole data set. For the needs of qualitative analysis at the current stage we have examined the prediction results visually. As it is demonstrated in Fig. 5, such an approach approximates transmission variance very well although for higher levels one can observe inevitable delay.

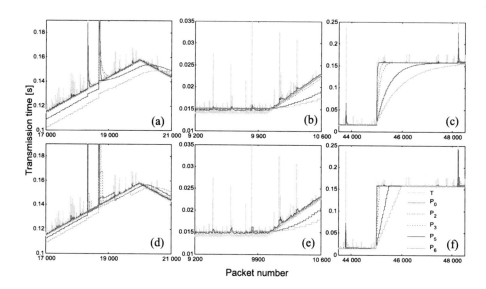

Fig. 5. Examples of MBRT based transmission time prediction: (a)–(c) EWMA, (d)–(f) MA

3.3 Real Life Case

The second data set taken for testing MBRT is data set B with no artificial additions as it contains all four types of jitter. The results were again visually examined although the task was not as simple as in previous case due to the fact that boundaries of episodes of slow delay change or short term delay change were not so clearly identifiable. However, the results (Fig. 6) were again visually very consistent with the input data.

3.4 Quantitative Testing

Finally we performed quantitative analysis of prediction. As a quality measure we have used mean average error between prediction and real transmission time:

$$D(k) = \frac{1}{N} \sum_{n=1}^{N} |P_k(n) - T(n)|$$

where: $P_k(n)$ is predicted value for n^{th} packet using k level predictor, $T(n)$ is real transmission time, N is number of packets. We tested both (Sect. 3.1) raw data sets (A_{real}, B_{real}) and as semi-synthetic (B_{syn}) set. The results are in Table 2.

3.5 Testing Summary

One can note that prediction on average is quite accurate regardless of the tree level. Only scenario with sudden and excessive transmission time changes cause

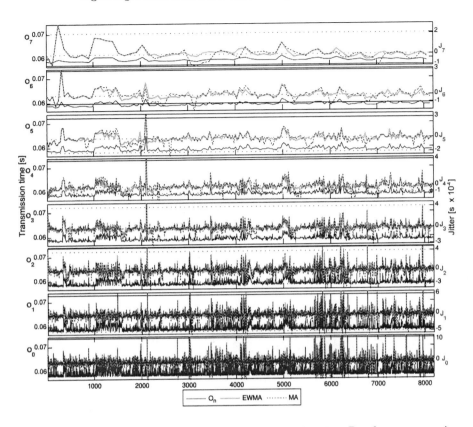

Fig. 6. Experimental results of jitter analysis in MBRT using D_{pp} for one way ping (OWAMP) real data

Table 2. Mean average prediction error D_k in miliseconds

set	estimator	$k=0$	$k=1$	$k=2$	$k=3$	$k=4$	$k=5$	$k=6$	$k=7$	$k=8$	$k=9$	$k=10$
B_{syn}	EWMA	2.97	3.67	3.89	4.62	5.57	7.53	11.33	18.50	29.82	40.68	48.40
B_{syn}	MA	2.88	3.52	3.74	4.19	4.68	5.69	7.61	11.57	19.41	33.71	52.33
B_{real}	EWMA	2.48	2.93	3.02	3.34	3.35	3.41	3.36	3.27	3.35	3.29	3.20
B_{real}	MA	2.36	2.85	3.02	3.30	3.35	3.42	3.39	3.30	3.37	3.36	3.29
A_{real}	EWMA	1.44	0.94	1.41	1.83	1.10	0.98	1.05	1.31	1.45	1.04	1.12
A_{real}	MA	1.17	0.98	1.25	1.59	1.02	0.98	1.05	1.20	1.39	1.04	1.12

large gap between prediction and real value (Fig. 5c,f) for higher analysis levels in MBRT. Such a behavior is caused by delayed responses at higher levels for sudden changes. The lower levels are more responsive to the sudden changes but at the expense of oversensitivity (Fig. 5a,d) to the incidental excessive peaks.

For testing purposes a prototype implementation was coded in Matlab environment and tests were performed using off-line traces but for real life on-line applications there would be no *a priori* knowledge on the transmission time so the proposed prediction method (Eq. (4)) should be improved by repetitive computation of C parameter. Another interesting and positive property is that despite the fact of the iterative computation of the prediction we haven't observed cumulation of errors.

4 Conclusions

The proposed algorithm of multiscale binary rectangular tree seems to be potentially very flexible and elastic solution. As it was demonstrated it is able to predict transmission times precisely but the prospective applications are not limited to jitter analysis. It might be applied in the whole area of transmission analysis – it is just a matter of analysis function (D, J). Due to elastic design it is possible also to overcome the drawbacks (like aforementioned oversensitivity or late response) by using different functions or function constants at the different levels. Another advantage of the proposed solution is the small computational complexity, although one should be aware that MBRT performance might be degraded by complex analytic functions used in the tree.

References

1. Burt, P.J., Adelson, E.H.: The Laplacian Pyramid as a Compact Image Code. IEEE Trans. on Communications 3l(4), 532–540 (1983)
2. Morton, A., Claise, B.: Packet Delay Variation Applicability Statement, IETF RFC5481 (2009)
3. Clark, A.: Analysis, Measurement and Modelling of Jitter. ITU-T Delayed Contribution COM 12 – D98. ITU, Geneva (2003)
4. Skurowski, P., Wójcicki, R., Jerzak, Z.: Evaluation of IP Transmission Jitter Estimators Using One-Way Active Measurement Protocol (OWAMP). In: Kwiecień, A., Gaj, P., Stera, P. (eds.) CN 2010. CCIS, vol. 79, pp. 153–162. Springer, Heidelberg (2010)
5. Do, M.N., Vetterli, M.: Framing Pyramids. IEEE Trans. on Signal Proc. 51(9), 2329–2342 (2003)
6. One-Way Ping, http://www.internet2.edu/performance/owamp/
7. PlanetLab, http://www.planet-lab.org/

Scheduling Algorithms for Different Approaches to Quality of Service Provisioning

Agnieszka Brachman and Jakub Mieszczanin

Silesian University of Technology, Institute of Informatics,
ul. Akademicka 16, 44-100 Gliwice

Abstract. IP network provides only best effort delivery meaning, that data is transmitted at unspecified variable bit rate and delivery time is unknown, depending on the current traffic load. Nowadays, real-time traffic occupies significant percentage of the available bandwidth and Internet must evolve to support new applications. Therefore one of the main and crucial objective of the future Internet is to change best effort network into Quality of Service controlled network.

Authors believe that virtualization may be an important component of the Future Internet architecture as well, therefore we search for scheduling policy, that will be implementable as a physical network adapter scheduler in virtual monitor, capable of QoS provisioning. The main purpose of this paper is to review the existing scheduling algorithms and to consider their usage in virtual monitor with the aforementioned assumptions.

Keywords: quality of service, scheduling, hierarchical scheduling, service curve.

1   Introduction

IP network provides only best effort delivery meaning, that data is transmitted at unspecified variable bit rate and delivery time is unknown, depending on the current traffic load. For newly developed applications and services such as VoD (Video on Demand), VoIP (Voice over IP), VTC (Video-Teleconferencing), interactive games etc., such delivery is unacceptable, since in case of congestion the Quality of Experience (QoE) may decline to unsatisfactory level.

Nowadays, real-time traffic occupies significant percentage of the available bandwidth and Internet must evolve to support new applications. Therefore one of the main and crucial objective of the future Internet is to change best effort network into Quality of Service controlled network. Various applications may have different, sometimes stringent requirements in terms of packet losses and delays. The simplest way to provide different transmission parameters for each application, is to deliver a separate network for each new application or to strictly dedicate part of the existing network to it.

Although the idea to build a new, dedicated network sounds unrealistic, the practical solution may be feasible – virtualization. Virtualization of networking

A. Kwiecień, P. Gaj, and P. Stera (Eds.): CN 2011, CCIS 160, pp. 135–143, 2011.

resources has several advantages. The most important is, that several overlay networks can use the same underlying physical infrastructure, being unaware of it. Virtualization allows coexistence of multiple networking technologies in the network layer and offers a possibility to deploy new architectures, protocols and services. As a matter of fact, it is considered a key component of the Future Internet architecture.

Unfortunately, available virtualization techniques do not provide resource virtualization mechanisms required for Future Internet needs, namely for QoS provisioning. Virtual links may require supporting the services with different Quality of Services requirements ranging form best-effort to fixed loss and delay. To satisfy those guarantees and provide isolated and dedicated virtual network, effective and adequate scheduling algorithms are necessary for each network element.

Network virtualization allows sharing hardware and software resources by several independent, isolated networks – virtual networks. Network virtualization requires virtualization platform, which provides resource virtualization. The most common software virtualization platforms are Xen (OracleVM, Citrix), KVM, VmWare ESX. In those platforms, access to each physical device is provided by a scheduler responsible for allocating device to the virtual machines.

Virtual network consists of virtual nodes and links. Virtual links require provisioning of services with different Quality of Service requirements. Therefore, the problem of scheduling traffic coming from different virtual networks into one physical adapter, is similar to the problem of scheduling packets in the network supporting differentiated services.

The main goal of the scheduler is to divide the total output link capacity between existing virtual networks with the assumption of the optimal usage of link capacity and providing defined QoS requirements. Aforementioned platforms does not provide suitable network card virtualization mechanisms, since they offer only basic sharing parameters. Therefore to enable QoS provisioning in network virtualization, designing schedulers that allow achieving the desired parameters and optimal resources usage is required. The problem of scheduling mechanisms in virtual networks is widely discussed in [1,2,3,4]. Authors indicate the lack of the performance isolation, underutilization of the resources and high cost of the context switching. The presented work concerns the overall problem of scheduling.

The rest of this paper focuses on the existing schedulers, designed to support QoS in network with different traffic classes and considering their application for network card scheduler in virtual monitor. The rest of the paper is organized as follows. Section 2 reviews the Quality of Service related issues and architectures for QoS provisioning. In Sect. 3, different scheduling algorithms are presented, designed for real-time service, link-sharing service provisioning or for both. Finally, the paper is concluded in Sect. 4.

2   Quality of Service in IP Network

When it comes to providing Quality of Service, the first question is "how to define the QoS"? Term Quality of Service refers to the network capability of providing some transmission parameters to existing connections. Therefore, depending on the service class the connection belongs to, QoS parameters usually comprise a subset of the following parameter set:

- Minimal Transmission Rate (throughput),
- Packet Delay,
- Packet Delay Variation (delay jitter),
- Packet Loss Ratio.

Real time traffic has the most stringent QoS requirements, which are very low packet delay and delay jitter as well as very low toleration to packet losses. Data transmission require guaranteed bit rate. ITU-T standardization group is involved in determining the service appropriate values of QoS parameters for network QoS classes [5] and application services [6]. Satisfying QoS requirements involves several stages:

- Marking – to distinguish between different service classes,
- Router policy – to treat packets accordingly,
- Provisioning of protection (isolation) for one class from other classes,
- Efficient use of resources while providing isolation,
- Admission Control – network may block the call if there are no resources to satisfy the needs.

To aid QoS provisioning on an IP network, the Internet Engineering Task Force (IETF) has defined two models: Integrated Services (IntServ) and Differentiated Services (DiffServ). The short description of both models is presented below.

2.1   Integrated Services

The IntServ [7] model relays on the reservation protocol for allocating resources and negotiating the transmission parameters. This functionality is performed using RSVP protocol (resource ReSerVation Protocol) [8]. The negotiation and reservation is performed for each connection or a group of connections.

There are three classes of service:

- Best Effort – without any guarantees,
- Controlled-load Service – better than best effort, for low delay and loss sensitive applications,
- Guaranteed Service – for applications with stringent delay constraints and assured bandwidth requirements.

IntServ uses end-to-end signaling, reservation, admission control and packet scheduler at each network element. All network devices must support RSVP protocol along the path from the source to the destination. Reservations must be refreshed periodically. Admission control at each hop is required. The packet scheduler manages the forwarding of packets belonging to different classes, using queues and other mechanisms. All those requirements increase the complexity of each network node along the path. IntServ has proved to work, however its main disadvantage is the requirement to store information concerning reservations at every router, which is impossible in large scale network.

2.2   Differentiated Services

Differentiated Services (DiffServ) [9,10] architecture provides different types of service for transmitted traffic. The DiffServ domain consists of edge (boundary) routers and DiffServ capable core routers. Flows are aggregated in the network and the core routers distinguish only a defined number of traffic classes, called Class of Service (CoS). The QoS is provided for a traffic class not for a particular flow. The DiffServ model has two major components: packet marking and PHBs.

To mark the CoS, six bits in IP header are used [9]. PHBs (Per Hop Behaviors) refer to the packet scheduling, queuing, policing or shaping behaviors of a node. Edge routers do traffic conditioning, perform per aggregate shaping and policing as well as marking packets. Core routers process packets based on packet marking and defined policy. Detailed definitions of PHBs can be found in [9,11,12].

Since classification and shaping is already done at the edge routers, the core router should forward the packages according to the transmission requirements of the CoSs. In comparison to IntServ, DiffServ model is much more scalable. DiffServ provides also more flexibility, because it allows defining own Classes of Service.

DiffServ was not motivated by real-time applications but economics and simplicity. It does not store any per flow information, therefore it cannot provide QoS guarantees. If there is no admission control or traffic policing there is also possibility that network gets congested.

2.3   QoS for Future Internet

None of the presented model of QoS architecture has been introduced in the current IP network, however the growing need for QoS guarantees will undoubtedly induce some changes in the nearest future. Regardless of Future Internet architecture, QoS provisioning will be its key component.

We believe that network virtualization is the most promising solution for Future Internet architecture, though it prompts reconsidering of existing approaches to support QoS. The efficient scheduling policy for network card in virtual monitor, capable of QoS provisioning is its key component. Good scheduling policy should be flexible, provide efficient bandwidth utilization along with transmission parameters' guarantees, fair bandwidth sharing and isolation between traffic belonging to different virtual networks and should be relatively easy to implement. Since the most difficult transmission parameter to satisfy is the experienced delay, we search for algorithm which provides strong support for real-time traffic.

3   Scheduling Algorithms

Scheduling algorithms can be categorized into one of the three major classes:

- GPS – Generalized Processor Sharing [13,14,15,16,17,18],
- RC – Rate-Controlled [19,20],
- SC – Service-Curved [21,22,23,24,25].

Two types of scheduler can be considered the work-conserving and non-work-conserving. Non-work-conserving algorithms are simpler, much less scalable and do not provide full network utilization, therefore work-conserving solution is more desirable. Most algorithms have been studied to provide a link-sharing service, i.e. transmission rate guarantees, however some of them provide a real-time service as well.

3.1 Generalized Processor Sharing Algorithms

GPS (Generalized Processor Sharing) algorithm [13,14] works as follows. All traffic is classified into so-called traffic classes i. Classes can be either individual flows or bunch of flows with similar transmission requirements. Each class is assigned a positive weight ϕ_i, which specifies the minimum share of the available bandwidth C. This weight is also used for distribution of the excess capacity, when a particular class doesn't fully use its bandwidth's share. Each backlogged traffic class, i.e. class, that has packets waiting for transmission in its queue or class which packet is in service, receives the guaranteed service rate r_i:

$$r_i = \frac{\phi_i}{\sum \phi} C \ ,$$

where $\sum \phi$ is the sum of the weights for all traffic classes.

GPS offers protection among traffic classes, along with full statistical multiplexing. GPS is an idealized scheduler, based on the assumption, that the capacity is infinitely divisible, which means that several packets can be served at the same time. Since in reality traffic is composed of discrete packets send in sequence, GPS cannot be implemented in real system.

WFQ (Weighted Fair Queuing) [13] and WF^{2}Q (Worst-Case Fair Weighted Fair Queuing) [16] closely reassemble the GPS scheduler. For every incoming packet, the departure time d_i^k is calculated, as if the packet would have completed service under GPS, with the restriction that no additional packets were to arrive after it. Packets with the smallest departure times are transmitted first. The difference between WF^{2}Q and WFQ is, that WF^{2}Q only considers the sets of packets that have started receiving service in the corresponding GPS system, whereas WFQ does not.

WF^{2}Q-M (Worst-Case Fair Weighted Fair Queuing with Maximum Rate Control) [17] uses the fluid model GPS-M (Generalized Processor Sharing with Maximum Rate Control) as a reference model. GPS-M is an extension of GPS in that every traffic class i may be assigned a maximum rate $r_{max}(i)$. A traffic class with assigned maximum rate does not receive service above the defined threshold. This scheduler may operate in non-work conserving mode.

WF^{2}Q-M provides both the performance similar to WF^{2}Q as well as restriction of maximum transmission rate. WFQ and WF^{2}Q can guarantee the minimum service rate for a session.

H-GPS [15] is another fluid model, which can be viewed as a hierarchical integration of multiple one-level GPS. H-GPS supports hierarchical link sharing for different traffic classes. Authors of [15] propose also an approximation of the aforementioned model – HPFQ (Hierarchical Packet Fair Queue). HPFQ gives the highest priority to guaranteeing the required minimum bandwidth share, therefore it can neglect the real time services in case of high incoming transmission rate.

HFQ (Hierarchical Fair Queuing) [26] is another approximation of the H-GPS. The algorithm allows achieving tighter maximum delay bounds than HPFQ.

The presented disciplines are different in terms of fairness and complexity. Their main disadvantage is that they provide identical delays for similar traffic rates.

3.2   Rate-Controlled Algorithms

Rate-controlled algorithms consists of regulators and a packet scheduler (see Fig. 1). Two types of schedulers may be used, namely SP (Static Priority) scheduler or EDF (Earliest Deadline First) scheduler. Usage of EDF scheduler [19] requires a regulator for each session. The regulator restricts the outgoing rate to the defined value and calculates the departure time for each packet. The EDF scheduler transmits packets in increasing order of theirs deadlines. In opposition to GPS algorithms, the RC-EDF can provide different delay bounds to the traffic with identical transmission rate.

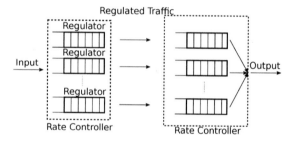

Fig. 1. Rate-control service discipline

The RC-SP scheduler [20] holds a fixed number of priority groups. The session is classified into a priority group during the admission control or basing on the predefined rules. Compared to RC-EDF, the algorithm is much more scalable but may suffer from low bandwidth utilization. EDF provides high network utilization, however it is not scalable because it requires regulators for each session. Both methods are non-work-conserving due to the presence of regulators.

3.3   Service-Curved Algorithms

Service curve indicates the minimum service amount required for a traffic class during time intervals. The SC algorithm performance strictly depends on the adopted service curve. The SC service disciplines are work-conserving. Their complexity depends mostly on the selection of the service curve.

SCED (Service Curve Based Earliest Deadline First Policy) [21,22] is developed for networks with fixed packet size. It is also based on the assumption that packets arrive synchronously in a time slot. In [27] authors proposed service curve for SCED for network with variable packet size however at the very high implementation costs.

HFSC (Hierarchical Fair Service Curve) [23] enables proportional sharing of available bandwidth as well as controlling and allocating latencies. HFSC reserves bandwidth for each session independently of the delay bounds and gives higher priority to guaranteeing the real time traffic delay constraints. HFSC uses the service curve model for allocating the bandwidth. Service curve represents the amount of service received $S(t)$ in bits at time t. The curve's slope represents the transmission rate.

In HFSC priorities are dynamically assigned basing on the service curve. HFSC differentiates between real time and link sharing services. Traffic class can be assigned both curves, the inner classes (aggregates) can only have link sharing curve. In [24] authors present HFSC improvement to support VBR (Variable Bit Rate) applications by using accurate traffic characterization for VBR sessions.

SCED and HFSC guarantee the service curve for each session using deadline-based discipline. The choice of service curve influences the network utilization. If it is constructed considering only traffic rates, the achieved level of outgoing transmission rate is the same as for the GPS. When both delay bounds and traffic rates are considered, the bandwidth utilization may drop to the same level as for RC-EDF.

Pyun et al. present SC-EDF algorithm in [25], which achieves very high network utilization, comparable to RC-EDF's performance. The algorithm doesn't require any regulators, which provides better scalability than the original RC-EDF. It considers variable-sized packets.

4   Conclusions and Future Work

Real time data occupies significant part of the network transmission. Supporting a large number of real time applications at the same time requires efficient bandwidth sharing. Generally, the real time services are guaranteed with bandwidth reservation, however such solution is hardly scalable, therefore alternative approach is required.

To provide real time services and link-sharing services at the same time several hierarchical algorithms have been proposed, including HTB, HPFQ, HFSC. Hierarchical schemes provide guarantees of requested bandwidth share for each traffic class, additionally they provide that the excess bandwidth is shared proportionally by active classes.

Hierarchical disciplines can guarantee a share of bandwidth according to organizations, protocols, applications type or virtual networks. We believe that virtualization will be an important component of the Future Internet architecture, therefore we search for scheduling policy, that will be implementable as a physical network adapter scheduler in virtual monitor, capable of QoS provisioning.

The work presented in this paper concludes the first step in the task of designing effective scheduling algorithm for the network virtualization. Further work includes:

- Implementation of hierarchical scheduling algorithms in virtual monitor,
- Evaluation of the proposed scheduling algorithms by simulation and analysis.

Acknowledgement. This work was supported by the European Union from the European Social Fund.

References

1. Ongaro, D., Cox, A.L., Rixner, S.: Scheduling I/O in virtual machine monitors. In: Proceedings of the fourth ACM SIGPLAN/SIGOPS International Conference on Virtual Execution Environments. VEE 2008, pp. 1–10. ACM, New York (2008)
2. Liao, G., Guo, D., Bhuyan, L., King, S.R.: Software techniques to improve virtualized I/O performance on multi-core systems. In: Proceedings of the 4th ACM/IEEE Symposium on Architectures for Networking and Communications Systems, USA, pp. 161–170. ACM, New York (2008)
3. Lin, B., Dinda, P.: Vsched: Mixing batch and interactive virtual machines using periodic real-time scheduling. In: Proceedings of the ACM/IEEE SC 2005 Conference, Supercomputing 2005, p. 8 (2005)
4. You, X., Xu, X., Wan, J., Jiang, C.: Analysis and evaluation of the scheduling algorithms in virtual environment. In: Second International Conference on Embedded Software and Systems, pp. 291–296 (2009)
5. ITU-T: Y.1541, network performance objectives for IP-based services (2002)
6. ITU-T: G.1010 end-user multimedia QoS categories (2002)
7. Braden, R., Clark, D., Shenker, S.: Integrated Services in the Internet Architecture: an Overview. RFC 1633, Informational (1994)
8. Braden, R., Zhang, L., Berson, S., Herzog, S., Jamin, S.: Resource ReSerVation Protocol (RSVP) – Version 1 Functional Specification. RFC 2205 (Proposed Standard) (1997)
9. Nichols, K., Blake, S., Baker, F., Black, D.: Definition of the Differentiated Services Field (DS Field) in the IPv4 and IPv6 Headers. RFC 2474 (Proposed Standard) (1998)
10. Blake, S., Black, D., Carlson, M., Davies, E., Wang, Z., Weiss, W.: An Architecture for Differentiated Service. RFC 2475, Informational (1998)
11. Heinanen, J., Baker, F., Weiss, W., Wroclawski, J.: Assured Forwarding PHB Group. RFC 2597 (Proposed Standard) (1999)
12. Jacobson, V., Nichols, K., Poduri, K.: An Expedited Forwarding PHB. RFC 2598 (Proposed Standard) (1999)
13. Parekh, A., Gallager, R.: A generalized processor sharing approach to flow control in integrated services networks-the multiple node case. In: Proceedings of Twelfth Annual Joint Conference of the IEEE Computer and Communications Societies, INFOCOM 1993. Networking: Foundation for the Future, vol. 2, pp. 521–530. IEEE, Los Alamitos (1993)

14. Parekh, A., Gallager, R.: A generalized processor sharing approach to flow control in integrated services networks-the single node case. In: Eleventh Annual Joint Conference of the IEEE Computer and Communications Societies, INFOCOM 1992, vol. 2, pp. 915–924. IEEE, Los Alamitos (1992)

15. Bennett, J.C.R., Zhang, H.: Hierarchical packet fair queueing algorithms. SIGCOMM Comput. Commun. Rev. 26, 143–156 (1996)

16. Bennett, J., Zhang, H.: WF2Q: worst-case fair weighted fair queueing. In: Proceedings of IEEE Fifteenth Annual Joint Conference of the IEEE Computer Societies, INFOCOM 1996. Networking the Next Generation, vol. 1, pp. 120–128 (1996)

17. Lee, J.F., Chen, M.C., Sun, Y.: WF2Q-M: Worst-case fair weighted fair queueing with maximum rate control. Computer Networks 51, 1403–1420 (2007)

18. Zhang, H., Zhao, Y., Guan, H.T.: HPFQ-M: Hierarchical packet fair queuing algorithm with maximum rate control. In: Arabnia, H.R., Mun, Y. (eds.) PDPTA, pp. 110–115. CSREA Press (2008)

19. Ferrari, D., Verma, D.: A scheme for real-time channel establishment in wide-area networks. IEEE Journal on Selected Areas in Communications 8, 368–379 (1990)

20. Zhang, H., Ferrari, D.: Rate-controlled service disciplines (1994)

21. Cruz, R.: Quality of service guarantees in virtual circuit switched networks. IEEE Journal on Selected Areas in Communications 13, 1048–1056 (1995)

22. Sariowan, H., Cruz, R., Polyzos, G.: SCED: a generalized scheduling policy for guaranteeing quality-of-service. IEEE/ACM Transactions on Networking 7, 669–684 (1999)

23. Stoica, I., Zhang, H., Ng, T.: A hierarchical fair service curve algorithm for link-sharing, real-time, and priority services. IEEE/ACM Transactions on Networking 8, 185–199 (2000)

24. Pyun, K., Song, J., Lee, H.K.: A generalized hierarchical fair service curve algorithm for high network utilization and link-sharing. Computer Networks 43, 669–694 (2003)

25. Pyun, K., Song, J., Lee, H.K.: The service curve service discipline for the rate-controlled EDF service discipline in variable-sized packet networks. Computer Communications 29, 3886–3899 (2006)

26. Jun, A.S., Choe, J., Leon-Garcia, A.: Hierarchical fair queuing: single-step approximation of hierarchical-GPS. In: Global Telecommunications Conference, GLOBECOM 2002, vol. 3, pp. 2405–2409. IEEE, Los Alamitos (2002)

27. Le Boudec, J.-Y., Thiran, P.: Chapter 1: Network calculus. In: Thiran, P., Le Boudec, J.-Y. (eds.) Network Calculus. LNCS, vol. 2050, p. 3. Springer, Heidelberg (2001)

Assessment of the QoE in Voice Services Based on the Self-Organizing Neural Network Structure

Slawomir Przylucki

University of Economics and Innovations, 7/9 Melgiewska Str, 20-209 Lublin, Poland
spg@spg51.net

Abstract. The quality of the transmitted voice in the Voice over IP (VoIP) service should be investigated from the end-user perspective, by estimating perceptional metrics like Mean Opinion Score (MOS). The research methodology of that kind is a particular transfer of the specific technical parameters, related to the IP data transmission, to level of service acceptance by an end-user. The article presents the research results obtained by the simulation of the developed MOS estimation algorithm based on the modified neural Self-Organizing Maps (SOM) structure.

Keywords: VoIP, speech quality, MOS, self-organizing neural networks.

1 Introduction

Research methodology on the quality of experience for multimedia services, including Voice over IP (VoIP) service, usually base on the objective criteria. Transaction between these objective measures of quality of transmitted voice and independent, individual end-user assessment is possible by introduction of proper evaluation metric [1]. There are several factors that affect the perceived quality of a voice stream running over a packet network. The metrics and corresponding quality-affecting factors, used in case of the IP networks can be divided on tree main groups. namely:

- packet level metrics – network related factors,
- connection level metrics – environmental factors,
- end-user level metrics – application related factors.

Unfortunately, the multimedia services in the modern Internet are unreliable and, in general case, provide no Quality of Service (QoS). This means that packets do not necessarily arrive at end-user location, and even if they do, they do not necessarily arrive in proper fashion in terms of their order and a timeline. Taking above into account, in most practical cases, a some way of mapping between subjective quality assessment and Quality of Service parameters has to be applied.

A. Kwiecień, P. Gaj, and P. Stera (Eds.): CN 2011, CCIS 160, pp. 144–153, 2011.

2   Subjective Quality Assessment

The process of subjectively assessing the quality of voice samples is a complex and time-consuming one. There are several types of assessment techniques of that kind, and they can be divided on two main classes, namely:

- Qualitative assessment [2],
- Quantitative assessment.

The quantitative techniques provide a more concise approach to quality assessment, and are more widely used in the literature than qualitative ones [3]. The results of these tests are normally summarize the group's assessment of the perceived quality and are presented as metrics. The most popular one is a Mean Opinion Score (MOS). There exist several ways, defined by international organization, like The Internet Engineering Task Force (IETF) or International Telecommunication Union – Telecommunication Standardization Sector (ITU-T) of subjectively assessing the quality of media and metrics definitions. Among these recommendations, one can find recommendation of the methodologies of proper network parameters measurement in case of wide range multimedia services. From the viewpoint of the article topic, worth mentioning are ITU standards such as ITU-T P.800 [1] for voice transmission and ITU-T P.920 [4] for interactive multimedia.

One of the most used metric when the quality of voice service in the IP network has to be evaluate, is the MOS metric. That metric belongs to end-user level metrics. It contains five main values, from 1 to 5. The MOS value represents quality of voice which was coded and transmitted through a network. The meaning of each value is as below:

- Value: 5 – QoE: excellent, voice distortion: unnoticeable,
- Value: 4 – QoE: good, voice distortion: noticeable but not annoying,
- Value: 3 – QoE: fair, voice distortion: a bit annoying,
- Value: 2 – QoE: poor, voice distortion: annoying,
- Value: 1 – QoE: bad, voice distortion: not acceptable.

The MOS metric has gained relatively high popularity among specialists responsible for realization and maintenance of voice services in the IP networks. The value of that metrics clearly describes the end-user experience when multimedia service is used. A good practical example of utilization of above metric are research results published by Cisco [5]. Many assessment setups are discussed in the literate, as well [6,7]. These result clearly assign MOS values to most popular voice codes and specific network conditions. Discussion on the MOS metric was the starting point to more detailed distinction of voice/speech transmission quality, which finally lead to definition of nine groups of QoS metrics [3]. The mentioned distinction took into account if one estimate the quality of one-direction or two-ways voice transmission. Depends on situation, the following metric classes were proposed: LQ – Listening Quality and CQ – Conversational Quality. For each of those class, next distinction has been made and next tree sub-classes were defined. Those subclasses are connected to the way on which level of the QoE metric has to be estimated and they are named as follow:

– subjective (MOS-LQS, MOS-CQS) – based on end-user assessment,
– objective (MOS-LQO, MOS-CQO) – the MOS value is estimated by comparison the voice samples, respectively: on sender side and receiver side – ITU P.862 (Perceptual evaluation of speech quality – PESQ),
– estimated (MOS-LQE, MOS-CQE) – the value of the MOS metric is obtained based on delay, jitter, packet loss, codec type etc. – ITU G.107 (E-model) [8].

There are great number of reports and scientific publications, which proposed the measurement algorithms for all mentioned above QoE metrics. The short review of most popular and promising approaches in that field can be found in [3,5,6].

3   Objective Quality Assessment

Subjective quality assessments are time-consuming and rather complex processes and that motivated the development of objective quality assessment mechanisms. The performance of these objective metrics is generally evaluated in terms of their correlation with subjective scores. The correlation coefficient CC of two random variables A and B is calculated as the ratio between the covariance of A and B and the product of their respective standard deviations

$$CC_{AB} = \frac{\mathrm{cov}\,(A,B)}{\delta A\,\delta B}\ . \tag{1}$$

An ideal quality metric and so ideal mapping should have a correlation of 1 with subjective scores.There many proposals of the objective assessment techniques for speech quality. Among them the most wide-used are [9]:

– Signal-to-Noise Ratio (SNR),
– Perceptual Speech Quality Measure (PSQM),
– Measuring Normalizing Blocks (MNB),
– Perceptual Evaluation of Speech Quality,
– ITU E-model.

The most popular objective measurement method is E-model that belongs to Non Intrusive Methods (NIM). The NIM measurement is the technique that do not require the original speech signal. This means, that the ITU E-model does not need the access to the original signal to compute a quality estimation. Therefore, it is the only available, according the today knowledge, measure which is computationally simple and can be used in real-time applications. It is different from other methods because it represents also a network simulation tool and so it should be treated rather as a network planning technique than a quality assessment [10].

E-model is a computational method based on the assumption that each quality degradation type is associated to a certain type of damaging factor. It uses transmission parameters to predict the subjective speech quality of packetized voice. The primary output from the E-Model is the Rating Factor (R), and R can be further transformed to give estimates of customer opinion by mapping it to the MOS scale. The damage factors involved in the process of the R factor computation are as follows: noise factors (both sender and receiver room noise, background noise), noises derived from the microphone and loudspeaker, loudness factors (sending, receiving and overall loudness rating), quantizing distortion, equipment impairment factor, packet-loss probability, mean one-way delay, absolute delay, receiver side factors (Side Tone Masking Rating, Listener Masking Rating, Talker Echo Loudness Rating), transmission path factors (Weighted Echo Path Loss, Round-trip Delay). Each of mentioned above factors are described in details in the ITU-T G.107 document [8,11]. The R factor can be translated to MOS metric scale, according to ITU-T G.109 [12], using the following formula:

$$MOS = \begin{cases} 1 & \text{for } R < 0 \\ 1 + 0.035R + 7.1 & \text{for } 0 \le R \le 100 \\ 4.5 & \text{for } R > 100 \end{cases} . \qquad (2)$$

4   ANN Techniques in the QoE Assessments

As it was mentioned above, there is not one way to asses the value of MOS. Moreover, the two serious problem arise from the analysis of wide-used methods. The first one is connected with developing the non-intrusive methods when reference samples are unknown. Except for the ITU E-model, all metrics propose different ways to compare the received signal with the original one. It is obvious, this feature precludes their use in on-line quality-control applications. Second problem comes from the fact that most of wide-used techniques try to answer the question how to describe and measure the voice degradation and from other hand, how to associate obtained metrics with an end-user quality assessment. Many of the objective metrics described above were originally developed to measure the voice degradation mostly when it is encoded without taking into account network factors. In case of VoIP streams, it has significant influence on the metrics correlation with subjective assessment results. The degradation of signal can occurs at the VoIP terminals as well as inside the network structure. Descriptions of both causes are difficult, especially in the dynamic environment of packet network.

That is why, there is growing interest in modeling and real-time monitoring the relation among the network parameters (packet loss, delay, jitter, codec, etc.) and subjective QoE assessment for given digital voice processing schemas (codding, serialization, buffering, decoding, etc). Simple solution based on the regression models or the layered backpropagation Artificial Neural Network (ANN) proved that they can be useful in predicting MOS value in the system where only the basic network parameters are used [13,14]. From other hand, there are a few articles showing that more sophisticated model can be promising in estimating the proper MOS value for whole transmission path, i.e. for user-user approach [15]. The proposed solution, described below, uses the modified Self-Organizing Map (SOM) [16] to map traffic conditions to quality metrics, ie, it concentrates on network-level factors to predict the MOS value in the same manner the non-intrusive methods do.

4.1   The Structure of Proposed System

The proposed solution belongs to QoE evaluation method based on MOS-LQE metric. The core of the system is the multiwinner SOM artificial neural network and it constitutes the first layer of the ANN structure. The mechanism inside this modified SOM allows avoid the typical disadvantages of the vector quantization, i.e. the dilemma of proper evaluation of the deviation between input and reference patterns represented by neurons weights [17]. Furthermore, the new learning algorithm, which determines the optimal Kohonen layer size was proposed. That algorithm allows proper feature separation and thanks that improves accuracy of the MOS estimation. This learning algorithm was named Regularized Growing Grid (RGG) and served as a fundamental tool for teaching the multiwinner SOM (MWSOM) layer [18].

The classical feedforward neural structure is followed by the Self-Organizing Map. It constitute the output layer. The aim of this layer is to transform the selected features set (inside the SOM) into the human readable numeric value of the MOS metric. Learning process inside the output layer based on the well-known backpropagation algorithm. Figure 1 presents logical schema of the proposed system for the QoE estimation based on SOM neural structure.

4.2   The Multi-winner Self-organizing Neural Network

The ability to approximate information during learning process permits the SOM structure to obtain particular organization of the self-organizing map, which is characterized by even distribution within each subarea. The proper regularization of the grid of neurons which forms the SOM improves that even distribution of weights values and consequently leads to good approximation of data set probability density . The Growing Grid algorithm is the standard way to gain proper balance level between these two features, approximation and regularization [17]. To illustrate and measure the improvement of the SOM characteristics with the increase in its size, the approximation regularization indexes were defined. Approximation index, AP was defined as average distance (by means of Euclidean measure), between consecutive of input data set X and corresponding with them reference vector in the form of neuron weight of neuron-winner w_r. The index is expressed with an equation:

$$AP = \frac{1}{N} \sum_{k=1}^{N} \left| X^k - w_r^k \right| \tag{3}$$

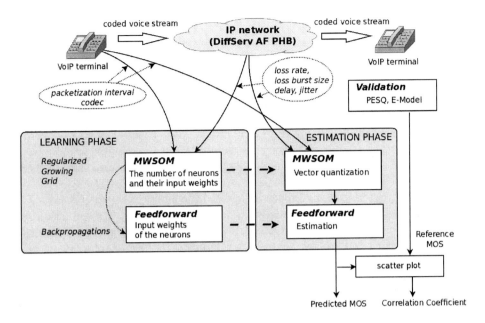

Fig. 1. The logical structure of the proposed system for evaluation of QoE in the VoIP service

where:

N – number of vectors in input data set,
$X(k)$ – k-th qualities vector,
$w_r^{(k)}$ – vector of winner weights r after the presentation of k-th learning vector.

Regularization index RG was defined by estimation of quantity of local distortion inside Kohonen map.The estimation was conducted by comparison of location each neuron belonging to SOM net with location its neighbors.This index is expressed with an equation:

$$RG = \frac{1}{m_k} \sum_{i=1}^{m_k} |wp_i - w_i| \qquad (4)$$

where:

m_k – number of neurons,
wp_i – perfect location of i-th neuron from regularity point of view,
w_i – real location of i-th neuron.

Ability of estimation of internal SOM organization by means of approximation index and regularity index is not enough to design SOM estimator whose characteristic ere suitable for signal mapping and quantization in the VoIP service. After the series of studies, the modified algorithm of competitive learning ot the

Winner Takes All (WTA) was proposed. That modification enriched standard WTA with two additional algorithms. First one is the Regularized SOM Training (RSOMT) [17], wchich in addition, treats the defined above indexes as boundary condition for the process of the determination of the final SOM dimensions. The second modification allows not only one neuron inside the SOM to win. Other words, the belonging of the input vector to given class is represented by not only one neuron, but by group of neurons. The neural estimator with hidden layer acting according to above schema can be named as MultiWinners Self-Organizing Map (MWSOM) [19]. In opposition to standard WTA, that modification allows recognition of more classes then number of neurons in the hidden layer (other words, it is possible to estimate the metric value with higher precision).

Summarizing, the learning process of MWSOM consists of the map dimension definition to solve generalization-approximation dilemma and determination of the group of neuron-winners. Combining the modified Growing Grid (GG) algorithm with RSOMT one give rise to development the new leaning algorithm called Regularized Growing Grid (RGG) [19]. The structure of the whole neural estimator is presented on Fig. 2.

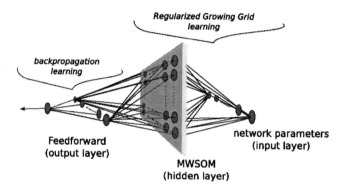

Fig. 2. The structure of the proposed neural estimator (for clarity, only a few connections among neurons are shown)

5   Verification of the Proposed Algorithm

In order to asses the properties of the proposed QoE estimation algorithm, the network parameters and the corresponding MOS value were collected. The testbed for the voice transmission measurements and emulation of possible speech distortions was implemented based on two components Cisco NAM module [20] and WAN emulator WANem [21]. NAM module detects and monitors Real Time Protocol (RTP) streams and computes the R-Factor MOS based on the ITU-T G.107 [8]. WANem is a Wide Area Network Emulator over a LAN environment. It allows setup a transparent application gateway which can be used to simulate WAN characteristics like network delay, packet loss, packet corruption, disconnections, packet re-ordering, jitter, etc. The structure of the testbed is presented on Fig. 3.

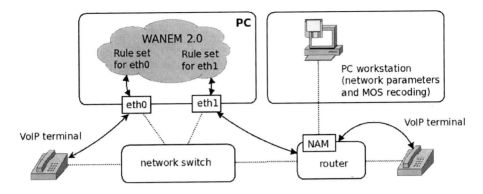

Fig. 3. The structure of the testbed

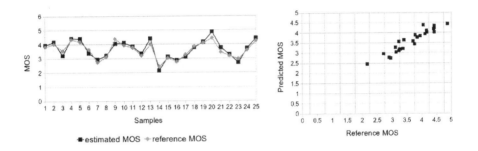

Fig. 4. The MOS estimation for 25 validation data sets (left) and scatter plot (right)

The MOS values recorded by NAM module were used as reference ones during learning phase.The network parameters were grouped into the data vectors required during either the learning and validation processes. The learning and validation data sets consist of 150 and 50 vectors, respectively. The data inside each data vector contain the following elements:

- Codec (G.711, G.729a, G.723),
- Packetization interval (20, 30, 40 and 50 ms),
- Loss rate (0%, 0,5%, 1%, 5%, 10%),
- Loss burst size (0.5, 1.0, 1.5, 2.0, 2.5) [15].

The Figure 4 presents performance of the proposed neural estimator for 25 validation data sets and the corresponding scatter plot.

The Correlation Coefficient for whole validation data set was equal to 0.89. That value is comparable with the results published in the literature [7].

6 Conclusion

Even though QoE analysis in the VoIP service is widely discussed in the scientific publications, is worth mentioning that analysis methods based only on the network parameters are in the minority. Proposed system treated the self-organizing neural network as the referenced database and thanks to this, the knowledge of initial voice samples during evaluation process is not required. The presented simulations results proved that introduction of multiwinner schema significantly improve the accuracy of the process of mapping signal features to MOS metrics. Simultaneously, modified gowning neural structure algorithm (MWSOM) assures that the final SOM size is accurate as far as specific analysis is concerned. Taking all mentioned above facts is clearly seen that proposed system can by apply in many different measurements configurations.

It should be noted at this point, that presented approach does not take into account the influence of Forward Error Correction (FEC) techniques on the estimation precission thus it should be the direction for further research.

References

1. ITU-T Recommendation P.800: Methods for Subjective Determination of Speech Quality. ITU-T (1996)
2. Bouch, A., Sasse, M.A.: Why value is everything: A user-centered approach to internet quality of service and pricing. In: Wolf, L., Hutchinson, D.A., Steinmetz, R. (eds.) IWQoS 2001. LNCS, vol. 2092, p. 59. Springer, Heidelberg (2001)
3. Cole, R., Rosenbluth, J.: Voice over IP Performance Monitoring. ACM Computer Communication Review 31(2) (April 2001)
4. ITU-T Recommendation P.920: Interactive test methods for audiovisual communications. ITU-T (2000)
5. Understanding Codecs: Complexity, Hardware Support, MOS and Negotiation. CISCO (2007),
   http://www.cisco.com/warp/public/788/voip/codec_complexity.html#mos
6. Colomes, C., Varela, M., Gicquel, J-C.: Subjective Audio Tests: Quality of Some Codecs When Used in IP Networks. In: Proceedings of the Measurement of Speech and Audio Quality in Networks, Prague (June 2004)
7. Mohamed, S., Rubino, G., Varela, M.: A method for quantitative evaluation of audio quality over packet networks and its comparison with existing techniques. In: Proceedings of the Measurement of Speech and Audio Quality in Networks, Praque (2004)
8. ITU-T Recommendation G.107: The E-model, a Computational Model for Use in Transmission Planning. ITU-T (2000)
9. Wang, S., Sekey, A., Gersho, A.: An Objective Measure for Predicting Subjective Quality of Speech Coders. IEEE Journal on Selected Areas in Communications 10(5) (1992)
10. Hall, T.A.: Objective Speech Quality Measures for Internet Telephony. In: Proceedings of SPIE, vol. 4522 (2001)
11. Estepa, A., Estepa, R., Vozmediano, J.: On the Suitability of the E-Model to VoIP Networks. In: Seventh International Symposium on Computers and Communications, IEEE ISCC 2002, Taormina (July 2002)
12. ITU-T Recommendation G.109: Definition of categories of speech transmission quality. ITU-T (1999)
13. Sun, L., Ifeachor, E.: Learning Models for Non-intrusive Prediction of Voice Quality for IP Networks. IEEE Transactions on Neural Networks (2004)

14. Mohamed, S.: Automatic Evaluation of Real-Time Multimedia Quality: a Neural Network Approach. PhD thesis, INRIA/IRISA, Univ. Rennes I (2003)
15. Rubino, G., Varela, M., Bonnin, J-M.: Controlling Multimedia QoS in the Future Home Network Using the PSQA Metric. The Computer Journal 49(2) (2006)
16. Kohonen, T.: Self-Organizing Maps. Springer Series in Information Science. Springer, Heidelberg (1995)
17. Goppert, J., Rosennstiel, W.: Regularized SOM-Training; A solution to the Topology-approximation dilemma. In: Proceedings of International Conference on Neural Networks, Washington (1996)
18. Przylucki, S., Wojcik, W., Plachecki, K., Golec, T.: An analysis of self-organization process for data classification in multisensor systems. In: Proceedings of SPIE, Optoelectronic and Electronic Sensor V, vol. 5124 (2003)
19. Przylucki, S., Plachecki, K., Duk, M.: New algorithm for self-organizing neural classifiers suitable for easy hardware implementation. In: Proceedings of SPIE, Photonics Applications in Astronomy, Communications, Industry, and High-Energy Physics Experiments, vol. 5125 (2003)
20. Monitoring VoIP with Cisco Network Analysis Module. White Paper, Cisco System, Inc. (2009)
21. WANem 2.0 Wide Area Network Emulator. TATA Consultancy Services, Performance Engineering Research Centre (2008)

Coloring VBR Streams Inside the DiffServ Domain

Slawomir Przylucki and Daniel Sawicki

Technical University of Lublin, 38A Nadbystrzycka Str, 20-618 Lublin, Poland
spg@politechnika.lublin.pl

Abstract. Video traffic is supposed to account for a large portion of future wired and wireless network traffic. The evaluation of different video coding standards for their effects on the network traffic, and the resulting requirements for networks have attracted great interest in the research community. Simultaneously, the numerous test and users' experiences proved that the limited quality of service (QoS) features available in both IPV4 and IPv6 cannot accommodate the various degrees of requirements needed by multimedia traffic and in particular, the video traffic. This paper investigates the influence of various packet markers on VBR video streams inside the DiffServ domain. Simulations based on NS-2 network simulator and Evalvid-RA framework and follow the IETF recommendations for video traffic shaping in the IP networks.

Keywords: DiffServ markers, streaming media, VBR video, IP network simulation.

1   Packet Coloring in DiffServ Architecture

Generally, packets coloring is a way of packets marking by setting of particular bits in the IP header. In case of the Differentiated Services (DiffServ), marking process takes place inside the mechanism of classifying traffic or after passing through the monitoring mechanism inside router on the edge of DiffServ domain. Packets can be colored in green, yellow and red. From the point of view of multimedia services, attention should be paid to DiffServ AF class [1]. In the case of that class green means AFx1, yellow Afx2 and red AFx3 [2]. The three algorithms of packets coloring were defined by Internet Engineering Task Force (IEFT):

– Single Rate Three Color Marker (srTCM) [3],
– Two Rate Three Color Marker (rtTCM) [4],
– Rate Adaptive Shapers (RAS) [5],
– The Time Sliding Window Three Color Marker (TSW3CM) [6].

1.1   Single Rate Three Color Marker

The Single Rate Three Color Marker (srTCM) is a combined metering algorithm that is able to set multiple conformance levels (not only in or out of traffic shaping

A. Kwiecień, P. Gaj, and P. Stera (Eds.): CN 2011, CCIS 160, pp. 154–163, 2011.

profile). The srTCM consists of two token buckets and one token accumulation rate. When the token bucket which has a token accumulation rate is full, further tokens "overspill" into the excess token bucket. The parameters of the srTCM are:

- Committed Information Rate (CIR),
- Committed Burst Size (CBS),
- Excess Burst Size (EBS),
- Color-mode flag (a boolean attribute).

Due to the two token buckets, the srTCM is able to declare three conformance levels:

- Green – when sufficient tokens are present in bucket B1,
- Yellow – when B1 has insufficient tokens, but B2 has sufficient tokens,
- Red – when neither B1 nor B2 have sufficient tokens.

The meaning of B1, B2 buffers and srTCM algorithm parameters are explained on Fig. 1.

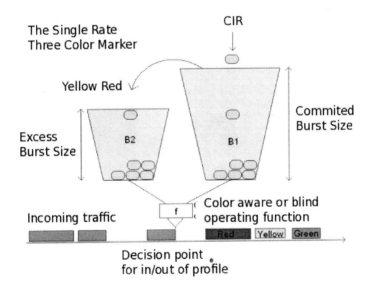

Fig. 1. The idea of the srTCM

The srTCM has two operating modes: color aware and color-blind. In color blind mode all incoming packets are treated equal. In color-aware mode packets arrive pre-colored to the marker. Algorithms of both operating modes are presented on Fig. 2.

The algorithm presented on Fig. 2, in case of color-aware mode, refers only to situation when arriving packet is market as green. It is not always the true.

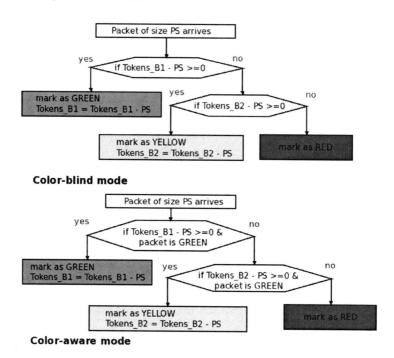

Fig. 2. Color-blind and color-aware mode algorithms for srTCM

Generally, packet of any of three colors can arrive thus color-aware algorithm can be described as follows:

- if a packet arrives Red, it will remain red and no tokens will be removed,
- if packet arrives Yellow, it will be checked only against the yellow bucket; in the absence of sufficient tokens in B2, the packet color is downgraded to Red, else remains yellow and only B2 is,
- if packet arrives as Green, it will be checked against B1 first. In case of sufficient tokens, the packet remains Green and only B1 is decremented. Otherwise, B2 is checked, and if there are sufficient tokens then the packet is downgraded to Yellow, and only B2 is decremented. If B2 does not have sufficient tokens neither then the packet is downgraded immediately to Red.

The srTCM is useful, for example, for ingress policing of a service. However, in such a policing scheme, only the length, not the peak rate, of the burst determines service eligibility.

1.2   Two Rate Three Color Marker

The idea of Two Rate Three Color Marker (trTCM) [4] is the extension of previously presented srTCM and can be summarized as follows:

- a packet is marked Red if it arrives with a rate exceeding PIR,

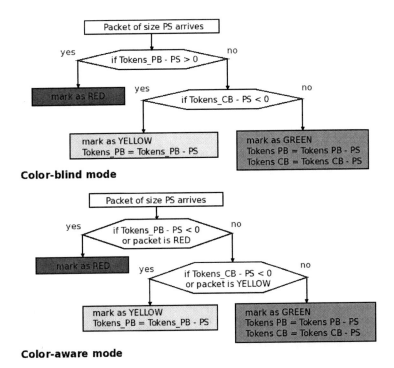

Fig. 3. Color-blind and color-aware mode algorithms for trTCM

- a packet is marked Yellow if the rate is between CIR and PIR,
- a packet is marked Green if the rate is below or equal to CIR.

The trTCM is useful, for example, for ingress policing of a service, where a peak rate needs to be enforced separately from a committed rate. The difference in the metering behavior between srTCM and trTCM is that in the case of the trTCM, the token buckets operate with different rates. The token bucket labeled PB has Peak Information Rate (PIR) and the token bucket CB has CIR. PBS (Peak Burst Size) is used as the size of the bucket P and CBS is used as the size of the bucket C. Bucket CB is incremented with a rate CIR (bytes per second) while bucket PB is incremented with a rate PIR. The trTCM can operate in color blind mode in which it assumes that the packet stream is uncolored, or in color aware mode in which the marker assumes that the packets have already been colored by some previous entity. The color is coded in the DS field of the packet, same way as in case of the srTCM, in the PHB specified manner. Algorithms of both operating modes are presented on Fig. 3.

1.3   Adaptive Shaper

Single Rate Three Color Marker (srTCM) and Two Rate Three Color Marker (trTCM) are the most prominent solutions. Specific extension of algorithms discussed above is Rate Adaptive Shaper (RAS) [5]. RAS can be used in combination with the single rate Three Color Markers (srTCM) and the two rate Three Color Marker (trTCM). The main objective of the shaper is to produce at its output a traffic that is less bursty than the input traffic, but the shaper avoids discarding packets in contrast with classical token bucket based shapers. The shaper itself consists of a tail-drop FIFO queue that is emptied at a variable rate. The shaping rate, i.e. the rate at which the queue is emptied, is a function of the occupancy of the FIFO queue. If the queue occupancy increases, the shaping rate will also increase in order to prevent loss and too large delays through the shaper. The shaping rate is also a function of the average rate of the incoming traffic. There are two types of rate adaptive shapers defined. The single rate rate-adaptive shaper (srRAS) will typically be used upstream of a srTCM while the two rates rate adaptive shaper (trRAS) will usually be used upstream of a trTCM.

1.4   The Time Sliding Window Three Color Marker

Markers from different group that discussed in the previous subsection, estimate the transient averaged throughput and use the current estimate for marking decision. This idea is apply to the Time Sliding Window Two/Three Color Marker (TSW2CM/TSW3CM) [6]. The marking is performed based on the measured throughput of the traffic stream as compared against the Committed Target Rate (CTR) and the Peak Target Rate (PTR). The TSW3CM is designed to mark packets according to following schema:

- packets contributing to sending rate below or equal to the CTR are marked Green,
- packets contributing to the portion of the rate between the CTR and PTR are marked Yellow,
- packets causing the rate to exceed PTR are marked with Red color.

The algorithm of estimating the average traffic rate and sliding window marking process is presented on the Fig. 4.

Many solutions based on TSW3CM have been proposed for last few years. One of them Improved TSW Three Color Marker (ItswTCM) that differs from TSW3CM in the characteristic of the marking probability as a function of the estimated averaged traffic rate. Additionally, so called intelligent rate estimator based markers using some additional knowledge on the traffic were proposed. Enhanced Time Sliding Window (ETSW) and Intelligent Traffic Conditioner use several TCP characteristics for computation of the marking probability. Unfortunately, these improvement are addressed to connection-oriented traffic so they are not very useful from the video transmission point of view. Comparison of performance of several less popular markers, namely TSW, PME, MBM, ACT, VS-ACT and ARM, can be found in [7].

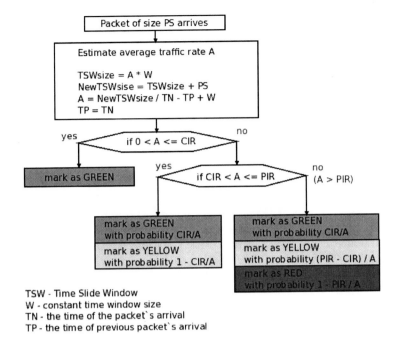

TSW - Time Slide Window
W - constant time window size
TN - the time of the packet`s arrival
TP - the time of previous packet`s arrival

Fig. 4. Marking algorithm of TSW3CM

1.5   IETF Recommendations

Based on the information contained in [2,8], the transmission of video data across DiffServ domain should use AF class. The open question remains, how to properly use that AF class to fulfill the requirements of video transmission. The answer is not simple mostly because the concept of video transmission covers wide range of possible end-user service configuration. IETF has noticed that gap between existing recommendation and ISP practice of everyday life. The response was the RFC4594 [9], describing commonly used scenarios for DiffServ domains. Considering the issues of the video transmission, the IETF recommends multimedia streaming service class for applications that require near-real-time packet forwarding of variable rate elastic traffic sources and are not delay sensitive. This service class should use the AF DiffServ PHB and be configured to provide a minimum bandwidth assurance for AF31, AF32, and AF33 marked packets.

Additionally, the multimedia streaming service class should be configured to use rate queuing like Weighted Fair Queuing (WFQ) or Weighted Round Robin (WRR). IETF also recommend, the applications or IP end points should pre-mark their packets with DSCP values or the router topologically closest to the end point should perform Multifield Classification and mark all packets as AF3x. The algorithm of this procedure is presented on Fig. 5.

If Random early Detection (RED) algorithm (this is the case for presented research results) is used as an Active Queue Management (AQM) algorithm,

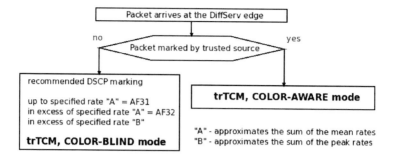

Fig. 5. IETF recommended marking and coloring algorithm

the min-threshold specifies a target queue depth for each Differentiated Services Codepoint (DSCP), and the max-threshold specifies the queue depth above which all traffic with such a DSCP is dropped. This schema can be summarized as following set of recommendation [9,8]:

- min-threshold AF33 < max-threshold AF33,
- max-threshold AF33 <= min-threshold AF32,
- min-threshold AF32 < max-threshold AF32,
- max-threshold AF32 <= min-threshold AF31,
- min-threshold AF31 < max-threshold AF31,
- max-threshold AF31 <= memory assigned to the queue.

2   Simulation Results

As encoded video traffic is dependent to the content, the encoding standard, and the encoder settings, no independent video source model can be easily developed. For this reason to facilitate the network performance evaluation, quality of service categorizations, and service designs, the real-life video traffic has to be utilized. On the other side, that causes difficulties in modeling the behavior of video sequences based on software network simulators. A large portion of research in the field of video traffic analysis is thus concentrated on video traces analysis [10]. That is also why the our testbed for evaluation the influence of packet marking on the video transmission is based on simulation tools and traffic traces. The configured testbed consists of two basic elements: a NS2 simulator [11] and a video quality evaluation tool-set Evalvid-RA [12]. The NS2 software packet is the network simulator which allows (among many other possibilities) DiffServ configuration with three kinds of nodes (respectively, ingress, core and egress routers). All tested coloring schemes and RED based AQM were implemented on the NS2 ingress node. Also, all mentioned earlier IETF recommendations are included in the NS2 DiffServ domain configuration. Evalvid-RA is the complete framework and tool-set for evaluation of the quality of video transmitted over a real or simulated communication network, provides packet/frame loss

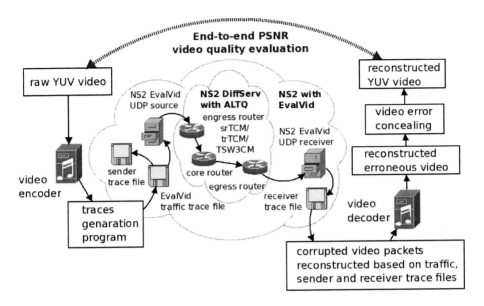

Fig. 6. The structure of developed testbed for QoS evaluation of video transmission through DiffServ domain

rate, packet/frame jitter, Peak Signal-to-Noise Ratio (PSNR) and Mean Opinion Score (MOS) metrics assessment. The overall simulation model is shown in Fig. 6.

The test video trace was a Highway CIF format sequence [10], which has 2000 frames. The encoded stream has a mean bit rate of 412 kbps and a peak rate of 1116 kbps. Each frame was fragmented into packets of 1000 bytes before transmission. This video flow competed with one on-off background traffic flow, which has an exponential distribution with mean packet size of 1000 bytes, burst time of 500 ms, idle time of 0 ms, and rate of 64 kbps, and one FTP traffic flow of 64 kbps (NS2 ftp source). The corresponding meters parameters were set as follows:

- SRTCM – CIR, CBS, and EBS parameters of 512 kbps, 1000 bytes, and 1000 bytes, respectively,
- TRTCM – CIR, CBS, PIR, and PBS parameters of 512 kbps, 1000 bytes, 1100 kbps, and 1000 bytes, respectively.

The core router implemented the Weighted Random Early Detection (WRED) mechanism for active queue management. The WRED parameters include a minimum threshold, a maximum threshold, and a maximum drop probability. In the presented simulations, these parameters were specified respectively as 2, 4, 0.1 for Red packets, 4, 6, 0.05 for Yellow packets, and 6, 8, 0.025 for green packets. The final assessment of video quality based on two very popular metrics: PSNR and MOS. During all QoS metric assessments, a frame was only

Table 1. The results obtained for different markers during video transmission through DiffServ domain (AF PHB)

Marker	Packets	GREEN		YELLOW		RED		PSNR	MOS
	Total	Total	Lost	Total	Lost	Total	Lost	dB	
srTCM	158 940	17 676	0	32	0	132 279	8 954	24.18	2.9
trTCM	158 915	17 676	0	17 661	0	114 663	8 916	32.25	4.2
TSW3CM	158 945	18 027	0	18 066	0	113 907	8 945	27.68	3.5

considered decodable if and only if all of the frames upon which it depended were also decodable. The simulation results are shown in Table 1.

3   Conclusions

In this paper the effects of transporting MPEG video stream over DiffServ AF class has been studied. The fundamental feature of DiffServ is metering and marking process. There are two possible configurations of both of them. First one is when incoming packets are pre-marked (color-aware mode) and second, when packets are not associated with any color (blind mode). Pre-marking should be apply at end-user side (application side) and it requires changes inside the standard coder structure. Moreover, the most popular video coding schema, like cosec, can operate in many different modes (called level and profiles). That means that simple statement that three kinds of frames (I,P,B) inside coded video stream have different importance in terms of reception quality in the presence of losses is not enough to build universal marker. Among particular profile and levels there are fundamental differences in the arrangement of frames inside so-called Group Of Pictures (GOP). From other side, taking into account the structure of the GOP and it combining the process of per-marking seems to be a promising direction of the future research. Thus, new color-aware marker ideas should be compared to the best existing blind mode algorithm. The presented results aim to answer which one standard blind-mode marker is the best.

Conducted simulations proved that the use of srTCM could degrade the quality of received signal. The recommended by IETF, trTCM clearly improves the quality of transmitted stream in comparison to srTCM and it was the best of all tested markers. Unfortunately, obtained PSNR and MOS values confirm that simultaneously it is not the ideal solution. The results for the third discussed coloring algorithm, the TSW3CM should be treated as preliminary. The problem with that method resulted from the difficulty in choosing the value of the Time Slide Window (TSW) for VBR source. The correct solution to this problem requires a statistical analysis of the encoder and video content. This strongly limits the use of that algorithm as a real-time marker. During performed tests TSW was equal to RTT on the path between sender and receiver. For that TSW value, the results proved to be worse that in case of trTCM.

References

1. Heinanen, J., Baker, F., Weiss, W., Wroclawski, J.: Assured Forwarding PHB Group. RFC 2597 (June 1999)
2. Recommendation ITU-T Y.1541: Applicability of the Y.1221 transfer capabilities and IETF differentiated services to IP QoS classes. Appendix VI, ITU-T (2006)
3. Heinanen, J., Guerin, R.: A single Rate Three Color Marker. RFC 2697 (September 1999)
4. Heinanen, J., Guerin, R.: A Two Rate Three Color Marker. RFC 2698 (September 1999)
5. Bonaventure, O., Cnodder, S.: Rate Adaptive Shaper for Differentiated Services. RFC 2963 (July 2000)
6. Fang, W., Seddigh, N.: Time Sliding Window Three Color Marker. RFC 2859 (March 2000)
7. Chang, X., Muppala, J.K.: On improving bandwidth assurance in AF-based Diff-Serv networks using a control theoretic approach. Computer Networks 49(6) (2005)
8. Baker, F., Polk, J., Dolly, M.: A Differentiated Services Code Point (DSCP) for Capacity-Admitted Traffic. RFC 5865 (May 2010)
9. Babiarz, J., Chan, K.: Configuration Guidelines for DiffServ Service Classes. RFC 4594 (August 2006)
10. Fitzek, F., Reisslein, M.: MPEG4 and H.263 Video Traces for Network Performance Evaluation. IEEE Network 15(6) (2001)
11. The ns Manual (formerly ns Notes and Documentation). The VINT Project (May 2010)
12. Lie, A., Klaue, J.: Evalvid-RA: trace driven simulation of rate adaptive MPEG-4 VBR video. Multimedia Systems 14(1) (2008)

Content Identification in PI CAN Network

Mateusz Nowak, Sławomir Nowak, Piotr Pecka, and Krzysztof Grochla

Institute of Theoretical and Applied Informatics,
ul. Bałtycka 5, 44-100 Gliwice, Poland
{mateusz,emanuel,piotr,kgrochla}@iitis.pl
http://www.iitis.pl

Abstract. Content addressing is one of the basic issues while design of CAN architecture and solution. The paper is devoted to the problem of choice of identifier format, length and characteristic. Basic assumptions of CAN as one of Parallel Internets in IIP (Inżynieria Internetu Przyszłości) project are presented and requirements for content identifier are shown in this context. Discussion of possible solutions is presented and proposal of final identifier format is provided.

Keywords: CAN, content aware networks, Future Internet Engineering.

1 Introduction

The significant increase of different kind of media content that is available in the Internet led to the concept of a CAN (Content Addressable Networks or Content Aware Networks), are also known as CCN (Content Centric Networks) [1,2].

These networks use the new paradigm of "content-centric network" as opposed to used in the current TCP/IP networks "host-centric" paradigm. Traditional networking architectures concentrate on the problem of providing a connection between terminals and hosts, while users are typically interested in reaching a particular destination object (*content*). When the user request delivery of a file using HTTP protocol, a particular file is identified by URL, containing host address and file name within this host. When the file is moved from host to host, determining the location of the requested object becomes a problem. A broken web link is a common problem in such a case. The problem is solved by introducing the less location dependent addressing schemes (e.g. URL), however, these solutions are not always sufficient (for example, do not support possible replication of the same content). In CAN the user requests a particular file, while the network layer is responsible for its location and the transmission.

CAN networks treat the searching, identification (content resolution) and delivery of content as the base functionality. The content in the CAN network is uniquely identified by an identifier, which consequently acts as a user level address.

The CAN network requires developing a new architecture that supports content searching, content localization (resolution), and content delivery with respect to specific demand connected to specific content's instances (taking into account content type and mode, network capabilities as well as server conditions).

A. Kwiecień, P. Gaj, and P. Stera (Eds.): CN 2011, CCIS 160, pp. 164–172, 2011.

In the current Internet some applications use similar concept as CAN. The most popular example are the p2p (*peer-to-peer*) applications for file sharing, like BitTorrent, which create overlay networks built on top of current TCP/IP network and operating in the application layer. The p2p solutions provide much functionality assumed also for CAN networks. P2p networks, however, must use the core network infrastructure (mainly TCP/IP) and have no influence on the process of connecting and managing connections at the network layer, making impossible to ensure proper quality of service (best effort mode only).

On the other hand, well-known p2p solutions are now developed and widely exploited, providing a source of solutions and experiences that can be used in designing the architecture of the CAN network. Based on that the revolutionary approaches can be investigated, by developing a complete CAN network architecture.

The paper discusses possible content identifier formats and their consequences for specific CAN architecture design. This work has been done within the context of Future Internet Engineering project (IIP) [3], which tries to design new networking architectures, including the CAN network. The IIP Project assumes multiple different "Internets", having distinct network protocols, working in common hardware resources (nodes and links) thanks to virtualisation technique [4]. Both network nodes (routers) and network links are virtualised, only the physical layer is common for all network traffic in IIP System. Even though we use in the paper some of the naming convention or object functions defined within the project, we aim to formulate general guidelines and rules how to define the content identifier in CANs.

2 Functions Provided by the CAN

The Content Addressable Network is designed for delivering the content to end-users. Typically, the single content object in CAN network shall have the form of:

- *plain file* containing the content – content provided in form of single file for best-effort download and off-line use; plain file may contain any data – image, audio or video file for off-line reproduction at end-user's workstation, 3D mesh for rendering by user's application etc;
- *off-line stream* (stream-on-demand) – audio or video stream, pre-recorded and available on user request, forwarded with streamed media protocol in unicast mode;
- *live media stream* – forwarded with streamed media protocol in multicast mode.

Although a particular CAN implementation may specify other types of content, they may be easily mapped to the three types listed above. Subbiah and Uzmi [2] distinguish four roles within the CAN: Content Consumer, who requests and receives the data, Content Service Provider, who provides search and location services, Content Provider, that creates and owns the content and Content Broker that delivers the data. In the IIP project four similar roles has been defined, but different names has been used: Content Consumer, Content Server (which stores the data), Content Mediator (provides search and location functions) and Content Forwarder, which is CAN router.

In CANs the content may be replicated in multiple locations (servers) among the network, to improve the speed of the delivery and minimize the network load. The identifier must define the particular set of data in unique way, no matter where is it stored at the moment. The user requests the content by its identifier and the CAN locates a particular server that stored the requested set of data and starts the transmission. The delivery must be preceded by the location of the server which will transmit the data to the client. The selection of the server may be determined e.g. by the distance between the client and the server, network load. The content may be also searched by some metadata or its attributes – in this case the whole process is started by the search request, which translates the metadata into the ID of the content.

Basis for content identification in all CAN implementations is the *identifier*, serving both as object name and object address at application level. An end-user of the CAN is able to demand (and get delivered) a content object of given identifier (ContentId), without pointing (in any way) at the place where the content is stored (server address, file path, transmission protocol and other elements which must be provided in current Internet).

The content may be associated with additional information related to it (such as author or originator, title, semantic descriptions, technical requirements, etc.). That information can be stored in description file, related to the content (meta-data file). The search function translates a query based on this additional information into the identifier.

3 Choice of Naming Scheme

To realize the functions described in the Section 2 the identifier must be compliant with the following requirements:

- must be unique within the network,
- must be long enough to allow addressing of all content in the network,
- should be as short as possible to minimize the overhead,
- must support the content localisation algorithms used in the network.

The open issues which have to be answered during the CAN architecture design are, whether the identifier:

- has any internal structure or is completely flat (and what the internal structure shall be),
- has constant or variable length,
- is human-readable or is not,
- is assigned locally or globally, and consequences for identifier structure (e.g. prefix of an entity granting the identifier),
- does include any content attributes – some security tokens, virtual network id, publisher prefix and many other options are possible.

The problem of choosing a specific "naming scheme" involves the selection of specific software mechanisms – protocols and algorithms. These are the key issues when designing the architecture of the CAN, because they will affect the performance and scalability and should be analyzed at different levels: the user, content provider and network-level mechanisms.

3.1 Identifier Uniqueness

The requirement of identifier uniqueness is obvious. The identifier is the only way to identify the content in the CAN, as no other addressing scheme is used. However, if virtual networks (vCAN) are planned in CAN design, the decision whether identifiers must be unique in the whole CAN or only in single vCAN must be taken.

The space of possible identifier values must be large enough to address all objects (files and live streams) which can be ever available in the network. Unfortunately, any estimations of maximum number of content objects in CAN are very hard and heavily depend on the scale of planned design – e.g. when an solution of small scale deployment is planned, tens of thousands of possible values may be enough, but when a scalability up to a world-wide network is planned, the space of possible values must include all possible files created by all possible users. Although the rule "the bigger the better" applies to CAN identifier, we should take into consideration size of frame and size of header in it. The bigger is the header, the less the payload will be.

While designing Content Forwarding Plane in IIP's CAN, responsible for content delivery, the assumption was taken that the identifier is put in the header of every content delivery transmission unit. The identifier should be as short as possible then, to limit the overhead imposed. The size of a data packet on the network layer is limited by size of maximum transfer unit (MTU). In most of the cases it is 1536 bytes (if ethernet links are used), but it may vary between few hundred bytes to tens of kilobytes (when jumbo frames are used). The ContentId is significant part of CAN Content Forwarding plane header, so its size should be small enough so as not to add a large overhead to the network. The plot on Fig. 1 presents the calculation of the overhead (in percent of packet size) for different ContentId sizes and different packet sizes, assuming that the ID is transmitted within each packet. The plot was generated by authors using Matlab. As can be seen, for smaller packet sizes (1000 bytes and smaller) the overhead is considerable even for IDs of size 12 bytes (more than 1%), and can grow up to 4% for larger ID size. Please note that the overhead shown concerns only identifier, disregarding other elements of header.

The 128-bits (16-bytes) long identifier seems to be a reasonable compromise. 128 bit seem to be capacious enough to assign unique identifier to every file which could appear in CAN. However, all values from the range $[0, 2^{128})$ should be allowed, or only a small range of values should be reserved. The analysis presented above shows that this size does not introduce large overhead even for small packets.

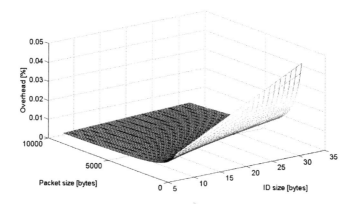

Fig. 1. Overhead of ContentID for different packet sizes and different ContentID lengths

3.2   Identifier Structure

Problems of choice of identifier format and object localisation algorithm in CAN are tightly connected. The structure of an identifier is tightly coupled with content resolution algorithm, used in CAN for content localization (described in general below). Localisation algorithm must be fast and reliable, in order to be useful. In practice, two groups of localisation methods can be taken into account – hierarchical and from DHT-family, because flooding all nodes with a request is not scalable [5]. Every algorithm forces its own format of identifier.

Hierarchical algorithms extend the idea of DNS, and the process of localisation of CM storing desired media-record is very similar to processing queries by current DNS. For hierarchical localisation identifier must be of variable size, and its internal structure reflecting network hierarchy will limit its capacity.

The Distributed Hash Tables methods originate from p2p applications. The logical structure of the network using DHT method for node localisation is flat, and identifiers have no particular structure. Lack of internal structure means maximum capacity of identifier of particular size, as all combination of bits are possible to use and new identifiers can be chosen freely from the whole identifier-space (if only given identifier is not already used), with no limitations like domain-name.

Most of the concepts quoted above were already considered by authors engaged in working out CCN concepts. In [1] hierarchical, context-dependent names are proposed. Part of the name is publisher identifier, in the form of server address. The latter part identifies the content more precisely. The content name proposed is long, not designed for sending in every network packet. Examples of names are: `/parc.com/videos/WidgetA.mpg`, or `/ThisRoom/projector`. Main advantages of presented format are: human-readability and possible context-dependency.

Another approach is shown in 4WARD report [6]. Naming Framework is security-oriented, and basic name structure includes three fields: type, hash of public key and label. Such a solution facilitates developing of trust and security mechanisms. The header length is still too long to be included in every packet's header.

For the resolution algorithm it is important to ensure the uniqueness of the identifier however the way it was created is not important at this level. The identifier need not to have any internal structure, as resolution algorithm proposed does not require it. Placing some fields inside is potentially possible (when other processes will require this, e.g. identifiers of original publisher, vCAN identifier, content profile, type of transmission – best effort/unicast stream/multicast stream).

It should however be borne in mind that the structuring of ID significantly reduces the number of content addresses space and still the most descriptive information will be placed in meta-data. Important notice is, that assuming any structure within identifier space will decrease range of usable identifier values. For example, we may consider splitting Content ID into two parts – 4-byte publisher id and 12-byte file id. We would have space available for 2^{32} publishers (over $4 * 10^9$). Every publisher will be able to publish 2^{96} objects. The numbers look to be big enough, but most of publishers will not use the whole address space. If particular publisher will publish N objects, $2^{96} - N$ addresses (identifiers) will never be used. This is big waste of resources, and we should avoid it, learning even from lack of addresses in IPv4 networks we face nowadays. Therefore our proposal is to use unstructured ContentId, having length of 16 bytes (128 bits).

Identifier assignment may be performed locally by every publisher, or globally. Global content ID allocation involves the additional mechanism at network level, and a global ID management. In local mechanism, in turn, a problem arises to generate a global, fully unique ID. The easiest way is to add the prefix, associated with the given content publisher. However, as it was mentioned above, it is recommended that the identifier has no internal structure.

The proposed solution presume that the process of determining the identifier will belong to the entity that adds the content to the network – the *content publisher*. At this level it can assign any ID value and try to register it. Registration will consist of verifying whether the ID is unique (by trying to search for the identifier in the network). If the content with the same ID is already present in the CAN, the content publisher must assign a different ID or cancel the content addition process. Resolving content based on ID is a procedure that still must be implemented as a basic functionality. There is therefore no need to implement additional mechanisms for the ContentId uniqueness verification at the global level.

Content publisher may propose any 128 bit ID for new content intended to be registered, but the specifications will provide a recommended, general mechanism for generating identifiers.

As a method for generation of ID one of the existing hash function should be considered, in particular MD5 [7], or GUID/UUID [8]. MD5 hash from binary content is the most appropriate, as it generates 128-bit result and assures required level of uniqueness probability. In the case of live content, where binary stream is not known in the time of registration, some version of GUID or UUID algorithm should be used.

Both methods – MD5 and GUID – assure enough level of uniqueness probability. In both methods little probability of Id repetition is possible, and final verification of uniqueness will be done while registration.

3.3   DHT as the Algorithm for Content Resolution

DHT algorithms allow to fully utilize of the assumed space of possible identifier values, as no internal structure of identifier is required. DHT solutions do not require any network hierarchy, so there is no need to designate any nodes having special role (e.g. first-level nodes). Speed of operation of DHT methods also is satisfying, as typical pessimistic complexity of localisation algorithm, counted as number of "hops" which given query performs between nodes, is $O(\log n)$ [9], where n stands for total number of nodes in localisation devices network (not all nodes in the network need to be engaged in resolution process). DHT content localisation algorithms were designed for p2p networks, being characterised by high level of lability of network topology. As the only nodes in the network were user's workstations, leaving and re-joining the network often, localisation algorithms dealing with query routing had to be flexible enough to deal with such a rapidly-changing network. This attribute of p2p networks came from the fact, that the networks worked in application layer of the networking stack, so no routers and other network-infrastructure nodes were aware of their existence.

Due to best utilisation of identifiers space and lack of any major disadvantages, DHT-based solution will be used for content localisation in CAN being designed in IIP project. CAN network in IIP is build from scratch, so localisation algorithms can be operated by devices forming network infrastructure, being much more stable than end-users devices, which are tend to change their state frequently. Therefore new localisation algorithm will be developed, but they still be based on DHT solutions. First research carried out by the authors show, that having relatively stable network it is possible to develop a localisation algorithm, based on above assumptions, with constant complexity $O(1)$.

4   Identifiers in Virtualized CANs

The network virtualization is a paradigm that gains a lot of attentions lately. The support for virtualization in the CAN would allow to use the same networking infrastructure to transmit separate sets of data, building e.g. a separate content addressable network for different clients or different applications. The virtualization of CAN is done by building multiple virtual CANs (vCAN) over a single physical set of links, routers and servers. The security profiles may be defined separately for each of the vCANs, granting the user access only to some of them. We assume that each of the virtual CAN must be identified by a unique number, a vCAN ID.

In network supporting virtual CAN there are two possible solutions for the identifier space – the common space of IDs for all vCANs or separate space for each vCAN.

Introduction of the vCAN ID as the part of content identifier makes the process of obtaining globally unique content identifier easier, however it would be checked only by the vCAN in which it is published. Thanks to globally unique identifier only one mechanism for content resolution is needed (e.g. DHT). At the level of content ID, this solution has drawbacks similar to the introduction of the content providers, described above. In addition it reduces isolation between virtual networks and is connected with some organizational problems (Content Mediation servers need to store the content IDs from vCANs which they do not belong to).

The proposed solution is to assume an independent space of identifiers in each of the vCAN networks. Different content can have the same ContentId, if it is available in different vCANs. On the other hand, given content, if it is to be available in many vCANs, can have different identifiers in particular vCANs.

5   Summary

The paper presents the review of possible solutions to identify (address) the content in CAN networks. Assumptions were analyzed for the specific CAN network architecture, as one of the basic parallel internets architectures in Future Internet Engineering project. Based on these assumptions the convention for content naming and co-search algorithm was proposed. Use of unstructured ContentId, having constant length of 128 bits was recommended, as well as DHT-based content localisation method. The solution will be part of the specification, which will be implemented in the next step and proven in a test environment. The related research work is detailed design and the performance evaluation of content resolution algorithm (based on DHT) and a solution of the problem of finding the content on the base of on specific attributes (in conjunction with the semantic description of the contents contained in the meta-data file). For these issues the authors provide a separate publication.

Acknowledgements. This work was supported by the European Union, European Funds 2007–2013, under contract number POIG.01.01.02-00-045/09-00 *Inżynieria Internetu Przyszłości*.

References

1. Jacobson, V., Smetters, D.K., Thornton, J.D., Plass, M.F., Briggs, N.H., Braynard, R.L.: Networking named content. In: Proceedings of the 5th International Conference on Emerging Networking Experiments and Technologies, CoNEXT 2009, pp. 1–12. ACM, New York (2009)
2. Subbiah, B., Uzmi, Z.A.: Content aware networking in the internet: issues and challenges. In: IEEE Int. Conf. on Communications, ICC 2001, vol. 4, pp. 1310–1315. IEEE, Los Alamitos (2001)

3. Z2.1. Specification of Parallel Internet 3: Content Aware Network. Future Internet Engineering (IIP) report, EU Funds 2007–2013, contract no. POIG.01.01.02-00-045/09-00 (March 2011), https://www.iip.net.pl/en
4. Z2.1. Architecture of System IIP – preliminary version. Future Internet Engineering (IIP) report, EU Funds 2007–2013, contract no. POIG.01.01.02-00-045/09-00 (March 2011), https://www.iip.net.pl/en
5. Ratnasamy, S., Francis, P., Handley, M., Karp, R., Shenker, S.: A scalable content-addressable network. In: SIGCOMM 2001, August 27-31, pp. 161–172. ACM, San Diego (2001)
6. D-6.2. Second netinf architecture description. EU 7th Framework Programme, The Network of the Future Project 216041: 4WARD – Architecture and Design for the Future Internet
7. Rivest, R.: The md5 message-digest algorithm. IETF RFC 1321 (April 1992)
8. Leach, P. et al.: A Universally Unique IDentifier (UUID) URN Namespace. IETF RFC 4122 (July 2005)
9. Maymounkov, P., Mazières, D.: Kademlia: A peer-to-peer information system based on the XOR metric. In: Druschel, P., Kaashoek, M.F., Rowstron, A. (eds.) IPTPS 2002. LNCS, vol. 2429, pp. 53–65. Springer, Heidelberg (2002)

Evaluation of Chaotic Internet Traffic Predictor Using MAPE Accuracy Measure

Leszek Borzemski and Marcin Wojtkiewicz

Institute of Informatics, Wroclaw University of Technology, Wroclaw, Poland
{leszek.borzemski,marcin.wojtkiewicz}@pwr.wroc.pl

Abstract. The main aim of this article is to show that the presented prediction algorithm is accurate enough to perform good forecast of network traffic. The algorithm was presented in [1,2] as forecasting the stock market. This publication presents the results of appliance of this predictor for the internet traffic forecasting. It will be used in the network traffic prediction system so therefore the need of its exploration. The main contribution of the authors is exploration of the algorithm by measuring its accuracy using the MAPE (Mean Absolute Percentage Error) that is commonly used to assess the accuracy of prediction algorithms. It means gathering the data from the laboratory setup, elaboration of dedicated functions that control the algorithm and realization og the experiments. In the article we show only hypothetical results but essential. Our results show that the MAPE error of the predicted data is less than 10%, what gives very good result taking into account that MAPE between 20 and 30 percent means good prediction.

Keywords: chaotic, predictor, network traffic, self-similarity, time series.

1 Introduction

Internet traffic prediction is very important in network design, management, control, and optimization processes [3]. There is widely proved that the Internet traffic, that is generated by many sources, has self-similar characteristics. This feature has been shown in many publications concerning network traffic characteristics [4,5,6,7]. The most important are facts that the reasons of appearance of self-similar characteristics lie in structure of a network infrastructure, distribution of available files and also in users behavior. Also traffic, coming from many workstations, that is the result of superposition of many information streams could be self-similar. There are many models explaining the cause of appearance of such a feature, the ON-OFF model is one of them. This model is presented in detail in [5,6]. The crucial goal of this article is to show that the algorithm, used for forecasting of such a network traffic, is accurate enough to perform prediction on acceptable level. The authors show this using the MAPE error. Why didn't the author of the algorithm analyse the MAPE error? Supposedly he didn't have such a need as the algorithm was realized for educational purposes.

In this publication the second section describes the laboratory setup, which was used to generate and capture the data. The third one describes the algorithm

A. Kwiecień, P. Gaj, and P. Stera (Eds.): CN 2011, CCIS 160, pp. 173–182, 2011.

that is the subject of the research. Next two sections describe the process of selection of the data which were used in the research and the MAPE error. The last one describes the experiments, the results and conclusions.

2   The Laboratory Setup

The network traffic was gained from the network infrastructure of one of the companies that provides the Internet for the housing estates in Wrocław city in Poland. To say more precisely, the data were gathered from the one of the network segments. The network infrastructure (Fig. 1), the network traffic was captured from, has about 1200 workstations. Each workstation provides a network traffic generated by its user. Workstations are connected to the network switches by 100 MB bandwidth links. Switches create a cascade structure. Then the traffic from the switches is redirected to the main Fast GB/Ethernet switch, from which is sent to the router through the 1 GB interface. For each client there is the bandwidth range – from 384 to 2048 KB. The traffic that was monitored was coming from the Internet to the router and vice versa. In each gained sample there is information about amount of IP packets and amount of bytes. For the sake of the analysis the traffic that comes to the router and was received by users was filtered out.

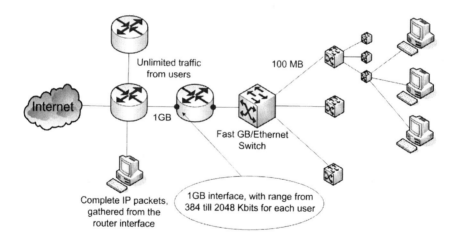

Fig. 1. Infrastructure used for generating of the self-similar network traffic

2.1   Why Such an Environment

As was stated earlier the latest research show that a network traffic could have self-similar characteristics. It concerns also the traffic that is the result of a superposition of many data streams. The infrastructure consisted of many network traffic sources can help gain the self-similar network traffic.

2.2   Details of the Network Traffic

Figure 2 visualizes the network traffic. The period during which the traffic was gathered is five days. The traffic collection begins at 11 o'clock on April the 11th, 2007 and ends at 11 o'clock on April the 16th, 2007. The graph visualizes the dependence of the intensity of the network traffic in bytes per second in time. It's easy to see that the intensity is high during the day time and decreases in the night time. The graph also shows that the router interface wasn't maximally limited, so the link hadn't any limitations and could send a traffic having two times higher intensity.

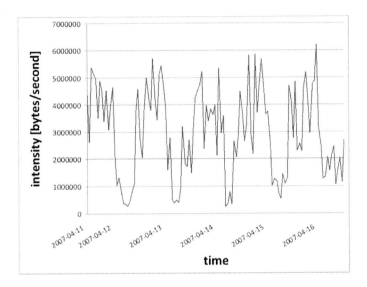

Fig. 2. The intensity of the network traffic in bytes per second during the assumed time period

2.3   Users

The traffic is generated by an ordinary Internet user, that uses the Internet in a typical way – browses internet pages, sends and downloads files, mails and uses communicators.

2.4   Characteristics of the Tool for Gathering the Data

Data were gathered using the script. It's the "light" tool, it doesn't charge the processor. The script had a high priority. A workstation on which it was ran was capable to manage more intense traffic, so its influence on the process of gathering the data was minimized. Moreover the machine was equipped with a lot of memory and had the unnecessary processes turned off. The script contains one main loop which calculates the timestamp, reads the system counter and zeroes them. Then script waits half a second. In the end the loop the output is written in the log file. The data in the log are stored in the following format:

```
1176281006.493985000 in 22 15644
1176281007.005317000 ou 3958 3207207
1176281007.005317000 in 4102 2608834
1176281007.516314000 ou 3540 2664676
```

The records contain data concerning the amount of packets and the traffic intensity in bytes. Below there is the description of particular fields:

– timestamp in the Unix time format. Unix time, or POSIX time, is a system for describing points in time, defined as the number of seconds elapsed since midnight Coordinated Universal Time (UTC) of January 1, 1970; for example the number 1297655407 means the date 2011-02-14 03:50:07;
– in – data received from the Internet;
– out – data sent to the Internet;
– amount of packets in the IP layer;
– amount of bytes.

3   The Prediction Algorithm

The research concerns the predictor algorithm that original purpose is predicting of the stock market data [1]. It uses the self-similar features of a data in connection with nearest neighbor technique to calculate the predictor coefficients and then to forecast the subsequent data. This section describes the algorithm. For further details please refer to [1] and [2]. Similar approaches are also presented in [8,9,10].

The algorithm was created in Matlab by Marcelo Scherer Perlin [2], however it was evaluated using the MAPE accuracy measure at first time in this article.

– Let's assume we have defined a training period, where value of T is the number of its observations. In the beginning the defined training period should be divided into different vectors y_t^m of size m, where $t = m, \ldots, T$. In this case value m defines embedding dimension of the time series. Moreover we define the last vector available before the forecasted observation. y_T^m. The remaining pieces used during the prediction are defined as y_i^m.
– The next step is to search for the k pieces most similar to y_T^m. The similarity is determined by the absolute Euclidian correlation $\|\rho\|$, between y_i^m and y_T^m. Each piece has m observations.
– Having the k vectors it's possible to calculate the predictor coefficients and construct the forecast in point $t + 1$. One of the methods is locally adjusted linear autoregressive prediction. The predictor is defined as:

$$\hat{y}_{T+1} = \hat{\alpha}_0 + \hat{\alpha}_1 y_{T-1} + \hat{\alpha}_2 y_{T-2} + \ldots + \hat{\alpha}_m y_{T-m} \ . \tag{1}$$

The coefficients $\hat{a}_0, \hat{a}_1, \ldots, \hat{a}_m$ are estimated using linear regression method with the dependent variable as y_{i_r+1} and the explanatory variables as $y_{i_r}^m = (y_{i_r}, y_{i_r-1}, \ldots, y_{i_r-m+1})$ where r goes from 1 to k. The regression equation (2) is as follows:

$$
\begin{bmatrix} y_{i_2+1} \\ y_{i_3+1} \\ \vdots \\ y_{i_k+1} \end{bmatrix} = \hat{a}_0 + \hat{a}_1 \begin{bmatrix} y_{i_2} \\ y_{i_3} \\ \vdots \\ y_{i_k} \end{bmatrix} + \hat{a}_2 \begin{bmatrix} y_{i_2-1} \\ y_{i_3-1} \\ \vdots \\ y_{i_k-1} \end{bmatrix} + \ldots + \begin{bmatrix} y_{i_2-m} \\ y_{i_3-m} \\ \vdots \\ y_{i_k-m} \end{bmatrix} + \begin{bmatrix} \varepsilon_2 \\ \varepsilon_3 \\ \vdots \\ \varepsilon_k \end{bmatrix}. \quad (2)
$$

- The values y_{i_k+1} – pieces observations one period ahead the of pieces chosen by the correlation criteria,
- y_{i_k-m} – the first values from chosen k vectors,
- y_{i_k} – the last values from chosen k vectors,
- the number of explanatory series is m and each one has k observations,
- $\hat{a}_0$, equation (2), is the coefficient aggregated to the last observation of the chosen series and $\hat{a}_2$ is the coefficient for all the second last observations of all k series. The values of the coefficients on equation (2) are estimated with the minimization of the sum of the quadratic error $\sum_{i=1}^{k} \varepsilon_k^2$.

– The steps above are executed in a loop until the point that all forecasts on $t+1$ are created. As the result of applying of the algorithm we receive a set of forecasted data.

4   Selection of the Time Series Fragments

The data, generated by the laboratory setup showed above, were divided into pieces of lengths: 1000, 2000 and 5000 samples, and named respectively: in144, in51 and in20. Then these subseries were analyzed using four self-similarity assessment methods: R/S analysis, variance-time plot, autocorrelation chart and periodogram. To further analysis were chosen only the pieces for which the Hurst exponent was greater than 0.5, what means that the series are self-similar. Figures 3 and 4 presents the results of the analysis for one of three chosen series – in51. This serie was chosen because the analysis showed that it is the one with largest Hurst exponent from these three.

In R/S analysis the Hurst coefficient is determined by the slope in the log-log scale, and it has value 0.823. This value reveals that the level of probability is high. The line that comes through the points of the Variance-time plot has slope 2H-2. For these data the Hurst coefficient is 0.76, what means that the series have the features of self-similarity. The slope of the line in Autocorrelation chart shows that the series are self-similar. On the basis on a periodogram we can deduct that series are self-similar. The slope of this line determined using the linear regression method, based on the values of points of the periodogram has the slope coefficient 2H-2. Having this value, H could be easily calculated and in this case it amounts to 0.59.

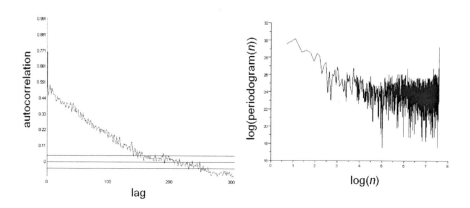

Fig. 3. Autocorrelation chart and periodogram for in51 series

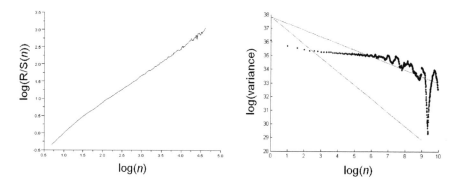

Fig. 4. R/S analysis and variance-time plot for in51 series

5   The MAPE Error

Accuracy of the predictors can be assessed by using the MAPE (Mean Absolute Percentage Error). This error is typically used to assess the accuracy of prediction algorithms. It is calculated as a sum of substractions of the original and forecasted value, divided by the original one. The sum of absolute values is then divided by the number of values, n.

$$MAPE = \frac{\sum_{t=1}^{n} \left| \frac{X_t - F_t}{X_t} \right|}{n}$$

where:

- X_t – original value,
- F_t – forecasted value,
- n – the number of values.

MAPE shows how much, percentage-wise, the forecasted values deviates from the real values. The MAPE error less than 10% means very good prediction. The MAPE between 20% and 30% is quite common [11].

6   Experimental Evaluation of Prediction Accuracy

The main task of the experiments is to use the algorithm for prediction of data sets, for which the proportion of the learning set and the predicted one is 70:30 percent. Then the MAPE error is calculated basing on the comparison of predicted and original data. On the basis of the error, the accuracy of the algorithm is assessed.

6.1   Moving Window

This experiment was performed using all data series and with using dedicated testing routines that are written in Matlab by the authors. In this case the window is created, that has starting point on 200th sample and length 600 samples. The window is moved till the end of the serie in steps, by 20 samples

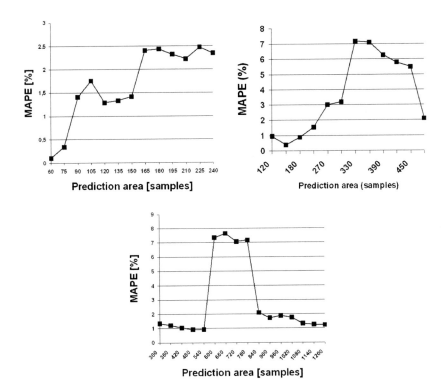

Fig. 5. Changes of the MAPE error according to increase of the window and prediction area length for series in144, in51 and in20 (at the bottom)

in each step. After each movement step, prediction is made for proportion of learning and prediction area – 70:30. For each prediction the MAPE error is calculated. The graphs below show the results of the experiment.

6.2   Expanding Window

The purpose of this experiment is to investigate how the MAPE error behaves, when the prediction window increases. The experiment proceeds as follows:

- The start point is defined.
- The initial size of the widow is defined.
- Adjusting of the final size of the window and amount of samples by what the window increases after each iteration.

The MAPE error is one of the outputs of the experiment. Changes of the MAPE error according to increase of the window and prediction area length are depicted in Fig. 5 respectively for series in144, in51 and in20.

7   Conclusions

The first experiment shows, that there isn't any regularity in the distribution of the MAPE error for particular pieces of data series (Fig. 6 and 7). The large MAPE error is caused by peaks, which appear as a result of the predictor inaccuracy. Large values, sometimes having order of magnitude three times higher than the original value significantly influence on the error. Minimal error appears generally for fragments of the traffic for which predicted values don't vary significantly from the original ones. Predicted values have the same or one time higher order of magnitude. Generally the MAPE error oscillates on good level, lower than 10, that means very good accuracy. The second experiment shows that MAPE is also dependent on deviations of forecasted value from the predicted one. The main conclusion is that the MAPE error is greater for parts of

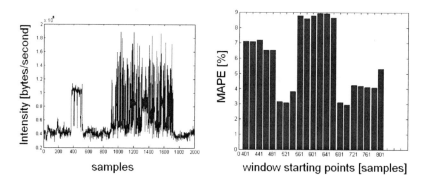

Fig. 6. The in51 data series and distribution of the MAPE error. The minimal MAPE error has value 2.925397 for the window with start and end points: 721, 1920. The maximal MAPE error is 8.932366 for the window with start and end points: 641, 1840.

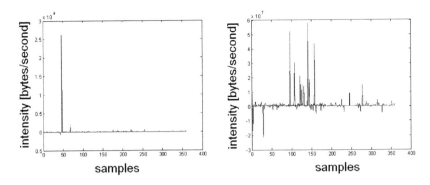

Fig. 7. Comparison of the original and forecasted data in the range for which the MAPE error is maximal and minimal. On each graph there are two superposed lines – darker with small peaks – original data, more light with huge peaks – predicted data.

the traffic that intensity reveals higher value diversity. When window becomes wider, and contains more diverse part of the traffic, the MAPE increases (serie in51 – Fig. 6 and 5). Decrease of the MAPE for the higher window sizes means that the high diverse area finishes and there are some low diverse one that makes the MAPE smaller. Generally the error holds on very good level (less than 10%) what means very good prediction.

References

1. Fernandez-Rodriguez, F., Sosvilla-Rivero, S., Garcia-Artiles, M.D.: Using Nearest Neighbour Predictors To Forecast The Spanish Stock Market. Investigaciones Economicas XXI(1), 75–91 (1997)
2. Perlin, M.S.: Details About Nearest Neighbour Algorithm
3. Ostring, S.A.M., Sirisena, H.: The Influence of Long-range Dependence on Traffic Prediction
4. Eland, W.E., Taqqu, M.S., Willinger, W., Wilson, D.V.: On the Self-Similar Nature of Ethernet Traffic. Journal IEEE/ACM Transactions on Networking 2(1) (February 1994)
5. Kubassa, W.: Creation of the Workload Generator, http://metis.weia.po.opole.pl/~d18616/generator/generator.html
6. Park, K., Willinger, W.: Self-Similar Network Traffic: An Overview
7. Smith, R.D.: The Dynamics of Internet Traffic: Self-Similarity, Self-Organization and Complex Phenomena. African Physical Review
8. Garroppo, R.G., Giordano, S., Pagano, M., Procissi, G.: On traffic prediction for resource allocation: A Chebyshev bound based allocation scheme. Computer Communications Journal 31, 3741–3751 (2008)
9. Hanias, M.P., Curtis, P.G.: Time Series Prediction of Dollar/Euro Exchange Rate Index. International Research Journal of Finance and Economics (15) (2008)
10. Arroyo, J., Espinola, R., Mate, C.: Different Approaches to Forecast Interval Time Series: A Comparison in Finance. Comput. Econ. 37, 169–191 (2011)
11. IPredict company web site, www.ipredict.it

12. Crovella, M.E., Bestavros, A.: Self-Similarity in World Wide Web Traffic: Evidence and Possible Causes. IEEE/ACM Transactions on Networking 5(6), 835–846 (1997)
13. Zacharewicz, A.: Metody Analizy Długozasięgowej (Methods of Long Range Dependence Analysis). Hugo Steinhaus Center (1999-2002)
14. Garroppo, R.G., Giordano, S., Lucetti, S., Procissi, G.: On Chaotic Prediction and Application to Resorce Allocation Strategies. In: IEEE International Conference on Communications 2004, vol. 2, pp. 1156–1160 (2004)
15. Garoppo, R.G., Giordano, S., Laschi, F., Pagano, M., Procissi, G.: On Classical and Chaotic prediction of broadband network traffic. In: Proceedings of First Workshop New Trends in Modelling, Quantitative Methods and Measurements, Zakopane, Poland (June 2004)
16. Williamson, C.: Network Traffic Self-Similarity. Powerpoint Presentation
17. Williams, G.P.: Chaos Theory Tamed. Joseph Henry Press, Washington, D.C (1997)
18. Karagiannis, T.: SELFIS: A Short Tutorial (November 2002)
19. Badford, P., Crovella, M.: Generating Representative Web Workloads for Network and Server Performance Evaluation. In: Proceedings of the 1998 ACM SIG-METRICS International Conference on Measurement and Modeling of Computer Systems, pp. 151–160 (July 1998)
20. Time Series (in polish),
    http://g.m.statystyk.w.interia.pl/metody/metody.htm
21. Loomis, D.: Evaluating Forecasting Models. Powerpoint Presentation

Generating Bursty Web Traffic
for a B2C Web Server

Grażyna Suchacka

Chair of Computer Science, Opole University of Technology,
Sosnkowskiego 31, 45-272 Opole, Poland
g.suchacka@po.opole.pl

Abstract. The paper deals with the problem of emulating highly bursty
Web traffic that can be observed at inputs of Web servers hosting online
Web stores. This problem is related to the broad issue of Web server
performance prediction and evaluation through simulation experiments.
Based on up-to-date results on real Web server workload analyses a workload model has been proposed. It combines a model of a user session at a
Business-to-Consumer (B2C) Web site with HTTP-level workload models for business and non-business Web servers. The proposed model has
been implemented in a workload generator. Based on statistics registered
during a simulation experiment, a burstiness factor has been computed
for the generated workload, which has proven to be highly variable and
bursty.

Keywords: Web traffic, burstiness, Web server, e-commerce, B2C,
Business-to-Consumer, simulation.

1 Introduction

Web performance prediction and evaluation is currently a hot research issue. Due
to the problem of the quality of Web service (QoWS), perceived by Internet users
mainly through long response times, there has been a lot of research aiming at
improving quality of service both in Web server nodes and in the network. This
paper addresses some QoWS issues on the Web server side – they are related
to modeling and generating Web traffic typical of Web servers hosting online
stores, i.e. Business-to-Consumer (B2C) Web sites.

In reality, Web traffic is characterized by some unique properties having a
significant negative impact on Web server performance. In particular, designing
a workload model for a B2C Web server requires including user navigational
patterns at B2C Web sites [1,2,3]. One needs also to take into consideration
unique characteristics and invariants typical of real Web traffic, especially its
high variability – so-called "burstiness". Real Web traffic has been proven to be
bursty across several time scales, i.e. self-similar. Burstiness means that peak
HTTP request rates during bursts exceed the average request rate by factors of
five to ten and thus can easily surpass the server capacity [4,5,6,7].

Section 2 discusses two main approaches applied to generate Web traffic for
a Web server. Section 3 presents a workload model proposed for a B2C Web

A. Kwiecień, P. Gaj, and P. Stera (Eds.): CN 2011, CCIS 160, pp. 183–190, 2011.

server, i.e. for the server hosting a retail store Web site. Burstiness of the Web traffic generated in a simulation experiment according to the proposed workload model is evaluated in Sect. 4. The results are summarized in Sect. 5.

2   Approaches to the Web Server Workload Generation

There are two main approaches to generate a stream of HTTP requests for an evaluated Web server system. The first one is a *trace-based* approach which consists in reproducing workload data recorded in a real Web server log file. Such workload is characteristic of only one actual Web site and may not be representative in general. It is also a kind of a "black box" and thus recognition of reasons for the system behavior and adjustment of the workload to different scenarios may be difficult. Moreover, Web server traces for e-commerce traffic are not publicized because of a sensitive financial aspect of companies' revenues.

Due to the aforementioned reasons we decided to apply a *distribution-driven* approach. It consists in specifying key Web workload characteristics by probability distribution functions and generating a workload according to parameters of the workload model. Distributions are the result of a detailed workload characterization for a few representative Web sites. The resulting sequence of requests has a synthetic nature but one can easily modify workload conditions by changing individual distributions or their parameters.

Research on Web traffic characteristics has resulted in developing a number of benchmarking tools, i.e. computer programs used to evaluate performance and scalability of highly accessed Web servers. Web benchmarks can generate a representative Web workload (usually allowing to customize the workload model) and collect some statistics on simulation results. However, the analysis of popular, freely available benchmarking tools, such as httperf, SPECweb99, SURGE, S-Clients, WebBench and WebStone, has indicated their low suitability for e-commerce Web servers, mainly due to very simplified workload models and their incapability of providing session- and business-oriented performance metrics [8,9]. Therefore, we decided to work out a workload model typical of B2C Web sites based on the up-to-date literature and to develop a new workload generator.

3   Workload Model of a B2C Web Server

Many studies have characterized Web server workload at the HTTP level, i.e. they described key workload characteristics (such as the number of objects per Web page, object sizes and requests interarrival times) by the most adequate probability distribution functions. Thanks to applying heavy-tailed distributions, such as Pareto or lognormal ones, the resultant Web traffic usually reflects an extremely variable and self-similar nature of a real Web traffic.

On the other hand, few studies for e-commerce Web servers characterize their workload at the high level. They identify and model different types of customers

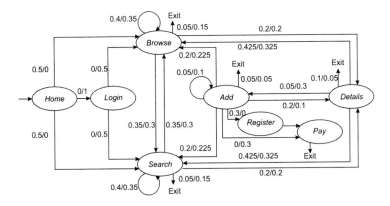

Fig. 1. Modified CBMG used to model *occasional buyer* session/*heavy buyer* session

and customer navigational patterns at the e-commerce site, i.e. a structure of a user session at the site [1,2,3]. Two user session models are well-established in the literature: a state transition graph called Customer Behavior Model Graph (CBMG) [1] and a Web interaction diagram specified in TPC-W benchmark [10], recommended by Transaction Processing Performance Council [11]. Both models specify e-commerce workloads which mimic activities of a retail bookstore Web site. They are based on a workload analysis for representative B2C Web sites and have been widely used in up-to-date research in the QoWS area.

In order to emulate highly variable Web traffic typical of B2C Web sites, we have proposed combining some results on HTTP-level Web workload characterization with a user session model based on the modified CBMG [12].

We decided to use the CBMG because it models two different customer profiles (a *heavy buyer* profile and an *occasional buyer* profile), as well as is more legible and easy to extend. Our modified graph is presented in Fig. 1. Beside six session states distinguished in the original graph (*Home, Browse, Search, Details, Add* and *Pay*), two additional states have been introduced: *Login* and *Register*. Thus, there are eight possible sessions states in our session model:

- *Home* – Entry to the home page of a retail store Web site;
- *Login* – User's logging into the site;
- *Browse* – Browsing the site contents, e.g. browsing items in various categories, bestsellers or new products;
- *Search* – Searching for products according to specific keywords;
- *Details* – Viewing a page containing detailed information on a selected product;
- *Add* – Adding a selected product to a shopping cart;
- *Register* – User's registration at the site;
- *Pay* – Finalizing a purchase transaction, including operations involved in purchase confirmation and making a payment online.

We assume that every occasional buyer navigates through the site without being logged on. Only when he/she decides to finalize a purchase transaction does he/she have to register. On the other hand, every heavy buyer in our session model logs on straight away after entering the site.

Each node of the graph corresponds to one session state. Each arrow between two states k and l means a probability $p_{k,l}^c$ of transition from state k to state l for customer profile $c \in \{heavy\ buyer,\ occasional\ buyer\}$. Arrows labeled with *Exit* mean a user's decision to leave the site without any specific reason. For given customer class c, each transition from state k to state l is characterized by a mean value of server-perceived user think time $u_{k,l}^c$. This is the time interval the user needs to analyze a downloaded Web page and to issue the next page request. User think time is modeled according to an exponential distribution with a maximum of 10 times the mean [10]. Its mean value is equal to 15 seconds for all transitions with the following exceptions [1]: $u_{Search,Details}^c = 30\,\mathrm{s}$, $u_{Details,Add}^c = 45\,\mathrm{s}$, $u_{Add,Pay}^c = u_{Add,Register}^c = 25\,\mathrm{s}$, $u_{Register,Pay}^c = 60\,\mathrm{s}$, for $c \in \{heavy\ buyer,\ occasional\ buyer\}$.

Each single Web interaction corresponds to a single Web page request, which can be assigned to one of the eight sessions states. All Web pages are modeled as dynamic pages with static and dynamic objects. Execution of each Web page request requires processing many HTTP requests, namely the first hit for an HTML page and following hits for all objects embedded in it. Since, to the best of our knowledge, there is no B2C workload model at the HTTP level, we decided to combine results of several workload studies for business [13,14] and non-business [15,16,17] Web servers in our model. We believe this combination is well justified given a common base of these studies, which is a Web server.

E-commerce traffic analyses have not shown a significant dependence of page sizes on a method type (e.g. GET or POST) or on a session state [4], so we model a composition of a Web page apart from the session state. The number of static objects per page (including the base HTML file) is modeled by a Pareto distribution with the scale parameter equal to 1.33 and the shape parameter equal to 2. The number of dynamic objects per page is obtained by a geometric distribution with the success probability 0.8 and then is incremented by 1 in order to ensure at least one dynamic object for a page. Sizes of HTML files are obtained from a hybrid function, where a body follows a lognormal distribution with the mean 7.63 and the standard deviation 1.001, while a tail follows a Pareto distribution with the scale parameter equal to 1 and the shape parameter equal to 10 240.

Sizes of embedded static objects are obtained from lognormal distribution with the mean 8.215 and the standard deviation 1.46. Sizes of embedded dynamic objects are obtained from Weibull distribution with the scale parameter equal to 0.0059 and the shape parameter equal to 0.9. Interarrival time of hit requests at the Web server is modeled by a Weibull distribution with the scale parameter equal to 7.64 and the shape parameter equal to 1.705.

4   Evaluating Burstiness of the Generated Web Traffic

Web traffic burstiness has been evaluated after carrying out simulation experiments and using an approach described in [6] for request arrival rates registered during the experiment in subintervals of duration 100 milliseconds and 1 second.

The proposed workload model has been implemented in a workload generator, written in C++. The workload generator is an integral part of a simulation tool, which allows one evaluating a B2C Web server system performance under different scheduling policies for different server load levels. The workload generator is responsible for generating and transmitting to the Web server system a stream of HTTP requests emulating the session-based server workload. Based on some input parameters it generates user sessions at a given session arrival rate λ_s, i.e. it initiates the given number of user sessions per minute. A pre-specified parameter Δ_{KC} denotes a percentage of generated heavy buyer sessions in the observation window (so a percentage of occasional buyer sessions is $100 - \Delta_{KC}$).

The experiments discussed here have been carried out for a session arrival rate of 100 sessions per minute ($\lambda_s = 100$), where 10% of all user sessions were generated according to the heavy buyer profile ($\Delta_{KC} = 10$). The generated workload was monitored in a 3-hour observation window after a 10-hour preliminary phase of the experiment (this time means the internal simulation time which differs from the "real world" time). HTTP request arrival rates at the Web server input have been registered for 100 milliseconds and 1 second intervals.

A visual inspection of the number of HTTP requests arriving at the Web server system confirms the high variability of the generated Web traffic. Figure 2 presents Web traffic bursts in slots of 100 milliseconds for a 3 minute period and Fig. 3 presents bursts in slots of 1 second for a 30 minutes period. High variations in request arrival rates in the figures indicate a significant burstiness of the generated traffic on fine time scales.

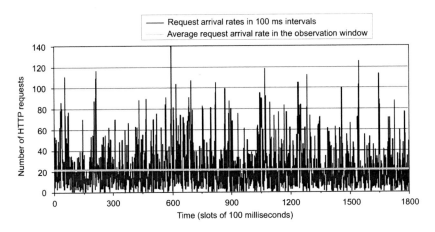

Fig. 2. Web traffic bursts in slots of 100 milliseconds (session arrival rate is equal to 100 sessions per minute)

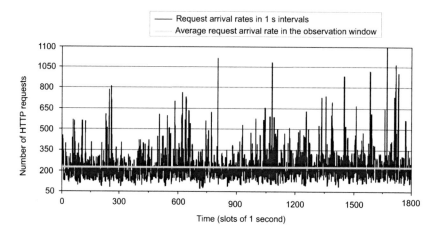

Fig. 3. Web traffic bursts in slots of 1 second (session arrival rate is equal to 100 sessions per minute)

Let L be the total number of HTTP requests generated during the simulation experiment in the interval of $T = 3$ hours $= 10\,800$ seconds. Let also λ be the average arrival rate of requests registered in the experiment, given by:

$$\lambda = \frac{L}{T} \ . \tag{1}$$

We consider the time interval T divided into n equal subintervals of duration t, called epochs. Let l_k be the number of HTTP requests that arrive in epoch k and λ_k be arrival rate of requests during epoch k, given by:

$$\lambda_k = \frac{n \times l_k}{T} \ . \tag{2}$$

Let also l^+ be the total number of HTTP requests that arrive in epochs in which the epoch arrival rate λ_k exceeds the average arrival rate λ registered in the interval T in the simulation experiment.

The burstiness parameter b is defined as the fraction of time during which the epoch arrival rate exceeds the average arrival rate λ:

$$b = \frac{Number\ of\ epochs\ for\ which\ \lambda_k > \lambda}{n} \ . \tag{3}$$

If generated Web traffic is not bursty, it is uniformly distributed over all epochs and so:

$$l_k = \frac{L}{n} \ \text{and} \ \lambda_k = \frac{\frac{L}{n}}{\frac{T}{n}} = \frac{L}{T} = \lambda \ . \tag{4}$$

Such situation means that that there are no epochs in which $\lambda_k > \lambda$ and thus $b = 0$.

For the Web traffic generated according to our workload model, the burstiness factors for epochs of 100 milliseconds and 1 second were equal to 0.34 and 0.39, respectively, which indicates a significant degree of variability and confirms results illustrated in Fig. 2 and 3.

Experiments performed for other levels of load intensity have shown that a degree of burstiness is slightly lower for higher session arrival rates, i.e. for higher server workloads. However, in all cases significant burstiness of traffic at the Web server input was observed.

5   Concluding Remarks

In the paper, a proposed workload model typical of B2C Web servers has been discussed and evaluated with respect to the variability in request arrival rates at the Web server input. The model combines a high-level model of a user session at a B2C Web site with HTTP-level workload characteristics identified for business and non-business Web servers. The model has been implemented in a workload generator integrated with a Web server system simulator. Simulation experiments have been carried out, in which request arrival rates at the server were registered for subintervals of duration 100 milliseconds and 1 second. A burstiness factor computed for the registered data indicates that the Web traffic generated according to the proposed workload model is highly variable and thus it can be applied to generate input traffic in experiments evaluating performance of e-commerce Web server systems.

References

1. Menascé, D.A., Almeida, V.A.F., Fonseca, R., Mendes, M.A.: Business-Oriented Resource Management Policies for E-Commerce Servers. Performance Evaluation 42(2-3), 223–239 (2000)
2. Song, Q., Shepperd, M.: Mining Web Browsing Patterns for E-commerce. Computers in Industry 57(7), 622–630 (2006)
3. Wang, Q., Makaroff, D.J., Edwards, H.K.: Characterizing Customer Groups for an E-commerce Website. In: ACM Conference on Electronic Commerce, pp. 218–227. ACM Press, New York (2004)
4. Kant, K., Venkatachalam, M.: Transactional Characterization of Front-End E-Commerce Traffic. In: IEEE GLOBECOM 2002, vol. 3, pp. 2523–2527 (2002)
5. Makineni, S., Iyer, R.: Performance Characterization of TCP/IP Packet Processing in Commercial Server Workloads. In: IEEE WWC-6, pp. 33–41 (2003)
6. Menascé, D.A., Almeida, V.: Capacity Planning for Web Services: Metrics, Models and Methods. Prentice Hall, Upper Saddle River (2002)
7. Vallamsetty, U., Kant, K., Mohapatra, P.: Characterization of E-Commerce Traffic. Electronic Commerce Research 3, 167–192 (2003)
8. Andreolini, M., Cardellini, V., Colajanni, M.: Benchmarking Models and Tools for Distributed Web-Server Systems. In: Calzarossa, M.C., Tucci, S. (eds.) Performance 2002. LNCS, vol. 2459, pp. 208–235. Springer, Heidelberg (2002)
9. Suchacka, G.: Generowanie obciążenia o specyfice e-commerce dla serwera webowego. Nowe Technologie Sieci komputerowych 2, 183–193 (2006)

10. García, D.F., García, J.: TPC-W E-Commerce Benchmark Evaluation. IEEE Computer 36(2), 42–48 (2003)
11. Transaction Processing Performance Council, www.tpc.org
12. Borzemski, L., Suchacka, G.: Web Traffic Modeling for E-commerce Web Server System. In: Kwiecień, A., Gaj, P., Stera, P. (eds.) 16th Conference on Computer Networks, CN 2009, Wisła, Poland. CCIS, vol. 39, pp. 151–159. Springer, Heidelberg (2009)
13. Shi, W., Collins, E., Karamcheti, V.: Modeling Object Characteristics of Dynamic Web Content. Journal of Parallel and Distributed Computing 63(10), 963–980 (2003)
14. Xia, C.H., Liu, Z., Squillante, M.S., Zhang, L., Malouch, N.: Web Traffic Modeling at Finer Time Scales and Performance Implications. Performance Evaluation 61(2-3), 181–201 (2005)
15. Barford, P., Bestavros, A., Bradley, A., Crovella, M.: Changes in Web Client Access Patterns: Characteristics and Caching Implications. WWW 2(1-2), 15–28 (1999)
16. Cardellini, V., Casalicchio, E., Colajanni, M., Mambelli, M.: Web Switch Support for Differentiated Services. ACM Performance Evaluation Review 29(2), 14–19 (2001)
17. Casalicchio, E., Colajanni, M.: A Client-aware Dispatching Algorithm for Web Clusters Providing Multiple Services. In: 10th International WWW Conference, pp. 535–544 (2001)

DDoS Detection Algorithm Using the Bidirectional Session

HeeKyoung Yi[1], PyungKoo Park[2], Seungwook Min[1], and JaeCheol Ryou[1]

[1] Department of Computer Engineering, Chungnam National University
{yikari,andor,jcryou}@home.cnu.ac.kr
[2] Future Network Research Dept. ETRI
parkpk@etri.re.kr

Abstract. Due to the proliferation of smartphones and wireless internet, the number of DoS/DDoS attacks has increased significantly, and it creates a lot of network traffic. The DoS/DDoS attacks consume the resources of the service server so that the network and the continuity of service cannot be guaranteed [1,2,3]. Current studies on DoS/DDoS focus on a radical change of total traffic or traffic pattern. Results of these type of studies cannot react to ever changing attack patterns and service types [4,5]. This paper proposes a new algorithm to detect DoS/DDoS attacks based on the session information of the service. In this paper, we propose BSDDA(bidirectional session aware DDoS detection algorithm) that detects DoS/DDoS attacks by analyzing the session information that contains service requests as well as service replies. Since the algorithm consideres session information of service requests and responses, its effectiveness is experimentally shown the algorithm effectively responds to the ever changing attack patterns.

Keywords: DoS/DDoS, bidirectional session.

1 Introduction

A DoS (Denial of Service) attack is an attack on the structural defects of the network or on the system to deteriorate or block normal service. The DDoS (Distributed Denial of Service) attack is carried out by numerous attackers on the internet that focus the attack to a specified server to (dry out) the resource of the server to (impossiblize) the service. The malicious attacker who starts DDoS attacks utilizes malicious programs to infect un-intended users so that these un-intended users generate overwhelming request to the target system [1].

As the network environment evolves, a DDoS attacker can control more systems and employ more diverse methods to attack a target system. The majority of the DDoS attacks were mainly done by exploiting the network layer; however, recently, DDoS attacks employ methods that span over the network layer to the application layer [6,7,8].

To defend against wide variety of the DoS/DDoS attacks, current studies collect, analyze and process enormous data on the network including data such as data packet transfer delay.

A. Kwiecień, P. Gaj, and P. Stera (Eds.): CN 2011, CCIS 160, pp. 191–203, 2011.
© Springer-Verlag Berlin Heidelberg 2011

To defend against DDoS attacks that exploits features from the network layer to the application layer, new defense mechanisms are needed at each layer. On the network layer, the IP address should be checked if it is spoofed; on the transport layer, the TCP header options should be inspected if they are properly set. Also on the application layer, the authenticity of the HTTP or FTP requests should be checked [9,10,7]. Inspection or checking at each layer imposes additional burden to detect DDoS attacks. The DDoS attack detection method proposed in this paper define a single service type that covers network activities of all network layers. It reacts to service request messages and the service response messages in order to inspect the state change if the request of a step is legitimate. The state is maintained with a Pseudo State machine to guarantee the speed of the state management. The performance of BSDDA(bidirectional session aware DDoS detection algorithm) is tested with NS2 (Network Simulator Program).

This paper is composed as below. Section 2 describes the related works to describe BSDDA, Sect. 3 defines the concept of the Session Information, Sect. 4 explains how BSDDA works, Sect. 5 discusses the experiments and its result and Sect. 6 concludes the paper.

2   Related Works

As the network environment progresses, DoS/DDoS attacks evolve from a simple form of bandwidth consumption to the form of IP Spoofing, Slowris Attack and Application Layer Attacks [6,7,8].

Current studies on DoS/DDoS attack detection include QoS (Quality of Service) study [11], PPM (Probabilistic Packet Marking) method [12,13], and Hop-Count method [14,15].

The DoS/DDoS attack detection mechanism utilizing QoS information monitors the traffic to detect abrupt changes in traffic, and if it detects an attack, it controls the traffic to aid continuous network service. And, to cope with unknown attacks, the QoS mechanism from the traffic measurement information, it can act to the attack irrespective of the attack patterns [11,16].

However, as the mechanism is based on the total traffic volume not the traffic pattern information, it cannot be claimed to gain high score on the basis of FNR (False Negative Ratio), FPR (False Positive Ratio). Also since the traffic shaping defense decision is not based on the analysis of individual packets, the NPSR (Normal Packet Survival Ratio) rate is not high. In the case of Slowris attack, which does not use a lot of bandwidth but creates a lot of sessions, the traffic changes is very small; thus, the attack may not be detected using methods based on the total traffic volume [5,11,16].

The PPM (Probabilistic Packet Marking) mechanism focuses on overcoming back tracing problem induces by fragmentation by minimizing marking size to minimize system over-head compared to the case of back tracing mechanism. In the PPM mechanism, a packet is marked with constant probability by near-by network system pair in order to determine the attack origin by the analysed marks if the DoS/DDoS attack is detected. Since not all packets are marked, the router overhead is minimized. PPM mechanism is robust since it is simple, cost-effective and by back tracing the origin of the attack can be traced [12,13].

The PPM mechanism, however, requires a minimum number of packets to reassemble the attack routes. Also if the number of attackers increases, it is hard to detect the attack and the marking field can be spoofed [12].

Hop-Count Filtering utilizes the hop count information to detect an attack. It utilizes the face that the hop count from source to destination cannot be changed even if the packet header is altered by the attacker. It also relies on the fact that hop count remains fairly constant from source to a given destination. The Hop count is calculated from the difference of the TTL (Time to Live) field of each packet at the destination (final TTL) and the value of the packet at the source (initial TTL). Even though the IP header including source address and initial TTL can be changed by the attacker, the value of the final TTL is determined by the network infrastructure and the routing protocol, and cannot be changed by the attacker. Therefore, if the network infra is not changed drastically between two hosts, the hop count is invariable so the packet with abnormal hop count can be classified as spoofed [14,15].

However Hop-Count Filtering cannot be effectively applied if the victims path is changed while attack is under way [14,15].

Current studies require extensive change to the equipments and a lot of information. The QoS mechanism is not (possible) with small number of DDoS traffic, while the PPM methods cannot deal with a huge volume of data. Also TTL based Hop-Count mechanism can only detect attacks using spoofed IP packets.

In this paper we propose a DDoS attack detection mechanism based on Pseudo State Machine of service level information extracted from service requests and responses to resolve above mentioned issues.

3   DoS/DDoS Detection Alogorithm

Network activity refers to the situation where two or more hosts exchange messages following pre-defined protocols. To understand the flow of messages exchanged between two or more hosts, request messages as well as response messages should be captured and analyzed. Normal network (flow) follows the procedures defined in the protocol; however, the abnormal network flows caused by DDoS attacks do not follow the protocol.

Application services are composed of service request messages and service response messages, and these messages form a session. The session information defined in this paper is comprised of source address, destination address, source port, destination port and protocol type, and it is extracted from the packet. The session information is composed of bi-directional activities between service requester (client) and service provider (server). Information of that packet flowing one direction is composed of reflected information of source address, destination address, source port and destination port of the packet flowing to the other direction.

BSDDA (bidirectional session aware DDoS detection algorithm) proposed in this paper utilizes Bidirectional Session information to determine DDoS attack situation by monitoring and analyzing message exchanges between the client and server.

3.1   Extract of Bidirectional Session Information

The Figure 1 shows how the session information is extracted from the procedure of session creation between a client and a server. The client sends request message to start a service session. After receiving the request message from the client, the server sends corresponding response message to the client. BSDDA extracts 5-tuple (source IP, destination IP, source port, destination port, protocol type) information of the session from the messages between client and server, and the information is used to determine the legitimacy of the session in progress.

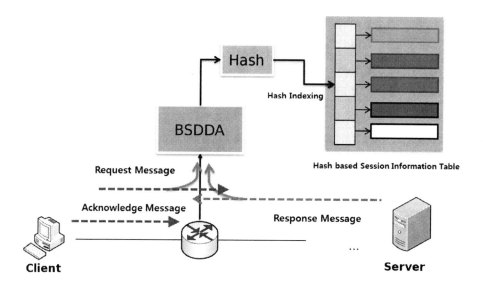

Fig. 1. Bidirectional session

In BSDDA, the request session and the response session have the same hash value. As the first service request packet from the terminal arrives, BSDDA extracts session information to calculate the hash index, and the hash table is looked up. If the information of the request packet is not found, a new record is added to the hash table. Also the current message status is added. If the service utilizes TCP, the status is one of these: SYN, SYN-ACK and ACK Message. The current message state and the message that should be received at the next stage are constructed.

If the service server sends response message, the source and the destination address of the packet are changed but have the same hash index and is stored in the same hash table to be examined if the message is expected at this stage.

In the case of TCP SYN flooding attack, instead of the required message, SYN messages arrive repeatedly, and such attack can be detected.

Also for most of UDP based protocols, such as SIP (Session Initiation Protocol), DNS (Domain Name Service) or TFTP (Trivial File Transfer Protocol), the client and the server exchange messages in a pre-defined order; and by utilizing this behavior, malicious packets can be detected.

3.2   Using the Pseudo State Machine for States Management

It is time consuming if the session information composed of real-time messages is used to detect DDoS attacks. The most efficient method to detect DDoS attack utilizing session information is to use peudo state machine. The signature based message processing is very fast but is not very flexible in the case of dynamic information processing. It is also possible to use statistical methods to process dynamic information but it is very hard to apply to the case of attacks that generate small traffic such as Slowloris Attack [17,18,19].

But if Pseudo State Machine is used, only the services that follow legitimate message exchange procedures are allowed and malicious traffic as well as attack traffic can be blocked effectively. Also attacks such as Slowloris Attacks that generates small traffic can be detected since they do not follow legitimate procedures.

The Figure 2 depicts the message exchange procedure between client and server in session based protocols such as TCP. The client sends request session message to the server to initiate a session. After receiving the request session message, the server sends acknowledge message. The client sends a complete message to the server after it receives acknowledge message from the server. This procedure sequence can be re-defined as a Pseudo State Machine as shown in Fig. 3.

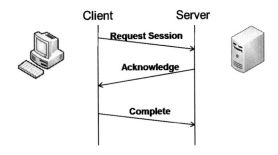

Fig. 2. Message exchange of a session based protocol

In Figure 3 the session protocol in Fig. 2 is added as a new rule to the Pseudo State Machine. As a new rule is added to the Pseudo State Machine, the protocol type is determined by the data header information. If incoming data is a session

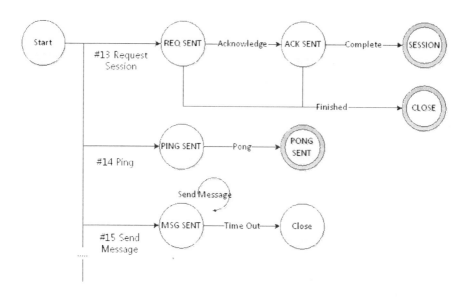

Fig. 3. Pseudo State Machine

protocol, request session message is checked to change the state to REQ SENT. Afterwards if data of the same session, the corresponding 5-tuple information can be quickly looked up with the hash value.

Attackers can carry out scanning, Fuzzing, DDoS attacks to the target host utilizing the session protocol. The malicious actions can be blocked by the Pseudo State Machine. If the attacker sends session request packets repeatedly, the Pseudo State Machine considers it as illegal packet. Also the case which the attacker sends acknowledge or finish packets at the first can be detected as abnormal session by Pseudo State Machine.

Figure 4 shows that it is possible to detect abnormal situation by monitoring message exchange even after the session is defined. The session creation procedure in Fig. 3 shows the session connection process between the start and the end of sessions.

If the Pseudo State Machine is not defined as in Fig. 4, the attacker can benefit in the following situation. The attacker can establish a legitimate session with the server and send request message to request for data. The server sends response message after it receives a request message. After receiving the Response Message, the attacker has to send a confirm message but he/she may send request message repeatedly. In this situation, the server cannot close the session because it has not received a confirmation message. If multiple sessions behave in this manner, the server would be overwhelmed. (i.e. the queue for the sessions will be full).

Table 1 shows the session information structure and the structure is updated as data flows into the system. The session information is comprised of the hash index value of the 5-Tuple, current status, next legitimate state and the arrival time of the packet. The next legitimate state information can have multiple

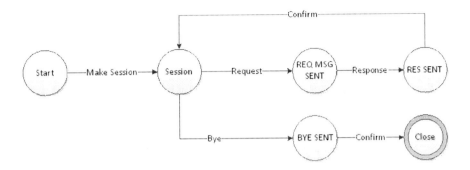

Fig. 4. Extended Pseudo State Machine

Table 1. Bidirectional session information

5-Tuple hashed value	Current States	Next message	Next Message	Arrived Time	Rule No
XXW2S2	—	—	—	12:00:00	#13
XXW2S2	REQ SENT	ACK SENT	Close	12:00:01	#13
XXW2S2	ACK SENT	SESSION	Close	12:00:02	#13
XXW2S2	REQ SENT			12:00:04	#13

fields. If a client has sent a request session message to the server as in Fig. 3, the current state of the client is "REQ SENT" and the next states can be either "ACK SENT" or "Close". The sever sends acknowledge message to the client after it receives request session message. After the client receives acknowledge message, it can send either "complete message" or "Finished Message". If it has sent a message that is not one of the two messages, it can be considered as illegal. In Table 1, we can determine abnormal behavior has occurred at 12:00:04.

To expand the coverage of the Pseudo State Machine to take the new service into account, a new protocol shown in Fig. 5 is included. Authentication process is added to the protocol for the client to use the service as shown in Fig. 2. Before sending request message, the client sends authentication message to the server to begin the authentication process. The server sends message with nonce after receiving authentication message from the client. After receiving nonce, the client encrypts password and nonce to send to the server. The server checks these values to authenticate the client.

Figure 6 shows part of the fields shown in Fig. 5. Some text fields of the protocol are used in constructing the Pseudo State Machine. Some fields of the message represent the current state of the session and are very important. For example, ID or nonce field of the response message is used to prevent packet re-use or to determine if the password and nonce is properly hashed to be exchanged between the client and server.

Figure 7 represents the authentication procedure of Fig. 5 as a Pseudo State Machine. In the authentication procedure of the Fig. 7, the session state pro-

Client
Server
Authentication
Nonce
Response
OK
192.168.0.2
192.168.0.5

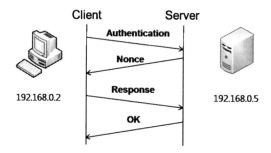

Fig. 5. Authentication procedure

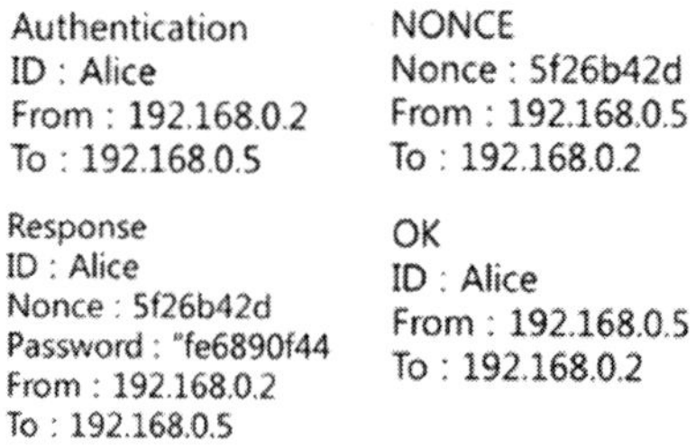

Authentication
ID : Alice
From : 192.168.0.2
To : 192.168.0.5
NONCE
Nonce : 5f26b42d
From : 192.168.0.5
To : 192.168.0.2
Response
ID : Alice
Nonce : 5f26b42d
Password : "fe6890f44
From : 192.168.0.2
To : 192.168.0.5
OK
ID : Alice
From : 192.168.0.5
To : 192.168.0.2

Fig. 6. Message Fields

gresses by referencing the message fields of Fig. 6. Authentication protocols have time out conditions unlike other protocols. Since it can prevent brute force attack or fuzzing attack, the request to dynamic information that uses database can be blocked. Similarly if a client requests contents by adding cache-control options in case of HTTP GET request, we can determine if the requests are part of an attack.

3.3 BSDDA: Bidirectional Session Aware DDoS Detection Algorithm

The DDoS attack detection mechanism presented in this paper consists of three parts: hash table construction, BSDDA application and abnormal traffic processing. In the first part of the process, if a new message comes to the system, hash indexing is processed from the 5-tuple information of the packet. If the hash index value is not present in the hash table, it is added with the session information to the hash table. After the hash indexing, the session information is applied to BSDDA. Current message is examined against the Pseudo State Machine defined in BSDDA to determine if it is part of an attack. If the current network traffic is normal, corresponding session information is updated and penalty points of the session information is not increased. Otherwise, the network traffic of interest turns out to be malignant, the penalty points for the session is increased (the penalty points are shared for all sessions, if they have same IP

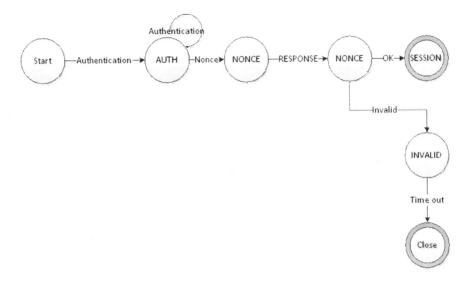

Fig. 7. Authentication protocol

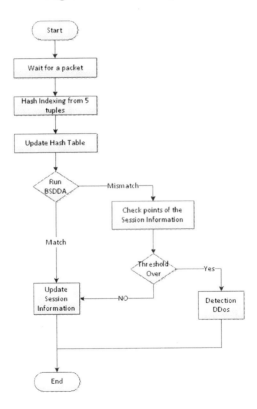

Fig. 8. Flow chart

address). If the penalty point exceeds certain threshold value, the corresponding network traffic is considered as DDoS attack traffic.

4   Implementation and Evaluation

To implement and test the algorithm, an experiment environment is set utilizing NS2 as shown in Fig. 9. IP and TCP, UDP and HTTP in NS2 are different from mechanism of real world. So we had to customize some of NS2 Kernel modules. Specifically, TCP and HTTP protocols are implemented based on the UDP protocol. TCP and HTTP protocols were designed in the simplest manner just enough to generate legitimate traffic.

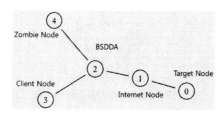

Fig. 9. NS 2 experimental environment

250 clients are setup at the client node side and 250 zombie systems are setup at the zombie node. The target node and the client nodes are connected with a series of routers and a network device with the BSDDA algorithm is placed at the network core.

Table 2. Input traffic

Per zombie node	18.5 KB/s
TCP Syn	7 KB/s
TCP RST, ACK, FIN	3.6 KB/s
HTTP Connection	1.4 KB/s
UDP Flooding	1.5 KB/s

Attack profile is given in Table 2. The zombie nodes are set to create random attack traffic. They send TCP SYN packets, HTTP connection requests or UDP flooding packets. Especially, zombies could change their port number for TCP Syn Attacks or the others, therefore BSDDA need to check for session timeout. If a session is not closed and expired, BSDDA impose penalty points.

The result shows that as soon as the attack is initiated the traffic began to increase explosively. Once BSDDA detects the attack, it applies the countermeasures and the traffic is decreased to the normal level. The simulation result is shown in Fig. 10 which represents the traffic between the internet node and the target node.

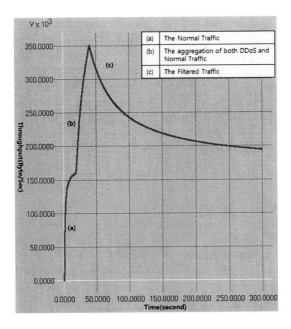

Fig. 10. Throughput between the Internet node and the target node (input traffic)

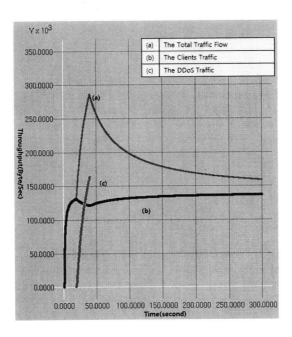

Fig. 11. Output traffic of the Internet node and target node: (a) the total traffic, (b) the clients traffic, (c) the DDoS traffic generated from the zombie node

To determine if the attack traffic is blocked, the output traffic of clients and DDoS is studied. The Figure 11 shows the DDoS traffic increases explosively and decreases after the attack is blocked by the algorithm. The attack traffic is completely blocked, but it does not appear on this figure as the figure has been cut off.

Through the experiment, we found the algorithm works against attacks that generate various types of traffic such as TCP, UDP or HTTP and the network traffic returns to normal after the malicious traffic is blocked.

5   Conclusion

In this paper, session information is calculated from the bi-directional messages to detect DDoS attacks. The session information is used to determine if a network traffic is part of DDoS attacks. The algorithm of the paper is examined experimentally to determine it can cope with numerous DDoS attack traffic patterns. Also the algorithm is tested if it works irrespective of traffic volume.

Acknowledgement. This research was supported by the MKE (Ministry of Knowledge Economy), Korea, under the ITRC (Information Technology Research Center) support program supervised by the NIPA (National IT Industry Promotion Agency) (NIPA-2010-(C1090-1031-0005)).

References

1. Mirkovic, J., Reiher, P.: A Taxonomy of DDoS Attack and DDoS Defense Mechanisms. Computer Communication Review 34, 39–53 (2004)
2. Khan, S., Loo, K.-K., Naeem, T., Khan, M.A.: Denial of Service Attacks and Challenges in Broadband Wireless Networks. IJCSNS International Journal of Computer Science and Network Security 8(7) (July 2008)
3. Arbor Networks, Worldwide Infrastructure Report, vol. V
4. Xie, Y., Yu, S.-Z.: A Large-Scale Hidden Semi-Markov Model for Anomaly Detection on User Browsing Behaviors. IEEE/ACM Transactions on Networking 17(1) (February 2009)
5. Kuzmanovic, A., Knightly, E.W.: Low-Rate TCP-Targeted Denial of Service Attacks and Counter Strategies. IEEE/ACM Transactions on Networking 14(4) (August 2006)
6. Dittrich, D., Dietrich, S.: P2P as botnet command and control: a deeper insight. In: 3rd International Conference on Malicious and Unwanted Software, MALWARE 2008 (2008)
7. Yatagai, T., Isohara, T., Sasase, I.: Detection of HTTP-GET ?ood Attack Based on Analysis of Page Access Behavior. In: IEEE Pacific Rim Conference on Communications, Computers and Signal Processing, PacRim 2007 (2007)
8. Lesk, M., Stytz, R., Trope, L.: The New Front Line: Estonia under Cyberassault. Security & Privacy IEEE 5(4), 76–79 (2007)
9. Network Ingress Filtering: Defeating Denial of Service Attacks which employ IP Source Address Spoofing. RFC 2827 (May 2000)

10. Wang, H., Zhang, D., Shin, K.G.: Detecting SYN Flooding Attacks. In: Proceedings of the IEEE Infocom, pp. 1530–1539 (2002)
11. Garg, A., Narasimha Reddy, A.L.: Mitigation of DoS attacks through QoS regulation. In: Proceedings of ACM SIGCOMM 2001 (August 2001)
12. Park, K., Lee, H.: On the effectiveness of probabilistic packet marking for IP traceback under denial of service attack. In: Proc. IEEE INFOCOM 2001, pp. 338–347 (2001)
13. Song, D.X., Perrig, A.: Advanced and Authenticated Marking Scheme for IP Traceback. In: Proc. Infocom, vol. 2, pp. 878–886 (2001)
14. Jin, C., Wang, H., Shin, K.G.: Hop-Count Filtering: An Effecitve Defense Against Spoofed DDoS Traffic. In: Proceeding of the 10th ACM Conference on Computer and Communications Security, Washington, DC (October 2003)
15. Paxson, V.: End-to-End Routing Behavior in the Internet. IEEE/ACM Transaction on Networking, 601–615
16. Specification of Guaranteed Quality of Service. RFC 2212 (September 1997)
17. Roesch, M.: Snort-Lightweight Intrusion Detection for Networks. In: Proc. of the USENIX LISA 1999 Conf. (November 1999)
18. Kumar, S., Spafford, E.: A Pattern Matching Model for Misuse Intrusion Detection. In: Proc. of the 17th National Computer Security Conf., pp. 11–21 (October 1994)
19. Feinstein, L., Schnackenberg, D., Balupari, R., Kindred, D.: Statistical Approaches to DDoS Attack Detection and Response. In: DARPA Information Survivability Conference and Exposition (DISCEX 2003), (April 22-24, 2003)
20. BBC News: New "cyber attacks" hit S Korea (2009-07-09)
21. Internet Protocol. RFC 1349 (1992)
22. Bellovin, S.M.: ICMP Traceback Messages. Internet Draft draftbellovin-itrace-00.txt (March 2000) (work in progress)
23. Park, K., Lee, H.: On the effectiveness of route-based packet filtering for distributed DoS attack prevention in power-law internets. In: Proceedings of ACM SIGCOMM 2001 (August 2001)
24. IP Router Alert Option. RFC 2113 (1997)
25. SIP: Session Initiation Protocol. RFC 3261 (2002)
26. El-Moussa, F.A., Linge, N., Hope, M.: Active router approach to defeating denial-of-service attacks in networks. IEEE, Los Alamitos (2007)
27. Mirkovic, J., Arikan, E., Wei, S., Thomas, R., Fahmy, S., Reiher, P.: Benchmarks for DDoS defense evaluation. In: Military Communications Conference (2006)
28. Li, M., Li, J., Zhao, W.: Experimental study of DDOS attacking of flood type based on NS2. International Journal of Electronics and Computers 1, 143–152 (2009)
29. Xie, Y., Yu, S.-Z.: Monitoring the Application-Layer DDoS Attacks for Popular Websites. IEEE/ACM Transactions on networking 17(1) (February 2009)

Analyzing Outbound Network Traffic

Mirosław Skrzewski

Politechnika Śląska, Instytut Informatyki, Akademicka 16, 44-100 Gliwice, Polska
miroslaw.skrzewski@polsl.pl

Abstract. Conventional security solutions monitor network communication without paying much attention to outgoing traffic, due to high processing cost of packet level network traffic analysis. Outgoing network communication, originating from typical system's application has common properties, which can be used for traffic selection in security related analysis. The paper presents the concept of outbound network traffic classification based on temporal characteristics of network flows and shows the results of experiments identifying traffic patterns of common user's application and values of classification parameters.

Keywords: network flow patterns, web flow, application traffic analysis.

1 Introduction

Conventional security solutions attempts to monitor network traffic, trying to identify and block any signs of malicious intended communication. Typically these systems analyzes mostly incoming traffic as potentially dangerous, paying less attention to outgoing, user initiated communication, assumed as secure from definition. This paradigm of security operation changes in last years due to arrival of stealth malware programs (trojans, bots) capable of exporting user's data over network and so the properties of outbound network traffic became the subject of research interest.

Most of the present client-server applications utilize HTTP protocol for request – result delivery, due to security imposed network communication constrains. Typical LAN access router/firewall configuration allows for incoming communication on ports 80 and 443 and blocks nearly all other lower TCP ports. Therefore many application use web browser as their user interface (mail, messengers), and others (voice, stream) use http ports for communication initialization.

The HTTP traffic, due to origin from typical applications, has some common properties on TCP connection or flow levels, so there should be possible to derive patterns of typical applications traffic, and use them to separate user initiated communication from remaining network flows, potentially requesting more attention from security monitoring systems. The paper presents results of analysis of outbound network communication for some typical applications and resulting models of network flow traffic, aimed on selection of user initiated packet flows in network outbound communication.

A. Kwiecień, P. Gaj, and P. Stera (Eds.): CN 2011, CCIS 160, pp. 204–213, 2011.

2   Related Work

Since the mid-1990s a lot of works analyses properties of HTTP network traffic. Its authors analyze the content of downloaded web pages, numbers of requested objects, amount of transferred data and on this basis attempt to derive statistical models of web related traffic and describe requirements on network throughput. Most of this works [1,2,3,4,5] were done on the network edges, on the campus external connections, and attempt to describe network traffic properties on the basis of relatively small traffic samples (of up to few hours duration) recorded on network access links.

Recorded traces of web communication were analyzed applying different models of web interaction, based on *Page-request* (single web page transfer) or *Web-request* (one or multi-page transfer in response to the user action) models. A set of parameters describing details of analyzed data exchange were defined for simulation models of web traffic and best fit probability distributions for model parameters were presented. The values of parameters were based on the analysis of communication on HTTP or TCP level, and in [4] also on Web-flow level.

The levels of analysis were described as follows: HTTP conversation represent single HTTP request and response transaction. In early (HTTP 1.0) times request and response pair use single TCP connection, from HTTP 1.1 due to persistent connection more then one pair of request and response may be transported in TCP connection (network flow). HTTP communication may use many concurrent TCP flows on the link, initiated by the same or different hosts.

A Web-flow was defined [4] as a group ot TCP flows with the same source IP address with parameters *TCP connection count* (number of TCP connections in Web flow) and *Interval of TCP connections* (interval between the starts of two consecutive TCP connection in a Web flow).

The notion of network flow is often used in monitoring of network usage, where it simple means IP data stream. There are two versions of network flow definition, one originating from Cisco and others vendors (NetFlow) says [6]: "a network flow is a sequence of packets between a given source and destination in one direction only" , the other used in *argus* program [7] ommits the words "in one direction only" so the flow is described by 5-tuple: IP source and destination addresses, source and destination ports and IP protocol number. This basic data are generally suplemented with timing (origin, closing time) and volume (number of transmitted packet, transmitted bytes) information.

3   System Network Activity Monitoring

Most of works devoted to HTTP traffic monitoring is based on data recorded at the network edges and due to amount of processing they are not well suited for real-time operation. To obtain the solution capable of real-time operation one must move the analysis near the source of the outgoing traffic – to user system, and base it on locally available traffic.

User systems generate a lot of outgoing network traffic induced by daily users activity, due to interaction with diferent types of web sites (informational, social, commercial etc.) or services (email, messengers, voip) and not containing any hazardous contents. It's full real time analysis on packet level may be very expensive in terms of computer power and processing time.

Instead we propose the concept of system network activity monitoring, based on analysis of network flows – network conversation between given pair of source and destination IP addresses/ports treated as a unit of communication. This approach is loosely modeled on bidirectional argus [7] flows. The flows, recorded locally on monitored system, with the additional information about the process and account responsible for communication and flow timing information are passed through origin analysis process, filtering out all users' application initiated traffic.

3.1   Data Collection

To capture network activity data we use custom program, recording communication events on Windows system's TDI (transport driver interface) kernel API (*TDIlog*). Acquired event's data recorded in text file delivers continuous picture of all system network activity – opening and closing of ports by active processes, reception and transmission of data on active UDP and TCP ports, source and destination IP addresses, with the amount and the direction of transmitted via given connection and port data. Each operation on TDI interface is recorded with suitable timestamp, so it is possible to compute diffrent statistics describing network communication of given application or system processes.

Our idea is to move with the flows recording near to the source of the outgoing traffic – to user system, and to use additional, locally available, information to classify outgoing traffic on user (aplication) intended communication, composing most of computer network activity, probably safe from security point of view, and on remaining, smaller part, requesting more detailed analysis.

We focused our attention on outbound communication, mostly user initiated outside of computer system. We don't want to analyze traffic contents nor traffic destinations, as this properties are constantly changing with user activity. We are searching for properties connected with communication algorithms embedded in application design, related to temporal relationship between application generated flows.

3.2   Developing Network Activity Patterns

To capture necessary flow data we record with *TDIlog* network activity of the test system with installed selected application. Because most of user's application operates in client-server model, with the usage of HTTP protocol, we focused our attention on the operation of web browsers, as the basic user tools. In our experiments we record flows generated by selected web browsers (Internet Explorer, FireFox, Opera and Chrome) opening the same, selected url's.

To have other variables of experiment constant, we installed all browsers on the same system, so the network operation background (operating system network activity) was identical in all tests. For comparison we also recorded operation of messenger communication (gadu-gadu messenger, skype), web mail applications (gmail) and the system's background network activity. We analyzed also recorded operation of database (PostgreSQL) client and CAD systems.

Selection of tested web pages may influence the test results, especially with limited page list, so we attempt to select diverse types of websites, situated in different distance from our system. The list of tested sites and their approximated localization are presented in Table 1. The test were run in a way similar to Web-flow analysis model [4].

Selected url was activated in chosen browser with one mouse click and all network activity connected with presenting the content of the web page were recorded. After some pause (1–3 minutes) the test was repeated with the other browser or the next url. We start all browsers before tests and don't close them during the test because of various network activity of the starting browsers (contacting search engines, company web site, restoring visited pages etc.) adding to recorded test traffic.

Recorded data were inserted into database and a set of queries were run to derive the TCP flows. Exemplary picture of user's network activity is portrayed on Fig. 1 as a plot of consecutive net flows in time. A group of net flows with small flow start to flow start span compose *Web-flow*, a unit of network activity

Table 1. Tested websites and their localization

Website url	Localization	Protocol	Comments
cn.polsl.pl	on campus	http	
cordis.europa.eu	Brussels	http	portal
www.techrepublic.com	San Francisco, California	http	portal
gmail.com	Mountain View, California	https	webmail

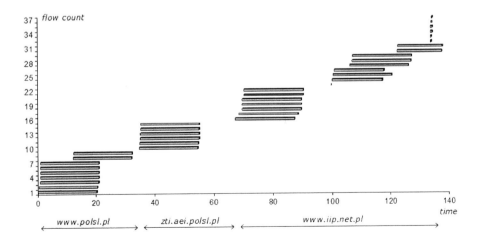

Fig. 1. Example of browser web-flow activity

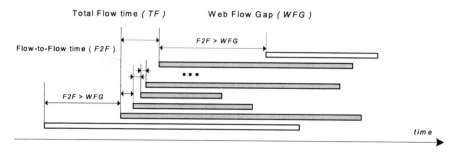

Fig. 2. Web-flow and net flows relationships

responding to user action. Detailed definition of parameters we use for temporal flows characterization is presented on Fig. 2.

TCP net flows were represented on the figure as the long narrow rectangles. Flows temporal characteristics depends on the values of interval between two next flow starts (*Flow-to-Flow* or *F2F*) times. A group of consecutive net flows with small F2F times constitute the *Web-flow*. Adjacent Web-flows are separated by F2F time greater then *Web Flow Gap* time (WFG). Duration of Web-flow or *Total Flow* time is equivalent to the sum of F2F times of N belonging net flows (grayed on Fig. 2).

The aim of our test was to find the values of F2F and TF times constituting Web-flows for given web sites and their dependency on the type of used browsers. From our test procedure the inter Web-flow interval (WFG time) will be forced to be greater then 10 to 30 seconds.

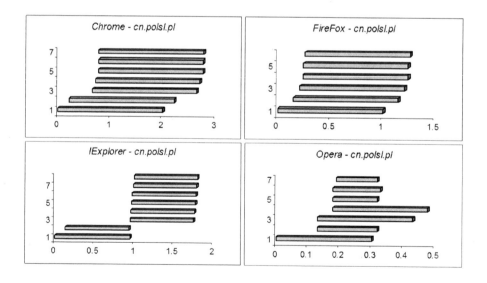

Fig. 3. Web-flow for cn.polsl.pl

3.3   Web Flow Analysis

Results of our test were presented graphically as plots of the same Web-flows obtained with selected browsers, side by side, and resulted temporal parameters of the Web-flows are presented in tables. The Fig. 3 presents the process of opening conference website `cn.polsl.pl`. The initial web page requires 6–7 net flows for completion. Nearly all plotted net flows were strongly shortened from original 3–5 minutes to 1–2 seconds, for plot resolution clarity. The Table 2 shows the values of flow parameters.

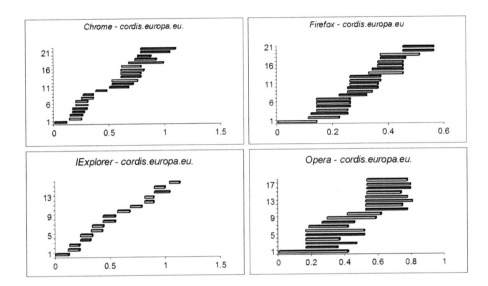

Fig. 4. Web-flow for cordis.europa.eu

Table 2. Web flow parameters for page cn.polsl.pl

Parameters	Chrome	Firefox	IExplorer	Opera
$F2F$ mean	0.130	0.209	0.143	0.0270
$F2F$ variance	0.028	0.115	0.089	0.0024
TF time	0.781	0.261	1.001	0.1880
N (flows number)	7	6	8	7

Next figure presents the Web-flows related to the opening the link of `cordis.europa.eu` site located in Belgium. The download of page require many TCP connections. The Figure 4 presents the plots of Web-flows, the Table 3 contains derived Web-flow parameters.

The next set of flow plots (Fig. 5) presents the operation of `techrepublic.com` site, located in California. Presumably due to longer transport delays the single click Web-flow splits in parts separated by inter flow gaps (WFG) bigger then 1-1.5 seconds. The Table 4 presents parameters of selected Web-flows. The web

Table 3. Web flow parameters for the page cordis.europa.eu

Parameters	Chrome	Firefox	IExplorer	Opera
F2F mean	0.036	0.022	0.067	0.032
F2F variance	0.043	0.0011	0.003	0.003
TF time	0.781	0.450	1.051	0.661
N (flows number)	21	20	17	21

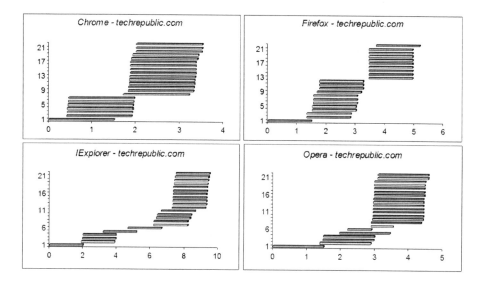

Fig. 5. Web-flows for `techrepublic.com`

Table 4. Parameters for the Web flow of `techrepublic.com`

Parameters	Chrome	Firefox	IExplorer	Opera
F2F mean	0.172	0.168	0.341	0.140
F2F variance	0.185	0.194	0.359	0.102
TF time	2.013	3.685	7.491	3.085
N (flows number)	22	22	22	22

mail applications make use of regular browsers, so their network activity looks very similar to previous cases. Figure 6 presents the flows related to user login to the `gmail.com` site, and derived flow parameters contain Table 5.

Comparing the obtained values of F2F parameter from this exemplary cases of web browsers operation one can notice that mean value of F2F is smaller then 400 ms, (in most cases much smaller then 200 ms), and the variance of F2F is generally smaller then mean value. The values of total flow time (*TF*) and the number of net flows in Web-flow are sometimes difficult to define and was chosen somewhat arbitrary. If web page contains any animations, the download

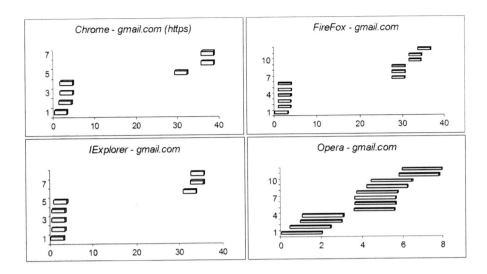

Fig. 6. Web-flows of login proces to `gmail.com`

Table 5. Parameters for the Web flow of `gmail.com`

Parameters	Chrome	Firefox	IExplorer	Opera
$F2F$ mean	0.497	0.156	0.178	0.347
$F2F$ variance	0.378	0.090	0.034	0.053
TF time	1.492	0.781	0.711	1.041
N (flows number)	4	6	5	4

continues through many TCP connections (30–50), without any clearly visible WFG gap.

There were many other then browser applications generating outbound network traffic. Two of them, communicators of the client-server type, *gadu-gadu*, and peer-to-peer type, *Skype* were also tested, and their behavior looks different. Figure 7 presents flow activity of both communicators. *Gadu-gadu* behaves like browser with web page containing animation, with F2F mean time of 0.078 s and F2F variance of 0.0022 s. The *Skype* HTTP communication is totally different. Single net flows arrives at random moments, and are probably connected with user textual communication. Similar activity is presented also on connections directed to port 443.

From other common system application similar to web browsers network activity manifests anti-virus programs, which continously periodically contacts their known sites. Figure 8 presents the operations of two such programs: *ESET NOD32 Antyvirus* and *COMODO AntiVirus*. The *F2F* time parameter has for NOD32 program values from 0.286 to 0.717 s.

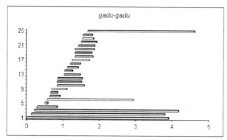
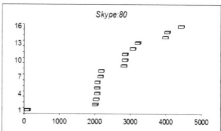

Fig. 7. Messengers net flows activity

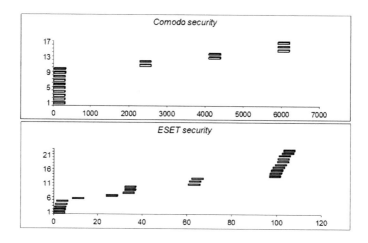

Fig. 8. Network flows of AntiVirus software

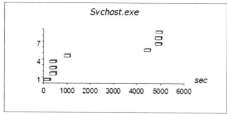
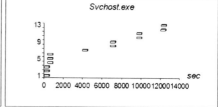

Fig. 9. Network HTTP activity of system services

The operating system network activity is also visible as HTTP outbound flows, however do not shows signs of regularity. On Fig. 9 there are presented network flows related to two different days of *svchost* service activity. The connections occures in unregular times, and their random, rather short (less then 500 ms) duration was, for visibility, extended on plot to about 500 seconds.

4   Conclusion

The concept of outgoing network traffic classification based on Web-flow model flows analysis was presented. Results of experiments confirm the ability of user initiated traffic selection based on the properties of outgoing network flows of typical user applications. Some initial values of flow-to-flow time (*F2F*) parameter intended as the basis for network traffic classification were identified. The tests results depend on application's embedded communication algorithms, so normal user activity has no influence on classification results (don't change minimal (*F2F*) times, chosen as the basis for application flows characterization). Examples of other types of system's network behavior were also presented.

In the future the examination of the effectiveness of Web-flow traffic classification model in the detection of malware generated network traffic is planned, for incorporation as additional way of improving the efficiency of N-IDS system in network threats detection.

References

1. Choi, H.K., Limb, J.O.: A Behavioral Model of Web Traffic. In: ICNP 1999 Proceedings of the Seventh International Conference on Network Protocols, pp. 327–334. IEEE Press, Washington (1999)
2. Hernandez-Campos, F., Jeffay, K., Smith, F.D.: Tracking the Evolution of Web Traffic: 1995-2003. In: Proceedings of the 11 th IEEE/ACM International Symposium on Modeling, Analysis, and Simulation of Computer and Telecommunication Systems (MASCOTS), Orlando, pp. 16–25 (2003)
3. Lee, J.J., Gupta, M.: A new traffic model for current user web browsing behavior, `http://blogs.intel.com/research/` `HTTP%20Traffic%20Model_v1%201%20white%20paper.pdf`
4. Shuai, L., Xie, G., Yang, J.: Characterization of HTTP behavior on access networks in Web 2.0. In: International Conference on Telecommunications, ICT, pp. 1–6 (2008)
5. Kim, M.S., Wona, Y.J., Hong, J.W.: Characteristic analysis of internet traffic from the perspective of flows, `http://dpnm.postech.ac.kr/papers/` `Comp-Communications/06/flow-based-traffic-analysis.pdf`
6. What is netflow? `http://www.caligare.com/netflow/netflow.php`
7. ARGUS – Auditing Network Activity, `http://www.qosient.com/argus`

Numerical Performance in the Grid Network Relies on a Grid Appliance

Dariusz Czerwinski

Lublin University of Technology, 38A Nadbystrzycka Str, 20-618 Lublin, Poland
d.czerwinski@pollub.pl

Abstract. The author of this paper will introduce the issues related to performance of the numerical calculations carried out on non-homogeneous Grid network. Created Grid Network is running the Grid Appliance, which is based on a network operating system Ubuntu 9.04. The author performed the series of tests of this system. Performed tests demonstrated how the single node is working under different Grid configurations as well as what is the efficiency of the numerical calculations in a Grid network.

Keywords: computer networks, grid networks, Grid Appliance, numerical calculations.

1 Introduction

The purpose of a grid technology is to create a simple, but having great capabilities, virtual computer. The Grid Appliance is a self-configuring system for creating an ad-hoc pool of computing resources in both LAN and WAN networks. It is mainly used to perform tasks requiring high performance and which are long lasting.

Another application of a grid is to create a virtual cluster for education and training. In the Grid Appliance, systems are connected via a virtual peer-to-peer network using private IP addresses called IPOP. The Grid Appliance uses GroupVPN, easy to configure, group-oriented implementation of IPOP. After starting the system, it is automatically connected to the pool of resources and is able to send and carry out tasks using the Condor scheduler application [1].

2 Virtual Grid Network Built with the Grid Appliance

The Grid Appliance consists of three technology elements: virtual machines, virtual networks and grid scheduler. Virtual machines allow the entire virtual computer, working under Linux OS and the Grid Appliance software, act as a guest in our existing system (Windows, Linux or MacOS for Intel). All we need to do it is just to install the virtual machine hypervisor and the Grid Appliance.

The second element is a virtual network. The virtual networks are built using a technique IPOP routing peer-to-peer ACIS developed in the laboratory for self-configuring resource pool, even if the nodes are behind firewalls and NAT routers.

A. Kwiecień, P. Gaj, and P. Stera (Eds.): CN 2011, CCIS 160, pp. 214–223, 2011.

The last element is a grid scheduler. The author used the middleware Condor from the University of Wisconsin. Condor is a reliable system that continuously supports hundreds of thousands of machines and performs their tasks [2].

Condor scheduler is a software that creates high-performance computing environment called High-Throughput Computing. The software effectively uses the computing power of workstations that communicate over a network. The scheduler can manage the grouping of workstations.

The idea of the scheduler, which can detect the grid topology and can be flexible in the meaning of determination of the minimum job criteria for workers is discussed in the literature [3,4,5].

Condor scheduler meets these requirements. The user sends a job to Condor.

Condor diagnoses, which machines are available on the network and sends the next task to chosen machine. Condor is able to detect whether the device is working and whether it is available in the Grid network. It also determines the appropriate separation of tasks and can migrate the job to another machine in the case when the first worker does not meet the particular job criteria. Condor continues to work on a new machine from this point exactly where the last one was completed. We can configure the Condor manager in such a way that if the pool does not have any resources, such as all the other individuals are disabled or have suffered damage, the manager starts a job to do on the same machine. Such configuration of the manager is called personal Condor.

Hosts in the Grid Appliance can be configured as client or worker. Client is a host which sends the tasks for calculations and the workers are making calculations. Worker hosts can also be configured in owner mode or dedicated mode.

Configuration in dedicated mode assumes that host is making calculations despite of the keyboard activity. In the owner mode Condor stops the calculations on host on which the keyboard activity was detected for 15 minutes.

The experimental network of computers linked together in a logical system acting as the Grid (Fig. 1) was built basing on required grid elements.

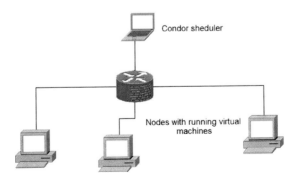

Fig. 1. The physical architecture of the Grid Appliance network

3   Tests of the Grid Network

This physical configuration allowed to build the logical Grid network using virtual machines. Oracle's VirtualBox V.3.2 software supporting hardware virtualization implemented in the processor was used for this purpose.

There were running up to three instances of virtual machines on the workstations. Finally this gave the infrastructure consisting of a maximum of three clients and six stations called Workers (Fig. 2).

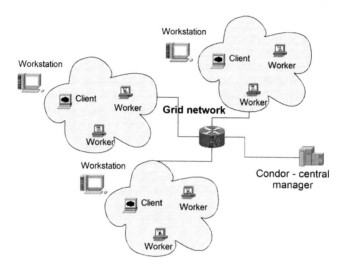

Fig. 2. Logical architecture of the built Grid Appliance network

During the tests configuration of hardware, software and network grid as well as the prevailing conditions in the local network remain unchanged.

After the test configuration changes are made (for example number of computers, configuration as customer or worker) and another test is performed.

The first step of the tests consisted in downloading and installing the application for testing at the terminals. Then the cron script was prepared to run every few / several seconds (depending on how long is the benchmark). The script is designed to store the necessary information to a text files for future analysis.

The next step was the selection of a benchmark, which can run on the built grid network. Benchmarking of the grid networks and techniques used for this purpose, are widely discussed in literature [6,7,8,9].

There are a lot of benchmark suites, which may be chosen (i.e. linpack, hpl, sparsbench, Dhrystone, nas, Whetstone). Because of the future destination of the grid network for numerical computations, the author decided to select a Whetstone benchmark.

4   Tests Carriage

The individual tests were conducted under similar conditions in order to produce a reference to earlier data. During the test the nodes were not loaded additionally. Benchmark, which has been implemented in the test is written in C language by Robert Richard Painter belonging to the IEEE (English Institute of Electrical and Electronics Engineers). Algorithm included in that benchmark was written in 1972 at the National Physics Laboratory in the UK [10]. Benchmark consists of the following modules:

1. Simple variables,
2. Matrix elements,
3. Matrix as a parameter,
4. Conditional jumps,
5. Integer arithmetic,
6. Trigonometric functions,
7. Procedure calls,
8. References to the matrix,
9. Standard functions.

The results are given in the unit of MIPS calculated by the Whetstone algorithm. Other variables included in the output file are: the number of repetitions of calculations, the number of iterations and execution time of the program on a single instance.

Furthermore the following parameters were monitored during tests: processor load, RAM memory utilization and network traffic in a virtual private network.

Condor (from the University of Wisconsin) was used as the main tasks scheduler. It is a set of services for parallel task execution management. Running Condor in a dedicated mode enforces the unconditional acceptance and execution of tasks by the host. The following conditions are determined in the works acceptance condition for owner's default mode: no keyboard activity within fifteen minutes, and processor usage in the background lower than 5%.

Hardware configuration of nodes was as follows:

- A: Intel® Core™ Solo T1300 (2 MB Cache, 1.66 GHz, 667 MHz FSB) – reserved 512 MB RAM for VM,
- B: Intel® Pentium® 4 (1 MB Cache, 3.00 GHz, 800 MHz FSB) – reserved 256 MB RAM for VM,
- C: Intel® Pentium® 4 (1 MB Cache, 3.60 GHz, 800 MHz FSB) – reserved 1024 MB RAM for VM,
- D: Intel® Pentium® E5300 (2 MB Cache, 2.60 GHz, 800 MHz FSB) – reserved 2048 MB RAM for VM.

The operating systems used for the tests are: Ubuntu Linux 9.04 in virtual machines. The virtual machines were running on the hosts computers described above. Oracle VirtualBox version 3.2.0 was used as the Hypervisor for virtual machines. The configuration of the nodes during test is shown in Table 1.

Each test consists in the addition of ten benchmark computational instances to the queue of Condor manager.

5 Tests Results

Performed tests of grid network gave the interesting results. For comparison of performance, time values for each configuration presented in Table 1, are shown on Fig. 3.

The best performance of the calculations in the grid network has been obtained in the test number 1 and 6. Grid configuration during these tests is almost the same, the only difference is that in test number 6 grid was configured with owner mode, but there was no keyboard activity and consequently no blackouts were observed. We can compare these tests with the test number 2 without any keyboard activity and we can observe blackouts during calculations.

Let us compare the nodes CPU performance on the basis of information shown in Table 2.

Table 1. Configuration of the nodes during tests

Test number	Host A	Host B	Host C	Host D	Comments
1	client	worker	worker	worker	dedicated mode
2	client	worker	worker	worker	owner mode
3	personal Condor	X	X	X	
6	client	worker	worker	worker	owner mode, no keyboard input
7	X	personal Condor	X	X	
8	X	X	X	personal Condor	
9	X	X	personal Condor	X	

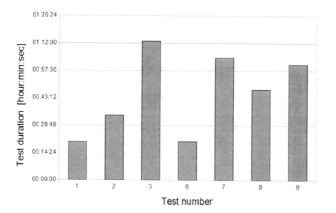

Fig. 3. Comparison of the tests duration

Table 2. Configuration of the nodes during tests [11]

CPU performance	Host A	Host B	Host C	Host D
Dhrystone 2.1 (VAX MIPS)	2296.61	2362.07	2874.10	4143.43
Linpack 100x100 (MFLOPS)	922.31	924.61	1066.58	1374.18

Taking into consideration Linpack tests we can see that Host A is the weakest host, Host B performs 0.25% better than A, Host C performs 15.64% better than A and Host D performs 48.99% better than A.

Host A during tests made all calculations (test number 3 in Fig. 3) in 73 minutes. If we consider that we have three additional hosts which performed better than Host A the duration of test in grid network should be much shorter. Making calculation with the differences between hosts assumed by the author, the final numerical tests time should be equal to 15 minutes 42 seconds.

Comparing calculated time with measured time (19 minutes 25 seconds) we have 3 minutes 43 seconds of difference (i.e. about 19%). Therefore the conclusion can be made that we can predict the numerical calculation time but with the 20% margin.

Let us take a look at test number 1 and 3 on Fig. 3. In test number 3 we have the slowest machine Host A performing numerical calculations in the time of 1 hour 12 minutes 59 seconds and in test number 1 we have additional three faster machines. We expected that the final time should be 4 times shorter, but in fact it was 3.1 shorter.

Grid network did not perform as we expected owing to additional tasks resulting from the Grid Appliance functioning.

To discover how calculations are made in the grid let's take a look at the Fig. 4 showing the nodes CPU utilization during test number 1. We can notice that not all machines are making numerical calculations.

Machine with central manager Condor does not make calculations. Hosts which are making calculations have short time breaks needed for sending a part of calculations to central manager and obtaining a new portion (Fig. 4).

Comparing this information with network traffic presented on Fig. 5 we can see maximum network traffic during the short time periods where CPU usage drops below the value of 35%.

The lowest CPU usage in host running central manager Condor we can observe during test number 1, a little bit higher during other tests. CPU usage is very low in comparison with the nodes configured as workers.

The following graph (Fig. 5) shows the traffic vs. time for test number 1.

We can therefore conclude that the fundamental difference in the configuration refers to the rules for the adoption of tasks, not their execution.

The hosts taking the task made the calculations using the maximum processing power regardless of the configuration.

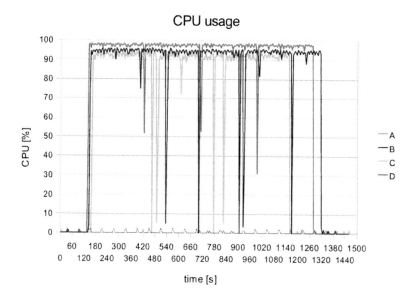

Fig. 4. Nodes CPU usage during the test No. 1

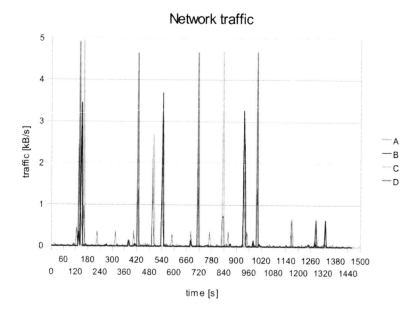

Fig. 5. Network traffic versus time for test No. 1

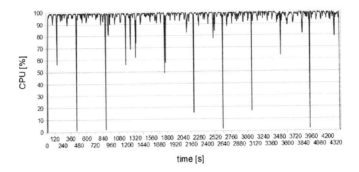

Fig. 6. Host A CPU usage during test No. 3

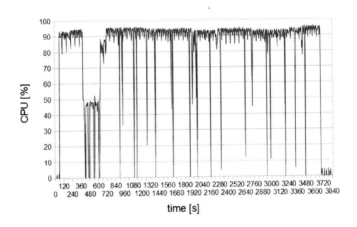

Fig. 7. Host C CPU utilization during test No. 9

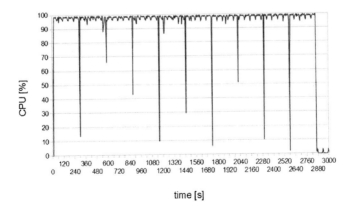

Fig. 8. Host D CPU utilization during test No. 8

Another aspect of the tests was to observe the CPU usage for the stations configured in the personal condor mode. In this mode we can see what is the performance of the single station for the whole benchmark. Let us compare three workstations called host A, host C and host D (weakest, medium and the strongest).

In Fig. 6 we can see the CPU usage of host A the weakest one in the pool.

The average utilization of the CPU of this host during the whole benchmark was about 95.7%. At the Fig. 7 we can see the CPU utilization of the host C.

The average utilization of the CPU of host C during the whole benchmark was about 84%. At the Fig. 8 we can see the CPU utilization of the host D (the strongest one).

The average utilization of the CPU of host D during the whole benchmark was about 91.7%.

Observing these figures, we can see that the instantaneous CPU utilization changes dynamically in the moments when the hosts are running additional processes and when data packages for the calculations are collected and returned.

6   Conclusions

In this paper the author presented the results of the numerical performance tests performed in non-homogeneous grid network.

The benchmarking process is based on the execution of the Whetstone benchmark suite, with an appropriate grid configuration, to emphasize the computational capabilities of the testbed.

The execution of benchmark with the critical problem size, has been used to analyze the potential gain in performance that a grid site could obtain.

We can also obtain the speedup that can be expected when executing High Throughput Computing applications on the Grid. Overall performance of the grid network in numerical tests is equal to about 7100 VAX MIPS.

Even such a small grid network enabled to obtain promising results and significantly reduced the numerical problem calculation time.

Installed central manager (Condor) can recognize the efficiency of the single nodes in grid network and assign more tasks to host with higher resources.

Due to the fact that the number of nodes available in the Condor pool is variable, we should plan on dynamically adjusting the number of workers to approximately match the number of nodes available in the pool at run-time.

The author has shown, that the implementation of the non-homogeneous Grid network largely improves the numerical calculations even when the hardware resources are limited.

References

1. Wikipedia Grid Technology, http://pl.wikipedia.org/wiki/Grid_(system)
2. Manual of the Grid Appliance, http://www.grid-appliance.org

3. Mastroianni, C., Talia, D., Verta, O.: A super-peer model for resource discovery services in large-scale Grids. In: Future Generation Computer Systems, vol. 21, pp. 1235–1248. Elsevier, Amsterdam (2005)
4. Brugnoli, M., Heymann, E., Senar, M.A.: Grid Scheduling Based on Collaborative Random Early Detection Strategies. In: 18th Euromicro Conference on Parallel, Distributed and Network-based Processing, Italy (2010)
5. Gorawski, M., Bańkowski, S., Gorawski, M.: The Software Agents in a Database Grid. In: Proceedings of the International Multiconference on Computer Science and Information Technology, Poland (2005)
6. Tsouloupas, G., Dikaiakos, M.D.: GridBench: A Tool for the Interactive Performance Exploration of Grid Infrastructures. Journal of Parallel and Distributed Computing 67, 1029–1045 (2007)
7. Dikaiakos, M.D.: Grid benchmarking: vision, challenges, and current status. Journal Concurrency and Computation: Practice & Experience Archive 19(1), 89–105 (2007)
8. Bailey, D.H., Barszcz, E., Barton, J.T., Browning, D.S., Carter, R.L., Dagum, D., Fatoohi, R.A., Frederickson, P.O., Lasinski, T.A., Schreiber, R.S., Simon, H.D., Venkatakrishnan, V.S., Weeratunga, K.: The nas parallel benchmarks. The International Journal of Supercomputer Applications 5(3), 63–73 (1991)
9. Nadeem, F., Prodan, R., Fahringer, T., Iosup, A.: Benchmarking Grid Applications. CoreGRID Technical Report Number TR-0104, CoreGRID – Network of Excellence (2007)
10. Benchmark Programs and Reports, `http://www.netlib.org/benchmark`
11. CPU World, `http://www.cpu-world.com`

Use of Holt-Winters Method in the Analysis of Network Traffic: Case Study

Maciej Szmit and Anna Szmit

Technical University of Lodz, ul. Zeromskiego 116, 90-924 Lodz, Poland
Maciej.Szmit@gmail.com

Abstract. The article presents the results of analysis of a few kinds of network traffic using Holt-Winters method in the analysis of network traffic. The data were obtained from five real computer networks using Snort intruder detection system and preprocessor AnomalyDetection.

Keywords: anomalies detection, IDS, Holt-Winters method.

1 Introduction

Intruder Detection Systems (IDS) are software or hardware solutions used for detection of intrusion trials to a protected network or a host. It is done by monitoring of network traffic, usage of resources of a protected computer system or by the analysis of system logs in order to detect suspicious actions and then take appropriate steps, which in the majority of cases is generation of an alert that communicates a detected danger. As to the way of detecting attacks, misuses detection systems and anomaly detection systems can be distinguished.

Misuse detection is the detection of defined behaviors which prove that an attack occurred whereas an anomaly detection takes for granted the existence of a predictive pattern of behaviors where their deviations are regarded as actions which can prove that a protected system was attacked. Misuse detection has, in the majority of cases, deterministic character (the rules matching the observed phenomena or action were found or not) and it is easier for algorithmization, whereas anomaly detection must refer more often to uncertain observations and has to use statistical methods[1].

One of the obvious areas in which predictive behavior patterns can be used is the anomaly-oriented analysis of computer network behavior, which in the literature is defined as NBAD – Network Behavioral Anomaly Detection, where single packages or a network traffic can be examined. The operation of

---

[1] Statistical measures have been used in IDS systems since 1987 and the first IDS in which they were implemented was "Haystack" project conducted in Los Alamos National Laboratory (compare e.g. [1] p. 432).

A. Kwiecień, P. Gaj, and P. Stera (Eds.): CN 2011, CCIS 160, pp. 224–231, 2011.

AnomalyDetection preprocessor which is used in this paper is based on the last approach[2] (also known as the network traffic analysis or network flow analysis[3]).

2 Research Area

The article presents research results of four small and middle-size networks in which the information on network traffic was collected during at least one month (in each of them) with 10 minutes intervals. Descriptions of networks are presented in the form of a table (Table 1).

Table 1. Description of examined networks. Source: [6] (network W1), [7] (networks T1 and T2), own study (network M4).

Net	Description
W1	Amateur campus network consisting of circa 25 workstations. Snort has worked on the router which acts also as the gateway to the Internet and as the following servers: FTP, Web, SAMBA, TeamSpeak. Data were collected from 13th September to 5th December 2006 with a ten minute interval (a total of 11 969 measurements).
T2	Campus network provided by a mid-size Internet Access Provider (about 400 clients). Data were collected from 3rd January to 16th March 2007 with ten-minute intervals (a total of 10 001 measurements) on the link between the network and the Internet in housing estates.
T3	A network in a block of flats; one of the subnetworks mentioned in the examples T2 containing about 20 clients. The data were collected from 20th November 2006 to 16th March 2007 with ten-minute intervals (a total of 16 402 measurements) on the same link as above (T2) but with address filtering.
M4	Home network connected to the campus amateur network (with maximum speed of inbound traffic set on the bandwidth manager to 4 Mbps. Home network consists of five computers protected by corporate firewall and two intranet servers (ftp and PrintServer). The network has no servers providing outside services and there is no remote access to the home network from the outside. IDS was placed on the link to the campus network before the firewall. The data were collected from 12th November to 2nd January 2011 with ten-minute intervals (a total of 7 453 measurements).

---

[2] Anomaly detection mechanism is also used by pre-processors such as SPADE (Statistical Packet Analysis and Detection Engine), after commercialization it was developed under the name Spice and then abandoned, it was using a so called correlation of packets, or Snort+AI that uses artificial neural networks to detect scanning of ports PHAD (Packet Header Anomaly Detection) – see e.g. [2,3,4].

[3] See e.g. [5,2].

3   Research Methodology

Anomaly detection is a complex notion taking into consideration a complex character of mechanisms operating in contemporary networks, different characters of networks and irregularity of users' behaviors. There are a lot of researches applying different statistical and artificial intelligence-based methods[4] in IDS systems. It is necessary to implement a mechanism of "standard-behavior" (predictive pattern) recognition and kind of learning in anomaly detection-bases IDS.

AnomalyDetection[5] is a preprocessor for popular IDS Snort, which enables analysis of different kinds of network traffic in order to detect its anomalies. The first version of AnomalyDetection preprocessor was created in a master thesis [6]. Its current version with a symbol 2.5 gathers information on network traffic, and more precisely on twenty nine traffic components (individual packets types, for example ARP-request or ICMP).

In the first version of the preprocessor generation of the so-called profiles of network was implemented on the basis of data collected for a period in question describing their behaviors (by mean and standard deviation of a given parameter) in weekly intervals. Nowadays it is being tried to implement more complex and better methods of statistical Time Series Analysis. Use of Winters model described below is one of such trials common in the literature[6]. The purpose of the presented tests was to analyse the applicability of Holt-Winters models to the empirically obtained time series, and in particular to check whether this applicability (measured with MAE error) depends on the type of modelled traffic.

Holt-Winters model, known also as a triple model of exponential smoothing[7] was defined as a version of model of simple exponential smoothing and Holt model designed for trend estimation and seasonality[8]. In the additive version it is a simplified version of time series y_t as the sum of three elements:

$$\hat{y}_t = S_t + F_t + C_{t-r} \tag{1}$$

---

[4] E.g. Bayesian conditional probability (see e.g. [1], p. 422 and further), entropy measurement, the so-called package correlation, Principal Component Analysis, support vector machines, algorithms of adaptive thresholding and cumulative sums, data clustering, k-NN, K Nearest Neighbors Methods, decision trees, artificial neuron networks, induction of decisional rules, immune algorithms, genetic algorithms, fuzzy logic.

[5] Preprocessor can be downloaded from the following address
http://anomalydetection.maciej.szmit.info

[6] See e.g. [8].

[7] See [9], p. 248.

[8] Please note that in computer networks a phenomena of overlaying of several types of seasoning may occur, and then the Winters method in its basic version may prove insufficient. It would then be advisable to consider methods that take the multiple seasonality into account, for example the extended Winters method proposed by Taylor [10]. In the series gathered so far, besides the daily seasonality one could suspect a weekly seasonality, but the series were too short to attempt its modelling.

where

$$F_t = \alpha(y_t - C_{t-r}) + (1 - \alpha)(F_{t-1} + S_{t-1}) \qquad (2)$$

is responsible for the smoothing of the deseasonalized component

$$S_t = \beta(F_t - F_{t-1}) + (1 - \beta)S_{t-1} \qquad (3)$$

is responsible for estimate of the trend

$$C_t = \gamma(y_t - F_t) + (1 - \gamma)C_{t-r} \qquad (4)$$

is a seasonal component series, where α, β and γ are parameters of smoothing estimated for series. These parameters are chosen in the iterative way taking a minimization of errors measurement as a criteria[9]. In case of described models the sums of absolute value of residuals were minimized.

4   Results and Conclusions

Table 2 presents the results obtained for the network traffic[10] from four networks described in Table 1. The network traffic was analyzed within single protocols and not in the way it is often done- as a totality of network traffic (total number of frames). Taking the substantial part into consideration seems to be justified by the fact that single protocols were different as far as their characters (unreliable & reliable, connection-oriented & connectionless) and applications are concerned. It can be expected that ICMP communicators will be more common in anomalous situations[11] but TCP incoming traffic intensity will increase in case of connection problems (as a result of the closure of sliding window and in return the increase of the number of acknowledgments and negative acknowledgements) whereas UDP traffic intensity can simply decrease when parts of datagrams are lost.

The table presents respectively:

– Value of autocorrelation factor (Pearson's correlation coefficient) with the value of variable obtained 24 hours earlier ϱ_{-24},
– value of the test of significance of this correlation (for the hypothesis that $E(r) = 0$),

---

[9] "It is common to choose such a value of parameter (...) so that the measurement of accuracy of ex post prognosis was as small as possible" [11] p. 187; "(...) and then the prognosis is compared against a real realization of a variable (...) and a constant is chosen by which, according to the adopted criteria, the prognosis best approximates the real realization of a predicted variable" [12] p. 226; "values of these parameters can be chosen (...) using the experiment method, minimizing the average of mean squared error of ex post prognosis for prognosis with one-period advance" [13] p. 76–77.

[10] For cumulative traffic i.e. a traffic which includes a sum of single parameters of traffic for the whole hour (six periods of ten minutes).

[11] There are two kinds of ICMP reports- information reports and error reports. Compare: [14] p. 17 and further.

Table 2. Results achieved (source: own study)

		ϱ-24	U test	p-value	Naïve method (-24 hours)		Winters Model				
					MAE/M [%]	MAE	MAE/M [%]	MAE	α	β	γ
W1	TCP	0.200	8.18	2.2e-16	82.19	535 610.5	59.09	385 113.7	0.4632	0.0084	0.0957
	UDP	0.210	8.82	0	96.76	44 138.0	68.72	31 347.5	0.5090	0.0027	0.2779
	ICMP	0.010	0.39	0.69	135.83	1 184.4	75.80	660.9	0.7975	0.0208	0.3410
T2	TCP	0.581	28.68	0	15.47	993 930.9	9.47	608 595.2	0.7967	0.0141	1.0000
	UDP	0.698	39.17	0	32.10	242 623.5	23.57	178 160.4	0.9109	0.0120	0.5837
	ICMP	0.571	27.90	0	39.63	77 267.4	18.79	36 625.8	0.8118	0.0028	1.0000
T3	TCP	0.586	29.31	0	14.99	937 742.2	7.34	459 533.6	0.8725	0.0010	1.0000
	UDP	0.758	47.12	0	30.28	288 926.9	20.88	199 214.5	0.7141	0.0042	0.1895
	ICMP	0.540	25.99	0	42.62	67 065.3	19.29	30 349.1	0.9291	0.0169	1.0000
M4	TCP	0.003	0.10	0.92	176.84	39 283.7	183.05	40 664.1	0.7062	0.0054	0.5419
	UDP	0.747	39.20	0	36.60	927.2	29.13	738.2	0.5428	0.0205	0.2812
	ICMP	0.278	10.10	0	17.17	50.5	14.86	43.7	0.5719	0.0336	0.3534

- p-value for the whole test,
- Mean Absolute Error referred to the average traffic in the whole test period[12] (MAE/M) and the values of mean absolute errors (MAE) for a naïve method (predicting that current traffic will be equal to the one which was 24 hours earlier),
- Values of the same statistics for Winters model,
- Values of α, β and γ parameters for these models[13].

In the examined networks, in two cases, there is no autocorrelation with the 24 hours delayed variable (ICMP traffic in the network W1 and TCP traffic in network M4).

In other cases the autocorrelation coefficients are significant, which proves (especially when taking into account the shape of a graph) the seasonality of series in all these cases.

Additionally, the quality of naïve method as well as Winters models for different kinds of networks and different kinds of traffic were significantly different. The best results were achieved by Winters model for TCP traffic in T2 network and naïve prognosis for TCP in the network T3. The last case is presented[14] in Fig. 1. As it can be observed, apart from three cases connected with rapid decrease of network traffic[15] the values of errors were really small.

TCP traffic in the network M4 (see Fig. 2) proved to be the second extreme of the quality of models: errors received for Winters model were bigger even than the ones received on the basis of naïve method. It is evident because TCP traffic in this network had an irregular character. It is doubtful whether it is possible

---

[12] Since in some observations the traffic of a given type of network traffic was close to zero, it was impossible to calculate the Mean Absolute Percentage Error.

[13] Parameters of Winters model were selected individually for each network and type of traffic so that to limit the average error for this data series.

[14] The figures present the real traffic in time, traffic resulting from Winters model and error value, respectively. All figures present 24-days period.

[15] A general evaluation would lead to a conclusion that one deals with anomaly of network traffic.

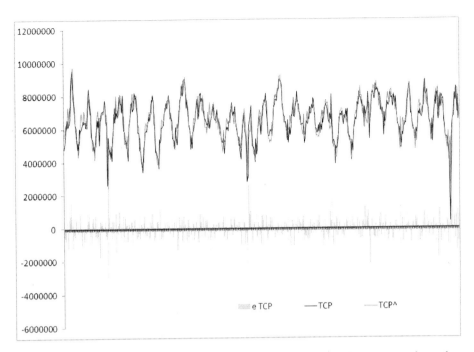

Fig. 1. TCP traffic in the network T3. Source: own study (TCP – measured number of TCP packets per time unit; TCP^ – value resulting from the Winters model; $e =$ TCP – TCP^ – residuals).

to create any predictive pattern with reasonable prognosis of errors for this kind of traffic. On the other hand, ICMP traffic in the network M4 comparing with ICMP traffic in other networks was characterized by much bigger regularity, and both a naïve method and Winters model had smaller errors in comparison with the same models of ICMP traffic in other networks. We can expect that it is an effect of a relatively high level of ICMP traffic (oscillating around 250 packages per hour) and unprofessional character of this network administration; it seems probable that in the network there was at least one source of ICMP traffic, operating all the time (e.g. error in router configuration, zombie participating in DDoS attack and so on). A good quality of the model does not have to mean lack of activities requiring the attention of a security specialist.

Beside situations in which there were no ICMP messages, there were packet storms which probably meant the abnormal situations which should implicate generating an alarm for the network administrator. In this case and in situation presented in the Fig. 2 Winters models prognosed a negative traffic of packages, which of course has no physical sense. In reality, it is necessary to apply at least one condition in order to make an estimated traffic negative[16].

---

[16] Different ways of realization of this constraint can be imagined – e.g. by adding big constant value to the observed value (which would allow to maintain the sense of the model) or by replacing forecasted negative values with zeros (which would correspond better to reality) etc.

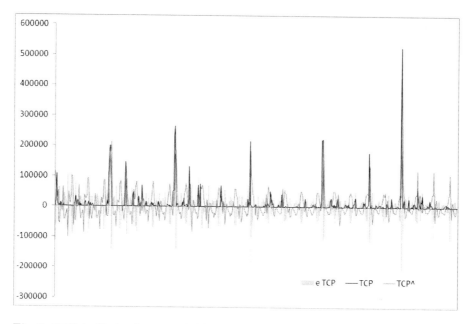

Fig. 2. TCP traffic in the network M4. Source: own study (TCP – measured number of TCP packets per time unit; TCP^ – value resulting from the Winters model; $e =$ TCP – TCP^ – residuals).

Also for UDP traffic the Winters models had different quality. Starting from an error below 21% in the network T3 up to 68% in the network W1.

The following conclusions can be drawn from the research presented above:

1. While analyzing network traffic, the analysis should not only refer to the whole traffic (which is in the majority of cases dominated by TCP packages), as it happens in many cases concerning traffic modelling. Although when this kind of traffic is characterized by high level of regularity, it enables the creation of models with formally good parameters but it will cause the loss of valuable information on anomaly visible in the different kinds of traffic.
2. Characteristics of networks can be very different. Kinds of traffics in the same network are different as well. Winters method can bring both: relatively good (with error below 10%) and poor effects (with tens of percents of errors), even excluding a case of irregular M4 network). The model applicability and adequacy should be analyzed individually in each case. Obviously this level of model errors may be considered unsatisfactory (though these are several dozen percent better than the results achieved in a naïve method), but it may form a reference level for other models that are under development.
3. The fact that network traffic in a tested period is regular and that it is possible to build a predictive pattern of behaviour or model with low MAE is not equal to the statement that there are no alarming phenomena in the network. Particularly high intensity of certain types of packets (ARP-reply,

DNS-response, ICMP-redirect and so on) may indicate attacks (e.g. ARP-spoofing or DNS cache positioning), especially when frequency of appearing of this kind of packets is regular and high.

References

1. Pieprzyk, J., Hardjono, T., Seberry, J.: Teoria bezpieczeństwa systemów komputerowych. Helion (2005)
2. Skowronski, M., Wezyk, R., Szmit, M.: Detekcja anomalii ruchu sieciowego w programie Snort. Hakin 9(3), 64–68 (2007)
3. Skowronski, M., Wezyk, R., Szmit, M.: Preprocesory detekcji anomalii dla programu Snort. In: Sieci Komputerowe, Aplikacje i zastosowania, vol. 2, pp. 333–338. Wydawnictwa Komunikacji i Lacznosci, Gliwice (2007)
4. Mahoney, M.V., Chan, P.K.: PHAD: Packet Header Anomaly Detection for Identifying Hostile Network Traffic. Florida Institute of Technology Technical Report CS-2001-04, http://citeseerx.ist.psu.edu/viewdoc/download?doi=10.1.1.15.4041&rep=rep1&type=pdf
5. Szmit, M., Wezyk, R., Skowronski, M., Szmit, A.: Traffic Anomaly Detection with Snort. In: Information Systems Architecture and Technology. Information Systems and Computer Communication Networks. Wydawnictwo Politechniki Wroclawskiej, Wroclaw (2007), http://maciej.szmit.info/documents/szmit_wezyk_skowronski_szmit_ebook.pdf
6. Skowronski, M., Wezyk, R.: Systemy detekcji intruzow i aktywnej odpowiedzi. Master thesis prepared In Computer Engineering Department of Technical University of Lodz, tutored by Maciej Szmit, typescript, Lodz (2006)
7. Tynenski, A.: Bezpieczeństwo sieci komputerowych. Autorska dystrybucja systemu Linux. Master thesis prepared In Computer Engineering Department of Technical University of Lodz, tutored by Maciej Szmit, typescript, Lodz (2008)
8. Brutlag, J.: Aberrant behavior detection in time series for network monitoring. In: Usenix 14th System Administration Conference, LISA (2000), http://www.usenix.org/events/lisa00/full_papers/brutlag/brutlag_html/
9. Guzik, B., Appenzeller, D., Jurek, W.: Prognozowanie i symulacje. Wybrane zagadnienia. Wydawnictwo AE w Poznaniu, Poznan (2004)
10. Taylor, J.W.: Exponentially weighted methods for forecasting intraday time series with multiple seasonal cycles. International Journal of Forecasting 26, 627–646 (2010)
11. Gajda, J.B.: Prognozowanie i symulacja a decyzje gospodarcze. C.H.Beck, Warszawa (2001)
12. Zelias, A., Pawełek, B., Wanat, S.: Prognozowanie ekonomiczne. Teoria, przykłady, zadania. Wydawnictwo Naukowe PWN, Warszawa (2004)
13. Cieslak, M. (ed.): Prognozowanie gospodarcze. Wydawnictwo AE, Wroclaw (1998)
14. Postel, J.: Request for Comments 792: Internet Control Message Protocol. DARPA (1972), http://www.rfc-editor.org/rfc/rfc792.txt

Bandwidth Efficient TCP Frame Design without Acknowledgment Number Field

Asjad Amin, Kanwal Afreen, Abida Shaheen,
Tayyabah Nadeem, and
Nida Rashid

Department of Telecommunication and Electronic Engineering,
The Islamia University of Bahawalpur, Pakistan
asjad.amin@iub.edu.pk, kanwal.afreen@gmail.com, abida.rao01@gmail.com,
tayyabah84@yahoo.com, nida-malik1@live.com

Abstract. This paper presents a novel design of a TCP frame. Unlike the original design, proposed design does not include 32 bit acknowledgment number field. This modified TCP design is discussed with the help of state diagrams, pseudo code, general equations and computer simulations. A comparison is then made between suggested and original design for simplex, duplex and pipelined case. The result clearly indicates that our design provides same kind of functionality for any case but with reduced header size. This reduction of header size decreases transmission time, increases bandwidth efficiency which in return increases throughput.

Keywords: TCP, simplex, duplex, pipelining.

1   Introduction

TCP provides core functionality for almost every application running on any kind of network. The Transmission Control Protocol (TCP) is the de-facto standard used by the internet community to handle bulk transfers [1]. Transmission control protocol (TCP) has become the dominant communication protocol suite in today's multimedia applications [2]. From old but reliable Ethernet to complex sensor networks, reliability of efficient and accurate communication heavily depends on the performance of TCP.

Communication networks have evolved greatly in the last decade [2]. An ignored factor affecting end-to-end TCP performance is the transmission time of ACK packets [3]. The influence of ACK packets on the throughput is also usually neglected when analyzing TCP [3–5] due to its small size compared to DATA packets. Reducing the size of header but keeping the original functionality in place is achieved by our new design that is proposed in this research paper. It does not involve any complex algorithms rather some small but intelligent modifications, at sender and receiver end, have made it possible. Careful designing

A. Kwiecień, P. Gaj, and P. Stera (Eds.): CN 2011, CCIS 160, pp. 232–241, 2011.
© Springer-Verlag Berlin Heidelberg 2011

assures that all the functionality that was with the acknowledgment field is still there with reduced header size even if the field is removed in our new design.

The paper is organized as follows: Sect. 2 presents the modified TCP frame structure, sender and receiver design for the modified system, Sect. 3 presents the TCP frame design for simplex system, Sect. 4 presents the TCP frame design for duplex and pipelined Duplex system, Sect. 5 presents conclusion remarks.

2 Modified TCP Frame Structure without Acknowledgment Field

In this research paper we present a new design for TCP frame that does not include Acknowledgment Number field. We save 32 bits in each packet which were used for acknowledgment in original design. With this design we can save thousands of bits for a large file. Original design and modified design is shown in Fig. 1 and Fig. 2 respectively.

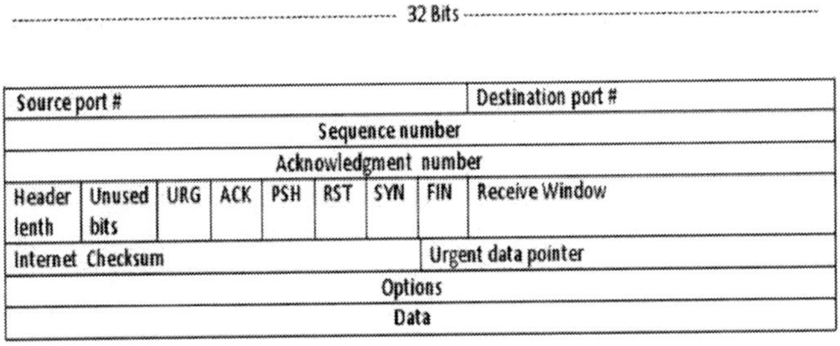

Fig. 1. TCP frame structure with 32 bit Acknowledgment Number

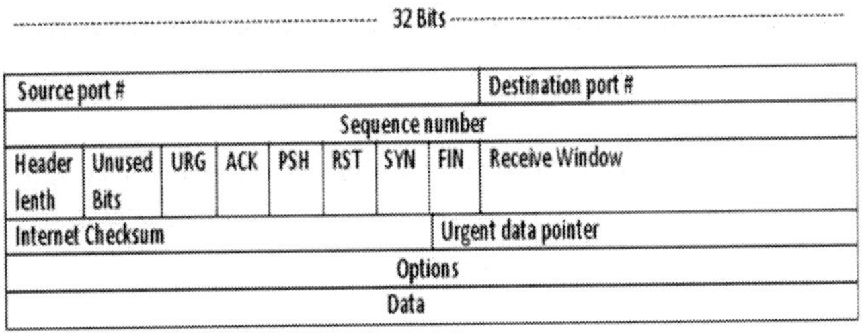

Fig. 2. TCP frame structure without 32 bit Acknowledgment Number

2.1 Receiver Design for TCP without Acknowledgment

Acknowledgment number is used to notify sender that data has been received successfully. We have therefore kept the functionality of acknowledgment in our new design even if the 32 bit acknowledgment field is removed. We achieve so by introducing two timers, one at sender and other at receiver end. Since acknowledgment field is removed, we use one bit ACK flag for a new purpose. Two events that can occur at receiver are:

Packet Received Successfully. A timer is placed at receiver. Transport Layer at receiver end receives packet from lower layers. In case of successful transmission receiver does not notify sender. Receiver simply extracts data, stop timer for received packet and start new timer for next packet.

Packet Received Unsuccessfully. In case if packet is lost or received in corrupted form the receiver discard corrupted packet and wait for timeout event. After timeout receiver prepares a response packet with ACK flag bit set to 1. Receiver then borrows the 1st 32 bits of options field and inserts the missing or corrupted sequence number in these 32 bits. An example of such packet is shown in Fig. 3.

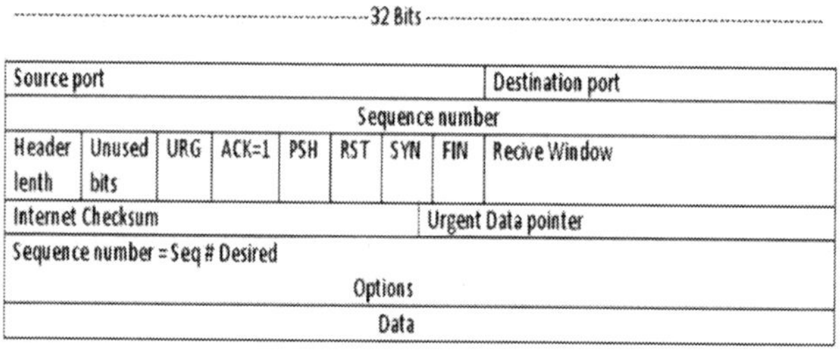

Source port								Destination port		
Sequence number										
Header lenth	Unused bits	URG	ACK=1	PSH	RST	SYN	FIN	Recive Window		
Internet Checksum							Urgent Data pointer			
Sequence number = Seq # Desired										
Options										
Data										

Fig. 3. TCP response packet for unsuccessful transmission, ACK=1

2.2 Sender Design for TCP without Acknowledgment

Sender sends a single or multiple packets depending on Window size and then waits for a certain time. In our design we have proposed Wait Time = One RTT. After one RTT sender can again start transmission. In case of successful transmission sender does not expect any acknowledgment. In opposite case, sender receives a packet with ACK bit = 1 which indicates that transmission of certain packet has not been successful. Sender then extracts the 1st 32 bits of option field that is the sequence number of missing packet. A packet with missing sequence number is sent again. Figure 4 and Fig. 5 show the state diagram for sender and receiver.

Receiver receives a packet and automatically start timer for next packet so a timer may be started even after receiving the last packet. It happens mainly because receiver has no knowledge if the packet received is last or not. To resolve the problem, an end packet is sent after the transmission is completed. Sender makes a special end packet by setting 1st 32 bit of option field equal to 32 0's and data field is set to 64 1's. When receiver receives a packet with such settings, it understands that transmission has ended and stops timer.

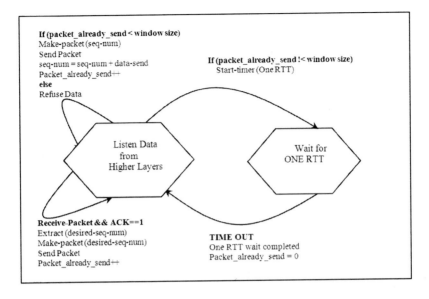

Fig. 4. State diagram for sender

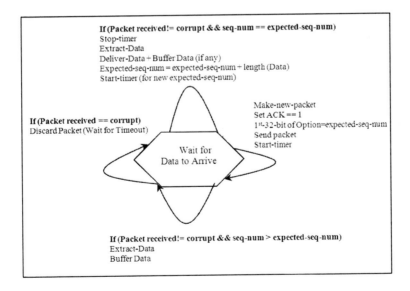

Fig. 5. State diagram for receiver

2.3   Pseudo Code for Sender and Receiver

```
*****    Sender   *****
while (! End data())
{
if (event == 1)
Collect data from above
Create TCP segment with sequence number
if (data-already-send < n)
Give TCP segment to network layer for transmission
Data-already-send++
Seq-num = seq-num + length(data-transmitted)
else
Data-already-send = 0
Wait for (one RTT)
if (event == 2)
Packet received
if (ACK == 1)
Desired-seq-num = Get(1st-32bit-option)
if (desired-seq-num <= last-seq-num-data)
Create TCP segment with desired-seq-num
Data-already-send++
else
Create TCP segment with seq-num= "000000..." 32 0's
Set the data field to " 1111111111111111111111" 64 1's
}


*****    Receiver   *****
while (forever)
{
if (event == 1)
Collect data from below
if (receive-packet != corrupt && receive-seq-num ==  expected-seq-num)
Stop timer ()
Extract-data
Deliver data to upper layers
Expected-seq-num = expected-seq-num + length(data-received + data-buffered)
Start-timer ( ) (for next packet)
if (receive - packet != corrupt && receive-seq-num > expected-seq-num)
Extract-data
Send data to buffer
if (receive-packet !=corrupt && receive-seq-num= "0000000000000000000000000000000000")
Extract-data
if (1st-64bit-data = "1111111111111111111" 64 1's )
Stop-timer ()
if (receive-data == corrupt)
Discard-packet
if (event == 2)
TIME OUT
Set ACK=1
Set 1st-32bit-option= expected-seq-num
Send
Start-timer ( )
}
```

3   TCP Frame Design for Simplex System

A simplex system indicates when one host sends and other receives. We consider a simplex system with two hosts Host A and Host B. Host A sends N number of packets to Host B. Host B only receives packets and does not send anything unless an unsuccessful transmission happens. In case of an unsuccessful transmission Host B sends a response packet with ACK = 1 and missing sequence number. Host A retransmits the missing packet.

3.1 TCP with Acknowledgment Field for Simplex System (Original Design)

$$Tr = [N * M]/B \tag{1}$$

The above equation gives transmission time if we use the original TCP frame structure. M is the size of packet and B is the link bandwidth. If C number packets get corrupted during transmission then

$$Tr = [((N + C) * M) + (C * M)]/B \ . \tag{2}$$

3.2 TCP without Acknowledgment Field for Simplex System

$$Tr = [(N + 1) * (M - 32)]/B \tag{3}$$

The above equation gives transmission time if we use the TCP frame structure without acknowledgment field. If C number packets get corrupted during transmission then

$$Tr = [(N + 1 + C) * (M - 32) + C * (M - 32)]/B \ . \tag{4}$$

For $M = d + h$, where d are the data bits and h are header bits, the throughput comes out to be

$$Tr = [N * d]/[(N + 1 + C) * (M - 32) + C * (M - 32)] \ . \tag{5}$$

4 TCP Frame Design for Duplex Pipelined System

A system where both the hosts transmit and receive is a Duplex system. We consider a system where Host A and Host B both transmits N number of packets to each other. In case of unsuccessful transmission, no separate response packet is generated. The next data packet to be sent is created with ACK flag bit equal to 1 and 1st 32 bit of option are filled with missing sequence number. These settings enable sender to learn about the unsuccessful transmission.

4.1 TCP with Acknowledgment Field for Duplex System (Original Design)

M is the size of packet and B is the link bandwidth. TrA is the time to transmit N packets from Host A to Host B and TrB is the time to transmit N packets from Host B to Host A. If $C1$ number of packets get corrupted during transmission form Host A to Host B and $C2$ number of packets gets corrupted from Host B to Host A then

$$TrA = [((N + C1) * M) + 32 * C1]/B \tag{6}$$

$$TrB = [((N + C2) * M) + 32 * C2]/B \ . \tag{7}$$

4.2 TCP without Acknowledgment Field for Duplex System

$$TrA = [(N + C1 + 1) * (M - 32) + 32 * C1]/B \qquad (8)$$
$$TrB = [(N + C2 + 1) * (M - 32) + 32 * C2]/B \ . \qquad (9)$$

The above equation gives transmission time if we use the TCP frame structure without acknowledgment field. For $M = d + h$, where d are the data bits and h are header bits, the throughput comes out to be

$$TrA = [N * d]/[(N + 1 + C1) * (M - 32) + 32 * C1] \qquad (10)$$
$$TrB = [N * d]/[(N + 1 + C2) * (M - 32) + 32 * C2] \ . \qquad (11)$$

4.3 Duplex System with Pipelining

Pipelining allows sender to send multiple packets simultaneously. Number of packets that can be sent collectively depends on Window size. After sending one set of packets our system wait for one RTT and then start transmitting again. Congestion control is mainly achieved through varying window size as per different scenarios.

4.4 TCP with Acknowledgment Field for Pipelined System (Original Design)

M is the size of packet, W is the window size and B is the link bandwidth. TrA is the time to transmit N packets from Host A to Host B and TrB is the time to transmit N packets from Host B to Host A. If $C1$ number of packets get corrupted during transmission form Host A to Host B and $C2$ number of packets gets corrupted from Host B to Host A then

$$TrA = [((N + C1) * M) + 32 * C1 + ((N + C1)/W) * RTT]/B \qquad (12)$$
$$TrB = [((N + C2) * M) + 32 * C2 + ((N + C2)/W) * RTT]/B \ . \qquad (13)$$

4.5 TCP without Acknowledgment Field for Pipelined System

$$TrA = [\ (N + C1 + 1) * (M - 32) + 32 * C1 +$$
$$((N + C1 + 1)/W) * RTT \,] \, / \, B \qquad (14)$$
$$TrB = [\ (N + C2 + 1) * (M - 32) + 32 * C2 +$$
$$((N + C2 + 1)/W) * RTT \,] \, / \, B \ . \qquad (15)$$

The above equation gives transmission time if we use the TCP frame structure without acknowledgment field. Figure 6 compares transmission time for full Duplex system for different number of packets, N. Figure 7 compares transmission time for full Duplex system for different packet sizes, M. For $M = d + h$, where d are the data bits and h are header bits, the throughput comes out to be

$$Throughput(A) = [\,N * d\,]\,/\,[\,(N + 1 + C1) * (M - 32) + 32 * C1 +$$
$$((N + C1 + 1)/W) * RTT\,] \tag{16}$$
$$Throughput(B) = [\,N * d\,]\,/\,[\,(N + 1 + C2) * (M - 32) + 32 * C2 +$$
$$((N + C2 + 1)/W) * RTT\,] \;. \tag{17}$$

Figure 8 presents throughput for old and new design with Packet size, M and number of transmitted packets, N. Figure 9 presents throughput for TCP without acknowledgment against N and M with different probabilities of error, Pe.

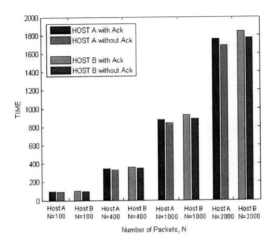

Fig. 6. Simulation results for full duplex system with different number of packets, N

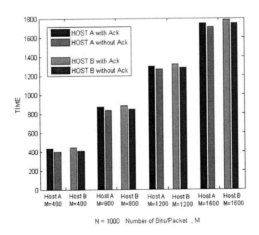

Fig. 7. Simulation results for full duplex system with different size of packet, M

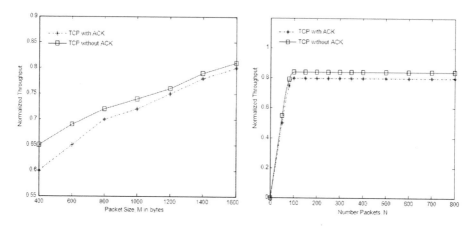

Fig. 8. Simulation results for full duplex system with different size of packet, M

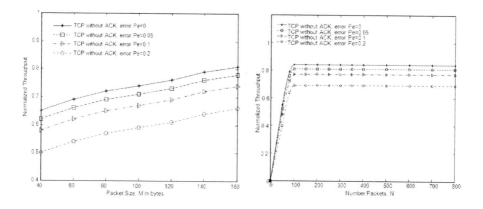

Fig. 9. Simulation results for full duplex system with different size of packet, M

5   Conclusion

A new TCP design has been discussed in detail with the help of sender and receiver state diagram, pseudo code and simulation results. The results, when compared with original design, clearly suggest that it gives better throughput and an increase in bandwidth efficiency. Further more the new design does not demand a lot of changing in existing system, rather an introduction of two small timers, one at sender and other at receiver will help us achieve the desired design. Still some work is needed to be done on the congestion control of this new system to make it more efficient in any kind of network.

Acknowledgments. We would like to thank our family for all the prayers and support. A very special thank to Shumaila for all the unasked motivation. A special thank to Dr. Rauf Baig as his presence even a couple years back made a big difference today. A special thank to te-b for giving enough confidence to convert a small thought to reality.

References

1. Talal, A., Guan, E.L., Oikonomou, G., Phillips, I.: Higher Order Delay Functions for Delay-Loss Based Congestion Control. In: 6th International Conference on Wireless Advanced, WiAD, pp. 1–6 (June 2010)
2. Xu, K., Tian, Y., Ansari, N.: TCP-Jersey for Wireless IP Communications. IEEE Journal on Selected Areas in Communications 22(4), 747–756 (2004)
3. Ding, L., Zhang, W., Yu, H., Wang, X., Xu, Y.: Incorporating TCP Acknowledgments in MAC Layer in IEEE 802.11 Multihop Ad Hoc Networks. In: IEEE Conference on Global Telecommunications, pp. 1–5 (2009)
4. Li, X., Kong, P.-Y., Chua, K.-C.: TCP performance in IEEE-802.11 based ad hoc networks with multiple wireless lossy links. IEEE Trans. on Mobile Computing 6(12), 1329–1342 (2007)
5. Padye, J., Firoiu, V., Towsley, D., Kurose, J.: Modelling TCP throughput: A simple model and its empirical validation. In: ACM SIGCOMM 1998 (1998)
6. Transmission Control Protocol. IETF, RFC 793 (1981)
7. Lefevre, F., Vivier, G.: Understanding TCP's behavior over wireless links. In: IEEE Symposium on Communication Vehicular Technology, SCVT, pp. 123–130 (2000)

Incorporating Small Length Data Cells in TCP Frame to Reduce Retransmission of Corrupted Packets

Asjad Amin, Danyal Shafi, Zeeshan Ahmed, Waqas Anjum,
Muhammad Owais, and Faheem Akram

Department of Telecommunication and Electronic Engineering,
The Islamia University of Bahawalpur, Pakistan
asjad.amin@iub.edu.pk, engrdanyal@hotmail.com, enge.shani32@yahoo.com,
waqas.anjum@iub.edu.pk, muhammadowais49@live.com, faheemovert@yahoo.com

Abstract. This paper presents a new scheme to reduce retransmissions of corrupted packets in TCP. The data segment of TCP frame is divided into small length unit we call as cells. A separate checksum is attached with each cell. In case of a corrupt packet, all the data cells are checked separately. Only corrupt cells are asked for retransmission instead of full packet. This helps us retransmitting the corrupt data of multiple packets in a single TCP packet which saves a lot of bandwidth. Extra bits attached with each cell increases redundancy but it reduces a lot of retransmissions. The proposed system has been explained with the help of pseudo code, general equations, comparative charts and simulation results. It has been further tested for different cases that include low noise environment, medium noise environment, high noise environment, and system with different BER and for full duplex system. Simulation results clearly indicate a significant improvement in throughput for all the scenarios especially for high noise environment.

Keywords: TCP, data cells, duplex, throughput.

1 Introduction

Transmission control protocol (TCP) provides a reliable connection-oriented in-order service to many of today's Internet applications [1].TCP is a reliable window-based flow control protocol where window is increase until a packet loss is detected. Here the source assumes that the network is congested and reduces its window. Once the lost packet is recovered, the source resumes its window increase [2]. However, in the recent years it has become clear that it can perform very poorly in networks with high bandwidth products (BWP) paths [3]. Recently many multimedia applications start to deploy over the internet due to its popularity. As the Internet becomes replaced with high-speed links and routers, further-more, more applications requiring real-time transmission with few packets loses are expected to appear and consume more bandwidth [4].

A. Kwiecień, P. Gaj, and P. Stera (Eds.): CN 2011, CCIS 160, pp. 242–252, 2011.

In TCP the data is send from one end system to other end system or from server to end system in the form of packets that may be of variable length, m bytes. If a packet gets corrupted during transmission then a retransmission of such packet is mandatory. Therefore extra bandwidth and extra time is consumed for such retransmissions. With more number of corrupted packets more retransmissions are required. These retransmissions consume extra time and overall transmission is slowed down. This reduces systems efficiency and throughput.

In case of corrupted packet it is found that each packet is not fully corrupt, infarct some of its bits are corrupt. Four corrupt packets with size 1100 to 1500 bytes are analyzed. Figure 1 show a comparison between total data bits in a packet and average bits getting corrupted in a packet for four chosen scenarios. Even with the corruption of a few bits we need to retransmit the complete packet. We propose a new idea in this paper which suggests that if we divide data segment of each packet into small cells of length say 50 bytes, and attach a separate checksum with each cell. Each packet will now contain n number of cells with each sell having its own checksum. Now if a packet gets corrupted, the receiver will verify each cell with the help of its checksum. All the correct cells will be separated from corrupt cells and will be saved in buffer. Unlike the previous case, only corrupted cells will be retransmitted instead of whole packet. In this method we save a lot of bandwidth with the help of cells arrangement within the packet and also we save the time.

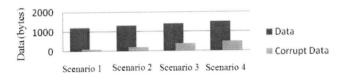

Fig. 1. Comparative chart of total data and corrupted data in a packet

The paper is organized as follows: Sect. 2 presents the modified TCP data segment with insertion of cells, sender and receiver design for the modified system, Sect. 3 presents system design and performance for various cases, Sect. 4 presents conclusion remarks.

2   Modified TCP Data Segment with Insertion of Cells

2.1   Modification at Sender for TCP with insertion of cells

In cell configuration case, the first and the core most step is that we divide data of each packet into small cells so that in case of any error, only corrupt cells may be retransmitted. For our case we have taken the size of each cell = 50 bytes. A size of 50 byte is chosen for each cell as too small size will increase a lot of processing overhead. Next we attach an 8 bit checksum to each cell. This checksum helps in distinguishing at receiver of which cells are corrupt and which are not. For a maximum of 1500 bytes, there can only be 1470 data bytes and 30 bytes for checksum. Unlike the original case, the last 30 bytes of data are shifted to the next packet in order to make space for checksum bytes associated with each cell. This may result in an increase in total number of packets that are transmitted. A maximum of only 30 cells can be formed and in case of a retransmission each cell number can be represented by only 5 bits. The header bits are kept unchanged and length of header remains the same as in original case. Now a packet is formed by attaching the cells and their respective checksums to the header {header, cel#1 + checksum, cell#2 + checksum...cell#n + checksum}. A modified TCP packet is shown in Fig. 2.

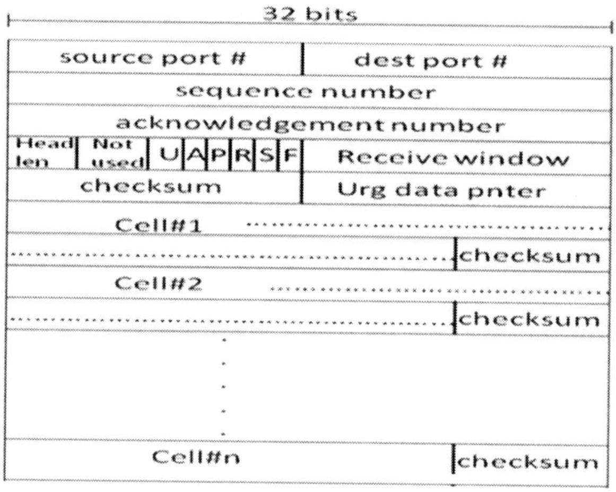

Fig. 2. TCP Frame with Data segment divided into cells

In case if data is not in an integral multiple of 50 bytes then the size of last cell can be varied depending on the bytes of data that are left. A receiver does not need the exact information of the size of last cell as it will extract all the bits of last cell except last 8 bits which represents the checksum. Consider a case where n numbers of packets are to be transmitted from one system to another. The size of each packet is $h + d$ bytes where h is the length of header and d is the length of data in each packet. So the total data dt to be transmitted is

$$dt = n * (h + d) . \tag{1}$$

If c number of packet gets corrupted then transmitted data dt becomes

$$dt = n * (h + d) + c * (h + d) = (n + c) * (h + d) . \tag{2}$$

The transmission time Tr, for the above case, on a link of bandwidth B is

$$Tr = [(n + c) * (h + d)]/B . \tag{3}$$

By inserting cells in data field, the size of each packet is increased. This is due to extra checksum bits that are needed to be attached with each cell. The size of a packet m in bytes is given by

$$m = (h + d) + (d/50) = h + 1.02d \qquad (4)$$

where size of each cell is taken as 50 bytes. For n number of packets, the total data dt to be transmit is

$$dt = n * (h + 1.02d) \ . \qquad (5)$$

The transmission time Tr, for the above case, on a link of bandwidth B is

$$Tr = [n * (h + 1.02d)]/B \ . \qquad (6)$$

If c number of packet gets corrupted and Nc number of cells are found erroneous in each corrupted packet then transmission time Tr becomes

$$Tr = [n * (h + 1.02d) + ((c * Nc)/k) * (h + d)]/B \qquad (7)$$

where k is the average number of cells that are retransmitted in a single packet.

2.2   Modification at Receiver for TCP with Insertion of Cells

When a packet is received, the receiver evaluates checksum to ensure if the transmission has been successful. In case of a successful transmission data is extracted and delivered to the higher layers. In case if a packet does not reach receiver and is lost completely during the transmission then receiver informs transmitter about the lost packet and complete packet is retransmitted. The concept of cell comes in case when a packet is received in corrupted form. The receiver extracts all the cells. Correctness of each cell is verified by its checksum. All the correct cells are stored in buffer. For each corrupt cell, the cell number is saved along with the sequence number of packet. The receiver then waits for some time. If another corrupt packet arrives during the wait time interval, the receiver again saves the cell number of all the corrupt cells along with the sequence number packet. This process is then repeated for every corrupt cell that arrives at receiver until a time out is reached. After timeout the receiver prepares a request packet. All the cells that have been corrupted so far, even if they belong to different packets, are requested for retransmission. Each cell is identified by its packet sequence number and its own cell number. Therefore receiver adds the sequence number and cell number of all the corrupted cells in the request packet. Figure 3 shows a request packet where different cells belonging to different packets are requested in a single request packet.

When a sender receives a request packet, it extracts the data field. Data field contains the sequence number and cell number of all the missing cells. Sender then prepares a response packet with all the corrupted cells added to it. This single response packet contains the corrupted portion of multiple corrupted packets.

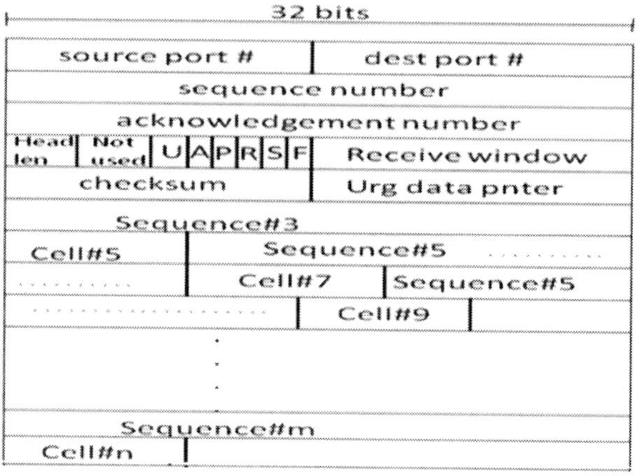

Fig. 3. TCP Request packet for multiple corrupt packets

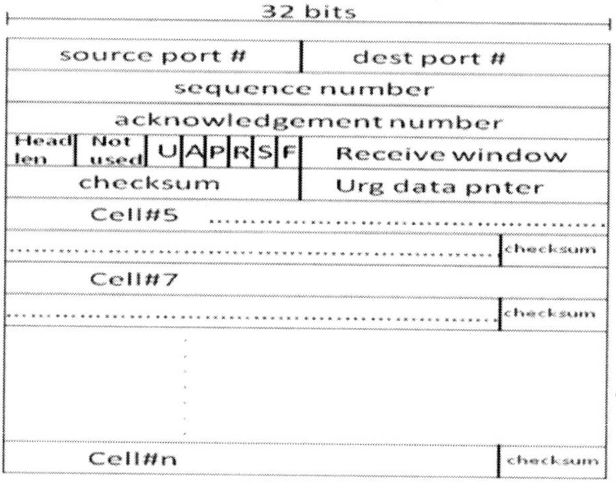

Fig. 4. Packet containing retransmitted data of multiple corrupt packets

Unlike the original case, a lot of retransmissions can be saved by introducing this new system. A response packet prepared for the Fig. 3 request packet is shown in Fig. 4. On receiving this response packet, the receiver extracts all the missing cells. It then places all the cells to their respective location in buffer where rests of the cells are placed. Complete data of each packet is then delivered to higher layers in sequence.

Figure 5 shows a complete system for two Hosts A and B where Host A is transmitting and Host B is receiving.

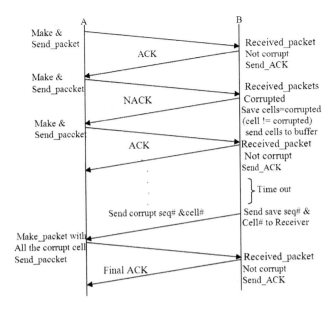

Fig. 5. Operation of complete TCP model with insertion of cells

2.3   Pseudo Code for Sender and Receiver

```
*****   Sender   *****
Case A:
Collect data from higher layers
Divide data into 50 bytes small cells
Calculate 8-bit checksum for each cell
Make packet
Send packet
Case B:
Packet received
If (ACK received & ACK-number! = sequence-num)
Extract Acknowledgment number
Make-packet (Acknowledgment)
Send-packets
Case C:
Packet received
If (1st_32_bit_option == "11111111111111111111111111")
While (! End-data-received)
Sequence-num = data (i -> i+31)  //start i with zero (i=0)
i = i+31
Cell-num = data (i -> i+4)
i = i+4
Data-to-be-send = Add-cell-with (sequence-num, cell-num)
Make-packet (1st-32-bit-option = "00000000000")


*****   Receiver   *****
Collect data from lower layers
If (data-received != corrupt && receive-sequence-num == expected-sequence-num)
Extract data
Deliver data to higher layers
Expected-sequence-num = expected-sequence-num + length (data)
Case B:
Collect data from lower layers
If (data-received != corrupt && receive-sequence-num > expected-sequence-num)
```

```
Extract data
Buffer data
Send-packet (Acknowledgment = expected-sequence-num)
Case C:
Collect data from lower layers
If (data-received == corrupt)
For   i=1 -> number-of-cells
Check checksum for each cell
If (cell == corrupt)
          Save (sequence-number, cell-number)
If (timer is not running)
Start-time
If (cell != corrupt)
Send cell to buffer
Case D:
Collect data from lower layers
If (1st-32-bit-option == "000000000")
Extract data
While (! end of data)
Extract (cell)
Send-cell-to right location in buffer
Case E:
Time-out
Add all the saved sequence-num, cell-number to a request packet
Make-packet (1st_32_bit_option = "11111111111111111111")
Send packet
```

2.4 Overhead of Proposed Scheme

Computation of 8 bit checksum for each cell requires extra computation as compared to original design. This tend to increase processing time which effects the system overall efficiency. Extra bytes are also needed for checksum which forces to move some of the data portion of one packet to the next packet. This increases the total number of packets that are transmitted. Therefore the proposed scheme only performs better where the ratio of corrupt packets is high. In small towns of under developed countries like Pakistan and Bangladesh, this design can be useful as the quality of links is very poor.

3 System Design and Results for Various Environments

We run this system for different scenarios to analyze its performance. It is clear though in ideal case where there are no corrupt packets, this new system under performs as more processing is involved in computing checksum and extra checksum bits attached to each cell increases redundancy and a decline in throughput is observed.

3.1 System Performance for Links with Different BER

We consider a scenario where there are links with different BER. Therefore the number of corrupt packets cvar is also different for each case. The links chosen have BER ranging from 1E-6 to 1E-3.5. We see that a considerable increase in throughput is observed as the number of corrupt packets increases which saves a lot of bandwidth. This is mainly due to reduced retransmissions. Therefore total data transmitted dt without insertion of cells is given by

$$dt = (n + cvar) * (h + d) . \tag{8}$$

The data transmitted for the above case with insertion of cells is

$$dt = n * (h + 1.02d) + ((cvar * Nc)/k) * (h + d) \tag{9}$$

where Nc is the average number of cells that are corrupted in a single packet and k is the average number of cells that are retransmitted in a single packet. Figure 6 shows Packet Loss for different BER and throughput for packets transmitted for a 1000 kb link with BER 1E-3.7.

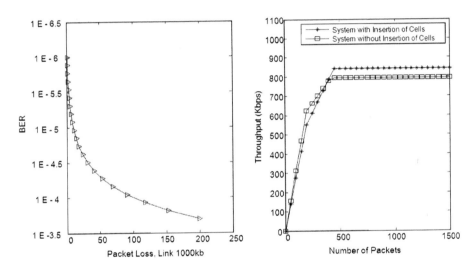

Fig. 6. Packet Loss for 1000 kb link for different BER, Throughput for different number of transmitted packets for 1000 kb link with BER = 1E-3.7

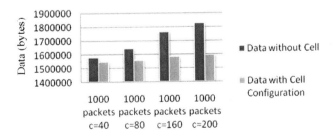

Fig. 7. Data transmitted for low noise, medium noise, high noise and very high noise environment

3.2   Low Noise, Medium Noise and High Noise Scenarios

In this scenario, we fix the number of transmitted packets to $nfix$ and size of data segment in each packet is also fixed to $dfix$. Now we test our system for low noise, medium noise and high noise environment. We observe that number of corrupted packet varies in each case. cvar denotes the number of packets that are corrupted in different noisy environments. We see a very small improvement in case of low noise, more improvement is observed in case of medium noise and a significant increase in throughput is observed for high noisy environment. Total data transmitted dt without insertion of cells is given by

$$dt = (nfix + cvar) * (h + dfix) \ . \tag{10}$$

The data transmitted for the above case with insertion of cells is

$$dt = nfix * (h + 1.02dfix) + ((cvar * Nc)/k) * (h + dfix) \tag{11}$$

where Nc is the average number of cells that are corrupted in a single packet and k is the average number of cells that are retransmitted in a single packet. Figure 7 shows the data transmitted and Fig. 8 shows throughput for low noise, medium noise, high noise and very high noise environment.

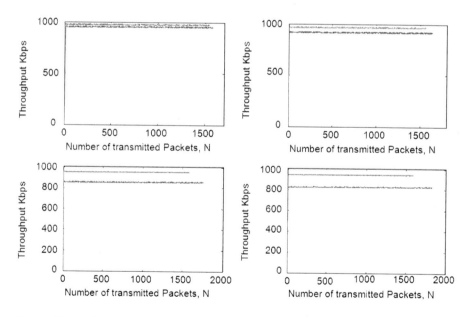

Fig. 8. Throughput for low noise, medium noise, high noise and very high noise environment

3.3   Duplex System

We consider a system with two hosts A and B transmitting data to each other. Both transmit n number of packets to each other. We run this system for different values of n. Figure 9 shows the scenario of a Duplex transmission. Figure 10 shows data transmitted between two hosts for different number of transmitted packets.

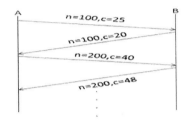

Fig. 9. A full Duplex system with Host A and Host B

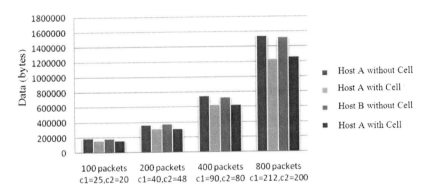

Fig. 10. Data transmitted for a full duplex system with different number of transmitted packets, n

4   Conclusion

TCP frame with insertion of cells has been discussed in detail with the help of pseudo code, comparative charts and simulations. A minimal change is required in existing system to achieve the suggested design. Only sender and receiver are modified as rest of network will consider the extra checksum bits as part of data. Results for various cases show a significant improvement in throughput. This improvement is highly notable for the case of medium, high and very high noise environment. The proposed algorithm is most suitable for environment where the ratio of corrupted packets is high. For an ideal case with no corrupt packets, the proposed system show a decline in performance due to extra bits attached with each cell for checksum and extra processing power involved.

References

1. Barakat, C., Altman, E., Dabbous, W.: On TCP Performance in a Heterogeneous Network: A Survey. IEEE Communications Magazine (January 2000)
2. Altman, E., Avrachenkov, K., Barakat, C.: A Stochastic Model of TCP/IP With Stationary Random Losses. IEEE/ACM Transactions on Networking 13(2) (April 2005)
3. Li, Y.T., Leith, D., Shorten, R.N.: Experimental Evaluation of TCP Protocols for High-Speed Networks. IEEE/ACM Transactions on Networking 15(5) (October 2007)
4. Na, S.-G., Ahn, J.-S.: TCP-like Flow Control Algorithm for Real-time Applications. In: IEEE International Conference on Networks (September 2000)
5. Mathis, M., Heffner, J., O'Neil, P., Siemsen, P.: Pathdiag: Automated TCP diagnosis. In: Claypool, M., Uhlig, S. (eds.) PAM 2008. LNCS, vol. 4979, pp. 152–161. Springer, Heidelberg (2008)
6. Mathis, M.: Reflections on the TCP Macroscopic Model. ACM SIGCOMM Computer Communication Review 39(1) (January 2009)
7. Wu, H., Peng, Y., Long, K., Cheng, S., Ma, J.: Performance of Reliable Transport Protocol over IEEE 802.11 Wireless LAN: Analysis and Enhancement. In: 21st Annual Joint Conference of the IEEE Computer and Communications Societies INFOCOM 2002, vol. 2, pp. 599–607 (2002)
8. Viéron, J., Guillemot, C.: Real-Time Constrained TCP-Compatible Rate Control for Video Over the Internet. IEEE Transactions on Multimedia 6(4), 634–646 (2004)
9. Barré, S., Bonaventure, O., Raiciu, C., Handley, M.: Experimenting with Multipath TCP. In: Annual Conference of the ACM Special Interest Group on Data Communication SIGCOMM (2010)
10. Wang, R., Yamada, K., Sanadidi, M.Y., Gerla, M.: TCP With Sender-Side Intelligence to Handle Dynamic, Large, Leaky Pipes. IEEE Journal on Selected Areas in Communications 23(2) (February 2005)

Information Protection Based on the Theory of Ateb-Functions

Ivanna Dronjuk, Mariya Nazarkevych, and Oleksandra Myroniuk

Automated Control Systems Department, Institute of Computer Science
Lviv National Polytechnic University
ivanna.droniuk@gmail.com, nazarkevich@mail.ru,
oleksandra.myroniuk@gmail.com

Abstract. The authors developed a new data protection method, which is based on the theory of Ateb functions. This method can be employed for protecting financial documents such as banknotes and securities in general. The protection method creates hidden messages or images, which become visible on counterfeited documents.

Keywords: information protection, Ateb-functions, protection securities.

1 Introduction

From the beginning of printing technology the thin graphics was one of the most common defenses. The group protection of thin graphics now based on the difficult reproduction of graphics elements, grids, rosettes, vignettes, hidden items and micrography also. Difficulties of reproduction associated with complicated geometry and the minimal thickness of a thin line elements graphics.

One of the first ways to protect documents from being copied in the stage of design technology was "hidden message" [1]. In accordance with these, a hidden warning message, such as *VOID* or *COPY*, is printed in a halftone within a halftone background on a substrate. If the consumer sees on paper manufactured hidden words, it can be argued that the product has been rigged. This effect is achieved in two ways. A small color difference between background and hidden words, that can not be achieved by using available printers or photocopiers. And the second effect is achieved by using non-standard shape points that the scanner can not recognize, so leaves empty areas, that form a words. This method is also sometimes used by reversing the screen values of the hidden warning message and the background, such that the elements of the hidden warning message are not reproduced, and the elements of the background are reproduced when photocopied or scanned [2].

Another type of graphical method of protection printed products is micrography [3]. It's based on the effect of latent image with high-resolution lines. Micrography visually perceived as a continuous line, although composed of the signs and symbols that can be seen only at a considerable increase. There are

A. Kwiecień, P. Gaj, and P. Stera (Eds.): CN 2011, CCIS 160, pp. 253–260, 2011.

two subspecies of this method of protection: NaNOcopy and LogoDot [4,5]. Description of the first protection subspecies is to use symbols and characters for building lines. The second is to use some selected images.

Common to most existing methods of hidden image is encoded structure of embedded information. It requires a specially designed software to create images and detect hidden parts. Another disadvantage is the high requirements for precision printing and difficulty reading the image.

Nowadays, in computerized world the technology continues to evolve. Therefore, the possibility of equipment, which often create counterfeit products, such as copy machines, printers and scanners are also improving. Every year, copy machines are using more and more colors, printers improves print quality, and scanners recognize elements of all higher resolution. So, there is always occurs a necessity for a new graphics technology protection.

In this paper, a proposed method is based on the theory Ateb-functions. It is similar to the methods proposed in [3,4,5], but is based on other ideas.

2   Introduction to the Periodic Ateb-Functions Theory

Let us consider the expression:

$$\omega = \frac{n+1}{2} \int_0^v \left(1 - \bar{v}^{n+1}\right)^{-\frac{m}{m+1}} d\bar{v} \tag{1}$$

n, m – determined by the alignment:

$$n = \frac{2\theta + 1}{2\xi + 1} \ , \quad m = \frac{2\zeta + 1}{2\varsigma + 1} \ , \quad (\theta, \ \xi, \ \zeta, \ \varsigma = 0, 1, 2, \dots) \tag{2}$$

In formula (1) ω is a function of v, n and m. To create Ateb-functions considering the inverse dependence v on ω, which at one time is a function depends on n and m it is called Ateb-functions sine and indicated [6]:

$$\nu = sa(n, m, \omega) \ . \tag{3}$$

Similary we obtain the alignment:

$$\omega = \frac{m+1}{2} \int_{-1 \le u \le 1}^{1} \frac{d\bar{u}}{\left(1 - \bar{u}^{m+1}\right)^{\frac{n}{n+1}}} \tag{4}$$

Dependence u of ω for integral (4) is a function of n and m, it is called Ateb-functions cosine and indicated

$$u = ca(m, n, \omega) \ . \tag{5}$$

P.M. Senyk [7] proved relations for periodic Ateb-functions:

$$ca^{m+1}(m, n, \omega) + sa^{n+1}(n, m, \omega) = 1 \ . \tag{6}$$

Also in [7] proved that introduced Ateb-functions are periodic with period $\Pi(m, n)$ where

$$\Pi(m, n) = \frac{\Gamma\left(\frac{1}{n+1}\right)\Gamma\left(\frac{1}{m+1}\right)}{\Gamma\left(\frac{1}{n+1} + \frac{1}{m+1}\right)} . \tag{7}$$

In (7) $\Gamma\left(\frac{1}{m+1}\right)$, $\Gamma\left(\frac{1}{n+1}\right)$ is gamma function.

So, if necessary calculation of functions is enough for the argument ω that changes on the interval

$$0 \leq \omega \leq \frac{1}{2}\Pi(m, n) .$$

Using the periodicity properties, we can continue the obtained value for the whole period.

3   Converting Periodic Ateb-Functions in the Numerical Values

In Formulas (1), (4) periodic Ateb-functions are represented by inappropriate inversion integrals. This is a mathematical representation of analytical writing, but is difficult to obtain numerical values. Therefore, a mathematical model which use a Taylor series was proposed for constructing a method of numerical representation Ateb-functions. Considering (6), we are making a conclusion that it is enough to identify only one of Ateb-functions. We'll search the function $ca(m, n, \omega)$.

From expression (4) we'll consider the function

$$\Phi(\omega, u) = \omega + \frac{m+1}{2} \int\limits_{0 \leq u \leq 1}^{1} \frac{d\bar{u}}{\left(1 - \bar{u}^{m+1}\right)^{\frac{n}{n+1}}} . \tag{8}$$

To determine the value of the function $ca(m, n, \omega)$ for each fixed parameter ω is found such u, for which the function (8) becomes small quantity of the given order. We'll decompose function (8) in series by powers u^{m+1}.

We'll get [7]

$$\Phi(\omega, u) = \omega - \frac{1}{2}\prod(m, n) - \frac{m+1}{2}uF(a, b, c, z) + \ldots . \tag{9}$$

Here $F(a, b, c, z)$ – hypergeometric row,

$$F(a, b, c, z) = 1 + \frac{ab}{c}\frac{z}{1!} + \frac{a(a+1)b(b+1)}{c(c+1)}\frac{z^2}{2!} + \ldots , . \tag{10}$$

where we introduced notification

$$z = u^{m+1} , \quad a = \frac{1}{m+1} , \quad b = \frac{n}{n+1} , \quad c = \frac{m+2}{m+1} . \tag{11}$$

Considering (11), we'll have $0 \le z \le 1$, and

$$a + b - c = -\frac{1}{n+1} < 0 \ . \tag{12}$$

4   The Method of Numerical Representation of Periodic Ateb-Function Based on the Taylor Series

Numerical method of presentation we will describe at the example of the function $u = ca(m, n, \omega)$. At the beginning declare variables and assign constant values, namely: set the precision for calculation of the full Beta-function; declare variables of cycles. On the first stage we create a text file for writing calculated numeric data. On the second stage calculate the constant values for $u = ca(m, n, \omega)$, this includes the period Ateb-function by formula (7), values a, b, c according to formula (11). Calculation is carried out with precision $\varepsilon = 10^{-10}$. The next stage is the main calculation. Let's describe it in detail. We organize a series by ω on the interval $[0, 1]$ with a step 0.01.

Then conduct the calculation by formula (7), z – by formula (11). Calculate $\Phi(\omega, u)$ that corresponds to the formula (9). Results are shown in Fig. 1.

5   Development of Protection Method Based on Ateb-Functions

The proposed method of protection based on creating lines with different thickness corresponding graphs of periodic Ateb-functions. We have developed a method of numerical and graphical representation of Ateb-functions. As has been proven, appearance of Ateb-functions depends from two reasonable options. Change of parameters of Ateb-functions leads to another kind of graphical representation which we choose for a single graphic element. On the basis of individual graphic elements guilloche motives are built. On the next step the hidden message is built in guilloche motive by changing the thickness of the line.

To ensure the quality of the protected document software has been developed using a language PostScript. The default coordinate system starts on the left top corner of the page. PostScript language reference system consider the origin as the left bottom corner of the page. We consider that the x-axis runs horizontally, and the axis y – vertically. Each point of the document has clearly defined coordinates (x, y).

Development implements a method of changing width of the line to construct a hidden message. Submitted document consists of a large number of repeating lines, built by Ateb-sine function, which forms guilloche motive. Larger area of the document is formed by continuous lines of given thickness, for the output of which is the procedure is designed. At the places of letters of the word $COPY$ we replace a single line by a smaller one with double thickness, for which a special procedure is also developed (Fig. 2 and 4).

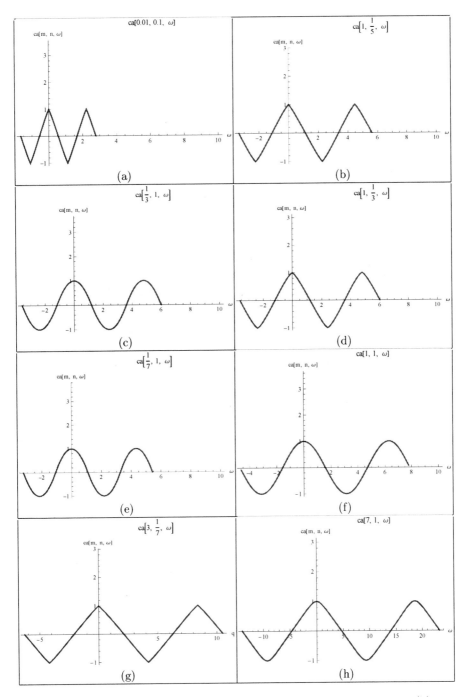

Fig. 1. A graphical representation $ca(m, n, \omega)$ for: (a) $m = 0.01$, $n = 0.1$; (b) $m = 1$, $n = \frac{1}{5}$; (c) $m = \frac{1}{3}$, $n = 1$; (d) $m = 1$, $n = \frac{1}{3}$; (e) $m = \frac{1}{7}$, $n = 1$; (f) $m = 1$, $n = 1$; (g) $m = 3$, $n = \frac{1}{7}$; (h) $m = 7$, $n = 1$

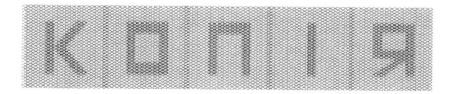

Fig. 2. View a secure document

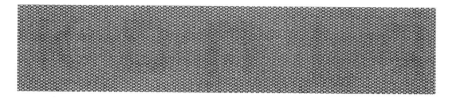

Fig. 3. Scanned document view

Fig. 4. The increased scale of the letter "K" of a secure document

Fig. 5. The increased scale of the letter "K" from a scanned document

Let us describe the principle of both procedures. Verifies the current coordinates of the document (x, y) on getting into the space of hidden words. If the coordinates fall within the area of hidden words, then call the procedure for constructing a double line, otherwise build a Single line. In the procedure is passed one parameter – the current coordinate x. When developing the single line in the body functions calculate values for the y coordinates of x, and then build a line from an earlier point to this. The function of the double line a little more complicated. Originally, recorded in the current coordinates of local variables and find the coordinates of the previous point, then finds slipped on some constants in the axis of ordinates and the new coordinates of the previous point between the transmitting line. There are two lines – one shifted up and the other – down.

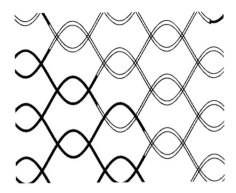

Fig. 6. Fragment guilloche motive in the transition letter-background

Thus, for increasing clarity the word *COPY* on the original document, reducing the thickness of lines 2 times (Fig. 6).

As each letter has its own display settings (width, position, etc.), then the output of each letter was created a separate procedure, which passed two parameters – the x and y position of the lower left corner of letters on paper. Thus, the body maintain current procedures set graphics mode (which also includes a point of reference coordinates), the starting point of reference set by changing the coordinates, and construction is already against them. At the end of the procedure restores the saved state of graphics mode, allowing the main body of the program precisely position the characters relative to one point. The main body of the program cycle is implemented by which the word *COPY* is positioned on the axis of ordinates. Scanned images have poorer quality (Fig. 3 and 5).

In this paper, the work method is illustrated for Ateb-cosine of the parameters $m = \frac{1}{7}$, $n = 1$. But we have created a library of different guilloche motives based on various Ateb-periodic functions.

6   Conclusions

This paper analyzes the document prepress stage. We demonstrate that one of the most promising and effective methods of document protection is micrography. The paper considers different ways of implementing micrography. As an example of micrography implementations, we discuss a method, which is based on line thickness variations. We propose a document security method, which is based on the idea of line splitting. The lines built correspond to the graphs of Ateb-periodic functions. Based on the proposed method, we developed our software using the Post Script language, which ensures the high quality of printed documents. We provide a number of examples to demonstrate how the system works. Lastly, to emphasize that our method can indeed be used to efficiently protect documents, we first scan the protected document. Then, we show that the electronic copy of the document does, in fact, reveal the hidden text. Overall, our protection method can be used to effectively protect the securities.

References

1. Kyrychok, P.O.: Protection securities. In: Kyrychok, P.O., Korostil, Y.M., Shevchuk, A.V. NTUU KPI (2008) (in Ukrainian)
2. Field, G.G: Color and It's Reproduction. Graphic Arts Technical Foundation Reprinted 1992, ch. 2, 3 (1992)
3. Konshyn, A.A.: Protection printing documents. Synus (1999) (in Russian)
4. Phillips, G.K.: New Digital Anti-Copy/Scan and Verification Technologies Verify First Technologies. P.O. Box 7001, Paso Robles, CA 93447 USA
5. Phillips, G.K.: Document Security System Having Thermo Activated Pantograph and Validation Mark. Patents 5,873,604 and 6,665,406
6. Rosenberg, R.: The Ateb-functions and their proporties. Quart. Appt. Math. 21, 1 (1963)
7. Senyk, P.M.: About Ateb-functions. Dopovidi AN URSR no 1, pp. 23–26 (1968) (in Ukrainian)

Revocable Anonymity in Network Monitoring Systems

Krystian Baniak

Institute of Telecommunications, Warsaw University of Technology
K.Baniak@elka.pw.edu.pl

Abstract. Ensuring subscriber's privacy in a network security monitoring system is usually in the conflict with security and accountability controls that are imposed by the security policy. This balance between subscriber's anonymity and visibility is often a dilemma for service providers and enterprises. This paper presents results of author's research in the field of distributed network security monitoring architectures and the proposal of such a monitoring system that incorporates cryptographic protocols and a group signature scheme to deliver privacy protecting, network surveillance system architecture that provides subscriber's accountability and controlled, revocable anonymity.

Keywords: anonymity, revocable anonymity, group signatures.

1   Introduction

The Internet has grown to become a major communication platform for economy, industry, education, politics as well as for people that tend to increasingly rely on it as the primary source of information and the mean of staying connected with other individuals. The other side of on-line activities are the risks of being the victim of cyber crime and threats that emerge from the complexity and vulnerabilities embedded in applications and networks. The network security monitoring is one of the essential means of control that allows security professionals to comprehend the nature of threats and to successfully prevent it. A network security monitoring is also one of the vital elements that provide visibility and accountability for network owners or service providers. Concisely, typical network monitoring system shall satisfy the following functional requirements:

- ensuring visibility for network maintenance and operations processes [1],
- network traffic measurement on purpose of service level agreements and quality of service tracking,
- providing evidence data for security incident management [2],
- providing data for investment planning and services management.

The network traffic monitoring has, however, some serious implications on the subscriber's privacy and thus the privacy-aware property is very important especially in case of Internet service providers and mobile incumbents. Authors

A. Kwiecień, P. Gaj, and P. Stera (Eds.): CN 2011, CCIS 160, pp. 261–270, 2011.

of PRIsm framework [1,3] were among the first to address this problem in the professional literature and they have also proposed appropriate standardization proposals. The author's research summarized with this paper showed that it is possible to use autonomous distributed agents in a way that protects subscriber's privacy and allows to satisfy security monitoring principles by using combination of behavioral profiling based on the frame system and privacy protecting evidence recording.

This paper presents the network security monitoring architecture proposal that provides conditional anonymity for monitored subjects and provides subject's accountability in case of the security incident.

2   Privacy Aware Network Security Monitoring Architecture

The Multi-Agent Network Surveillance Framework (MANSF) is designed for packet networks running the Internet protocol suite and leverages the distributed passive network traffic analysis with aid of autonomous agents. A passive interception ensures that no alteration is imposed on inspected network flows. The packet interception is performed in key network locations in order to achieve the maximal visibility and accountability (see Fig. 1). The target audience for this platform are Internet service providers, mobile operators, enterprise security and management teams or the security incident management organizations. The proposed platform is designed to satisfy security monitoring and network measurement goals at the same time with ensuring that no network subscriber experiences anonymity degradation. This requirement is also essential for satisfying legal regulations in the field of privacy and anonymity like EU directive 95/46/EC [4]. Key functional requirements behind this design are computation of network baseline behavioral profile, subscriber's behavioral profiles and retention of evidence data in case of identified security incidents. Service providers' networks are characterized by complex topologies and large traffic rates, therefore they are no match for centralized monitoring systems. The proposed solution assumes the application of specialized autonomous agents that collect traffic related events in key network locations thus enabling to monitor the activity of targeted group of subscribers. The frequently used [5,6,7] concept of autonomous agents has been combined with the hierarchical multi-agent structure, where raw traffic data is transformed into knowledge about the monitored network environment in a number of stages. The MANSF framework consists of three types of agents: collecting agents (AGC), processor agents (AGP) and the Central Repository (CR).

agent collector is a network sensor that discovers network topology, evaluates network baseline behavioral profile and persistently tracks subscribers' profiles and records security incidents,

agent processor is a second layer type of agent that analyzes network baseline and subscriber's profiles in order to produce an aggregated information about the network,

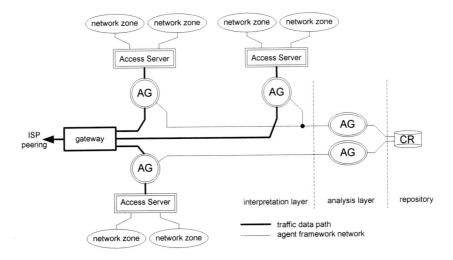

Fig. 1. Distributed network security monitoring architecture. Access Server i.e. is a GGSN in the mobile network scenario or a DSLAM in a broadband one.

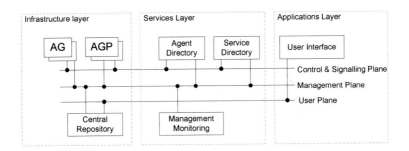

Fig. 2. MANF communication platform architecture

central repository is a knowledge repository agent and the placeholder for evidence data of recorded security incidents.

The concept of the hierarchical, multi-layer agent framework is used to partition and facilitate the knowledge mining process as well as to support anonymity protection controls. The MANSF's multi-agent framework, consists also of support nodes like the Agent Directory (AD), that is the repository of all known agents and the Service Directory (SD), that is the repository of all advertised agent framework services. Those nodes provide maintenance services for the multi-agent framework. The communication subsystem of the MANSF, presented in Fig. 2, is decomposed into layers and planes [8] to facilitate the security design and to limit the penetration scope for a potential attacker. The security monitoring engine is based on behavioral profiles and it has to learn the baseline of the network or alternatively has to be provisioned with a set of the initial profile data. The network environment observations are represented in a compound model consisting of profiles that include both network traffic statistical information as well as individual subscriber's profiles. Network events and subscriber profiles are calculated using a frame system [9] that recognizes stereotyped activity patterns like i.e. "news page browsing" or a "software update". Security incidents are detected as anomalies to the baseline or expected bias of a subscriber's profile. In order to satisfy accountability, system retains evidence data associated with an security incident in the encrypted form stored at the Central Repository. The frame system elements include a hierarchy of frames that contain slots and activators. During the network event analysis, a most specific frame that is activated, may trigger certain actions like for instance the evidence recording for a given detected scenario.

The subscriber's anonymity protection is realized with a set of architectural and cryptographic controls, that combined provide robust compromise in a form of the revocable anonymity scheme. This scheme is further discussed in the next section.

3   Anonymity Controls

Network monitoring system's goals and privacy requirements can only be satisfied with application of the conditional anonymity. The conditional anonymity [10] is understood in this context as a revocable anonymity, due to the fact that subscriber's identity may be revealed to a legal authority when given subscriber violates some security policy. The MANSF system uses pseudonyms to represent data records that are linked to the specific subscriber and provides pseudonymity [11]. For example it is an individual behavioral profile or an evidence record that contains details pertaining to the suspicious security incident. The pseudonym is an important anonymity control that represents the subscriber within the network security monitoring system. A pseudonym is linked to a subscriber's unique identifier in the customer management system of the service provider. In that way the monitoring system presents personalized reports or evidence data preserving the real identity of a user. Clearly, it is important to limit possibilities to reverse engineer this linkage in a case when somebody wants to leverage this information in a malicious way. The MANSF system anonymity controls consist of a set of architectural, procedural and cryptographic techniques that are summarized in Fig. 3. Anonymity controls are applied to all important elements of the system like network data retrieval, security event generation, security event storage and anonymity control.

data retrieval is performed in a distributed way by multiple agent collectors that broadcast results to associated processor agents in order to avoid linking the message's pseudonym with a given agent,

message generation where agent collectors sign a message with the group signature in order to authenticate to the agent processor,

event storage is encrypting privacy sensitive information of the evidence data,

anonymity control with revocation is realized by the dynamic group signature scheme and the secure shared secret scheme used for group signature system's keys access protection,

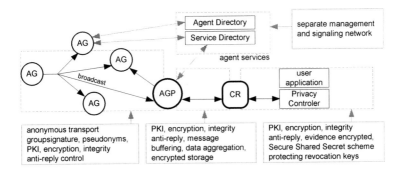

Fig. 3. MANSF key anonymity controls

communication platform for the multi-agent framework is protected with an
encryption, integrity checks and anti-reply with timestamps. Authentication
mechanism for a non-broadcast exchange is based on a public key infrastructure system and digital certificates.

3.1   Revocable Group Signature Scheme

The major cryptographic primitive that supports the privacy protection is the
dynamic group signature scheme, secure with assumption of existence of trapdoor permutations. This scheme is based on the formal description and the
rigorous security model of BSZ05, first proposed in the paper [12]. The set of
procedures available for this scheme consists of: `Issue`, `Join`, `Judge`, `Open`,
`Remove`, `Sign`, `Verify`. The original BSZ05 scheme has been extended with the
`Remove` procedure that allows a group member removal and the Group Member
Revocation List (`GMRL`) that allows to verify signatures depending on the cadence
of a group member. Additionally, the set of group signature scheme procedures is
partitioned into public and protected classes thus limiting the number of oracles
available for a potential attacker in an internal or external perspective. The key
elements of the MANSF group signature framework are the following:

Group Manager (GM) – that is responsible for the provisioning of group members and maintenance of the secret database of member certificates. The
Group Manager has a *gmsk* key used to provision new members and implements group signature scheme procedures like `Join`, `Judge`, `Revoke` and
`Verify`. It is located on the Central Repository and provides the following
public services for the multi-agent framework:
- `Verify`, used by Agent Processors and the Central Repository to verify
  the authenticity of agent collector's messages,
- `Remove`, used to disable compromised or decommissioned agent collector,
- `Judge`, used by an user-plane application like the Privacy Controller,
  performing a revocation of subscriber's anonymity.

Group Opening Manager (GOM) – implemented on the Agent Directory.
GOM owns the *gomk* private key that is used to open a signature and reveal

the identity of a signer. Provides the `Open` procedure and hosts the Group Member Revocation List (abbr. `GMRL`) that is used to verify whether the signature is issued by authorized group member without disclosing the identity of a signer.

Group Controller (GC) – implemented on the monitoring system of the MANSF and used to decommission agent collector in case of its malfunction. The GC uses the Agent Directory as the reference to the list of agent collectors and uses the `Remove` procedure hosted on the Central Repository.

Group Member – any agent collector agent within the MANSF multi-agent platform, implements `Sign` procedure.

The Privacy Controller (PRC) is not a part of the group signature scheme, but it plays the important role within this framework. It is an application layer module, responsible for evidence inspection and subscriber incident's reporting. It may revoke the identity of a subscriber based on the decision of an operator and the authority responsible for privacy protection. Agent collector as a member of the group signature scheme uses the `Sign` procedure to certify that message is generated from trusted source and broadcasts it to associated Agent Processor. Broadcast communication is used to enhance resistance to the traffic analysis. In general, the signature is constructed over the digest of an exchanged message and a time stamp to record the time of sending a message. Signature also contains a revocation token that is used to check expiration status of the source agent. This token is padded with random value and encrypted with public key of Agent Directory to avoid leaking information that may lower anonymity of the sender. Following the group signature construct proposed in [12], the result of the `Open` procedure may be verified with the second procedure `Judge` that is hosted on a separate system: the Central Repository. This solution is necessary to eliminate the scenario when one of the key group signature scheme members, like GM or GOM, is compromised. The Privacy Controller is used to revoke the anonymity of a given subscriber. It follows the `Open` procedure and then checks the validity of results with the `Judge` procedure. The procedural flow of the `MANSF` group signature scheme is presented in Fig. 4. Due to the fact that most of anonymity risks are connected to the group opening manager the secret key *gomk* is protected with the Secure Shared Secret scheme, where a k–quorum of key partition stakeholders needs to participate in a `Compose` procedure to revoke the anonymity of a subscriber or to decommission one of the agent collectors.

3.2   Adversary Model

The anonymity protection level is analyzed in the scenario that mostly resembles the real life case where the attacker tries to disclose an identity of some monitored subscriber. Due to the fact that the group signature opening manager and the revocations list are protected with a secret sharing scheme it is not enough for an attacker to obtain access to the `Open` oracle. The most promising strategy for the attacker is to use the traffic analysis or acquire access to the evidence log. We assume that there are two scenarios where attacker knows the total

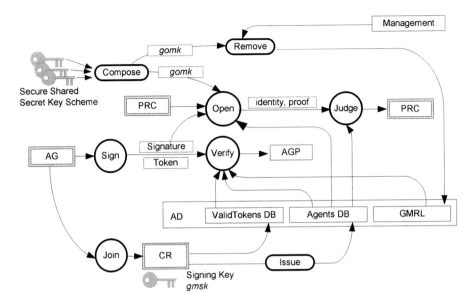

Fig. 4. Group Signature Scheme details

number of active subscribers in a time t and when attacker knows the exact set of active subscribers $n = (n_1, \ldots, n_i)$ in a time t. We assume that this knowledge comes from the network management system and that the attacker is unlikely to be able to successfully capture raw network traffic (in busy service provider's aggregation points it is almost impossible as this would be service affecting). The anonymity evaluation scenario is presented in Fig. 5

3.3 Anonymity Evaluation

Generally, the MANSF framework leverages frame system logic rules to produce the network baseline in a form of network and subscriber behavioral profiles. The subscribers' network activity may trigger generation of network security events.

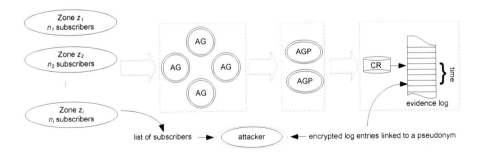

Fig. 5. Anonymity evaluation scenario

Agent collectors generate updates that contain behavioral profile transactions and security events that are linked to subscribers via pseudonyms. The traffic analysis is prevented with use of anonymous, group authenticated transfer protected with confidentiality and integrity controls. Subscribers belong to different zones managed by various agent collectors. Updates are collected by agent processors and placed in the repository log of the Central Repository. A potential attacker that may threat the anonymity property has to have an access to the evidence log file thus the best candidate is the system operator. The evidence log is the only usable part of the system that can be leveraged by such an adversary as the remaining security related knowledge retained by the system are the behavioral profiles and frame system rules that are used to produce new security events on course of network traffic analysis. The entries in the evidence log contain the event type, subscriber's pseudonym and the time of recording. Eventual incident's payload is encrypted therefore not usable by the attacker.

Each of the network zones has a known cardinality of subscribers. The number of possible scenarios that has to be considered by the attacker is implied by the MANSF architecture. The zones that group subscribers are assigned an event generation intensity level as the ratio of total events observed by the system. This ratio is averaged for every zone in the system. Let $Z = \{z_1, z_2, \ldots, z_n\}$ be the set of zones managed by the agent collectors and z_i is the number of registered subscribers in each zone and $|Z| = r$. All zones together consist of n subscribers. The attacker observes, in given time t, that there is k distinct event sources identified by pseudonyms in a log file. The number of possible allocations C_z of k pseudonyms to subscribers is the given by the partitioning of k events into compartments $A_i = a : a \in z_i$ where t_i is the number of events coming from zone z_i and $\sum_i t_i = k$. The number of events coming from given zone has to be less than the cardinality of given zone. The numbers $t_1, \ldots, t_r$ are based on system observation or some uniformly distributed values if the first data is not known.

The anonymity level provided by the MANSF framework has been examined and quantified with use of the entropy measure, which denotes the level of uncertainty the attacker has while analyzing a average situation in some time interval. In case of the local attacker's perspective, where adversary has only information about the total number of active subscribers, the level of uncertainty is given by entropy $log_b \frac{n!}{(n-k)!}$ and in the global perspective, where attacker knows the exact number of active subscriber set, the uncertainty drops to $log_b C_z$. In conclusion the anonymity level A_{MANSF} is bounded by:

$$log_b C_z \leq A_{\mathsf{MANSF}} \leq log_b \frac{n!}{(n-k)!} \quad ,$$

where

$$C_z = \frac{k! \cdot z_1! \cdot z_2! \cdot \ldots \cdot z_r!}{t_1! \cdot t_2! \cdot \ldots \cdot t_r! \cdot (z_1 - t_1)! \cdot (z_2 - t_2)! \cdot \ldots \cdot (z_r - t_r)!} \quad .$$

Clearly, the uncertainty grows with the number of events appearing in time t and the cardinality of subscriber groups for each zone. In simple case when $k = 1$ the number of potential candidates is minimal and the probability of given subscriber to be the source of an event is $1/n$. It has to be underlined that in case when an adversary is able to build a posteriori distribution based on the event types versus a given zone this may lead to further decrease on the anonymity level. This however requires traffic analysis to be performed in critical parts of the busy network thus limiting the probability of such an attack.

4 Summary

In conclusion, the formal concept of the network surveillance system's architecture, proposed in this paper, may be implemented in a efficient way based on layered architecture, proven cryptographic primitives and anonymity core based on dynamic group signature scheme conforming to strict security models like those in BSZ05 [12,13]. Thus it is applicable in a practical solution of the network monitoring system. The current advancements in the bilinear maps have delivered new group signature constructs offering even more rigid security properties and practical k-security parameter sizes, allowing the use of existing message digest functions like SHA-2 [13] and not relying on random oracles or trapdoor permutations [14,15]. The additional security controls and restrictions in the adversary models allow also for more robust CPA-anonymous group signatures that have constant public key and short signatures [16,13]. Those group signatures constructed using the pairings cryptography and elliptic curves over finite fields, offer very fast signature and verification procedures costing a few milliseconds on contemporary hardware.

From the practical point of view, security functions of this framework, are beneficial in order to comprehend the nature of the monitored network environment, merely due to the application of behavioral analysis. The accountability principle is satisfied by recording of data like packets or other admissible evidence, that is associated with security incidents identified on course of the analysis done with use of the frame system and deviations from behavioral baselines. Of course this kind of a system may not replace lawful intercept solutions mostly due to the fact that it is recording only anomalous events and security incidents. However, it has to be noted that the revocable anonymity core of the solution can be easily extended to support other types of security monitoring solutions like the aforementioned lawful intercept or classical signature based incident prevention.

References

1. Bianchi, G., Boschi, E., Kaklamani, D.I., Koutsoloukas, E.A., Lioudakis, G.V., Oppedisano, F., Petraschek, M., Ricciato, F., Schmoll, C.: Towards Privacy-Preserving Network Monitoring: Issues and Challenges. In: Personal, Indoor and Mobile Radio Communications, PIMRC 2007, pp. 1–5 (September 2007)
2. Xu, K., Zhang, Z.-L., Bhattacharyya, S.: Internet Traffic Behavior Profiling for Network Security Monitoring. IEEE/ACM 16(6), 1241–1252 (2008)

3. Gogoulos, F., Antonakopoulou, A., Mousas, A.S., Lioudakis, G.V., Kaklamani, D.I., Venieris, I.S.: Privacy-Aware Passive Network Monitoring. In: Panhellenic Conference on Informatics, pp. 171–175. IEEE Computer Society, Los Alamitos (2009)
4. European Commission: Directive on protection of individuals with regard to the processing of personal data and on the free movement of such data (1995), http://eur-lex.europa.eu/LexUriServ/ LexUriServ.do?uri=CELEX:31995L0046:EN:HTML
5. Wooldridge, M., Jennings, N.R.: Intelligent agents: Theory and practice. The Knowledge Engineering Review 10(2), 115–152 (1995)
6. Jennings, N.R., Sycara, K., Wooldridge, M.: A roadmap of agent research and development. Autonomous Agents and Multi-Agent Systems 1(1), 7–38 (1998)
7. Nguyen, N. Ganzha, M., Paprzycki, M.: A Consensus-Based Multi-agent Approach for Information Retrieval in Internet. In: International Conference on Computational Science, ICCS 2006, pp. 208–215 (2006), http://dx.doi.org/10.1007/11758532_29
8. ITU-T Study Group 17: ITU-T Recommendation X.805. ITU-T (2003), http://www.itu.int/itudoc/itu-t/aap/sg17aap/history/x805/index.html
9. Minsky, M.: Minsky's frame system theory. In: Theoretical Issues in Natural Language Processing, TINLAP 1975. Association for Computational Linguistics, Morristown, USA, pp. 104–116, (1975)
10. Chatzikokolakis, K.: Probabilistic and Information-Theoretic Approaches to Anonymity. PhD thesis, pp. 35–36, Laboratoire d'Informatique (LIX), École Polytechnique, Paris (October 2007), http://www.lix.polytechnique.fr/~kostas/thesis.pdf
11. Pfitzmann, A., Hansen, M.: Anonymity, Unlinkability, Undetectability, Unobservability, Pseudonymity and Identity Management – A Consolidated Proposal for Terminology v0.33 (April 2010), http://dud.inf.tu-dresden.de/Anon_Terminology.shtml
12. Bellare, M., Shi, H., Zhang, C.: Foundations of group signatures: The case of dynamic groups. In: Menezes, A. (ed.) CT-RSA 2005. LNCS, vol. 3376, pp. 136–153. Springer, Heidelberg (2005)
13. Groth, J.: Fully anonymous group signatures without random oracles. In: Kurosawa, K. (ed.) ASIACRYPT 2007. LNCS, vol. 4833, pp. 164–180. Springer, Heidelberg (2007)
14. Bellare, M., Duan, S.: New Definitions and Designs for Anonymous Signatures. In: Cryptology ePrint Archive, Report 2009/336 (2009), http://eprint.iacr.org/
15. Nguyen, L., Safavi-Naini, R.: Efficient and provably secure trapdoor-free group signature schemes from bilinear pairings. In: Lee, P.J. (ed.) ASIACRYPT 2004. LNCS, vol. 3329, pp. 372–386. Springer, Heidelberg (2004)
16. Ateniese, G., Camenisch, J., Hohenberger, S., de Medeiros, B.: Practical Group Signatures without Random Oracles. In: Cryptology ePrint Archive, Report 2005/385 (2005)

Flow Based Algorithm
for Malware Traffic Detection

Mirosław Skrzewski

Politechnika Śląska, Instytut Informatyki, Akademicka 16, 44-100 Gliwice, Polska
miroslaw.skrzewski@polsl.pl

Abstract. Detection of malware operation on user's system was always a difficult task. With modern trends in stealth malware design (meta- and polymorphism modified code, multiple short series) monitoring of network traffic becomes one of the surest ways of malware operation detection. The paper presents the concept of outbound net flows analysis for malware traffic exposure to facilitate its operation detection. System network activity monitoring, algorithm for user's flows detection in recorded net flows traffic and some results of it operation on clean and malware infected test systems are described.

Keywords: malware detection, network flow monitoring, outbound web-flows.

1 Introduction

The term *malware* become the common name for malicious computer programs like viruses, trojans, worms and bots designed to exploit users' computer systems for nefarious purposes. Such programs use various techniques to hide themselves in victim systems, and their existence may often remain unknown for a long time to systems users. Antivirus software, regarded as the primary countermeasures against all types of threats, proves insufficient [1] for system protection and due to relaying mainly on signature detection, has significant shortcomings [2] detecting new threats.

Most of the current antimalware technologies are focused on the malware of the past – active internet or email worms, generating big spikes of network traffic, with mostly static codebase, easily detectable by proper signatures. The current picture of malware looks quite opposite – low activity worms, trojans, malware programs building botnets, hiding their presence on infected systems, constantly modifying via meta- and polymorphism their codebase [3,4] to avoid signature detection.

Due to high activity of malware authors and their malware generating systems (up to few thousand of new malware versions per day [5,6]) it is predicted that no one antivirus program can detect and stop all possible malware infections.

For users' protection against long unnoticed malware operation on their systems the additional lines of defense are necessary, independent of the analysis of malware samples. Because the network communication is the only way malware

A. Kwiecień, P. Gaj, and P. Stera (Eds.): CN 2011, CCIS 160, pp. 271–280, 2011.

may contact its author, the traces of these communication in recorded network traffic should allow for detection of malware operation and one of these defense lines may be based on the monitoring of the network activity.

2   Monitoring of the Network Operation

Monitoring of the network operation on packet level is based on analysis of traffic treated as a stream of separated packets and is the duty of the Network Intrusion Detection Systems (NIDS), operating on the network edge, by which all traffic passes through. In many cases the monitoring process resembles the operation of the antivirus system – detection of the signs of threats in the stream of network packets is often signature based, with its all inconveniences and dependence on malware samples analysis.

Another level of monitoring the network operation depicts the network traffic as a set of flows – streams of packets exchanged in TCP/UDP connections between connected systems. Flows recording may takes place also on the network edge, on the routers or on dedicated monitoring systems running e.g. *argus* [7]. Flows recording may also take place locally on any system, as system's network activity monitoring, and record all network connections originating from or destined to the monitored system.

Many discussed new methods of bots/malware detection attempt to identify operational characteristics common to malware activity in network traffic and later use it for malware detection. A big hassle of these attempts is amount of benign, user generated traffic, the method must cope with and which may mask any signs of malware network operation.

The paper describes the concept of definition of traffic properties common to user's application operation for benign traffic selection, for simplification of malware traffic detection. The local activity monitoring system *tdilog* [8], proposed flow based algorithm for malware presence detection in network activity data and results of it implementation on recorded data from selected user systems are presented.

3   Malware Network Traffic Analysis

Subject of malware detection on the basis of network traffic properties analysis was presented in many research papers. Most of them discussed variants of network-wide anomaly detection [9] and attempt to apply some statistical tools to recorded packet flow data to identify deviation from steady flow level as signs of malware activity. Fernandes et al. [10] used time series of traffic volume metrics obtained for short time slots in recorded flow data for traffic classification and then applied set of signatures for detection of different class of anomalies.

Zaparelao et al. [11] used routers snmp MIB objects sample series for traffic classification and anomaly detection. Barford et al. [12] applied wavelet-based signal analysis to Netflow and SNMP monitor link volume data to define some classes of anomalies. These and other works (ex. [13]) were focused on cases where malware activity introduces measurable changes in network traffic, characteristic for active network worms, massive spam distribution and DoS attacks.

Most of modern malware now exhibit different, rather stealth behavior [14,15] and is nearly invisible on packet traffic intensity monitoring level, so their detection must follow different path. However, this stealthy malware (botnets, spyware) also communicate over the network to deliver stolen data to the attacker, to receive attacker's commands or execute them, but this communication attempts to hide in normal network traffic.

The landscape of malware communication channels also has changed significantly. Due to widespread use of corporate and personal firewalls, better and better configured by default, most of remote access channels over arbitrary selected open ports to victim systems are now blocked. But these firewalls generally do not block the outgoing connections, so malware writers changed to *call home* mode of communication, starting connections outbound via mostly user used channels: email, web, messengers and peer-to-peer networks.

This change has found reflection in works focusing on analyzing outgoing communication for identification of peer-to-peer traffic [16,17] and botnet traffic detection [18]. Monitoring outgoing traffic may impose restriction on types and destinations of users network activity [19], in other cases (Huijun et al. [20]) to verify potentially suspicious traffic destinations some forms of user cooperation is anticipated.

These outgoing communication paths are heavily used, so search for signs of malware communication in massive user generated traffic resembles the quest for a needle in a haystack. It is possible to derive some hints from the descriptions of known malware behavior. Since malware rarely infiltrates single system, there are chances, that *call home* communication should emerge from many infected hosts, and follow similar timing and destination, and also other traffic properties. Yen et al. [18] use traffic aggregation of argus recorded data flows from campus edge router for selection of systems possibly infected with malware.

4   Detection of Signs of Malware Operation

Our work is aimed at the design of the malware operation warning system. We assume that current malware protection tools may miss some new types of stealth malware, so we want to check for signs of malware operation on the system. We search the algorithm, which helps us to identify these signs without the knowledge of malware code or details of operation.

We assume, that each type of malware attempts to reach its creator over the network to deliver results of own operation, and we want to expose the traces of this communication. Instead of monitoring combined network traffic on network gateway we move the traffic acquisition point to user system, to record system's network activity. This way we reduce amount of recorded information to system's network flows and we may have access to additional, internal parameters related to network communication.

According to this assumption a dedicated program, monitoring all events on Windows kernel Transport Driver Interface (TDI) API (*tdilog*) was designed, recording all TCP/UDP protocols stack event's data, with additional information (time stamp, communicating process PID, path, process context, type of event and amount of transmitted / received via given port data). Data recording was modeled after argus flows, with pair of records (port open, closed) describing data exchange in network flow (over network connection).

To further reduce the amount of analyzed traffic data we expected that communication algorithms embedded in typical user's applications (ex. web browsers, email clients, messengers) influenced the properties of outbound network traffic and results in some similarities in outgoing flows properties, which may help us to filter out big part of network flows associated with legal users' activity.

Because *tdilog* records contain additional information's about the processes responsible for the given network communication and the volume of transmitted data in both direction, we may consider further constrain of our search to flows originating rather from system than the user accounts, taking place in moments unrelated to user activity and during which more data leaves the system than comes in.

4.1   Benign Traffic Reduction Algorithm

From analysis of network activity patterns [21] of selected user's application a set of temporal relationships between outgoing flows (Fig. 1) was derived. A model of *Web-flow* (a set of network flows generated by web browser in reaction to user single action – mouse click) was assumed for user initiated flows selection and flows related timing parameters were measured.

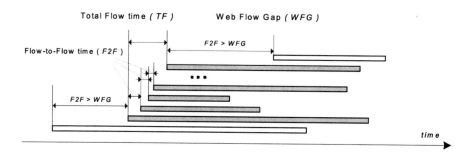

Fig. 1. Web-flow parameters definition

A set of network flows with the *Flow-to-Flow* start (F2F) time values smaller than *Web Flow Gap* (WFG) creates the web-flow. For the sake of our algorithm we assume, that destination IP addresses (end points) of net flows belonging to given web-flow are intentionally contacted in user initiated web browser connection, so these IP addresses may be marked as user-known and all tdilog records containing these addresses may be removed from further analysis as not related to searched malware communication.

Thus the algorithm for user initiated flows reduction consists of the following steps:

- For each start of outgoing flows (*tdilog* record of the type CONNECT), identified by process PID and destination port *dport* compute F2F time (time to the next CONNECT event with the same PID and *dport* values) and append it to the current record.
- If the computed F2F time is smaller than selected threshold value, read the destination IP address value from the record and save as temp.IP.
- Check the values of destination IP address in all *tdilog* records and mark each occurrence of the value stored in temp.IP with the flag *user-known address*.

Repeat these steps for each process PID and destination port *dport* value recorded in *tdilog* logs. Then select the remaining flow records without the *user-known address* flag set for next step of the analysis.

Result of algorithm operation depends on the selected value of threshold parameter, and this in turn, should reflect the properties of traffic patterns of web-flows generated by given user applications. The tests run in [21] show that mean value of F2F time depends slightly on the efficiency of web server and distance between server and user systems, and in more visible way on the type of web browser, and measured mean values span from 0.02 to about 0.35 seconds.

4.2   Web-Flows Detection Tests

To check the procedure operation on the real data some sets of *tdilog* logs were analyzed. At first the logs recorded on a test system used for web browsers flows analysis [21] were processed. The test system opens selected web sites using four popular browsers (internet explorer, firefox, chrome and opera), the same site was visited sequentially by all browsers with visit margin of about 30–90 seconds and no other applications were run on test system.

The value of threshold was gradually incremented from 0.023 to 0.615 seconds. After each run of procedure with selected threshold value some statistics related to remaining (not marked as user-known) flows were recorded. Results are contained the Table 1. Threshold value *none* represents initial flows number.

All programs included in table make their own secure outbound connections (dport 443) to some external systems (in tests only normal http pages were contacted), and at least part of this connections was rather unrelated to web-flows (F2F time > then 0.615 seconds). Most of the web flows were marked in first program runs, and probably optimal threshold value lie between 0.085 and 0.125 second.

In next step, the network activity of some users' systems were analyzed. The first one operates only in working hours and daily is switched on/off. Results of its outbound flows analysis is presented in Table 2.

The other system operates in lab in continuous mode, 24 hours a day. For the test, the data from one day, 11 February 2011, was selected. Because of continuous operation, *tdilog* logs contain multiple instances of the same programs

Table 1. Numbers of non marked flows for given threshold value – test system

Programs	dport	Flows count								
google/chrome.exe	80	179	19	15	14	7	7	6	4	4
settings/chrome.exe	443	5	1	1	1	1	1	1	1	1
google_update.exe	80	5	3	3	3	3	0	0	0	0
iexplore.exe	80	112	26	20	17	12	12	10	7	5
iexplore.exe	443	3	2	2	2	2	2	2	2	2
firefox.exe	80	158	24	20	20	12	6	4	4	4
firefox.exe	443	2	1	1	1	1	1	1	1	1
opera.exe	80	250	33	25	17	5	5	4	3	3
opera.exe	443	16	9	6	6	0	0	0	0	0
svchost.exe	80	9	9	9	9	7	7	7	6	6
svchost.exe	443	2	2	2	2	2	2	2	2	2
Threshold:		none	.023	.050	.085	.125	.185	.275	.430	.615

Table 2. Numbers of non marked flows for given threshold value – user system

Programs	dport	Flows count								
C:/Program Files/iexplore.exe	80	2801	266	220	175	175	72	63	40	35
C:/Program Files/iexplore.exe	443	407	4	4	4	4	1	1	1	1
C:/Program Files/iexplore.exe	1935	2	2	2	2	2	2	2	2	2
C:/Program Files/firefox.exe	80	41	20	18	18	18	9	8	8	8
C:/Program Files/firefox.exe	443	45	2	2	2	2	1	1	1	1
C:/Program Files/realplay.exe	80	4	4	4	4	4	4	3	3	3
C:/Program Files/trueplay.exe	80	1	1	1	1	1	1	1	1	1
C:/.../system32/spoolsv.exe	515	2	2	2	2	2	2	2	2	2
C:/.../system32/svchost.exe	80	2	2	2	2	2	2	1	1	1
C:/.../system32/svchost.exe	443	11	11	11	11	11	11	11	11	11
Threshold:		none	.050	.085	.125	.185	.275	.410	.615	.930

with different PID's, and sometimes with different behavior. Results of flow analysis are presented in Table 3.

All tables (Tables 1–3) show correct behavior of our algorithm, most of the recorded web-flows were marked at first tested (smallest) value of the threshold, at 0.050 second, and probably optimal threshold value is somewhere between 0.185 and 0.275 second.

Algorithm reduces mainly the number of unmarked outbound system connections to port 80 and 443 (web traffic) and preserve nearly all outgoing connections done by system software and installed applications (ex. realplayer, trueplayer, svchost from Table 2 or driverscan, googleupdater in Table 3).

Analyzed logs show also some interesting facts about browsers behavior – programs make sporadic connections to some high ports e.g. internet explorer to port 1935 (Table 2) and google chrome to ports 54 680 and 54 709 (Table 3). IP addresses remaining on the list after web-flows marking were also analyzed. Most of them belong to search service providers (google.com); software updates services – Microsoft, Mozilla, Opera, Skype and some of them to web monitoring

Table 3. Numbers of remaining for analysis flows – lab system

Programs	Proc.ID	dport	Flows count								
chrome.exe	2784	21	2	2	2	2	2	2	2	2	2
chrome.exe	2784	80	705	43	36	32	32	18	13	10	10
chrome.exe	2944	80	3	3	3	3	3	3	3	3	3
chrome.exe	2784	443	9	9	9	9	9	9	9	9	9
chrome.exe	2784	54680[a]	2	2	2	2	2	2	2	2	2
googleUpdate.exe	2784	80	6	6	6	6	6	6	6	6	6
DriverScan.exe	3084	80	4	4	4	4	4	4	4	4	4
iexplore.exe	3376	80	13	10	4	4	4	2	0	0	0
iexplore.exe	3376	443	2	2	2	2	2	2	2	2	2
iexplore.exe	2924	80	295	56	44	32	32	19	13	13	10
iexplore.exe	3936	80	232	79	61	57	57	24	12	6	2
iexplore.exe	3936	443	15	5	5	5	5	2	2	2	2
iexplore.exe	2924	8080	60	0	0	0	0	0	0	0	0
iexplore.exe	3936	8080	29	0	0	0	0	0	0	0	0
pg_ctl.exe	1716	5432	2	2	2	2	2	2	2	2	2
skype.exe	3992	80	8	8	8	8	8	8	8	8	8
skype.exe	3992	443	14	13	10	10	10	10	10	9	9
skype.exe	3992	52657[b]	8	8	8	8	8	8	8	8	8
svchost.exe	1136	80	2	1	1	1	1	1	1	1	1
svchost.exe	1136	443	2	2	2	2	2	2	2	2	2
rundll32.exe	952	80	1	1	1	1	1	1	1	1	1
Threshold:			none	.050	.085	.125	.185	.275	.410	.615	.930

[a] Chrome makes single connections to ports 54680 and 54709 ports.
[b] Skype makes separate single connections to 5698, 12221, 15532, 34308, 39228, 41537, 52657 and 65298 ports.

services like Akamai Technologies. There were no intentionally visited web sites addresses on this list.

4.3 Some Malware Operation Tests

To check our assumptions about algorithm ability to enhance visibility of malware operation traces in recorded outbound network flows were necessary to run on the examined algorithm with data recorded on systems infected with some malware programs. To get such data we decided to intentionally run some malware on virtual machine test system. From installed on unprotected research network honeypot system *dionaea* [22] we captured some new malware samples daily.

The problem was to find some malware operating in an expected way. Many of the captured samples operate like the active internet worms, generating a lot of visible scanning traffic or are totally unknown to Internet search engines. Our goal was to find low activity sample, which can be left operating on test systems for some time and allows the normal usage of the system on the network, to fill logs with normal user web activity.

Table 4. Numbers of remaining for analysis flows – infected system

Programs	dport	Flows count								
Opera/opera.exe	80	302	19	15	11	11	10	0	0	0
Opera/opera.exe	80	120	9	8	7	7	7	6	6	4
Opera/opera.exe	443	113	69	65	62	62	60	60	14	14
/Explorer.exe	25	1044	214	214	214	214	33	33	24	24
/Explorer.exe	25	957	41	41	41	41	8	8	8	8
/Explorer.exe	8800	101	101	101	101	101	101	101	101	101
/Explorer.exe	8800	81	81	81	81	81	81	81	81	81
/svchost.exe	80	4	4	4	4	4	3	3	3	3
/svchost.exe	443	1	1	1	1	1	0	0	0	0
Threshold:		none	.050	.085	.125	.185	.275	.410	.615	.930

Started malware has MD5 sum f273d1283364625f986050bdf7dec8bb and the size of 57 344 bytes. After infection VM system was responsive and there was possible to use it web browser and visit some web sites. Infected system operated approximately six hours and after that *tdilog* logs were exported for analysis. The results of algorithm's operation are presented in Table 4.

The started malware turned out to be an e-mail worm, and operated in the system under the name of Explorer.exe program. During the test the system was restarted, and therefore there are two instances of operating programs in the logs. Malware divided its operation between an attempt to contact mail servers of America Online (...mx.aol.com) and probably proxy system 174.122.138.154 (ISP *theplanet.com* in Huston, TX) on 8800 port.

Program's network activity was rather moderate, with F2F time of about 30 seconds and generally unsuccessful – there was no data transfer in the network connections. The program do not attempt to contact web servers, so its operation was clearly visible in *tdilog* logs. Opera browser generated network flows were successfully marked at threshold value about 0.085–0.125 second. The operation of program email service was irregular, attempts to contact many times only few IP addresses were made, and some connections had very short F2F time, so algorithm treated them like web-flows.

5   Conclusion

In this paper a concept of system local network activity monitoring, based on recording system's network communication was presented and it's usage for outbound flows monitoring for malware operation detection was described. An algorithm for user's outgoing web-flows selection on the basis of the net-flows properties of installed application programs and web browsers were defined. For web-flow definition a flow-to-flow start time (F2F) was selected and a group of net flows with F2F time's smaller than selected threshold value constituted the web-flow.

User activated transmissions generated in response to user actions (mouse clicks) are shaped by communication algoritms embedded in installed applications and web browsers in the form of web-flows. Detected user's web-flows in the outbound system's network activity may be marked as probably safe and may expose this way potential signs of malware hidden traffic. Some results of web-flows detection in recorded logs of system's network activity from clean and infected systems were also presented.

The result of tests proves that proposed method of enhancing visibility of non-user initiated outgoing traffics in network activity logs works according to our expectations, and improves chances for malware traffic detection.

References

1. Higgins, K.J.: Lab Test Results: Detect The Most Zero-Day Attacks...,
   `http://www.darkreading.com/security/antivirus/222002625/index.html`
2. Cyveillance testing finds AV vendors detect on average less than 19% of malware attacks, `http://www.cyveillance.com/web/news/`
   `press_rel/2010/2010-08-04.asp`
3. Bilar, D.: Flying below the Radar: What modern malware tells us,
   `http://cs.wellesley.edu/~dbilar/papers/Bilar_ModernMalware_HGI2007.pdf`
4. Q1 2007 Malware Outbreak Trends: Server-Side Polymorphic Malware Explodes Across Email, `http://www.altn.com/Literature/WhitePapers/Other/`
   `Alt-N_Commtouch_2007_Q1_Malware_Trends_Report.pdf`
5. Annual Report PandaLabs 2010, `http://press.pandasecurity.com/wp-content/`
   `uploads/2010/05/PandaLabs-Annual-Report-2010.pdf`
6. Rozas, C., Khosravi, H., Sunder, D.K., Bulygin, Y.: Enhanced Detection of Malware, `http://www.infoq.com/articles/malware-detection-intel`
7. Carter, B.: Argus – auditing network activity, `http://www.qosient.com/argus/`
8. Skrzewski, M.: Wykrywanie działania niepożądanego oprogramowania. In: 14th Konferencja Sieci Komputerowe, Zakopane (2007)
9. Detecting Botnets with Network ADS, `http://blog.damballa.com/?p=547`
10. Fernandes, G., Owezarski, P.: Automated classification of network traffic anomalies,
    `http://www.docstoc.com/docs/29514548/`
    `Automated-Classification-of-Network-Traffic-Anomalies/`
11. Zaparelao, B., Mendes, L., et al.: Three levels network analysis for anomaly detection, `http://netgna.it.ubi.pt/pdfs/2009-SOFTCOM2.pdf`
12. Barford, P., Plonka, D.: Characteristics of network traffic flow anomalies,
    `http://citeseerx.ist.psu.edu/viewdoc/download?doi=10.1.1.74.7539.pdf`
13. Gu, Y., McCallum, A., Towsley, D.: Detecting anomalies in network traffic using maximum entropy estimation, `http://conferences.sigcomm.org/imc/2005/`
    `papers/imc05efiles/gu/gu.pdf`
14. Sophos: Security threat report: 2010, `http://www.sophos.com/sophos/docs/eng/`
    `papers/sophos-security-threat-report-jan-2010-wpna.pdf`
15. Blue Coat Systems Inc.: The alarming shift in cybercrime,
    `http://www.bluecoat.com/doc/7993`
16. Sendil, M.S., Nagarajan, N.: An Optimized Method for Analyzing the Peer to Peer Traffic, `http://www.eurojournals.com/ejsr_34_4_09.pdf`
17. Karagiannis, T., Broido, A., Faloutsos, M., Kcclaffy: Transport Layer Identification of P2P Traffic, `http://www.caida.org/publications/papers/2004/`
    `p2p-layerid/p2p-layerid.pdf`

18. Yen, T.F., Reiter, M.K.: Traffic Aggregation for Malware Detection,
    http://www.ece.cmu.edu/~tyen/TAMD.pdf
19. Wippich, B.: Detecting and Preventing Unauthorized Outbound Traffic,
    http://www.sans.org/reading_room/whitepapers/detection/
    detecting-preventing-unauthorized-outbound-traffic_1951
20. Huijun, X., Prateek, M., Deian, S., Chehai, W., Danfeng, Y.: User-Assisted Host-
    Based Detection of Outbound Malware Traffic, http://www.cs.rutgers.edu/
    research/technical_reports/report.php?series_id=1&report_id=658
21. Skrzewski, M.: Analyzing Outbound Network Traffic. In: Kwiecień, A., Gaj, P.,
    Stera, P. (eds.) 18th Conference on Computer Networks, CN 2011, Ustroń, Poland.
    CCIS, vol. 160. Springer, Heidelberg (2011)
22. Dionaea catches bugs, http://dionaea.carnivore.it/

Intercepting Mobile Phone Calls and Short Messages Using a GSM Tester

Iosif Androulidakis

Jožef Stefan International Postgraduate School
Jamova 39, Ljubljana SI-1000, Slovenia
sandro@noc.uoi.gr

Abstract. In this paper, we present and explain both the theoretical and the practical background of mobile phone interception using a GSM tester, providing valuable security advice. A live demonstration during the conference, featuring an actual implementation of the proposed setup will further convince the readers about the feasibility of the task.

Keywords: GSM, interception, GSM tester, IMSI catcher, mobile phone security.

1 Introduction

Interception of mobile phone calls used to be a simple radio-scanning exercise back in the era of the first analog systems. Digital systems such as GSM proved to be a lot more secure, encompassing encryption and difficult to overcome complexity. As it is the case with every other technology however, the scientific community soon started theoretical discussions about the algorithms' security. Following, attackers managed to mount practical attacks too. There are many papers discussing crypto attacks to the GSM standard itself or to its various implementations by different vendors. GSM mobile phone communications can easily be intercepted, without performing any cryptanalysis, using a fake base station. The main shortcoming of GSM specification in that respect is that there is no provision for the network to authenticate itself to the user. Only the user has to authenticate himself in order to gain access to the network. Secondly, encryption is not mandatory and if present the algorithm can be negotiated In case the base station does not support encryption, then the mobile phone can proceed to the call without it. As such, a fake base station in the proximity of a user, without encryption supported (or disabled) is all that is needed to intercept his communication using a simple man in the middle approach.

2 Interception Risks

The necessary setup ideally consists of an industrial base station, the same as the ones used by the network operators. However, this expensive setup can easily be substituted using just some advanced GSM testing equipment. These equipments

A. Kwiecień, P. Gaj, and P. Stera (Eds.): CN 2011, CCIS 160, pp. 281–288, 2011.

provide all the necessary signaling for the operation of the handset and can also demodulate voice out of the digital signal. They can also intercept the IMSI (International Mobile Subscriber Identity) of the user's SIM (Subscriber Identity Module) card and the IMEI (International Mobile Equipment Identity) of his handset. At the same time, they can read the short messages (SMS) that the user is trying to send. The malicious user further can initiate calls or send messages to the victim, choosing freely any caller identity he pleases. A very interesting fact is that not only plaintext messages but also specific binary ones can be send towards the handset. Such messages are normally restricted only for provider's usage and blocked in case a simple user tries to send them. Using the equipment and the setup presented in this paper, this check is circumvented and the attacker can indeed send such messages.

3   Experimental Setup and Tools

The tools needed to conduct the experiment are:

1. A GSM tester [1,2,3] such as the one seen in Fig. 1,
2. An antenna (GSM testers usually are connected with a special cable directly to the antenna of the handset under test, but in our case we will transmit in the open air using the antenna),
3. A GSM repeater [4] (optionally, in order to increase the effective distance of the interception),
4. A mobile handset with monitoring software installed or enabled (further explained below),
5. A second mobile phone or land line in order to "channel" the interception communication through it. This phone is connected to the audio out/audio in output of the demodulator, as seen to the right of Fig. 1.

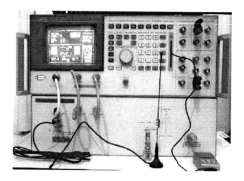

Fig. 1. A typical GSM tester

A PC with IEEE488.2 and serial port connectivity would enable the full automation of the process. In any case, the connection details are straight forward and need not be presented here.

4   Theory and Implementation

ITU-T E.212 [5] defines a list of Mobile Country Codes (MCCs) for use in identifying mobile stations in wireless telephone networks, particularly GSM and
UMTS networks. There are also Mobile Network Codes (MNCs) that further
discriminate operators in a given country. As such the MCC/MNC combination
is universally unique for each operator. This information is freely available, and
can even be accessed by Netmonitor.

The first step in our demonstration is to set into the base station-GSM tester
the MCC and the MNC of the operator of the SIM of the mobile phone to
intercept. Table 1 shows the relevant entries for Greece.

Table 1. MCC and MNCs for Greece

MCC	Country	MNC	Network
202	Greece	01	COSMOTE
202	Greece	05	VODAFONE
202	Greece	10	WIND

Netmonitor (or Engineering Menu) which was mentioned previously is a special mode in GSM mobile phones, used to measure network and phone operating
parameters and status [6]. When activated, a new, additional menu usually appears, providing a wealth of information. It must be noted that each phone has
different capabilities in regards to Netmonitor and there are different methods
of activation.

Continuing the process, the most important clue that Netmonitor provides for
the needs of the experiment is the ARFCNs (absolute RF channel numbers) that
near-by GSM base stations BCCHs transmit in. In Figure 2, such a Netmonitor phone screen is presented, providing information about BCCHs (broadcast
control channels) in the vicinity of the phone.

BCCH is a signalling channel that carries information about the identity, configuration and available features of the base station. Mobile phones continuously
"listen" to that broadcast signal in order to be able to communicate with the

Fig. 2. Netmonitor showing the neighboring channels

Fig. 3. Victim phone has camped-on to the fake base station

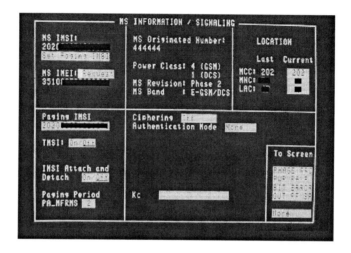

Fig. 4. Details of IMSI, IMEI and calling number of the victim, available to the GSM tester

GSM network. This channel also provides a list of ARFCNs used by neighboring BTSs.

So, the second step towards launching the attack would be to instruct our fake base station to transmit into one of these RF channels, effectively masking the legitimate signals and seizing control of the nearby mobile phones.

As it can be seen in Fig. 3, a few moments after the operation of the GSM tester, the "victim" phone camps on to our fake base station according to GSM standards procedures [7,8,9]. Namely, the GSM tester is transmitting in channel 84 (which was the already selected channel by the mobile phone before the "intrusion" as was seen in Fig. 2). The received signal from the GSM tester, overpowers the legitimate signal since our transmitter is far closer than the antenna of the base station of the network provider. It is also interesting to note, that in the specific setup we have instructed the BCCH from the GSM tester not to advertise any other BCCHs (hence the rest of neighboring channels is full of 00).

Following this point, every call attempt originating from the cell phone will be logged by our equipment. In Fig. 4, we can see among other things, that IMSI, IMEI and the number that the user is trying to dial are decoded. One has merely to dial the number requested (444444 in our example) by the "victim" phone, using the second phone which will actually dial the call, channelling the communication, as in the classical concept of the man in the middle attack.

5   Problem Solution

GSM engineers suggested that the lack of encryption, being a tell-tale that the phone is under a possible interception should be mentioned to the user. This could be achieved with a special mechanism via an indicator (Fig. 5).

Fig. 5. The (lack of) ciphering indicator

As we will see, it apparently took many years for that mandatory feature to mature and, even today, not all manufacturers comply with it. Most of the handset vendors implement this mechanism using an icon or a cryptic symbol that the user has to figure out its meaning (an exclamation mark i.e, or an unlocked pad). Even worse, users themselves (more than 80% of them) are completely unaware of the existence of this indicator [10].

During the long history of GSM standards, the first occurrence of this mechanism appeared in prETS 300 977 (GSM 11.11 V5.5.0) [11] in May 1997. In paragraph 10.3.18 of this standard, Elementary File (the equivalent of data files in SIM) 6FAD includes a cryptic "OFM bit" (Fig. 6). The meaning of OFM wasn't mentioned in the abbreviations nor elsewhere in the text.

A few months later, in July 1997, GSM 02.09 V4.4.0 [12], paragraph 3.3.3 states for first time the "ciphering indicator", referencing back to GSM 11.11 (which still used the term OFM at the moment): "The ME has to check if the user data confidentiality is switched on using one of the seven algorithms as defined in GSM 02.07. In the event that the ME detects that this is not the case, or ceases to be the case (e.g. during handover), then an indication is given to

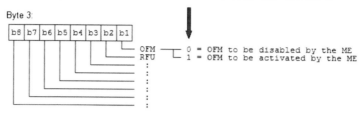

Fig. 6. The first occurrence of OFM bit in the standards

the user. This ciphering indicator feature may be disabled by the SIM (see GSM 11.11). In case the SIM does not support the feature that disables the ciphering indicator, then the ciphering indicator feature in the ME shall be enabled by default. The nature of the indicator and the trigger points for its activation are for the ME manufacturer to decide".

Then, in January 1998 there is an addition in ETS 300 505 (GSM 02.07 version 4.8.2) [13], paragraph B.1.22 that re-states the functionality of the ciphering indicator: "The ciphering indicator feature allows the ME to detect that ciphering is not switched on and to indicate this to the user, as defined in GSM 02.09. The ciphering indicator feature may be disabled by the home network operator setting data in the *administrative data* field (EFAD) in the SIM, as defined in GSM 11.11. If this feature is not disabled by the SIM, then whenever a connection is in place, which is, or becomes unenciphered, an indication shall be given to the user. Ciphering itself is unaffected by this feature, and the user can choose how to proceed".

Descendants of GSM 11.11 are 3GPP 51.011 and then 3GPP 31.102. In 3GPP 31.102 V6.5.0 [14] (March 2004) the notion of OFM gets at last abandoned in the description of EFAD in paragraph 4.2.18 in favor of the more straight forward term of Ciphering Indicator Feature (Fig. 7).

As described, the operator can disable the ciphering indicator. 10 years after 3GPP's 22.101 first occurrence of Ciphering Indicator, with 3GPP 22.101 V8.11.0 [15] of March 2009, there are some "Clarification and enhancement of ciphering indicator feature" as stated in the new phrasing, in paragraph 14: "However, terminals with a user interface that can allow it, shall offer the possibility for the user to configure the terminal to ignore the operator setting data in the SIM/USIM. If this feature is not disabled by the SIM/USIM or if the

Byte 3 (second byte of additional information):

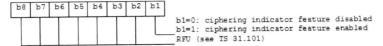

Fig. 7. OFM gets abandoned in 3GPP 31.102 V.6.5.0

terminal has been configured to ignore the operator setting data in the SIM/USIM, then additional information may be provided about the status of the ciphering. Ciphering itself is unaffected by this feature, and the user can choose how to proceed".

This standard seems to be the first step towards actually empowering the user to overcome the control of the Operator, in regards to the Ciphering Indicator. Sadly, our research didn't find any handsets that implement the feature of manually configuring the terminal to ignore the operator's setting of Ciphering Indicator [16].

Apart from the possible presence of the ciphering indicator, another clue that something is wrong is the fact that, while the victim's phone is under surveillance it cannot accept any calls or messages since it is effectively cut out of its home network. The phone under attack can however initiate calls and text messages which are intercepted as described earlier. The quality of the voice might also give a hint since it will usually be worse than normal.

Taking into consideration these facts, there are at least two ways to mitigate the problem. The first one involves clear and easy understand messages and icons, informing the user about the situation. The second, in regards to the protocol suite, is to have a mandatory authentication of the network to the handset as is the case with 3G networks.

6   Conclusion

As it was shown in this paper and the relevant demonstration, an attacker with a limited knowledge of GSM details can easily intercept nearby cell phones' communications (voice and sms). Furthermore, he can initiate phone calls and short messages choosing any identity he pleases, effectively masquerading himself. The main problem of lack of network authentication which stems from the standard itself is arguably difficult to be solved. The notification issue that is so weekly implement can however easily be improved in order to alert users when such an attack is taking place. Further research [16] presenting results from current handsets of the market will hopefully be the basis of an effort to prompt the industry to move towards better designed handsets and graphical user interfaces, which even if not completely secure would at least be informative enough when being under attack.

References

1. Agilent Technologies 8922M/S GSM Test Set User Guide. Agilent 08922-90211, UK (1998)
2. Racal 6103B Digital Radio Test Set User Manual. Racal Instruments Ltd, UK (1999)
3. Rohde & Schwarz, Digital Radiocommunication Tester CMD52/55, Operating Manual, Germany
4. Qixiang Electron Science & Technology Co. Ltd.: AnyTone AT-400 GSM. Repeater User Manual, China (2006)
5. ITU-T E.212: The international identification plan for public networks and subscriptions (May 2008)
6. Marcin's Page On-line, http://www.mwiacek.com/ (visited November 1, 2008)
7. Digital Cellular Telecommunications System (Phase 2): Mobile Radio Interface Layer 3 Specification (GSM 04.08). Doc. ETS 300 557 (1997)
8. Digital Cellular Telecommunications System (Phase 2+): Radio Subsystem Link Control (GSM 05.08 v. 8.5.0 Release 1999). Doc. ETSI TS 100 911 v. 8.5.0 (2000-10) (1999)
9. Digital Cellular Telecommunications System (Phase 2+): Functions Related to Mobile Station (MS) in Idle Mode and Group Receive Mode, (GSM 03.22 v. 8.3.0 Release 1999). Doc. ETSI TS 100 930 v. 8.3.0, (2000-01) (1999)
10. Androulidakis, I., Kandus, G.: Users' state of awareness and practices regarding mobile phones security, a quantitative survey in 10 countries and 17 universities (under submission, 2010)
11. European Telecommunications Standards Institute, Digital cellular telecommunications system (Phase2+): Specification of the Subscriber Identity Module Mobile Equipment (SIM ME) interface. ETS 300 977 (GSM 11.11 version 5.5.0) (May 1997)
12. European Telecommunications Standards Institute, Digital cellular telecommunications system (Phase 2): Security aspects. ETS 300 506 (GSM 02.09 V4.4.0) (July 1997)
13. European Telecommunications Standards Institute, Digital cellular telecommunications system (Phase 2): Mobile Stations (MS) features. ETS 300 505 (GSM 02.07 version 4.8.2) (January 1998)
14. 3rd Generation Partnership Project: Technical Specification Group Terminals, Characteristics of the USIM application. 3GPP TS 31.102 V6.5.0 (March 2004)
15. 3rd Generation Partnership Project: Technical Specification Group Services and System Aspects Service aspects, Service principles (Release 8). 3GPP TS 22.101 V8.11.0 (March 2009)
16. Androulidakis, I., Kandus, G.: Mobile phones' GUIs against man-in-the-middle attacks (or the history of the cryptic OFM bit) (under submission, 2011)

On Scalable Security Audit for Web Application According to ISO 27002

Wojciech Bylica and Bogdan Ksiezopolski

Institute of Computer Science, Maria Curie-Sklodowska University,
pl. M. Curie-Sklodowskiej 5, 20-031 Lublin, Poland

Abstract. The security audit is the process of checking compliance of the IT systems with information security managements system policy. The IT audit process according to full ISO 27002 standard is very complex issue. In this article we introduce the guidelines that point out which parts of ISO 27002 are selected for creating role based questionnaires which are used to check web application standard compliance. We present the process of formal questionnaire ordering method for web application security audit. The presented process scales security issues depending on the asset character.

Keywords: web application security, security audit, security standards, audit methodology.

1 Introduction

In the past few years internet has become dominant source of information and entertainment for modern society. People make transactions, socialise, gamble and do day to day work using countless applications, protocols and systems, which have serious problems with security [1].

One key aspect of Internet popularity are web applications. Web applications are client-server programs that are accessed via a web browser. Application itself is available thanks to working http server. Http architecture leaves a gap [2,3] in security that must be filled by security oriented approach in administration and development of webapps. There are some key problems that make it difficult.

- Developers are forced to decrease costs of web application so the security issues are omitted.
- New technology solutions used in web application that emerge on the market create new threats and presents new vulnerabilities [4].
- The free access to web application creates potentially big groups of attackers.

All of these make applications difficult to secure and because of that internet is limited by worldwide state of accepted insecurity on web pages [5,6]. Industry needs a solution that would bring new quality and show the difference between well made applications and those that are not.

The best way to show users that security is taken seriously is to apply a known and developed security standard such as ISO 27002 [7] or COBIT [8]. It is a very

A. Kwiecień, P. Gaj, and P. Stera (Eds.): CN 2011, CCIS 160, pp. 289–297, 2011.

difficult [9,10,11,12] task to comply with regulations and recommendations from the standard. The problem is that standards cover the full aspect of organisation security, involving fire exits, hardware protection and a lot other aspects they are not necessarily most important for a web application oriented organisation.

In such situation a careful selection must be applied on the standard with web application security in mind. By narrowing the perspective in such a way we achieve a set of rules that used for a specific organisation radically increase it's security, because we focus on the main problem which is the web application, it's environment and the way it's handled. This both instantly improves information protection and partially prepares organisation to achieve full standard compliance.

Such approach is foundation for webapp security auditing and gives wider perspective than traditional methods such as penetration tests. It is because standards have been developed over the years by groups of professionals and, even though stripped for web application use, they cover every aspect of organisation security [13].

In this article we would like to present the selection of the issues from the standard ISO 27002 [7] which refers to the web applications. After this selection the auditor has to define the questions which are relevant to selected issues. We would like to introduce the process of defining signification of these questions according to organization security. Thanks to this methodology the auditor can prepare the web application audit in scalable way [14] where the most important security issues will be extracted automatically.

2   Questionnaires According to ISO 27002

The security auditing process is twofold. One part concerns analysis of technical solutions used in application and the other covers formal compliance with rules defined in the standard. The first one is beyond the scope of this article. The formal compliance with the standards requires a defining set of questions that will check whether application and organisation complies with the standard. Such questionnaire is the main tool for an auditor and it's completeness and sophistication reflects upon whole audit quality.

During preliminary audit stages questionnaires are distributed between the staff who fill them out to their best knowledge. This way auditor learns about the system organisation is working in and it's flaws. Analysing all questionnaires is essential to find problems within the system and it must be done at some point.

One of the most important aspects of the described audit is a valid selection of issues from the standard. In this article we have chosen the standard ISO 27002 [7] because of it's popularity and that it is more compact in comparison to other standards or frameworks in this field [15].

Guidelines for questionnaire selection are presented below.

1. Organisations security itself is less important than applications, however it is still partially checked.

2. Every case of failure in application implementation, design, administration or security policy must be detected.
3. Each part of the standard which refers to application security directly or significantly must be checked.
4. Each real life situation that involves application and it's environment protection must be covered by appropriate questions.

The standard ISO 27002 is grouped into 12 type of issues, they are numbered from 4 to 15. In this group of questions we distinguish three sets of issues which refer to the web applications. The first one includes those which do not refer to web application. The second one refers partially and the third one refers to application security or makes it easier to do it's further checks therefore it is considered relevant for web application as a whole.

The First Group: Not Relevant to Web Applications. The system elements such as hardware, human resources and compliance with legal requirements are not taken into consideration. Therefore we omit points 8, 9 and 15.

- *Part 8: Human Resources Security* is a part completely devoted to personnel, and includes processes completely irrelevant from application security point of view.
- *Part 9: Physical and Environmental Security* fully describes important issues from the hardware point of view. It covers security of devices, cabling, working areas etc. These points are very important for application protection, however limiting security perspective from organisation to application requires that we assume proper work of these elements and do not analyse it further.
- *Part 15: Compliance* with legal requirements is irrelevant for application security. Policies and standards compliance or audit considerations don't relate directly to application security.

The Second Group: Partially Relevant to Web Applications. The points 6, 10 and 11 are the core of the standard and contain most of its requirements. It is important to emphasise the way we are limiting ISO perspective from organisation to application. Each point described in the standard that we choose to use is applied to both organisation and application. All excluded points from 10 and 11 are concerning hardware or web connection security and are not important for this audit. Every other element is key for application security and must be investigated thoroughly. This means that questions from these groups should have higher weights than others.

- *Part 6: Organising information security* describes approach the organisation has towards security. It is important to consider this especially in preliminary stages of the audit. In this part all issues must be examined except: 6.1.1, 6.1.6, 6.1.7, 6.1.8, 6.2.2, 6.2.3.

- *Part 10: Communications and operations management.* In this point one has to take care of every aspect of communication regarding both application and application staff. In this part all issues must be examined except: 10.6, 10.7.1, 10.7.2, 10.8.3.
- *Part 11: Access Control.* This issue needs no explanation as violation of access mechanisms is one of the more common events in web application security. Together with Part 10 it checks the core of technical compliance of the system. In this part all issues must be examined except: 11.3.2, 11.3.3, 11.4, 11.7.1.

The Third Group: Fully Relevant to Web Applications. The next group of issues are examined as a whole, however still with web application security in mind.

- *Part 4: Risk Assessment and Treatment* is the basis of weighing questionnaires. It defines part of the process described here.
- *Part 5: Security Policy* is also a basic requirement for further processing. It gives the auditing team information on how security is treated, how available is this information. What are managements aims, what are the consequences of policy violation etc. How it was revised and whether it was done with proper input data. Did upgrades in policy produce results? This gives context for further research.
- *Part 7: Asset Management* gives information on what resources organisation holds, which of them are used as a part of application and what are acceptable ways of their use etc.
- *Part 12: Information systems acquisition, development and maintenance.* This point doesn't need explanation. Every point in this chapter affects application life cycle directly. More than that it gives information on how sensitive data is being used and what are accepted methods of it.
- *Part 13: Information security incident management.* Proper handling of security incidents is one of more important points of application defence. It is impossible to achieve full security for any system, and the accessibility of web based programs make them even more susceptible for an attack.
- *Part 14: Business continuity management* is another important point particularly for web applications. Any attack that spreads throughout application and affects critical data may be basis for temporary application shut down. However auditing process must validate that it is done in adequate situations, and that methods of indicating such situations are safe and that methods of blocking use are effective and inaccessible for an attacker.

3   A Scalable Security Audit Approach

In this article we would like to present something more than selection of issues which are relevant to web application. We would like to present the process of defining signification of these questions according to organization security. Every selected question within the questionnaire is weighted by it's relevance to the system issues. However, every organisation has different priorities and goals and that is reflected in its asset analysis (if there one exists). Auditor on the other hand does have his own point of view and knows what are typical problems and downfalls of web application security. Both of these have to be included in the auditing process, and at some point flaws in client asset analysis have to be pointed out and described.

On the Fig. 1 one can see the diagram of scalable security audit process:

– Dashed lines indicate optional data flow and that the results of this flow are not essential for further processing.
– Arrows that split only signify that particular container data is required equally in two or more processes.
– Identical containers that are found on different places in the diagram have been placed there to increase readability. Element that does have tag *[copy]* and no input arrows does not influence data flow, and is only a reference to another element on the diagram.

In the round brackets the references to the diagram elements will be indicated. Firstly, auditor extracts useful information regarding web application security from ISO standard (Question Extraction). As the result of this step, auditor forms the sets of questions (Questionnaires for web application) and additionally refers them into the roles of employees, it could be for example: database administrator, front end developer. Optionally after reading clients organisation asset analysis the auditor can create additional questions regarding to assets defined by the client (Including specific questions regarding client assets). In the next step, the defined questionnaires are distributed to employees in the organisation. After this, during asset analysis [16] the client and auditor are defining the weights of assets of the organization ($W_j^{\text{significance}}$ and W_j^{impact}) each in their own asset analysis documents. The weights are defined according to the Formula (1):

$$W_j = W_j^{\text{impact}} * W_j^{\text{significance}} \tag{1}$$

where:

j – the id of the asset;
$W_j^{\text{significance}}$ – importance of the asset j, $W_j^{\text{significance}} \in < 0, 1 >$;
W_j^{impact} – the impact according to successful attack for the asset
   j, $W_j^{\text{impact}} \in < 0, 1 >$;
W_j – the weight of the asset j.

Later the auditor is setting asset weights for Merged Asset Analysis from the auditor's and clients asset analysis' by comparing the common asset weights according to Formula (2) (Merging Asset Analysis):

$$W_j^{\max} = \begin{cases} W_j^{\text{client}} & \text{for} \quad W_j^{\text{client}} > W_j^{\text{auditor}} \\ W_j^{\text{auditor}} & \text{for} \quad W_j^{\text{client}} \leq W_j^{\text{auditor}} \end{cases} \tag{2}$$

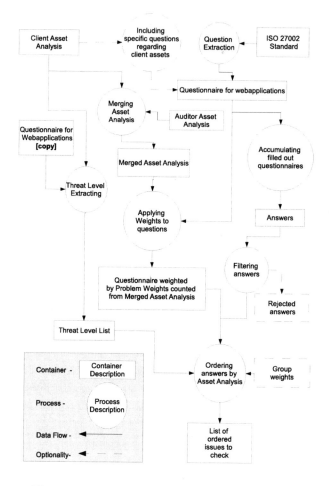

Fig. 1. The process diagram of scalable security audit

where:

j – the id of the asset;
W_j^{client} – the weight of the asset j defined by the client;
W_j^{auditor} – the weight of the asset j defined by the auditor;
W_j^{max} – the maximum weight for the asset j defined by client and auditor.

Applying weights to questions according to Formula (3) produces a list of problem weights associated with each question (applying weights to questions):

$$PW_i = \max(W_{ij}^{\text{max}}) \qquad (3)$$

where:

i – the id of the question from questionnaire;
j – the id of the asset, j=(1,. . . ,n) (n – the number of assets associated with the question);
$W_{ij}^{\max}$ – the maximum weight for the asset j, for the question i;
PW_i – the problem weight for the question i, $PW_i \in< 0, 1 >$.

Another factor that influences security issue is threat level, and it is extracted from Clients Asset Analysis according to Formula (4) (threat level extracting):

$$TL_i = \max(TL_{ij}) \qquad (4)$$

where:

i – the id of the question from questionnaire;
j – the id of the asset, j=(1,. . . ,n) (n – the number of assets associated with the question);
$\max(TL_{ij})$ – the maximum threat level of the asset j and for the question i;
TL_i – the global threat level for the question i, $TL_i \in< 0, 1 >$.

At this point it is important to stress that this work doesn't define a strict methodology of creating asset assessments. It is only pointed out that such elements are necessary for the described process. However it should be pointed out that Auditors Asset Analysis must be influenced by current security trends, statistics and any other sources chosen by the auditor. Threat level list on the other hand is extracted strictly from clients risk analysis. Any security events that have happened in the clients system will form an overall opinion about security threats and particular threat levels. Such list is a guarantee that each audit is designed specifically for a given system.

At this point all that is needed are staff answers. By acquiring filled out questionnaires from employees (Accumulating filled out questionnaires) we get information about vulnerabilities and protection. Each question reflects to some set of elements from asset analysis and it's weighted by maximum value of them all (Formula (3)). After the employees have answered all the questions (Answers), auditing team can filter questionnaires (Filtering answers). As the effect of this auditors can optionally rejected some questions in case of for an example low trustworthiness of a given answer (Rejected answers).

Optionally auditor can introduce another element that would reflect competence of each particular role in creating the final questionnaire order (group weights). Ideally each role an answering employee represents should have a corresponding weight applied in specific parts of the questionnaire (ω in Formula (5)). However to keep the process simple each answer may have the same significance ($\omega = 1$). This is included in Formula (5):

$$P_i = \frac{1}{4z} \sum_{n=1}^{z} a_n * \omega_{ni} \qquad (5)$$

where:

i – the id of the question from questionnaire;
n – the id of employee which answered the question i;
a_n – the answer for the question i from the employee n;
z – the number of employee which answered the question i;
ω_{ni} – weight of role n for question i;
P_i – the protection level of the assets associated with the question i.

At this point all that needs to be done is counting security issue value (SI) for each question according to Formula (6) and order by result values.

$$SI_i = (1 - P_i) * (TL_i * PW_i) \tag{6}$$

where:

i – the id of the question from questionnaire;
TL_i – the global threat level for the question i;
PW_i – the problem weight for the question i;
P_i – the protection level of the assets associated with the question i;
SI_i – the security issue of the question i, $SI_i \in\, <0, 1>$.

Formula 6 is a simple representation of security issue. Threat level corresponds to probability of security event occurrence and it is know from client asset analysis. Protection is a value between 0 and result of threat level and problem weight multiplication. It is known from the questionnaire answers which correspond to numeric values in the following way:

– yes – 4,
– rather yes – 3,
– rather no – 2,
– no – 1,
– no data – 0.

4   Conclusions

In modern days web applications need more than security. They need security governance, monitoring and upgrades [17]. It is very hard to achieve security level that would be fully compliant with ISO 27002. It can be done partially with great profit to the organisation, application and it's users. In the article we introduced a method of quick selection of important security issues from audit questionnaires.

The proposed scalable audit process gives the auditor knowledge about which assets are not properly protected, and in what particular way organisation fails to do that. The introduced process allows to focus on the most important security issues while including organisation priorities.

References

1. Web Application Security Trends Report Q1-Q2 (2009),
   http://www.cenzic.com/downloads/Cenzic_AppSecTrends_Q1-Q2-2009.pdf
2. Chau, J.: Application security – it all starts from here. In: Computer Fraud and Security, pp.7–9 (June 2006)
3. Morgan, D.: Network Network security and custom Web applications. Security 2000(4), 15–17 (2004)
4. Ritchie, P: The security risks of AJAX/web 2.0 applications. Network and Security (March 2007)
5. Ollmann, G.: Application Security – A Serious Pitfall. Network Security 9, 7 (2002)
6. White, L.: Internet security is the killer application for campus cards. Card Technology Today, 13–14 (November/December 2001)
7. ISO/IEC 27002 Information technology – Security techniques – Code of practice for information security management (2005)
8. IT Governance Institute Control Objectives for Information and related Technology (COBIT 4.0) (2005)
9. Kenning, M.J.: Security management standard – ISO 17799/BS 7799. BT Technol. J. 19(3) (July 2001)
10. von Solms, B.: Information Security – A Multidimensional Discipline. Computers and Security 20, 504–508 (2001)
11. Coles, L.: Kemp Information Security management: An entangled reasearch challenge. Information Security Technical Report 14, pp. 181–185. Elsevier, Amsterdam (2009)
12. Eloff, J.H.P., Eloff, M.M.: Information Security Architecture. Information Security Technical Report 14, pp. 181–185. Elsevier, Amsterdam (2009)
13. Johnson, E.C.: Security awareness: switch to a better programme (2006)
14. Ksiezopolski, B., Kotulski, Z.: Adaptable security mechanism for the dynamic environments. Computers & Security 26, 246–255 (2007)
15. von Solms, B.: Information Security governance: COBIT or ISO 17799 or both? Computers and Security 24, 99–104 (2005)
16. Information technology - Security techniques (ISO/IEC JTC 1/SC 27) (2003)
17. King, S.: Applying application security standards. Computers and Security 23, 17–21 (2004)

DNS Pseudo-Random Number Generators Weakness

Maciej Szmit and Anna Szmit

Technical University of Lodz, ul. Zeromskiego 116, 90-924 Lodz, Poland
Maciej.Szmit@gmail.com

Abstract. In article [1] we presented the results of analysis of well-known weakness of some DNS servers[1]: poor quality of pseudo-random numbers generators (PRNG), which makes it possible to hack them using the birthday attack. In this article we present extended analysis of current DNS servers: DNS build in Windows 2003 server with SP2, DNS from Windows 2008 server with SP2 and Bind ver. 9.0.p1, comparing the old ones. The analysis included the following tests of randomness: Median Runs Test, Quartile Runs Test, Runs Test for Characters and Symmetry Test and tests of autocorrelation: significance of first order autocorrelation and the test χ^2 of conformity with uniform distribution as well as test of frequency of occurrence of particular values and frequency of occurrence of pairs of values.

Keywords: DNS, pseudo-random numbers generators, birthday attack.

1 Attacks against DNS

The birthday attack described in [2] is an attack against weak authentication of DNS-querying process[2]: an attacker forces the attacked DNS to send a series of requests to authoritative domain name server and then sends a series of fake replies (with spoofed sender's IP address) with several DNS ID numbers[3], hoping one of them will be accepted by attacking DNS (this would happen if the attacker managed to select proper ID number). Comparing to a classic DNS-spoofing (when attacker sends only one reply to only one DNS-request), birthday attack[4] has a higher probability of success. Classic attack success probability (one request, n fake responses) is given by equation

---

[1] There were four DNS: djbdns, DNS build in Windows 2003 server, bind ver. 8 and DNS from NetWare 5.1 operating system.

[2] See: [3] and [4].

[3] DNS ID number is 16-bit unsigned random number which is used as authentication method for DNS response.

[4] Birthday attack owes its name to birthday paradox: how many people should we chose to achieve more than 50% probability to have at least two people born on the same day of the year (one of 365 possibilities). The answer is a very small number: 23 people. In a birthday attack when the number of possibilities is 65 536 the answer would be only 302.

A. Kwiecień, P. Gaj, and P. Stera (Eds.): CN 2011, CCIS 160, pp. 298–305, 2011.

$$P_{s1} = \frac{n}{65\,536} \ .$$

(1)

In case of birthday attack (n fake replies to n forced requests) the probability of success is given by the equation:

$$P_{s2} = 1 - \left(1 - \frac{1}{65\,536}\right)^{\frac{n(n-1)}{2}}$$

(2)

where obviously $65\,536 = 2^{16}$ is a number of possible values of 2 bytes DNS request ID.

Of course if DNS IDs were generated with poor quality Pseudo-Random Numbers Generators the IDs are easy to predict, the probability of attacker's success would increase rapidly[5]. For instance in NetWare 5.1 PRNG generates series of ID by adding (or subtracting) 1 from last ID and from time to time really generates new starting ID. If an attacker forces an attacked DNS to send him a request (it can be done by attacker spoofing client ID or if he can convince "legal" DNS client to send a query to server i.e. sending him an e-mail with link to the attacker's site) he knows current ID and can easily find out what will be next.

So there are a few characteristics that should be analyzed in process of comparing generators build in DNS servers – like a number of too-frequently appearing numbers or a number of repeating sequences (pairs at least). They are not widely used in tests of PRNGs generally but they can be very useful in this context. The mechanism of both attacks bases on DNS-cache concept: after client's DNS recognized searching IP address it put it in cache memory and when other client asks about the same symbolic address he gets the IP address from cache, so one effective attack can affect many clients until cache expiry time elapse. For this reason the attack is sometimes named "DNS cache poisoning"[6].

2   Subject, Methodology and Research Results

The aim of performed tests was to find out the statistical characteristics of the behaviours of pseudo-random numbers generators used by DNS software in view of their possible susceptibility to attacks consisting in DNS forgery. For this purpose we have performed statistical analyses of the empirically gathered series of subsequent requests generated by servers to the root servers. We generated series of 65 535 requests for each DNS and observed ID included in queries which DNS generated to the root servers. The test was conducted in the following way: in an isolated network, on a client machine we have activated a script generating successive requests to the tested server and on the third machine we have captured the traffic directed from the server to root servers. In order to avoid unnecessary flooding of root servers with successive requests, what could be considered as attacks, the tests were carried out in an isolated network: requests generated by

---

[5] See [5,6].

[6] See [7].

the servers were not sent to the Internet. It prolonged the test duration because in case of the lack of reply the servers must have waited for a certain time and then repeat the requests if necessary, but it allowed to gather complete data without concerns about the impact of external factors. The researches presented in the paper were aimed at the PRNG used in Domain Name Servers quality assessment. In the investigation we choose relatively actual[7] servers from operation systems: Windows 2003 with Service Pack 2, Windows 2008 with Service Pack 2 and Bind 9.0.p1 (respectively w2k3.SP2, w2k8.SP2, bind9). In the following tables we also included the results of old servers (described in article [1]): Windows 2003, BIND version 8 and djbdns (respectively w2k3, bind8 and djbdns) were chosen for the investigation.

3   Descriptive Statistics

Behaviour of bind9 server differed significantly from the behaviour of the servers operating in Windows family systems when the servers were sending two single queries addressed to the first and the alternate address of the top-level domain server (both queries of the same ID) and in the case of not receiving a response they returned the requestor a negative result, BIND kept sending a series of several queries to both addresses, where ID in the queries were different, which on one hand shows the care of generating truly random ID, but on the other hand facilitates attacking; it is enough for the false response to have the same ID as any of the queries. Additionally, generating such a large number of queries to the root servers caused overload of the DNS itself, that could not had kept up with processing of requests from requestors and omitted some of them[8]. This is why, the research was performed for two series: a series, containing the ID of the first generated queries only (marked as bind9.f) and a series containing IDs of all consecutive queries (marked as bing9.a) including those repeated.

Table 1 collects the basic descriptive statistics of all of the researched series.

Theoretical range of possible results is from 0 to 65 535 for all the generators, though in series from w2k3 and w2k3.SP2 in practice values from one fourth of this range have been obtained (series maximum was equal to 16 383). This combines directly lower median, quartiles and arithmetic average with these series. In the remaining series these quantities are very alike, as well as variation (CV) expressed as standard deviation, which for all series was 57 and 58% of average, that is desirable in this case of shape of distribution (in uniform data set distribution with value ranges beginning from zero the standard deviation ought to be 57.7% of average). It was also regarded as proper, when all series were

---

[7] All servers were patched and updated up to 15th of January 2011.

[8] For obvious reasons (the necessity of generating long sequences with consecutive value IDs) the situation of extreme system overload, generated for the research purposes (ten clients requesting simultaneously for resolving of subsequent unique addresses in the period of nearly two days) is rather improbable in reality, at least in networks where using DNS installed on a single PC is an acceptable solution. Thus, it does not seem to be any especially sensible problem.

Table 1. Basic statistics of all tested series (source: own study)

	bind8	w2k3	w2k3.SP2	w2k8.SP2	bind9.f	bind9.a
Series length (n)	65535	65535	65535	65535	65535	65535
Median	32674	8271	8217	32664	32893	32808
First quartile (Q1)	16566	4153	4086	16318	16574	16369
Third quartile (Q3)	48875	12312	12303.5	49022	49312	49166
Arithmetic average	32684.4	8236.5	8203.2	32674.9	32887.0	32734.5
Standard deviation	18843.5	4730.8	4736.8	18897.7	18912.1	18944.7
Coefficient of variation (CV)	0.577	0.574	0.577	0.578	0.575	0.579
Skewness	0.0088	-0.0078	-0.0069	0.0034	-0.0077	-0.0058
Minimum	2	0	0	1	0	0
Maximum	65535	16383	16383	65535	65531	65533
Spread	65533	16383	16383	65534	65531	65533
Number (a) of non-recurrent numbers	12701	9924	10865	41429	41508	41608
Diversity number percentage (a/n)	0.1938	0.1514	0.1658	0.6322	0.6334	0.6349

characterized by low symmetry – the asymmetry index was close to zero. It is worth noticing (in the last row), that in the series obtained by use of older DNS servers (Win.03 and bind8) a number of drawn numbers did not extended 20% of possible values from range $\{0, \ldots, 65\,535\}$, in the newer the results of drawing were much more varied (more than 63% of possible ones), that apparently shows considerable improvement in randomness.

4   Randomness Tests

Randomness has been researched with an aid of the quantile test in two variants: median test and quartile test[9]. According to the test conditions, for large samples of series generated in a random way the statistics

$$u_1 = u_2 = \frac{k - 0.5(n+1)}{\sqrt{0.25(n-1)}} \tag{3}$$

has standard normal distribution $N(0,1)$, where n corresponds to sample length, while k is a number of series (in the median test elements that are bigger and smaller than median, in the quartile test those, that are situated between the first and the third quartile and beyond them). Too small or too big number of series is considered as non-random.

   Another carried test of randomness was the runs test for characters[10]. The series are in this case monotone sequences (for which '+' corresponds to the increasing and '−' for the decreasing) of series values. Test

---

[9] See [8] pp. 37–39.
[10] See [9] vol. 56, p. 156-9.

$$u_3 = \frac{k - \frac{2n-1}{3}}{\sqrt{\frac{16n-29}{90}}} \tag{4}$$

has standard normal distribution.

For symmetry test the statistics is:

$$u_4 = \frac{w_i - 0.5}{\sqrt{\frac{0.25}{n-1}}} \tag{5}$$

where w_i is percentage of numbers less than average.

Table 2 presents results of randomness tests for the investigated series[11].

Table 2. Randomness tests results of the investigated series (source: own study)

	bind8	w2k3	w2k3.SP2	w2k8.SP2	bind9.f	bind9.a
Median Runs Test						
Test result value (u_1)	0.025	-0.018	-0.002	-0.002	-0.010	-0.017
p-value (p)	0.980	0.985	0.998	0.998	0.992	0.986
Quartile Runs Test						
Number of series (k)	32572	32718	32584	32781	32536	32869
Test result value (u_2)	-1.531	-0.391	-1.438	0.102	-1.813	0.789
p-value (p)	0.126	0.696	0.151	0.919	0.070	0.430
Runs Test for Characters						
Number of series (k)	43503	43006	43106	43826	43565	43686
Test result value (u_3)	-1.729	-6.334	-5.407	1.263	-1.155	-0.034
p-value (p)	0.0837	2.39e-10	6.39e-08	0.2066	0.2481	0.9729
Symmetry Test						
Number of values less than average	32792	32635	32712	32783	32761	32689
Percentage of numbers less than average (w_i)	0.500	0.498	0.499	0.500	0.500	0.499
Test result value (u_4)	0.191	1.035	0.434	0.121	0.051	0.613
p-value (p)	0.848	0.301	0.665	0.904	0.959	0.540

In the quantile tests all of the series achieved $p > 0.05$, that is, they positively passed the quantile runs tests (median and quartile). Similarly, good result was achieved in symmetry test investigating whether proportion less or greater than average differs significantly from 0.5, however in series generated by DNS from Window 2003 was not enough of monotone series (as a result there were, too long) to regard these series as random in the light of these tests.

---

[11] Besides test result values the table presents the values of maximum significance levels, for which it is not possible to reject the null hypothesis for a given test. For the most commonly assumed significance level 0.05 the tests with test value u have threshold value $= 1.959963985$.

5   Autocorrelation Test

The very important feature characterizing random series is lack of their auto-correlation, because existence of essential autocorrelation in principle facilitates prediction of values of series to come on the basis of known past values. This is why the significance of autocorrelation index has been researched (limiting it to first order autocorrelation). For series without first order statistic

$$t = \frac{\sum_{i=2}^{n}(y_i - \bar{y})(y_{i-1} - \bar{y})}{\sum_{i=1}^{n}(y_i - \bar{y})^2}\sqrt{n} \tag{6}$$

has Student's t-distribution with $(n-1)$ degrees of freedom[12].

The next test carried out was the test χ^2 of conformity with uniform distribution. For variables with uniform distribution statistic

$$\chi^2 = \sum_{i=1}^{r}\frac{(n_i - \frac{n}{r})^2}{\frac{n}{r}} \tag{7}$$

has distribution χ^2 with $r-1$ degrees of freedom, where r is the number of classes, the set of data has been split into (for this test $r = 10$). The Table 3 presents – besides the calculated tests values – the values of maximum significance levels, for which it is not possible to reject the null hypothesis for a given test. For the most commonly assumed significance level 0.05 the t-test (autocorrelation significance) for $65\,535 - 2$ degrees of freedom has a threshold value equal 1.960000129 while the threshold value of test χ^2 of conformity with uniform distribution for 9 degrees of freedom equals to 16.91898.

Table 3. Significance test for first order correlation and test of conformity with uniform distribution (source: own study)

	bind8	w2k3	w2k3.SP2	w2k8.SP2	bind9.f	bind9.a
First order autocorrelation significance						
r Pearson's corr. coefficient	-0.0042	0.0242	0.0162	-0.0009	0.0054	0.0123
Test r	-1.077	6.191	4.150	-0.235	1.375	3.143
p	0.282	6.01e-10	3.32e-05	0.814	0.169	0.0017
uniform distribution test						
χ^2	42.28	147515.4	147465.8	5.319	4.394	7.665
p	2.9e-06	0	0	0.806	0.884	0.568

The value of linear correlation coefficient in relation to observation delayed by 1 was in all cases small (close to zero for coefficient within range $< -1; 1 >$), thus no strong relation with the previous values in any of the series was affirmed. However in the three cases (w2k3.S2, w2k8.SP2, and bind9.a) this coefficient has value significantly different from 0.

---

[12] See [10].

Differences in the results of shape of the distribution test reflected the division between the old and the new generators. Bind8 and w2k3 distributions as well as w2k3.SP2 cannot be regarded as consistent with uniform distribution; the remaining ones do not differ from it significantly.

6   Occurence Frequency Test

As mentioned before, peculiarly significant characteristics in case of research of DNS servers is, the typical to appear, recurring pairs (series) of numbers, since their occurrence can in an obvious way considerably facilitate the attacks. The frequency of occurrence of particular values, that the series may have, has also been researched. The biggest frequencies of appearance of the particular values occurring for each of series have been found, as well as proportion of elements, occurring in the series (on the level of significance 0.05) more often, than the expected value of frequency. Test results are presented in Table 4.

Table 4. Test results of the occurrence frequency test of numbers and pairs of numbers (source: own study)

Recurrence of numbers		bind8	w2k3	w2k3	w2k8	bind9.f	bind9.a
The biggest number of occurrence of the particular value		6	56	46	8	8	8
Number of values appearing too often		10517	7457	7395	1257	1251	1231
Number of values appearing multiple times, correspondingly	4	440	2402	1734	1013	1009	982
	5	676	166	1463	202	201	205
	6	9401	1755	1139	39	29	39
	7–8	0	1156	1284	3	12	5
	9–10	0	720	650	0	0	0
	11–15	0	644	588	0	0	0
	16–20	0	281	215	0	0	0
	21–30	0	189	169	0	0	0
	31–40	0	108	140	0	0	0
	41–50	0	32	13	0	0	0
	51–56	0	4	0	0	0	0
Recurrence of pairs of numbers							
Number of non-recurrent pairs		26436	32607	56722	65533	65534	65534
Number of recurrence of pairs		39098	32927	8812	1	0	0

In all series there were numbers that recurred significantly more often than they should, it is at least 4 times. In series generated in the newer DNS servers there were numbers, that recurred as many as 8 times, but the biggest problem presented few dozen times recurrences in series generated by the use of Windows 2003 both with and without the service pack. It is also worth noticing, that while in the newer generator series in majority of these situations recurrences were equal to circa 4 times (for 65 535 trials), for the DNS server from Windows 2003 more than 10% of all drawn values recurred more than 10 times.

In the newer series the problem with the pairs of number recurring one after another disappeared. In older of the researched series this phenomenon caused big problems, indeed every second pair was recurring. It is worth mentioning, that this characteristics has significantly improved in Windows 2003 after installation Service Pack 2, though it seems to be the only significant improvement of this generator.

7   Conclusions

New versions of the DNS servers use the pseudo-random sequences generators generating numbers in a definitely better way that it use to be in the older versions of servers. At the same time, it is noticeable, that although many patches and corrections were introduced in the Windows 2003 operating system (this version is still officially supported by Microsoft), only some of the weaknesses of the generator embedded into the DNS server were corrected. It should be noticed, that there are differences in numbers and in the way of generating consecutive queries by the servers installed in the default settings, used by various operating systems. In the hypothetical case, when a DNS will have to serve a very large number of users, these differences could have influence on the efficiency of the particular solutions. Based on the conducted tests we may state that in practice the issue of predictability of generated IDs was eliminated in the latest versions of server operating systems.

References

1. Szmit, A., Tomaszewski, M., Szmit, M.: Domain Name Servers' Pseudo-Random Number Generators and DNS Cache Poisoning Attack. Polish Journal of Environmental Studies 15(4C), 184–187 (2006)
2. Stephard, J.: DNS Cache Poisoning – the Next Generation,
   http://www.lurhq.com/dnscache.pdf
3. Mockapetris, P.V.: Domain Names: Concepts and Facilities. RFC 882,
   ftp://ftp.rfc-editor.org/in-notes/rfc882.txt
4. Mockapetris, P.V.: Domain Names: Implementation Specification. RFC 883,
   ftp://ftp.rfc-editor.org/in-notes/rfc883.txt
5. Zalewski, M.: Strange Attractors and TCP/IP Sequence Number Analysis,
   http://lcamtuf.coredump.cx/newtcp/
6. Tian, J., Gu, D., Lu, H.: A Solution for Packet Validity Check Against DNS Cache Poisoning. Communications Technology, 43(08(224)), 146–151 (2010)
7. Dagon, D., Antonakakis, M., Day, K., Luo, X., Lee, C.P., Lee, W.: Recursive DNS Architectures and Vulnerability Implications. In: NDSS Symposium 2009, San Diego (2009)
8. Domanski, C.: Statystyczne testy nieparametryczne. PWE Warszawa (1979)
9. Edington, E.S.: Table for Number of Runs of Signs of First Differences in Ordered Series. Journal of the American Statistical Association (1961)
10. Hanke, J.E., Reitsch, A.G.: Business Forecasting (Hardcover). Prentice-Hall, Englewood Cliffs (1998)

Using HTTP as Field Network Transfer Protocol

Arkadiusz Jestratjew and Andrzej Kwiecień

Silesian University of Technology, Institute of Informatics,
Akademicka 16, 44-101 Gliwice, Poland
{arkadiusz.jestratjew,andrzej.kwiecien}@polsl.pl
http://www.polsl.pl

Abstract. Increasing popularity of Ethernet-based field networks is an opportunity to integrate heterogeneous automation devices and systems. To achieve this goal, a universally adopted open communication protocol is required. In general computing, Hypertext Transfer Protocol (HTTP) performs that role. In this paper, the HTTP is evaluated as a core data transfer protocol of industrial field networks, and compared to a proprietary Ether-S-Bus communication protocol of Saia Burgess PCD Series programmable logic controllers.

Keywords: distributed, industrial, network, fieldbus, Ethernet, HTTP, Ether-S-Bus, integration.

1 Introduction

Modern industrial automation systems rely heavily on data exchange over industrial networks. During past years, a variety of network protocols were developed for specific application areas, that can be roughly categorized as follows.

1. Low cost networking solutions designed for simple field devices (pushbuttons, position sensors, pressure sensors etc.) such as AS-Interface [1] or HART [2].
2. Low latency, high speed networking solutions for motion control applications such as Ethernet PowerLink (EPL) [3] or Profinet IO [4].
3. General purpose field networks for robust data exchange in distributed industrial automation systems. Many industrial networking solutions, either proprietary or "open", fit in this category, e. g. Modbus [5], Profibus [6], Profinet CBA [4], Ether-S-Bus [7], EGD or SRTP [8], to name just a few.
4. Vertical communication solutions designed to integrate industrial automation and enterprise management systems, such as OPC [9], OPC Unified Architecture [10] or Internet protocols, namely HTTP [11] and FTP [12].

Many industrial networks use dedicated physical layer hardware. However, during several past years, one can observe an increasing popularity of Ethernet-based field networks. Besides high bit rate and relatively low cost, Ethernet-based field networks are able to carry several unrelated protocols at once, to provide a way to interconnect automation devices coming from independent vendors. While

A. Kwiecień, P. Gaj, and P. Stera (Eds.): CN 2011, CCIS 160, pp. 306–313, 2011.

interconnection is not equivalent to *integration*, a common physical layer hardware makes integration much easier. There are several popular communication protocols for field networks based on Ethernet and TCP/IP protocol stack, such as Modbus/TCP [13] or Profinet, that could be used as integration platform, however none of them are universally adopted.

In general computing, HTTP protocol is *lingua franca* for integration of heterogeneous systems. HTTP is used to access an abstract or physical resources globally identified by URIs (Universal Resource Identifiers) [14] and to execute operations provided by Web Services, based on SOAP [15] or REST [16,17]. Vendors of automation devices acknowledge this fact by providing limited support for HTTP protocol in modern devices as follows.

1. Programmable Logic Controllers (PLC) may include HTTP server software, serving typically static content (html pages, Java applets etc.) and live process data from PLC memory [18]. In rare cases (e.g. [19]), PLC memory can be written to via HTTP protocol.
2. Human-Machine Interface (HMI) devices may include Web browser application [20,21]. Such devices are sometimes called *Web Panels*.

On-board HTTP server software available in PLCs can be used in vertical communication solutions, providing data when requested by management and supervisory systems. However, reversed approach that PLC requests services via HTTP, can also be profitable as shown in previous work [22,23]. At the time of writing, there is no automation devices vendor known to the authors that provide HTTP client software in PLC devices. Therefore HTTP client software must be implemented in PLC application software. Such implementation was created for Saia Burgess PCD Series devices [19].

Having HTTP client and server software running on a PLC, HTTP-based field network can be created. In this paper, HTTP is evaluated as a core protocol of industrial field network and compared to proprietary Ether-S-Bus protocol, that is a native (built in the firmware) field network protocol of Saia Burgess PCD Series PLCs.

2   Experiment Setup

The automation system consists of two Saia Burgess PCD3.M5540 controllers with firmware 1.10.16 (station A) and 1.14.23 (station B) connected via typical 100 Mbps Fast Ethernet switch. Station A is a *master* that issues requests to *slave* station B. These requests, sent with either HTTP or Ether-S-Bus protocol, are handled entirely in firmware of station B. Application software of station B executes no network-related code.

Firmware of station B executes network requests immediately after reception. Neither Ether-S-Bus nor HTTP requests are synchronized with slave station sweep. Therefore impact of station B sweep time on network exchanges is considered negligible. Such approach can be advantageous in typical Saia PCD applications where independent process values (e.g. temperature or pressure measurements) are transferred. However, one must take precautions if complex data structures shall ever be transferred, to avoid access to possibly inconsistent values.

Application software of station A manages Ether-S-Bus network exchanges with standard communication library available for Fupla programming language. HTTP data exchanges are processed by experimental HTTP communication library. All exchanges are processed synchronously, therefore station A sweep time has measurable impact on exchange duration. A parametrized delay loop is included in application software of station A to achieve desired sweep time.

A single network exchange can spread over several PLC sweeps. Ether-S-Bus telegrams are encapsulated in UDP and are able to transfer up to 32 signed long (32 bit) integer values. At most 16 383 values can be transferred by a single exchange. Such long exchanges are automatically split into several telegrams.

HTTP data stream is processed in chunks no longer than 1460 bytes, that is a maximum length of data buffer supported by Saia PCD Ethernet Open Data Mode API [24]. At most one data chunk is processed during a PLC sweep. At most 16 383 values can be transferred by a single HTTP exchange. Total number of data bytes is highly dependent of transferred values. Each 32 bit value is encoded as text, therefore a sequence of single digit positive numbers $(0 \ldots 9$, *short numbers*) may fit in lower number of chunks than a sequence of negative ten-digits numbers $(-2^{31} \ldots -1\,000\,000\,000$, *long numbers*).

Each experiment consists of three sets of measurements taken for HTTP (both short and long numbers) and Ether-S-Bus protocols, holding all else equal. Measurements of time are based on internal PLC system clock running with resolution of 1 ms. Each data series consists of 1000 individual measurements.

3   Results of Measurements

Maximum exchange duration vs. PLC sweep time is shown on Fig. 1, 2 and 3. Results obtained for 16 383 and 1024 transferred values are quite reasonable. However maximum durations of HTTP exchanges that transfer 32 values, measured for ≈ 5 ms sweep time are unexpectedly high. A closer investigation (Fig. 4, 5) reveals that there are less than 5% exchanges that last for several seconds. These unusual long exchanges increase average exchange duration to approx. 350 ms for exchanges of less than 1024 values, while a typical exchange lasts around 100 ms (Fig. 6).

This strange behavior was further tracked down to a limited pool of TCP connections that is being exhausted by experimental HTTP client implementation. Therefore, a connection cannot be open anymore until one of closing TCP connections that stays in TIME-WAIT state [25] is finally closed.

Performance of HTTP communication is compared with Ether-S-Bus on Fig. 7 and Fig. 8 for sweep times ≈ 50 ms and ≈ 100 ms respectively. Such sweep times are more typical for real world PLC applications and are also long enough to avoid exhausting of TCP connection pool.

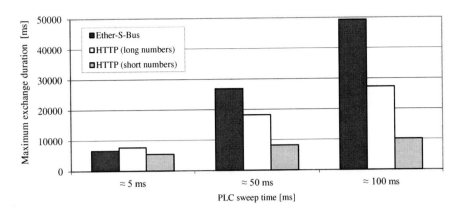

Fig. 1. Temporal properties of data exchange of 16 383 32-bit integer values

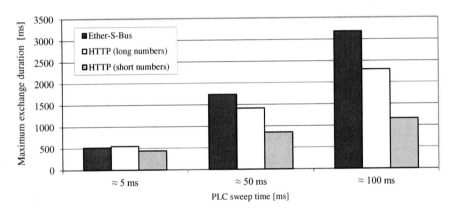

Fig. 2. Temporal properties of data exchange of 1024 32-bit integer values

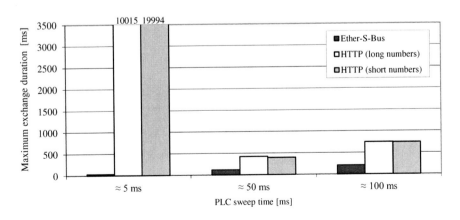

Fig. 3. Temporal properties of data exchange of 32 32-bit integer values

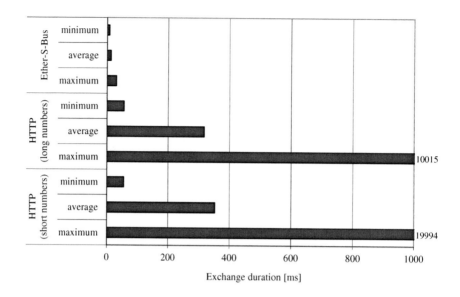

Fig. 4. Temporal properties of data exchange of 32 values for sweep time ≈ 5 ms

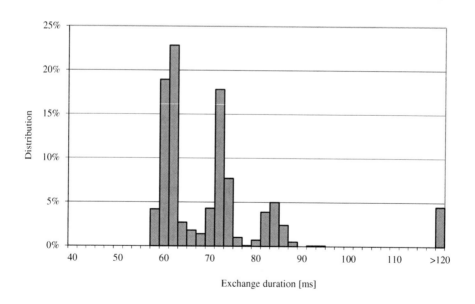

Fig. 5. Distribution of duration of data exchange of 32 values for sweep time ≈ 5 ms

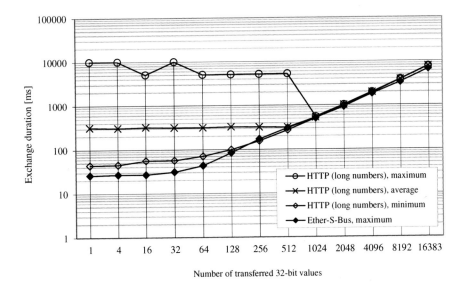

Fig. 6. Temporal properties of data exchange for sweep time ≈ 5 ms

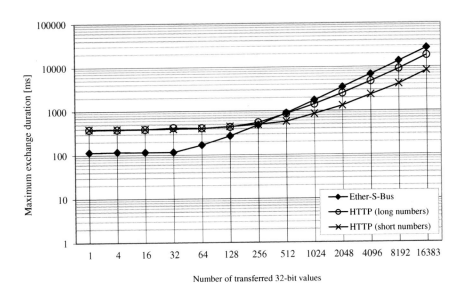

Fig. 7. Temporal properties of data exchange for sweep time ≈ 50 ms

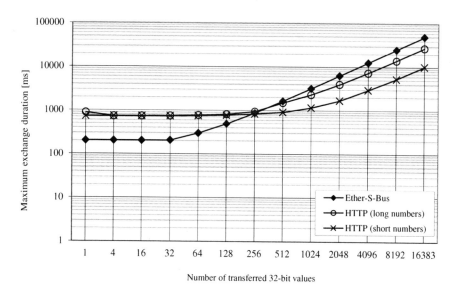

Fig. 8. Temporal properties of data exchange for sweep time $\approx 100\,\mathrm{ms}$

4   Conclusions

HTTP communication involves some overhead related to TCP connection management and request/response processing. That overhead can be relatively large, especially for short data exchanges that are typical for horizontal communications in field networks. However, even relatively large overhead may not prevent the use of HTTP in many real-world applications, as measured durations of short exchanges do not exceed 8 PLC sweeps.

The measurements reveal an issue that may exist in a simple HTTP client implementation that use new TCP connections for each data exchange. The pool of available TCP stack resources can be exhausted if connections are opened and closed at a very high rate. This issue is implementation specific and presents no inherent limits in HTTP applications in field networks, as it can be avoided by a more sophisticated HTTP client software that reuses TCP connections for multiple data exchanges with the same remote peer.

Master station executes data exchange processing synchronously with PLC sweep. Thus increasing PLC sweep time lead to lower exchange rate, especially when several frames are required to transfer data. If the sweep time is moderate to large, HTTP takes advantage over PLC native communication protocol (Ether-S-Net) as significantly lower number of telegrams must be processed.

Based on the results of measurements, HTTP seems to perform well enough to be applicable as a field network transfer protocol in some of the distributed industrial control systems. Implementing HTTP client as a PLC application software encounters difficulties in both code complexity and execution time. However further development work, especially native support for HTTP client communications by means of firmware implementation, shall greatly improve performance and ease of use of HTTP protocol in field networks.

References

1. Becker, R., et al.: AS-Interface – The Automation Solution. AS-International Association (2002)
2. HART Communication Foundation: HART Communication Application Guide (2010)
3. EPSG Draft Standard 301, Ethernet PowerLink Communication Profile Specification Version 1.1.0. EPSG (2008)
4. Popp, M., Weber, K.: The Rapid Way to PROFINET (2004)
5. MODBUS-IDA: MODBUS Application Protocol Specification v1.1b (2006)
6. PROFIBUS Nutzerorganisation e.V.: PROFIBUS System Description – Technology and Application (2010)
7. Saia-Burgess Controls Ltd.: S-Bus Manual for the PCD family. Document 26/739, Edition E4 (2000)
8. GE Fanuc Automation: TCP/IP Ethernet Communications for PACSystems^{TM} User's Manual. Document GFK-2224H (2008)
9. OPC Foundation: OPC Overview (1998)
10. OPC Foundation: OPC Unified Architecture Specification. Part 1: Concepts (2006)
11. RFC 2616 Hypertext Transfer Protocol – HTTP/1.1. Internet Engineering Task Force, The Internet Society (1999)
12. RFC 959 File Transfer Protocol (FTP). Internet Engineering Task Force, The Internet Society (1985)
13. MODBUS-IDA: MODBUS Messaging on TCP/IP Implementation Guide (2006)
14. RFC 3986 Uniform Resource Identifier (URI): Generic Syntax. Internet Engineering Task Force, The Internet Society (2005)
15. SOAP Version 1.2 (Second Edition). W3C Recommendation (2007)
16. Fielding, R.T.: Architectural Styles and the Design of Network-based Software Architectures. PhD thesis, University of California, Irvine (2000)
17. Fielding, R.T., Taylor, R.N.: Principled design of the modern Web architecture. ACM Trans. on Internet Technology 2(2), 115–150 (2002)
18. GE Fanuc Automation: PACSystems^{TM} CPU Reference Manual. Document GFK-2222K (2007)
19. Saia-Burgess Controls Ltd.: Hardware Manual for the PCD3 Series. Document 26/789 Edition E8 (2007)
20. GE Fanuc Intelligent Platforms: 12" QuickPanel^{TM} View & QuickPanel Control Loaded Color TFT. Document GFK-2284C (2008)
21. Steib, P.M.: Web technology in automation. Whitepaper. Saia-Burgess Controls Ltd., Document 26/260, Edition E2 (2009)
22. Jestratjew, A.: Improving Availability of Industrial Monitoring Systems through Direct Database Access. In: Kwiecień, A., Gaj, P., Stera, P. (eds.) CN 2009. CCIS, vol. 39, pp. 344–351. Springer, Heidelberg (2009)
23. Jestratjew, A., Kwiecień, A.: Using Cloud Storage in Production Monitoring Systems. In: Kwiecień, A., Gaj, P., Stera, P. (eds.) CN 2010. CCIS, vol. 79, pp. 226–235. Springer, Heidelberg (2010)
24. Saia-Burgess Controls Ltd.: Ethernet Manual for the PCD Series. Document 26/776 Edition E5 (2010)
25. RFC 793 Transmission Control Protocol (1981)

Genius Network Communication Process Registration and Analysis

Andrzej Kwiecień and Jacek Stój

Silesian University of Technology, Institute of Informatics
Akademicka 16, 44-100 Gliwice, Poland
{andrzej.kwiecien,jacek.stoj}@polsl.pl
http://www.polsl.pl

Abstract. The estimation of the information exchange cycle duration in industrial networks is an essential issue, because the knowledge of this parameter allows answering several questions related to satisfying of assumptions of the real-time system or the redundant systems design. The characteristic features of systems with communication link redundancy are the delays in switching the redundant buses. This may require a registration of the time values, preferably in "on-line" mode. The authors discussed this very issue, trying to achieve the objective of registration of the communication process and the value of network sweep time in an exemplary Genius network, using standard computer tools.

Keywords: distributed real-time system, communication, data flow, genius network.

1   Introduction

The main objectives set to designers of industrial systems is to meet the requirements and restrictions resulting from assumptions, which are typical in real-time systems. In architectures with a single communication bus, namely without the redundancy of transmission channel, the project calculations are limited to the estimation of the network time cycle T_c in accordance with the accepted model of protocol, taking into account the so-called "worst case" [1,2]. In most cases this is sufficient to determine the conditions of an appropriate operation, in accordance with the requirements of real-time systems. The problem of proper selection of system parameters to be a real-time system becomes more complicated when it includes a backup (redundant) communication bus. Then, there are additional calculation problems, related to the transient state of the redundant elements like the moment of switchover of the buses when one of them fails [3]. As a matter of fact, in many, if not most, contemporary solutions of redundant systems, both buses are active, which means that transmission takes place both by "normal" and "standby" bus. Nevertheless, here it refers to switching the buses in the network coprocessor. It is not possible to model or describe analytically all activities occurring between CPU and the coprocessor. Is is because of the fact, that the designer has access neither to electrical schematic nor software that resides

A. Kwiecień, P. Gaj, and P. Stera (Eds.): CN 2011, CCIS 160, pp. 314–321, 2011.
© Springer-Verlag Berlin Heidelberg 2011

on the coprocessor card. In these circumstances, only the empirical experiment which involves the registration of switching times of redundant communication buses in transition state can be conducted. This temporary (transient) state begins when a failure is detected and ends at the moment when full software and hardware control is taken over the redundant bus. The experiment is also related to observation of the network activity for the presence of subscribers and the data they send. Moreover, this process should allow to estimate the value of duration of the information exchange cycle in the network, which is fundamental for designing the real time systems. For that purpose the Genius network communication process registration and analysis laboratory set-up was built and programmed.

2 Genius Network

Genius network is a token based real-time communication network. However in this solution, the transmission right is passed over using "implicit token" as no datagrams are being sent during that process. The token passing operation is done in the means of Time Division Multiple Access mechanism.

In the Genius network up to 32 devices may be addressed. The token is always passed in turn from the subscriber with SBA00 address (Serial Bus Address) to the SBA01 subscriber and so on. The subscriber with the token may transmit data for a specified period of time. When subscriber SBA31 finishes its transmission, the token is passed back to the SBA00 starting the next network operation cycle (sweep). The SBA31 subscriber is always GBC (Genius Bus Controller). There may be up to 3 GBC subscribers and they always occupy the highest addresses.

Token passing process starts when subscriber with the token ends its data transfer. After detecting the end of transmission of one network subscriber, every other subscriber starts counting down its own time delay based on the address number. A given subscriber starts transmitting data the moment the calculated period of time elapses, on condition that no other device is transmitting. The time delay is equal to the time constant (called "skip time") multiplied by the the difference between its SBA address and the last SBA address received (the address of last transmitting subscriber). For example the time delay between data transmissions of SBA05 and SBA15 subscribers would be $(15-5) \cdot T$, where the T constant is equal 0.025 ms for the 153.6 kb/s bus frequency.

2.1 Bit Coding

The logical "0" value is sent in the Genius network as a series of three AC pulses. No pulses for a specified time is recognized as the logical "1" value, as shown on Fig. 1

The pulse frequency is three times the baud frequency, for example 460.8 kHz at 153.6 kb/s. Another baud frequencies for the Genius network are 38.4 kb/s and 76.8 kb/s. The duration of one bit it a multiplicative inverse of the baud rate (eg. $1/153.6$ s).

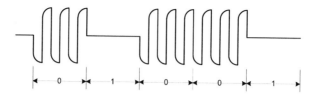

Fig. 1. Genius network bit coding

2.2 Byte Coding

One Genius character consists of 11 bits. Apart from one data byte in the character are included: one control bit, one start bit (always "0", i.e. three pulses) and one stop bit (always "1"). The bytes are sent in little endian order. It is important to note at this point, that as experiments prove the control bit is sent after the data byte. Whereas, according to the available Genius brief description, it should be sent before the data bit. Detailed specification for that network protocol is not published.

A minimum transmission has a start character, one or more data characters, anda stop character. The start character data byte contains the SBA address and whether the transmission is directed to a specific address or is a broadcast to all. The stop character contains the CRC-6 checksum. Complex transmissions may have additional start and end of block characters to break up the message into blocks of data [4].

3 Genius Communication Process Registration

For the needs of Genius communication process registration National Instrument USB Data Acquisition module was used (NI USB-6251). The communication bus was connected to one of the module's analog input with a maximum sampling rate 1.25 MS/s.

The communication bus consisted of three Genius subscribers as shown on Fig. 2. One of them was GBC (IC687BEM731 by GE Fanuc) module mounted in a PLC. The other two subscribers were remote input/output stations based on VersaMax NIU modules (Network Interface Unit, IC200GBI001 by GE Fanuc). Between GBC and every NIU was exchanged the same set of data: 16 binary inputs and outputs, 4 analog inputs and 2 analog outputs. The sum of user data being transmitted in the network was 32 bytes.

For the needs of Genius communication process registration LabVIEW environment was used. Registered data that were to be analyzed in off-line mode were stored in HWS files (Hierarchical Waveform Storage) using LabVIEW Signal Express.

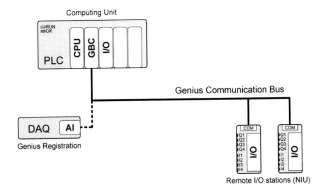

Fig. 2. Genius distributed system with acquisition module

4   Off-Line Genius Communication Process Analysis

For off-line Genius network communication process analysis HWS file is used as data input. The HWS file are being loaded with created for that purpose "HWS to Waveform" VI (VI – National Instruments program diagram, see: Fig. 3). It gets as an input the HSW file name and the path and other parameters. As an output it produces waveform signal to be analyzed.

The analysis is based on a trigger detecting the first genius character bit (always "0"). The start trigger condition is defined as falling edge. The trigger stops at the character end. In other words, it stops after a constant sample count as the character has always the same length in the means of time. The triggered signal is then passed over for the analysis (see: Fig. 4).

The analysis of the triggered signal (one Genius character) starts with two tests of the first and the last character bits, which are supposed to have the value of logical "0" and "1" accordingly. If that condition is satisfied, then other character bits are being checked (8 data bits and one control bit). In order to perform bit testing a VI created by authors is used (see: Fig. 5, 6).

"Check signal state" VI is used for the testing of individual Genius character bit. At the first step during the VI operation a part of input signal is extracted and then tested for two possible bit states. The immediate result of that tests is stored to "State is ON" and "State is OFF" output parameters. The binary "State" is also calculated and a simple consistency check is conducted ("Undefined state" output). At the end of analysis of every Genius characters the required bit order is applied. In case of Genius communication network the "little endian" order is used. With that operation the acquisition of the Genius character finishes and the character is passed over to a "Genius chars" array. In Figure 7 the front panel of the described VI is shown.

On the front panel of the Genius communication process analysis VI, an "Acquired signal" wavegraph is visible (see: Fig. 7) where the change of analog input value is presented. In this case 6 communication frames are shown with different

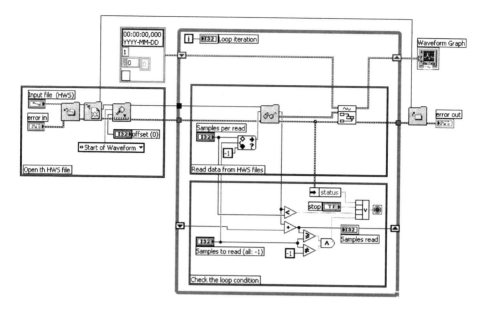

Fig. 3. "HWS to Waveform" VI diagram

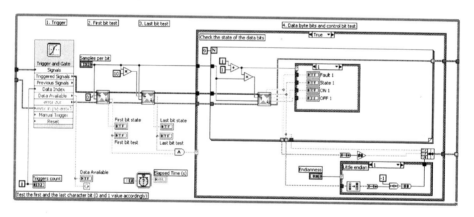

Fig. 4. The main part of Genius character analysis VI diagram

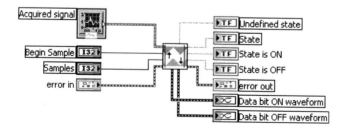

Fig. 5. "Check signal state" VI inputs and outputs

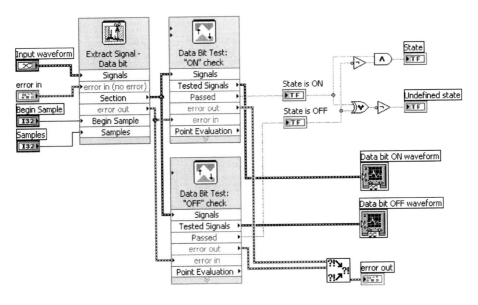

Fig. 6. Genius bit analysis "Check signal state" VI diagram

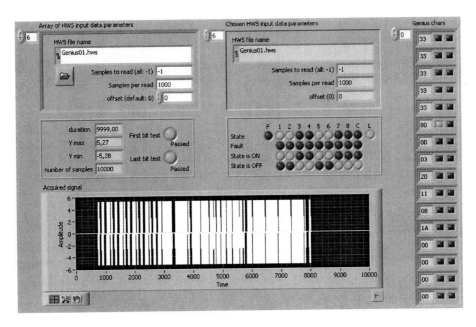

Fig. 7. Front panel of the Genius communication process analysis VI

Table 1. Genius communication frames example

| Genius | | NIU frame | | | GBC frame | |
		SBA 05	SBA 16	Description*	SBA 31	Description*
Genius	01	33_0	33_0	- nd -	55_0	- nd -
characters	02	33_0	33_0	- nd -	55_0	- nd -
	03	33_0	33_0	- nd -	55_0	- nd -
	04	33_0	33_0	- nd -	55_0	- nd -
	05	33_0	33_0	- nd -	55_0	- nd -
	06	28_1	80_1	Src_SBAxx	2C_1	Dest_SBA05
	07	6C_0	DC_0	DI01-08	F8_0	Src_SBA31
	08	80_0	80_0	DI09-16	8B_0	DQ01-08
	09	C0_0	C8_0	AI01LSB	7C_0	DQ09-16
	10	12_0	12_0	AI01MSB	D2_0	AQ01LSB
	11	88_0	60_0	AI02LSB	04_0	AQ01MSB
	12	05_0	00_0	AI02MSB	2E_0	AQ02LSB
	13	00_0	00_0	AI03LSB	16_0	AQ02MSB
	14	00_0	00_0	AI03MSB	01_1	CtrlWord
	15	00_0	00_0	AI04LSB	84_1	Dest_SBA16
	16	00_0	00_0	AI04MSB	F8_0	Src_SBA31
	17	17_1	07_1	CRC-6	9B_0	DQ01-08
	18				65_0	DQ09-16
	19				B9_0	AQ01LSB
	20				08_0	AQ01MSB
	21				67_0	AQ02LSB
	22				11_0	AQ02MSB
	23				7D_1	CtrlWord
	24				F8_1	Src_SBA31
	25				2F_1	CRC-6
Frame length		17 bytes		—	25 bytes	—

*Not defined, no Genius network specification available.

"skip times" for each frame type. As 3 subscribers were present in the system, there are 3 types of frames. The longest one was transmitted by Genius bus controller module.

5 On-Line Genius Communication Process Analysis

At the beginning of the research on-line Genius communication process analyzes were planned to be done. Implementation of the off-line analysis showed however that it is not such a feasible task. The operation of the off-line analysis of 6 sample Genius communication frames took about 6 seconds whereas the frames were sent in approximately 53 milliseconds. For the on-line analysis the method of the Genius communication process analysis still needs to be developed.

6 Genius Communication Frames

In Table 1 there are 3 sample Genius communication frames are shown. They were detected in the network. The description of characters in the frames is based on experimental laboratory research.

In the brief Genius description that is published, it is said that a Genius frame consist of one start character, a number of user data bytes and one stop character with CRC-6 checksum. However, every registered frame was preceded by 5 more Genius characters with the same data byte. For NIU subscribers it was the value of 33h. For GBC subscriber it was 55h. The meaning of this characters is unknown to the authors. It may be used for synchronization of the transceiver of the Genius subscriber.

Another piece of research done by the authors shows that the control word being sent by GBC after every data block (characters 14 and 23 in the Table 1) may consist of some kind of control sum. Measurement of the response time of the Genius network based system suggests that for the NIU units reception of the data block and the control word is enough to process the data as valid system outputs. For more information see [3].

7   Final Notes

During the described research a LabView application for Genius network communication process analysis was implemented, which was based on National Instrument USB data acquisition module. The goal was to make it possible to work on off-line data (HWS files) as well as on-line allowing for Genius analysis in the real-time. Former operation mode (off-line analysis) was implemented successfully. However, implementation of the latter operation mode seems to the authors not possible at this moment because of the complexity of the code and too lengthy execution time. More research is needed in order to decide whether the on-line analysis is possible after some code optimization.

The implemented application allows its users to determine the number of subscribers present in the Genius network as well as the Genius network sweep time. The inspection of data sent over the network is possible too. The application may be useful during experimental research associated with temporal characteristic of real-time systems and, among others, the transient states of real-time systems with communication bus redundancy. Nevertheless some more work is still required on the presentation of the data to make it more user-friendly.

Acknowledgment. This work was supported by the European Community from the European Social Fund.

References

1. Stój, J.: Wpływ redundancji na zależności czasowe w rozproszonych informatycznych systemach czasu rzeczywistego. Doctoral dissertation (2009)
2. Gaj, J.: Pessimistic useful efficiency of EPL network cycle. In: Kwiecień, A., Gaj, P., Stera, P. (eds.) CN 2010. CCIS, vol. 79, pp. 297–305. Springer, Heidelberg (2010)
3. Kwiecień, A., Stój, J.: The Response Time of a Control System with Communication Link Redundancy. In: Contemporary Aspects of Computer Networks, vol. 2, ch.19. WKŁ, Warszawa (2008)
4. VersaMax™System Genius® Network Interface Unit. GE Fanuc Automation, Programmable Control Products, document no. GFK-1535A (November 2000)

Network Integration on the Control Level

Błażej Kwiecień and Jacek Stój

Silesian University of Technology, Institute of Informatics,
ul. Akademicka 2A, 44-100 Gliwice, Poland
{blazej.kwiecien,jacek.stoj}@polsl.pl
http://www.polsl.pl

Abstract. In the following paper the authors analyze the problem of the network integration on the lowest level of industrial computer system which is the control level. Exchange of information between different levels in integrated pyramid of enterprise process is fundamental with regard to an efficient enterprise operation. Communication and data exchange between levels for different systems are not always the same because of a variability of the used network protocols, communication mediums, system response times, etc. That makes the problem of network integration an important aspect for research.

Keywords: real time system, PLC, network, SCADA, integration, response time.

1 Introduction

The development of computer technologies supports creation of new solutions or optimizations of those that already exists. Contemporary industrial computer systems are usually distributed over wide plant areas, thus computer networking is essential – Fig. 1. On account of the operation features of those systems, the exchange of data between nodes most often must be determined in time. Character of the network operation and the bandwidth of the communications medium are forcing application of appropriate time deterministic communication protocols.

The need of increasing data transfers and reliability is stimulus for Ethernet network standard to become more and more popular in this area. In spite of its lack of temporal determinism, Ethernet is often applied in computer industrial installations [1]. It is possible to justify it by the fact that both the software and the hardware connected through the Ethernet network are spread widely and are present in industrial technologies in many branches [1,2]. The usage of Ethernet is not limited only to control, regulation and monitoring. It concerns also production management systems MES [3] (Manufacturing Execution System) and managing of whole production plant with ERP systems [4] (Enterprise Resources Planning). For MES systems the information exchange in the real time is essential in order to maintain production process supervision. Only then it is possible to react quickly to the state and parameters of the industrial computer

A. Kwiecień, P. Gaj, and P. Stera (Eds.): CN 2011, CCIS 160, pp. 322–327, 2011.

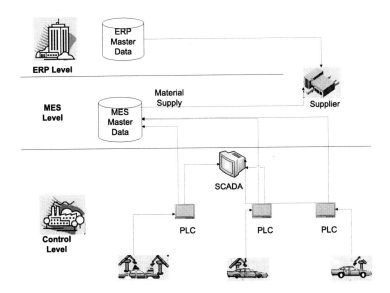

Fig. 1. Model of distributed computer systems

object [3]. A MES system also supports ERP systems which integrates the data coming from the industrial computer object with the business data. It delivers in the real time information about the current state and parameters of production and enables accurate analysis of the profitability and costs of the production [5]. A typical, hierarchical model of management and control enterprise is shown Fig. 2.

The goal of network integration process on the lowest level of a distributed computer system, i.e. the control level, is to make possible the exchange of information between two of more independent segments of the network. The segments may be in heterogeneous or homogeneous relation to each other. The described integration plan relates to the extensions of the information exchange between nodes of the network in the same level and between nodes of the network in the various levels. The result of integration should be a fulfillment of the requirements of the communication system and should pay special attention to the time determinism. Time determinism is associated with following parameters:

- the sweep time of the network, which is the time span between any given subscriber following transmissions,
- the information exchange time, which is the minimum, necessary time needed for the exchange of all user data between all subscribers in the network. It is the multiplicity of the sweep time of the network,
- the communication network access time, which is a maximum guaranteed time after which any given subscriber will have the possibility to transmit at least a part of the user data,

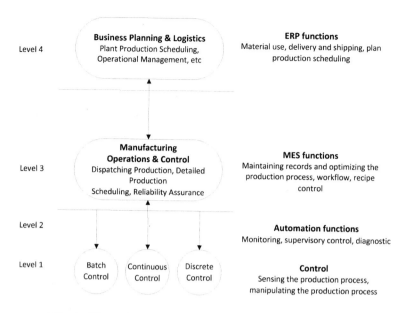

Fig. 2. Hierarchical model of industrial computer object [5]

- network capacity, which is defined as quotient of number of usable data in a single exchange transaction to the length of the single exchange transaction,
- network efficiency, which is defined as quotient of usable data transmission time in the single exchange transaction to whole time of single exchange transaction.

2   Network Integration

On the control level, the most essential factor that has influence on the way of integration is access time to the communication medium.

Figure 3 shows an integration example on the lowest network level of two existing network segments with additional pressure sensor, which should be accessible to different network segment. Usually the network A and the network B are autonomic communication subsystems and do not require an information exchange between them. However, future development of the systems may result in the necessity of some data exchange. It may happen for example when new data sources are added to one of the systems (like pressure meter on Fig. 3) and the data is also needed in the other system. Then the network integration is necessary. The most important thing that has to be taken into account is the temporal parameters of both systems. It is crucial to carry out a temporal analysis of the possibility of network integration in order to assure time determinism of the integrated systems. Program code which realized integration is not universal. The guaranteed information exchange time is the main characteristic of industrial networks. On the scheme of an integration device shown on Fig. 4 it can be noticed that the time necessary for programmable integration depends on the protocol conversion time, the number of data buffers and the network operation time [1]:

$$T_{\text{INT}} = f\left(T_{\text{CONV}}, T_{\text{BufIn}}, T_{\text{BufOut}}, n_{\text{A}} * T_{\text{NetA}}, n_{\text{B}} * T_{\text{NetB}}\right) \tag{1}$$

where:

T_{INT} – integration time,
T_{CONV} – protocol conversion time,
$T_{\text{BufIn}}, T_{\text{BufOut}}$ – buffers operation time,
$T_{\text{NetA}}, T_{\text{NetB}}$ – network A and network B cycle time,
$n_{\text{A}}, n_{\text{B}}$ – number of network A and network B cycles.

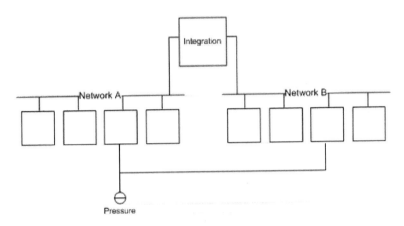

Fig. 3. The lowest level network integration [1]

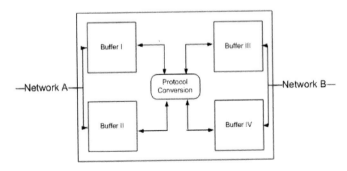

Fig. 4. The structure of interconnection device [1]

3 Data Exchange

In all production companies the acquisition and management of information is a crucial element in decision-making process. It makes production more efficient and reliable. In addition, it is a great aid for the functioning companies based on production on all production levels – from machines and production lines, through engineering departments, all the way to administrative departments. In the lowest levels are applied superior systems of control and data acquisition – SCADA, industrial arrangements of CNC control (Computer Numerical Control), PLC (Programmable Logic Controller), IPC (Industrial PC), sensors, executive elements and different devices of industrial automation. They constitute a specific computer system that is active in a real time, of which controlling machines and production lines are basic elements [6]. In the highest levels of the industrial enterprise there are applied two kinds of systems – MES and ERP systems. MES systems which effective leading a production process on the basis of accurate and current production data coming from systems of control and data acquisition. ERP systems which managing supplies of materials, human resources, finances, enterprise resource planning. An essential element of the modern MES system is a possibility of a simple integration with systems of industrial automation (PLC, SCADA) and with databases in which production data is stored. MES systems join the control of the production departments, keeping the logistic departments, qualities departments and different sources of data into a uniform computer system, using provided standard components software as: OPC (OLE for Process Control) Client, OPC Server and ActiveX. These modern computer technologies in the considerable way reduce the total cost of MES integration with systems of automation and databases. However, the design of communication systems is not a simple task and it requires many technical parameters of the computer network, communications protocols,

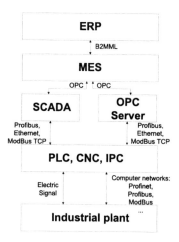

Fig. 5. Data acquisition

interfaces linking computer systems, as well as consideration of time requirements, the safety of the data transmission and limitations resulting from the bandwidth of the network and technical requirements [6]. The data acquisition in industrial plant is shown on Fig. 5.

4 Conclusions

Usually the process of information exchange is realized by software. So, it is obvious that the network integration is associated with deterioration of parameters relating to the time of the information exchange in the system. As every type of the network has own transmission protocol, while integrating various network protocols it is necessary to create a mechanism which realizes the information flow management between subscribers in different networks. Usually the mechanism relates to the process of data buffering during transmission and finding the addressee and the sender of the information. With the growth of the number of subscribers and the vastness of the network system, temporal characteristics of the mechanism realization has essential meaning for efficient operation of the processes of control being hold on the industrial object. To sum up, the process of communication systems design for the automation of production are applied computer systems, applications, interfaces, systems of control, computer networks, databases and functional requirements of final users. One should pay extra attention to analysis of requirements concerning the time constraints of the data transfer between applications. Industrial communication systems like OPC are very well fulfilling their objective in production area where they require transmission of data in the short time e.g. 1 second. These stringent time requirements do not have to be fulfilled in computer applications as MES or ERP systems. It is possible to imagine a situation, in which generating the report for the manager cockpit will be a second longer, because of load the computer network, and this delay will be acceptable and unnoticeable for the end user.

References

1. Kwiecień, A.: Analiza przepływu informacji w komputerowych sieciach przemysłowych. Wydawnictwo pracowni komputerowej J. Skalmierskiego (2000)
2. Cupek, R.: Protokół TCP/IP w systemach wizualizacji procesów przemysłowych. Studia Informatica 22(3) (2001)
3. Kletti, J.: MES – Manufacturing Execution System. Springer, Heidelberg (2007)
4. Lech, P.: Zintegrowane systemy zarządzania ERP/ERP II. Wykorzystanie w biznesie, wdrażanie; Wydawnictwo Difin, Warszawa (2003)
5. Zaborowski, M.: Sterowanie nadążne zasobami przedsiębiorstwa. Wydawnictwo pracowni komputerowej J. Skalmierskiego (2008)
6. Skura, K., Smalec, Z.: Integracja systemów informatycznych w automatyzacji procesów produkcyjnych. Pomiary, Automatyka, Robotyka, no. 7-8/2005 pp. 6–11 (2005)
7. Cupek, R.: Akwizycja danych z sieci PROFINET CBA do systemów klasy MES. In: Sieci Komputerowe. Aplikacje i zastosowania, vol. 2, pp. 389–399. WKŁ, Warsaw (2007)

The Concept of a Multi-network Approach for a Dynamic Distribution of Application Relationships

Piotr Gaj

Silesian University of Technology, Institute of Informatics,
ul. Akademicka 16, 44-100 Gliwice, Poland
`piotr.gaj@polsl.pl`
`http://www.polsl.pl`

Abstract. In the current highly urban zone, home and personal computer devices are implanted in a highly communicative environment. There are computer networks of any kind almost everywhere around us. A potential user can, without any special effort, establish an access to a local network via a wireless or a cable interface in practice anywhere within the public zone. In a given location such access can be run with a good likelihood for more than one local network and via more than one media type. This phenomenon can be observed by an average user. However, please notice that a similar communicative environment was developed in highly industrial zones, and, curiously enough, with easier access. In this article a concept of the utilization of the available communication resources in order to execute communication tasks, depending on various criteria, such as time and safety is being used.

Keywords: industrial, virtual, network, real-time, Ethernet, fieldbus, transaction, exchange, time, safety, reliability, efficiency, redundancy, multi-network, relationships.

1 Introduction

There are two general points of view of computer networks usage within industrial computer systems: internal needs of physical node distribution within a system and requirements of systems' interconnection.

Distributed systems in industry are physically dispersed. It means that devices are located in separate places positioned near to a given part of technological process. Such system nodes have to exchange their data and synchronize. Therefore, they have to be connected via a computer network. The network is a bottleneck of the whole system from the efficiency of data transfer point of view, and it is the weakest link from the reliability point of view. In other words, the speed of internal data exchange in a computer device is considerably higher than the speed of useful data passing via a local network. Moreover, the network is the only common highway designated to perform such an exchange. The conclusion is that useful data has to wait sometimes on its way between application levels

A. Kwiecień, P. Gaj, and P. Stera (Eds.): CN 2011, CCIS 160, pp. 328–337, 2011.

of involved nodes, while the exchange process is of a discrete type with a given frequency of state updates. Additionally, an unpredictable malfunction of a network (e.g. a forklift integrated with a cable tray) can disturb part of or even the whole mechanism of system data passing.

Not so long ago, a distributed computer system in automation was a pretty modern solution, especially contrary to the centralized super-power and super-wired ones. Now, it is pretty hard to find technological lines with only one system involved in the production process. The set of information collected and processed within one system is likely to be useful in the other. So, the natural consequence is a need of integration of available systems [1], mainly of data exchange and sometimes of processing support. It applies to the same type of systems, on the similar horizontal level of integration as well as to the vertical integration, e.g. with a sort of factory management systems. Nowadays, a typical technologist has two main reasons for doing this. The first reason is an interconnection of systems due to the necessity of common and mutual collaboration and the second one is system multiplication to increase the general safety level.

The main goal related to the issues mentioned is to establish a reliable connection between system nodes. A necessary mechanism shall exist to assure the execution of all communication tasks in normal and failure conditions of networking [2]. Let us consider a simple analogy. Probably, if one wants to avoid a street flooding, one could build two sewers with two grates or one big drain. Additionally, if we want to evade the unpredictable choking possibility, the drain multiplication is a better choice. Let us consider the same problem according to computer networks. On the one hand, a high-speed and high efficiency network can be made up, implemented and used. On the other hand, there is a possibility to use many networks at the same time with a special application layer which could dynamically control a given network usage depending on error status, delays, timeouts, utilization, and other instantaneous parameters. This approach is good for non-real-time networks because of accepted risk of using network with various protocols and different usage context. Nevertheless, the deterministic networks can also be controlled by a multi-network layer, especially when errors are detected or when a crash occurs. One additional thing is good to think about. Contemporary PLC devices and other computing devices [3,4,5] which are used to control process are mostly multi-network supplied. Unfortunately, there is no control layer to be designed for the management of the available network coprocessors as one communication system. Therefore, in this paper the mechanism of internal data routing within a node is signaled.

In Fig. 1 the schema of a distributed system is presented. It is based on a virtual communication layer founded on physical networks of three types and with internal data passing among them inside each node. The virtual layer represents the logical connection between applications. Not each node is covered by each physical network in this example. Application's abstract entities can be connected by a fixed association to the physical network or networks can be dynamically selected to serve the application relationships established within a system.

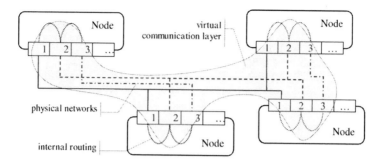

Fig. 1. Idea of a distributed system with a multi-network environment

In the following paragraphs it is discussed what can be used to determine a network selection, how the control mechanism can work and where it can be located as well as a simple example is presented.

2   Logical Connections within a Distributed System

The main goal of a communication layer in industrial distributed computer systems is to pass useful data from one application to another. Computer networks are the only reasonable means that are currently available to do this job. In order to execute data exchange between system nodes, the network infrastructure and protocol are needed. Nevertheless, it is important to emphasize that the main task in industrial distributed systems is to enable the communication between applications but not physical interfaces of nodes themselves. Thus, to enable a proper synchronization and communication during system processing, there is a necessity to define relationships between applications, of which the whole system consists: namely, between some kinds of abstract objects defined on the application level, such as variables, modules, slots, etc. Such associations are commonly used in contemporary industrial network protocols and are well documented in literature [6,7,8].

Typically, application relationships are established between applications located in different network nodes but through one given network. Precisely, via one type of networks or a network system based on a given network solution, because instead of a single network, a redundancy architecture could be used with multiplied networks and coprocessors within nodes [9,10]. In the presented approach there are many different networks considered. It is not defined how many – generally, at least two different networks. In practice, it could be physically the same type of network or completely different networks, but it is assumed that independent computer networks and autonomous interfaces exist to be used as a communication channel for the purpose of a given distributed system [11].

A given logical connection between applications can be serviced by various communication mechanisms. What is typical for data processing in industry is cyclic data transactions and aperiodic transactions for events, data, messages, and other information units [7,12,13,8]. A communication activity executed in the context of an application relationship can be considered a network task. The task shall be performed with time limitations coming from the technology process requirements. The temporary status of its execution can be described by a special descriptor of run quality. In this case the most important factor associated with the quality is time. Such a time descriptor can be assigned to each connection, application's abstract element or just to a network task. In a simple case it could be a time-status or an exchange-counter describing the time-related quality of data passing. For instance it could be a binary flag calculated as a ratio of the designed lifetime of a variable and its real production period completed by the application in a given moment in time. It also could be a discrete status related to the initialization of a network variable or passing time of data between variables allocated in different levels of a protocol stack. Such status mechanisms and data management models are also commonly known [14,15]. Nevertheless, they are only used to estimate an application data quality within a given industrial network, mostly of a fieldbus sort. Beside the fieldbus systems, time descriptors can be used to express the quality of data passing within an integration node (e.g. specialized gateway), a heterogeneous system in general, or a system working in a multi-network environment. In the last case, a continuous analysis of a time descriptor can be used to produce a decision which network shall be used to run a given task.

In Figure 2 simple time dependencies related to basic timeouts are presented. The production and consumption statuses refer to the time coherency between an application and a network cycle of data exchange. The reply status refers to the expected reply time to a given network event, e.g. a request. For instance, the condition for network selection can be $T_{RP} \geq T_{RP\_MAX}$, $T_R \geq T_{R\_MAX}$, or $T_W \geq T_{W\_MAX}$.

Presented dependencies in a physical channel are only a sample. In practice there are more complex dependencies which could be used to calculate the threshold point for changing the physical connection within the logical one. A good example, to describe a time quality of data passing observed from the application point of view, is utilization of a stochastic process [16]. For instance,

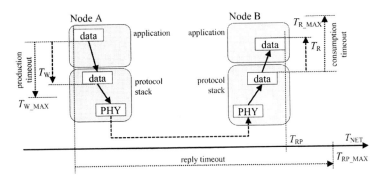

Fig. 2. Examples of time descriptors of a sample network exchange

a real-time analysis of changes of the reply time distribution can bring information that is useful for making a decision of network selection. The distribution of this type is usually stationary in real-time networks and should be stationary in non-deterministic solutions. So it is easy to detect any disturbances, but not yet downs, of running tasks, and thanks to that put the execution of the task in the other network context.

Generally, the mechanisms used to determine a temporary status of a given physical network activity can be useful for detecting any malfunctions [17,2] of a logical connection, especially when more than one network cycle operates within a logical connection.

3   Control Layer

In order to design a multi-network node with an internal routing of useful data, a special virtual application layer has to be designed [18,19]. This layer acts as an overriding protocol responsible for data passing from the node application to a given real network and from the real network to the node application. The control mechanism located in a virtual network layer does not refer to a simple switching of data among networks. The switching activity is too general and cannot be done in practice for a logical connection. The layer has two important responsibilities. The first one is to establish an interface to the node application and the second one is to control all available network protocols. The provided interface should allow the user to define a set of typical network tasks to be found in industrial systems. The basic set consists of activities known from the typical communication models, such as: confirmed and unconfirmed transactions based on cyclic and acyclic updates (e.g. requests, acknowledgements, responses, pushes, pulls, etc.). The typical communication relationships to be created within application relationships are Client-Server, Producer-Consumer, and Master Slave [7]. The control job refers to actions such as: starting and stopping a given task, redirecting useful data to become a payload in given cyclic transactions, executing acyclic exchanges/transactions, etc. Details of the control job depend on connected networks and their protocols.

Generally, during the nodes activity, while a logical connection is active, some events can occur that signal a need of making changes in physical connections. To clarify this issue, the mentioned changes are not welcome at all. They are time-consuming and may lead to time changes, characteristic to a given connection. But the proposed mechanism is designated to avoid going wrong with the communication. The most important reasons for such an action are the following:

(a) *A network temporary malfunction or a communication timeout.* It could operate on real-time networks as well as on non-real-time ones. The main benefit is to avoid a communication down or evading the growth of the detected disturbance. An additional benefit appears when timeout occurs during the cyclic real-time transactions. In that case the specific time holes are detected with the idle state of the medium. If the timeout is a result of a node fault, the time holes reduce the throughput, but if the timeout is a symptom of a bad configuration, a delayed reply can disturb other exchanges. In both cases withdrawing the transaction from the damaged physical connection is valuable for other connections of the considered network.

(b) *A network overload*. It could operate on non-real-time networks. The advantage is to evade an overload increase. A part of network traffic can be directed to the other physical connection.

(c) *A network fault*. It could operate on any kind of network. The extended functionality in this case is increasing safety by a redundancy appliance. The other physical connection can take the logical connection on.

(d) *The increase of communication efficiency*. It could operate with any kind of network. This case is not connected with network faults. The mechanism can be used in order to utilize both (or more) networks to establish one application link. Thanks to that the maximum throughput of one network could be exceeded in the whole logical channel.

For a dynamic task assignation to the real interface, the mechanism based on the mentioned time descriptors becomes a pretty good solution. A simple routing algorithm based on a delay status and on a limited exchange withdrawal is presented below in C++ language. The example refers to two networks named A and B. The Channel variable identifies a physical connection used to pass the application variable carrying useful data from and to the application layer of the nodes involved in the logical connection. The value of the variable is unique in time, so a given usage in the channel context concerns the same variable but not the same value; the value is from a given moment in time.

Example of the Channel Selection Algorithm

```
if (Channel==1) {//in case on channel A is active
  if (LimitA>0 && Withdraw==0) {//withdrawal service A
    Channel=2;//change the channel
    Withdraw = LimitB;}//set the limit of withdrawal
  else {
    Withdraw--;//counting down the task execution in A
  }
  if (ReplyTime>=ThresholdA) {//threshold point for A
    Channel = 2;//change the channel
    Withdraw = LimitB;//set the limit of withdrawal
  }
}
else if (Channel==2) {//in case on channel B is active
  if (LimitB>0 && Withdraw==0) {//withdrawal service B
    Channel=1;//change the channel
    Withdraw = LimitA;}//set the limit of withdrawal
  else {
    Withdraw--;//counting down the task execution in B
  }
```

```
if (ReplyTime>=ThresholdB) {//threshold point for B
  Channel = 1;//change the channel
  Withdraw = LimitA;//set the limit of withdrawal
 }
}
```

This algorithm is designed for a system which refers to the usage reasons (a) and (b) where there is one base network (A) and one reserved network (B). Network B is used limited times only when the time descriptor signals trouble in the channel A. In case of a network fault (c), the channel change is permanent. In that case (d) both channels shall be used mutually, e.g. for the cyclic transaction on (A) and for the acyclic one via (B). Instead of examining the characteristic of each logical connection, the multi-network system can be also designed with a fixed service association. In such a case a given service, e.g. a cyclic update, message passing, or alarm signaling could be assigned to a given physical interface. For instance, the cyclic exchanges with high time requirements shall be associated with a high-efficiency real-time network, but acyclic updates shall be associated with other non-real-time network. Thanks to a fixed assignation, the whole band can be used for a critical data service. In other words, the significant network cycles can be designed without time reservation for a less important network activity.

4   Example of Connections

Let us consider an example of a simple monitoring system collecting data from remote devices. The system is based on telemetric devices and a PC computer with a DB (database) and SCADA (Supervisory Control and Data Acquisition) software. The communication in the system has no time-critical constraints. A connection is established via a Modbus protocol [20] both on a cellular network (GPRS) and a cable local Ethernet along the Internet. Only one logical connection is considered. The used protocol is deterministic, but physical connections introduce unpredictable disturbances which break the real-time character of the main protocol. The physical network changes can also have influence on the time characteristic of the logical connection if response times on both networks differ considerably and one of the physical timeouts impacts the timeout of the logical connection. The example is only an illustration of the issue. The used protocols, physical networks and their number are not important in this case so any solution can be used, including pure real-time protocols and networks. The condition is to design a control layer corresponding properly with used networks. The schema of the tested system is presented in Fig. 3. The used control layer is based on the algorithm presented previously. Several malfunctions of the considered link were tested according to the points mentioned above.

The reply time was regarded as an authoritative time descriptor of the connection and, depending on its value, the implemented algorithm in the control layer selected the physical network. The measured times with comments are presented in the graphs below (Fig. 4). The consecutive exchanges are presented on

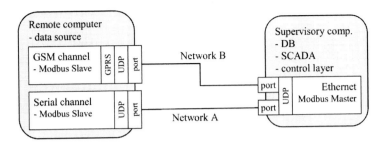

Fig. 3. Schema of the monitoring system example

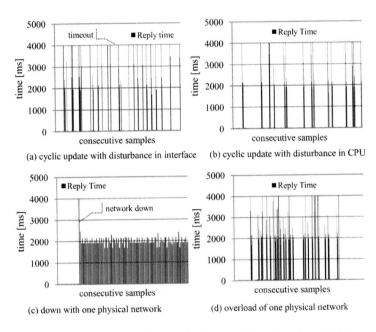

Fig. 4. Samples of reply time during specific networks activity

the abscissa. The samples are taken in same time interval, so generally time is presented on the axis. In the graphs (a) and (b) the reply time is presented. The time values of about 30 ms are derived from the network (A) and represent a normal network activity. The values of 4000 ms are a global timeout for a logical connection and if such values occur, it means that the device is not responding on a given network. The disturbances were specially introduced in the network interface (a) and in CPU of the device (b). The values of thresholds points for a given network are set to 50 ms and 3500 ms. The withdrawal of exchanges to network (B) is set to 4 times. So, it could be observed that in case of a timeout on network (A), the second network is activated and communication is performed for a few times via network (B) with a much longer reply time. However, the global cycle of the considered variable exchange is set to 5000 ms and the global cycle is not disturbed.

In the graph (c) the moment of a down of the base network is presented. The communication is automatically passed to the network (B) and the base network (A) is activated a few times to check the communication ability. In the graph (d) there is a sample of overloading the network (A). In case of reaching the threshold point calculated from a delay of the reply time, the channel through the network (B) is activated. After the withdrawal limit the communication channel is restored to the network (A).

In the presented simple example it is shown that the idea of using many networks in order to establish a single logical connection is possible and can be useful.

5   Conclusions

The current network environment in industry is ambient and composite. There is a possibility of using all available communication ways instead of a selected one, especially when abstract relationships as communication tasks can be distinguished and descriptors of transmission quality on application level can be calculated. The presented idea is related to network integration issues. However, instead of data passing from one system to another, the proposed internal routing is designated to use many networks within one system.

Producers should take into consideration the ambient character of the network environment and consider a creation of a common control layer in their devices with multi-coprocessor interfaces. The implementation of much more complex algorithms seems to be possible. Nevertheless, even simple mechanisms dedicated to routing the useful data on the application layer are valuable, especially for monitoring systems and any other systems aimed at data collecting [21]. The main advantages of such solutions lay in static or dynamic control of networks' utilization as well as it can be useful wherever backup communication should be assured.

References

1. Kwiecień, B.: Data Integration in Computer Distributed Systems. In: Kwiecień, A., Gaj, P., Stera, P. (eds.) CN 2010. CCIS, vol. 79, pp. 183–188. Springer, Heidelberg (2010)
2. Won, Y.J., Choi, M.-J., Lee, J.J., Lee, J.H., Hwang, H.W., Hong, J.W.-K.: Detecting Network Faults on Industrial Process Control IP Networks. In: Medhi, D., Nogueira, J.M.S., Pfeifer, T., Wu, S.F. (eds.) IPOM 2007. LNCS, vol. 4786, pp. 184–187. Springer, Heidelberg (2007)
3. CX1000 Embedded PC Hardware documentation, manual version: 1.1. Beckhoff Automation GmbH (2006)
4. Programmable Automation Controllers (PACs). GE Fanuc Automation (2005)
5. Saia® PCD3.Mxxx0 – compact programmable CPUs. Saia-Burgess Controls Ltd. P+P26/397 E5 05 (2005)

6. Borangiu, T., Balibrea, L.-M.T., Contreras Gonzales, L.A., Nis, C., Manu, M.: Object-oriented model of an open communication architecture for flexible manufacturing control. In: Moreno-Díaz, R., Pichler, F. (eds.) EUROCAST 1997. LNCS, vol. 1333, pp. 292–300. Springer, Heidelberg (1997)
7. EPSG Draft Standard 301: Ethernet POWERLINK Communication Profile Specification Version 1.1.0. EPSG (2008)
8. Popp, M., Weber, K.: The rapid way to Profinet. PNO (2004)
9. Kwiecień, A., Stój, J.: The Response Time of a Control System with Communication Link Redundancy. In: Contemporary Aspects of Computer Networks, vol. 2. WKŁ, Warszawa (2008)
10. Kwiecień, A., Sidzina, M.: Dual bus as a method for data interchange transaction acceleration in distributed real time systems. In: Kwiecień, A., Gaj, P., Stera, P. (eds.) CN 2009. CCIS, vol. 39, pp. 252–263. Springer, Heidelberg (2009)
11. Karmouch, A., Galis, A., Giaffreda, R., Kanter, T., Jonsson, A., Karlsson, A.M., Glitho, R.H., Smirnov, M.I., Kleis, M., Reichert, C., Tan, A., Khedr, M., Samaan, N., Heimo, L., El Barachi, M., Dang, J.: Contextware research challenges in ambient networks. In: Karmouch, A., Korba, L., Madeira, E.R.M. (eds.) MATA 2004. LNCS, vol. 3284, pp. 62–77. Springer, Heidelberg (2004)
12. Gaj, P.: Pessimistic Useful Efficiency of EPL Network Cycle. In: Kwiecień, A., Gaj, P., Stera, P. (eds.) CN 2010. CCIS, vol. 79, pp. 297–305. Springer, Heidelberg (2010)
13. Gaj, P., Kwiecień, B.: Useful efficiency in cyclic transactions of Profinet IO. Studia Informatica, Gliwice (2010)
14. Lee, D.C.: Real-Time Data Management for Network Information System. In: Sloot, P.M.A., Abramson, D., Bogdanov, A.V., Gorbachev, Y.E., Dongarra, J., Zomaya, A.Y. (eds.) ICCS 2003. LNCS, vol. 2660, pp. 614–625. Springer, Heidelberg (2003)
15. Lee, K.B.: Smart Transducer Interface Standards for Condition Monitoring and Control of Machines. In: Condition Monitoring and Control for Intelligent Manufacturing. Springer Series in Advanced Manufacturing, pp. 347–372 (2006)
16. Wideł, S., Flak, J., Gaj, P.: Interpretation of dual peak time signal measured in network systems. In: Kwiecień, A., Gaj, P., Stera, P. (eds.) CN 2010. CCIS, vol. 79, pp. 141–152. Springer, Heidelberg (2010)
17. Rrushi, J., Kang, K.-D.: Detecting Anomalies in Process Control Networks. In: Critical Infrastructure Protection III. IFIP Advances in Information and Communication Technology, vol. 311, pp. 151–165 (2009)
18. Neumann, P., Poeschmann, A., Messerschmidt, R.: Architectural Concept of Virtual Automation Networks. In: 17th IFAC World Congress, July 6-11, Seoul, Korea (2008)
19. Zezulka, F., Beran, J.: Virtual Automation Networks – Architectural Principles and the Current State of Development. In: Proceedings of the 34th Annual Conference of the IEEE Industrial Electronics Society, Orlando, Florida, pp. 1545–1550 (November 2008)
20. Pereira, C.E., Neumann, P.: Industrial Communication Protocols. Springer Handbook of Automation, pp. 981–999. Springer, Heidelberg (2009)
21. Jestratjew, A., Kwiecień, A.: Using Cloud Storage in Production Monitoring Systems. In: Kwiecień, A., Gaj, P., Stera, P. (eds.) CN 2010. CCIS, vol. 79, pp. 226–235. Springer, Heidelberg (2010)

OPC Historical Data Access – OPC Foundation Toolkit Improvement Suggestions

Michał Bochenek[1], Marcin Fojcik[2], and Rafał Cupek[1]

[1] Silesian University of Technology, Institute of Informatics
`michal.m.bochenek@gmail.com`, `rcupek@polsl.pl`
[2] Sogn og Fjordane University College
`marcin.fojcik@hisf.no`

Abstract. Industrial computer systems require not only current measurement data but also data from previous periods of time called "historical data". Apart from many corporate solutions there is a "standard" named OPC HDA (Openness, Productivity, Connectivity Historical Data Access). It describes a server as well as many options of accessing the data made accessible by the server. At the moment, OPC HDA Software Development Kit increases openness and versatility, unfortunately, at the expense of efficiency. This article shows the structure of the toolkit, efficiency tests and some possibilities of changes that would increase the effectiveness.

Keywords: OPC; Historical Data Access; OPC Foundation Software Development Kit; historian servers; COM/DCOM; client-server data exchange.

1 Introduction

In distributed industrial steering systems the basic principle of proper functioning is the data exchange. It touches measurement data as well as steering commands. Many different software solutions have been introduced since the beginning of using this type of applications. Very first systems of this type revealed the necessity of possessing not only current but also previous data along with their timestamps. One of the reasons was the analysis of efficiency, the other was the production planning. Variety of steering applications and the lack of communication standard effected in historical data stored in many different ways, very often with the use of auxiliary programs like databases. This variety caused the fact, that historical data could be in different form, built in different structures, making grouping and simple data calculations possible. Important difference was also the timestamp. It had not been defined whether it should be the moment of change detection (e.g. by the sensor, inside the Programmable Logic Controller) or the moment of data write (e.g. into the database). It all caused to introduce many conversions of historical data while connecting different systems with each other. In the same time when industrial communication was trying to be standardized (OPC), historical data standard specification was created – OPC

A. Kwiecień, P. Gaj, and P. Stera (Eds.): CN 2011, CCIS 160, pp. 338–347, 2011.

HDA. Although OPC standard for current data (OPC DA) quickly became popular, OPC HDA standardization did not make any spectacular success. Authors' experiences show that many times, regardless of using OPC DA and technical possibilities of applying OPC HDA, companies refuse to take this opportunity, installing own (custom) historical data handling software. The aim of this article is to try to explain this phenomenon by means of selected research made to rate the efficiency of OPC HDA Software Development Kit and to present some possibilities of actions that would improve the standard. Research was mostly based on analysis of internal kit's operations and comparison tests with other methods of data gathering and presenting (SQL server database). The difference here is that, OPC HDA is the standard of data processing and transmission, but data can be stored in various data sources (in our research it was the database), while SQL client application is able to make access to data in the storage without dedicated OPC HDA protocol.

2   Protocol Description

OPC Data Access protocol is used worldwide in many different systems to provide access to real-time data for various purposes. OPC DA is not a real-time communication protocol but time stamping mechanism provides consistent: Value, Time Quality (VTQ) information about process variables and gives precisly data and time of its production. From this reasons it is used mainly in SCADA (Supervisory Control and Data Acquisition) and HMI (Human Machine Interface) systems. Today MES (Manufacturing Execution Systems) became a very important part of industrial computer systems. It must be kept in mind that many times requirements of a specific product include product genealogy tracing, quality analysis as well as widely understood maintenance. For this kind of activity, there must be some amount of historical data gathered and available for further processing. This is the reason why the OPC Historical Data Access protocol became more and more important as an industrial standard. OPC Historical Data Access is one of the OPC (Opennes, Productivity and Connectivity) standards [1,2,3,4,5,6]. The OPC HDA specification accommodates a number of applications that need to provide Historical data. Servers that are connected to a specific data source, like for instance to a database, are called "historian servers". There are different types of Historian servers. OPC HDA standard supports some main types of them like for instance Simple Trend data servers and Complex data compression and analysis servers, which are capable of providing summary data or data analysis functions. In particular, there are multiple levels of capability for handling historical functionality, from the simple to the sophisticated. From one point of view OPC HDA can be applied to MES systems, where on the other hand historical data might be a common data repository for distributed control stations. The gain we make at this point is data consistency and ease of management which is hard to obtain in systems based on copying data (distributed systems) or data replication in local repositories. Of course, there are some disadvantages, like for instance the necessity of transferring gathered data in order to present it to the client. This article focuses on the communication aspects between OPC HDA client application and OPC HDA server, created by OPC Foundation [7], in means of efficiency, to application being a regular SQL client.

The OPC HDA protocol uses similarily, like in SQL, data structures for requests but includes start and end time.

OPC HDA client application is able to connect to OPC Historical servers manufactured by different vendors. Provided code determines the data to which each server has access, the data names, and the details about how the server physically accesses that data. Vendors may also provide other OPC servers along with their OPC Historical Data server, but they are not required to. Figure 1 illustrates an example of OPC Vendor server configurations, showing that client applications can establish connections to servers coming from different vendors but also that each connection can lead to a different kind of server (data, alarms or historian server).

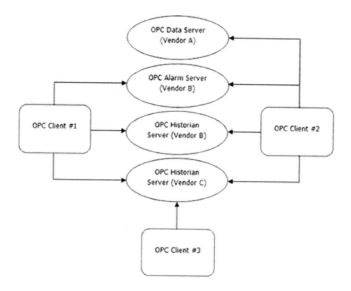

Fig. 1. Possible OPC server interactions [8]

Any client application that needs access to the OPC HDA server should cooperate with all kinds of servers. In case there is another OPC server (e.g. Data Access server) required as part of the system, client should be working properly even in absence of this additional server.

The OPC Historical Data Server provides a way to access to or communicate with a set of Historical data sources. The types of sources available are a function of the server implementation. The server may be implemented as a standalone OPC Historical Data Server that collects data from an OPC Data Access Server or another data source. It may also be a set of interfaces that are layered on top of an existing Proprietary Historical Data Server. The clients that reference the OPC Historical Data server may be simple trending packages that just want values over a given time frame or they may be complex reports that require data in multiple formats.

Client application performs the communication with the server through specified interfaces. There are two main types of such classes: custom and automation interfaces. The custom interface implementation is mandatory for historical data server but automation interface is optional. OPC Specification lists COM interfaces, but not the implementation of those interfaces. Component Object Model is a binary-interface standard for software componentry introduced by Microsoft in 1993. It is used to enable interprocess communication and dynamic object creation in a large range of programming languages. Within the OPC Specification developer is able to find specification of the behavior that the interfaces are expected to provide to the client applications that use them.

The OPC Historical Data Server objects provide the ability to read data from a historical server and write data to a historical server. The types of historical data are server dependent. All COM objects are accessed through Interfaces. The client sees only the interfaces. An OPC historian client application must implement a callback interface to support a shutdown request. The client may also implement interfaces for the various asynchronous connections that a server may provide. If the client expects to use (and the server provides) a particular asynchronous interface, the client must implement the matching callback [8].

3   Data Exchange Mechanism

As mentioned in the previous part, the OPC HDA protocol is used in client-server architecture. Data exchange in this particular solution can be described just like in a traditional system built on this type of topology. Client application represents software which aim is to acquire data for a period that certain user is interested in, given as raw data or processed data, according to the selected algorithm and supported by the particular system. Decision, which kind of data will be returned is made by the client application's user. Software Development Kit supplied by the OPC Foundation includes some implementations of data processing algorithms, described in the OPC HDA specification. The server part is often placed on a remote machine and it is responsible for fulfilling queries received from clients. Server must have a certain connection to the data source established, however the type of data source can vary from simple text files to complex databases and client does not need to know where data is stored. The OPC HDA address space is available for clients by OPC HDA Browser interfaces.

Every OPC HDA server must implement the Browse method that informs the client which OPC tags' historical data is available to be queried. User of the client application is able to specify (provided that the specific client/server implements these functionalities) the tag name, time period, processing algorithm

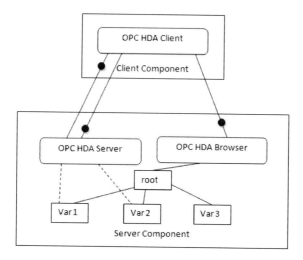

Fig. 2. OPC HDA SDK client-server data exchange mechanism

(e.g. standard deviation, sum, average) for the data that should be returned by the server, and the client sends proper request to the server. The interaction between main OPC HDA components is presented in Fig. 2. There are four main ways to access historical data:

- Read: the client can read raw values, processed values, values at a specific point in time, modified values, or value of attributes by synchronous or asynchronous calls;
- Update: the client can insert or replace values in synchronous or asynchronous calls as well;
- Annotation: the client can read and insert annotations;
- Playback: the client reads values with a defined frequency for a defined time frame, for both raw and aggregated data [9].

After receiving the data request, server application connects to the data source and sends requested records back to the client. From the point of view of the case depicted in this article, client-server data exchange mechanism can be illustrated like in Fig. 2. When user of client application request data for specified period to be presented as a trend, the SyncRead() method is invoked, in which there is a Trend class object, from which the COpcHdaServer ReadRaw() method is called. This particular method tries to invoke the ReadRaw() COM method (placed in the COM Wrapper) which eventually relates to the ReadRaw() method included in the COpcHdaHistorian class. Then, historian's ReadRaw() method starts to operate, inside of which the COpcHdaItem object is present, which method Load-Data() and LoadDataFromFile() perform the actual fetching data from the data source.

4 Protocol Efficiency Analysis in Context of Downloading/Sharing Data

The OPC HDA specificacion defines client and server interfaces. The specification doesn't define how the data are collected and stored. Different systems are able to provide data read or write in some specified ways. It leads to make an effort of finding of criteria that could be measured in order to compare the efficiency offered by a number of systems, every one of which uses a different mechanism of acquiring data from the data source. One of many ways to juxtapose functionalities provided by systems standing based on various protocols would be to measure the time required to gather different amount of data from the database. Testing environment has been presented in the Fig. 3.

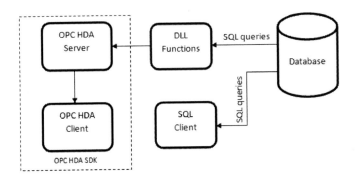

Fig. 3. Testing environment

Test presented here gives the opportunity to see measurements made for an application using regular SQL statements (stored procedures) and sample OPC HDA client. There were twenty attempts of measurements in each case. Numbers that represent minimum, maximum and average measured time given in milliseconds were gathered in Table 1. Measurement were taken for the same period of time in each case, however there was a different number of records to be loaded from the database which represented various frequencies of acquiring the data from the field.

All measurements were taken by using functions for time counting provided by C# language in every involved application. The SQL client mentioned in the Table 1 is the description for the simple application, using which the user is able to view data already stored in the database.

Analysis of numbers leads to following conclusions. In the SQL client case results are coherent with expectations. This means that the time for retrieving data from the database is raising linearly with the amount of records that are supposed to be loaded. More interesting is, however, the amount of time needed by the OPC HDA client. It is necessary to explain that after every measurement the client application was restarted to provide the same set of operations, as

Table 1. Summary of time test results (all times in milliseconds)

Record number		HDA client time	HDA client time (after modifying)	SQL client time
8000	MAX	17121	25941	430
	MIN	16565	20034	225
	AVG	16679.6	24693.9	281.9
4000	MAX	7002	8015	204
	MIN	5347	5349	123
	AVG	5682.4	5606.15	158.85
2000	MAX	2003	1509	212
	MIN	1439	1409	77
	AVG	1553.5	1455.95	120.3
1000	MAX	1689	842	128
	MIN	771	397	48
	AVG	937.7	739.65	82.7

normally client places acquired data in the memory using it as a kind of cache which minimizes time of presenting data to the user. Compared to the regular SQL client, using OPC HDA protocol to load large amount of data seems unprofitable. If there were 8000 records (which approximately stands for one measurement per hour during one year) to be loaded from the database, user would have to wait up to twenty five seconds to use required data which is unacceptable. And it should be obvious that this number of records is very little if we consider that majority of systems collect data more frequently than once per hour. For larger amount of data it is better to use simple SQL queries or stored procedures as they provide quicker data loading. The usage of OPC HDA protocol for smaller data packages can be taken under consideration.

This led to making some modifications to the server application so that it would load only data for a time period specified in the OPC HDA client interface. After analysis of gathered results (Table 1) it can be noticed that time needed for loading different amount of data is a little shorter for larger sets of data, but, surprisingly, is longer for smaller sets of data. However, compared to measurements taken before changing the structure of the application code, gain that could have been achieved had not been satisfactory enough. One of the reason for the fact that time measured for OPC HDA client differs so much from other results that authors describe in the next section (Improvement Considerations), along with some conclusions about correctness of the work of sample OPC HDA client.

5 Improvement Considerations

Although SQL client proved to be more suitable for usage in acquiring data stored in a database it will not provide data processing mechanism (e.g. standard deviation, regression lines) unless software developer makes an effort to supply an application with these mechanisms described in the OPC HDA specification. Using the OPC HDA client application, like for instance the sample client included in the software development kit (SDK) prepared by OPC Foundation [7], user possesses these functionalities from the beginning, however the data acquiring part has to be modified. It has to be mentioned that the sample client application operates on data stored in CSV (Comma separated values) files and the solution mostly used is having data stored in a database.

After some modifications to the library standing in the testing environment between OPC HDA client and database had been made, meaning that only data for the period of time specified in the OPC HDA client were loaded, additional conclusions were drawn. Client application did not work properly, as any change in specifying required time period for historical data gathering gave wrong results. It is related to the fact that OPC HDA client connects to the server only in the beginning and any further data request is performed on data stored in the memory of the client machine. So, if there had been request for data from a month period in the beginning, and later user wanted to gather data from a year period only the data from a month would be shown as there was no other data in the memory. Time required to process demanded data is only a bit different than it was before making the changes to the DLL, because data acquired from the database is stored in an array and then copied record by record to a list structure in the memory, which increases the time of data processing. Another field for improvements can be noticed in the way data is transferred from the OPC HDA server to the client. Whatever the amount of data to be transferred was, it was sent from server to the client as a character string, containing value, timestamp, quality and, optionally, any additional information required by the specific implementation. With a large amount of data requested, exceeding a few thousands of records, mentioned character string's length can be estimated as more than 100,000 bytes.

However, it is not the data transmission time that is the issue here, but the amount of time required to process gathered data from character string to the array, then into the list, then again to sorted array and then to the appropriate grid on the Graphical User Interface (Fig. 4). Moving data from one structure in the memory to another also should not become a problem, because even if the amount of data becomes larger modern processing units will be capable of handling this task. However conducting some measurements show that it really is a problem. In relation to results gathered in the Table 1, it can be said that 80 percent of each number is the time needed to transfer required data from one structure in the memory to another. In details, it can be seen in Fig. 4.

There are some possibilities of improving or extending the functionalities given by the original SDK. Author suggests the solution of omitting those parts "in the middle" (marked "I" and "II" in the Fig. 4) on the basis of applying the database as the data source. As it was mentioned earlier, in the SDK data had been stored in CSV files, which caused the necessity of additional data sorting before it would be inserted into the returned structure. Using database, we are not obliged to apply additional data sorting as it can be done by the

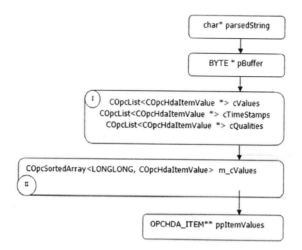

Fig. 4. Data flow in the OPC HDA server

database engine, at the stage of executing a query (containing ORDER BY phrase). According to that, OPC HDA server would receive already sorted data and the only thing to be done, would be to place it the structure passed to the method invoking data fetching. OPC HDA taken "as is" currently can be treated as a standard. Current implementation of the OPC HDA standard in the SDK from OPC Foundation is not effective enough which can be the cause of the fact that it is not very popular solution, in relation to the OPC DA standard. Unfortunately, OPC HDA efficiency is highly limited in comparison to corporate solutions. If the main criteria, when using historical data, were openness and versatility, HDA would be used in the system. However, if the great efficiency of operations was needed, it would not be the best solution. Changes mentioned in this article show that there are some possibilities of making improvements that could increase effectiveness of data transmission by optimizing the model and customizing it to suit the characteristics of information available through OPC HDA protocol.

6   Summary and Conclusions

In the current shape, OPC HDA might be used in systems, which require the highest level of openness and standardization. In other cases it might be considered as too slow in comparison to some corporate solutions, which might be the cause of its rare usage in industrial applications. There are some possible improvements described in the Sect. 5 of this article, which could increase the usability. It is not enough, however, to make OPC HDA competitive with other systems, in the area of speed. To make further considerations about the usage of this standard possible, the efforts for accelerating its performance should be continued.

Acknowledgement. This work was supported by the European Union from the European Social Fund.

References

1. Iwanitz, F., Lange, J.: OPC, Fundamentals, Implementation and Application, 2nd edn. Huthing Verlag, Heilderberg (2002)
2. Mahnke, W., Leitner, S.H.: OPC Unified Architecture, pp. 1–66 (2009)
3. OPC Unified Architecture Specification Part 11: Historical Access, Version 1.00 (January 2007)
4. Son, M., Yi, M.: A study on OPC specifications: Perspective and challenges. Sch. of Comput. Eng. & IT. Univ. of Ulsan, Ulsan, South Korea (2010)
5. Hong, X., Jianhua, W.: Using standard components in automation industry: A study on OPC Specification. Institute of Electrical Engineering. Xi'an JiaoTong University, Xi'an, China (2005)
6. Yoo, D.-S., Van Tan, V., Yi, M.-J.: A universal data access server for distributed data acquisition and monitoring systems. In: Huang, D.-S., Jo, K.-H., Lee, H.-H., Kang, H.-J., Bevilacqua, V. (eds.) ICIC 2009. LNCS, vol. 5754, pp. 762–773. Springer, Heidelberg (2009)
7. OPC Foundation Website, http://www.opcfoundation.org
8. OPC HDA 1.20 Specification, Version 1.20. (released December 10, 2003)
9. Iwanitz, F., Lange, J.: OPC-Opennes, Productivity, and Connectivity. In: Zuravski, R. (ed.) The Industrial Information Technology Handbook, pp. 62_1–62_30. CRC Press, Washington (2005)

Efficiency of OPC UA Communication in Java-Based Implementations

Kamil Folkert[1], Marcin Fojcik[2], and Rafał Cupek[1]

[1] Silesian University of Technology, Institute of Informatics
kamil@folkert.pl, rcupek@polsl.pl
[2] Sogn og Fjordane University College
marcin.fojcik@hisf.no

Abstract. Nowadays communication in industrial computer systems needs to be standardized. One of the promising possibilities is usage of OPC UA protocol, which assures common set of data and functions for every system node. Next step of standardization may be unifying communication modules development for diverse platforms in Java. In theory, Java implementation of OPC UA allows to use homogeneous industrial network interface completely independent from hardware and software used in a system. On the other hand, is this kind of implementation of communication able to fulfil some time constraints? Is it possible to estimate connection parameters? Does such complex unification have any negative influence on communication parameters? The article is an attempt of realization and tests of this type of connection.

Keywords: OPC UA, Java, stack adaptations, communication latency.

1 Introduction

Contemporary manufacturing systems trend away from central control structures to distributed local units. The Ethernet based real-time communication networks are used in all levels of automation. In the meantime more and more open IT standards are used in automation. We can say that IT and automation world are growing together.

Rapid development of market of electronic devices and services caused multiply repercussions in the area of standardization in IT. One of the best examples of such a normalization is set of standards defined for local and global computer networks. Unfortunately, it is not present in industrial computer systems. Many companies define their own so-called "standards" designed for specific types of applications. The situation is caused by very broad aspect of usage of industrial computer networks. In some cases time resolution of milliseconds is needed. In other situations the number of system variables becomes an issue (e.g. in intelligent building projects, where the number of sensors and actuators may be greater than several thousands). Finally, in different case we have to assure communication between nodes of distributed system, which is not an easy operation (e.g. in geological measurements systems) [1].

A. Kwiecień, P. Gaj, and P. Stera (Eds.): CN 2011, CCIS 160, pp. 348–357, 2011.

Thanks to industrial electronic devices development and lowering prices of fieldbus components today we can find many examples of devices equipped with fieldbus communication modules placed on factory field level. Examples of fieldbus devices are: switches, valves (e.g. solenoid, pneumatic), drive, position encoders, operating devices, display devices, measurement and analysis devices, protective devices, robots, safety engineering (light barriers, emergency off).

There is an international standard IEC 61158 *Digital data communications for measurement and control – Fieldbus for use in industrial control systems*, which defines services for communication between distributed electronic devices, but it was created against 18 different existing fieldbus standards [2]. This situation causes that today standardized electronic devices are mutually incompatible. Nowadays there are many efforts to move well established IT standards to the industrial electronic device domain. One of the toughest trends is OPC UA solution [3,4,5,6]. OPC UA is based on widely used OPC DA vertical communication standard. Because OPC DA was based on Microsoft DCOM it was very difficult to use directly on the electronic device level. OPC DA servers are mainly installed on the PC computers and different industrial networks communication protocols are used for direct communication with electronic devices. This situation introduces serious delays and may be the source of data inconsistency [7]. The newest specification, OPC Unified Architecture, defines new platform-independent model of communication and may be applied on various devices and hardware platforms. Other feature of OPC UA standard is meta data based on defined model to vertical communication. The raw process information is supported by meta information available on OPC UA server which supports clients access to big data sets by hierarchical and object-oriented standardization [8]. Another important feature of OPC UA is possibility of usage of programming language which is not bound to any hardware platform (e.g. Java), which allows to develop application in one form and deploy it on diverse environments. The goal of this article is to show how standardization of various systems (monitoring, controlling, visualisation, etc.) may be realized.

Due to usage of Java and OPC UA features it become possible to apply communication standards not only on level of desktop computers and servers, but also on level of embedded devices and process control layer devices, like programmable logic controllers or data concentrators. Cardinal benefit of this solution is independence from specific data transfer protocols in favour of system-wide usage of TCP/IP (in some cases in its industrial variety) – due to that the whole system is strongly homogeneous. It facilitates data exchange with higher layers without additional delay in communication.

In theory, there should be no problem even if the communication mediums are diverse (GPRS, WiFi, Ethernet). Practical implications of this kind of situation, especially latencies in communication, are described in this article.

2   Rapid Development of OPC UA Applications

Nowadays software developers are expected not only to implement computer systems accordingly to the engineering project, but also to the business development plan. In many cases it means that they are under pressure for increasing their productivity, with keeping all planned features of the project implemented. For that reason RAD (Rapid Application Development) became very popular methodology of software development.

Because RAD reduces planning in favour of prototyping, some actions must be performed to prevent from deprecation of software quality. The solution for achieving this goal is usage of SDKs (Software Development Kits), which are implementing most of the core functionality of considered project in a language-dependent or platform-specific manner, allowing to create stable and easily maintainable applications. SDK hides lower layers functionality from the developer and makes him able to use only specified interfaces of given components. This attitude allows to reduce both time of software development as well as amount of possible mistakes, but in some cases is unacceptable for the developer as he may need access to some more specific parameters.

OPC UA standard defines many complex features which may be implemented in various ways. To shorten time of developing OPC UA applications some SDKs were implemented also in this area. OPC UA does not favour any system platform or programming language. In the same moment it guarantees interoperability between various implementations of the standard. However, the popularity of some programming languages determined the SDK vendors to use those languages. Therefore there are three well-known OPC UA SDKs, each developed by another vendor:

- .NET OPC UA SDK (OPC Foundation),
- C/C++ OPC UA SDK (Unified Automation),
- Java OPC UA SDK (Prosys) [9].

OPC UA SDK may be provided as set of utilities for creating only client or server application, or as bundle package. Each OPC UA SDK consists of two main parts: OPC UA Stack and specialized API (Application Programming Interface), which provides interfaces for the application developer. OPC UA specification does not define how the API should be implemented – it only determines how it should work. Typical view of software layers in an OPC UA system is shown in a Fig. 1 below.

OPC UA standard defines mechanisms for client-server data transfer model, enabling connectivity between applications using communication Stacks from different vendors, developed on diverse platforms. Compatibility of the

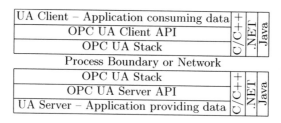

Fig. 1. OPC UA Software Layers [10]

communication is great feature of OPC UA and allows to connect different system nodes, from simple devices to complex servers, into on enterprise-wide system.

OPC UA Stack is responsible for tasks related with handling the TCP/IP-based communication between peers, like message encoding, transport and security. It is developed by the OPC Foundation (in some cases with cooperation with outer vendors). As the Stack implements functionalities on OS (Operating System) boundary, it may be considered as the most platform-specific part of the OPC UA application. However, it is not a rule. Despite that, currently there are stacks for three most popular programming languages and environments:

- ANSI C Stack,
- .NET Stack,
- Java Stack.

While Stack implements the protocol, OPC UA SDK encapsulates Stack into more complex objects and implements some higher layer operations (which may be considered as services). In many cases it completely hides the lower software layers, depending on platform-specific communication handling. This situation is slightly different when considering Java OPC UA SDK, as Java itself is defined as platform-independent as long as no native code is used. Moreover, Java enables various options of adapting the Stack, as it is described in Sect. 3. Whichever programming language is used for implementation, the OPC UA SDK should implement following features:

- methods of information modelling,
- node management,
- subscription management,
- session management,
- identity management.

Using SDK for developing OPC UA applications is almost indispensable. There is no another way of creating OPC UA servers and clients in a reasonable time and without great engineering effort. Usage of SDK assures that developed application will be compatible and interoperable with another OPC UA products and allows to focus on desired functionality instead of communication handling, server-side data modelling methods, and many more.

3   Java-Based OPC UA Implementation

Choosing a programming language for developing a software is always a hard task. Considering OPC UA application development it is more specific than in case of regular desktop software, although still some area for maneuver exists.

OPC UA strongly impacts on object-orientedness of the data model. Undoubtedly it is easier to implement object model in a programming language that is object-oriented. For that reason Java and .NET SDKs have some advantage over

ANSI C SDK. On the other hand, for low-end devices it is not necessary to implement complex object model. Moreover, significant majority of them does not support .NET framework, which is designed for Windows OS. Luckily, more and more vendors develop their implementation of JVM (Java Virtual Machine) for the low-end devices. Since that, Java seems to be golden mean between severity of ANSI C and complexity of .NET [11].

Portability of Java may be a great advantage, but in some cases performance is far more important then platform-independence. Despite performance issues were well-known problems in older versions of Java, nowadays some basic data operations are still far more effective when implemented in native, low level ANSI C code. In case of OPC UA applications it may be cleverly used for improving performance of communication handling operations, like serialization and deserialization of transferred data. Due to possibility of embedding native code in Java it is possible to resign from portability in favour of better performance of communication stack's operations. Continuing, the developer is given three options:

- ANSI C Stack encapsulated via JNI (Java Natice Interface) or JNA (Java Native Access),
- ANSI C communication handling and serialization of data in Java,
- Complete implementation in Java.

First and second option may introduce some acceleration into data processing, but in the same moment they cause platform-dependency of the application, because it must be recompiled for every platform it is going to be run on. Third option maintains portability of the software, but all data processing is done not on the level of OS, but is performed by JVM.

As it was described in Sect. 2, process of developing OPC UA applications may be significantly accelerated with usage of SDK. Java is not an exception in this area. Prosys OPC UA SDK, also mentioned in Sect. 2, is a composite set of Java classes, provided as source code or precompiled libraries, depending on the edition:

1. Client Binary (without the source code),
2. Client Source (with the source code),
3. Client & Server Binary (without the source code),
4. Client & Server Source (with the source code),
5. Evaluation editions.

Prosys OPC UA Java SDK is uses Java Stack licensed by OPC Foundation. However, the Stack is developed mainly by Prosys as a main contributor of Java-based OPC solutions.

Despite Prosys SDK accelerates the process of developing UA applications, it may cause several problems because of its complexity. The number of classes and their mutual affiliations and relations may be the source of consternation. To avoid problems with multiple invoking the same functions the API provided by the SDK was encapsulated into own methods. They are enclosed to OpcUaServer object provided by the SDK, and that made further implementation much easier. The client application is also implemented using Prosys SDK and includes methods for delay communication measuring.

4 Handling OPC UA Communication in Diverse Mediums

Since Prosys OPC UA SDK hides implementation of the Stack from the software developer, it is also based on some significant principles. One of them is that Java Stack does not use any native code, so the implementation is portable and platform-independent. It means that both communication sockets' handling and data serialization/deserialization is performed in Java. Moreover, we may assume that the SDK and the Stack use as much from core Java functionalities as possible. This assumption is true, we can notice that communication is handled using Java NewIO API. What does it mean for the final application developer? That low level TCP communication is handled by the JVM itself and is not visible for the higher layers (like the Stack or the SDK). Continuing, we do not have to care about the communication medium, because Java handles it as it is.

In theory, that situation is very comfortable. Application is not only portable, which means that it may be deployed on any type of hardware (the only constraint is that JVM for that platform must be available), but also is independent from the network layer and should operate properly in case of any TCP-based communication. Of course, it is a simplification. It is possible to imagine situation when server application is built and deployed on a computer that is connected to the Internet, but its IP address is covered by NAT – it is visible only in local network area. In practice, it makes the server useless for remote clients because it cannot be accessed from the outside network as long as TCP port on the router is not redirected and provide an IP address that is discoverable from outside (or VPN is configured to connect to the inside network, but it causes additional overhead to the data exchange). It is not always possible, because not always redirection of the transmission may be applied (e.g. in case of GPRS connection the server is covered the NAT of GSM operator). The SDK guarantees the portability of the application, but it does not guarantee proper network configuration, which must be done beforehand.

Moreover, network configuration has cardinal importance also on the client side. The server creates and shares some endpoints, which may be accessed for the OPC-based communication. The SDK allows the developer to specify if the endpoint should be created on each network interface available or not. In both cases expected behaviour of the server is that it creates endpoint which consists of the name of the computer (and the rest of the endpoint address in OPC format: `opc.tcp://serverNameOrIP:portUsed/applicationName`), which not always may be resolved by the client. Ultimate portability of the application will be useless without proper DNS configuration.

As it was mentioned, the SDK does not access the network directly, but it makes use of Java core APIs. For that reason, the type of connection is known

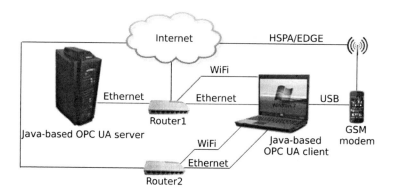

Fig. 2. Research environment

during runtime, not earlier. It implies that the Stack and the SDK should be prepared for various types of connection bandwidth, which determines speed of data transfer. Obviously, correct configuration of connection timeouts and another high level connection parameters may be crucial.

To test how the SDK handles OPC UA communication via diverse mediums the client and server applications were implemented. They were deployed and run on two separate standard personal computers. Figure 2 presents the research environment. The server was accessible through the port redirection and the client could resolve the name of the server's machine. The computers' clocks were synchronized using NTP (Network Time Protocol). During the experiment the latencies in communication were measured. As a data model `double` primitive was used to avoid distortion of the results by complex model data serialization process, which probably would be . Security mode used during the connection was `SecurityMode.None` (without encryption and authorization) to assure minimal amounts of bytes are being serialized and transferred in each transaction. Server was updating tag every 1 second with accuracy of 1 ms. Also client's subscription interval was set to 1 ms.

Scenario of the experiment was defined as follows:

1. Client connects to the server,
2. Client browses address space,
3. Client chooses a node for subscription,
4. Client subscribes for `value` property of chosen node,
5. Each time the data is refreshed, the latency is measured.

This scenario was applied to seven rounds of measurements. Each round consisted of 5000 measurements and was conducted using different interface. The average results for each round of the experiment are presented in the Fig. 3.

According to OPC UA Specification, part 6 "Mappings", amount of bytes used for encoding data value exchanged during subscription is at least 34 B (depending on data model). However, latency is not directly dependent of amount

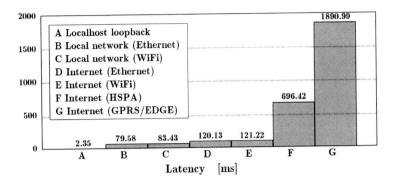

Fig. 3. Results of the experiment

of data, because some asynchronous communication handling data frames are being transferred as well [12].

When client and server instances were running on the same machine and OPC UA endpoint was created on the localhost loopback interface the latency was no longer than 3 ms. In local network it was about 80 ms, regardless of communication medium used (Gigabit Ethernet or 802.11g WiFI). Additional 40 ms were result of routing the packets through the outside network. Despite this is not very convincing result because we do not have any control over the true route of the packages, it gives some general overview. The most interesting are latencies in GSM network. For HSPA (3.5G) it was almost 700 ms, while for Enhanced GPRS (2.5G) it was almost 1900 ms (almost 2 times more then updating interval). Those results were expected, because they correspond to the results of another experiment, described in [1]. OPC UA overhead seems to be acceptable even in case of slow GSM connection, of course with assumption that we do not need real-time data transfer.

The stability of the connection managed by the SDK is solid and firm. Even the reconnection is not performed automatically, some server object events are generated and may be handled to perform reconnection. Identifier of the node is kept and after reconnection the subscription does not have be set up again.

5   Summary and Conclusions

Based on the experiment results it is possible to state that Java implementation of OPC UA communication is an effective solution for rapid development of OPC UA client and server applications. Moreover, created applications are almost always portable between completely different devices. This feature facilitates the process of testing the software, especially in context of industrial devices. However, at least two main problems exist:

1. Network configuration must allow the server to be discoverable by the clients (if the server is behind NAT communication on listening port must be redirected);

2. Device the application is deployed on must be equipped with JVM for Java SE 6 or newer (communication stack libraries are compiled for this version). This requirement is not always fulfilled, especially in case of low-end devices. In some cases it is possible to use built-in OPC UA server, but deploying custom software is always a pain.

However, if these problems are solved, it seems that Java implementation of OPC UA is one of the most universal manners to arrange communication in an industrial computer system without hard real-time requirements.

Despite the results are promising and allow to expect that standardization process in the area of industrial automation will be continued, some further researches must be done to confirm this statement. It seems that in case of simple objects the overhead of the OPC is almost negligible, but OPC UA was designed for complex data modelling, so time of this kind of objects serializing and transferring also should be measured. Furthermore, OPC UA defines more security modes, which also may affect the communication process. Combination of all of those parameters may change the outlook of the universality of Java implementation of OPC UA applications. Nevertheless, stability of the connection and predictable transmission delays are great advantages of Java-based OPC UA communication and determine solid base for further development of this kind of homogeneous industrial computer systems.

Acknowledgement. This work was supported by the European Union from the European Social Fund.

References

1. Folkert, K.: Communication in a distributed system of geological data acquisition. Gliwice (2010)
2. Felser, M.: The Fieldbus Standards: History and Structure. Technology Leadership Day, Luzern (2002)
3. Renjie, H., Feng, L.: Research on OPC UA based on Electronic Device Description. In: 3rd IEEE Conference on Industrial Electronics and Applications, ICIEA (2008)
4. Hannelius, T., Salmenpera, M., Kuikka, S.: Roadmap to adopting OPC UA. In: 6th IEEE International Conference on Industrial Informatics (2008)
5. Yamamoto, M., Sakamoto, H.: FDT/DTM framework for field device integration. In: SICE Annual Conference (2008)
6. Suzuki, K., Ideguchi, T.: Proposal of device capability profiling for manufacturing application service interface. In: Proceedings of the 2009 IEEE International Conference on Industrial Technology, ICIT 2009. IEEE Computer Society, Washington DC, USA (2009)
7. Cupek, R., Huczała, L.: Passive PROFINET I/O OPC DA Server. In: 14th IEEE International Conference on Emerging Technologies and Factory Automation

8. Cupek, R., Fojcik, M., Sande, O.: Object Oriented Vertical Communication in Distributed Industrial Systems. In: Kwiecień, A., Gaj, P., Stera, P. (eds.) CN 2009. CCIS, vol. 39, pp. 72–78. Springer, Heidelberg (2009)

9. Prosys OPC website, http://www.prosysopc.com

10. Mahnke, W., Leitner, S.H., Damm, M.: OPC Unified Architecture. Springer, Heidelberg (2009)

11. Hannelius, T., Shroff, M., Tuominen, P.: Embedding OPC Unified Architecture, Automaatio XVIII Seminari, Helsinki (2009)

12. OPC Unified Architecture Specification

Field Level Industrial Ethernet Network Data Analysis

Rafał Cupek and Łukasz Huczała

Silesian University of Technology, Institute of Informatics
{rcupek,lukasz.huczala}@polsl.pl

Abstract. This paper describes the PROFINET I/O field level industrial network data analysis idea that was realized as a research tool at the Institute of Informatics, Silesian University of Technology. The authors describe the method of accessing industrial network real-time data (RT) from the level of widely known data analysis environment MATLAB. The attached tests and results proof MATLAB as an efficient and flexible tool which may be used for RT Ethernet networks analysis support.

Keywords: real-time Ethernet, network monitoring, MATLAB, data analysis, Profinet IO.

1 Introduction

The real-time industrial network area is now changing from solutions based on standard serial communication into area of dedicated real-time Ethernet based solutions. Another fact is the increasing size of new applications in the area of industrial networks. Distributed industrial control systems become more and more complicated. The new network monitoring tools which will support RT Ethernet low level industrial network: start-up, diagnosis and maintenance activities become very important element of distributed industrial computer systems area. Despite of some good examples of general purpose Ethernet network monitors and network analyzers, rapid development of real-time Ethernet field level network domain enforces new scientific works on real-time communication systems. Industrial informatics systems are created as strongly heterogeneous structures in most of cases. There are many different RT Ethernet protocols used in one factory location.

The main goal of presented solution is to create open and universal platform for network monitoring and network diagnosis tools. Another goal is to create solution which will be useful in education process focused on industrial network protocols. This paper presents the practical example of open network analyzer built on the base of MATLAB environment adopted for field level industrial network analysis. The presented solution is dedicated for Profinet IO network but it may be easy adapted to any RT Ethernet communication protocol. The concept of usage open WinPcap software library and switch mirroring port allows for an easy creation of another RT protocol plug-ins. No dedicated hardware for

A. Kwiecień, P. Gaj, and P. Stera (Eds.): CN 2011, CCIS 160, pp. 358–366, 2011.

such solution is necessary. The frame analyzing part may be easily modified to fulfil another protocols structure and provide a various kind of data to the digital laboratory.

2   Profinet IO Data in MATLAB

There is no need to convince anybody how useful MATLAB can be when it comes to data analysis. The great number of various mathematical, statistical and data processing functions together with advanced data presentation tools and many professional toolboxes speak for itself.

Our goal was to create an easy to use MATLAB extension to analyse real-time Ethernet network data supporting creation, startup and maintenece process for PROFINET I/O based distributed control systems. The biggest advantage of the method is that we can get any data from Ethernet frames and we get it straight into the mathematical laboratory what means we can easly create a logical model for real time communication in a given distributed industrial control system.

From a MATLAB user point of view there is only one new PNIOmat() function with proper parameters for setting and controlling the data capturing process. The first parameter is always a command, the other are the command attributes. The input and output parameters due to MATLAB rules are matrices or arrays. To avoid too many unnecessary details a simple usage diagram of the function parameters is presented in Fig. 1.

The general requirement of the interface is to adjust custom MEX-function input/output data to MATLAB data format, that means: arrays or matrices. To do so, proper MATLAB libraries containing data conversion and creation functions have to be included in a custom program. Then just few application building settings in a development environment need to be done and a new function for MATLAB is ready for use. As MEX-files are widely described in manuals or on Internet let's focus on the other part of the problem, on how to get PROFInet IO data into the MEX function.

Since PROFInet IO protocol is based on Ethernet, it is possible to reach process data by capturing and decoding Ethernet network frames [1]. To get the frames from the PROFInet system network a switch device with "mirroring" feature is needed. The mirroring feature allows copying all network traffic from one port to the other.

Most of the accessible industrial switches have the mirroring capability for only one port but if the mirrored port is a controller port we have a possibility to "listen to" the network frames exchanged between the controller and all devices connected to the controller. In such case the solution is limited to one controller system. The general application architecture is presented in Fig. 2.

To capture and decode the network frames WinPcap library was used. The library is free and open for developers and is applied in theEthernet network monitors like Wireshark or Ethereal.

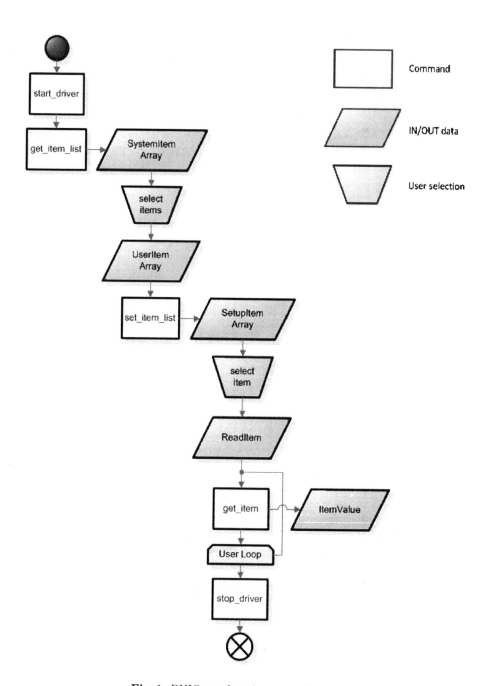

Fig. 1. PNIOmat function usage diagram

WinPcap consists of a driver, which is installed inside the networking portion of Win32 kernels to provide low-level network access, a low-level dynamic link library (packet.dll) and a high-level and system-independent library (wpcap.dll). The biggest advantage of WinPcap is the access to the "raw" data on the network without the interposition of protocol processing by the operating system [2].

The PROFInet data is captured by two channels. Through the one of them real-time IO data is accessed. The second channel is used to capture RT Alarms frames and the rest of network traffic like configuration data and connection events. Such division is made due to a great load of data in the RT IO data channel, so we can be sure that all process control data is registered and no alarm or event is missed. To create the two processing channels two instances of WinPcap driver are created. The basic packet filtering is done at the driver level. Here the appropriate frames are directed to different dumping threads. Next the packets are passed to application level decoding threads where the information requested by user is read and forwarded to the data buffers.

The next step is to make the captured and filtered data accessible to the MEX function. As the MATLAB function is intended to give us a current process data in a respectively short time the whole process of creation and configuration capturing threads cannot be started and terminated by every call. The data needs to be ready to be fetched.

The solution to that problem is a standalone capturing process writing filtered and initially processed data to the interprocess shared memory segment. As it is shown at Fig. lukhuc:fig:3 that function is served by CaptureAgent process.

To configure and control the state of the process an interprocess message queue is implemented, therefore the MEX function process and capturing process can communicate. For both the shared memory segment and the message queue implementation the Boost.Interprocess libraries were used.

The configuration of CaptureAgent consists of two steps. At the process initialization an XML file containing all accessible data description is loaded. In particular, the information structure contains of:

- Local station information (interface to be used);
- IO Device network identification;
- IOCRs (IO data exchange channels);
- AlarmCRs (Alarms channels);
- Modules parameters;
- Sub modules parameters.

Knowing the particular IO Devices configuration that together with an IO Controller goes into the making of an industrial network we are able to decode the data straight from frames exchanged in the system [3]. Such information can be read from IO Controller configuration or by means of an external tool like Profinet Analyzer which was developed during a students' project at our university [4].

In the very first version of presented application there are three types of data items available:

- PNIO Item – device input/output process data;

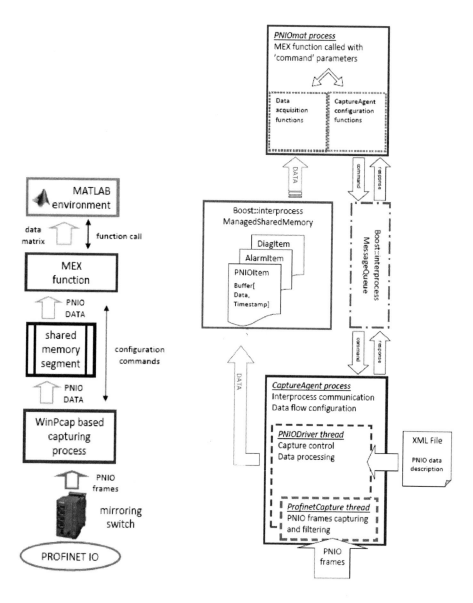

Fig. 2. General application idea

Fig. 3. Data flow architecture

- Alarm Item – PROFInet IO alarms;
- Diag Item – communication diagnostic data, in particular: data exchange cycle counter.

The item list is accessible to MATLAB user by means of calling PNIOmat function with the input parameter *get_item_list*. After calling the function with the command *set_item_list*. and array of selected item ids CaptureAgent process creates the items. objects in the shared memory segment and sets proper data filters up. Every item consists of data source identification fields, buffer for filtered data signed with capture timestamp and data decoding function.

When the data items are created capturing threads start up. The data buffers are updated cyclically as the PROFInet frames are coming in. The call of PNIOmat function with the command *get_item*. and an item id parameter allows for getting captured data directly from the buffers allocated in the memory segment. The software structe of presented solution is presented in Fig. 3.

3   Tests and Results

For testing the functionalities and performance of the tool a simple research environment was created. The installation consisted of Simatic PNIO CPU317 IO Controller, ET200S IO Device (2 input and 2 output modules), Scalance X200 Ethernet switch with mirroring functionality and a dedicated Xlinix FPGA board for injecting disturbances into the network.

The controller had a simple program loaded: there was a cyclic counter from 0 to 255 (1 byte) incremented every 20 ms, the current value was split into low and high 4-bit parts of the byte and sent accordingly to the Output 1 and Output 2 of the IO device. The data exchange cycle time was set to 1 ms. The application run at standard PC platform with Windows 7 system.

The first test was to check if we are able to get all IO real-time data into MATLAB. The parallel call for item of Output 1 and Output 2 in a loop was executed. After analyzing the data captured into result arrays it showed up that there are always 20 values per value change at Output 1 and respectively 320 (16×20) values per change at Output 2. The results generated in MATLAB are presented in Fig. 4 and 5. It is obvious that we cannot expect that the PROFInet IO data can be accessed by MATLAB exactly in the same moment when it occurs in the network, there is always some delay caused by processing. However; the most important thing for us is a reliable time interval between captured frames what can gives us delayed but still true image of network events. For that reason timestamp of the captured IO data, which makes the most of PROFInet IO network traffic, was analyzed [5]. The results, presented in Fig. 6, are satisfying.

The measured cycle time deviation period was less than 0.2 ms what is consistent with the PROFInet IO standard and reality [6]. In fact, PROFInet IO Cycle Counter, which serves as RT IO data transmission watch, is incremented by value of 32 every 1 ms and any less frame transmission delay is not noticeable in the system.

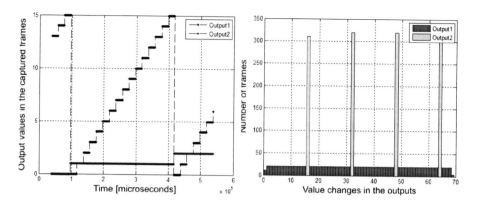

Fig. 4. Recorded values   **Fig. 5.** Number of captured frames

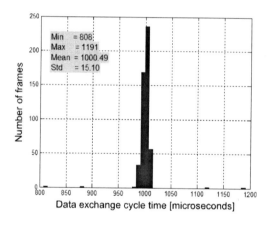

Fig. 6. RT IO data timestamp

The Cycle Counter was a subject of the next test. Thanks to the mentioned FPGA board with two Ethernet interfaces we were able to control network traffic. In this particular case our goal was to delay PROFInet IO RT data exchange frames by various time: starting from 1 μs up to 1 s. The forced time crack was not recognized in the system up to the value of 1 ms. The Cycle Counter difference between consecutive RT IO data frames presented in Fig. 7 was always constant and did not signaled any cycle time disturbance.

The situation, however; looked quite different when we checked the recorded timestamp. The frame transfer delay can be clearly noticed. In Fig. 8, one can also learn how the protocol manages the problem. After the disturbed frame, in the next two transfer cycles, frames were sent much faster to make up for the lost time.

The next step was the delay of 10 ms. In this case the disturbances caused a connection break and PROFInet IO alarm was generated by the IO Controller.

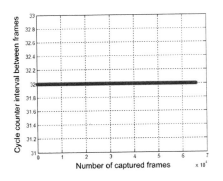

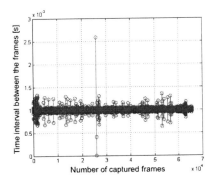

Fig. 7. RT IO data timestamp (1 ms crack)   **Fig. 8.** Cycle Counter interval

That time the Cycle Counter value significantly point to a communication problem. In Fig. 9, the difference of consecutive frames cycle counter is presented. There were two connection breaks and the two high values represents a time of about 1.5 s break what, taking into account a restart process of the transmission, corresponds to the forced time crack event.

The mentioned RT Alarm frame was also captured. The decoded fields: Alarm-Type, ErrorCode, ErrorDecode, ErrorCode1 and ErrorCode2 had the corresponding values: [4, 207, 129, 253, 2]. The values, according to the standard, mean: Alarm High, PNIO RTA Error, RTA_ERR_CLS_PROTOCOL, instance closed (RTA_ERR_ABORT) [6]. Such values are typical for connection break between IO Controller and IO Device.

In every test case the data was captured and stored using the PNIOmat function called within a MATLAB loop. The speed of data access and performance of the tool can be described by inspecting the item buffers load. The result is presented in Fig. 10.

In the test the MEX function was called 30 000 times continuously. The great majority of the calls returned from 1 to 2 values in array (please notice that the

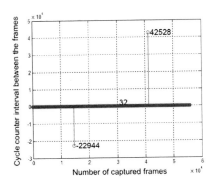

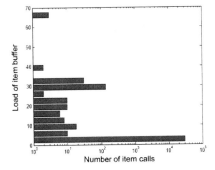

Fig. 9. Cycle Counter – connection break   **Fig. 10.** Load of the item buffers

X-axis scale is logarithmic). Taking into account the fact that the research was done using standard PC platform it can be stated that the access to PROFInet IO data is fast enough and the tool can give us a reliable image of real-time data and events.

4   Conclusions

As the results show the presented PNIOmat plug-in satisfies the technical and methodological requirements. The performed tests show the best how valuable conclusions can be drawn out of the captured data with a help of a professional analysis tool.

Although the Ethernet based industrial real-time networks are becoming more and more popular, the knowledge about how the protocols works is still under a cover. Most of the diagnostic tools are producer dependent and concentrate on process data send by means of real-time network rather than on the network.s communication technology matters.

At the moment the presented solution provides an access to the most time critical data of PROFInet IO system. This is because at first we wanted to proof that the available component tools are efficient enough to build such kind of industrial networks laboratory. The scope, though, can be easily extended thanks to the implemented XML item description.

Following the idea our future works will concern data analysis in Ethernet industrial networks independently of protocol.

Acknowledgements. This work was supported by the European Community from the European Social Fund.

References

1. Siemens: PROFINET Technology and Application. Karlsruhe (2005)
2. Risso, F., Deogianni, L., Varenni, G.: Profiling and Optimization of Software-Based Network Analysis Application (2001)
3. Cupek, R., Huczała, Ł.: Passive PROFINET I/O OPC DA Server. In: 14th IEEE International Conference on Emerging Technologies and Factory Automation, ETFA 2009 (2009)
4. PInternational: GSDML Specification for Profinet IO, Version 2.16. PROFIBUS Nutzerorganisation e.V., Karlsruhe (2008)
5. Kleines, H., Detert, S., Drochner, M., Suxdorf, F.: Performance Aspects of PROFINET IO. IEEE Transactions on Nuclear Science 55(1) (February 2008)
6. Popp, M., Weber, K.: The Rapid Way to PROFINET. PROFIBUS Nutzerorganisation e.V., Karlsruhe (2004)

Industrial Networks in Explosive Atmospheres

Andrzej Kwiecień and Karol Opielka

Silesian University of Technology, Institute of Informatics
Akademicka 16, 44-100 Gliwice, Poland
{andrzej.kwiecien,karol.opielka}@polsl.pl
http://www.polsl.pl

Abstract. The paper presents a review of selected existing ways of realizing distributed computers systems in explosive atmospheres. It points out the problems that must be considered during designing of the system. It evaluates the influence of specific installations architecture on data flow of the control network. Also the possibility of early detection of potential errors in the system associated with incorrect operation of network components was analyzed. Particular attention was given to diagnostic issues because the preventive actions aiming to reduce the number of failures in the hazardous installation are of utmost importance.

Keywords: distributed real-time system, hazardous area, ATEX.

1 Introduction

Carrying out of an industrial process in conditions where it is possible for flammable substances in the form of gases, dust or vapour to accumulate is particularly hazardous. As a result of the accumulation of flammable substances an explosive atmosphere may form. If the ignition occurs, it may cause an explosion, which constitutes a danger to people and the installation itself. Such possibility of an ignition results in an array of requirements and restrictions with which used devices must comply. ATEX Directive [1] is the basic document that includes requirements and guidelines for those devices within the European Union. It lists requirements that must be met by any equipment used in hazardous areas. It consolidated the conditions across all EU countries. This directive classifies areas according to the type and timing of the occurrence of hazards, describes in detail the requirements for each of these zones, and precisely defines the process of approval of the device to operate within the zone. Equipment approved for use is properly categorized as presented in Table 1.

Equipment categorized under the corresponding risk group can only be operated in designated areas. It is necessary to undergo a certification process for each new appliance to be operated. Outlined requirements also apply to computer systems that are used in such areas. This paper provides an analysis of industrial computing solutions used for the Ex (EXplosive atmosphere) zone; it also presents the proposed solutions to the functional extension of such systems for their maintenance and diagnostics requirements.

A. Kwiecień, P. Gaj, and P. Stera (Eds.): CN 2011, CCIS 160, pp. 367–378, 2011.

Table 1. Equipment's classification within ATEX directive

Group	Group description	Subgroup	Subgroup description
I	Equipment designed to operate in underground and those over-ground parts of the mining facilities that are threatened by explosion	—	Risks of methane or coal dust explosion
II	Equipment designed to operate on the surface in areas subjected to gases, vapours, mists or dusts explosion	A B C	Propane group Ethylene group Hydrogen group

2   Fulfilment of the Requirements

Nowadays, using computer systems in areas where there is a risk of explosion became a standard solution. However such practices necessitate a number of restrictions with respect to monitoring and control systems installed in hazardous areas [2]. There are particular hardware and software demands for industrial networks working in these conditions. Adherence to these requirements is a prerequisite for the use of computer systems in the described area. Only the absolute compliance with these requirements ensures the safety of the system's operation. In addition to the standardized design process, complementary studies and tests that verify compliance with existing requirements must also be performed. One of the most important elements is to analyze the level of energy emitted by the each component. Energy emission in an operating device must be limited to a level making it impossible for it to ignite the potentially explosive mixture. Consequently such equipment must be constructed according to certain principles of the ATEX Directive and a number of supporting standards. The rules clearly define the nominal parameters for electronic devices such as inductance, capacitance, resistance and power. An absolute practical application of the requirements is essential to ensure the safe operation of the system. The individual components have to undergo a series of tests before being admitted to be used. These tests are carried out by certification units, in order to confirm safety of those components. Only certified equipment can be legally incorporated into real installation. There are several known solutions dedicated for industrial networks working in potentially explosive areas, e.g. RS-485-IS, FISCO or Profibus-PA [3]. Such solutions are based around reducing the emission of energy by reducing the level of voltage, reduce the maximum number of nodes or only passive clients connections. Principal requirements for the Ex zones are not always suitable for fieldbuses due to their specific design and operational requirements. It is particularly true for example in the mining industry, where known solutions are not generally applicable.

It should be stressed that in order to ensure the required level of security is not necessary to build new intrinsically safe devices [4]. One possible solution is to separate standard equipment from the external environment by placing it in flameproof case. These cases provide isolation from the outside atmosphere. Energy generated in the device is contained within the case, hence there is no danger of initiation of an explosion. Standard industrial devices can be used in that way, but only if they exclusively operate in the described case and before each opening they are switched off or disconnected. This solution also requires approval by the entire system certification body, but allows for the use of standard components within a dedicated case. Designed systems typically utilize a hybrid of the outlined solutions. When there is no device certified to operate in the Ex zone, then the device is placed in a dedicated case utilizing solutions based on separation of the signals to exchange information with the external environment. An example of such installation is presented in Fig. 1, where PLCs are placed in a flameproof cases connected to the bus by barriers. A control panel is the only element that is directly connected to the bus, it is possible because it is an Ex component.

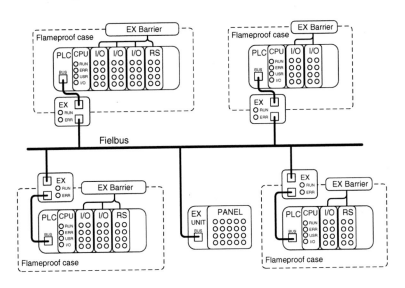

Fig. 1. Industrial network in Ex zone

Presented model should be analyzed in terms of design of the industrial control network. The use of additional components such as barriers has a significant impact on the operation of the entire control network. In presented case in order for the device to communicate with the external environment the use of barriers is required. They ensure isolation of the external circuits and allow for internal signals' transmission to the external environment and the introduction of the required signals to the device. It is the most common practice in designing and implementing industrial computer networks that operate in hazardous environments. This is due to the limited number of intrinsically safe devices with industrial communication interfaces. Therefore, designing Ex control networks requires prior consideration of the need for separation of the signals and consequences associated with it.

3 Data Flow in Ex Network

Mentioned above factors necessitate a need for analysis and verification of data flow in the network considering its structure and nature of operation. Such constructed network is composed of more components. It may consist of intrinsically safe components and elements which are standard industrial solutions separated electrically and installed in explosion-proof containers. The collection of such components makes out a part of the entire network. Impacts of the use of separating signals on system's operation must be analyzed first. Their application alone increases the complexity of hardware, and also is an impediment in the diagnostics and maintenance. Taking into consideration that barriers often include digital circuits, their application's impact on the transfer time was analyzed. First step was to measure the transmission delay introduced by the separator and analyze the process of exchanging information between two network nodes. In both cases, the study was conducted on the RS485 barriers due to their popularity in the studied systems.

Measurement of separators' delay time was approximately equal to the time needed to send a single character. The time exchange cycle of messages between the two drivers was the second analysis. Study was based on the time comparison between the nodes connection with and without the separation. Both cases are presented in the Fig. 2. One exchange time cycle consisted of the executing of PLC program, sending data and receiving a response from the second PLC. The scheme is a classic example of a Master-Slave communication. Cycle time of such a networks is expressed by the formulas:

$$T_1 = T_{\text{Master}} + T_{\text{Barrier}} + T_{\text{Send}} + T_{\text{Barrier}} + T_{\text{Slave}} + T_{\text{Barrier}} + T_{\text{Send}} + T_{\text{Barrier}} \quad (1)$$

$$T_2 = T_{\text{Master}} + T_{\text{Send}} + T_{\text{Slave}} + T_{\text{Send}} \quad (2)$$

where:

T_1 – cycle time for safety network;
T_2 – cycle time for normal network;
T_{Master} – PLC Master: program time, I/O time and network coprocessor time;
T_{Barrier} – Barrier processing time;
T_{Slave} – PLC Slave: program time, I/O time and network coprocessor time;
T_{Send} – network transmission time.

Time cycle was measured in the master controller, in a separate high priority thread. Results indicated that the tested separators affect the transmission time.

Results showed that an average network cycle was longer by about 1ms for 57 600 bps and about 3 ms for 19 200 bps in a network configuration with barriers. It is approximately equal to the delay introduced by the four barriers for this baudrate. Similar results were obtained for other baudrate. It should be noted

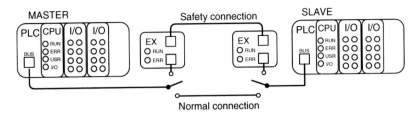

Fig. 2. Analysis of communication between two Ex nodes

that these are relatively insignificant differences in relation to the entire network cycle. The Table 2 lists the time values for both cases, the average measured value was calculated for 10 000 random samples. Based on the presented results, it is evident that when designing an industrial network for potentially explosive areas utilizing digital separating elements, incurred delay has to be taken into account, despite it not being significant for majority of applications.

Table 2. The network cycle for data exchange between PLCs

	Ex Network		Normal Network	
Baudrate [bps]	19200	57600	19200	57600
Avarage network cycle [ms]	69	54	66	53
Max network cycle [ms]	87	75	85	76
Min network cycle [ms]	48	35	44	35

Secondary important aspect is a greater complexity of the system. As previously discussed greater number of components complicates the analysis and maintenance. Increased complexity also transcends to a greater probability of damage and failure. Furthermore inability to monitor the physical state of the communication bus is an additional disadvantage. The reason for this is that the external bus is completely separated from the communication devices by the separators. Taking into account difficult and dangerous conditions of systems' servicing their diagnostics become a paramount. This lead to a more extensive analysis of diagnostics' aspect.

4 The Operational Reliability and System Maintenance

Operational reliability of networks operating in hazardous areas should be considered from a few perspectives. Problems may occur with wiring, control units, barriers or software. The analysis of data generated during process's operation is one way of analyzing the operational reliability of the network. Study conducted during the research [5] based on the use of data mining algorithms for mining diagnostics of industrial processes has shown that the data analysis process not only allows to analyze of the operations of the equipment itself, but also for determination of the nature of industrial network's operation. On such basis it is possible to provide mechanisms increasing the reliability of the installation. Coal mining systems, which the presented study relates to, are an example of systems where there is a risk of explosion, and where all the previously described Ex requirements are applicable. Equipment operating underground is in the first group according to the ATEX Directive, while the demands for this group are among the most stringent. Conducting analysis of mining systems has allowed to determine several solutions that can be applied to the development and maintenance of Ex systems.

The fundamental thing is to maximize the use of diagnostic possibilities of communication protocols. The Profibus DP protocol will serve as an example here. This protocol has standard cycles replacement scenario but it is possible to add to this scenario an acyclic data transfer, containing diagnostic information [6]. Individual nodes add information about availability of additional diagnostic data in periodic data frame. This data can be received and then interpreted by the master controller. A suitable configuration of I/O modules can provide a complex characteristics of the installation operation. It often enables the causes analysis in the event of a failure, however the complexity of such system makes such a solution not always sufficient. In case of Ex systems additional components further complicate its operations' monitoring. The possibility of extending the system should be consider as a solution providing additional information. Typically control devices are separated from the environment by separators, which are passive elements in the communication network. This makes it impossible to diagnose all the elements connected to the bus, also making it impossible to monitor the physical layer's parameters. Additionally, barriers are often mounted outside the cases for which reason they are more exposed to damage. Obtaining information about operational status of barriers and the condition of communication layer is extremely valuable for maintenance.

4.1   Extended Protocol

Due to the outlined factors, the possibility of extending the applied transmission protocols was analyzed. One option is the introduction to the protocol an extended diagnostics concerning data's route in the network. Its principle is based on extending the digital barriers by an interface allowing them to transfer data. It was assumed that the barriers would be equipped with a system capable of decoding transmitted frames and if necessary sending feedback. Such barrier, while operating, can monitor the transmission line and decode queries addressed to it on the basis of a simple Slave node. In such case it is possible to diagnose each physically connected network's element. The monitoring process should, wherever technically possible, ensure analysis of communication protocols and the quality of signal's transmission at the physical layer. Monitoring of the physical layer requires the use of intrinsically safe measuring unit with the signal converter connected to the bus. Barriers equipped with elements monitoring the physical layer parameters will allow to decode the various states of transmission line; including: decoding short circuit, an interruption in data lines, the line impedance and signal value measurement. In the logical layer its monitoring aim should be to analyze the protocol and the format of transmitted data frames. The barrier after encoding query directed at it can send in a response the diagnostic information about its operating, link-state and other parameters. Information about whether the barrier responds or not is extremely valuable in itself. It provides an opportunity to specify which part of the line connecting units is defective. Ability to determine causes of problems where there is danger of explosion without any physical human intervening into the systems is a big advantage [7]. Outlined procedure while it is not being able to precisely determine the root of a problem it supports its localization. A study on data transmission through the digital barriers has shown that such a barrier in most cases does not significantly affect the transfer time, therefore such expansion can be made without adversely affecting the operating network. However it is necessary to take into account the time required by the proposed communication. In this case network cycle time should accommodate for time required to receive data through the barriers, analysis, and then feedback transfer time. To illustrate that, time analysis of data flow was conducted for a Master-Slave network structure like in Fig. 1. The cycle time of the network is expressed by the presented formulas.

$$T_N = 3 * T_{PLC} + T_{Panel} \tag{3}$$

$$T_{EX} = 3 * T_{PLC} + T_{Panel} + 4 * T_{Barrier} \tag{4}$$

where:

T_N – cycle time without barriers' communication;
T_{EX} – cycle time with barriers' communication;
T_{PLC} – communication time with PLC;
T_{Panel} – communication time with Panel;
$T_{Barrier}$ – communication time with Barrier.

This analysis was conducted on a Profibus DP; where Profibus DP cycle time [6], can be determined from the formula (5) (retransmission and transmission of diagnostic data have been omitted for analysis purposes).

$$T_{Profibus} = \sum_n (T_{SYN} + T_{ID1} + T_{SDR} + T_{Header} + 11 * I_n + 11 * O_n)\, Tbit \tag{5}$$

where:

$T_{Profibus}$ – Profibus cycle time;
T_{SYN} – Synchronization Time – 33 Tbit (Tbit – bit time);
T_{ID1} – Master idle time – 75 Tbit;
T_{SDR} – Slave delay – 11 Tbit;
T_{Header} – overhead in the request and response telegram – 198 Tbit;
I_n – number of data sent to the nth node;
O_n – number of data sent from nth node.

The presented calculation assumes that the master controller communicates by sending and receiving 20 bytes with slave controller and Panel, and sending 2 and receiving 5 bytes from the barriers.

$$T_N = 3 * T_{PLC} + T_{Panel} = 4 * (317 + 220 + 220) = 3028 \, \text{Tbit} \qquad (6)$$

$$T_{EX} = 3 * T_{PLC} + T_{Panel} + 4 * T_{Barrier} = 3028 + 4 * (317 + 22 + 55) = 4604 \, \text{Tbit} \quad (7)$$

Proportion of cycles has been determined for the data exchange system with and without barriers.

$$p = \frac{T_{EX}}{T_N} \approx 1.52 \qquad (8)$$

where p – proportion of cycle time.

Such significant increase in cycle time for the network, in many cases may prove to be unacceptable. In order to avoid prolongation of the cycle, a concept where the master controller is not sending inquiries to barriers during the normal cycle, but only at the time when it is found necessary seems justified. For example in case of exceeded slave PLC response time, the Master can sent a query to each of the barriers, which are on the way to not communicating station, like in Fig. 3. This situation should be treated as a state of emergency, where time determinism is not met. At that time this status should be determined as a diagnostic network mode.

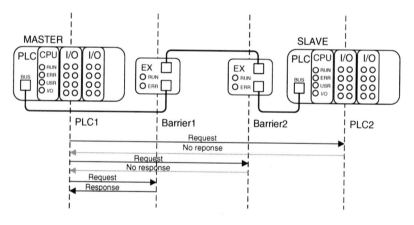

Fig. 3. Network diagnostics after decoding non-response Slave

Acyclic communication with the barriers in a free fieldbus time or communication with the single barrier per one cycle of the network only is another solution to the problem of extending the cycle time. Selecting one of the proposed exchange scenarios should depend on the requirements and possibilities of an installation. The issue of selecting the optimal scenario of exchanges in the industrial real-time network can be found in reference list [8]. The idea of using separators as active nodes necessitates a broader analysis of requirements and a proper preparation of an network components, but it allows to obtain valuable diagnostic information in the course of operating installations.

4.2   The Analysis of the Obtained Data

Acquiring the data is the first step, though in order to obtain the maximum quantities of useful information, the data must be analyzed. Some information can be processed on controllers' PLCs, but as their main task is to control the system therefore the data processing should be moved to the external node. For that, such data must be transmitted to an external computer system, where it will be processed and archived. For research purposes a testing system was constructed. It included industrial controllers, pre-test barriers and the digital units implementing the proposed functionality of the barrier at the logical protocol layer. Functionality of used units constituted of decoding the correct format protocol, checking transmitted frames, logging information in internal memory and sending feedback status on request. Master controller sent data to the external computer station through a dedicated interface. The described earlier exchanging scenario was later implemented. Master PLC communicated only with a single barrier in a single cycle and in case of communication break ran its full diagnostics. In such network a predetermined cycle time has been maintained, while additionally obtaining the useful diagnostic information. The network diagram used in the study is presented in Fig. 4. The applied digital communication units were treated as an integral part of the separators. Data collected by the master controller was later transmitted to an external server.

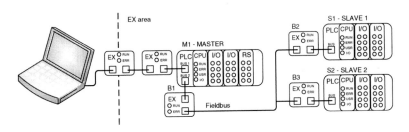

Fig. 4. Transmission of diagnostic data to an external system

Parameters were registered and then analyzed while in operation. By using the diagnostic protocol mechanisms and extended barriers functionality the following events were registered: the number of timed out communication instances between nodes, number of retransmission queries, the number of frames discarded because of incorrect structure or length, the number of additional diagnostic data transmitted on demand and barriers' statuses. A number of pieces of information collected in such way gives an overview of the structure and operation of the network.

Abnormal states of the system were simulated by disconnecting or short-circuiting the bus, stopping the program, sending bad data, disconnecting the nodes and their components. Then that data was processed and results analyzed.

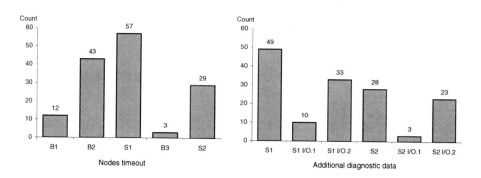

Fig. 5. Nodes timeout and additional diagnostic data

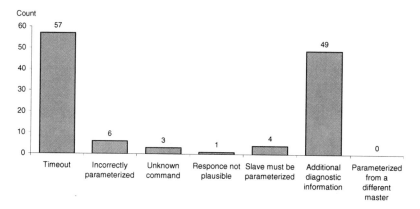

Fig. 6. Slave 1 – work analyze

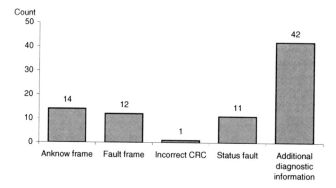

Fig. 7. Barrier 2 – work analyze

The results presented are only demonstrative, because the data was obtained from simulations carried out in a laboratory rather than from a real industrial object. The first chart (Fig. 5) shows the number of registered timeouts of individual controllers and barriers. The second one (Fig. 5) shows the number of diagnostic data collected from each of the I/O PLCs modules. Summary in the third (Fig. 6) and fourth (Fig. 7) represent respectively decoded alarm states for the controller S1 and the barrier B2. It is possible to carry out system's analysis based on this data compilation. From the presented diagrams, lack of response of S1 controller caused by the B2 barrier failure can be observed. There were 43 communication brakes with B2 barrier corresponding to 57 S1 timeouts, representing 75 per cent of cases. Analyzing the operation of S2 controller it can be observed, that most of the diagnostic information is concentrated in the second I/O module. These conclusions confirm the origin the most of the simulated crashes. Correct interpretation may be used to determine actions required to eliminate the decoded errors.

5   Conclusion

Due to associated risk and danger, presented issue illustrates the field of possible applications of computer network equipment in the extreme working conditions. Designing dedicated systems for use in hazardous areas should consider many conditions specific to this type of installation. The proposed solutions are one of the development directions for Ex systems. The potential use of these solutions is the coal mining equipment, where factors such as difficult access to wiring, distances between the devices, installation elements in flameproof cases complicates underground maintenance. Service works performed in such conditions are burdened by additional risks. All these elements significantly prolong a failure removal time, and therefore the introduction of additional mechanisms supporting diagnostics seems to be extremely valuable; it increases safety of work. Conducting system's data analysis can determine failure prone elements and reasons for their failures. For instance analysis of the use of redundancy of individual components can be made on this basis. A lot of issues are still to be considered, such as the possibility of the obtained information's comparison of the work of the network with data describing the industrial process itself. The problem to be addressed in this case is synchronization of all the collected data. If such a summary proves possible, then by the use of data mining algorithms lots of new, relevant information about the correct operation of the system could be obtained. Research area in this matter is extensive and it is advisable to conduct further analysis of computer systems operating in the hazardous areas.

Acknowledgment. The research was conducted as project of the European Social Fund *Aktywizacja społeczności akademickiej jako element realizacji Regionalnej Strategii Innowacji* POKL.08.02.01-24-019/08.

References

1. Directive 94/9/WE – ATEX
2. Schram, P., Benedetti, R., Earley, M.: Electrical Installations in Hazardous Locations. Jones and Bartlett, National Fire Protection Associate, Sudbury (2009)
3. Profibus RS 485-IS User and Installation Guideline. Profibus Guideline v1.1 (2003)
4. McMillan, A.: Electrical installations in hazardous areas. Butterworth-Heinemann, Oxford (1998)
5. Opielka, K.: Metody eksploracji danych jako środek wspomagający diagnostykę przemysłowych systemów czasu rzeczywistego. WKŁ, Warszawa (2010)
6. IEC-61158 and EN 50170-2 standard
7. Directive 99/92/EC
8. Kwiecień, A.: Analiza przepływu informacji w komputerowych sieciach przemysłowych. Wydawnictwo Politechniki Śląskiej, Gliwice (2002)

The Method of Reducing the Cycle of Programmable Logic Controller (PLC) Vulnerable "to Avalanche of Events"

Andrzej Kwiecień[1] and Marcin Sidzina[2]

[1] Silesian University of Technology, Institute of Informatics
[2] University of Bielsko-Biala, Department of Mechanical Engineering Fundamentals
andrzej.kwiecen@polsl.pl, msidzina@ath.bielsko.pl

Abstract. Reducing the cycle duration of PLC (Programmable Logic Controller) is one of the methods for increasing the access frequency of nodes in the real time distributed system into the transmission medium. The authors presents in this paper one of the methods developed by themselves for a rather specific use of a cases of avalanche of events.

Keywords: PLC, distributed real time system, industrial computer network, time cycle of exchange data, PLC programming, avalanche of events.

1 Introdution

The basic parameter of the design of industrial real time systems is the maximum time (T_G) defined [1] as the maximum amount of time which elapses from the moment of detection of an event or sequence of events, until the appropriate system response to these events. It is obvious, [1] that the shorter time the better properties expressed even by the quality of controlling or monitoring and further reporting of events. Through the analysis of the node work, which is usually the PLC, it is clear (Fig. 1) that the duration of the user application executed by the processor has a huge impact on the frequency of access to the transmission medium.

From the principles of PLC work result (Fig. 1), that values such as T_{IC}, T_{WE}, T_{WY}, T_K are constant. The only one value, variable in time, is the duration of application realization T_{AP}. The sum of all listed values consists of the so-called machine cycle time (time of basic cycle PLC). Therefore, through manipulation of the value of the cycle duration, it is possible to influence on the access frequency of the system node to the communication network coprocessor, and thus gain the frequent access to the medium.

The increase in the frequency of access to the network, influences basically on such parameters as the efficiency of communication system (n) and its practical throughput (P), and thus on the time T_G. [1,2] Therefore, the very high attention is given to the appropriate software development, in accordance with the rules of software engineering, and also new ways and methods designed for reducing

A. Kwiecień, P. Gaj, and P. Stera (Eds.): CN 2011, CCIS 160, pp. 379–385, 2011.

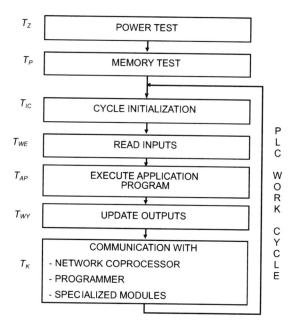

Fig. 1. The basic processes realized during PLC cycle [2]

the duration of the basic cycle of user application are explored. Several methods prepared by the authors have already been published [3,4]. Another one is the subject of consideration in this paper.

2   The Idea of Shortening the Duration of Controller Cycle

The idea of shortening the controller cycle depends on sharing of the application program in such a way, so that in each cycle of program loop (Fig. 1) which is executed in controller (PLC) only a part of it was realized. Thus, a fragmentation (division) of a program into parts is achieved, of which only some are executed in a particular cycle. The realisation of parts in a particular cycle depends on many elements. In general, the division results from the fact whether a particular part (function) is supposed to be executed in each cycle (fixed functions), or whether its execution can be delayed or postponed without any negative effects for the controlled process (reducible functions) . Duration of a machine cycle for the structure of application fragmentation from the (Fig. 2) is described by the dependence (1). The entire execution of cycle is the realization of control algorithms, placed in the fixed and reducible functions, but in the shortened cycle only the algorithms placed in fixed functions are executed,

$$T_{\mathrm{AP}} = T_{\mathrm{S1}} + T_{\mathrm{R}} + T_{\mathrm{S2}} \;\; or \;\; T_{\mathrm{AP}} = T_{\mathrm{S1}} + T_{\mathrm{S2}} \tag{1}$$

where:

T_{AP} – time for program realization;
T_{S1}, T_{S2} – time for fixed functions realization;
T_R – time for reducible functions realization.

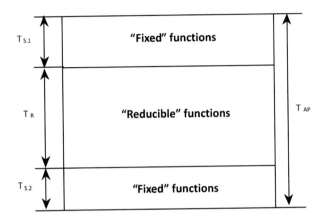

Fig. 2. Fragmentation of the application [2]

The constant part of a program is divided into two segments. The first segment is at the beginning of application and it consists of some functions used for taking a decisions that refer to the shortening the duration of control application, these are counters of exchanges, conditions for finishing the shortened cycle. The shortened cycle or idle cycle refers to the cycle which does not execute any control algorithms placed in the part of reducible functions, that is the application omits the reducing part, and realizes only the part of fixed function. The simple logical issues decide about activating and deactivating of shortened cycle [4]. The way of activation of a shortened cycle can be as follows:

- the cycle of PLC controller is executed;
- at some point an exchange data is required (which can be the result of the action of control algorithm, or this request will be called from outside of the system);
- a request is sent to the network as a result of program response;
- the program sets a state 1 for condition CS a shortened cycle, if the state of this condition is 1 it skips the part of the reduced application;
- after the exchange, the state of variable CS is reset. The execution of control algorithm can be continued.

In the constant part of application the following elements should be included:

- queue of cyclic exchanges;
- queue of acyclic exchanges;

– the condition for the beginning of shortened cycle (if the condition is realised, the cycle is permanently shortened until further notice).

3   The Method Description

One of the rules that prevailed during the development of a method, was the concept of shortening the duration of the controller cycle, while ensuring the proper realization of control algorithm. If it is possible that in the control system many states which trigger the shortening the controller cycle occur, it was then necessary to prevent the starvation of certain parts of the program by introducing the rank order of the transitions. The authors introduced the principle, that an item omitted from the last time is directed at the end of the list of skipped items.

Using a mechanism for temporary cessation of control algorithm realization it is possible to shorten significantly the machine cycle, thus enhancing the frequency of coprocessor access to the memory of central unit. This operation will shorten the duration of individual exchanges in the network.

It should be noticed that the method being the subject of this paper, is characterized by another feature, which accepts dynamic rather than static division of applications. It means, that the range of application executed in a particular cycle depends on the fact whether the network service request appears or not. Obviously, the fixed functions are executed always. Another fundamental feature of this method is that it includes the emergence of an avalanche of events. This phenomenon will certainly cause the delays in realization of reducible functions as a result of increased frequency of transmission request. When many events occur then the segmentation can be presented as in the Fig. 3.

The discussed method work in the following way:

– In case of avalanche of transaction requests, transition to the end of shortening part should be performed in such a way in order to ensure to all segments the execution of control algorithm for a some impassable time;
– To avoid the "starvation" of the control algorithm of some reducible functions, it is necessary, in case of many requests to implement a flag informing that a particular segment of the control algorithm cannot be omitted;
– This mechanism should ensure the execution of each program segment in case of avalanche of events. It will guarantee the increase of minimum frequency of access to the network. $\dot{f}_{ACS}$

The minimum frequency of the coprocessor access to the network during a complete cycle of the controller is:

$$f_{ACS} = \frac{1}{T_A} = \frac{1}{T_{APS} + T_{APR} + T_{INST\dot{R}}} \qquad (2)$$

where:

T_A – duration of basic PLC cycle;
T_{APS}, T_{S2} – realization time of fixed functions;

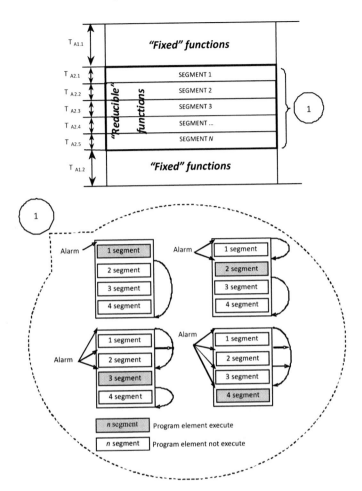

Fig. 3. The mechanism preventing the "starvation" of application segments, in case of many exchange data requests [3]

T_{APR} – realization time of reducible functions;
T_{INSTR} – realization time of all constant cycle elements such a:
 – Time of inputs data acquisition – physical states of PLC inputs;
 – Time of coprocessor operation;
 – Time of updating the physical states of PLC outputs.

In the division of the n segments of program in case of avalanche of events, the average frequency of access to the network is:

$$\dot{f}_{\text{ACS}} = \frac{1}{\frac{T_{\text{APR}}}{n-1} + T_{\text{INSTR}}} \, . \tag{3}$$

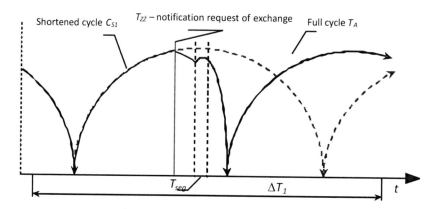

Fig. 4. Illustration of time delay ΔT_1 during the realization of reducible functions for the discussed method

Delay ΔT during the avalanche of events for the entire application program realization is:

$$\Delta T = \dot{T}_A - T_A = n\left(\frac{T_{AP}}{n} + T_{INSTR}\right) - T_{AP} - T_{INSTR} = (n-1)\,T_{INSTR} \quad (4)$$

where: n refers to the number of reported events.

This value may deteriorate realization of control process, as well as parameters of real time system. However, it can prevent the starvation of control algorithm through execution of following part of algorithm one after another. Figure 4 presents the time course with forcing the realization of one segment of program.

The method, as already mentioned, is quite specific in comparison with other already presented methods [4]. The main goal of the method is to reduce the duration of data exchange transaction through reduction of basic control cycle (PLC) duration, so that in case of avalanche o events not to cause the control algorithm realization to be blocked. Thus, the essential condition, which must be implemented is the guarantee of continuous realization at least of a part of control algorithm.

4   Conclusions

The presented method requires further research, which the authors are going to conduct in the Genius [5] network. Based on the single tests it can be presume that this method will be effective in shortening the cycle duration, and thus increasing the frequency of access to the transmission medium. The essential issue is that the method presented in the paper allows in a dynamic way, depending on the network load and application to reduce the cycle duration. Thus, the time of realization of a program will be change depending on requirements of control algorithm and the network load. The authors hope that thanks to the presented method the PLC cycle time reduction on the one hand, improves the parameters of transmission and data exchange, and on the other will not deteriorate the control quality.

References

1. Kwiecień, A.: Analiza przepływu informacji w komputerowych sieciach przemysłowych. Studia Informatica, Gliwice (2002) (in Polish)
2. Kwiecień, A., Sidzina, M.: Metody skracania wymian wyzwalanych w sieciach przemysłowych typu Master-Slave. In: Współczesne Problemy Systemów Czasu Rzeczywistego. WKŁ, Warszawa (2004) (in Polish)
3. Sidzina, M.: Dynamiczne modyfikacje programu aplikacji sterownika swobodnie programowalnego celem zwiększenia częstości wymian komunikatów w przemysłowych systemach rozproszonych czasu rzeczywistego. Doctor thesis, Silesian University of Technology, Gliwice (2008)
4. Kwiecień, A., Sidzina, M.: Metody skracania czasu trwania cyklu sterownika swobodnie programowalnego i ich podstawowe badania. In: Systemy Czasu Rzeczywistego. Projektowanie i aplikacje, vol. 2. WKŁ, Warszawa (2005) (in Polish)
5. Kwiecień, A., Sidzina, M., Rysiński, J.: Analiza wymiany danych w sieci Ethernet dla sterowników swobodnie programowalnych. In: Systemy Informatyczne z Ograniczeniami Czasowymi. WK, Warszawa (2006) (in Polish)

Secure Position-Based Selecting Scheme for WSN Communication

Pawel Szalachowski[1], Zbigniew Kotulski[1,2], and Bogdan Ksiezopolski[3]

[1] Institute of Fundamental Technological Research of PAS,
Pawinskiego 5B, 02-106 Warsaw, Poland
[2] Institute of Telecommunications of WUT
Nowowiejska 15/19, 00-665 Warsaw, Poland
[3] Institute of Computer Science, Maria Curie-Sklodowska University,
pl. M. Curie-Sklodowskiej 5, 20-031 Lublin, Poland

Abstract. Wireless Sensor Networks (WSNs) found applications in different hostile environments. Addressing messages to a given node or a group of nodes in these situations is a very important and difficult task. Often one should address all nodes from a given area.

In this paper we propose a new approach to the addressing problem. Our proposal is primarily destined for broadcast networks but it can be also used in other networks with specific routing protocols. The scheme is based on identification of the spatial position of a node and it is realized by fast cryptographic hash functions. Such a solution makes it possible to address all sensors from a given connected area in an easy, fast and secure way.

Keywords: position-based selecting, addressing, cryptographic protocols, wireless sensor network.

1 Introduction

Addressing is a basis in network communication. Each participant of communication, when receives any message, must check its sender. Afterwards he can relay, reject or process the message. Usually the network's nodes are addressed by unique numbers. The method of addressing depends on a protocol, a standard or a network's layer. Examples of such numbers are MAC addresses or IDs of nodes. usually we must know an ID of the node to which we want to send a packet. In a WSN that method can be inconvenient, especially when information must be delivered to a group of sensors in a given area. Based on unique numbers each sensor should map the terrain with position of nodes and address messages by this map. However, we must keep in mind that WSNs are usually dynamic networks. Moreover, sensors' resources are highly constrained, so this solution requiring a lot of memory is unacceptable.

Another aspect worthy of mentioning is localization of sensors in a WSN. In many WSN's applications location of a given sensor is the crucial problem. Except of the problem remarked above, such applications of WSNs as weather

A. Kwiecień, P. Gaj, and P. Stera (Eds.): CN 2011, CCIS 160, pp. 386–397, 2011.
© Springer-Verlag Berlin Heidelberg 2011

observations, earthquake detections or a lot of military systems require knowledge about nodes' positions. Approaches that address this problem are briefly reviewed in the next section.

Next important issue is security. WSN's nodes use an open medium (broadcast) to communicate each other. So, everyone can easily eavesdrop, inject, jam or modify packets. Therefore each protocol and other technology applied in WSN must be designed with adequate protection. Furthermore, as we already remarked, sensors are very constrained in term of hardware performance. In production applications a regular member of a WSN (a node) has about 8 MHz CPU and 8 KB RAM. It does not suffice to take advantages of standard cryptographic solutions. Thus, the security methods applied should be not only robust and secure but also light. Each cryptographic primitive, like a block cipher or a hash function must be implemented for sensors' applications in an efficient way.

In this paper we propose a novel addressing scheme for WSNs which is fast, secure, flexible and position-based. The rest of the paper is organized as follows. In the next section we present related work concerning localization of sensors in WSNs. Section 3 outlines the method proposed and following section extends method and presents an example of its application. We comment and conclude the results in Sect. 5.

2   Related Work

Routing in WSN is one of the most important challenge and it is exact connected with our scheme. In [1] there is a survey on routing techniques in WSNs. The paper [2] introduces the interesting multi-cast routing protocol called GMR (geographic multi-cast routing). Next, in [3] there is presented another mechanisms for secure group communications in WSNs. This approach for achieving goals, uses Logical Key Hierarchy and directed diffusion. In [4] the authors introduce secure and reliable broadcasting method using multi-parent trees.

Majority of WSN applications need identity management. SIDA [5] is interesting self-organized method for ID assignment. It is dedicated for WSN and ID in this solution is variable-length. It influences scalability, flexibility and energy efficiency. Other approach is presented in [6]. Authors of this solution try to reduce overhead connected with traditional MAC address by replacing it by novel scheme for MAC address assignment. In [7] Doss describes a dynamic addressing mechanism for event-driven wireless sensor networks. Next interesting addressing scheme for WSNs is presented in [8]. Approach is based on energy maps and Huffman coding. Furthermore author presents simulation and results.

In paper [9] is presented a survey on secure localization in WSNs. [10,11] introduces relative location estimation algorithms. In [12], for the same goal, probability grid is defined. Next, in [13] authors, in new way, use hop-count values to localize nodes in WSN. Papers [14,15,16] use additionally cryptography techniques for estimate localization of the nodes. ROPE [15] addresses the problem of secure localization and location verification. SeRLoc presented in [14] is the algorithm for secure localization. It is robust against many WSNs attacks (wormhole attack, the Sybil attack, compromise of network entities). The scheme introduced in [16] works in two ways. First, it can filter out attacker beacon signals, while the second method tolerates attacker signals and puts them into voting. It is interesting solution, because WSN can detect attacker, even when he bypass authentication process.

3   New Selecting Scheme

Analyzing WSN applications which gather data from some given terrain we come to an obvious conclusion that many packets are useful only for sensors in a particular subarea. It is very important in a hostile environment. For example, a request for data near a volcano should be processed only by the nodes near this volcano. Thus, selecting scheme must be able to address only a subgroup of sensors within the whole network.

A natural place in a packet to locate the destination address information is its header. The receiver interpreting the header decides to process the message only if the address is correct. In WSNs it is crucial. As we already mentioned in Introduction, each routing protocol implemented in a WSN must be secure. In common use, security can be realized by encryption, see [17]. However, strong cryptography is computationally expensive and the sensors should encrypt/decrypt data only if it is indispensable. Our selecting scheme makes it possible.

Requirements for the approach proposed in this paper are the following:

- selecting is realized by nodes' positions,
- the selecting protocol is cryptographically secure,
- it is possible to assign the address to a given subarea of the terrain covered by WSN,
- each sensor in WSN can quickly check if it is a correct receiver,
- for an attacker from outside of the network it is impossible to determine what is the correct receiver,
- for an attacker inside the network it is difficult to determine what is a correct receiver.

To achieve these goals we must be able to analyze headers of packets in a fast and secure way. We decided to use cryptographic hash functions, which are usually faster than symmetric ciphers. However, in cases when it is more convenient to use ciphers (when they are built-in or they are more efficient) we can turn them to appropriate hash modes (e.g., Davies-Mayer, Miyaguchi-Preneel, CMAC mode, etc.).

For further considerations we introduce the following notation:

- $\|$ is concatenation of two blocks of bits,
- x is a receiver's position information (in one dimension),
- n is a tolerance (known to the receiver),

- $f(x, n)$ is a function, which converts each value $\hat{x} \in \{x - n, \ldots, x, \ldots, x + n\}$ to one value $f(\hat{x}, n)$ and which satisfies the following condition

$$f(x, n) \neq f(x + k, n) , \tag{1}$$

for all integer k such that $|k| > n$,
- $H()$ is a cryptographic hash function,
- K is a secret shared by communicating nodes (the common secret key).

The secret K may be shared within the whole WSN. The numbers n describe positions from $x - n$ to $x + n$ (in one dimension) which are treated as recipient sensors' positions.

The sender sensor, when it wants to send a message to sensors located at positions from $x_s - n_s$ to $x_s + n_s$, only computes:

$$H_{x_s} = H(K\|n_s\|f(x_s, n_s)) \tag{2}$$

and attaches the result to the message being sent. Next, a receiver can in the same, easy and fast way check if it has a destination receiver position. It calculates the hash of its own position (x_r). Next, if

$$H(K\|n_s\|f(x_s, n_s)) \neq H(K\|n_s\|f(x_r, n_s)) \tag{3}$$

it is not a right recipient and it can drop the whole message. When hashes are equal the node decides to process the whole message packet.

An important property of this solution is secrecy of the destination address information. Even nodes or attackers that know the shared secret K must perform the exhaustive search attack to determine which area is addressed. In case of wide WSNs such an attack is very compound.

The selecting scheme presented above is vulnerable to replay attacks. A communication protocol based on this approach needs to use nonces or other freshness methods, see e.g. [18]. For legibility we pass over this aspect in the whole paper.

Another case is delivery of the messages. The presented approach assumed that nodes within the addressed area always can receive messages easily. Basically it can be realized by an appropriate routing protocol [1]. Protocols like the flood protocol or the gossip protocol in WSNs are inefficient. Acceptable are efficient broadcast protocols, geo-cast or multi-cast protocols. This aspect is very important. As a requirement for our method, we assumed that for an attacker from outside the network it is impossible to determine who is the receiver. In traditional multi-hop routing, an attacker who eavesdrops WSN traffic is able to determine the route and as a consequence, to detect the receiver's position. When broadcast communication is enabled, this is impossible, because the message is sent to all sensors.

4   Case Study

In this section we extend, presented above, approach and introduce it on real scenario. Through this section we use notations from previous section. Our goal is to address all sensors in given area. Area is specified as rectangle in $2D$.

An important element of the presented construction is function $f()$. As mentioned in Sect. 3, $f(x, n)$ converts any $x - n, \ldots, x, \ldots, x + n$ to one value. The crucial property of $f()$ is:

$$f(x, n) \neq f(x + k, n) \ , \tag{4}$$

for $k < -n$ or $k > n$.

Now we must define the function which satisfies the above-mentioned properties and which is suitable for our applications. Since in this paper we consider the nodes' selecting in $2D$ area, an appropriate function $f(x, n)$ can be defined as:

$$f(x, n) = \begin{cases} \frac{x}{p}, & r = 0 \\ \frac{x-r}{p}, & r \leq n \\ \frac{x+p-r}{p}, & r > n \end{cases} \ ,$$

where $p = 2n + 1$ and $r = x \mod p$.

The function $f(x, n)$ converts any of $x - n, \ldots, x, \ldots, x + n$ to one value. So, to address with tolerance n the position s, we must shift the arguments of the function $f()$. We define the parameter $offset$ as:

$$offset = s \mod p \ . \tag{5}$$

To obtain the address we first compute $f(s - offset, n)$ and then the hash value of the concatenation of all the required parameters:

$$hash_s = H(K\|n\|offset\|f(s - offset, n)) \ . \tag{6}$$

Of course, this construction identifies the sensor's location in one dimension only, so for $2D$ selecting we need two $f()$ values with parameters. In the next section we consider our example in more details.

5   Example Scenario

Now we define a conceivable scenario for our solution. We assumed that WSN is observing objects over some given terrain. Once in a while the Base Station (BS) sends a request for the sensors' results. That WSN is event-driven and the request is intended for the specific area which is defined by the rectangle. This rectangle is constructed by hashing two $f()$ function values presented above. One $f()$ value is for X-axis and the other for Y-axis. Each node is equipped with $2D$ position sensor. When a packet is received, the node verifies by computing the hash if its own position is inside the rectangle. Of course, if the hash value is invalid then processing remaining part of message may be omitted.

BS specifies the area under interest on $2D$ axes. The middle point of the rectangle is (x, y). Tolerances t_x and t_y determine dimensions of the edges of the addressing rectangle. Next, BS must compute the hash. In our example BS uses the function $f()$ defined above. The secret K is shared within WSN. Calculations for X axis are as follows:

$$p_x = 2t_x + 1 \ , \tag{7}$$

$$offset_x = x \mod p_x \ , \tag{8}$$

$$f_X = f(x - offset_x, t_x) \ . \tag{9}$$

For Y axis the calculation is analogous:

$$p_y = 2t_y + 1 \ , \tag{10}$$

$$offset_y = y \mod p_y \ , \tag{11}$$

$$f_Y = f(y - offset_y, t_y) \ , \tag{12}$$

$$hash_{XY} = H(K \| t_x \| t_y \| offset_x \| offset_y \| f_X \| f_Y) \ . \tag{13}$$

The values $hash_{XY}$, $offset_x$, $offset_y$ are the elements of the packet's header. Tolerance values are knows to network nodes. The layout of the packet for the our selecting solution is presented in Fig. 1. Behind the header, the packet contains encrypted data (request or other information) for the sensors located in the rectangle area.

header		payload
$hash_{XY}$	$offset_x$	crypted message
	$offset_y$	

Fig. 1. Packet layout in our example

This way we addressed specific area in the WSN. Such an area is presented in Fig. 2.

Each node, which received a packet checks the hashes and if its position is correct, it decrypts the message. This construction guarantees that each sensor in the demanded rectangle passes the hashes verification and each sensor outside the rectangle need not decrypting the payload.

An important issue is communication overhead. The most popular WSN standard (ZigBee) defines the maximum length of the packet at 1024 bits. Popular and secure cryptographic hash functions produce hashes with lengths of at least 128 bits. But this length is unnecessarily and in most cases it may be truncated. The length of the hash in the header should be exactly determined by the scale of the WSN and the tolerance arguments we used. For small networks short hashes are suitable but in the case of wide networks longer hashes should be considered.

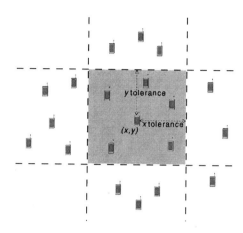

Fig. 2. Multi-cast communication in specific area

6   Analysis

The approach presented in a novel way solves the problem of group communication in networks based on nodes' positions. It has many advantages and it is designed for WSNs. Especially it is interesting for some applications of the event-driven network model. First of all selecting in our scheme is fast and computationally simple. In our example it needs only one hash calculation. Additionally $f()$ can be reconstructed, e.g., for a circle or for a square. Thus, it needs low computational overhead [19], what is very important for WSNs. In Table 1 we present popular representatives of methods, which can be used for our scheme. AES-CMAC is MAC scheme based on the block cipher AES and MD5 is the widely-used cryptographic hash function. We assumed different input lengths for MAC or hash function. It consist of K length (K_{len}), two $f()$ outputs lengths (f_{len}) and two offsets lengths (o_{len}). All lengths are expressed in bits. We present time needed to create or verify header with these parameters. Measurements have been performed on IRIS Xbow mote equipped with AtMega1281 Processor and 8 KB of RAM. For details about measurements and implementations we send to [19]. These methods operates on different blocks size. 128 bits for AES and 512 bits for MD5. Additionally in AES-CMAC algorithms we do not need to merge K directly into message, so we save space in inputs. Amount of free space in block is also presented in table. This space may be used to authenticate even whole payload of a packet, without any significant computational overhead. As we can see, in most cases, AES-CMAC should be applied for our scheme. It is very fast and for short payloads it may authenticate all message in one cryptographic operations. Moreover, CMAC-AES used implementation of AES which can be used for encryption of data.

Another crucial issue of the solution presented is security. A MAC scheme or cryptographic hash function is a kernel of our construction. It must be chosen and verified carefully to prevent secret key breaking attacks. When hash function

Table 1. Performance and space availability for AES-CMAC and MD5

Algorithm	$K_{len} = 128$ $f_{len} = 32$ $o_{len} = 8$	$K_{len} = 96$ $f_{len} = 32$ $o_{len} = 8$	$K_{len} = 64$ $f_{len} = 16$ $o_{len} = 8$	$K_{len} = 48$ $f_{len} = 16$ $o_{len} = 4$
AES-CMAC	0.4 ms 48 bits left	0.4 ms 48 bits left	0.4 ms 80 bits left	0.4 ms 88 bits left
MD5	1.7 ms 304 bits left	1.7 ms 336 bits left	1.7 ms 400 bits left	1.7 ms 424 bits left

is secure, then the best known attack is birthday attack. For hash function $H()$ we define collision as messages m_1, m_2 such that: $m_1 \neq m_2 \wedge H(m_1) = H(m_2)$.

In Table 2 is presented how many (in average) hashes must be computed to find a collision with given probability and hash length (h_{len}). Bases on this numbers, knowledge about topology and traffic in network we can adjust length of the hash to achieve acceptable probability of collision occurrence.

Table 2. Probability of the birthday attack for a given hash (part of the header) length

Prob.	$h_{len} = 96$	$h_{len} = 64$	$h_{len} = 48$	$h_{len} = 32$
25%	2.134×10^{14}	3.258×10^{9}	1.273×10^{7}	4.971×10^{4}
50%	3.314×10^{14}	5.057×10^{9}	1.975×10^{7}	7.716×10^{4}
75%	4.686×10^{14}	7.152×10^{9}	2.793×10^{7}	1.091×10^{5}

However, our specification pass over the aspect of freshness of packages. Now an attacker can perform the replay attack. A sensor in the addressed area, when it receives the same well-addressed packet again, it computes hashes and next decrypts the whole payload. It is the expensive operation. So, the replication of the same packets in loop by attacker imitating BS could result in a Denial-of-Service attack. As a countermeasure, we suggest to apply one of the freshness methods [18]. Another issue is possible determination of location of legitimate receivers by an attacker. When we broadcast packets or use routing protocols like flooding/gossiping, an attacker outside the network cannot find the addressed area. The attacker inside the network (when he knows the shared key K) must perform the search attack over all terrain. It is consequence of using cryptographic hash function.

He computes hashes for the whole addressing area. In case of a wide network or a small tolerance parameter such an attack may be time-consuming. Table 3 shows how many (average) hashes attacker, which knows K, must compute to identify addressed rectangle. This computations must be executed for each packet with different header. It is presented for $10\,000 \times 10\,000$ unit area and different tolerances (t_x, t_y). In some cases it could be difficult for attacker to determine receivers of all packets, even when the shared key K is compromised.

Table 3. Average number of hashes needed to determine receiver of a message

Area	$t_y = t_x = 1$	$t_y = t_x = 5$	$t_y = t_x = 15$	$t_y = t_x = 50$
10 000×10 000	12 500 000	500 000	55 555	5 000

7   Circular Selecting Scheme

In some applications selecting of circle is more appropriate that rectangle.

On Figure 3 example of circular selecting is presented. We identify circle as middle point (x_m, y_m) and radius, which is equal to tolerance parameter (n). For these reasons we must modify $f()$ from Sect. 4. Auxiliary function, which help us determine middle of the circle can be realized as follows:

$$g(x, n) = \begin{cases} x, & r = 0 \\ x - r, & r \leq n \\ x + p - r, & r > n \end{cases},$$

where $p = 2n + 1$ and $r = x \mod (2n + 1)$.

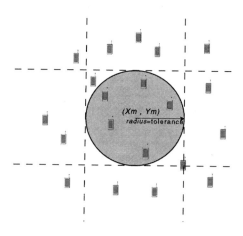

Fig. 3. Circular selecting

For selecting given circle, we must specify middle (x_m, y_m) and offsets for X and Y axises:

$$offset_x = x \mod p, \tag{14}$$

$$x_m = g(x - offset_x, radius) \tag{15}$$

$$offset_y = y \mod p, \tag{16}$$

$$y_m = g(y - offset_y, radius) \tag{17}$$

Next, we when we have parameters for the circle, we need to code it as a unique number, which will be hashed. This can be realized by function:

$$S(x, y) = \frac{(x + y + 1)(x + y)}{2} + y + 1 \tag{18}$$

$S(x, y)$ assigns unique value to each (x, y) point, as showed on Fig. 4. We want to express circle (middle point and radius) as unique number so we achieve this by simple computing $S(S(x, y), n)$. Now, the sender computes hash:

$$hash_s = H(K \| offset_x \| offset_y \| S(S(x_m, y_m), n)) \tag{19}$$

and broadcasts it with n and the offsets parameters.

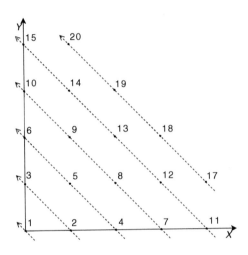

Fig. 4. $S(x, y)$ function

Then, when a node receives the message, it performs foregoing computations (to achieve a corresponding middle point) with its position and the given parameters (n, offsets). But he must also check if his position belongs to circle region. So we introduce function $F()$:

$$F(x, y, x_{mr}, y_{mr}, n) = \begin{cases} S(S(x_{mr}, y_{mr}), n) & \text{for } (x - x_{mr})^2 + (y - y_{mr})^2 < n^2 \\ 0 & \text{otherwise} \end{cases},$$

We denote (x_r, y_r) as node's position, and (x_{mr}, y_{mr}) as the nearest circle middle point (according to offsets). So now, the node can compare

$$hash = H(K \| offset_x \| offset_y \| F(x_r, y_r, x_{mr}, y_{mr}, n)) \tag{20}$$

with the received $hash_s$ to determine if it is the right recipient.

The security and efficiency analysis of the scheme presented above is analogous to the one in Sect. 5, so we omitted it here.

8   Conclusions and Future Research

As the above considerations shown, the proposed selecting scheme proved to have such properties that are indispensable in sensor networks. It is quick, scalable, efficient and secure. The most time-consuming operation is tagging with cryptographic hash function or MAC scheme. But as shown in paper and references, even in high-constraint environment like WSN, it can be realized in efficient way. Security of presented solution strongly depends on chosen hashing method and parameters values. But in general and rational usage, scheme seems to be secure and robust.

Our approach is also flexible. We can fit the header's length to our network, e.g., applying selecting in $3D$ by adding only one more $f()$ calculation. Additionally scheme may be enhanced by adding tolerance values to a header. It influences on scalability but it needs additional bits in a header. All parameters of solution should be fixed with carefully consideration of network topology, applications, hardware capabilities and traffic profile. The presented approach, with small modifications, can be applied for other network communication or network security purposes. Noteworthy is the issue of freshness/time-synchronization in WSN realized with the similar construction.

References

1. Al-Karaki, J.N., Kamal, A.E.: Routing techniques in wireless sensor networks: a survey. IEEE Wireless Communications 11(6), 6–28 (2004)
2. Sánchez, J.A., Ruiz, P.M., Liu, J., Stojmenovic, I.: Bandwidth-Efficient Geographic Multi-cast Routing Protocol for Wireless Sensor Networks. IEEE Sensors Journal 7(5), 627–636 (2007)
3. Pietro, R., Mancini, L., Law, Y., Etalle, S., Havinga, P.: LKHW: A Directed Diffusion-Based Secure Multi-cast Scheme for Wireless Sensor Networks. In: Proc. of IEEE International Conference on Parallel Processing Workshops (2003)
4. Srinivasan, A., Wu, J.: Secure and Reliable Broadcasting in Wireless Sensor Networks using Multi-Parent Trees. Security and Communication Networks 2(3), 239–253 (2008)
5. Liu, J., Liu, Y., Ni, L.M.: SIDA: self-organized ID assignment in wireless sensor networks. In: Proceedings IEEE International Conference on Mobile Ad-hoc and Sensor Systems, MASS 2007, Pisa, October 8-11 (2007)
6. Schurgers, C., Kulkarni, G., Srivastava, M.B.: Distributed On-Demand Address Assignment in Wireless Sensor Networks. IEEE Transactions on Parallel and Distributed Systems 13(10), 1056–1065 (2002)
7. Doss, R.C., Chandra, D., Pan, L., Zhou, W., Chowdhruy, M.: Address reuse in wireless sensor networks. In: Tucker, R. (ed.) Proc. of the Australian Telecommunication Networks & Applications Conf., pp. 329–333. ATNAC, Melbourne (2006)
8. Kronewitter, F.D.: Dynamic Huffman Addressing in Wireless Sensor Networks Based on the Energy Map. In: Military Communications Conference, IEEE MILCOM 2008, pp. 1–7 (November 16-19, 2008)
9. Srinivasan, A., Wu, J.: A Survey on Secure Localization in Wireless Sensor Networks. In: Furht, B. (ed.) Encyclopedia of Wireless and Mobile Communications. CRC Press, Taylor and Francis Group (2008)

10. Patwari, N., Hero, A.O., Perkins, M., Correal, N.S., O'Dea, R.J.: Relative location estimation in wireless sensor networks. IEEE Transactions on Signal Processing Processing 51(8), 2137–2148 (2003)
11. Nasipuri, A., Li, K.: A Directionality based Location Discovery Scheme for Wireless Sensor Networks. In: Proceedings of the First ACM International Workshop on Wireless Sensor Networks and Applications (WSNA 2002), in conjunction with ACM Mobicom 2002 (September 28, 2002)
12. Stoleru, R., Stankovic, J.: Probability grid: a location estimation scheme for wireless sensor networks. In: First Annual IEEE Communications Society Conference on Sensor and Ad Hoc Communications and Networks, pp. 430–438 (2004)
13. Ma, D., Er, M.J., Wang, B., Lim, H.B.: Range-free wireless sensor networks localization based on hop-count quantization. Telecommunication Systems. Springer, Heidelberg (2010)
14. Lazos, L., Poovendran, R.: SeRLoc: Robust localization for wireless sensor networks. ACM Transactions on Sensor Networks (TOSN) 1(1), 73–100 (2005)
15. Lazos, L., Poovendran, R., Čapkun, S.: ROPE: robust position estimation in wireless sensor networks. In: Proceedings of the 4th International Symposium on Information Processing in Sensor Networks, Los Angeles, California, April 24-27 (2005)
16. Liu, D., Ning, P., Liu, A., Wang, C., Du, W.K.: Attack-Resistant Location Estimation in Wireless Sensor Networks. ACM Transactions on Information and System Security (TISSEC) 11(4), 1–39 (2008)
17. Szalachowski, P., Ksiezopolski, B., Kotulski, Z.: CMAC, CCM and GCM/GMAC: Advanced modes of operation of symmetric block ciphers in wireless sensor networks. Information Processing Letters 110(7), 247–251 (2010)
18. Gong, L.: Variations on the Themes of Message Freshness and Replay or, the Difficulty of Devising Formal Methods to Analyze Cryptographic Protocols. In: 6th IEEE Comp. Security Foundations Workshop, pp. 131–136 (1993)
19. Szalachowski, P., Ksiezopolski, B., Kotulski, Z.: On Authentication Method Impact upon Data Sampling Delay in Wireless Sensor Networks. In: Kwiecień, A., Gaj, P., Stera, P. (eds.) CN 2010. CCIS, vol. 79, pp. 280–289. Springer, Heidelberg (2010)

Data Acquisition Server for Mini Distributed Control System

Dariusz Rzońca, Andrzej Stec, and Bartosz Trybus

Rzeszow University of Technology, ul. W. Pola 2, 35-959 Rzeszów, Poland
{drzonca,astec,btrybus}@kia.prz.edu.pl
http://www.prz.edu.pl

Abstract. The paper describes PACQ, a distributed control mini system. WWW and data acquisition functionality of PACQ server is presented from the user perspective together with a discussion on security issues. The communication between the server and control modules is modelled with hierarchical timed coloured Petri net. Programmability of the control modules using CPDev environment and their system software is also characterized.

Keywords: CPDev, DCS, HTCPN, Petri nets, data acquisition.

1 Introduction

PACQ is a prototype small distributed control and measurement system (mini-DCS) developed in Rzeszow University of Technology. It consists of multiple control modules and the main data acquisition and WWW server (Fig. 1). The control modules equipped with inputs and outputs are programmed in CPDev environment in ST, FBD or IL languages [1]. Process variables are exposed by the modules to PACQ server via a custom, Modbus-like communication protocol. The collected data is stored in the server database. WWW interface is used to access the data from the Internet.

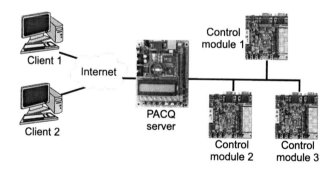

Fig. 1. Structure of PACQ distributed system

A. Kwiecień, P. Gaj, and P. Stera (Eds.): CN 2011, CCIS 160, pp. 398–406, 2011.

2   PACQ Data Acquisition and WWW Server

PACQ server (*microserver*) is used to record measurement data transmitted from the control modules via RS-485 interface. A dedicated master-slave protocol similar to Modbus is used to communicate with the modules, as described in Sect. 4. The collected data can be viewed using a web browser.

PACQ server prototype has been developed on EVBnet02 evaluation board (Fig. 1, center) [2]. The board is equipped with ATmega128 microcontroller, RAM and DataFlash memories, 10 Mbit/s Ethernet controller, UART, RTC, LCD display and 4 buttons. WWW and FTP services run under Nut/OS operating system [3].

Software for PACQ server has been written in C. The application part consists of three major components (Fig. 2):

– serial communication subsystem for acquiring data from control modules,
– archiving service for storing the data in a database,
– web server CGI extensions generating dynamic web pages.

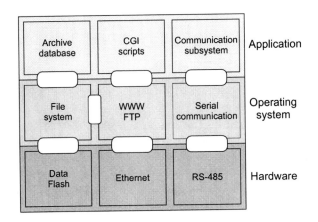

Fig. 2. Software and hardware components of PACQ server

Web pages are written in HTML with addition of JavaScript and CSS. Dynamic web pages are generated by CGI scripts. GET and POST methods are used for processing HTML forms. Because of limited performance of the server as well as to reduce the size of transferred pages, the server sends raw data from the database to the browser. The final processing is done on the client by JavaScript.

PACQ server web page can present both current (on-line) and archived data (Fig. 3). The server periodically acquires data from control modules and stores it in the archive database located in DataFlash memory. The update interval is configured independently for each module.

The most important features available to the web user are:

– monitoring of current data,

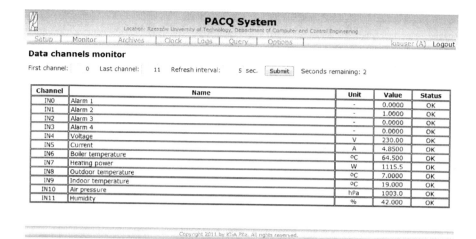

Fig. 3. Browsing data on the PACQ web page

- browsing archived data,
- customizing the user interface,
- managing of the server configuration,
- setting the real-time clock (RTC),
- viewing server logs.

A user enters login information (username and password) on the startup page. According to the granted privileges, appropriate pages are presented by the browser. A common user is allowed to view the data, while an administrator is also able to modify some parameters of the system. For example, the configuration and RTC management is available only for admins.

Moreover, some settings of the system can only be changed by a special management software. Due to security issues, the software communicates with the server locally (via the serial port). FTP protocol can be also used to modify configuration files. However, this possibility is blocked by default. Unblocking requires pressing a button on PACQ board and lasts only for a short period of time (e.g. 10 minutes) or until the server reset.

PACQ server has been designed primarily for local networks (LAN). Such networks are the most common in the industry. If remote access is needed to a particular network within a plant, creating a secure VPN tunnel is the preferred solution to get sufficient security.

3   Control Modules

Control modules in PACQ system are small programmable controllers equipped with analog or binary inputs and outputs. The module prototype is based on

ARM7 microcontroller development board AT91SAM7S-EK from Atmel [4] (Fig. 1, right). The board has been equipped with extra I/O hardware and RS-485 bus.

Each module can be programmed to perform process control. Programs are written in CPDev (*Control Program Developer*) engineering environment developed in Rzeszow University of Technology [1]. CPDev integrates tools for programming, simulation, hardware configuration, on-line testing and running control applications. Programs can be written in ST and IL textual languages (*Structured Text, Instruction List*) and in FBD graphical one (*Function Block Diagram*), according to IEC 61131-3 standard [5]. Main window of CPDev environment with programs in ST and FBD is shown in Fig. 4

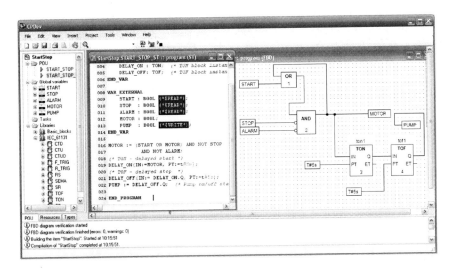

Fig. 4. Main window of CPDev programming environment

Programs for PACQ control modules are able to process several elementary data types defined in the IEC standard i.e. BOOL, BYTE, SINT, INT, WORD, DINT, LINT, DWORD, LWORD, REAL, LREAL, TIME, DATE, TIME_OF_DAY, DATE_AND_TIME. The elementary types may be used to define derived types such as arrays and structures.

Data can be processed with functions defined in IEC standard. Examples are:

- numerical functions: ADD, SUB, MUL, DIV, SQRT, ABS, LN,
- Boolean and bit shift functions: AND, OR, NOT, SHL, ROR,
- selection and comparison functions: SEL, MAX, LIMIT, MUX, GE, EQ, LT,
- type conversions: INT_TO_REAL, TIME_TO_DINT, etc.

A portion of code can be used as a *function block*. The CPDev package provides two standard libraries containing IEC-61131 blocks (flip-flops, counters, timers, edge detectors) and basic blocks (pulsers, filters, signal analysers). User-developed functions, function blocks and programs can be stored in custom libraries. *Native blocks* are components of the user program providing hardware dependent functions internally. They are written in C/C++ and linked to CPDev. A library of such blocks has been created for PACQ modules providing read/write of program variables into non-volatile memory and handle I/O.

CPDev programs are compiled into the intermediate, universal code executed by the runtime interpreter, called *virtual machine* [1]. The machine is written in C, so it may run on different hardware platforms, from 8-bit microcontrollers up to 32/64-bit general purpose processors. It has also been adapted to PACQ control modules with their ARM7 microcontroller.

Software for the control modules is run under FreeRTOS real-time operating system [6]. FreeRTOS is an open source, time-sharing multitasking operating system, what means that the CPU time is shared among running processes. It is also preemptive, so if a higher priority process becomes ready to run, the currently running process is suspended.

FreeRTOS in PACQ modules runs several tasks (processes) including:

- CPDev virtual machine executing control programs,
- communication subsystem exchanging data with PACQ server,
- handlers of native blocks.

FreeRTOS tasks exchange data via *queues* and use *mutexes* for mutual exclusion when accessing shared resources such as virtual machine data area [6]. The machine control cycle is kept constant by FreeRTOS task delay facility.

4   HTCPN Model of PACQ Communication

Hierarchical Timed Coloured Petri Net (HTCPN) [7] model of communication between PACQ server and control modules is shown in Fig. 5. Upper left part of the model represents PACQ server communication subsystem, upper right part is related to the transmission link, and bottom part models behaviour of the control modules.

Communication between PACQ server and the control modules relies on a custom master-slave protocol. The server is continuously acquiring data from the slaves. Although common Modbus protocol could have been used, the customized one turned out to be better suited, because the control modules provide not only the actual values of data, but also their timestamps.

In every communication cycle, the master (PACQ server) chooses next slave to read process variables from. This behaviour is modelled by *Counter* place and related inscriptions on the arcs. This place stores the number of the next message to be sent. According to the value of the 1 variable, the appropriate message is chosen from the *Messages*. When the transition *Sending* fires, the selected message is put to the *Outgoing buffer* and the value of the token stored in the *Counter* is appropriately changed. Additionally, a token is put into *Waiting for response* place, with timestamp delayed by tout units of time. Thus, *Timeout* transition will not be ready until this time passes. However, the transition *Microserver processing* can be fired earlier (immediately after receiving the

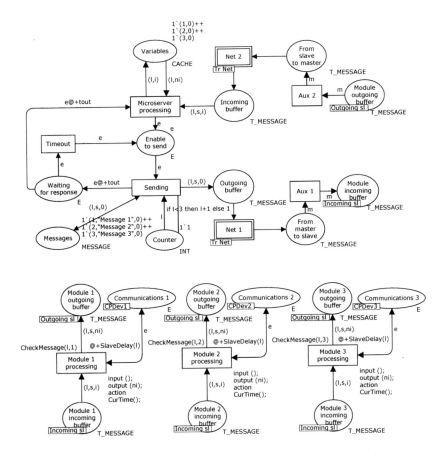

Fig. 5. HTCPN model of PACQ communication

response token in the *Incoming buffer*), because the inscription on the arc from *Waiting for response* to *Microserver processing* allows this token to be consumed without delay.

The message put into the *Outgoing buffer* is transmitted to the slaves. The transition *Net 1* is a substitution transition, introducing to the model hierarchy an instance of *Tr net* subnet (a subpage). This way many different models of the transmission link can be used if necessary, without a change of the main superpage. It has been shown in [8], that various parameters of the transmission link can be easily modelled in such subnet, e.g. additional delay (transmission time) related to the message type, or a packet loss with assumed probability. Similar technique has been applied here.

The message which has been successfully transmitted through the network is put to *From master to slave* place, and finally, by the auxiliary transition *Aux 1* to the *Module incoming buffer*. This place is a *fusion place*, tokens here are shared by all *Module 1-3 incoming buffer* places (lower part of Fig. 5), belonging to the

Incoming sl fusion. Thus many slave modules can be easily modelled, although only three of them are presented here for simplicity.

Function CheckMessage in the guards of *Module 1-3 processing* transitions enables only one transition, depending on the target of the message. This function is defined as follows:

```
fun CheckMessage(no:INT, addr:INT) = (no=addr)
```

As a result only the module addressed by the message is able to respond. However, the transitions *Module 1-3 processing* will not fire unless a token in the appropriate *Communications 1-3* place is put. The place (fusion) is connected to CPDev virtual machine model (not shown, see [8]). Each control module involves the machine to execute programs so receiving the message will cause reading process variables. However, this is possible only during time windows i.e. in every cycle after the program execution. Consequently, processing of the message is delayed until such time window is reached. Additional delay related to the processing time is modelled by the SlaveDelay function, when the transition *Module 1-3 processing* fires.

Besides modifying the timestamp of the token, the transition records *current model time* for further analysis. The value represents timestamp of the response, i.e. the point in time when the values of process variables have been determined and considered as valid. This timestamp is held in ni part of the token put into *Module 1-3 outgoing buffer* place. Its value is calculated by the following function:

```
input ();
output (ni);
action
CurTime();
```

where the CurTime is defined as:

```
fun CurTime() = IntInf.toInt(time())
```

The response from the *Module outgoing buffer* through the auxiliary transition *Aux 2* reaches the place *From slave to master* (upper right part of Fig. 5). Subsequently the response is transmitted through the *Net 2* (another instance of the *Tr net* subnet mentioned earlier) to the *Incoming buffer*. When *Microserver processing* transition fires, the timestamp of the received response (i part, not the timestamp of the token) is recorded in the *Variables* place. Additional token is put into the place *Enable to send*, activating *Sending* transition. This way another message to the successive module can be handled.

5   Model Analysis and Results

Simulation of HTCPN model can be used for simple performance analysis at the design stage. Therefore potential problems, like bottlenecks can be predicted and avoided. One of the performance parameters, which can be estimated on the basis of the described model, is latency time of on-line variable values.

As mentioned, PACQ server periodically acquires data from the control modules. After every readout, the *variable buffer* in the server is updated to store current values. However, when on-line data view is presented on the server web page, values of the variables from the buffer may be slightly outdated. HTCPN model can be used to estimate maximum and typical delay according to the number of control modules, transmission time, program cycle, update interval, etc. helping to achieve optimal performance. Such analysis has been performed to determine average latency time depending on the number of connected control modules and CPDev program execution time t_{prog} in each module. It has been assumed for simplicity, that CPDev program cycle time t_{cycle} is equal in each module and set to 200 ms. The simulation results of the model are shown in Table 1.

Table 1. Average latency of variable values

No. of boards	t_{prog} [ms]				
	20	60	100	140	180
3	43	52	80	113	160
5	62	84	121	185	261
7	84	112	165	250	362

The results have been compared to theoretical calculation. It has been stated in Sect. 4 that each control module procesess the received message only during time window after the program execution. CPDev program cycle time t_{cycle} is set by the user during development of the program. However, actual CPDev program execution time t_{prog} is shorter, and may vary between cycles. The virtual machine has to wait before starting the next program cycle to keep CPDev program cycle constant. The probability that the message will be received during program execution is $\frac{t_{\text{prog}}}{t_{\text{cycle}}}$. Processing of such messages will be delayed by average time of $\frac{t_{\text{prog}}}{2}$. The message will be received during the time window with the probability of $\frac{t_{\text{cycle}} - t_{\text{prog}}}{t_{\text{cycle}}}$. In this case, the machine will be ready for answering and the message will be processed immediately.

Thus average delay time caused by a module not being ready t_{wait} is:

$$t_{\text{wait}} = \frac{t_{\text{prog}}^2}{2t_{\text{cycle}}} \; . \tag{1}$$

The average time used by the server to handle each module will be denoted $t_{\text{avg\_1}}$. Apart from t_{wait}, it should also incorporate the delay caused by the network (transmission time) t_{net} and the message processing time t_{proc}. The components have been assumed equal for all modules and messages for simplicity.

$$t_{\text{avg\_1}} = t_{\text{wait}} + 2t_{\text{net}} + t_{\text{proc}} \; . \tag{2}$$

Total communication time (i.e. time of acquiring all variables from n control modules) $t_{\text{avg\_n}}$ will be n times larger. Average latency of variable values in local buffer t_{lat} will be:

$$t_{\text{lat}} = \frac{t_{\text{avg\_n}}}{2} + t_{\text{net}} \ . \tag{3}$$

The latency calculated from the equation above corresponds to the simulation results shown in Table 1. The differences are caused by additional parameters introduced into the HTCPN model but omitted in the above calculations, like transmission time depending on message size, processing time modelled by the SlaveDelay function (Fig. 5), etc.

6   Summary

New distributed control mini system PACQ has been described in the paper. Central unit of the system is PACQ server with data acquisition and WWW capability. The control modules can be programmed in IEC-61131 languages in CPDev engineering environment.

Formal HTCPN nets have been used during development to model the communication between the server and control modules. Simulation and performance analysis of the model have been made with CPN Tools [9]. The results have been compared to theoretical calculations.

Future extensions of the PACQ system are developed to provide secure connection between PACQ server and a web browser.

References

1. Rzońca, D., Sadolewski, J., Stec, A., Świder, Z., Trybus, B., Trybus, L.: Mini-DCS System Programming in IEC 61131-3 Structured Text. Journal of Automation, Mobile Robotics & Intelligent Systems 2(3), 48–54 (2008)
2. EVBnet02 User's Manual,
   http://www.propox.com/download/docs/EVBnet02_en.pdf
3. Nut/OS Software Manual, http://www.ethernut.de/pdf/enswm28e.pdf
4. AT91SAM7S-EK Evaluation Board User Guide,
   http://www.atmel.com/dyn/resources/prod_documents/doc6112.pdf
5. IEC 61131-3 Standard: Programmable Controllers. Part 3. Programming Languages, IEC (2003)
6. Barry, R.: Using the FreeRTOS Real Time Kernel – A Practical Guide
7. Jensen, K.: Coloured Petri Nets. Basic Concepts, Analysis Methods and Practical Use. Springer, Heidelberg (1997)
8. Rzońca, D., Trybus, B.: Hierarchical Petri Net for the CPDev Virtual Machine with Communications. In: Kwiecień, A., Gaj, P., Stera, P. (eds.) CN 2009. CCIS, vol. 39, pp. 264–271. Springer, Heidelberg (2009)
9. CPN Tools: Computer Tool for Coloured Petri Nets,
   http://www.daimi.au.dk/cpntools

Multicast Connections in Mobile Networks with Embedded Threshold Mechanism

Damian Parniewicz, Maciej Stasiak, and Piotr Zwierzykowski

Poznan University of Technology, Chair of Communications and Computer Networks
ul. Polanka 3, Poznań 60965, Poland
piotr.zwierzykowski@put.poznan.pl

Abstract. The paper presents a new analytical model of cellular network servicing multicast connections. In the model it was assumed that threshold mechanism was introduced in the Iub interface of the UMTS network. The proposed model is based on the model of the full-availability group servicing a mixture of different multirate classes. The presented analytical model is an approximate model and hence the results of the analytical calculations were compared with the results of the simulations, which confirmed the essential accuracy of the model. The calculation method presented in the paper can be further used for the analysis, optimization and dimensioning of UMTS networks or any other multiservice cellular networks such us the forthcoming LTE-Advanced standard.

Keywords: threshold mechanism, UMTS, multicast.

1 Introduction

In the present day world multimedia services are being introduced to many mobile networks, including UMTS networks. The rapid development of multimedia services in cellular networks is related to an increase in investments and influences the factors underlying operators's decisions related to optimization and dimensioning methods for multiservice mobile networks. Any analysis of mobile networks is usually and conventionally started by operators with a definition of the set of KPI (Key Performance Indicator) parameters that are based on predefined SLA (Service Level Agreement) parameters that can be further used as input data in the process of dimensioning and optimization of networks. On the basis of the KPI efficiency parameters it is possible to determine such parameters as the blocking probability or the average bit rate of the network, which, in turn, can be used in calculations for GoS (Grade of Service) parameters [1].

The process of dimensioning of the UMTS network should make it possible to determine such capacities of individual elements of a system that would ensure, in a given load of the system, a predefined level of the GoS parameters. The most characteristic constraints in the dimensioning of an UMTS system are: capacities of the radio and the Iub interface. In order to increase the capacity of the radio interface some other access technologies can be applied or, alternatively, an increase in the number of base stations can be introduced (NodeB). If, however,

A. Kwiecień, P. Gaj, and P. Stera (Eds.): CN 2011, CCIS 160, pp. 407–416, 2011.

the constraint to the capacity of the system is an insufficient capacity of the Iub interface (i.e. interface in the core data network), then a decision as to adding another node to the network may be financially ineffective. The literature of the subject is very extensive, reflecting the great variability in articles related to the process of traffic management in mobile systems with radio WCDMA interfaces such as, for example, [2, 3, 4, 5], and only a few titles related to the analytical modelling of the Iub interface, e.g. [1, 6].

With regard to the increasing significance of multicast connections in mobile networks, the paper considers an exemplary scenario for the execution of multicast connections in the UMTS network. The proposed analytical model takes into consideration the influence of multicast connections on traffic effectiveness of a mobile system in which the threshold mechanism has been introduced.

The paper is divided into seven sections. Section 2 presents two exemplary scenarios for setting up multicast connections in the UMTS network. Section 3 discusses a basic model of the Iub interface. Sections 4 and 5 present respectively the analytical models for multicast and k-cast connections. Section 6 includes exemplary numerical results, whereas the last section sums up the presented study.

2   Multicast Connections in the UMTS Network

Let us consider an UMTS network servicing multicast connections. Assume that the multicast connection is here understood as a connection in which one user gets a connection with a defined group of users. Our next assumption is that both the user that initiates the connection and the users that belong to the group of recipients can be linked to different base stations (NodeB)[1]. It is possible then to distinguish a number of scenarios for setting up multicast connections in the UMTS network with the application of radio interfaces and Iub interfaces. The present paper considers an exemplary scenario shown in Fig. 1, where RNC is the Radio Network Controller, WCDMA is the radio interface, and Iub is the interface linking NodeB with RNC [7, 8]. The scenario assumes that the users of the multicast connection are in different cells, which means that the radio resources of each of the cells service one connection, while the resources between RNC and NodeB stations carry multiple parallel connection. Each of the multicast connections has to be set up in multiple Iub interfaces concurrently. Thus, in this scenario, the service process to multicast traffic itself has to be taken into consideration at the level of the Iub interface. Therefore, setting up of a multicast connection requires setting up of a number of independent Iub-based connections. Let us assume that the Iub interface services a mixture of different traffic classes. For modelling multicast connections, the two analytical models presented in Sect. 4 and 5 will be used.

---

[1] The considerations presented in the paper are limited to the downlink direction only, with the assumption that a determination of given capacities of particular interfaces in the uplink directions will require the application of standard methods for dimensioning of the interface that services a mixture of many traffic classes with differentiated demands [1].

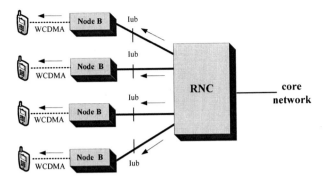

Fig. 1. Multicast connections in the UMTS network (downlink direction)

3   Analytical Model of the Iub Interface

The Iub interface in the UMTS network can be treated as a full-availability group that services a mixture of unicast and multicast multirate traffic [6]. Our next assumption is that the total capacity of the group is equal to V basic bandwidth units (BBUs) [9]. We also assume that the system under consideration is offered M traffic streams: and, additionally, that a Multi Threshold Model (MTM) is used in the system [10, 1].

We assume that individual Poisson call streams have the intensities: $\lambda_1, \ldots, \lambda_M$. The service times of particular classes have an exponential distribution with the parameters: $\mu_1, \mu_2, \ldots, \mu_M$. Thus, the mean offered traffic in the system by class i stream is equal to: $A_i = \lambda_i/\mu_i$.

Let us consider a discrete interface model. In such a system, the amount of resources demanded by calls of particular traffic classes offered to the interface has to be expressed in integer numbers [9]. In order to express the amount of demanded resources in bandwidth units we first have to determine the greatest common divisor for the resources demanded by all traffic classes serviced by the system:

$$R_{BBU} = \mathrm{GCD}(R_1, \ldots, R_M) \ , \tag{1}$$

where R_i is the number of demanded resources (expressed in kbps) by calls of class i, and M is the number of traffic streams serviced by the system.

Our assumption is that a threshold mechanism for traffic management has been introduced into the considered system [11, 12, 10]. In the threshold mechanism we define one the so-called *pre-threshold* area and q *post-threshold* areas for each class of traffic. All states n belonging to the set of states so that $0 \leq n \leq Q_{i,1}$ create a pre-threshold area for class i stream. The states n such that $Q_{i,p} < n \leq Q_{i,p+1}$ belong to the p-th post-threshold area of class i. In the pre-threshold area for class i, a call can be serviced with the assumed maximum number of BBUs equal to $t_{i,0}$. In the p-th post-threshold area, the control system makes the service of class i call with $t_{i,p}$ BBUs acceptable. In the last q-th post-threshold area $(Q_{i,q} \leq n \leq Q_{i,q+1} = V)$, the class i call can be serviced with minimum number of BBUs, equal to $t_{i,q}$. Therefore, the threshold mechanism makes the number of adopted BBUs for service of class i call dependent on the load of the system. The more overloaded systems, the smaller number of BBUs accessible for service of a given call.

In the case of the considered system with thresholds that services a mixture multirate streams, the generalized Kaufman-Roberts recurrence equation can be written in the following form [10, 1]:

$$n[P_n]_V = \sum_{i=1}^{M} \sum_{p=0}^{q} A_i t_{i,p} \sigma_{i,p}(n - t_{i,p})[P_{n-t_{i,p}}]_V , \qquad (2)$$

where $[P_n]_V$ is the state probability of n busy bandwidth units, and $\sigma_{i,p}(n)$ are the conditional transition coefficients that determine the pre- ($p = 0$) and the post-threshold ($0 < p \le q$) areas for calls of class i. The transition coefficient can be defined in the following way:

$$\sigma_{i,p}(n) = \begin{cases} 1 & \text{for } Q_{i,p} < n \le Q_{i,p+1} \\ 0 & \text{for other values of } n \end{cases} . \qquad (3)$$

Based on Formula (2), and taking into consideration the condition (3), the blocking probability B_i for the stream of class i can be written in the following form:

$$B_i = \sum_{p=0}^{q} B_{i,p} , \qquad (4)$$

where $B_{i,p}$ can be expressed as follows [10, 1]:

$$B_{i,p} = \begin{cases} \sum_{n=V-t_{i,p}+1}^{Q_{i,p+1}} [P_n]_V & \text{for } V - t_{i,p} < Q_{i,p+1} \text{ and } V - t_{i,p} > Q_{i,p} \end{cases} \qquad (5)$$

and

$$B_{i,p} = \begin{cases} \sum_{n=Q_p+1}^{Q_{i,p+1}} [P_n]_V & \text{for } V - t_{i,p} < Q_{i,p+1} \text{ and } V - t_{i,p} \le Q_{i,p} , \end{cases} \qquad (6)$$

where $Q_{i,q+1} = V$.

Most frequently, threshold areas are selected in such a way to let blocking states occur in the last post-threshold area. This means that for all states $0 < p \le q - 1$ the condition (5) is satisfied. In the post-threshold area q, however, the blocking probability is determined by the dependence (6).

4   Model of the System with Multicast Connections

Let us assume that a multicast connection is lost if it cannot be set up with at least one of the pre-defined receivers. The blocking probability of multicast calls of class i in the interface r can be thus expressed as a function of the intensities of all traffic classes M offered in the interface r [13]:

$$B_{i,r} = F[(A_{1,r}, t_1), \ldots, (A_{i,r}^e, t_i), \ldots, (A_{M,r}, t_M)] \ , \tag{7}$$

where $A_{1,r}$ denotes the traffic intensity of class 1 stream offered to the interface r, whereas $A_{i,r}^e$ is the intensity of this part of multicast traffic of class i that is offered to the interface r (effective traffic). Traffic $A_{i,r}^e$ forms such part of the total multicast traffic of class i (denoted by the symbol A_i) which is not blocked in the remaining interfaces involved in this connection (hence this traffic can be offered in the interface r). This dependence – combined with the fixed-point methodology [14] – can be written in the following way:

$$A_{i,r}^e = A_i \prod_{z=1, z \neq r}^{L_i} (1 - B_{i,z}) \ , \tag{8}$$

where L_i is the number of interfaces (resources of the Iub interface) that are involved in the multicast connection of class i. Function (7) can be determined on the basis of the modified Kaufman-Roberts distribution described in Sect. 3.

With the knowledge of the blocking probability for multicast calls of class i in each of the interfaces involved in this connection we can determine the total blocking probability of multicast calls of class i in the system. A computational method for determining this probability depends on the adopted definition of the blocking state. In the model under consideration we assume that any blocking in the connection occurs in a situation of a lack of free resources required for servicing of a given connection in at least one of the demanded interfaces. Therefore, the total blocking probability can be determined by the following formula:

$$B_i = 1 - \prod_{z=1}^{L_i} (1 - B_{i,z}) \ , \tag{9}$$

where B_i is the blocking probability of a multicast call of class i in the system.

The iterative calculation process, based on Equations (7), (8) and (9), is repeated in order to obtain the optimal values of the blocking probability determined with the assumed accuracy.

5   Model of the System with k-cast Connections

In Sect. 4 we adopt that the blocking probability events appear when at least one of the interfaces taking part in the multicast connection is blocked. In this section we assume that the system services the so-called k-cast connections [15]. In k-cast connection the blocking event appears if more than k interfaces, from among L_i interfaces required to set up a connection, are blocked. This means that the system can service a k-cast connection if at least k component connection form among L_i required connections is set up. It is assumed in [15] that a multicast connection for which this assumption has been defined will be called the k-cast connection.

Let us assume now that the blocking probability for each of the component interfaces, i.e. those that belong to a given k-cast connection, is equal to B_i^*. To determine the probability $P_B(k/L_i)$ of blocking of the k interfaces from L_i of component interfaces of the k-cast connection, the binomial distribution can be applied:

$$P_B(k/L_i) = \binom{L_i}{k}(B_i^*)^k(1 - B_i^*)^{L_i-k} \ . \tag{10}$$

To determine the blocking probability of the considered k-cast connection, we have to consider all events in which the connection will be blocked. Thus, we start with determining the maximum and the minimum number of interfaces required for setting up a k-cast connection of class i. These parameters will be denoted by L_i and k_i, respectively. We have already stated that a k-cast connection of class i is blocked when there is no possibility to set up $L_i - k_i + 1, \ldots, L_i$ connections. Thus, the blocking probability for a k-cast call of class i can be determined on the basis of Equation (10) in the following way:

$$B_i^{k\text{-cast}} = \sum_{z=L_i-k_i+1}^{L_i} \binom{L_i}{z}(B_i^*)^z(1 - B_i^*)^{(L_i-z)} \ . \tag{11}$$

In order to evaluate the blocking probability for a k-cast connection, the value of blocking probability in single component interface (parameter B^*) is to be known. This parameter can be approximated on the basis of the multicast call blocking probability in the following way:

$$B_i^* = 1 - \sqrt[L_i]{1 - B_i} \ , \tag{12}$$

where B_i is the blocking probability of a multicast call of class i which is determined on the basis of the model presented in Sect. 4.

To sum up, it is easily observable that to determine the blocking probability of multicast and k-cast calls serviced in a mobile network, it is necessary to determine the blocking probability for each traffic class in each interface involved in this connection. In line with the discussed scenario of connections, this value can be determined on the basis of the analytical model of the Iub interface, presented in Sect. 3.

6   Numerical Results

Assume that our objective is to carry out a traffic analysis of an access part of the UMTS network that is composed of RNC and 7 base stations (NodeB). The system services a mixture of traffic classes in the downlink direction. Our next assumption is that Realtime Gaming and Mobile TV services require multicast and k-cast connections, respectively. According to the scenario, multicast connections are serviced based on the resources of the Iub interfaces. To determine the blocking probability for multicast and k-cast calls, the dependencies presented in Sect. 4 and 5, are used.

The proposed analytical model of the UMTS system that services multicast connections is an approximate model and, hence, the results of the analytical calculations have been compared with the results of the simulation experiments.

The study was carried out for users that demanded the following set of traffic classes:

- VoIP – $t_1 = 16$ kbps,
- Realtime Gaming – $t_2 = 10$ kbps and $L_2 = 3$,
- Mobile TV – $t_3 = 64$ kbps, $L_3 = 5$, $k_3 = 3$,
- Web Browsing – $t_4 = 40$ kbps.

We also adopt the following assumptions:

- R_{BBU} is equal to 1 kbps,
- physical capacity of each of the Iub interface is equal to: $V_{Iub} = 8$ Mbps (8000 BBUs),
- traffic classes are offered in the following proportions:
  $A_1t_1 : A_2t_2 : A_3t_3 : A_4t_4 : A_5t_5 = 5 : 2 : 1 : 10$. Appropriately, the main part of traffic was occupied by Web Browsing and VoIP traffic. A relatively low part of traffic is formed by Realtime Gaming and Mobile TV,
- Realtime Gaming use multicast connections that demand, by default, three component connections,
- Mobile TV makes use of k-cast connections which demand, by default, five component connections but require setting up of at least three connections,
- threshold mechanism for Mobile TV with the following parameters: $Q_{3,1} = 7000$, $Q_{3,2} = 7500$, $t_{3,0} = t_3 = 64$ kbps, $t_{3,1} = 56$ kbps and $t_{3,2} = 48$ kbps is introduced.

The results of the study of the system are presented in Fig. 2–4. The graphs show the dependence of the blocking probability in relation to offered traffic per bandwidth unit in the system. It is clearly seen that along with an increase in the load of the system, blocking probabilities of all traffic classes offered to the system also increase. Figure 2 shows the results for the system in which Realtime Gaming and Mobile TV calls are treated as multicast calls. The values of blocking probabilities obtained for the Mobile TV traffic are the highest, whereas the values of blocking probabilities for Realtime Gaming traffic are higher than the values obtained for VoIP traffic (which requires higher number of BBUs) in a single interface. This phenomenon results from the way in which blocking for multicast connection is defined, according to which the blocking state occurs if only one of the demanded Iub interfaces lacks available free resources.

The blocking probabilities for Mobile TV class that use k-cast connections presented in Fig. 3 are markedly lower than those for the remaining traffic classes within the small loads of the system. It is also worthwhile to note that, in this

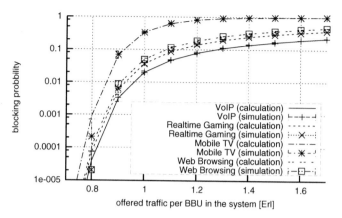

Fig. 2. System servicing Mobile TV calls as multicast calls

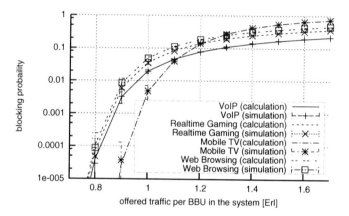

Fig. 3. System servicing Mobile TV calls as k-cast calls

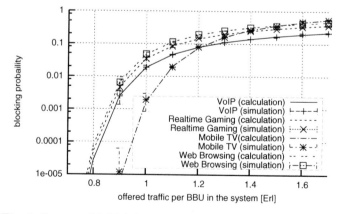

Fig. 4. System with Mobile TV k-cast, undergoing threshold, calls

particular case, along with an increase in the load of the system, the blocking probabilities are characterized by a highly pronounced growing tendency. This effect is related to the definition of the blocking state for the k-cast connection adopted in the study, according to which blocking occurs when there is no possibility of a concurrent setting up of a connection in four or five interfaces. This situation is statistically far more infrequent than a blocking situation in a single interface, but with an increase in the load of the system, is statistically more and more frequent. This is particularly observable when we compare the results presented in Fig. 3 with the results in Fig. 2. A comparison of the values of the blocking probability for Mobile TV traffic in Fig. 3 provides us with an observation that the growing tendency depends on the tolerance of k-cast connections on blocking states, i.e. on the difference between the number of demanded connections and the number of connections required for an execution of a k-cast connection. Mobile TV has a greater tolerance on blocking states in single interfaces and, therefore, a higher growing tendency in blocking probabilities.

Figure 4 shows the influence of the application of the threshold mechanism on the servicing process of Mobile TV calls. It is easy to see that the values of the blocking probability for calls of this class are lower than the analogous values presented in Fig. 2 and 3. This phenomenon is related to the operation of the threshold mechanism, according to which calls, after exceeding the threshold, decrease the number of demanded bandwidth units.

The results of the analytical calculations were compared with the results of the simulation experiments that based on a simulation program especially designed for the purpose. The simulator generates calls of individual classes according to the Poisson distribution. These calls, demanding the integer number of BBUs, are forwarded to the system. Service streams of individual classes are generated on the basis of exponential distributions. Each simulation point shown in the Fig. 2, 3 and 4, represents an average value of the 10 results obtained in 10 simulations series, each having 10,000,000 calls of this class which demands the highest number of BBUs. The results of the simulation are denoted in the form of markers with 95% confidence intervals calculated after the t-Student distribution.

7   Conclusions

The paper proposes a new method for a calculation of the blocking probability in a mobile system with a threshold mechanism servicing multicast connections. The proposed analytical method can be applied in an analysis of the core data network in mobile system which offers services, or in which they are planned to be introduced, that use interactive multicast connections.

The proposed computational method is characterized by a low computational complexity, which, combined with the acceptable accuracy of the method, makes it applicable in engineering calculations.

References

1. Stasiak, M., Głabowski, M., Wiśniewski, A., Zwierzykowski, P.: Modeling and dimensioning of mobile networks: from GSM to LTE. John Wiley and Sons, Ltd., Chichester (2011)
2. Iversen, V.B., Epifania, E.: Teletraffic engineering of multi-band W-CDMA systems. In: Network Control and Engineering for Qos, Security and Mobility II, pp. 90–103. Kluwer Academic Publishers, Norwell (2003)
3. Kwon, Y.S., Kim, N.: Capacity and cell coverage based on calculation of the erlang capacity in a WCDMA system with multi-rate traffic. IEICE Transactions on Communications E87-B(8), 2397–2400 (2004)
4. Subramaniam, K., Nilsson, A.A.: Tier-based analytical model for adaptive call admission control scheme in a UMTS-WCDMA system. In: Proceedings of Vehicular Technology Conference, vol. 4, pp. 2181–2185 (2005)
5. Vassilakis, V.G., Logothetis, M.D.: The wireless Engset multi-rate loss model for the handofftraffic analysis in W-CDMA networks. In: Proccedings of 19th International Symposium on Personal, Indoor and Mobile Radio Communications, Cannes, France, pp. 1–6 (2008)
6. Stasiak, M., Zwierzykowski, P.: Analytical model of the iub interface carrying HSDPA traffic in the UMTS network. In: Hong, C.S., Tonouchi, T., Ma, Y., Chao, C.-S. (eds.) APNOMS 2009. LNCS, vol. 5787, pp. 536–539. Springer, Heidelberg (2009)
7. Holma, H., Toskala, A.: WCDMA for UMTS. In: Radio Access For Third Generation Mobile Communications, John Wiley and Sons, Ltd., Chichester (2000)
8. Laiho, J., Wacker, A., Novosad, T.: Radio Network Planning and Optimization for UMTS, 2nd edn. John Wiley and Sons, Ltd., Chichester (2006)
9. Roberts, J., Mocci, V., Virtamo, I. (eds.): Broadband Network Teletraffic, Final Report of Action COST 242. Commission of the European Communities. Springer, Berlin (1996)
10. Glabowski, M., Kaliszan, A., Stasiak, M.: Modeling product- form state-dependent systems with bpp traffic. Journal of Performance Evaluation 67(3), 174–197 (2010)
11. Kaufman, J.: Blocking with retrials in a completly shared recource environment. Journal of Performance Evaluation 15, 99–113 (1992)
12. Vassilakis, V.G., Moscholios, I.D., Logothetis, M.D.: The extended connection-dependent threshold model for elastic and adaptive traffic. In: 5th International Symposium on Communication Systems, Networks and Digital Signal Processing, Patras, Greece(2006)
13. Parniewicz, D., Stasiak, M., Zwierzykowski, P.: Model of the cellular network servicing multicast connection in iub and WCDMA resources. In: Pióro, M., Szczypiorski, K., Rak, J., Gonzalez-Soto, O. (eds.) 14th International Telecommunications Network Strategy and Planning Symposium, Warszawa, Poland, Warsaw University of Technology and Polish Association of Telecommunication Engineers, pp. 273–278 (2010)
14. Kelly, F.: Loss networks. The Annals of Applied Probability 1(3), 319–378 (1991)
15. Parniewicz, D., Stasiak, M., Zwierzykowski, P.: Model of k-cast connections in mobile networks. In: Ghassemlooy, Z., Ng, W. (eds.) 7th IEEE&IET International Symposium on Communication Systems, Networks and Digital Signal Processing, Newcastle upon Tyne, United Kingdom, School of Computing, Engineering and Information Science, Northumbria University, pp. 911–915 (2010)

The Analysis of Microprocessor Instruction Cycle

Andrzej Kwiecień, Michał Maćkowski, and Krzysztof Skoroniak

Silesian University of Technology, Institute of Computer Science,
Akademicka 16, 44-100 Gliwice, Poland
{akwiecien,michal.mackowski,krzysztof.skoroniak}@polsl.pl
http://www.polsl.pl/

Abstract. Each microcontroller realizing the code saved in a program memory emits electromagnetic disturbances, both conducted that propagate through lines connected to the processor and radiated in the form of electromagnetic field. All of these undesirable signals emitted by the processor can be measured, received and interpreted by the appropriate methods. However, this subject requires a precise measurement and understanding of processes occurring inside the microprocessor during realization of the sequential instructions. The presented results of the influence of parameters such as data bus state, instruction argument, the result of operation on the voltage waveform on the power supply lines of microprocessor, enable to understand the processes occurring during the realization of following instructions by microprocessor unit.

Keywords: reverse engineering, program code, microcontroller, conducted emission, electromagnetic disturbances, electromagnetic interference.

1 Introduction

The analysis of microprocessor programme code on the basis of measurement of power supply changes, requires an accurate measurement of voltage or current draw by the processor during execution of the instruction cycle. Temporary changes in power consumption during the execution of following instructions are mainly due to having to reload the output capacity of gates within the structure of microprocessor [1]. Total current, used by all gates in the microprocessor unit when changes of the output state occur, can take very high values, and its amplitude and the waveform may enable the analysis and reconstruction of processes occurring in the considered system. The network controller placed in the network card can be also considered as a microprocessor unit, which is responsible for data processing of transmitted frames.

The microprocessor executing a program, performs certain repetitive activities consisting in getting instruction codes from the memory and loading them into the microprocessor control system, and then executing the fetched instruction. All these operations executed by microprocessor are synchronised by a clock signal, which result in an increased activity of elements constituting the central unit

A. Kwiecień, P. Gaj, and P. Stera (Eds.): CN 2011, CCIS 160, pp. 417–426, 2011.

in each machine cycle. Mainly, the activity of address and data buses, instructions decoder and arithmetic logic unit, causes the changes of outputs states of gates included in these elements, and thereby contributes to the dynamic power consumption from the power source. A precise analysis of voltage changes during the performance of particular machine cycles included in a single instruction cycle, presented in the paper, may allow to determine which instruction is currently executed [2,3,4].

2   Test Bench

The test bench presented in the Fig. 1 consists of microprocessor PIC16F84A produced by Microchip to which an 250 kHz external square waveform generator was connected. Programmer used in the research was connected to the microprocessor only while programming occurred, in order to avoid conducted disturbances. Otherwise, these disturbances can spread from the programmer on the microprocessor supply lines. During the research the test bench was placed in shielded environment – GTEM (Gigahertz Transverse ElectroMagnetic) cell, which ensured an entire isolation of measurement area from the external influences of electromagnetic fields. The microprocessor was powered with 5 V from Agilent power supply (E3649A). In previous studies a complete of batteries was used, however a long time of research resulted in discharging them, and as a consequence, caused a large error of measured voltage.

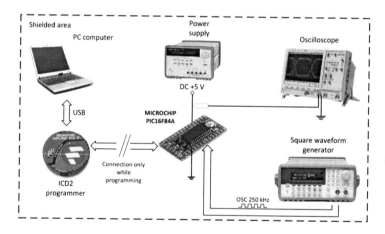

Fig. 1. The schema of research position

The analysis of microprocessor programme code based on the observation of power supply changes, requires a precise measurement of voltage or current draw by the processor. Each change of gate state determines a temporary change in power consumption by the microprocessor unit, meanwhile the total power drawing by all gates that execute a single instruction may indicate the kind of instruction, which is already executed.

Figure 2 presents three cases of the current/voltage measurements that were considered as follows:

- Measure 1 (Fig. 2a) – measured parameter is the voltage drop on the resistor placed on the processor ground circuit. Nevertheless, in this case the problem concerns an appropriate selection of resistance. Too little resistance causes that measured voltage has very little value (at the noise level),whereas too high a resistance value lowers the voltage that powers microprocessor itself, and as a result its incorrect work.
- Measure 2 (Fig. 2b) – measured parameter is the voltage drop on the secondary winding of the transformer. The primary winding is in the microprocessor ground circuit. An additional element in the form of transistor causes too much uncertainty of measurement therefore, this method was not taken into account during the research.
- Measure 3 (Fig. 2c) – an oscilloscope was connected to the supply line in order to observe the voltage drop on them. Despite of using the linear (stabilized) power supply, the voltage drops was observed in the oscilloscope, which were an accurate reflection of current flowing through power lines. The DC power supply was unable, in this case to ensure a constant level of voltage because of too low rate of output voltage stabilisation, in comparison with the transient and rapid changes in current drawn by the microprocessor, when the gate switching occurred. This method has proved to be the best, and therefore was used in the research. This approach was dictated by the difficulty in finding a proper current probe, which could measure the currents of a milli, and even microampere, with sampling frequency of 1 GHz.

3   The Research Procedure

The research procedure is as follows (Fig. 3):

1. Assignment of the value to the working register and accumulator.
2. Determination of the time flow of the microprocessor power supply voltage during the whole program.
3. Excision of part of the time flow which refers to the currently tested instruction.
4. Determination of influence of parameters such as: data bus state, instruction argument, the result of operation on the voltage flow measured on the microprocessor supply lines, when the instruction is executed.

Each program consists of 11 instructions:

- the instruction that initializes the microprocessor, realized implicitly – microprocessor initialization,
- the instructions that reset the value of accumulator and the working register (two instructions),
- the instructions that set the state of a working register and accumulator (three instructions),

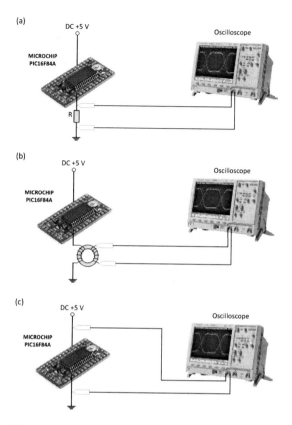

Fig. 2. The way of connecting the oscilloscope during the research

- the tested instruction,
- the instructions that set the state of a working register and accumulator (three instructions),
- the SLEEP instruction that was to switch the microprocessor into standby mode.

In order to execute the instructions that set the working register and accumulator on a certain value, it is necessary to use the data bus and arithmetic logic unit. Thus, before the tested instruction is executed, the state of the basic elements included in microprocessor results from the realization of previous instructions. There were two tests conducted during the research for six programmes (instruction arguments are presented in decimal system):

1. The influence of instruction argument and the state of data bus resulting from the previous operation on voltage waveform during the first machine cycle. This test concerns the MOVLW instruction (bold type in Table 1).

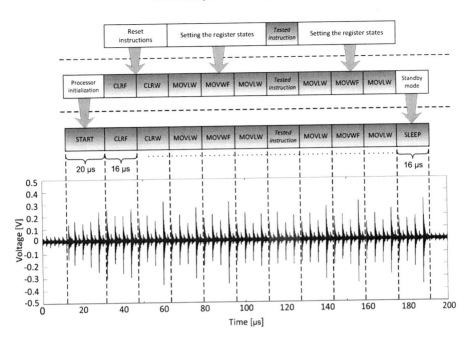

Fig. 3. The research procedure – microcontroller test program construction

2. The influence of instruction operation result and the state of data bus on voltage waveform during the third machine cycle. In this case the tested instruction is ADDLW (bold type in Table 2).

4   The Research Results

Figures 4, 5 and 6 present the voltage waveforms on the microprocessor supply lines in the middle of executing MOVLW . 0, MOVLW .12, MOVLW .15 instructions, respectively for programmes 1, 2 and 3 (Table 1). Comparing the voltage waveforms in the figures it can be seen that mainly the differences during the first machine cycle occur. The voltage shapes for 2, 3 and 4 cycle are the same for all considered instructions. In order to explain the differences observed during the first machine cycle, it is necessary to examine the state of microprocessor before and afterwards the first machine cycle execution.

Before the first machine cycle of the tested instruction is realized, a state resulting from the previous instruction is maintained on the data bus. In the following stage, an instruction is decoded, and instruction argument contained in the instruction code or retrieved from memory is set on the data bus, overwriting at the same time its previous state (Table 3).

Figures 7, 8 and 9 present the voltage waveforms on the microprocessor supply lines in the middle of executing ADDLW .63, ADDLW .12, ADDLW .85 instructions, respectively for programmes 4, 5 and 6 (Table 2). Comparing the

Table 1. Microprocessor test programmes – interaction on the first machine cycle

Program 1	Program 2	Program 3
CLRF 15	CLRF 15	CLRF 15
CLRW	CLRW	CLRW
MOVLW .0	MOVLW .0	MOVLW .0
MOVWF 15	MOVWF 15	MOVWF 15
MOVLW .0	MOVLW .3	MOVLW .240
MOVLW .0	**MOVLW .12**	**MOVLW .15**
MOVLW .0	MOVLW .0	MOVLW .0
MOVWF 15	MOVWF 15	MOVWF 15
MOVLW .0	MOVLW .0	MOVLW .0
SLEEP	SLEEP	SLEEP

Table 2. Microprocessor test programmes – interaction on the third machine cycle

Program 4	Program 5	Program 6
CLRF 15	CLRF 15	CLRF 15
CLRW	CLRW	CLRW
MOVLW .0	MOVLW .0	MOVLW .0
MOVWF 15	MOVWF 15	MOVWF 15
MOVLW .0	MOVLW .36	MOVLW .85
ADDLW .63	**ADDLW .12**	**ADDLW .85**
MOVLW .0	MOVLW .0	MOVLW .0
MOVWF 15	MOVWF 15	MOVWF 15
MOVLW .0	MOVLW .0	MOVLW .0
SLEEP	SLEEP	SLEEP

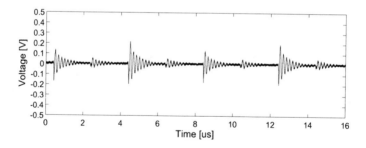

Fig. 4. The voltage waveform on the microprocessor power supply lines during the execution of MOVLW .0 instruction – program 1

Table 3. State of data bus before and after realization of the first machine cycle

	Program 1	Program 2	Program 3
The state of data bus before realization of the first machine cycle	0	3	240
The state of data bus after realization of the first machine cycle	0	12	15

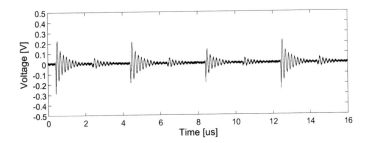

Fig. 5. The voltage waveform on the microprocessor power supply lines during the execution of MOVLW .12 instruction – program 2

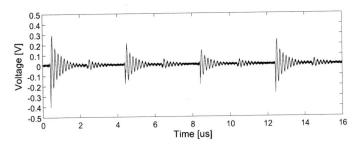

Fig. 6. The voltage waveform on the microprocessor power supply lines during the execution of MOVLW .15 instruction – program 3

voltage waveforms in the figures it can be seen the differences during the first and third machine cycle performance, whereas the voltage shapes for the second and fourth cycle are the same for all considered instructions. The rule of interaction on the first machine cycle can be explained as in the previous example, but it is not sufficient to explain the differences in the third machine cycle. Hence, it is necessary to examine the state of the microprocessor before and after the third machine cycle execution.

Before the third machine cycle of the tested instruction is realized, on the data bus is maintained a state that corresponds to instruction argument retrieved at the beginning of instruction cycle (the first machine cycle). Arithmetic Logic Unit operations are executed in the third machine cycle. In the considered example it is the summarizing operation. Next, the operation result is set on data bus, overwriting at the same time instruction argument, and then it is written into the accumulator W or to determined register in data memory (Table 4).

In order to explain the changes that occur in the voltage waveform during the first and the third machine cycle, it is helpful to use the parameter called Hamming distance (HD). In information theory, the Hamming distance between two strings of equal length is the number of positions at which the corresponding symbols are different. Put another way, it measures the minimum number of substitutions required to change one string into the other.

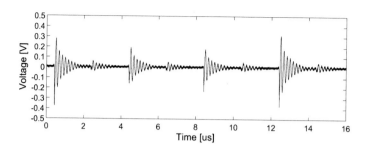

Fig. 7. The voltage waveform on the microprocessor power supply lines during the execution of ADDLW .63 instruction – program 4

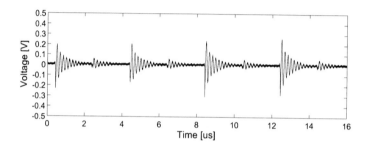

Fig. 8. The voltage waveform on the microprocessor power supply lines during the execution of ADDLW .12 instruction – program 5

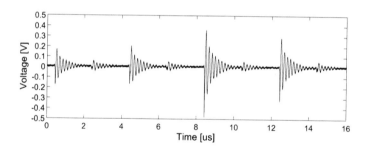

Fig. 9. The voltage waveform on the microprocessor power supply lines during the execution of ADDLW .85 instruction – program 6

Table 4. The state of data bus before and after realization of the third machine cycle

	Program 4	Program 5	Program 6
The state of data bus before realization of the third machine cycle	63	12	85
The state of data bus after realization of the third machine cycle	63	48	170

Table 1 illustrates test programmes for which the Hamming distance between the previous result and the argument of tested instruction (Table 3) was estimated from Equation (1), (2) and (3):

$$HD(0,0) = HD(00000000\text{b}, 00000000\text{b}) = 0 \qquad (1)$$
$$HD(3,12) = HD(00000011\text{b}, 00001100\text{b}) = 4 \qquad (2)$$
$$HD(240,15) = HD(11110000\text{b}, 00001111\text{b}) = 8 \ . \qquad (3)$$

As the equation results present, the larger number of positions with the difference between the instruction argument and data bus state, the higher voltage amplitude occurs during the first machine cycle. Table 2 presents test programmes for which the Hamming distance among the data buses state before and after realization of the third machine cycle (Table 4) was estimated from Equation (4), (5), and (6):

$$HD(63, 0 + 63) = HD(63, 63) = HD(00111111b, 00111111b) = 0 \qquad (4)$$
$$HD(12, 36 + 12) = HD(12, 48) = HD(00001100b, 00110000b) = 4 \qquad (5)$$
$$HD(85, 85 + 85) = HD(85, 170) = HD(01010101b, 10101010b) = 8 \ . \qquad (6)$$

As in the previous case, the equation results suggest that together with the increase of Hamming distance, being the result of difference between instruction argument set on data bus in the first machine cycle, and the result of instruction operation, the voltage amplitude during the third machine cycle also increases.

5   Conclusion

As mentioned above, the main goal of the research is to determine a currently executed instruction on the basis of the emission of conducted disturbances on the power supply lines. However this subject matter requires a precise measurement and understanding of processes occurring inside the microprocessor during realization of the sequential instructions.

The presented results of the influence on parameters such as data bus state, instruction argument, the result of operation on the voltage waveform on the power supply lines of microprocessor, enable to understand the processes occurring during the realization of following instructions by microprocessor. In the technical specification of microprocessor units no information presented in this research is given, or it has only an elementary character. As the research result illustrate, not only instruction code, but also arguments on which the operation is executed, affect the supply voltage waveform during the realization of the instruction cycle.

The conducted emission of disturbances of power supply voltage (via supply lines) can be called compromising emanation, and its precise analysis may allow for reproducing the program code executing by microprocessor (reverse engineering). These issues will be taken into consideration in further authors research.

References

1. Piotrowski, R., Szczepański, S.: Input gate current uses to differential power analysis cryptographic device. XI International PhD Workshop. Wisła (2009)
2. Bendhia, S., Labussiere-Dorgan, C., Sicard, E., Tao, J.: Modeling the electromagnetic emission of a microcontroller using a single model. IEEE Transactions on Electromagnetic Compatibility (2008)
3. Maćkowski, M., Skoroniak, K.: Electromagnetic emission measurement of microprocessor units. In: Kwiecień, A., Gaj, P., Stera, P. (eds.) CN 2009. CCIS, vol. 39, pp. 103–110. Springer, Heidelberg (2009)
4. Maćkowski, M., Skoroniak, K.: Instruction prediction in microprocessor unit based on power supply line. In: Kwiecień, A., Gaj, P., Stera, P. (eds.) CN 2010. CCIS, vol. 79, pp. 173–182. Springer, Heidelberg (2010)

Instruction Prediction in Microprocessor Unit

Andrzej Kwiecień, Michał Maćkowski, and Krzysztof Skoroniak

Silesian University of Technology, Institute of Computer Science,
Akademicka 16, 44-100 Gliwice, Poland
{akwiecien,michal.mackowski,krzysztof.skoroniak}@polsl.pl
http://www.polsl.pl/

Abstract. Protection of computer systems from an unauthorized access to the classified information is a very essential issue. The research deals with some aspect of this problem resulting from the fact, that for instance, an author of a software for embedded system is not aware that it is possible to identify partly or entirely, program code. It can be done in non-invasive way, without influence on the microprocessor internal structure and program memory. The authors intend to prove that it is possible to recognise the instructions executing by certain type of microprocessor, analysing only the character of disturbances in the power supply lines. The research results inspire to the more careful study of ways and methodology for developing software, which should highly hinder the software reverse engineering.

Keywords: reverse engineering, program code, microcontroller, conducted emission, electromagnetic disturbances, electromagnetic interference.

1 Introduction

The fast expansion of microelectronic in various fields of technology, which is the result of rapid technological development, caused that more and more people deal with the exploitation and development of devices based on a microprocessor unit. The maximum of costs, during the construction of devices based on a microprocessor unit, is related to system design and time spent on writing software which would execute the assumptions presented to the programmers. In this case, the manufacturer must be aware of the security of its product and program contained in the memory of microprocessor.

However, the lack of information about the security offered by a particular microprocessor is the reason for the wrong choice of the central processor unit which is not dictated by a security of a system, but a low price. Generally, each vendor of microprocessors can offer some methods of securing the program code and data from being accessed, in order to protect information. Though, there is no information on the level of such security and tests proving their effectiveness. In this situation, the manufacturer of a particular device should be aware of threats, which may arise when choosing the microprocessor, including the loss of classified information such as program code and encryption key.

A. Kwiecień, P. Gaj, and P. Stera (Eds.): CN 2011, CCIS 160, pp. 427–433, 2011.

Obtaining information about the operation of a device through the influence of its work or monitoring the parameters of its activity, is called side-channel attack. The existence of the "side" channel through which such information is obtained, is usually unintended and results from the construction of a device or technology, in which it was built. An example of this situation can be any electrical powered device – in this case electromagnetic signals result from the currents flow and existing voltages. Signals used to transfer information from one point to another by conduction or radiation in the form of electromagnetic waveforms, in a deliberate manner, create the transmission channel. On the other hand, the situation when the signals are unintentional and, what is more, carry the information about the state of device operation, refers to side channel and information passing. Emission of such signals is often called compromising emanation. Thus, all unintentional signals that can reveal information in the case of capturing and analyzing them, are considered as compromising emanation. The source of these signals can be any electrical device used to transmit, receive, store or process information. For example, in this case the network controller placed in the network card can be also considered as a microprocessor unit, which is responsible for data processing of transmitted frames.

Methods of analysis of the microprocessor program code based on registration of power supply changes presented in this paper, use the conducted compromising emanation for reconstructing processes occurring in the microprocessor. Such propagation of conducted signals is the result of instantaneous changes in current consumption from the power source, depending on the currently use of elements constituting the central unit [1,2].

2   Test Bench and Research Procedure

The test bench used in the research was presented and discussed in the authors paper *The Analysis of Microprocessor Instruction Cycle* [3]. That paper presents the ways of measurement of power supply disturbances and describe the elements constituting the test bench. The analysis of microprocessor program code on the basis of measurement of power supply changes, requires the knowledge on microprocessor architecture, instruction cycle organization and microprocessor instruction list.

The 8 bit processor PIC16F84A used in the research, is one of the very popular Mid-Range processors. Because of the fact that the simplest PIC16 family of processors is devoid of advanced peripheral blocks, authors could focus mainly on the analysis of microprocessor program code based on the measurement of power supply changes, without interfering into the construction and operation of peripheral circuit. PIC16F84A processor is made in the Harvard architecture, i.e. it has a separated data and program memory, and is characterized by a reduced instruction set RISC (Reduced Instruction Set Computers). The processor instruction list includes 35 commands, most of which are executed in one cycle. The exceptions are several jump and call subroutine instructions that are executed in two instruction cycles.

Microcontroller PIC16F84A instruction list contains:

- 1-cycle instructions (2 μs):ADDWF, ANDWF, CLRF, CLRW, COMF, DECF, INCF, IORWF, MOVF, MOVWF, NOP, RLF, RRF, SUBWF, SWAPF, XORWF, BCF, BSF, ADDLW, ANDLW, CLRWDT, IORLW, MOVLW, SLEEP, SUBLW, XORLW,
- 2-cycle instructions (4 μs): DECFSZ (1 or 2 cycles), INCFSZ (1 or 2 cycles), BTFSC (1 or 2 cycles), BTFSS (1 or 2 cycles), CALL, GOTO, RETFIE, RETLW, RETURN.

High performance of the used processor results from using instruction pipeline and 14-bit wide operation code, which, apart from instruction code can also include the argument. The microprocessor PIC16F84A used in the research has one executive stream, which means that during one command cycle only one instruction is realized. One instruction cycle (16 μs) consists of four machine cycles (4 μs):

- Q1 – instruction decode cycle,
- Q2 – instruction read data cycle,
- Q3 – process the data,
- Q4 – instruction write data cycle and fetching the next instruction from the program memory.

Due to the fact that in the last cycle (Q4) another instruction is fetched from the program memory, thus not only currently realized instruction but also next instruction has the influence on the current flow. In the research presented in this work all 1 and 2 cycles instructions were taking into account.

The way of receiving (writing) the instructions executed by microprocessor unit and the program structure during the test was presented in the previous authors paper [3] in the research procedure. In this paper the authors consider the completely different problem, that is they intend to predict the currently executed instruction on the basis of voltage disturbances in the power supply lines. To achieve these goals, first it is necessary to write each of the instructions in a certain way into the memory (Fig. 1). Thus, a database of instructions samples is created, which can be then compared with various instructions of test program (Fig. 2).

After determining the time waveform of processor voltage supply during the whole program operation, a part of the time waveform of a tested instruction is excised. Then, the minimum and maximum value of voltage for each machine cycle is saved – this includes six values that characterize a particular instruction. As it was mentioned when discussing the test bench, during the fourth machine cycle not only the result is written, but also another instruction is fetched from the memory. Therefore, the fourth machine cycle was not taken into consideration, because the address of another instruction in the memory influences also on the shape and level of voltage in this cycle.

In the previous research [4], each instruction was written with the use of amplitude spectrum designated for the voltage waveform while executing the

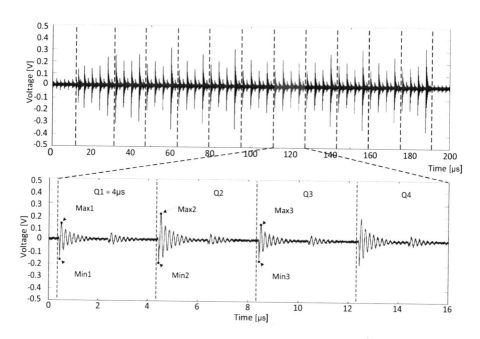

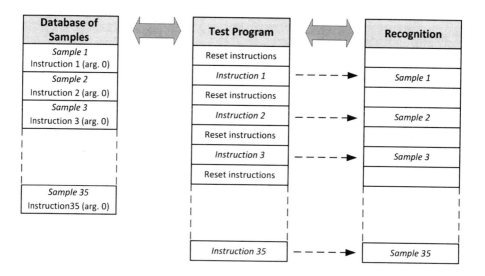

Fig. 1. The research procedure – microcontroller test program construction

Fig. 2. The process of instruction identification

instruction. However, the method of writing and comparing the instructions which applies the minimum and maximum value, developed by authors and presented in this paper, gives better effects.

Having created the database of samples, the authors then wrote a test program, used to determine the effectiveness of the method (Fig. 2). The program consisted of individual instructions separated by instructions that reset the register – the database included also instructions operating on arguments with zero value. Then, each of the instructions of a test program (in the form of 6 minimum and maximum values) was compared to all samples in database using the method of the least squares. It enabled to reveal that a sample from the database, which was the most similar to the tested instruction, was then typed as a recognized instruction.

3 The Research Results

According to the research procedure, each instruction of a tested program was compared to all samples included in the database. The first column of Table 1 presents the following instructions of a test program that consists of all 35 microprocessor instructions. The following columns illustrate 6 instructions, which obtained the minimum values, using the least squared method.

Because of the fact that the least squares method was used, thus the smaller value this method returns (the number in brackets in Table 1), the more relationship is between instruction in a test program and instruction in database. In consequence of using presented research method, 32 of 35 instructions were recognised correctly – the proper equivalents of instructions were marked in grey.

The instructions are considered to be correctly recognised, only when their equivalents in database of the samples was found at the first step (column 2 in Table 1). For three instructions the corresponding samples in database were found in the further place. This refers to COMF, SWAPF, and XORWF instructions. In case of COMF instruction (complementary operation) using the least squares method, instructions DECFSZ and DECF were returned at the first step (both of these instructions realize the argument decrementing). As it was previously mentioned, instructions in the test program as well as those saved in the database of samples, operated on arguments with zero value. In this situation the operation of COMF and DECF is similar and leads to change of value of 8-bit argument from 0 up to 255. The negation of all 8 bits of argument in case of these two instructions causes, that it is necessary to switch a certain number of gates inside the microprocessor unit, which results, in this case, in rapid and similar current consumption from the power supply – this may explain incorrect instruction recognition.

4 Conclusion

This paper presents the method developed by authors, which determines the currently executing instruction based on the disturbances of the voltage supply.

Table 1. The results of instruction recognise for the following instruction of tested program

The following instructions of test program	RECOGNISED INSTRUCTIONS					
	Instruction 1 (result of least squares method)	Instruction 2 (result of least squares method)	Instruction 3 (result of least squares method)	Instruction 4 (result of least squares method)	Instruction 5 (result of least squares method)	Instruction 6 (result of least squares method)
1 ADDWF	ADDWF (9.5)	RLF (12.2)	XORWF (13.0)	SWAPF (13.0)	RRF (15.2)	MOVWF (15.6)
2 ANDWF	ANDWF (2.2)	BTFSC (3.0)	BTFSS (7.4)	MOVWF (50.3)	XORWF (67.7)	BCF (70.3)
3 CLRF 15	CLRF (6.1)	MOVWF (8.7)	RLF (31.2)	SWAPF (31.2)	ADDWF (34.7)	RRF (43.0)
4 CLRW	CLRW (5.2)	SUBWF (109.4)	BCF (154.1)	BSF (220.5)	ANDWF (224.8)	BTFSC (245.7)
5 COMF	DECFSZ (5.2)	DECF (5.6)	COMF (11.7)	RETURN (6492.2)	RETFIE (6671.9)	BSF (7039.1)
6 DECF	DECF (10.0)	DECFSZ (12.2)	COMF (23.0)	RETURN (6549.2)	RETFIE (6728.3)	BSF (7072.0)
7 DECFZ	DECFSZ (10.0)	DECF (10.4)	COMF (17.4)	RETURN (6401.5)	RETFIE (6576.8)	BSF (6920.6)
8 INCF	INCF (3.5)	INCFSZ (16.5)	BSF (43.8)	CLRF (118.9)	CLRWDT (132.8)	XORWF (134.5)
9 INCFZ	INCFSZ (10.4)	INCF (11.3)	BSF (34.3)	CLRF (106.8)	CLRWDT (133.7)	MOVWF (147.6)
10 IORWF	IORWF (1.3)	MOVF (4.3)	XORWF (6.1)	RRF (10.0)	ADDWF (11.3)	SWAPF (22.6)
11 MOVF	MOVF (3.5)	IORWF (4.8)	XORWF (5.2)	ADDWF (6.9)	RRF (8.2)	SWAPF (14.8)
12 MOVWF	MOVWF (2.2)	CLRF (14.3)	ADDWF (16.9)	SWAPF (20.4)	RLF (21.3)	RRF (21.7)
13 NOP	NOP (5.2)	IORLW (78.1)	ADDLW (81.6)	XORLW (91.6)	CLRWDT (95.9)	ANDLW (108.1)
14 RLF	RLF (0.9)	ADDWF (3.5)	RRF (4.8)	SWAPF (6.9)	MOVWF (9.5)	MOVF (13.9)
15 RRF	RRF (1.7)	ADDWF (3.9)	RLF (4.8)	MOVF (6.5)	IORWF (8.7)	MOVWF (12.6)
16 SUBWF	SUBWF (3.0)	BCF (92.9)	CLRW (110.7)	ANDWF (115.0)	BTFSC (121.1)	BTFSS (136.7)
17 SWAPF	RRF (0.9)	ADDWF (1.3)	RLF (3.0)	MOVF (4.8)	SWAPF (6.9)	IORWF (7.4)
18 XORWF	MOVF (1.7)	RRF (2.2)	IORWF (3.0)	ADDWF (3.5)	RLF (9.5)	XORWF (9.5)
19 BCF	BCF (10.4)	BTFSC (61.2)	SUBWF (63.8)	BTFSS (64.7)	ANDWF (72.5)	GOTO (141.5)
20 BSF	BSF (13.0)	INCFSZ (13.5)	INCF (27.3)	CLRF (85.5)	MOVWF (133.2)	RLF (161.9)
21 BTFSC	BTFSC (10.9)	ANDWF (13.5)	BTFSS (19.5)	MOVWF (55.6)	BCF (59.0)	XORWF (63.4)
22 BTFSS	BTFSS (5.6)	BTFSC (6.5)	ANDWF (8.2)	BCF (53.8)	MOVWF (54.7)	XORWF (76.4)
23 ADDLW	ADDLW (13.9)	XORLW (18.7)	IORLW (27.8)	MOVLW (49.0)	ANDLW (54.3)	NOP (78.1)
24 ANDLW	ANDLW (6.5)	XORLW (64.7)	ADDLW (65.1)	IORLW (66.0)	SUBLW (74.7)	NOP (85.9)
25 CALL	CALL (7.8)	SUBWF (588.5)	GOTO (685.3)	CLRW (798.6)	ANDWF (947.0)	BTFSC (968.8)
26 CLRWDT	CLRWDT (1.3)	IORWF (36.5)	XORWF (51.6)	MOVF (51.6)	RRF (53.8)	ADDWF (57.7)
27 GOTO	GOTO (4.8)	BTFSC (145.0)	BCF (150.6)	BTFSS (154.5)	SUBWF (162.3)	ANDWF (167.5)
28 IORLW	IORLW (2.6)	XORLW (3.9)	ADDLW (6.1)	MOVLW (15.2)	ANDLW (58.6)	NOP (76.4)
29 MOVLW	MOVLW (7.4)	IORLW (8.7)	XORLW (16.1)	ADDLW (27.8)	NOP (112.8)	ANDLW (119.4)
30 RETFIE	RETFIE (9.5)	RETURN (11.3)	SLEEP (183.2)	INCF (204.4)	RETLW (208.3)	INCFSZ (247.8)
31 RETLW	RETLW (5.6)	SLEEP (76.0)	RETURN (135.0)	RETFIE (148.9)	CLRWDT (278.6)	INCF (289.9)
32 RETURN	RETURN (10.4)	RETFIE (11.3)	INCF (195.7)	SLEEP (204.9)	RETLW (223.1)	INCFSZ (249.6)
33 SLEEP	SLEEP (11.7)	RETLW (56.9)	RETFIE (147.1)	RETURN (154.1)	INCF (232.6)	INCFSZ (238.7)
34 SUBLW	SUBLW (6.1)	MOVF (54.3)	BTFSS (59.9)	IORWF (60.8)	BTFSC (66.8)	ANDWF (67.7)
35 XORLW	XORLW (1.7)	IORLW (4.8)	ADDLW (4.8)	MOVLW (11.3)	ANDLW (69.4)	NOP (89.8)

The methodology and conducted research that enable to determine and compare the spectrum of amplitude of a particular instruction were presented in the previous papers of authors [5,4]. The research conducted at that time was limited only to a one cycle instructions, and the result of a correctly recognised instructions was at the level of 80%. In this paper the authors focused mainly on improving the effectiveness of proper instructions recognition, and conducting the research for the entire microprocessor instruction list.

Enhancement of accuracy is achieved by placing the test bench in a shielded area (GTEM cell) so the test area was separated from the influence of external interference. The research procedure was also modified by changing the analysis of voltage disturbances in power supply lines in frequency domain into time domain. In consequence, this approach improved the instruction recognition.

In the conducted research it was possible to foreseen the currently executing instruction with the 91%. According to the research, 32 of 35 instructions for which the smallest value was obtained in the method of the least squares, have been correctly recognised. In the further research the authors intend to focus on developing the presented research method, in which also the instruction arguments will be considered.

References

1. Kocher, P.C., Jaffe, J., Jun, B.: Differential power analysis: leaking secrets. In: Wiener, M. (ed.) CRYPTO 1999. LNCS, vol. 1666, p. 388. Springer, Heidelberg (1999)
2. Piotrowski, R., Szczepański, S.: Input gate current uses to differential power analysis cryptographic device. XI International PhD Workshop. Wisła (2009)
3. Kwiecień, A., Maćkowski, M., Skoroniak, K.: The Analysis of Microprocessor Instruction Cycle. In: Kwiecień, A., Gaj, P., Stera, P. (eds.) CN 2011. CCIS, vol. 160, pp. 427–433. Springer, Heidelberg (2011)
4. Maćkowski, M., Skoroniak, K.: Instruction prediction in microprocessor unit based on power supply line. In: Kwiecień, A., Gaj, P., Stera, P. (eds.) CN 2010. CCIS, vol. 79, pp. 173–182. Springer, Heidelberg (2010)
5. Maćkowski, M., Skoroniak, K.: Electromagnetic emission measurement of microprocessor units. In: Kwiecień, A., Gaj, P., Stera, P. (eds.) CN 2009. CCIS, vol. 39, pp. 103–110. Springer, Heidelberg (2009)

Optimization for Database Migration Using Network Socket Option

Błażej Kwiecień

Silesian University of Technology, Institute of Informatics,
ul. Akademicka 2A, 44-100 Gliwice, Poland
blazej.kwiecien@polsl.pl
http://www.polsl.pl

Abstract. In this article the author analyzes a problem of the database migration using a socket option. Database migration always means a planned downtime and is a very special phase in the life of an SAP system. It is very important to reduce the downtime to the absolute minimum. The most efficient way to perform the database migration is to use the socket option, which works similarly to a network pipe and is realized with utilization of TCP/IP sockets.

Keywords: database migration, heterogeneous system copy, socket, downtime.

1   Introduction

Heterogeneous system copy (migration is another term for a heterogeneous system copy) describes a system copy where either operating system or database type will be changed during the copy. In this article the author focuses on the database migration. Database migration almost always requires an export and import of the database. This means that the old system must have the capacity to export the data and store it somewhere, where the new system can read it from. Briefly speaking, a heterogeneous system copy works as follows – Fig. 1:

1. The database of the source system is exported into a database and operating-system-independent format using SAP tools.
2. A new SAP system is installed, using the export from step 1 to load the database.

While exporting or importing, the SAP system must be offline. No SAP user activity is allowed.

As the migration always means a planned downtime and is a very special phase in the life of an SAP system, it is very important to reduce the downtime to the absolute minimum [2]. The most important recommendation we would like to provide is to use only the optimizations that are required to meet the downtime target. The best way to minimize downtime is to make the export in parallel with the import. This is possible by using a network socket option.

A. Kwiecień, P. Gaj, and P. Stera (Eds.): CN 2011, CCIS 160, pp. 434–438, 2011.

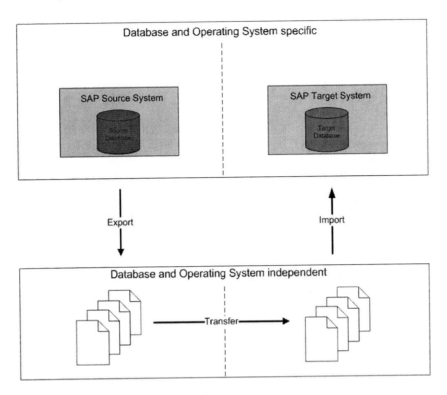

Fig. 1. SAP heterogeneous system copy overview [1]

2   Database Migration

According to the "Introduction" section, migration is a process during which the operating system or database system or both are changing – Table 1.

Table 1. SAP Migration Terminology

Migration Types	Change of Operating System OS	Change of Database DB
SAP OS Migration	Yes	No
SAP DB Migration	No	Yes
SAP OS and DB Migration	Yes	Yes

In this article the author focuses on database migration – Fig. 2. This means that only a database platform will be changed during migration process – operating system platform stays the same.

In some cases before executing the heterogeneous system copy, it might be necessary to upgrade the database or the operating system of the source system first. On old SAP releases even an SAP upgrade might be necessary. This

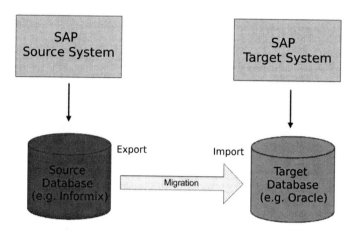

Fig. 2. Database Migration

might happen if the target platform requires a database version, which was not backward released for the SAP System release that is to be migrated. The decisive factors for performance in the SAP System are the parameter settings in the database, the operating system, and the SAP System itself (which in turn, depends on the operating system and the database system). During an OS/DB migration, the old settings cannot simply be transported unchanged. Determining the new parameter values requires an iterative process, during which the availability of the migrated system is restricted. The below mentioned points are the primary reasons for changing the operating system or the database [1]:

– hardware enhancements,
– performance improvement,
– availability of new technologies,
– administrative efficiency,
– cost reduction,
– guarantee against hardware/software obsolescence.

3   Network Socket Option

The data import phase is a long-running task. Together with the export, it influences the overall downtime phase of a heterogeneous system copy. Therefore, it is important to optimize the downtime by export in parallel with import. Data that is exported from the source system can be, for example, stored on a disk and then transported to the target server using one of the following methods:

– transportable device (disc, tape),
– network share,
– ftp.

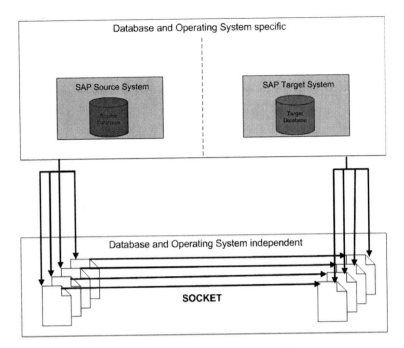

Fig. 3. Network socket option [1]

However, the most efficient way is to use the socket option, which works similarly to a network pipe and is realized by using TCP/IP sockets. The data is sent to the target server by the exporting process using the network sockets. The importing process receives the data and adds it to the target tables at once. This method saves time because it is not necessary to store the data on an external device and the import can be started immediately. To use this option it is necessary to have a stable network connection – Fig. 3.

An author makes a comparison of the socket method to the standard disk method with store disk dump on a device (disk, tape). A migrated database has 190 GB capacity and the operating system is AIX 5.3 version. An import and export servers (IBM eServer p5 Model 570) were similar with 4 CPUs (POWER 5) and 8 GB memory.

Figure 4 shows the comparison of the socket to the disk method. To a disk time the author added the time that is necessity to copy data dump between the servers, because during this time the SAP system is also turned off, and the database is not available. In test environment the author measured a reduction of the runtime by 40%. This can lead to a substantial reduction of downtime during a migration. In the socket-based migration, the export and the import are done in parallel. The advantage in the above case is that we can save nearly the complete export time. The CPU usage and the I/O transfer rate are the same in both methods.

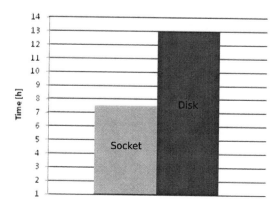

Fig. 4. Migration Method Comparison

4   Conclusions

Database migration is a process during which the SAP system and database is not available. This is a key moment because in the company focused on production, collecting and management of the information from database it is a crucial element of the decision-making process [3,4]. For this reason, minimization of the system downtime is essential to reduce costs of database being unavailable. It is possible by making the export parallel with the import utilizing network socket option. As it has been shown in the conducted experiment this solution can reduce downtime by 40% and minimize the cost associated with SAP system and the database unavailability.

References

1. Christian, A., Gaida, W., Moldowan, H.J., Rech, T.: DB2 Optimization Techniques for SAP Database Migration and Unicode Conversion, IBM Red Book
2. Kletti, J.: MES – Manufacturing Execution System. Springer, Heidelberg (2007)
3. Lech, P.: Zintegrowane systemy zarządzania ERP/ERP II. Wykorzystanie w biznesie, wdrażanie. Wydawnictwo Difin, Warszawa (2003)
4. Zaborowski, M.: Sterowanie nadążne zasobami przedsiębiorstwa. Wydawnictwo pracowni komputerowej J. Skalmierskiego (2008)

Self-adapting Algorithm for Transmission Power Control in Integrated Meter Reading Systems Based on Wireless Sensor Networks

Artur Frankiewicz

Silesian University of Technology, Institute of Computer Science
artur.frankiewicz@polsl.pl

Abstract. This paper describes algorithm used for computing optimal transmission power in battery powered wireless sensor networks. The algorithm is based on standard ATPC, but allows for further data consumption reduction in non-critical application. The algorithm keeps link quality at required level providing the lowest possible transmission power. With use of transmission power tables it provides reliable operation in networks, where no acknowledge signal is sent after transmitting data. The algorithm has been designed for integrated meter reading systems, where data is being sent over long distances on public radio frequency.

Keywords: wireless sensor networks, transmission power, ATPC.

1 Introduction

Wireless Sensor Network is a group of spatially distributed devices able to monitor physical values. All devices in WSN can analyze and pass messages. This ability allows directing measured values toward gateway node, which communicates with remote server. As the devices in WSN are randomly distributed, the distance from closest neighbor can vary from few meters to few hundred meters.

One of the examples of WSN usage is remote medium usage monitoring. Most of such networks are built on battery powered devices, where energy saving is one of the most crucial problems in network design and implementation. This paper presents modifications to a standard Adaptive Transmission Power Control algorithm that could provide better performance for this specific type of network. Additionally, proposed modifications allow for efficient long distance communication, where high data delivery ratio is hard to achieve.

This paper is organized in six sections, which gradually describe the problems and provide solutions. The following section explains existing studies in area of transmission power control in wireless sensor networks and gives a classification of related works. Next section describes test scenario and used equipment. This section also explains in detail the problems that transmission power control algorithm has to face. Section number 4 describes proposed algorithm and provides some suggestions regarding implementation. In the next section algorithm is validated by simulator using results from empirical studies. The paper is summarized by conclusions and proposal of future work.

A. Kwiecień, P. Gaj, and P. Stera (Eds.): CN 2011, CCIS 160, pp. 439–447, 2011.

2 Related Studies

Theoretical studies and simulations provide valuable solutions to specify the minimum transmission power level that achieves the required communication reliability at a best possible efficiency. However, such efforts may not be effective in real running systems. This is caused by simplifying the assumptions, for example, taking into studies static values of transmission power, transmission range or link quality.

Besides the theoretical studies, there are a number of empirical researches about communication reality conducted with real sensor devices [1,2,3]. They reveal the instability of the received signal power and the link quality for a specified transmission power and communication distance. However, they ignore the impact of the radio and link dynamics in the context of different transmission power settings.

In order to achieve the optimal transmission power consumption for specified link qualities, further researches have been based on Adaptive Transmission Power Control algorithm for wireless sensor networks. It results in proper transmission power level being used by every node for each of its neighbors as well as good link qualities between the nodes caused by dynamic adjustments of the transmission power through on-demand feedback packets. The topic of transmission power control has been discussed many times in various publications. Depending on the assumption made, the different solutions have been suggested.

Following are few groups of solutions that are based on different thesis:

- network-level solutions – propose use of a single transmission power for the whole network, even though it doesn't make the full use of the configurable transmission power provided by radio hardware to reduce energy consumption [4,5,6,7],
- node-level solutions – assume that each node chooses a single transmission power for all the neighbors [6,7,8,9,10],
- neighbor-level solutions – suppose that nodes use different transmission powers for different neighbors [11,12],
- adaptive neighbor-level solutions – provides the algorithm that analyzes history of transmission power levels and link quality to determine new transmission power [13].

Presented algorithm belongs to fourth group. It works similar to the one presented in [13] but is adapted to works in integrated meter reading systems.

3 Experimental Setup

The designed wireless sensor network will be used for integrated meter reading system measuring heat consumption. Each node in the network consists of radio transceiver, microcontroller, battery and sensor. Measured data as well as data received from other devices is sent to neighboring nodes according to specified routing protocol. Due to power constraints no ACK/NACK signal is sent by receiving devices at the end of transmission. Feedback notifications, which contain delivery status and measured received power level, are sent in synchronizing packets. Such packets are sent periodically and are used for system maintenance i.e.: synchronization of device clocks, establishing new related gateways etc.

3.1 Measurement Scenario

This paper is based on radio wave propagation empirical study conducted in September 2009 by AIUT Ltd. The devices were distributed in various locations in the area, where wireless sensor network for heat meter readings is going to be built. The area is extensively build-up with block of flats. Data transmitters were located at the highest buildings in order to provide proper communication range. The experiment was carried out on 19 devices located as shown on Fig. 1. Collected data was also used in publications [14,15] to create radio wave propagation model for wireless sensor networks.

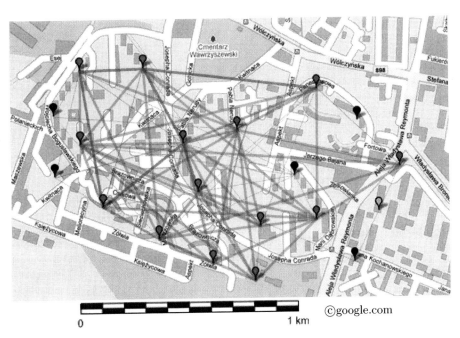

Fig. 1. Location of wireless sensor nodes in 24 hour test scenario. Data was gathered in Warsaw in Bielany district, where wireless sensor network is going to be built. Thickness of interconnection lines represents link quality between nodes.

3.2 Test Equipment

All nodes were based on AIR6050 radio transceiver (Fig. 2) and equipped with battery pack and data collection unit. Devices were manufactured by AIUT Ltd. and are widely used in wireless metering systems. Key features of single AIR device:

– RF output power: 500 mW,
– radio frequency: 869 MHz,
– modulation: GFSK,
– ability to measure received signal strength.

Fig. 2. AIR6050 radio transceiver

4 The Algorithm

4.1 Optimal Received Power

Minimum received power is the value that provides average packet reception ratio at required level. The algorithm assumes some tolerance in required packet reception ratio, what extends optimal transmission power from single point to specific range. In order to provide transmission power at possibly stable level, acceptable error has been implemented. Received power is a function of transmission power. For the purpose of simulation and analysis it is assumed that received power is proportional to transmitted power.

4.2 Optimal Transmission Power

Figure 3 shows that even using high transmission power the average Packet Reception Ratio will never reach 100% in our test scenario. Increasing transmission power above certain level will not increase packet reception ratio (PRR) significantly, but will increase overall power consumption. There might be a couple of reasons why PRR will newer reach 100%:

– 869 MHz radio frequency is commonly used by other devices which causes interference.
– The network consists of many nodes what makes collisions unavoidable.
– Data is transmitted over long distances (above 1 km) at relatively high transmission power, what causes propagation problems like multipath fading effects.

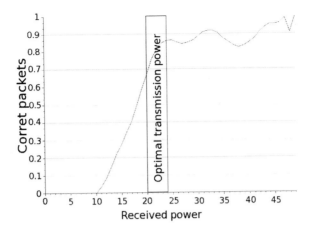

Fig. 3. Relation between measured power received and percentage of correctly received packets. Figure shows optimal received power for required PDR ~ 0.76 with acceptable error $= 0.1$. Graph was based on 22 995 packets collected from 18 transmitters in 24-hour test.

The local minimums around received power 28 and 38 are caused by non-ideal test environment and are neglected. For further simulation approximation function has been used instead of empirical data. Figure 3 also points out that in designing transmission power control algorithm the following should be taken into consideration – attempt to maintain packet delivery ratio at level higher that certain threshold would cause much more energy consumption with minimal PDR increase.

4.3   Principle of ATPC Based on Transmission Power Table

When Device A sends data to its neighboring device – Device B, it uses Transmission Power Table to determine required transmission power. Computed transmission power is saved to temporary cache to verify data delivery prior receiving synchronization packet from its neighbor. Device B receives data and writes to its received packet table transmission data CRC status. Next time Device B sends synchronization packet to device A, it adds information from Received Packets Table referring Device A. After sending synchronization packet back to device A data is being verified against temporary cache to find whether all packets were successfully delivered and new value is inserted into Transmission Power Table. Figure 4 ilustrates data flow in the algorithm.

4.4   Construction of Transmission Power Table

This is cyclic table – newly inserted values override existing values. It consists of two fields only: transmission power and boolean value representing delivery status.

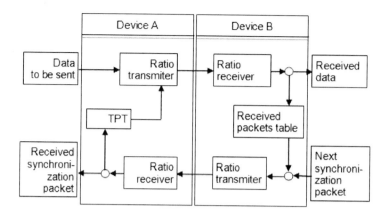

Fig. 4. Design of ATPC with Transmission Power Table

4.5   Implementation of the Algorithm

Computation of new transmission power takes the following parameters: Required packet reception ratio rrq – determines average percentage of successfully delivered packets. Choosing this value too high will cause devices to use maximum transmission power. Too low value will decrease overall link quality and will cause too many missed packets.

Correct delivery threshold – determines acceptable variations in PRR. Choosing this value to be too high will cause algorithm to be more stable at cost of higher PRR variations. Choosing too low value will make algorithm overactive. Empirical analysis shows that any value in range 0.02–0.1 will be appropriate.

Adjust Factor A_{f} – this value determines how fast the algorithm is going to react to environment changes like link quality degradation or increase in noise signals. Assuming maximum allowed number of consecutive missed packets will allow us to compute this value using the following formula:

$$A_{\mathrm{f}} = \frac{1}{2} n \frac{L_{\mathrm{TPT}}}{C_{\mathrm{MP}}} \tag{1}$$

where n is number of different transmission power settings, L_{TPT} is length of transmission power table and C_{MP} is number of missed packets after which device will use maximum possible transmission power. Transmission power is defined with the following formula:

$$P = \frac{\sum_{n=0}^{L_{\mathrm{TPT}}} P_n}{L_{\mathrm{TPT}}} + \left(\frac{\sum_{n=0}^{L_{\mathrm{TPT}}} D_n}{L_{\mathrm{TPT}}} - r_{\mathrm{rq}} \right) A_{\mathrm{f}} \tag{2}$$

where P_n is recorded transmission power at n^{th} position in TPT. D_n is 1 if n^{th} packet was delivered correctly and 0 otherwise. rrq is required packet reception ratio (PRR). The algorithm can also be presented by the following function:

```
function int ComputeNextTransmissionPower()
begin
  {required PRR}
  Const float RequiredPacketRatio := 0.7;
  {acceptable PRR error}
  Const float AcceptableError := 0.05;
  {determines adaption speed}
  Const float AdjustFactor := 40.0;

  float AvaragePower = Table.GetAvgTransmissionPower();
  float ReceptionRatio = Table.GetCorrectPacketRatio();

{keep constnt transmission power if average reception
ratio is within in acceptable error}
  if (
     ReceptionRatio + AcceptableError > RequiredPacketRatio &&
     ReceptionRatio - AcceptableError < RequiredPacketRatio)
     return AvaragePower;

  return (PowerAvg + (RequiredPacketRatio -
PacketRatioAvg) * AdjustFactor);
end.
```

5   Simulation Results

The algorithm has been implemented as a PC application. Packet delivery probability as a function of received power has been implemented using pseudo-random generator. In simulation 500 packets has been sent. After sending each packet TPT was updated. The delivery status was set using random generator based on distribution function (Fig 3). Other parameters for the simulation have been chosen as following: Required PRR = 0.7, A_f = 40, Table length = 15 entries, Acceptable error = 0.05.

Figure 5 shows simulation results. Packet Reception Ratio is the relation between number of packets with correct checksum and total number of packets sent. Transmission power is value currently computed by the algorithm. Figure 5 shows steady operation in samples 0–200, sudden increase in radio wave attenuation (sample 200) and sudden radio wave attenuation decrees (sample 400). The result shows that even though external conditions may change average packet, reception ratio is kept at constant level. Af value is set to 40 to allow maximum of 9 missed packets until full transmission power is reached.

Simulation results show that even in changing environment, effective packet reception ratio oscillates around specified value. Transmission power shows sudden variations, which is normal in closed control loops.

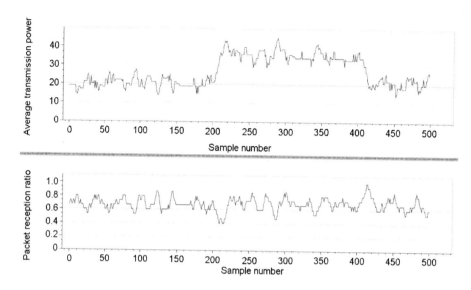

Fig. 5. Simulation results of packet reception ratio and current transmission power

6   Conclusion and Future Work

Even though the proposed algorithm may not be used in applications, where data reliability is crucial, it may be successfully applied in integrated meter reading systems. Keeping packet reception ratio at relatively low level allows to minimize transmission power, where further energy usage optimization in receiving node as well as neighboring nodes is possible by not sending acknowledge signal at the end of each packet.

The simulation based on real data has proved that the algorithm fulfilled the expectations in simulation environment. Further empirical tests with algorithm implemented in telemetric devices may prove this proposal to be applicable in real world scenario.

References

1. Zhao, J., Govindan, R.: Understanding Packet Delivery Performance in Dense Wireless Sensor Networks. In: ACM SenSys (2003)
2. Woo, A., Tong, T., Culler, D.: Taming the Underlying Challenges of Reliable Multihop Routing in Sensor Networks. In: ACM SenSys (2003)
3. Zhou, G., He, T., Krishnamurthy, S., Stankovic, J.A.: Impact of Radio Irregularity on Wireless Sensor Networks. In: ACM MobiSys, pp. 125–138 (2004)
4. Park, S.J., Sivakumar, R.: Quantitative Analysis of Transmission Power Control in Wireless Ad-hoc Networks. In: IWAHN, pp. 56–63 (2002)
5. Narayanaswamy, S., Kawadia, V., Sreenivas, R.S., Kumar, P.R.: Power Control in Ad Hoc Networks: Theory, Architecture, Algorithm and Implementation of the COMPOWProtocol. In: European Wireless Conference, pp. 156–162 (2002)

6. Bettstetter, C.: On the Connectivity of Wireless Multihop Networks with Homogeneous and Inhomogeneous Range Assignment. In: IEEE VTC, vol. 3, pp. 1706–1710 (2002)
7. Kirousis, L.M., Kranakis, E., Krizanc, D., Pelc, A.: Power Consumption in Packet Radio Networks. Theoretical Computer Science 243, 289–305 (2000)
8. Kubisch, M., Karl, H., Wolisz, A., Zhong, L.C., Rabaey, J.M.: Distributed Algorithms for Transmission Power Control in Wireless Sensor Networks. In: IEEE WCNC (2003)
9. Ramanathan, R., R-Hain, R.: Topology Control of Multihop Wireless Networks using Transmit Power Adjustment. In: IEEE INFOCOM, vol. 2, pp. 404–413 (2000)
10. Wattenhofer, R., Li, L., Bahl, P., Wang, Y.M.: Distributed Topology Control for Power Efficient Operation in Multihop Wireless Ad Hoc Networks. In: IEEE INFOCOM, pp. 1388–1397 (2001)
11. Xue, F., Kumar, P.R.: The Number of Neighbors Needed for Connectivity of Wireless Networks. In: Wireless Networks, vol. 10, pp. 169–181 (2004)
12. Blough, D., Leoncini, M., Resta, G., Santi, P.: The k-Neigh Protocol for Symmetric Topology Control in Ad Hoc Networks. In: ACM MobiHoc, pp. 141–152 (2003)
13. Lin, S., Zhang, J., Zhou, G., Gu, L., He, T., Stankovic, J.A.: Adaptive Transmission Power Control for Wireless Sensor Networks. In: Proceedings of the Fourth International Conference on Embedded Networked Sensor Systems
14. Brachman, A., Laskarzewski, Z., Chrost, L.: Measurement based error analysis in the 869 MHz 500 mW subband. In: HEAT-NETs 2010, pp. 391–404 (2010)
15. Brachman, A., Laskarzewski, Z.: Measurement based model for wireless propagation in the 869 MHz 500 mW band. In: HEAT-NETs 2010, pp. 405–418 (2010)

Simulating Performance of a BitTorrent-Based P2P TV System

Arkadiusz Biernacki

Silesian University of Technology, Institute of Computer Science, Gliwice, Poland
arkadiusz.biernacki@polsl.pl

Abstract. In this paper we describe a prototype of a simulation framework and some ideas which are to be used to study performance of a P2P TV system in a controllable and adjustable environment. We created a simplified model describing live video distribution in a P2P TV system. Using the model we analyse how some of the system parameters influence its behaviour. We present the preliminary results obtained at different granularity levels of measurements, describing the macroscopic system performance as well as the performance of its individual components.

Keywords: self-organizing system, computer network performance, P2P television.

1 Introduction

Traditional Internet TV services based on a simple unicast approach are restricted to moderate numbers of clients. The overwhelming resource requirements make these solution impossible when the number of users grows to millions. By multiplying servers and creating a content distribution network (CDN), the solution will scale only to a larger audience with regards to the number of deployed servers which may be limited by infrastructure costs. Finally, the lack of widespread deployment of IP-multicast limits the availability and scope of this solution for a TV service on the Internet scale. Therefore the use of P2P overlay networks to deliver live television in the Internet (P2P TV) is achieving popularity and has been considered as a promising alternative to IP unicast and multicast models [1]. The raising popularity of this solution is confirmed by the amount of new P2P TV applications that have became available, amongst them: PPLive, SOPCast, Tvants, TVUPlayer, Joost, Babelgum, Zattoo, and by constantly increasing amount of their users. As the P2P TV is not without drawbacks, currently the popularity are gaining solutions combining multicast, CDN and P2P approaches. However in certain performance evaluation scenarios, the components of such hybrid systems can be considered separately.

The nodes in a P2P TV network, called peers, self-organize themselves to act both as clients and servers to exchange TV content between themselves. As a result, with increasing number of network peers the number of servers in a network also increases leading to a smoother exchange process. Consequently, this approach has the potential to scale with a group size, as greater demand

A. Kwiecień, P. Gaj, and P. Stera (Eds.): CN 2011, CCIS 160, pp. 448–458, 2011.

also generates more resources. Thus it seems important to have an insight into some of performance aspect of such system. Since the most widely deployed commercial P2P TV software mentioned above have closed architecture and are proprietary, only an experimental behavioural (black-box) characterisation of such systems is in general possible. Reverse engineering of these systems may be costly and not give answers to all nurturing questions regarding their behaviour.

To avoid these disadvantages, we prepared an OMNeT++ based P2P TV simulation by means of which we observed how macroscopic behaviour of the system is influenced by its internal structure and rules describing the interactions between its elements. Our aim is to create a simulation framework for rapid P2P TV systems prototyping which will serve as a common platform for running and comparing different solutions. At the current stage of our works, the simulation will enable us to have a rough insight into some issues emerging while prototyping P2P TV systems and applications, e.g. what influence on the system have: performance and capacity of particular peers, audio-video stream forwarding capabilities of the peers, number of sources which are emitting the content and some properties of an overlay network topology.

2 Previous Works

While P2P TV has drawn interest from researchers, most studies have concentrated on measurements of real world data traces and their statistical analysis [2,3,4], reverse engineering [5,6,7], performance comparison of different systems [8,9,10,11], or crawling P2P systems [12]. These approaches has significant advantages with respect to the reliability of the extracted results however collecting representative global information from the complex and dynamic P2P overlay network is not simple and the data gathered may be incomplete. Thus some research works tend towards examination of the P2P system in controllable simulation environment. One of the obstacle in the way is availability of proper tools for this kind of experiments. Whereas there are simulators or simulation libraries dedicated for P2P systems, they rarely directly support simulation of P2P TV solutions. Nonetheless some of these tools may be adopted for this purpose. P2PTVSim is the P2P TV simulator initially developed by Polytechnic University of Turin, but then evolved to a more general P2P simulator and is used by P2P TV researchers [13]. The tool mainly simulates the flow of data traffic through a network of interconnected peers and aims to evaluate several, mainly push-based, chunk scheduling algorithms used for video streaming. It uses mostly chunk diffusion delay and an amount of lost chunks as an algorithm efficiency criterion. The simulator implements simplified coarse-grained representations of the underlying network and several predefined overlay topologies. Except of the type of simulated scheduling algorithm, one can configure such parameters as peers number, number of random neighbours that each peer is able to connect to, set of different bandwidth-classes of peers and upload bandwidth of the source peer. As a result, a user obtains information amongst others about the delay of every chunk and a statistics of uploaded and downloaded chunks for every peer. Another related simulator, SSSim [14], is dedicated for comparison of the streaming performance of different chunk and peer scheduling algorithms. The simulator is based on some simplifying assumptions, amongst them: all peers are synchronised and have the same output bandwidth and infinite input bandwidth. Additionally peers have the possibility to know the internal state of all the other peers in the system. Therefore both P2PTV and SS-Sim are primarily dedicated for fast prototyping of streaming algorithms for P2P systems. PeerSim [15] is a Java P2P simulator which main purpose and goal is an exploration of messaging protocols, gossiping and epidemic diffusion, and has not been dedicated to handle a continuous stream of information, so that it presents some scalability problems especially in streaming dimension (number of chunks), which characterise P2P TV applications. However, due to its focus on messaging and the large number of already implemented gossiping algorithms, it can be used to explore details of signalling traffic and overlay management of P2P TV systems. Some analysis of P2P TV systems were performed using PlanetLab environment, amongst them is [16], where the authors monitored SopCast application placed in 70 PlanetLab nodes.

The above mentioned simulators are flow based or application level simulators which means they work at an application level and disregard parts of underlay network stack. This give them good time and memory efficiency but simultaneously providing drawbacks in terms of simulation reality because of many simplified assumptions introduced e.g. knowledge of a system global state by its peers, coarse-grained representation of lower network layers or not including them at all, lack of the control traffic implementation. All the simulators are standalone, they are not based on any other general discrete simulator, thus simulating hybrid systems providing live video and TV may somehow be difficult.

Hence the main contribution of this work is presentation of our simulation solution based on OMNeT++, which in an assumption should take into account more realistic network scenarios. We plan to provide support for underlay and overlay layers using for this purpose INET and OverSim [17] libraries. Thus our framework will focus rather on more detailed implementation of a single TV streaming protocol than coarse-grained comparison of several protocols as in the works cited above. The work is an extension to [19].

3   Simulator

Due to number of different approaches to P2P TV distribution, it is impossible to simulate them all. Thus in our research we focus on the most popular and verified in practise BitTorrent-based (BT-based) solutions. Originally BT has shown to be very efficient in distributing large files, however currently it is also used for distributing video streams [20]. Amongst others, the most popular P2P TV systems like mentioned PPLive or SopCast are based on the BT protocol, with a channel selection bootstrap from a Web tracker, and peer download/upload video in chunks from/to multiple peers [12].

Generally there are four different types of components in a typical BT-based P2P TV system (e.g. GoalBit [21]), see Fig. 1(a) – a source (broadcaster), peers, superpeers, and a tracker. The source is responsible for content to be distributed i.e. for getting it from a storage or TV camera and to put it into the platform. The superpeers are highly available peers with a large capacity helping in the distribution of the content. The peers, representing the large majority of nodes in the system, are final users, who connect themselves to the streams for playout. The tracker is in charge of management of the peers in the system. For each TV channel the tracker stores a reference to the peers connected to it. The peer periodically learns about other peers connecting the tracker and parsing a peer list returned. The peer joins the swarm by establishing connections with some others peers.

All the above components were implemented in our simulator, however with functionality reduced to establishing and tearing down connections, monitoring the bandwidth status and basic control traffic exchange, see Fig. 1(b). While modelling data traffic we do not focus on individual packets (chunks), which does not make much sense in case of P2P content networks, but we model a stream of chunks. Every network node is described by several attributes, amongst them: performance, forwarding ability of audio-video stream, a maximum number of incoming and outgoing connections. Other globally controllable parameters involve a number of transmitted TV channels, a number of network nodes: peers, superpeers and sources. So far we have ignored an influence of underlying and overlying protocols and focused on an application logic. Another simplification is that simulation currently supports only a single tracker and does not use trackless DHT mode. All messages are responded immediately which implies that their simulation processing time is zero. In our approach we used an event driven approach, where a scheduler maintains a list of simulation events.

4   Theoretical Model and the Experiment Assumptions

For most of our experiment we simulated the system composed of a 1200 peers nodes, variable number of superpeers and sources, and a single TV channel. All the implemented overlay connections between the nodes in our simulation were directional. By outgoing connection for node P_a we denote a link between node P_a and any other node P_i by which P_a downloads data from P_i. By an incoming connection for node P_a we denote a link between node P_a and any other node P_i by which P_a uploads the data to P_i. When two nodes are connected by either type of the link we call them neighbours. We measure performance of single system nodes in terms of downloading and uploading content goodput (the application level throughput) which can be interpreted as packet stream intensity that a node is able to download or upload in a certain time unit.

The downloading goodput P_a^{DG} of node P_a is a sum of uploading goodput P_i^{UG} of all the directly connected nodes P_i to node P_a via its outgoing connections limited by its maximum download goodput $P_a^{\mathrm{DG_{max}}}$:

$$P_a^{\mathrm{DG}} = \min\left(\sum_{i=1}^{n} P_i^{\mathrm{UG}}, P_a^{\mathrm{DG_{max}}}\right) . \tag{1}$$

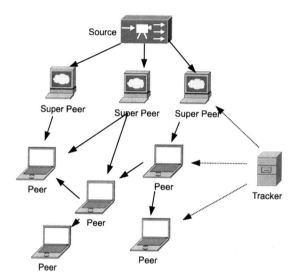

(a) BT-based P2P TV architecture, source [21]

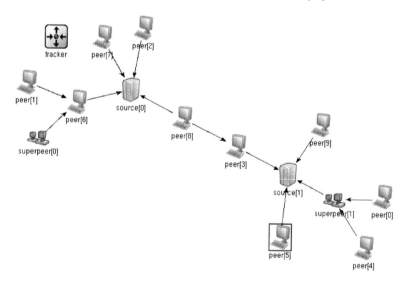

(b) Simulation

Fig. 1. System components

For the source nodes $P_a^{DG} = P_a^{DGmax}$ because they do not download any data from other nodes in the network.

The upload goodput for peers and superpeers is defined as

$$P_a^{UG} = RP_a^{DG}/n \quad 1 \le n \le N \;, \tag{2}$$

where R is the audio-video stream repeatability coefficient and n is number of incoming connections, see also Fig. 2. The download goodput of a single peer depends on P_a^{DGmax} parameter which in practise may be related to underlay network performance in which this peer is embedded. Our assumption is that a user is able to watch the channel if P_a^{DG} of its peer is greater than 0.5, otherwise he disconnects for certain time specified in the simulation configuration. Consequently, in our simulation we set P_a^{DGmax} parameter to a random value generated uniformly from a range 0.5 to 1.0. Upload goodput depends on an ability for repeating the received stream and may be interpreted as a result of asymmetry in download and upload capabilities of the underlying network. Generally, we assumed that for the common peers $R \le 1$ and $P_a^{DGmax} = 1$, for the superpeer $R \ge 1$ and $P_a^{DGmax} = 2$, and for the source peers $R = 1$ and $P_a^{DGmax} = 1.5$. Hence the superpeers are treated as servers with good upload abilities which can simultaneously distribute the same content to many peers using unicast method. Our implementation provides configurable upper bounds for the number of established both outgoing and incoming connections, which is regulated by the N parameter for every network node.

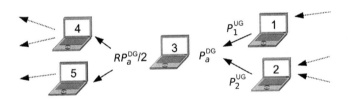

Fig. 2. Computation of the download and upload goodput

To clarify the theory behind the above mentioned coefficients we present a simple example. Our network has a topology as presented on Fig. 2. As all the nodes are common peers so, as we assumed earlier, for all of them P_i^{DGmax} parameter has a random value generated uniformly from a range 0.5 to 1.0. For the purpose of this example and simplicity of computation let us assume that for all five nodes $P_i^{DGmax} = 0.8, i = 1 \ldots 5$ and the repeatability coefficient $R = 1$. Let us also assume that upload goodput of the nodes 1 and 2 are $P_1^{UG} = 0.4$ and $P_2^{UG} = 0.3$ respectively. Thus, according to (1), the download goodput of node 3 will be

$$P_3^{DG} = \min\left(P_1^{UG} + P_2^{UG}, P_3^{DGmax}\right) = \min(0.4 + 0.3, 0.8) = 0.7 \;.$$

Node 3 forwards the stream to nodes 4 and 5 (so in this case $n = 2$) and, according to (2), its upload goodput is

$$P_3^{UG} = RP_3^{DG}/n = 0.35 \ .$$

Hence the nodes 4 and 5 receive from node 3 stream with upload coefficient 0.35.

The system topology is created dynamically from scratch. We implemented a random churn generator. In fixed time intervals a random number is drawn and depending on this number, a random node is either added or deleted. Peers and superpeers periodically query a tracker to obtain lists of their neighbours and the neighbours' parameters. Every peer creates a ranking of neighbouring peers and tries to connect to a peer with the highest upload goodput (2). After the connection, the peer monitors its download goodput in certain time intervals which is a parameter of the simulation. If the number of connections is equal to the maximum allowed number of connections, the peer disconnects from a neighbour which has the worst upload goodput and tries to reconnect to a better one, thus making network topology constantly evolve. At the current stage we do not implement the chocking – a popular BitTorrent mechanism involving temporary refusal to upload.

The main purpose of our work was to examine how the above mentioned parameters: the number of superpeers, the number of sources, R, and N will influence on its goodput represented by P_a^{DG} and P_a^{UG}. The results were presented at three different levels: the analysis of global values, where we summarised and aggregated multiple peers behaviour in a function of a few system parameters; the analysis of average values, where we compared the behaviour of a several peers; and the transient behaviour of single peers, where we monitored the behaviour of selected peers in the function of time. These simple analyses could be helpful for the P2P TV designers and developers facing the question of how many certain system special components like sources or superpeers should be used to provide the system users acceptable quality of audio-video transmission. From the other side, it can be also useful for the system access control – having defined the system infrastructure the system designer can assess the amount of users who can access the system simultaneously without degradation of its performance below an acceptable level.

5   Results

In the first experiments we obtained a macroscopic view of the system studying how upload to download ratio R (2) affects the system performance. Our system had 4 sources, 16 superpeers, the number of allowed connection for peers was set to 8 and, as it was mentioned earlier, the system had 1200 peers. We concluded that the decrease of R parameter from 1 to 0.9 provided relatively low impact on system performance, see Fig. 3(a), nonetheless another decrees from 0.9 to 0.8 resulted in dramatic reduction of our system performance measured both as upload and download goodput. An interesting question arises: for which value range of R the performance of the system deteriorates the fastest?

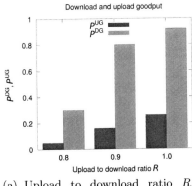

(a) Upload to download ratio R, $N=8$, 4 sources, 16 superpeers

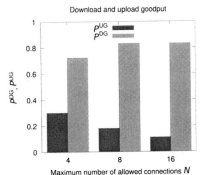

(b) Number of allowed connections, $R=0.9$, 4 sources, 16 superpeers

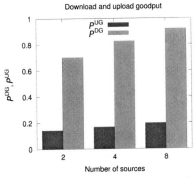

(c) Number of sources, $N=8$, $R=0.9$, 16 superpeers

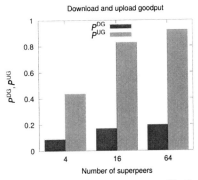

(d) Number of superpeers, $N=8$, $R=0.9$, 4 sources

Fig. 3. Aggregate goodput measurements in a function of different simulation parameters

In the second analysis we examine how the number of maximum allowed connections N (2) influence the system performance using the same set of parameters as in the first experiment. We claim that the parameter had minor impact on system download goodput however it affected upload goodput, see Fig. 3(b). Such behaviour has simple explanation, according to (2) there is an inverse proportion between the upload goodput and the number of incoming connections, thus with the increasing number of connections, the upload goodput decreases.

Increasing number of sources from 2 to 8 gradually increased the system goodput, see Fig. 3(c). However instead of adding content sources, which may be problematic due to synchronization of content transmission, we can increase the system performance by adding more superpeers. The system efficiency is quite sensitive to a number of superpeers, however adding more than 16 superpeers did not lead to any further improvement in the system goodput, see Fig. 3(d).

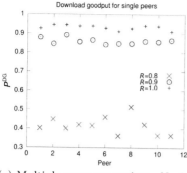

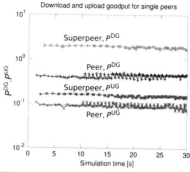

(a) Multiple peers comparison, $N=6$, 4 sources, 16 superpeers

(b) Transient analysis, $N=6$, $R=0.9$, 4 sources, 16 superpeers

Fig. 4. System goodput – detailed level

It should be recalled that the aforementioned values strictly depend on the others of the experiment parameters, amongst them the amount of peers.

The results of the simulation can be further analysed on more details levels. We extended the results presented on Fig. 3(a) obtaining the download goodput for a several selected peers separately, see Fig. 4(a). The values varied amongst the peers suggesting that in certain cases the global analysis might not be enough to achieve a reliable view of the examined system. In accordance with Fig. 3(a) there was a noticeable difference when stream repeatability coefficient R drops from 0.9 to 0.8. We could also observe that the last mentioned value of the repeatability coefficient tiggered the highest variation of download goodput for the examined peers. Taking one step further we were able to analysis a single scenario from Fig. 4(a) in terms of a peer transient behaviour. On Fig. 4(b) we presented download (1) and upload (2) goodput for randomly selected peer and superpeer. As expected the download goodput of the superpeer clearly surpasses the goodput of the common peer. However, the difference between upload goodput of the superpeer and the peer was not as dramatic, which proved that the the superpeer fulfilled its role distributing its content. Both upload and download goodput were characterized by small oscillations even though we did not observe any huge fluctuations.

6   Conclusions

In this paper we have presented a draft of an implementation of the BT-based P2P TV system using the OMNeT++ simulation environment. The preliminary results presented in this paper indicate that using the proposed simulator we are able to perform small-scale simulations of the simplified system showing its behaviour in micro- and macroscopic scale, which potentially may be helpful for fast prototyping of this kind of P2P TV systems. The results were obtained assuming a

number of simplifications in our modelled system, especially concerning chunk selection, chunk buffer management and underlay network modelling. However our
approach, i.e. a choice of popular discrete event simulator for the implementation,
allows us to gradually incorporate further details. In the future we plan to model
the P2P TV exchange protocol with greater attention to its details and provide
support for underlying and overlay layers using INET and OverSim libraries. In
an assumption our simulation framework should not only be dedicated to P2P
TV but also should provide the researches possibilities of testing hybrid scenarios
involving multicast and CDN solutions.

References

1. Liu, J., Rao, S.G., Li, B., Zhang, H.: Opportunities and Challenges of Peer-to-Peer
   Internet Video Broadcast. Proceedings of the IEEE 96(1), 11–24 (2008)
2. Liu, F, Li, Z.: A Measurement and Modeling Study of P2P IPTV Applications. In:
   International Conference on Computational Intelligence and Security, CIS 2008,
   vol. 1 (2008)
3. Vu, L., Gupta, I., Liang, J., Nahrstedt, K.: Measurement of a large-scale overlay
   for multimedia streaming. In: Proceedings of the 16th International Symposium
   on High Performance Distributed Computing, p. 242 (2007)
4. Wang, F., Liu, J., Xiong, Y.: Stable peers: Existence, importance, and application
   in peer-to-peer live video streaming. In: IEEE Infocom, USA (2008)
5. Agarwal, S., Singh, J.P., Mavlankar, A., Baccichet, P., Girod, B.: Performance and
   quality-of-service analysis of a live p2p video multicast session on the internet. In:
   IEEE IwQoS (2008)
6. Ali, S., Mathur, A., Zhang, H.: Measurement of commercial peer-to-peer live video
   streaming. In: Workshop on Recent Advances in Peer-to-Peer Streaming, Waterloo
   (2006)
7. Hei, X., Liu, Y., Ross, K.W.: Inferring Network-Wide Quality in P2P Live Streaming Systems. IEEE Journal on Selected Areas in Communications 25(9) (2007)
8. Alessandria, E., Gallo, M., Leonardi, E., Mellia, M., Meo, M.: P2P-TV Systems
   under Adverse Network Conditions: a Measurement Study. In: INFOCON 2009,
   pp. 100–108 (April 2009)
9. Ciullo, D., Mellia, M., Meo, M., Leonardi, E.: Understanding P2P-TV Systems
   Through Real Measurements. In: IEEE Global Telecommunications Conference,
   IEEE GLOBECOM 2008, pp. 1–6 (2008)
10. Horvath, A., Telek, M., Rossi, D., Veglia, P., Ciullo, D., Garcia, M.A., Leonardi, E.,
    Mellia, M.: Dissecting PPLive, SopCast, TVAnts. Technical report, NAPA-WINE
    project (2009)
11. Silverston, T., Fourmaux, O., Botta, A., Dainotti, A., Pescapé, A., Ventre, G.,
    Salamatian, K.: Traffic analysis of peer-to-peer IPTV communities. Computer Net-
    works 53(4), 470–484 (2009)
12. Hei, X., Liang, C., Liang, J., Liu, Y. Ross,K.W.: Insights into PPLive: A Mea-
    surement Study of a Large-Scale P2P IPTV System. In: Proc. of IPTV Workshop,
    International World Wide Web Conference (2006)
13. Kiraly, C., Abeni, L., Cigno, L., et al.: Effects of P2P Streaming on Video Quality.
    In: 2010 IEEE International Conference on Communications (ICC), pp. 1–5 (2010)

14. Abeni, L., Kiraly, C. Cigno, R.L.: SSSim: a Simple and Scalable Simulator for P2P Streaming Systems. In: IEEE 14th International Workshop on Computer Aided Modeling and Design of Communication Links and Networks, CAMAD 2009, Pisa (2009)
15. Montresor, A., Jelasity, M.: Peersim: A scalable p2p simulator. In: IEEE Ninth International Conference on Peer-to-Peer Computing, P2P 2009, pp. 99–100 (2009)
16. Lu, Y., Fallica, B., Kuipers, F.A., Kooij, R.E., Mieghem, P.V.: Assessing the quality of experience of sopcast. International Journal of Internet Protocol Technology 4(1), 11–23 (2009)
17. Baumgart, I., Heep, B., Krause, S.: OverSim: A flexible overlay network simulation framework. In: IEEE Global Internet Symposium, 2007, pp. 79–84 (2007)
18. Baumgart, I., Heep, B., Krause, S.: OverSim: A Flexible Overlay Network Simulation Framework. In: 2007 IEEE Global Internet Symposium, Anchorage, AK, USA, pp. 79–84 (2007), http://www.oversim.org/wiki/OverSimBibtex
19. Biernacki, A.: Simulation of P2P TV system using OMNeT++. In: Joint ITG, ITC, and Euro-NF Workshop "Visions of Future Generation Networks" (EuroView 2010), Würzburg, Germany (August 2010)
20. Dana, C., Li, D., Harrison, D., Chuah, C.N.: Bass: Bittorrent assisted streaming system for video-on-demand. In: 2005 IEEE 7th Workshop on Multimedia Signal Processing, pp. 1–4 (2006)
21. Bertinat, M.E., De Vera, D., Padula, D., Amoza, F.R., Rodrguez-Bocca, P., Romero, P., Rubino, G.: GoalBit: the first free and open source peer-to-peer streaming network. In: Proceedings of the 5th International Latin American Networking Conference, pp. 49–59 (2009)

Virtual Museum
as an Example of 3D Content Distribution
in the Architecture of a Future Internet

Arkadiusz Sochan, Przemysław Głomb, Krzysztof Skabek,
Michał Romaszewski, and Sebastian Opozda

IITiS PAS, Bałtycka 5, Gliwice, Poland
{arek,przemg,kskabek,michal,sebastian}@iitis.pl

Abstract. Digitisation of historical objects scattered among museums allows to create virtual exhibitions. Distributed Virtual Museum facilitates visualisation and arrangement of a digitised content in a 3D stereoscopic presentation environment. The system relies on a content-aware network (CAN) architecture created in the FIE project for content localization and delivery. Progressive mesh transmission is used to create adequate exhibition representations.

Keywords: virtual museum, progressive meshes, distributed models, CAN.

1   Introduction

Museums all over the world have unique historical objects, usually belonging to different collections indexed by e.g. epoch, culture, place, artistic or scientific significance. With respect to certain exposition theme (e.g. Flemish painting of the XV-th century) no museum has a complete set of objects so an organization of thematic exhibition requires gathering together objects from different places. This is a difficult operation with many logistic, technical, and legal problems. Yet such exhibitions are crucial among others for education, scientific research, or exploring our cultural heritage.

Our idea is to develop a system that aims to facilitate visualisation arrangement of a distributed 3D content in a virtual 3D presentation environment. Such system can also be useful in other applications including online shopping, virtual fairs and exhibitions.

1.1   Related Works

There are multiple projects concerning the 3D digitisation of cultural heritage. One of the pioneer research projects in this domain was called the Digital Michelangelo [1] and was conducted at Stanford University in collaboration with the producer company of a 3D scanner Cyberware. The project focused on the development of techniques for scanning large monuments. It utilised a calibrated

A. Kwiecień, P. Gaj, and P. Stera (Eds.): CN 2011, CCIS 160, pp. 459–464, 2011.

positioning device and the scanner which had both the depth and brightness sensors. Contractors attempted to overcome a number of research problems, starting from calibration of scanning devices to merging and mapping colors on 3D surface. This project was an inspiration to many studies in the field of 3D computer vision.

Construction of a digital 3D representation of architectural objects using scanner Cyrax 2500 was a subject of related projects concerning: the cathedral of Saint-Pierre in Beauvais [2], a monumental gate Porta Portello in Padule, Romanesque monuments and ruins in Tyre [3] or the statue of Buddha from Kamakura [4]. Also in Poland the National Centre for Research and Documentation of Monuments finances the 3D modeling work of the elevation in the Wilanów Palace [5].

Two EU projects were directly related to the task of using information technology in the protection of cultural property. The first is Virtual Heritage: High-Quality 3D Acquisition and Presentation (ViHAP3D) conducted in 2002–2005, aimed at the protection, presentation, sharing and promotion of a cultural heritage, using the interactive graphics of spatial quality. The second: European Research Network of Excellence in Processing Open Cultural Heritage (EPOCH) conducted in 2004–2008, focused on the effort of about 100 European cultural institutions, interchanging their efforts to improve the quality and effectiveness of information technology for purposes of communication and sharing a cultural heritage.

An interesting Polish initiative concerning digitisation of a cultural heritage is ARCO Center[1]. In this approach the exhibitions are presented as interactive 3D spaces or rich multimedia web presentations. All exhibitions can be accessed both locally in the museums and remotely over the Internet. Some virtual collections which incorporate the 3D interactive visualisation of exhibits include: Luovre[2], The Virtual Museum of Iraq[3], or the National Museum of Agriculture and Agro-Food Industry in Szreniawa (Poland)[4].

The works related to the digitisation of cultural heritage have also been implemented in the Institute of Theoretical and Applied Informatics PAS in the years 2007 to 2009 under the Grant No. N N516 1862 33. The research concerned the machine vision techniques for collecting, processing and sharing of spatial objects with multimodal hierarchical representation [6].

1.2   An Overview of the Distributed Virtual Museum Functionality

The system presents the user with an interactive 3D exhibition environment. The basic scenario contains three data structures that are exchanged between database servers and the user:

---

[1] http://www.virtual-museums.eu/

[2] http://www.louvre.fr/

[3] http://www.virtualmuseumiraq.cnr.it/

[4] http://szreniawa.wirtualne-muzea.pl/

- The exhibition description – a general definition of the virtual exhibition consisting of links to multiple scenes.
- The scene description – a presentation environment for single exposition room including links to 3D objects.
- 3D objects – the museum pieces used to instantiate them in the exposition room.

The presentation begins with a download of the exhibition description file and next scene description files, by the client application called 'Smart Exhibition Explorer' (SEE). After the current exhibition scene is reconstructed, museum pieces visible to the observer are downloaded and visualised using the stereoscopic presentation devices. Visitor sees the scene in the first-person perspective, with an ability to explore and interact with the scene during the presentation. Currently only common Human Input Devices (HIDs) (e.g. keyboard, mouse, joystick) will be supported but in the future, motion capture systems (haptic devices in particular) may be used.

2 The Development of a Distributed Virtual Museum

Preparation of interactive virtual exhibitions consists of several steps:

- Digitisation and further refinement of 3D objects (museum pieces).
- Preparation of an exhibition environment (e.g. a presentation scenery, object and light placements, optional sound effects).
- Network publication of both exhibition environment and museum pieces, for distributed access.
- Transmission of the prepared content using a progressive coding of 3D objects to present them with different level of details (LoD).
- Presentation of a selected content using the SEE.

2.1 Digitisation of Cultural Heritage Objects for Virtual Museum

Objects are digitised by an acquisition of measurement data in the form of 3D meshes covered with texture. The data is collected using 3D scanners (e.g. FARO Laser Scan Arm and Konica-Minolta VI-9i). After the triangulation process used to convert the data into the mesh representation, regularisation and registration is done (the process consist of placing the partial measurement grids into one common coordinate system and it can be repeated several times with different criteria, until an accurate surface matching is achieved). Next the partial grids for directional observations are merged into one mesh.

Further processing includes filling the surface holes, smoothing and remeshing, closing the mesh and making it a manifold, covering it with NURB surfaces and exporting to CAD format. Now the final decoration of the model surface and the rendering is performed. The model surface may also be covered with texture, obtained from object photographs.

2.2   Progressive Transfer of 3D Objects

Digitised 3D objects are stored into content provider databases using standard 3D mesh file formats (VRML, X3D). Since the stored 3D Mesh files are large (e.g. with a file size on the order of 1 GB) the progressive mesh transmission [7] may be used to deliver an object representation to the SEE.

The implementation of progressive meshes realises the concept of a hierarchical representation which reflects the human perception of shapes and spatial relationships. This representation is available as a collection of partial information from multiple imaging sensors and is enabled for reading at different levels-of-detail (LoD).

2.3   Content Distribution

Figure 1 presents the key elements associated with the distribution of virtual museum content. Three network object types can be distinguished:

- Exhibition and Scenes Servers (ESS) – contains an information about the exhibition, including compositions of scenes. The particular scenes of the exhibition may be located on different exhibition servers. A description of the scene contains general characteristics (description, audio commentary, etc.), information about the 3D appearance (mesh, lighting, texture, etc.), scenarios of interaction, and information about 3D objects necessary to instantiate them (localization, identifiers or metadata).
- StoreHouse Server (SHS) – contains an information about museum pieces placed in chosen scenes including its general characteristics and information on the 3D appearance (mesh, material, texture). Objects can be retrieved using progressive coding.
- Smart Exhibition Explorer (SEE) – client application used to explore the exhibition environment.

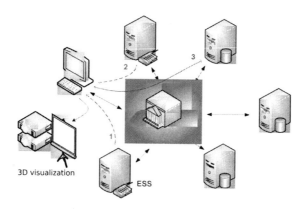

Fig. 1. The communication in the Distributed Virtual Museum

2.4   Network Environment

The main assumptions of the developed Distributed Virtual Museum are to achieve a functionality of a distributed virtual environment and to rely it on a CAN architecture created in the FIE project.

CAN, also known as Future Content Networks (FCN) or Content Centric Networks, support the content identification, searching, location, management and delivery operations. There are two approaches to their implementation: CAN operating in an application layer (e.g. p2p [8]) or a model that delivers a new architecture with functions supporting content distribution (content naming, identification, resolution, routing and consumption) e.g. Netinf [9].

The CAN mechanisms allow for conceptually simple and efficient retrieval of data by the SEE, while internal network management optimises the load balancing by replicating most often referred (popular) objects. The content registered on SHS and ESS (exhibition and scene files along with presented 3D objects) is uniquely identifiable. It can be retrieved using a unique descriptor or (optionally) an associated metadata (e.g. friendly name,version, creation date or description).

Fig. 2. Example museum objects and their representation using SEE prototype environment

2.5   Smart Exhibition Explorer

Open source Blender[5] [10] environment (version 2.5) along with an integrated Blender Game Engine (BGE) is used to create an application called 'Smart Exhibition Explorer' (SEE), responsible for an interactive exploration of the virtual museum (an early prototype screen example is presented in Fig. 2). Retrieving of an exhibition content consists of three phases (presented in Fig. 1): chosen exhibition is searched on the network and its description is downloaded (stage 1). Information about the first scene included in the exhibition is retrieved and 3D visualisation of the exposition room begins (stage 2). Depending on the requirements (e.g. a position of an observer), information about particular museum pieces is progressively retrieved and the 3D visualisation is performed (step 3).

---

[5] http://www.blender.org

Native BGE multi-platform '.blend' binary file format [BFF] is adopted to store information about a scene description including:

– Predefined 3D objects (meshes and their location, materials, textures),
– Light placement, scene physics,
– Logic of interaction with the scenario (e.g. collision detection, physics),
– Auxiliary information (text descriptions, audio commentary),
– The list of 3D objects available for downloading.

3   Conclusion

The goal of the developed system is to present a distributed 3D virtual environment based on a CAN architecture created in the FIE[6] project. The 3D stereoscopic visualisation of a museum exhibition may contain objects from multiple locations. The presentation may be further extended, e.g. by an introduction of haptic devices to interact with the 3D objects or an avatar for a curator functionality.

Acknowledgements. This work has been partially supported by the Polish Ministry of Science and Higher Education under the European Regional Development Fund, Grant No. POIG.01.01.02-00-045/09-00 Future Internet Engineering.

References

1. Marc, L., Rusinkiewicz, S., Ginzton, M., Ginsberg, J., Pulli, K., Koller, D., Anderson, S., Shade, J., Curless, B., Pereira, L., Davis, J., Fulk, D.: The digital Michelangelo project: 3D scanning of large statues. In: ACM SIGGRAPH Conference on Computer Graphics, pp. 131–144. Addison-Wesley, Reading (2000)
2. Allen, P.K., Stamos, I., Troccoli, A., Smith, B., Leordeanu, M.: New Methods for Digital Modeling of Historic Sites. IEEE Computer Society, Los Alamitos (2003)
3. Takase, Y., Sasaki, Y., Nakagawa, M., Shimizu, M., Yamada, O., Izumi, T., Shibasaki, R.: Reconstruction with laser scanning and 3D visualisation of roman monuments in Tyre, Lebanon. The International Archives of the Photogrammetry, Remote Sensing and Spatial Information Sciences, XXXIV (2003)
4. Nishino, K., Ikeuchi, K.: Robust Simultaneous Registration of Multiple Range Images. In: The 5th Asian Conference on Computer Vision, Melbourne (2002)
5. Gołembnik, A., Morysiński, T.: Na tropie ogrodowych alejek – badania architektoniczne w ogrodach wilanowskich. Archeologia Żywa 4(34) (2006)
6. Skabek, K., Tomaka, A.: Applications of Computer Vision in Medicine and Protection of Monuments. Theoretical and Applied Informatics 20(3), 203–223 (2010)
7. Hoppe, H.: Efficient Implementation of Progressive Meshes. Computers & Graphics 22 (1998)
8. Lua, E.K., et al.: A survey and comparison of peer-to-peer overlay network schemes. IEEE Communications Surveys & Tutorials 7(2), 72–93 (2005)
9. Ambrosio, M.D., et al.: Second NetInf architecture description. Deliverable 6.2 of project 4WARD, FP7-ICT-2007-1-216041-4WARD/D-6.2 (January 2010)
10. Mullen, T.: Mastering Blender. John Wiley & Sons, Chichester (2009)

---

[6] http://iip.net.pl

Author Index